HUMAN NATURE
A Critical Reader

HUMAN NATURE
A Critical Reader

Edited by
Laura Betzig

New York   Oxford
Oxford University Press
1997

Oxford University Press

Oxford   New York
Athens   Auckland   Bangkok
Bogota   Bombay   Buenos Aires   Calcutta
Cape Town   Dar es Salaam   Delhi
Florence   Hong Kong   Istanbul   Karachi
Kuala Lumpur   Madras   Madrid   Melbourne
Mexico City   Nairobi   Paris   Singapore
Taipei   Tokyo   Toronto

and associated companies in
Berlin   Ibadan

Library of Congress Cataloging-in-Publication Data
Human nature : a critical reader / edited by Laura Betzig.
       p.   cm.
    Includes bibliographical references and index.
    ISBN 0-19-509865-X
    1. Sociobiology.   2. Human behavior.   I. Betzig, Laura L., 1953–.
GN365.9.H84   1997
304.5—dc20   95-52160

9 8 7 6 5 4 3 2 1

Printed in the United States of America
on acid-free paper

For Bill, Bob,
and George

CONTENTS

II STUDIES OF MODERN SOCIETIES

III COMPARATIVE AND HISTORICAL STUDIES

PREFACE

DONE - THE END OF HISTORY !

It's happened. We have finally figured out where we came from, why we're here, and who we are.

How did it happen? It all started with Patrick Matthew, Alfred Russel Wallace, and—most of all—Charles Darwin, who, a hundred some years ago, came up with a theory of life. Its essence was simple. It said: traits for sterility die out; and traits for fertility spread.

But it wasn't enough. It took the Modern Synthesis—the merging of Mendelian genetics and Darwinian selection—to answer the question: Traits for fertility *of what?* The answer, arrived at in the last thirty-odd years by Ronald Fisher, William Hamilton, Robert Trivers, and George Williams was: The fertility of *genes.*

That answer started a revolution in the study of behavior. But people were timid at first. They looked at wasps. They studied ground squirrels and elephant seals, pied flycatchers and scrub jays, sunfish and sticklebacks, red colobus and red deer. In time, they got better and better data to test better and better models predicting everything—from the production of alarm calls to the production of sons—as means to the spread of genes.

It was 1979 when Duxbury, a little North Scituate, Massachusetts press, published the very first set of tests of Darwinian predictions on *us*. The book sold less than four thousand copies, and in less than five years it went out of print. But it left a lasting mark. *Evolutionary Biology and Human Social Behavior: An Anthropological Perspective,* edited by Napoleon Chagnon and William Irons, had neither a catchy title nor an attractive cover nor a big promotional budget. But it was the beginning of the end for every pre-1859 answer to the questions, what are we doing, and why?

This book is a record of that revolution. It reprints eighteen "classic" tests of Darwinian predictions about what people think, feel, or do. The first classic in the book, Bill Irons's "Cultural and Biological Success," comes out of *Evolutionary Biology and Human Social Behavior.* The rest come from a scatter of later sources. Six of these classics are field studies, done in "traditional" societies; six are studies done in "modern" societies; and six are library studies. These aren't the *best* tests of Darwinian predictions; the best tests are being done, as they should be done, *now.* But they're among the first. And every one was done by a pioneer.

Bill Irons lived with the Yomut in Persia for thirty months, on three trips, over a stretch of ten years starting in 1965. Napoleon Chagnon made his first trip up the Orinoco to study the Yanomamö in 1964; since then he's gone again at least twenty times; and he's compiled—in books, on film, and on the computer—one of the best records of demography, social organization, and warfare ever put together. Eric Smith lived with the Inuit in the Arctic in 1977 and '78, testing models of cooperative hunting, among other things, in one of the last foraging groups on earth. Kim Hill showed up at the Manduvi mission in eastern Paraguay on New Year's Day, 1978, and has returned to live with the Ache ten times or more since then; he has, with the help of Magdalena Hurtado, Hilly Kaplan, Kristen Hawkes, and other friends, put together some of the best data on hunting and gathering, sharing, and reproduction we're likely to get. Monique Borgerhoff Mulder has lived with the Kenyan Kipsigis for more than twenty-four months over the last ten years. And, though the data on bushman demography used in his classic article were borrowed from Nancy

Howell, Nick Blurton Jones has been to Botswana twice—in 1970 and 1988—and to Tanzania, with Kristen Hawkes, Jim O'Connell, and others to live with the big game–hunting Hadza several times since 1988. Since 1979 or before, every field-worker in this book has gathered data—by counting observations, counting calories, and counting babies—in order to test predictions derived from the theory of natural selection.

Tests of selectionist hypotheses in modern societies have gone on almost as long. Daly and Wilson's were the first. In 1981 they published their pioneering studies of child abuse and neglect, and they've been studying homicide ever since. The Thornhills's studies of rape date back to a 1983 paper. Doug Kenrick has been advocating evolutionary studies of mate choice in print since 1983, David Buss since 1984. Leda Cosmides's pathbreaking studies of cheater detection as an adaptation began as a doctoral dissertation in 1985. When Bruce Ellis, in the late '80s, pointed out that Don Symons's unprecedented *Evolution of Human Sexuality* was full of testable hypotheses, "my response, if I remember rightly, was to whine that since I had gone to all the trouble of thinking of those hypotheses, it didn't seem fair that I should have to test them." Bruce "quite sensibly replied that perhaps they should, but they hadn't." The classic in this book was the result.

The library moles were neither last, nor least. Mildred Dickemann, "the mother of Darwinian history," published a trilogy of breathtaking papers testing selectionist predictions in 1979 and 1981. Bobbi Low's first cross-cultural study, a look at "Sexual Selection and Human Ornamentation," came out in Chagnon and Irons's collection in 1979. Steve Gaulin started out with a comparative test of "confidence of paternity" hypotheses in 1980. John Hartung has done comparative work on inheriting wealth since his first, iconoclastic, 1982 piece. I've looked at despotism since 1982; and Sarah Hrdy, who studied langurs once, has been obsessed since 1987 with human maternal care.

What got these people started? Some studied monkeys. Hrdy made a major contribution testing Williams's gene-level theory of selection on infanticide in langurs. Gaulin looked at red howlers in the Columbian Andes (and now radiomonitors voles). Margo Wilson and Don Symons looked at sex and play in rhesus. Oth-

ers studied other species. Nick Blurton Jones started out, "one of the very last of Niko Tinbergen's students *not* to work on adaptiveness," looking at great tits. Martin Daly, working in the early seventies with John Crook at Bristol, went off to watch rodents in the Sahara; back on this continent, he looked at "the ecological equivalent"—Californian kangaroo rats. Monique Borgerhoff Mulder drove across Africa with (and eventually married) a cheetah biologist, and wrote up the first of her Kipsigis results at LARG, Tim Clutton-Brock's Cambridge "large animal research group." Mildred Dickemann inspected lizard eggs, coconut crabs, and cockroaches with her sister as a kid in Samoa. Bobbi Low did a dissertation on toad skin secretions, switched to digger wasps, and then "finally decided that rather than backpack a grumpy infant [her two-year-old son] into the mosquitoes, I'd better find something I could analyze on the computer." John Tooby and Leda Cosmides started out making major theoretical contributions on intragenomic conflict and the evolution of sex. Randy Thornhill, one of the world's best ethologists, has spent years studying sexual selection in scorpionflies. He grew up (like Ed Wilson) in Decatur, Alabama, and (like Wilson) collected plants, bugs, and lizards on the Tennessee River.

What else got these people started? Most read Williams. For some, *Adaptation and Natural Selection* was an epiphany. For Symons, who read it at Berkeley, it was "a profound meditation on the nature of adaptation"; Eric Smith read it "in the hiatus" between going to school at Santa Barbara and going to graduate school at Cornell. For Randy Thornhill, as for many others, it was part of the course that included fresh work by Hamilton, Trivers, and Maynard Smith. "With Williams's book, which I read first, came the staggering realization that nothing makes sense in biology except in the light of the history of differential reproduction." David Buss was at Berkeley in the late seventies when he "came across Trivers's 'Parental Investment and Sexual Selection' in a used book store, and found it more profound than anything I'd read in psychology." Mildred Dickemann, who'd been immersed in infanticide for years, rented a house in Lawrence, Kansas, from Richard Johnston, who edited *Annual Reviews of Ecology and Systematics*. "He came across something that might interest me

(Dick Alexander's prediction re status and female infanticide) and xeroxed it for me, but by accident xeroxed the wrong pages! I had to scurry to get the right copy to recognize Dick's idea." Bill Irons underwent a similar conversion: "I had a scales-falling-from-my-eyes experience when I read Alexander's 1974 paper in the Penn State library in 1975. I later read Williams." Napoleon Chagnon started out, in the early '70s, trying to analyze Yanomamö marriage and kinship using Sewall Wright's inbreeding coefficients. John Hartung, holed up in a tent in St. Thomas, tucked into Darwin: "Wondering what to read that might give me some understanding, I had the good fortune of not finding anything in the local library that might possibly be relevant except a dog-eared copy of Charles Darwin's *Origin of Species.* I spent six months reading *The Origin* and sent for a copy of *The Descent of Man.*"

Most of all, though, these people got started by other people. It was Symons, at UCSB, who got Eric Smith to pick up a copy of Williams. Symons, back in '64, had got his evolution from Sherwood Washburn—with a little help from Peter Marler and Richard Dawkins, then in biology at Berkeley. ("Although today it is a mystery to me why anyone would have ever supposed that the royal road to the human mind is the study of nonhuman primate behavior, in the midsixties this absurdity was simply taken for granted.") Washburn's lineage bore more fruit through another student, Irv DeVore, who went on to found his own empire in anthropology at Harvard. Hrdy, Gaulin, Hartung, Tooby, Cosmides (who was up the road in psychology), and a great many more all ended up there. Nick Blurton Jones got tied up with this group when he met Mel Konner, who "came to my lab to see how we were recording parent-child interactions and when he reached the field invited me to come visit the bushmen." David Buss was teaching at Harvard in the early eighties when he "was paid a visit" by Leda Cosmides, who invited him to DeVore's simian seminar. Daly and Wilson spent a sabbatical year at Harvard in 1984; then was the bond among Buss, Cosmides, Daly, Tooby, and Wilson formed.

Another lineage of sorts started up in Ann Arbor, in biology, under Richard Alexander. Randy Thornhill is the only one on this list who did a dissertation in Alexander's department. But Chagnon and Irons, who'd written dissertations in anthropology at Michigan, were both influenced by Alexander—in protracted discussions that followed their conversions. Along with a few others, Borgerhoff Mulder and I worked with Chagnon and Irons after they'd moved to Northwestern. Kim Hill and Magdi Hurtado studied anthropology at Utah with Kristen Hawkes; both came in contact with Eric Charnov in biology; Charnov had got his first dose of evolution at Michigan. Eric Smith (who, like more than one of these people, got it from both ends) took biology at Cornell from Steve Emlen; Emlen had done a dissertation at Michigan. In Arizona, Doug Kenrick and Ed Sadalla got together over a copy of Ed Wilson's *Sociobiology* in 1975: "We proceeded to conduct our first experimental studies of dominance and sexual attraction in 1976, but were unable to get them published for a decade." Eventually, across campus, Kenrick talked to John Alcock, who'd done a book with Randy Thornhill on the evolution of mating in insects. David Buss and Bobbi Low got hooked up with Alexander and others in the Evolution and Human Behavior Program in Ann Arbor (b. 1986, d. 1994). John Hartung saw the light in a Pennsylvania museum: "It was December of 1972 and I went on my motorcycle. Just as I thawed out, about fifty minutes into his talk, R. D. Alexander explained mother's-brother-sister's-son. There was hope."

One point of this book, then, is to collect some of the best of the first work that used natural selection to understand human action. The other point is to suggest how that work might be better. That's how science goes. In the Darwinian study of *Homo sapiens,* as in the Darwinian study of any other species, better data will make it possible to construct better models, and better models will make it possible to get better data. Knowledge, in science, builds on itself.

To that end, this is the plan of the book. "Classic" papers are grouped in three sections. The first section holds the "Studies of Traditional Societies," the second the "Studies of Modern Societies," the third the "Comparative and Historical Studies" done in libraries. But every classic is interspersed with critiques. Authors have been asked to update their work with "self-critiques" answering the simple question, "How could the science be better?" And, because biology is a cannibalistic endeavor—because, as Ed Wilson prophesized in *Sociobiology* in 1975, history, philosophy, political science, sociology, economics, anthropology, psychology, and every other human "science" will become a branch of biology as they turn, inevitably, to Darwinian theory—I've asked half a dozen of the best biologists I know to write sweeping critiques of each of the three sets of classics. Alex Kacelnik (who does elegant foraging studies) and John Krebs (who cowrote The Book on foraging and coedited The Book on behavioral ecology) have done the "traditional societies" critique; Paul Sherman (who pioneered the adaptationist study of animal cognition with his long-term studies of kin recog-

nition) and Kern Reeve (who studies kin recognition and despotism) have done the "modern societies" critique; and Ruth Mace and Mark Pagel (who've reinvented the comparative method in cross-cultural studies by applying Pagel and others' work on comparing species) have critiqued the library studies. Last, in order to round out the book and bring it up to date, I've written an introduction that covers the basics in evolutionary theory and reviews—comprehensively, I hope—cutting-edge tests of that theory on us.

Tube snaking in the wave of scientific revolution is fun. It is my profound hope that a few clever readers will come in and swim.

CONTRIBUTORS

Laura Betzig
  The Adaptationist Program
  Ann Arbor, Michigan

Nick Blurton Jones
  School of Education
  University of California, Los Angeles

Monique Borgerhoff Mulder
  Department of Anthropology
  University of California, Davis

James Boster
  Department of Anthropology
  University of California, Irvine

David Buss
  Department of Psychology
  University of Texas, Austin

Napoleon Chagnon
  Department of Anthropology
  University of California, Santa Barbara

Leda Cosmides
  Department of Psychology
  University of California, Santa Barbara

Martin Daly
  Department of Psychology
  McMaster University

Mildred Dickemann
  Richmond, California

Bruce Ellis
  Department of Psychology
  Vanderbilt University

Steven Gaulin
  Department of Anthropology
  University of Pittsburgh

Gary Groth
  Department of Psychology
  Arizona State University

John Hartung
  Department of Anesthesiology
  State University of New York at
  Brooklyn

Kim Hill
  Department of Anthropology
  University of New Mexico

Sarah Blaffer Hrdy
  Department of Anthropology
  University of California, Davis

Magdi Hurtado
  Department of Anthropology
  University of New Mexico

Bill Irons
  Department of Anthropology
  Northwestern University

Alex Kacelnik
  Department of Zoology
  Oxford University

Douglas Kenrick
  Department of Psychology
  Arizona State University

John Krebs
  Department of Zoology
  Oxford University

Bobbi Low
  School of Natural Resources
  University of Michigan

Ruth Mace
  Department of Anthropology
  University College London

Mark Pagel
  Department of Zoology
  Oxford University

Kern Reeve
  Department of Biology
  Cornell University

Edward Sadalla
  Department of Psychology
  Arizona State University

Catharine Salmon
  Department of Psychology
  McMaster University

Paul Sherman
    Department of Biology
    Cornell University
Eric Alden Smith
    Department of Anthropology
    University of Washington
Donald Symons
    Department of Anthropology
    University of California, Santa Barbara
Nancy Wilmsen Thornhill
    Department of Anthropology
    University of New Mexico

Randy Thornhill
    Department of Biology
    University of New Mexico
John Tooby
    Department of Anthropology
    University of California, Santa Barbara
Melanie Trost
    Department of Communications
    Arizona State University
Margo Wilson
    Department of Psychology
    McMaster University

HUMAN NATURE
A Critical Reader

1

Introduction: People Are Animals

LAURA BETZIG

> *Putting it negatively, the myth of eternal return states that a life which disappears once and for all, which does not return, is like a shadow, without weight, dead in advance, and whether it was horrible, beautiful, or sublime, its horror, sublimity, and beauty mean nothing.*
>
> —Milan Kundera, *The Unbearable Lightness of Being*

> *She stood to her knees in heavy mud, the red thick water closed below her shoulders. She looked up through the loose fronds of grass at the grey pit of the sky and heard a mutter of thunder. She was quite alone. A long swathe of grass had been beaten across the surface of the water, and around its stems trailed a jelly of frog spawn. . . . There she felt the crouching infant, still moving tentatively around its prison, protected from the warm red water by half an inch of flesh. Her stomach stretched and contracted; and the frog swam slowly across the water, with slow, strong spasms of its legs. . . . In the jelly spawn were tiny dark dots of life.*
>
> —Doris Lessing, *A Proper Marriage*

> *DNA neither knows nor cares. DNA just is.*
>
> —Richard Dawkins, *River Out of Eden*[1]

Is there a point to all this?

Yes.

There is a reason why dungflies copulate for 35.5 minutes; why big male reef fish turn into females but little male reef fish don't; why female swallows like males with elongated tails; why more promiscuous primates have bigger testes.[2] The reason is simple. Dungflies, reef fish, swallows, and promiscuous primates who do otherwise leave less DNA. The chemically encoded messages, "copulate for just 28 minutes," "if small, become female," "prefer somewhat shorter plumage," and "if promiscuous, grow a small scrotum" all get passed on to fewer bodies, and so all tend to die out. Messages, on the other hand, that make it easier for animals to grow, mate, and—this is the bottom line—*breed,* all tend to spread. The point of life is the proliferation of life.

THE END

As Darwin put it in *The Origin of Species* in 1859,

> As many more individuals of each species are born than can possibly survive; and as, consequently, there is a frequently recurring struggle for existence, it follows that any being, if it vary however slightly in any manner profitable to itself, under the complex and sometimes varying conditions of life, will have a better chance of surviving

—and of reproducing. By a simple process of descent with modification, Darwin explained the geographic distribution of species across space, and the geologic distribution of species over time. Darwin referred to that process as *natural selection.*[3]

But even *if* Darwin's theory fits a few bizarre facts about dungflies and reef fish, monkeys and swallows, what does it say about *us?* Do we cooperate and compete, have sex and raise babies the

who are 'we' & what is 'the way we do' ? revolution
e.g. pink & blue blankets

way we do because our ancestors out-cooperated, out-competed, out-mated, and (this is the bottom line) out-reproduced everybody else?[4]

Yes. From pregnancy complications, to the stress response, to the beauty in symmetry, to the attraction of money, to the historical tendency of the rich to favor firstborn sons, everything we think, feel, and do might be better understood as a means to the spread of our own—or of our ancestors'—genes.[5]   !!!

How unlock the mysteries of life? By asking one simple question: What's in it for my own, or for my ancestors', genes? How might, say, making my mother throw up if I'm a fetus, or pulling a baby from a burning building if I'm her big brother, or starting a revolution if I'm a laterborn son help me (or have helped my ancestors) survive, mate, and (this is the bottom line) breed? It seems deceptively easy at first. But by asking this simple question, people have begun to solve an astonishing variety of problems. And solving them is, of course, a good first step toward fixing them.   *? for example ?*

MOTHERS, FATHERS, AND BABIES

Take pregnancy. If anything in life approaches perfect loving kindness, it's the bond between a mother and child. Though they inevitably grow apart, they start out almost indistinguishably close. The fetus takes a part of every breath its mother takes, of every bite its mother eats. It carries, and will in turn transmit, its mother's DNA: it's her ticket to genetic immortality.

But, as Bob Trivers was the first to make clear, there's plenty of room for conflict between parents and offspring. Because life is fraught with risks, no parent on earth is meant to reproduce just once. All living things are designed to make more than one copy of their genes. Sibling rivalry is the result: parents are equally related to each of their offspring so, other things being equal, they have an interest in treating them all the same; offspring are more closely related to themselves than to their brothers and sisters so, other things being equal, they have an interest in getting treated better.[6]

The upshot is conflict from the moment of conception. Complications in pregnancy, as David Haig has very cleverly pointed out, can be seen as an effect of this maternal-fetal tug-of-war. Fetus often wants, and sometimes gets, more food than mother is prepared to give. In Haig's words, "Mother and fetus will compete after every meal over the share that each receives." Fetus wants food of higher quality and higher quantity. To these ends, it does two things. First, placental hormones, working on fetus' behalf, oppose the effects of insulin. This improves baby's food *quality* by keeping blood glucose levels higher for longer. Mothers

counter by raising insulin production. The result, where the conflict gets to be out of control, is gestational diabetes—a common complication in pregnancy. Second, the placeta, again on fetus' behalf, works to raise maternal blood pressure. This improves baby's food *quantity* by giving it access to a more voluminous supply of blood. Mothers counter with vasodilation of their peripheral circulation. But the result, where conflict escalates, is hypertension or, where conflict is out of control, preeclampsia—another common complication. Two key facts fit Haig's tug-of-war hypothesis: mothers with high blood glucose levels and mothers with high blood pressure tend to give birth to bigger babies.[7]

When might parent-offspring conflict get to be most intense? One answer is: When parents are in poor condition. Parents do best, in that case, to scrimp now and splurge later on child care. Another answer is: When mother's babies have different fathers, and when father's babies have different mothers.

First answers first. If would-be mothers in poor condition are evolved to conserve, then it should be harder to make a baby when times are bad. So, says Peter Ellison, it is. Women tend to lose weight, their salivary progesterone levels drop, and they ovulate less often during the preharvest dearth in Zaire's Ituri Forest; after the harvest, the trends are reversed. Across populations—from the Himalayas, to Poland, to Kenya, to Bangladesh, to the peanut-farming Lese of the Ituri—birth rates tend to peak around nine months after a relative feast and to bottom out around nine months after a relative famine. Even after she's given birth, a well-fed mother has an edge: she's likely to ovulate, to conceive, and to give birth again sooner than a lean one.[8]

Second answers second. *Do* babies by different fathers fight harder with mother? Enter, again, David Haig. Hypertension is, it turns out, more common in mothers who have already borne children by someone other than fetus' father. That makes sense, Haig says, since such a fetus is draining maternal resources away from its half sibs (brothers and sisters by the same mother but different fathers) rather than from its full sibs (brothers and sisters by the same mother and the same father). "Genetic imprinting," he suggests, may be the means to that end. Paternal genes, expressed in the fetus, might evolve to raise their demands where mother has had—or is likely to have—babies by other fathers. Interestingly, hypertension is *less* common in women who have lived with fetus' father for longer. As Haig says, sperm may differently imprint in the testes of men in short-term and long-term relationships.[9]

By the way, parents and offspring don't always conflict. That's true even when the effects are unpleasant. For instance, long before hypertension and high glucose levels kick in, pregnancy makes women sick. But "pregnancy sickness" may be an adaptation—and of mutual benefit to mother and child. As Margie Profet puts it, " 'Sickness' implies dysfunction, yet vomiting during early pregnancy is usually a sign of health." Women who feel seriously queasy or actually throw up during the first three months of pregnancy are less likely to miscarry. The reason, Profet suggests, is that nausea specifically inhibits mother's ingestion of toxins. Toxins that cause birth defects are widespread among the plants people eat. Pregnancy sickness starts at around two to four weeks after conception, peaks at around six to eight weeks, and then falls off; organogenesis—the forming of the fetus' heart, ears, eyes, genitals, limbs, and brain—starts at around twenty days after conception, and ends by about day 56. They coincide.[10]

KIN

So, conflict—even parent-offspring conflict—evolves by natural selection. So does cooperation. When, as a rule, should sharing evolve? Bill Hamilton answered this question with a simple inequality. He said, altruism should be favored by natural selection wherever

$$k > 1/r,$$

where k is the ratio of benefit to the receiver to cost to the giver, and r is the proportion of genes they have in common by descent. In short, it makes genetic sense for one body to come to the aid of another to the extent that both bodies carry the same genes.[11]

Who would you pull from a burning building? Gene Burnstein and collaborators asked that question of people in the United States and Japan. Guess what they found? That women were helped a little more often than men; that the young were helped more often than the old; that closer kin (e.g., "your three-day-old younger sister" or "your forty-five-year-old father") were helped more often than remoter kin (e.g., "your brother's ten-year-old daughter" or "your eighteen-year-old cousin"); and that any tendency to help "acquaintances" was slight.[12]

Other results are a little less intuitively obvious. Mark Flinn and friends have spent the last eight (not unpleasant) years collecting and analyzing 18,376 samples of spit from 247 children in a village on Dominica's east coast. They've been looking for cortisol—a key hormone produced in response to stress. And they've found three major determinants of variation in cortisol levels. The first is time of day: cortisol levels go down by around a factor of ten from sunup to sundown. The second is eating and drinking: cortisol levels show a predictable "postprandial" rise. The third, and most interesting by far from Flinn's point of view, is household composition. Children living in nuclear family households, in households with single moms plus close kin, or in grandparents' households all show moderate cortisol levels; kids living with stepfathers, half sibs, and distant kin tend to have abnormal cortisol profiles. They're under chronic stress. As Flinn and England conclude, "In contrast to their responses to most potential stressors, children do not seem to habituate readily to family trauma." Physical stressors—like working, playing, or eating—tend to be followed by a moderate (+10–100%) cortisol rise, then a quick attenuation. Social stressors—especially family conflict or change—are most likely to cue a (+100–2000%) cortisol spike. With calm, affectionate contact

$(-10–50\%)$ cortisol levels (reassuringly) go down.[13]

Stress is unpleasant; but it's more than that. It appears to affect immune system function. Flinn finds no evidence that better housing, better diet, or a more leisurely life substantially affects child health. Social stressors do. Chronically stressed kids with abnormal cortisol profiles are sick more often. They show evidence of immunosuppression: they have reduced cell-mediated (neopterin, microglobulin β_2), humoral (secretory-immunoglobulin A), and/or nonspecific (neutrophil recruitment via interleukin-8) immunity. In short, Flinn and England suggest, "Family stress, abnormal glucocorticoid response, and concomitant immunosuppression are important intermediary links between socioeconomic conditions and child health." More than anything else, mother appears to matter. Secure moms—with stable support from men or kin—can better care for their children.[14]

HUSBANDS, LOVERS, AND WIVES

Affectionate contact is not, of course, confined to kin. Before half sibs and full sibs, nieces and nephews, daughters and sons can be cared for, they have to be conceived. That means mating. For Darwin, mating was such an important source of adaptation that he devoted another book to the subject. He brought it out a dozen years after *The Origin*. And he called it *The Descent of Man and Selection in Relation to Sex.* In it he wrote, "It is certain that amongst almost all animals there is a struggle between the males for the possession of the female. This fact is so notorious that it would be superfluous to give instances. Hence the females have the opportunity of selecting one out of several males." The difference, he thought, had something to do with the fact that "the female has to spend much organic matter in the formation of her ova, whereas the male expends much force in fierce contests with his rivals, in wandering about in search of the female, in exerting his voice, pouring out odoriferous secretions, &c."[15]

This point was made clearer, a hundred years later, by Bob Trivers. The key difference between the sexes, he said, is in the "parental investment" they make. Trivers defined PI as "any investment by the parent in an individual offspring that increases the offspring's chance

The Wonder of You

Figure 1.1. The wonder of you

of surviving (and hence reproductive success) at the cost of the parent's ability to invest in other offspring." The effect is a difference in potential reproductive rates: the greater investor (usually, but not always, the female) is an object of competition; the lesser investor (usually, but not always, the male) competes.[16]

When people *are* choosy, what do they want in a mate? One answer is: "Good genes." Particularly, as Bill Hamilton has pointed out, genes good at building parasite-resistant hosts. Choosy people looking for genes of this sort should look for healthy—colorful, energetic, symmetrical—mates.[17]

Why symmetry? Because exposure to environmental flux of all sorts—like parasites, pollutants, or extreme climates—leaves its mark. Faces, torsos, and limbs all move away from left-right mirror images. Symmetry should be, as a result, "a reliable health certificate." In a spate of studies, Randy Thornhill, Steve Gangestad, and collaborators have found that New Mexico *men*, but not *women*, with more left-right body symmetry (that is, more equal left and right ankle, elbow, foot, hand, wrist, and ear breadth) have more attractive faces; that German students find symmetrical faces of men *and* women more attractive than asymmetrical faces; that U.S. and Spanish women with more symmetrical breasts have higher age-specific fertility; that in New Mexico, both male *and* female students with more left-right body symmetry say they've had sex with more partners; and that in New Mexico couples, *both* men and women with more left-right body symmetry are more prone to infidelity.[18]

As a rule, people haven't got eyes for equal-sized ankles, elbows, and so on to the nearest .1 or .01 mm. What index might they have evolved to track? For one thing, large body mass. Symmetrical men tend to be bigger men. Arguably, that's because being massive is condition-dependent: men with "good" genes better resist environmental stress. They grow more regular; and they grow larger.[19]

What—besides symmetry—should make a woman sexy? The "gynoid" look. High waist-to-hip ratios (above .85) in women are associated with high risk of hypertension, diabetes, endometrial cancer, breast cancer, ovarian cancer, and gallbladder disease. So low ratios, Dev Singh says, should appeal. He asked Texas college boys to rank sketches of women with low to high waist-to-hip ratios. Regardless of weight, they liked the lowest (0.7) ratios best and the highest (1.0) ratios least. Hourglass girls were rated healthier, younger, prettier, sexier, more anxious to have children, and better built to bear them.[20]

And what else—besides mass and symmetry—might make a man look healthy? An "android" body. Normal male waist-to-hip ratios run in the .80–.95 range. Low ratios (curvy figures) are more likely in men suffering from hypogonadism, Klinefelter's syndrome, or advanced cirrhosis—all associated with less testosterone and more estrogen. High ratios (straight up and down) are more likely in men with peptic ulcers, sociopsychological stress, fetal adversities, or retarded growth. Up to a point, Dev Singh concludes, thin hips and washboard abs should look good. He asked Texas college girls to rate line drawings of men with high to

low waist-to-hip ratios. They liked the medium-high (0.9, on a scale of 0.7 to 1.0) waist-to-hip ratio most.[21]

To sum up, "sexy" is, among other things, "healthy." And "healthy" is, among other things, balanced, big, and properly built. In choosing for good health, men's and women's tastes overlap. In other respects, though, their tastes are distinct.

Getting "good genes" may worry both females and males; getting "any genes" at all tends to be an exclusively male concern. Why is that? For one thing, a woman's ability to make babies is closely tied to her age; a man's is not. For another thing, maternity is guaranteed; paternity is moot. It follows that men, more than women, must monitor age; and men, more than women, should pay attention to chastity.[22]

Doug Kenrick and Richard Keefe found, six times, that men want young women. They looked at personal ads from the *Arizona Solo;* at 1986 marriage statistics from Seattle and Phoenix; at 1923 marriage statistics from Phoenix; at personal ads from Germany, Holland, and India; at marriage statistics from the island of Poro—five hundred kilometers southeast of Manila—for 1913–39; and at personal ads placed by "rich" women and men in the *Washingtonian*. The results were overwhelmingly redundant. Women, regardless of age, want mates their age or older. Young men want women a little older or a little younger; old men want younger women.[23]

Keying in on age is a good low-resolution solution to the "any genes" problem. But there are high-resolution tricks too. Ovulation is tough to pinpoint; that makes conception something of a guessing game even in cycling women. And, for the vast majority of women over the vast span of history, ovulation has been a rare event. Estimates are that in "natural fertility" societies a woman who lives past fifty has fewer than forty-eight fertile cycles in her entire life. The rest of the time she's premenarcheal, postmenopausal, pregnant, or with a baby at her breast.

How spot a "fecundable" female? Women in the narrow window endocrinologists call the "waiting time to conception" have been, as Beverly Strassmann points out, almost universally bound by taboos. In most (more than two-thirds of all) cases, these taboos are private enough to signal just to a husband and close kin. In some (less than one-third of all) cases, taboos are more generally known.[24]

Dogon women live in the Sahel on a 240-kilometer sandstone cliff; they give birth to an average of 8.6 children apiece; and, during the rare times they are not with a child in their wombs or a child at their breasts, they spend at least five nights a month at the *yapunduru,* or menstrual huts. These huts are conspicuous. They're cramped, out in the open, and round (every other village structure is rectangular). In Sangui, the village Strassmann lived in for two and a half years, huts are within twenty-three and twenty-five meters of—and in full view of—the shade shelters where Dogon men spend time. Huts stand on major village routes, and on principal paths to millet fields and the main water source. By meticulously drawing up their hormonal profiles, Strassmann found that when a woman stays in the huts, she is menstruating in fact. She is, in other words, honestly signaling the rare fact that she's cycling. But *to whom?* To Strassmann, huts promote the interests of Dogon *men,* because they're the ones who enforce the taboos. The point is defense *against* cuckoldry.[25]

In short, having found "any genes," a man's got to guard them. Jealousy may be one evolved means to that end. David Buss and friends found, three times, that men worry more than women about sexual rivals. They asked Michigan students to decide which would bother them more—"imagining your partner forming a deep emotional attachment" or "imagining your partner enjoying passionate sexual intercourse." Men chose (B); women chose (A). Next, they hooked students up to Ag/AgCl surface electrodes on their first and third fingers to measure electrodermal activity, to photoplethysmographs on their thumbs to tap pulse rate, and to electrodes over their brows to monitor electromyographic activity. Subjects were then "asked to relax." They were told to imagine either "walking to class"; their serious romantic partner "falling in love and forming an emotional attachment" to someone else; or their serious romantic partner "having sexual intercourse" with someone else. Again, men were more disturbed by sexual, and women by emotional, infidelity. In their third and last study, Buss *et al.* used another student sample to replicate their first study. This time, they found the

sex differences in both sexual and emotional jealousy more marked among those who had been or were really (rather than hypothetically) romantically involved.[26]

One last solution to the "any genes" problem completely contradicts, on the face of it, an obsession with chaste women. That is, an obsession with "fast" ones. These obsessions aren't really, as more than a few songwriters know, contradictory at all. Coyness counts when men invest a lot in their children; fastness counts when they don't. Richard Dawkins summed this up in a neat cost-benefit analysis of "the battle of the sexes." Depending, of course, on how the payoffs are assigned, natural selection can produce any mix of chastity and promiscuity as frequency-dependent strategies. Frequencies hinge, as always, on what everybody else is up to. In Dawkins's particular tabulation, "If you do the sums, it turns out that a population in which 5/6 of the females are coy, and 5/8 of the males are faithful is evolutionarily stable." That can mean: 5/6ths of the girls are coy all the time; or all of the girls are coy 5/6ths of the time.[27]

Jeff Simpson and Steve Gangestad think they've found evidence of a heritable behavioral trait they call "unrestricted sociosexual orientation," and have developed an instrument, the "Sociosexual Orientation Inventory," to measure it. The SOI is a composite of markers of what might, in colloquial terms, be referred to as "fastness." These markers include reported number of sexual partners in the past year; reported number of "one-night stands"; estimated number of partners in the next five years; frequency of fantasy with a partner other than the current one; and attitudes toward casual sex. "High scores reflect a relatively unrestricted sociosexual orientation." Interestingly, men are better at spotting "fastness" than women. Also intriguingly, fast women date more attractive and socially visible men; they date less responsible, less affectionate and loyal men; and they give birth to more sons. Maybe fast girls, Simpson and Gangestad suggest, are choosing "good genes" and giving birth, thereby, to healthier, more attractive, more promiscuous sons.[28]

Left-right symmetry, waist-to-hip ratio, chastity, and fastness aside, people don't just look for "good genes" when they mate. When people are choosy, what else do they want? The other answer is: A "good provider." Genes are the bottom line—you can't make a baby without them. But the code (DNA) goes nowhere without food. Genes—especially human genes—need nurturing, too. And good nurturers are, among other things, good providers.

Every girl's crazy 'bout a sharp-dressed man. John Marshall Townsend and friends put men in a Rolex watch, designer tie, and white dress shirt with a navy blazer thrown over the shoulder, *or* in a Burger King uniform. Then they asked New York college women how much or little they'd like to have coffee and conversation with such a person; to date them; to have uncommitted sex with them; to have a serious involvement with them; to have a serious, sexual involvement with them; or to marry them. Across the board, women preferred the Rolex to the Burger King man. And, as long as they found her pretty, New York college men preferred well-tailored women as well. Rolex girls, like Rolex boys, were better prospects for coffee, dates, sex, marriage, and romance. As Townsend and Roberts sum up: "Probably everyone would prefer a physically attractive partner who will have a successful career some day." Differences between men and women show up when they're forced to choose between cash and looks.[29]

This phenomenon doesn't just work in New York. Natives gave the Ashante Hene (their African Gold Coast king) credit for keeping 3,333 women in his harem. Montezuma II (the Aztec who met Cortés, in Mexico, in 1519) had 4,000. In Peru, Incan emperors kept "houses of virgins," crammed with 1,500 women apiece, in every principal province. In China, emperors kept *t'ang-shih,* "records made with the red brush," after the sexual contacts they made with hundreds of girls on their "correct" calendar days. In India, according to one *Jataka,* the royal seraglio in the fifth century B.C. held a record-holding 16,000. Even His Highness Maharaja Sir Bhupinder Singh, friend to Mussolini and George VI, died with 332 women in his harem—and liked to float them on ice blocks in transparent clothes.

In the past, power pretty much paralleled polygyny wherever you went. Aka, Ache, Efe, !Kung, Ifaluk, Yanomamö, Gabbra, Dogon, Mukogodo, Yomut, Kipsigis, Trinidadian, Bakkarwal, Mormon, Lancashire, Locknevi, Soknedal, Ostfriesland, Hungarian, Portuguese, Roman, medieval European, and modern English men with means (meat, land, cash, kin, or rank) have (reportedly) outreproduced men without. But do they here and now? Does, for instance, money still predict fertility?[30]

Figure 1.2. Feminine logic

For the past few years a small army in Albuquerque, New Mexico has stopped every man in the Bernalillo County Motor Vehicle Division waiting in line to get his driver's license photo. They've gotten 7,107 of those men to tell them about where and when they were born; their income, education, and religion; the number of women who had borne their children; the number of those children; and the number and fertility of their full and half sibs. They've found (and were not surprised to find) that income is *not* a good predictor of the number of a man's children. They've also found (and were somewhat surprised to find) that income fails to predict the number of a man's grandchildren. As Hilly Kaplan, Jane Lancaster, and coauthors put it, "In all cases, maximum fertility was associated with maximum number of grandchildren." Keeping fertility down in generation one has not, in this group, paid off in higher fertility in generation two. Are men in twentieth-century Albuquerque—are men in the twentieth century generally—breaking their backs to no genetic effect?[31]

They could be. But two things missing from the best of studies, like the Albuquerque study, are the "tails"—that is, the really rich, and the really poor. As Kaplan, Lancaster, and friends point out, "The elderly, disabled, institutionalized, transient, extremely poor, and criminal" are among men least likely to be seen in the MVD. And, though they don't point it out, rich men (and women) are somewhat more likely to decline being interviewed, generally.[32]

One thing we do know: Wilt Chamberlain claims to have had sex with twenty thousand women. "Yes, that's correct, *twenty thousand different ladies.* At my age, that equals out to having sex with 1.2 women a day, every day since I was fifteen years old." In his autobiography, *A View from Above,* he goes on: "I have a feeling a lot of you are saying, 'Come on, Wilt, stop all that bullshit.' " Magic Johnson might not. As he put it in *My Life,* "They say power is an aphrodisiac. Maybe so, but it's not the only one. So is success, and fame, and wealth, and winning." So are forty or fifty twenty-year-old girls waiting in a hotel lobby. Some basketball players—some extremely good, extremely rich basketball players—have had spectacular success with women. Frank Zappa had opportunities as well. Like the

"A.G.P.'s" *("assistant groupie person-ettes")* provided by the "F.G.P." *("Famous Groupie Person")* on a road tour in Dallas. Certainly, a few U.S. politicians have been promiscuous, too—though their motives for concealment, in an electoral democracy, are nontrivial.[33]

This question remains: What about the average man? For him, do mating success and reproductive success have nothing to do, anymore, with power, reputation, or cash? Not according to Daniel Pérusse. From October 1988 to April 1989, he dispersed detailed questionnaires to a representative sample of 433 French Canadian men. He found that "social status"—a composite of occupation, income, and education—*failed* to predict number of children. But he also found that social status *did* predict "number of potential conceptions" remarkably well. Men (especially single men) with more income, prestige, and power were having sex more often, and with more women.[34]

Robin Baker and Mark Bellis have found, they think, evidence of human "sperm competition." They've filmed "Kamikaze sperm"— among the 199/200 sperm estimated to be incapable of fertilizing an egg, some effectively "block" or "seek and destroy" sperm from other men; and they've measured out ejaculate sperm counts—which go up, predictably, with time spent apart from partner since last insemination. Sperm competition is a logical effect of what is generically known as "promiscuity," and known in the bird literature as "extra-pair copulations." Extra-pair conceptions are another. For the nearly four thousand women who answered Baker and Bellis's questionnaire, distributed in March and April 1989 by Britain's *Company* magazine, 5 to 10 percent of all copulations were "extra-pair"—that is, with somebody other than husbands or significant others. Baker and Bellis find that extra-pair copulations involve higher sperm retention, are more often timed to coincide with ovulation, and less often involve the use of a contraceptive device than in-pair copulations. They write, "The more fertile the female (i.e. in terms of stage of menstrual cycle and type of contraceptive), the higher the proportion of copulations that are double matings."

Blood tests for misassigned paternity in human societies yield rates ranging from a low of 1.4 percent in rural Michigan, to 2 percent among the Kalahari !Kung, to 2.3 percent in Hawaii, to 6 percent in West Middlesex, England, to 9 percent among the Venezuelan Yanomamö, to 20 to 30 percent in the "Liverpool flats." It's *probable,* though we'll never know for sure, that the men most responsible for extra-pair copulations are the men most responsible for extra-pair conceptions. These would be—to borrow Pérusse's categories—richer, more powerful, more prestigious men.[35]

DAUGHTERS AND SONS, FIRSTBORNS AND LATERBORNS

Enough about sex. Back to babies. Back, this time, to parent-offspring *cooperation.* When might parents' and babies' interests overlap most? One answer, you'll remember, is: When babies are full sibs rather than half sibs. Another answer, you'll also recall, is: When parents are rich enough to splurge on child care. A third answer is: When babies have terrific reproductive prospects.[36]

Enter, again, Bob Trivers—this time with Dan Willard, his mathematician friend. What makes a baby's reproductive prospects terrific? Among other things, Trivers and Willard say, sex. (There it is again.) A really reproductively successful son may grow up to father hundreds (thousands?) of children by hundreds (thousands?) of women. A really reproductively successful pre-*in vitro* fertilization daughter could never do as well. In other words people, like most other animals, are "polygynous"; and "polygyny" means many females mate with just one male. Given such a situation, Trivers and Willard say, "A male in good condition at the end of the period of parental investment is expected to outreproduce a sister in similar condition, while she is expected to outreproduce him if both are in poor condition." The effect is that, *other things being equal,* rich parents may be expected to favor sons; poor parents may be expected to favor daughters.[37]

Poor parents first. The Mukogodo are sheep, goat, and cattle herders living in Kenya. Until the 1920s and '30s they lived in caves, spoke a vanishing language called Yaaku, and ate wild foods and honey. They stand at the bottom of the local, regional hierarchy in wealth, status, and—this is the key issue—reproductive opportunities. Men from adjacent groups—Mu-

monyot, Digirri, and Ilng'wesi with more cattle, goats, and sheep—have more bridewealth to offer and outcompete Mukogodo men for Mukogodo wives. The result, says Lee Cronk, is that Mukogodo value their sons (whose reproductive prospects are poor) less than their daughters (whose reproductive prospects are better). They take little girls to the Catholic mission dispensary more often; daughters outsurvive sons in the first five years of life; the Mukogodo even report slightly more female than male births.[38]

Rich parents last. In England there are dukes and duchesses, lesser peers and gentry, and a great hoard (as Gregory King uncharitably put it in his *Scheme of the Income & Expence of the Several Families of England Calculated for the Year 1688*) of "labouring people, cottagers and paupers, vagrants, gipsies, thieves, beggars, &c." Once upon a time, not so long ago, dukes were much richer than gentry, who were in turn much richer than laborers. Accordingly—some evidence suggests—dukes' sons outreproduced, say, rich yeomen's sons, who outreproduced, say, cottagers' sons, by a wide margin. The upshots were patriarchy and primogeniture, says Ted Bergstrom.

The patriarchy—or, sons-favored-over-daughters—result follows straightforwardly from Trivers and Willard. Given that strictly monogamously *married* British dukes—like strictly monogamously married Incan, Aztec, Indian, and Chinese emperors—had plenty of opportunities to *mate* polygynously, they had "terrific" reproductive prospects compared with their sisters. Incan, Aztec, Indian, Chinese, and other emperors and lesser nobles kept hoards (dozens, or even hundreds) of guarded, young consorts—and (evidence suggests) often had sexual access to their subordinates' daughters and wives. English dukes, peers, and gentry kept housefuls (dozens, or even hundreds) of unmarried, late-adolescent maids—and (evidence suggests) often had sexual access to their subordinates' daughters and wives.

The primogeniture—or, firstborn-sons-favored-over-laterborn-sons—result follows from the simple law of "increasing returns to scale." To the extent, for example, that "it takes money to make money," or that "a divided estate is a conquered estate," it makes economic sense to pass on an inheritance intact. And, to the extent that rich Englishmen are reproductively successful Englishmen, it makes Darwinian sense as well. Sons of daughters, sons of laterborn sons, and sons of illegitimate children should get small shares of family estates; firstborn sons of firstborn sons should get the lion's share to themselves. In Bergstrom's words, "If expected rates of return to great fortunes are sufficiently larger than expected rates of returns to small fortunes, noblemen will maximize their reproductive value by concentrating inheritance on a single son."[39]

But when firstborns land on their parents' estates, where do laterborn sons end up? Far away, or dead. In medieval Portugal, for instance, the probability of death in war increased with birth order (firstborn sons' risk was low; fourth-born sons' risk was high); and laterborn sons were more likely to die far from home. As Jim Boone, who reviewed the *Peditura Lusitana,* a fifteenth- to sixteenth-century genealogy of the Portuguese nobility, sums up: "Younger sons who were killed were more likely to be killed much farther away, in India, than their elder brothers, who as youths participated in the nearby Moroccan campaigns, but soon returned to Portugal to take their place in society."[40]

Other younger-son revolutions have been relatively benign. They were, Frank Sulloway says, of the scientific kind. Sulloway has spent two decades reading biographies of the thousands of men (and handful of women) most responsible for "revolutions" in, among other things, science. These are the Copernicuses, the Newtons, the Einsteins, the Darwins—and scores, of course, of lesser (women and) men. Having plugged every datum he could think of into a computer, Sulloway found that just one overwhelmingly predicts revolutionary proclivity. The risk takers of the pen (abacus, lab), like the risk takers of the sword (rifle, Molotov cocktail), are overwhelmingly likely to have been laterborn.[41]

FRIENDS

Enough about babies. Enough about inheritance, other investments, and the lack thereof. Cooperation, like conflict, is not confined to kin. "Acquaintances" may not get pulled from burning buildings often; but friends help friends all the time. The essential question, for any theory of social life, must be: When? What, other than kinship or sex, makes us scratch each other's backs?[42]

Reciprocity. Darwin was cynical about that possibility. He mused, in *The Descent of Man,* that "as the reasoning powers and foresight . . . became improved, each man would soon learn that if he aided his fellow-men, he would commonly receive aid in return." Darwin thought reciprocity a "low motive" for lending somebody a hand. Bob Trivers was more upbeat. He attributed much we value in human emotion and cognition—including gratitude, sympathy, friendship, trust—to what he called "reciprocal altruism." That is, to the simple fact that one good turn deserves a return.[43]

What conditions make cooperation likely? Among other things, a big payoff, repeated interactions, and having somebody watch. Put strangers in a room and ask them to start sharing money. You'll find a surprising number of them are willing to make the first move. But, as Elizabeth Hoffman, Kevin McCabe, and Vernon Smith have found out, people are less likely to offer something if they're sure nobody's looking when they offer nothing. As Hoffman *et al.* point out, these results differ "strikingly" from experiments in which subjects are *not* carefully watched by the experimenters. They "demonstrate quite strongly the power of observability in enforcing social norms of equity and (implied) reciprocity."[44]

Cooperation didn't begin with money. Kristen Hawkes has spent the last twenty years on three continents stalking the origins of "collective action." The problem of collective action, in a nutshell, is this: "If one need not give to receive, why give?" It is, in short, *the* problem of human social life. And it has, as Hawkes's work more than anybody's makes clear, been with us for a very long time. Men have, for thousands of years or more, been bringing home big game. But every hunt raised this issue: How should the carcass get split up? The last of the big game hunters, the twentieth-century foragers studied by Hawkes and friends, share the spoils of these kills remarkably fairly. But the killing is done by remarkably few men. In Botswana, for instance, just one man, ∓ Toma, provided 78 percent of the meat for an entire !Kung bushman camp for a month; in Paraguay, among the Ache, good hunters provide up to six times as much meat as

Biography   Autobiography

Figure 1.3. Biography and autobiography

poor hunters; and in Tanzania, the range in Hadza meat acquisition rates is from 0 to about 27.25 kg/day. How do good providers get paid back? Not in kind, says Hawkes—there's no evidence of that—but maybe in other currencies. They may get more "social attention": more allies, better child care, more *mates.* In at least one of these groups, the Ache, good hunters are reported to have sex with more (if marginally more) women, and their children are more likely (if marginally more likely) to survive.[45]

There is another, sinister, solution to the collective action problem. Maybe good hunters are being coerced. The critical point is the ratio of effort expended to genes produced. If good hunters work no harder than necessary to feed themselves *and* their dependents—including their legitimate and illegitimate children—then there is no collective action problem. If, on the other hand, the extra food they bring in is feeding *somebody else's* dependents, then good hunters' hands may be forced. Big men (men with more allies, or strong men) may be getting little men (men with fewer allies, or weak men) to do their big game hunting for them. To the extent that good hunters' fitness returns (which appear to be marginal) fail to keep pace with their foraging returns (which appear to be

great), the solution to the problem of collective action may be exploitation.

HOSTILE FORCES

Enough is enough. Having begun (at the beginning) with conception, and got through politics and sex, we end (at the end) with death. Why do we die? Can natural selection account for death as well as birth? Of course.

When poorly provisioned mothers or fathers, indifferent acquaintances, or competitors for symmetrical mates don't get us, we can still get hit by falling rocks or devoured by predators or parasites. Parasites get all of us sooner or later. And a few simple, selective pressures determine how lethal or benign their assult will be. Paul Ewald, by taking a selectionist's-eye-view of the spread of parasite genes, has revolutionized the study of infectious disease. The severity of a pathogen's attack has to do with how the pathogen is borne. When parasites can replicate only by moving directly from host to host, their genetic fate is completely contingent on their host's mobility. A severely debilitated, bedridden body is unlikely to come in contact with lots of potential new carriers. In this case it makes sense for the pathogen to be less severe:

give host a runny nose, but don't lay him low. When, on the other hand, parasites can replicate through "vectors"—when they're carried by insects, say, or contaminated water—they lose less by knocking their hosts out flat. Clean up the water, says Ewald, and put screens on the windows, and the pathogens responsible for cholera and malaria will evolve to be more benign.[46]

Ewald's success with parasites has, in part, prompted Paul Turke to look at how hosts fight back. He's used evolutionary theory to unravel some of the immune system's complexity. Immune systems are involved in perpetual arms races. Their goal is to distinguish "self" from "non-self" while parasites try, in turn, to break into the system by mimicking hosts. To this end the immune system's T cells are screened by the thymus, which spares those adept at distinguishing "self" from "non-self" but induces inept cells to undergo apoptosis, a programmed death. This process, too, can be subverted—by parasites that manage to contaminate the thymus. Turke suggests that hosts have fought back by making T cells long-lived, and by doing the screening very early, even in utero, while still under the protection of mother's immune system. Having done its job, soon after the first year of life, the thymus begins "inexorably and rapidly" to involute—that is, to senesce. To Turke, "Thymic involution is proposed to be an undesirable, unavoidable consequence of strong selection for enhanced early thymic function."[47]

Even if we get lucky—and manage to survive attacks by parasites, predators, family members, and falling rocks—we will still slowly, but surely, wind down and die. Why? George Williams solved this last, but not least, problem. Senescence—the inevitable, intrinsic decline we all endure with age—is an unfortunate effect of extrinsic mortality rates. Because, again, life is fraught with risks—because predators, parasites, floods, famines, and other "hostile forces" must in the end cause death—any gene that spurs reproduction early in life will have an edge over a gene that spurs reproduction later on. The opposite should hold for genes with bad side effects; they should add up late in life and be culled early. The cumulative effect should be vigor in youth and decline with age. That prediction is borne out, among other things, by two facts. First, in species with high

adult death rates due to "hostile forces," senescence is generally quick. As Williams says, "Active adult insects have mortality rates of the order of ten percent per day, and maximum longevity is of the order of a few weeks. Mortality rates of adult man in extremely primitive situations probably never averaged more than ten percent a year, and man's maximum longevity may include as many years as that of the insects includes days." Second, in the risk-taking sex (usually male) senescence is generally faster than in the risk-averse (usually female) sex. Thus, "Throughout the animal kingdom it is a general rule that females are longer-lived than males."[48]

THE BEGINNING

A lot about life is nasty. There are absent fathers, wicked stepmothers, lopsided bodies, tight belts, disinherited children, and defectors. But they stand out in stark relief against a lot we take for granted. There are—and there always have been—fathers who stay up carrying crying babies all night, mothers whose hearts swell with love and pride every time they look at their daughters and sons, beautiful people, rewards for hard work, payoffs for risk taking and exchange wherever we look. We dwell on the nasty, in part, because we want to fix it.[49]

Fixing it will necessitate figuring it out. There have been more theories than any of us cares to remember about what people do and who people are. A hundred-odd years ago, Darwin came up with a good one. It's so good it has, in the last seventeen years, shed new light on human anatomy, physiology, emotions, cognition, and interaction. Can we get rid of preeclampsia? Stress? Child neglect? Infertility? Cholera and malaria? Social injustice? We can, if we can figure them out. Knowledge is power. And this theory—Darwin's theory—is the best route to knowledge we've got.

Darwin—the well-loved son of a successful doctor, husband of a Wedgewood heiress, and father of seven loving, surviving children—was sure the good outweighs the bad. In his *Autobiography,* written at the end of a wonderful life, he remarked: "According to my judgment happiness decidedly prevails, though this would be very difficult to prove." He went on:

Pain or suffering of any kind, if long continued, causes depression and lessens the power of action; yet it is well adapted to make a creature guard itself against any great or sudden evil. Pleasurable sensations, on the other hand may be long continued without any depressing effect; on the contrary they stimulate the whole system to increased action. Hence it has come to pass that most or all sentient beings have been developed in such a manner through natural selection that pleasurable sensations serve as their habitual guides.[50]

Whether or not Darwin was right about happiness, he was almost certainly right about natural selection. May his theory make more pleasurable sensations possible, and help put an end to suffering and pain.

NOTES

1. Epigraphs are from Kundera (1984:1); Lessing (1952:134–35); and Dawkins (1995:133).

2. Parker and Stuart (1976); Fricke and Fricke (1977); Møller (1994); Harcourt et al. (1981).

3. Darwin (1859, quote on p. 13). Recent works on geographic and geological distributions as products of natural selection include Grant (1986) and Weiner (1994); Gould (1989) and Wright (1990).

4. This is the gene's-eye-view of selection. Its central players have been Ronald Fisher, who in large part initiated it; George Williams, William Hamilton, and Robert Trivers, who developed it; and Richard Dawkins, who best advocated it. Key works include Fisher (1958); Williams (1957, 1966a, 1966b, 1975, 1992, 1996); Williams and Williams (1957); Hamilton (1963, 1964, 1966, 1967, 1971, 1972, 1980, 1996a, 1996b); Axelrod and Hamilton (1981); Axelrod (1984); Hamilton, Axelrod, and Tanese (1990); Hamilton and Zuk (1982); Trivers (1971, 1972, 1974); Trivers and Willard (1973); and Dawkins (1976, 1982, 1986, 1989, 1995). Cronin (1991) is a very nice history of science.

5. Several reviews of adaptationist approaches to human behavior have appeared in recent years, including Daly and Wilson (1983); Gray (1985); Harpending, Rogers, and Draper (1987); Betzig (1988a); Badcock (1991); Borgerhoff Mulder (1991); Cronk (1991a); Smith (1992a, 1992b); Voland (1993); Dahl (1994); Hippel (1994); Nielsen (1994); Buss (1995a, 1995b); and Thornhill and Gangestad (1995); collections of review essays include Maxwell (1991); Smith and Winterhalder (1992); and Crawford and Krebs (1996); new popular books include Batten (1992); Fisher (1992); Ridley (1994, 1996); Small (1995); and Wright (1994). Important essays on the study of adaptation include Tinbergen (1963); Mayr (1983); and Reeve and Sherman (1993).

6. Trivers (1974) is the original paper on parent-offspring conflict. Much of "life history theory" takes off in this mode. See Stearns (1992) and Charnov (1993) for recent reviews.

7. Haig (1993, quote on p. 496). On "giving birth to bigger babies": Evidence that mothers with high glucose levels have heavier birthweight babies is relatively solid; evidence that mothers with high blood pressure have heavier birthweight babies, in the absence of preeclampsia, is relatively tentative.

8. Ellison (1994a, 1996) and Wood (1994) are important reviews. Original work in "human reproductive ecology" includes Ellison, Peacock, and Lager (1989); Leslie and Fry (1989); Bailey et al. (1992); Panter-Brick (1991); Panter-Brick, Lotstein and Ellison (1993); Becker, Chowdhury, and Leridon (1986); and Jasienska and Ellison (1993), which show that fertility and/or ovarian function improve with ecology in Africa, Nepal, Bangladesh and rural Poland; and Prentice et al. (1983); Wood et al. (1985); Jones (1988); and Worthman et al. (1993), which link lactation and birth spacing to mothers' nutritional status. Male reproductive ecology has been studied by Campbell and Leslie (1995) and Bribiescas (1996). Other studies have shown that mothers in bad circumstances are forced to scrimp on child care after conception or birth. These include Bugos and McCarthy's (1984) finding that infanticide among Bolivan foragers almost always takes place after the child's father has deserted the mother, and Essock-Vitale and McGuire's (1985a) and Hill and Low's (1992) demonstrations that abortion is more common among single women.

9. Haig (1994, quote on p. 1633). Haig (personal communication) notes that "this of course is highly speculative at the moment." Alternatives include "the immunological hypothesis" and "the possibility that we are looking at maternal (rather than paternal) effects. The one I hear most commonly is that mothers near the beginning of relationships are more 'stressed.'"

10. Profet (1992, quote on p. 327, see also Profet 1995). Profet has extended her theory that toxin elimination is an adaptation to allergy (Profet 1991) and menstruation (Profet 1993); see Strassmann (1996a) for another view on the function of menstruation. This short jaunt through parent-offspring conflict has served to introduce the reader to the new field of "Darwinian medicine." Applications have already been made to cancer (Eaton et al. 1994); allergy (Profet 1991); immunology (Turke 1996b); aging (Rose 1991); fever (Kluger 1979); stress (Sapolsky 1994; Flinn and England 1995, 1996, and Flinn 1996); psychiatry (Wenegrat 1990; McGuire et al., 1992; McGuire and Triosi 1996); and infectious disease (Ewald 1980, 1994a, 1994b; Ander-

son and May 1991)—besides infertility and pregnancy. Important reviews of Darwinian medicine include Eaton, Shostak, and Konner (1988) and Nesse and Williams (1994).

11. Hamilton (1963, 1964). Important updates include West-Eberhard (1975) and Grafen (1984).

12. Burnstein, Crandall, and Kitayama (1994).

13. Flinn and England (1995, quote on p. 19). Other studies link kinship to proximity (Chagnon 1979b, 1980b, 1981; Hames 1979; Hurd 1983); child care (Hames 1987); adoption (Silk 1980, 1987a, 1990); abortion legislation (Betzig and Lombardo 1992); suicide (deCatanzaro 1980, 1981, 1991, 1995); child abuse and neglect (Daly and Wilson 1981a, 1985, 1988b; Lennington 1981; Lightcap, Kurland and Burgess 1982; Flinn 1988c; Malkin and Lamb 1994); incest (Van den Berghe and Mesher 1980); lying (Fredlund 1984); ax fighting (Chagnon and Bugos 1979); homicide (Daly and Wilson 1988b; Johnson and Johnson 1991; Dunbar, Clark, and Hurst 1994); fantasies about homicide (Kenrick and Sheets 1993); food sharing (Kaplan et al. 1984, Kaplan and Hill 1985a; Hames 1996, Betzig and Turke 1986a, Betzig 1988b); labor sharing (Hawkes 1983; Hames 1987; Berté 1988); exchanges of favors (Essock-Vitale and McGuire 1980, 1985b; Hager 1992; Euler and Weitzel 1996); wealth flows (Turke 1988, 1989; Hawkes, O'Connell, and Blurton Jones 1989; Hurtado et al. 1992; Kaplan 1994); and effects on survival, mating, and fertility (Chagnon 1982; Faux and Miller 1984; Turke and Betzig 1985; Turke 1988; Betzig, Harrigan, and Turke 1989; Flinn 1986, 1988a; Hewlett 1988; Hill and Hurtado 1991; Mace 1996a). Hughes (1988) is a thoughtful review.

14. Flinn and England (1996); see also Flinn (1996); Flinn and England (1995); and Flinn et al. (1996).

15. Darwin (1871), quote on pp. 571, 581. For more recent accounts of the evolution of gamete dimorphism, see Parker, Baker, and Smith (1972) and Hurst (1990).

16. Trivers (1972, quote on p. 55). Updates include Clutton-Brock and Vincent (1991); reviews include Trivers (1985) and Clutton-Brock (1991).

17. Hamilton (1980); Tooby (1982); Hamilton and Zuk (1982); Hamilton, Axelrod, and Tanese (1990). The "good genes" version of sexual selection has been updated by Møller and Pomiankowski (1993) and Johnstone (1994). Zuk (1992) and Watson and Thornhill (1994) are recent reviews.

18. Gangestad, Thornhill, and Yeo (1993) on symmetry and attractiveness in New Mexicans; Grammer and Thornhill (1994) on symmetry and attractiveness in Germans; Møller, Soler, and Thornhill (1995, quote on p. 208) on breasts; Thornhill and Gangestad (1994) on symmetry and promiscuity—Gangestad and Thornhill (1995) replicates this result for men but not for women; Gangestad and Thornhill (1996a) on symmetry and infidelity. Gangestad and Thornhill (1995) find men with more mass report more promiscuity; and Thornhill, Gangestad, and Comer (1996) find mates of more massive men report more frequent orgasms. Review in Gangestad and Thornhill (1996b). Related results include Low's (1990a) finding that, across cultures, polygyny correlates with parasite loads; Gangestad and Buss's (1993) finding that, across cultures, physical attractiveness is valued more where parasite loads are high; Singh's (1995a) replication of the finding that men like symmetrical breasts; a study by Wedekind et al. (1995) showing that women prefer the smell of dirty T-shirts worn by MHC dissimilar men (see also Hanschu 1996); and Singh's (1996) result showing that mother's complications in pregnancy significantly predict daughter's fluctuating asymmetry. Townsend and Levy (1990a, 1990b) find both women and men value attractiveness more in a lover than in a spouse.

19. Gangestad and Thornhill (1995) and Manning (1995) on mass and symmetry.

20. Singh (1993; see also 1993b, 1994, 1995a, Singh and Luis 1995, Singh and Young 1995); many of these studies replicate this result on samples of men of various ethnicities and ages. Anderson et al. (1992) have found, among other things, that fatter women are more attractive in food-starved cultures.

21. Singh (1995b).

22. Fisher (1958) and Williams (1966).

23. Kenrick and Keefe (1992). Related results include Buss and Barnes's (1986; see also Buss 1989b, 1994) and Feingold's (1990, 1991) findings that men rate attractiveness higher than women; Thornhill and Thornhill's (1990a) findings that young women are more traumatized by rape; Studd and Gattiker's (1991) report that young women report sexual harassment more often; Thiessen, Young, and Burroughs's (1993), Wiederman's (1993), and Greenlees and McGrew's (1994) lonely hearts ads surveys showing men more often seek attractiveness and women more often offer it; Bailey et al.'s (1994) finding that, regardless of sexual orientation (straight or gay), men rate youth in a mate more highly than women; and Pérusse's (1994) finding that young, single Canadian women report significantly more sex partners per year than older, single Canadian women. Cunningham (1986), Jankowiak, Hill, and Donovan (1992), Johnston and Franklin (1993), Jones and Hill (1993), Cunningham et al. (1995), and Jones (1995) show men prefer "neotenous" female faces (compare Cunningham, Barbee, and Pike, 1990, who find women prefer "neotenous" features in men). See also Symons (1979); Buss (1994); and Fisher (1989, 1992).

24. On menstrual taboos, see Strassmann (1992). On numbers of fertile cycles, see Short (1976a, also Strassmann 1992, 1996a). On concealed ovulation, see Alexander and Noonan (1979); Strassmann (1981); Turke (1984); Knight (1991), and Manning et al. (1996).

25. See Strassmann (1992, 1996a).

26. Buss et al. (1992). A number of studies have looked at the "confidence of paternity" problem. They include cross-cultural tests by Gaulin and Schlegel (1980), Flinn (1981), and Hartung (1985) showing husbands with little to invest have wives inclined to be promiscuous; comparative evidence reviewed by Dickemann (1981) on footbinding, veiling, infibulation, and other abominations as confidence of paternity mechanisms; studies of newly delivered couples finding babies are more commonly said to resemble fathers (especially newlywed fathers) than mothers (Daly and Wilson 1982; Regalski and Gaulin 1993); North American homicide studies and cross-cultural studies by Daly and Wilson (Daly, Wilson, and Weghorst 1982; Daly and Wilson 1988b) showing sexual jealousy to be the leading motive in killing a spouse; field studies by Flinn (1987, 1988b) showing mate and daughter guarding more common for fecundable women; an experimental study by Hill, Nocks, and Gardner (1987) showing men prefer scantily clothed mistresses and well-clothed wives; surveys by Buss (1988a, 1988b, 1989, 1991, 1994; Buss and Dedden 1990) suggesting women attract and keep mates by, for instance, lacking sexual experience, being loyal, and "playing hard to get"; surveys by Ellis and Symons (1990) showing male sexual fantasies to involve many, many more partners than female sexual fantasies; a cross-cultural study by Betzig (1989a) showing wife's adultery to be the most common cause of divorce; surveys by Symons and Ellis (1989), Buss and Schmitt (1993), and Kenrick et al. (1993) showing women want fewer partners, better-known partners, and fewer anonymous partners than men; a survey by Simpson, Gangestad, and Lerma (1990) showing that both men and women are less attracted to members of the opposite sex when they're already involved in relationships; field and comparative studies by Strassmann (1992, 1995b) suggesting menstrual hut visits assure paternity; interview studies by Cashdan (1993; see also Cashdan 1995) suggesting that women expecting low PI from their mates are more likely to wear sexy clothes and to have frequent sex; "lonely hearts" ads studies by Thiessen, Young, and Burroughs (1993), Wiederman (1993), and Greenlees and McGrew (1994) showing men more than women want casual sex; a survey by Wiederman and Allgeier (1993) showing men more than women are upset by their partner's one-night-stands; Einon's (1994) finding that women consistently report dramatically fewer sex partners than men; Greer and Buss's (1994) report that women are shy in promoting sexual encounters; a survey by Geary et al. (1995) showing, again, that U.S. and Chinese men report more sexual jealousy than women; and Campbell's (1995) finding that young women compete—sometimes physically—to defend themselves against accusations of promiscuity.

27. See Dawkins (1989, 151–53) on the "battle of the sexes"; see, more generally, Maynard Smith and Price (1973) on evolutionarily stable strategies.

28. See Gangestad and Simpson (1990, quote on p. 71); Simpson and Gangestad (1991); Gangestad et al. (1992); Simpson and Gangestad (1992); and Simpson, Gangestad, and Biek (1993). See Fisher (1958) and Pomiankowski, Iwasa, and Nee (1991) on "sexy" sons. Others involved in the budding business of the evolution of personality differences include Draper and Harpending (1982); MacDonald (1988); Draper and Belsky (1990); Belsky, Steinberg, and Draper (1991); and Mealey (1995).

29. Townsend and Levy (1990a); Townsend and Roberts (1993, quote on p. 513; see also Townsend 1989, 1993). In another study, Townsend and Levy (1990b) got similar results when subjects were asked how much or little they liked photographs paired with doctor/high school teacher/waiter biographical texts. Other studies relating men's status to mating success include Low's (1979) cross-cultural study showing men advertise wealth by ornamenting their wives; Buss and Barnes's (1986; see also Buss 1994) survey showing women rate a mate's earning capacity and ambition higher than men; Flinn and Low's (1986) cross-cultural study showing men pay directly for wives—for example, by brideprice—where inheritance is rare, and that they exchange women directly—for example, by cross-cousin marriage—where resources of any kind are scarce; Sadalla, Kenrick, and Vershure's (1987) videotapes showing women more than men want dominant mates; questionnaires suggesting men attract and keep mates by, for instance, having good financial prospects and buying gifts (Buss 1988a, 1988b, 1989, 1991, 1994; Buss and Dedden 1990; Tooke and Camire 1991; Wiederman and Allgeier 1992; B. Ellis 1995; Landolt, Lalumiére, and Quinsey 1995); Chagnon's (1988b) study showing Yanomamö men with high rank manipulate kinship categories so as to call more women sexually accessible "wives;" Thornhill's (1989, 1990, 1991) comparative studies showing men and women use inbreeding to concentrate wealth; Low's (1989) comparative study linking polygyny to status-striving in sons; Betzig's (1989) finding that men are divorced more than women for failing to provide; a survey by Kenrick et al. (1990) showing girls are choosier about partners' status than boys; Gaulin and Boster's (1990) comparative study linking stratification to dowry; Manson and Wrangham's (1991) comparative report that foragers say they fight for resources where they don't say they fight directly for women; Feingold's (1992) meta-analysis showing women weigh mates' status, ambitiousness, character, and intelligence more highly than men; Kenrick et al.'s (1993) questionnaires showing that, regardless of relationship duration, women value status and dominance more than men; Thiessen, Young, and Burroughs's (1993), Wiederman's (1993), and Greenlees and McGrew's (1994) lonely hearts ads studies showing women seek and men offer money; Mazur, Halpern, and Udry's (1994) ques-

tionnaire study showing dominant-looking teenage boys report more coital activity; Pérusse's (1994) survey showing high status predicts frequency of simultaneous partners and number of lifetime partners among Canadian men; Scheib's (1994) survey showing women select for wealth and good character even in sperm donors; Walters and Crawford's (1994) questionnaires showing status and resource advertisement are thought more effective in male-male than in female-female competition; Jensen-Campbell, Graziano, and West's (1995) survey showing women find dominant men attractive *as long as* they are agreeable ("nice guys"), too; Singh's (1995a) survey showing women prefer men with means, even when men's waist-to-hip ratio is controlled; and a survey by Townsend, Kline, and Wasserman (1995; see also Townsend 1987, 1995, and Townsend and Wasserman 1996a, 1996b) showing that, even among men and women high in "sociosexual orientation," women more than men want compensation. Sexual dimorphism in height (Alexander et al. 1979; Gray and Wolfe 1980; Gaulin and Boster 1985); risk-taking (Wilson and Daly 1985; Clarke and Low 1992; cf. Campbell 1995); and spatial ability (Gaulin and Hoffmann 1988; but see Silverman and Eals 1992; Silverman and Phillips 1993; Eals and Silverman 1994) have been explained as effects of greater male than female competition for mates. Clutton-Brock (1988) and L. Ellis (1995) are good cross-species reviews.

30. On the Ashante Hene-Bhupinder Singh: Betzig (1982, 1986, 1993). On Aka-Mormons: Hewlett (1988; see also Walker and Hewlett 1990) on Central African Republic Aka foragers; Kaplan and Hill (1985b) and Hill and Hurtado (1996) on Paraguayan Aché foragers; Bailey (1991) on Zairean Efe foragers; Pennington and Harpending (1993) on Kalahari !Kung foragers; Turke and Betzig (1985; also Betzig 1988b) on Ifaluk fishermen and taro farmers; Chagnon (1980b, 1988a, also Chagnon, Flinn and Melancon 1979) on Yanomamö hunters and small farmers; Mace (1996a, 1996b) on Kenyan Gabbra pastoralists; Strassmann (1996c) on Malian Dogon farmers; Cronk (1991b) on Kenyan Mukogodo pastoralists; Irons (1979a) on Iranian Yomut pastoralists; Borgerhoff Mulder (1987a, 1987b, 1988e, 1990; see also Borgerhoff Mulder 1988a, 1988c, 1995, 1996) on Kenyan Kipsigis pastoralists; Flinn (1986) on Caribbean farmers; Casimir and Rao (1995) on Indian Bakkarwal; Faux and Miller (1984) and Mealey (1985) on Utah Mormons; Hughes (1986) on eighteenth-century Lancashire farmers; Low (1991a) and Low and Clarke (1992; see also Forsberg and Tullberg 1995) on nineteenth-century Swedish farmers; Røskaft, Wara, and Viken (1992) on eighteenth- to twentieth-century Norwegian farmers; Voland (1990; see also Voland 1988) on eighteenth- and nineteenth-century Krümmhorn farmers; Bereczkei and Csanaky (1996) on modern Hungarians; Boone (1986) on sixteenth- to eighteenth-century elite Portuguese; and Betzig (1992c, 1995, 1996a) on imperial Romans, medieval Europeans, and modern Englishmen. Borgerhoff Mulder (1989c); Chisholm and Burbank (1991); Josephson (1993); and Hames (1996) deal with the "polygyny threshold" problem. Other comparative studies correlating wealth or rank with mating or reproductive success include Dickemann (1979a); van den Berghe (1979); and Hill (1984). Essock-Vitale (1984); Blurton Jones (1986, 1987a); Borgerhoff Mulder (1987b); Voland and Engel (1989, 1990); Strassmann (1996c); and Hill and Hurtado (1996) focus on wealth and fertility in women.

31. Kaplan et al. (1996, quote on p. 7); Kaplan (1996); see also Vining (1986). Bentley, Goldberg, and Jasienska (1993) have determined that, in traditional societies, forgers' and horticulturalists' fertility is lower, on average, than fertility among agriculturalists; that is, higher fertility is associated with the intensification of agriculture. Rogers (1990, 1996) has modeled the evolution of propensities to maximize fertility versus propensities to maximize wealth. That wealth and fertility no longer correlate positively is—to many economists, demographers, and others—an established conclusion. See Becker (1981); Bulatao and Lee (1983); and Turke (1990b) for reviews.

32. Kaplan et al. (1996). On sampling bias by status see, for example, Groves (1989).

33. Chamberlain (1991, 251); Johnson (1992, 277); Zappa (1989, 211); Betzig and Weber (1993).

34. Pérusse (1993).

35. Baker and Bellis (1988, 1989, 1993a, 1993b, 1995, quote on p. 198); and Bellis and Baker (1990). Oddly enough, Baker and Bellis (1995, 196) report EPCs more common among *older* women with *more* children. Also interesting are Grammer, Dittami, and Fischmann's (1994; also Grammer 1993a, 1993b) finding that German girls in a discotheque with higher estradiol levels in their saliva expose more skin; from this they conclude that "skin display is a display for active female choice" and "silent ovulation allows active female choice and might promote sperm competition." See Parker (1970) on sperm competition in general and R.L. Smith (1984) on sperm competition in humans. On the bird literature, Birkhead and Møller (1992) is a good review.

36. On reproductive prospects irrespective of sex: Daly and Wilson (1981a); Lightcap, Kurland, and Burgess (1982); Littlefield and Rushton (1986); Crawford, Salter, and Lang (1989); Hrdy (1992); Mann (1992); and Burnstein, Crandall, and Kitayama (1994).

37. Trivers and Willard (1973). Updates include Charnov (1982); Frank (1990); and Haig (1992).

38. Cronk (1989b). Sex allocation has been studied in Venezuelan Yanomamö (Chagnon, Flinn, and Melancon 1979), eighteenth- to nineteenth-century Germans (Voland 1984); Micronesian Ifalukese (Betzig and Turke 1986b), sixteenth- to eighteenth-century elite Portuguese (Boone, 1986); Kenyan Kipsigis (Borgerhoff Mul-

der 1988d); the Kalahari !Kung (Anderson and Crawford 1993); Kenyan Gabbra (Mace 1996c); Inuit eskimos (Smith and Smith 1994; Smith 1995); twentieth-century Canada (Smith, Kish, and Crawford 1987); and the twentieth-century United States (Mealey and Mackey 1990; Gaulin and Robbins 1991; Judge and Hrdy 1992a; Betzig and Weber 1995). Dickemann (1979b); Hartung (1976, 1982); Müller (1991); and Cowlishaw and Mace (1996) have done comparative studies. Hrdy (1987) and Sieff (1990) are good critical reviews.

39. Bergstrom (1994, quote on p. 20). On polygyny in modern British society, see Betzig (1996a); Gregory King's figures are reprinted in Laslett (1984). Compare Betzig (1992b, 1993, 1995); Hrdy and Judge (1993); and Ellison (1994b) on primogeniture.

40. Boone (1986, 1988a, quote on pp. 210–11).

41. Sulloway (1996). Newton and Einstein were firstborns. So am I.

42. This has traditionally been the stuff of economics. The new question, for the evolutionist, is currency. What's being maximized—money, mates, or (in the long run) reproductive success? Exciting new work bridging the gap between evolution and economics includes Becker (1976); Hirshleifer (1977, 1978, 1995); Maynard Smith (1982); Frank (1988); Bergstrom (1995); Bergstrom and Stark (1993); Rogers (1994); and Binmore (1994).

43. Darwin (1871, 499); Trivers (1971). Updates include Axelrod and Hamilton (1981); Stephens, Nishimura, and Toyer (1995); Connor (1995); and Dugatkin (1996).

44. Hoffman, McCabe, and Smith (1996a, quote on p. 35; see also Hoffman et al. 1994; Hoffman, McCabe, and Smith 1996b; and Smith 1994). This work—though done by economists—represents a sample of the thrilling new study of evolution and cognition. Other pioneering work includes Cosmides (1989; also Cosmides and Tooby 1989, 1992); Gazzaniga (1992); Orians and Heerwagen (1992); Pinker (1994, 1996); Gigerenzer and Hug (1995); Hauser (1996); Mealey et al. (1996); Miller (1996a); and Wang (1996, also Wang and Johnston 1993, 1996). Critiques include Davies, Fetzer, and Foster (1995).

45. Hawkes (1993, quote on p. 346); see also Hawkes (1990, 1991, 1992); Hawkes et al. (1985); and Hawkes, O'Connell, and Blurton Jones (1991). On the mating and reproductive success of Aché hunters, see Kaplan and Hill (1985b) and Hill and Hurtado (1996). The question: Is sharing an adaptation? was preceded by the question: Is foraging an adaptation? Work on optimal foraging includes O'Connell and Hawkes (1981, 1984) on Alyawara plant use; Winterhalder (1981; also Winterhalder et al. 1988) on Cree hunting and gathering; Hames and Vickers (1982) on Amazon hunting; E.A. Smith (1985, 1991) on Inuit hunting; Hawkes, Hill, Hurtado, Kaplan, and O'Connell on Ache hunting and gathering (Hawkes, Hill, and O'Connell 1988; Hill 1988; Hill and Hawkes 1983; Hill and Kaplan 1988; Hill, et al. 1987; Kaplan, Hill, and Hurtado 1990); Beckerman (1983) on Bari hunting and fishing; Keegan (1986) on Machigeuenga forager-horticulturalists; Kuchikura (1988) on Bari blowpipe hunting; Whitehead and Hope (1991) on Galapagos off-island whaling; Alvard (1993, 1995) on Piro hunting; and Bliege Bird and Bird (1996) and Bird and Bliege Bird (1996) on Meriam foraging and sharing. Cronk (1989a) and Mace (1993a, 1993b) focus on subsistence change; Cashdan (1994) has argued for an adaptive "sensitive period" in food learning in children. Kaplan and Hill (1992) is a good review. Classic works on optimal foraging include Charnov (1976) and Stephens and Krebs (1986).

46. Ewald (1980, 1994a, 1994b).

47. Turke (1996b). For a related theory of the evolution of the human lifespan, see Turke (1996a).

48. Williams (1957, quotes on pp. 404, 406). By the way, cooperation and conflict don't stop at the organismic level. Important work on intragenomic conflict includes Cosmides and Tooby (1981) and Hurst (1992). The standard works on levels of selection are Williams's great 1966 and 1992 books.

49. I've restricted this review to empirical tests. As a result, I've left out a couple of large, largely nonempirical, literatures. One covers culture. See, for example, Alexander (1979); Barkow (1989); Dawkins (1989); Cavalli-Sforza and Feldman (1981); Pulliam and Dunford (1981); Lumsden and Wilson (1981, 1982); Boyd and Richerson (1985); Cosmides and Tooby (1987); Tooby and Cosmides (1989, 1992); Durham (1991); Aunger (1994, 1995, 1996); Cronk (1995); Goodenough and Dawkins (1994); Goodenough (1995); and Leland, Kumm, and Feldman (1995). I, personally, find "culture" unnecessary. Another covers ethics. See, for example, Wilson (1975, 1978); Ruse (1982, 1995); Humphrey (1983); Alexander (1987); Masters (1987); Richards (1987); Tiger (1987); Williams (1989); Degler (1991); Irons (1991, 1996); Gibbard (1992); Holcomb (1993); Cronk (1994); Niteki and Nitecki (1994); Bradie (1995); Dennett (1995); Hurd (1995); and Roston (1995). I, personally, find "ethics" a matter of taste. Also interesting is the new evolutionary literary criticism; see, for example, Nesse (1995) and Carroll (1995).

50. Darwin (1887/1983, 51–52). Thanks to Theresa Duda of the University of Michigan Museum of Zoology for help with faxing, posting, and library services; and to Don Blaine, archivist extraordinaire, for finding the Abner Dean cartoons.

I
STUDIES OF TRADITIONAL SOCIETIES

2
Yanomamö Dreams and Starling Payloads: The Logic of Optimality

ALEX KACELNIK
JOHN R. KREBS

A HUNTING EXPEDITION

Picture this scene. A band of fierce-looking Yanomamö Indians marches through the jungle in a revenge expedition against a distant village. They started with high spirits, but fear mounts as they walk, and sometime before reaching their destination they turn back because somebody had a bad dream. What aspect of this enterprise is dictated by the maximization of inclusive fitness?

Well, calling the whole thing off possibly was a good thing, since as the saying goes, *Il soldato che fugge serve per un'altra volta.* There is some difficulty, however, in maintaining that starting the ill-fated march in the first place had been a good idea. The would-be warriors have lost six days that could have been used hunting or perhaps seeking sexual partners, and have ended with lower self-esteem and sore feet. To judge if what they did was the most advantageous behavior given the available options at the time is not easy, since on one hand fear had good reason to be selected for, and on the other fear does not always win: sometimes they go on to kill those that have imposed damage on their kin in the past, inhibiting further interference with the avengers' relatives in the future and earning social standing. A rigorous analysis of the adaptive value of this behavior would have to consider the universe of possibilities for what could have been done in the time devoted to this behavior (the "lost opportunity"). No mean task.

This example, taken from Chagnon's de-scription of Yanomamös' cultural practices (Chagnon 1992), illustrates the difficulties of evolutionary analysis of the behavior of humans and other animals. Humans do certain things that increase their fitness (such as engaging in sexual intercourse or restraining from eating their offspring) and others that appear to lower fitness (such as using birth control, ceasing ovulation thirty years before other physiological functions senesce, or remaining celibate to satisfy imaginary deities). Many differences among populations are hard to reconcile with an exclusively fitness-maximizing view. Take incest legislation, for instance. In Scotland it is illegal for a woman to have sexual intercourse with her great-grandson or with her former adoptive son (Incest and Related Offences Act [Scotland] 1986), while in England the law permits these presumably infrequent events if both parties are consenting adults (English Sexual Offences Act 1956). Both legal systems might have a kernel of genetic reasonableness, but the difference between these two practices can hardly be explained by the ecological conditions prevalent on the two sides of Hadrian's Wall. Similarly, religiously inspired celibacy may have a kernel of fitness-maximizing, kin-selected reasonableness in its origin, if once celibacy conferred exceptional fecundity on a priest's relatives, but it appears far-fetched to assume that the current pope or Mother Theresa might score as exceptionally high achievers in that front.

These observations pose a challenge for the development of evolutionary accounts of human behavior, and, we realize, sound very different from the upbeat review of evolutionary insights into human behavior of our editor (chapter 1, this volume). Indeed, far from being a coherent lot, we may all think rather differently about our own work. Readers should not be surprised to find lively epistemological differences among evolutionary biologists who do similar work. Most people (including scientists but perhaps not philosophers) are better at doing than they are at understanding or explaining what they do. Reflections about research programs are usually made years after the research programs take shape, and only after reflecting on what one and one's colleagues have done it is possible to say, "Gosh, *that* is what we were trying to do!" and to judge the degree of achievement. As animal behaviorists, at various stages we have reexamined our own past research and have been alternately dazzled by the proliferation of successes or disappointed by the apparent triviality or ephemerality of past findings. We intend to share some of these reflections comparing it with human evolutionary work.

The collection of field studies of traditional societies brought together in this section belongs in a research program whose core is linking evolutionary optimality to human culture and individual decision making. The boundaries of this research fade into a variety of disciplines, including ecology, ethology, psychology, anthropology, and even clinical medical research. Optimality comes into the picture as the method to infer or predict properties of organisms from the premise that natural selection has shaped the reality one sees today. We will illustrate our commentary and critique using experiences from our own research program in optimal foraging theory (OFT), starting by a brief glance at OFT itself. We pose, and suggest answers, to four general questions about the program of research in OFT. These four questions could equally be asked of any research program in which neo-Darwinian, adaptationist thinking has been applied.

1. *What is being tested?* Although optimality models use an evolutionary logic, they are not constructed to test the hypothesis that evolution has occurred. Nor do individual studies test the principle of making predictions about behavior using the notion of "design by natural selec-

tion." Instead, optimality models (or what might be called the *classical optimality program*) are aimed at testing very specific hypotheses underlining very specific explanatory models.

Let us briefly review the concept of a specific optimality model. We (and, of course, many others) have used various conceptualizations of optimal foraging models. In one, models are said to be formed by two hypotheses, one about currency and the other about constraints, with the addition of an identified decision variable (Stephens and Krebs 1986). A subject is expected to maximize the currency (which reflects Darwinian fitness) by modulating the decision variable, limited by constraints. Here we will follow an equivalent, more explicit concept (Kacelnik and Cuthill 1987), which has models as sets of three hypotheses, one about the relation between a measurable quantity (the currency) and fitness, another about the strategy set (the range of possible behaviors), and a third one about the feedback function, namely, a function determining the value of the currency resulting from each possible behavior. It is easy to see that both the currency and the feedback function include hypotheses about both the subject and its environment. Consider the most classical foraging currency: rate of energy gain. How this currency relates to long-term fitness depends on the species, the state of the subject and the time of the year. In turn, rate of gain as a function of foraging behavior (the feedback function) depends on food-handling ability and ecological circumstances such as abundance or patchiness of resources. The remaining hypothesis (the strategy set) has more emphasis on the subject, but is also a hypothesis because often one defines the range of what an animal can do by recording what it does.

Since all the components of the model are hypotheses, it follows that all three of them can be rejected by data. As we shall see, this happens often, and this is what makes the approach valuable. Failure of predictions of specific models never implies a rejection of the underlying rationale for optimality: that the system has been designed by natural selection. As we said, this is not what is being tested. Our view can be made clearer with an example.

The first version of the Marginal Value Theorem (MVT; Charnov 1976), which is a typical first-generation optimal foraging model, used (1) "overall rate of food intake" as the currency, (2) the ability to abandon patches at any value of the instantaneous capture rate as the strategy set, and (3) overall rate of food intake as a function of patch time as the feedback function. For each particular application, the feedback function depended on specific hypotheses such as distance between patches, travel velocity, and decline in instantaneous gains as a function of patch exploitation. One prediction that followed from this model was that if all patches were equal, foragers should exploit patches more thoroughly in habitats with greater distance between them. This qualitative relation has often been corroborated, but occasionally its quantitative predictions have failed (Stephens and Krebs 1986). What are the consequences of these successes and failures? In either case, we believe, the consequences are manyfold. First, they alter (up or down, respectively) our confidence in the set of hypotheses conforming the particular application of the model—namely, they lead to greater knowledge of the specific features of that species and its current habitat. Second, they change our confidence in the suitability of OFT as a guide for the study of foraging. Third, they affect our general belief that it is useful to make evolutionary assumptions to investigate behavioral mechanisms and the structure of natural habitats in general (i.e., in nonforaging contexts). What the evidence definitely does not do is to alter our confidence in the process of evolutionary change by natural selection.

2. How should optimality models be tested? A test is always a discrimination between competing hypotheses. In many early optimality studies, the optimality model was, in effect, tested against only a null hypothesis of random choice, random visiting of patches, or random search. However, later, more sophisticated analyses compared a range of models involving different hypotheses at the three levels. Let us illustrate this process by expanding on our OFT example. In a field study of brood provisioning by starlings, Joost Tinbergen (1981) found that when parents were exploiting patches at greater distance from the nest they brought back larger prey loads. This is what the MVT predicts. The finding provides a sound rejection of the null hypothesis that starlings be-

have at random with respect to patch distance. It tells us that the three hypotheses that formed the specific application of the MVT (that starlings maximize overall rate of capture, that they can terminate patch exploitation at any load size, and that overall food gain rate as a function of load size has a maximum whose position increases with distance) are viable. It would have been negligent, though, to rejoice on this rejection of the null hypothesis as if it had meant that the three hypotheses had been definitively validated by the finding. If we genuinely want to learn about starlings' behavior, we must accept the limitation of our finding and conclude: "With the inspiration of the set of hypotheses that form this implementation of the MVT, Tinbergen has succeeded in showing that starlings do not forage at random, and it remains possible that these hypotheses are actually true." But, of course, they may also be false and have still predicted the right trend. We may ask, for instance, if another reasonable hypothesis could replace each member of the set and let the model make the same prediction. Take the feedback function, for instance. The hypothesis was that patches were of the same value at different distances. But what if starlings were exploiting better patches when they flew farther away and simply brought back larger loads from better patches? The correlation with distance would have been the same, but the original hypothesis in the model would have been false. Or look at the currency hypothesis. What if instead of maximizing rate of food delivery per unit time the starlings had been maximizing food delivered per unit of energy spent in getting it? Same again, this time for the currency. Further, what if both feedback function and currency had been wrong? One could still find the same prediction.

Summing up: many different sets of hypotheses predict a rejection of the null hypothesis of random behavior. Showing that behavior has the predicted trend encourages further research into the hypotheses that conform the model; it does not prove them.

Studying all hypotheses at once is as difficult as trying to bite a hanging apple while standing on a skateboard. However, testing optimality models in natural circumstances in the field is doing precisely that. This is why experiments are often unavoidable, to fix some elements of the model in order to explore the others. For instance, in a follow-up to Tinbergen's work, one of us (Kacelnik 1984) fixed the feedback function by supplying the birds with identical artificial patches at various distances from the nests. Under these conditions, each different currency makes precise quantitative predictions. In this situation, observations can go beyond the mere rejection of the null hypothesis and help to discriminate among equally sensible currency hypotheses. In fact, the behavior of the starlings differed significantly from the predictions of maximization of energy gain per unit of energy spent and from gross rate of energy but did not differ from the maximization of net energy gain per unit time. This finding narrows down the set of possible hypotheses by rejecting some putative currencies, but let us emphasize what it does not do. It does not demonstrate the feedback function hypothesis because Kacelnik actually built it in his experiments, and it does not exclude other currencies that may make the same prediction as net rate of energy gain under the specific conditions of the test. The winning currency has, in fact, become a new null hypothesis by its own success. Testing a model is a progressive task by which its various elements must be examined one by one and refined using empirical data. The joy of a first rejection of the null hypothesis in the right direction is often short-lived. We have summarized our view of the process in our Figure 2.1.

To complicate matters even further, we must emphasize that a single modeling strategy is not enough. We have exemplified our points using a particular modeling technique, namely, a particular procedure for arriving at predictions from a given set of hypotheses. Foraging research found very early that some problems cannot be handled like that. A striking example is the search for optimal decisions when the appropriate currency depends on the state of the subject. Net rate of gain may be the right currency when you are underfed and you know your habitat, but safety from predators or acquiring knowledge by sampling may be more important when your tummy is full or you are in a relatively unknown place. State-dependent problems are best handled by dynamic techniques (Houston et al. 1988; Krebs, Kacelnik, and Taylor 1978; Mangel and Clark 1988) or even by computer simulations. We should avoid the temptation of oversimplifying the problems faced by our subjects to shoehorn them into the

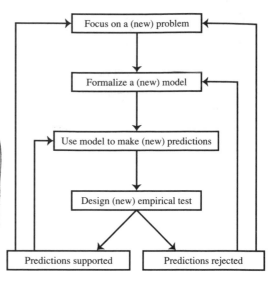

Figure 2.1. A scheme of the optimaity research program in biology. Notice that the crucial step of focusing on a new phenomenon is not dependent on any formal procedure: biological intuition and fashion are crucial at this step. In spite of the iterative process, there is progress in the program because new discoveries of biological facts occur all along, and later models incorporate the findings of earlier ones.

predictive tools we happen to have at hand at the moment.

Our main point here is that while in the early days of foraging theory great emphasis was placed on the success of predictions, foraging research evolved toward a recognition that once a discrimination between hypotheses becomes the main goal, prediction failures are often at least as informative as a guide for research.

3. *Laboratory experiments under controlled conditions or field observations under natural conditions?* Many classical foraging studies were carried out under laboratory conditions with caged animals and precise control over prey size, encounter rates, travel times, and so on. The great advantage of this approach is that the necessary control over the feedback function can be achieved. A possible danger is that the approach designs situations to fit models rather than designing models to fit the problems animals have faced during the species' evolutionary history. Demonstrating that in a contrived environment a particular model is consistent with the behavior of an animal says little

about the relation between the currency hypothesis and fitness, but exposes the mechanisms by which the properties of the environment control the behavior of the subject. No matter the extent to which our model is evolutionarily inspired, this form of testing models provides evidence about behavioral mechanisms and not about their evolution. We make this point here because the same applies to a lesser extent in field studies. Studying a species in a single environment exposes behavioral mechanisms, but unless we have evidence that the present environment (i.e., the feedback function) is that under which the behavioral mechanism evolved, this does not constitute direct evidence for claims about evolution.

So far we have considered the possibilities of predicting behavior using ideas about evolution; this is sometimes called a "backward" approach. A more direct strategy is to test currency hypotheses "forward," by measuring the fitness consequences of behaving in different ways (Sherman and Reeve, this volume). This sounds easier than it actually is. The reason this approach has difficulties is that unless behavior is imposed on the subjects by experimental manipulation, it is hard to disentangle why different behaviors subsist in the strategy set. A typical example in behavioral ecology is the issue of optimal laying date. Let us consider the hypothesis that there is an optimal laying date for a bird population, representing the best compromise between waiting enough to avoid the last frosts (when incubation is costly) while being early enough to allow sufficient time for the young to grow before the next winter. How could we test this idea?

We could formulate an explicit optimality model. Here the currency could be number of young recruited to the winter population; the strategy set the range of dates in the year when enough resources can be gathered to produce the eggs; and the feedback function the incubation costs, young growth rate, typical weather, and season length in the habitat. We could thus predict the optimal laying date (that date within the strategy set that maximizes young recruited under the present feedback function) and contrast it against the observed laying date distribution in the population. Failure of our prediction would clearly be informative: if most laying is at some time other than our prediction, we must revise out hypotheses.

But consider the consequences of finding a distribution with modal laying date at the predicted time but showing considerable variance. This is a common outcome that begs the question of why, if the hypotheses are correct, many individuals are showing different behaviors.

In the field we may test the model forward by looking at the model's component hypotheses. For instance, we may be tempted to use natural variance in laying date and ask whether birds who lay at the predicted date do actually recruit more young than earlier or later individuals. However, neither confirming nor failing to confirm this correlation solves the problem, because this sort of test has to live with the paradox of existence of variance in fitness in the first place. If one date is best, why do many individuals lay at suboptimal times? Maybe each animal has a different optimum taking its circumstances into account because strategy sets differ, but then we can never attribute a causal effect to laying date by itself: those who had a bad winter may have less fat, live in poorer territories, mate with poorer partners, lay later, and recruit fewer young. Since in most cases we cannot test the same individual under varying circumstances, we still do not know if it is true that each individual chooses its own personal optimum.

Sometimes it is possible to find ways around this problem by experimental manipulations (e.g., advancing the date of chick hatching by giving the parent previously incubated eggs), but this strategy is rarely available in humans. An alternative, which is discussed later by Mace and Pagel (this volume), is to use the powerful techniques developed for comparative studies across species to establish causal reasons for the differences among natural human populations.

In summary, regardless of whether a study is carried out in the field or in the laboratory, while it is possible to obtain definite information about decision mechanisms, it is usually extremely hard to discriminate hypotheses about the evolutionary history that led to these mechanisms.

4. *Where is the optimality program leading?*
The discussion of the preceding sections can be summarized by asking which of the following non–mutually exclusive outcomes is likely to result from an optimality research program in biology.

(a) *An improved understanding of evolution.* As we have argued, the optimality program in itself does not lead to an improvement in our understanding of evolutionary history or of processes such as speciation. However, if we find that under many situations our species fails to behave in a fitness-maximizing fashion we may be forced to revise our ideas of how selection has operated.

(b) *Improved understanding of mechanisms.* Optimality models, particularly those that lead to experimental manipulation, have been successful in leading to a greater understanding of many behavioral mechanisms, especially those involved in memory for foraging parameters such as prey locations, inter-prey intervals, perception of prey sizes, and so on. It remains an open question whether these questions about psychological mechanisms could have been addressed without an optimality approach or whether the optimality aspect gives a unique insight into an understanding of mechanisms.

(c) *An improved understanding of "design by natural selection."* Although a single optimality study says little about the general concept of design by natural selection, the accumulated result of many such studies might enhance our understanding of the kinds of currencies and constraints that influence behavior.

(d) *A sound basis for supraindividual modeling.* Even if optimality models fail in their detail, they may capture enough of the essence of behavior to give qualitatively successful predictions that act as "general rules of behavior." These rules may, in turn, be of use to others who wish to incorporate them into further models at the population level. Thus, for example, foraging models may lead to general rules about the distribution of predators between patches (the ideal free distribution). This could then become the input to an ecological model of the interactions between predators and their prey. As an input it would have more validity than an arbitrarily chosen "aggregation function" because it would be based on better understanding of individual and group behavior. We experienced this property when we tried to understand the factors leading to various frequency-dependent effects on mortality. This is a classical and important problem in ecology. In one simple scenario, one considers two interactive populations, a predator and its prey. Say that the prey population is sessile and het-

erogeneously distributed, so that some areas are denser than others. The predators are mobile and distribute themselves according to their foraging benefit, but they show interference, in that for a given prey density, individual predator's payoff drops with predators' density. One question of interest in relation to population stability is asking for the relation between density and mortality within the prey population. Is proportional mortality higher or lower in denser prey patches? If mortality is caused only by predation, the foraging rules of the predators should help in predicting this relation. In a series of modeling studies led by our colleague Carlos Bernstein we looked in some detail at the population consequences of more or less realistic assumptions for predators' foraging. We assumed that each predator followed a rule derived from the marginal value theorem: "If the payoff in your current patch is lower than your estimate of average payoff in the whole habitat, then move to another patch, else stay put." This deceptively simple rule led us to see that many more details needed to be specified: Over which time periods should you estimate payoffs? What operational definition can be given for "estimates"? How can your personal decision incorporate the anticipation of what other predators will do? What is the effect of prey depletion by exploitation? What is the effect of different degrees of mobility of predators with respect to patch size? We quickly found that small variations in these assumptions could completely reverse the results: for instance, we moved from positive to negative density dependence in mortality by simply changing the relative rates of learning and local prey depletion. Indeed, a number of surveys of density dependence in natural populations found the whole range of relations, but since learning rates in the wild are unknown, the reason for this diversity remains a mystery. Our theoretical application of optimal foraging to this issue tells us that we will probably only be able to predict the diversity among populations by studying behavioral mechanisms at individual level.

THE EVOLUTION OF EVOLUTIONARY BIOLOGISTS

The optimal foraging program has evolved. In part this occurred through a change of scientists and in part through a change in what each participant in the early times of the program has gone on to do. Here we pause to reflect on the way in which different individuals involved in classical foraging studies have developed their own research, as an informal aid in thinking about the developments one might expect among the participants on human evolutionarily inspired field studies.

Undoubtedly, some scientists have continued since the 1970s with the original program in which an abstract problem (how do predators exploit patches?) is built into a model (the marginal value theorem), and this is then illustrated with a successful test (starlings *do* bring greater loads from farther away). The emphasis for them is on problems rather than the problem solvers and on verification rather than hypothesis discrimination. This, as we said, was once very fashionable, but it has limitations. These people make contributions to a large variety of problems, but their contributions are not very deep because after each successful test of a prediction (a rejection of random behavior in the appropriate direction) they switch to a different issue, avoiding the normal disappointments that follow when one explores the nooks and crannies of real-life biology.

Others have gone on to develop ever more elaborate theory, pointing to inconsistencies between different models, benefits of state-dependent or dynamic models, and exploring the implications of more refined but still abstract assumptions. This group has a persistent and important function in intellectual leadership; they help many others to think correctly and to be aware of the many reasons why particular tests of models might not have been expected to succeed in the first place. For instance, while simple models do not predict any variance among subjects, state-dependent models describe how fitness may be maximized by doing different things if individuals differ in their state, and thus predict the variation among individuals in natural circumstances that is to be expected. They have been less successful, though, in developing a strong link to empirical research. Many of the crucial parameters identified in advanced models are not measurable in natural circumstances.

A third group has used foraging theory as a stepping-stone to understand problems at the population level, for example, in the stability of predator-prey systems, the coevolution of parasites and their hosts, or the interaction between nectar-feeding insects and pollination biology of plants. The main unsolved issue for this route is the extent to which evolutionary thinking remains an essential ingredient; population-level predictions depend on the behavior of individuals, but it is not obvious yet that ecological models benefit much by understanding how these responses were shaped by selection.

A fourth approach has been to move from the essentially adaptationist approach of classical optimality to a direct investigation of mechanisms at the psychological and neural level. For example, the expanding research in food-storing memory and the brain had its origins in optimality models of the evolutionary stability of food-storing behavior. Since the prevalent hypothesis of how hoarding worked was group selectionist, Andersson and Krebs (1978) hypothesized that it must have been wrong, and sought alternatives based on sound evolutionary principles: hoarding behavior must be of greater advantage to the actor than to others, or it would not have been selected. These sound alternatives made demands on individual spatial memory that did not seem probable at the time. It turned out that previous ideas about spatial memory were wrong, and this triggered a spate of studies on how memory for location actually works and how it differs among species (Krebs et al. 1989). In this fourth category, analysis of the processes underlying animal decisions, including the neural support of these processes, has become an end in itself, and the foraging models, having been used as a lever to enter the animal mind, have become ancillary.

Many unstated and often unconscious goals and assumptions of early foraging research, such as the hope that evolutionary insights offered a shortcut to replace psychological or neurophysiological research, have been left behind. We suspect that much of this may be mirrored by the evolutionary interpretation of humans in their natural (social) circumstances.

WE, PERSONALLY, FIND CULTURE NECESSARY

This brief section is motivated by our differences with a comment from our editor and the views about culture contained in some of the studies we comment. Laura Betzig writes: "I, personally, find 'culture' unnecessary" (chapter 1, this volume, n. 49).

What is meant, we suspect, is that we can test evolutionarily inspired optimality models of human behavior without reference to culture because the latter is very accommodating: it does not get in the way of fitness maximization. This relates to the notion that culture is the result of each subject struggling to maximize her own fitness, which, at a general level, we do not contest. The mechanism of evolution by natural selection applies to humans with the inexorable certainty of its logic: genetic traits for which there is variation change their frequency in the population if they impose variation on the inclusive fitness of their carriers, resulting in adaptations. Adaptation by natural selection may be smooth or jerky, fast or slow, but it will operate. Although this process occurs in parallel with random drift, no other credible process of directional change can be held responsible for shaping human genetic endowment. And it is this endowment that makes culture possible and to whom cultures must accommodate. However, we have repeatedly found in foraging studies how a mechanism evolved under some circumstances may generate inappropriate behavior in others. While attacking small moving objects is an adaptation for insect-eating trout, this mechanism evolved before the proliferation of fly fishing, and there is no reason to believe that present-day trout respond to these stimuli with the readiness that maximizes their fitness, taking into account the relative frequency of fishermen and real insects in each particular habitat. The system formed by an organism and its habitat is not in constant equilibrium. We would not understand trout behavior if we thought only about fitness maximization in present circumstances. To explain trout behavior we must identify its mechanisms and consider its evolution under past and present scenarios.

Genetic trends for cultural participation are likely to have evolved under circumstances that differed from those present in current human societies. Today's humans, like today's trout, use behavioral mechanisms to follow stimuli that sometimes are just but lures. In the optimality language we used for foraging studies, as the feedback function changes rapidly, subjects continue to use currencies that may or may not maximize fitness presently. This is more of

an obstacle in human studies than with other species because many models of human cultural evolution (Boyd and Richerson 1985; Cavalli-Sforza and Feldman 1981; Dawkins 1976; Sperber 1994; Tooby and Cosmides 1992) have shown that it is possible for cultural traits to spread even at the expense of direct genetic benefits to their carriers. Cultural evolution has its own dynamics, constrained but not fully determined by human evolutionary adaptations. A satisfactory understanding of human behavior requires examining the articulation of formerly adaptive traits with present cultural circumstances.

THE STUDIES

In this section we will discuss each of the studies in this collection to illustrate our points. Readers may prefer to make a break and return to this point after having read the original papers.

Irons

We start with the paper by William Irons because its explicit theoretical stand allows a direct comparison with the foraging research program. It is clear from the outset that Irons avoids a purely descriptive approach and sees his research as an attempt to test hypotheses using individual studies as instances. In this paper the hypothesis under test is clearly presented:

I suggest as a hypothesis that in most human societies cultural success consists in accomplishing those things which make biological success (that is, inclusive fitness) probable. (chapter 3, p. 37).

The reason for suggesting such a hypothesis is also clear:

This hypothesis is derived from the following more general principle: Human beings track their environments and behave in ways which, given the specific environments in which they find themselves, maximize inclusive fitness; what is observed as culture and social structure is the outcome of this process. (chapter 3, p. 37).

As it is the method suggested for empirical testing, summarized in these two quotes:

The proposition that cultural, or emic, success makes a high inclusive fitness probable can be tested by collecting demographic data in combination with data on degrees of success by the standards defined by the population under study. One can then analyze data to determine whether individuals who are emically successful have a higher inclusive fitness" (chapter 3, p. 37), and

The analysis presented here is a type of test which would falsify the hypothesis that striving for cultural success equates with striving for biological success, if the predicted relationship among variables did not emerge. It is suggested that replication of this type of test in many human societies would yield either strong support for the hypothesis, or would falsify it, depending on the outcome. (chapter 3, p. 37)

As happens in all empirical research programs, the general principle (our second quote) is not being tested by each particular study. Its validity is meant to be judged in two other ways: the long-term productivity of research inspired by the principle and the logical credentials of its formulation. We cannot offer an informed judgment on the former, but we can make at least a brief comment on the latter.

We are aware that there are still authors who deny any relation between humans and biology. Some people seem strangely comfortable with the contradiction of supporting a materialistic philosophical stand while denying that human attributes such as language have evolved by a blind, unguided process. Others claim that culture evolves with total independence from psychological processes that are themselves the result of natural selection. We find these views untenable and will not discuss them here. We assume that most readers have already accepted that nobody has guided the evolution of human nature and that natural selection is the only known process that can lead blindly to good design. From this starting point, we can argue with Irons's principle. Given that evolution by natural selection is not under question, we may ask if there is a logical alternative to his principle. It seems to us that one logical alternative would be something like this:

"Human beings *do not* track their environments and behave in ways which, given the specific environments in which they find themselves, maximize inclusive fitness; their behavior is controlled by mechanisms that must have maximized fitness over long periods of their history but that may lead to evolutionarily suboptimal behavior under changing circumstances. What is observed as culture and social structure is the outcome of individual behavior being controlled by these mechanisms

and of evolutionarily neutral historical change produced by the dynamics of cultural evolution."

In fact, the second formulation is not really very polemical. Not only we would choose it to fit our experience with foraging studies, but Irons himself, in his final discussion on the application of the principle to other populations, states that it may turn out that the hypothesis under test is not confirmed in post-demographic-transition societies, and that in that case this "would indicate that the novelty of modern social environments is such that the proximate behavioral mechanisms which were adaptive in pre-industrial societies are no longer adaptive" (chapter 3, p. 45).

This seems to us to embody a contradiction. The alternative principle that we presented, and with which Irons agrees in his reference to postindustrial societies, truly contradicts the original general principle. What this means is that we are skeptical of the generality of the "general principle" on which the hypothesis under test is based, but it does not question the possibility that it applies sometimes, or even often. In contrast with the status of natural selection, this principle is itself a hypothesis under empirical test.

The specific hypothesis proposed for empirical test (our first quote) is a statement about shared values in societies. It is not a strong logical derivation from the principle of natural selection, but it is an empirically testable proposition. So, let us turn to it.

Just as we did for foraging studies, we see the empirical task as a discrimination among hypotheses, and ask which are the hypotheses being discriminated by the methodology employed here. The following are two among many possible examples of alternative hypotheses:

1. In most human societies cultural success *does not* consist in accomplishing those things that make biological success (that is, inclusive fitness) probable.
2. In *a minority* of human societies cultural success consists in accomplishing those things that make biological success (that is, inclusive fitness) probable.

Both alternatives present logical difficulties. The obvious difficulty of (1) is that, contrary to Irons's suggestion, each instance of a negative result (lack of correlation between emic success and fitness within a culture) would not falsify the original proposition in favor of this alternative. Lack of correlations can result from many causes even if the hypothesis is true (for instance, small sample size). Using (1) as an alternative could never falsify the hypothesis under test. The second alternative is statistically sounder but is not very sexy. Even if it were to be rejected in favor of the proposal, namely, if it were to be shown that significantly more than 50 percent of human societies do show a correlation between emic and biological success, we would not have uncovered a human universal nor made a convincing case for the importance of this finding. In any case, alternative (2) can only be rejected by a study of a representative number of societies. A study of one culture, no matter how profound and accurate, would not make a substantial contribution.

We are left with a difficulty, because the hypothesis suggested is not derived from a strong general principle and because the conditions for its falsification or inferential acceptance are not immediately obvious. We have seen that in foraging studies the most convincing contributions are based on discrimination among sensible alternative hypotheses, but this is possible because the hypotheses are formulated at a more specific level. The claim that foraging is organized so as to maximize fitness in the habitat of evolutionary adaptedness is not seen as falsifiable, but the views that foraging is such that, say, energy per unit time or energy per unit of energetic cost are maximized can be distinguished with appropriate research, as can hypotheses about the feedback function or the strategy set. Perhaps the solution here would be to find a set of sensible proximate mechanisms of individual behavior and cultural evolution that could be pitched against each other.

In summary, we have expressed caveats with respect to the explicit theoretical goals of this program, but we must now make it clear that this does not mean a negative view of the detailed study of human societies uncovering specific functional relationships. On the contrary, testing the predictions of optimality models against null hypotheses may be an unavoidable first step until more specific mechanistic alternatives can be formulated. Irons's study of the Turkmen resulted in very specific and valuable findings that may make more specific hypothe-

ses possible. For instance, the finding that wealth-related variance in fitness increases with age in males but decreases in females is much more specific than the finding of a straightforward correlation between wealth and fitness. Focusing on this sort of finding and the mechanism by which it takes place may allow for the proposal of sensible alternative currencies that make different predictions in this respect.

Chagnon

Napoleon Chagnon studies one tribal society in great detail, in an attempt to develop an explanatory account of violent conflict among "primitive" people. Given the importance of warfare in these societies and of some form of violence in all human cultures, his theoretical framework has implications far beyond the study of a single culture. He explicitly agrees with Irons's stand:

"I do not assume that humans consciously strive to increase or maximize their inclusive fitness, but I do assume that humans strive for goals that their cultural traditions deem as valued and esteemed. In many societies, achieving cultural success appears to lead to biological (genetic) success." (chapter 9, p. 88)

Rather than commenting on the extraordinary achievements of his long-term study and on the indisputable value of his demonstration that reproductive interests must be included in explanatory models of human conflict, we will use this study as a foothold to expand on our general comments on the research program.

Chagnon's quote can serve for a reflection on human behavior in cultural settings. The proposition has two elements, one about individual behavior within a culture and another about the structure of cultures (what is it that is deemed to be valuable). Since both elements relate to multi-individual problems, an introduction of the language of game theory and evolutionarily stable strategies may be useful.

In many theoretical models of multiplayer interactions, each participant struggles for her own aims but is being conditioned by the behavior of the other players. Given a certain game, each group may be trapped in a different local equilibrium because of its history. In the equilibrium, everybody is doing their best but nobody is achieving an unconstrained individual optimum. It seems to us that it may be helpful to examine cultures from this perspective.

One feature of game theoretical analyses is that they often aim at finding the stable set of individual behaviors once the rules of the game have been established, and not at finding the reasons for the establishment of certain rules and not others. In cultural settings, one could ask what is it that individuals should do given that they live in a certain culture, and this is a different question from asking why that culture has a given set of shared values.

As a concrete example, consider the game of "chicken," in which two young males competing for female esteem drive their cars at high speed toward each other and the first one to swerve loses. Once the game becomes a cultural practice, participating in it may be the only way to obtain mates, and it may be justly argued that participants are maximizing their fitness by showing the appropriate degree of nerve in the game, even if the game itself is profoundly stupid. It is possible to some extent to derive stable states, namely, stable distributions of individual strategies, given that we know the rules of the game. It is not equally easy, however, to derive the nature of the game itself from the premise that each young male will always do what he can to maximize female esteem in any situation.

By extending this line of thinking, it seems to us that we might understand why individual Yanomamö engage in iffy undertakings by looking at how their culture conditions what is best for its members, so that all individuals may be doing something which is far from the unconstrained optimum but that is the best of a bad job given the culture in which they find themselves.

The rebels without cause that played chicken may have chosen the stupidest of possible conventional methods to settle relative merits, but once the convention is established each individual has to follow, and the practice is maintained. The warring habits of the Yanomamö may be equally at odds with the common good but still be maintained by the need of each individual to perform well given that tradition.

We do not think there is a discrepancy here, but we make the point as a warning against a possible misreading of the use of evolutionary ideas in human contexts. It would be wrong to believe that individual maximization criteria

(be they reproductive goals or some evolved proximate alternative such as maximization of sexual pleasure or reduction of pain) can explain the origin of cultural habits, because there may be infinite sets of cultural habits that might find some form of stability with subjects that struggle to maximize their own gains. In another game theoretical example, we may explore the stable distribution of strategies given that players are subject to the rules of the Prisoner's Dilemma, but we cannot predict that they will play this game from the fact that they maximize their gains.

A major difficulty with our game theory versus culture analogy is that while diversity of strategies is to be expected in most cases, it is not easy to explain variance in payoff. As a first approximation one would expect everybody to have the same payoff because individuals would change their strategy to achieve the maximum attainable. However, this approximation rarely applies. Say, for instance, that attempting to kill another man has a positive effect on fitness through the subject's increase in social standing, while it has a negative effect through its increased probability of dying himself in the attempt. There will be an optimal intensity of aggression. Nevertheless, both positive and negative fitness components may vary from individual to individual so that there will be as many optima as there are individuals in the population. This, in turn, will result in a potentially large variance in payoffs. We may find, for instance, that there is variance in the number of men attacked (and killed) by individuals and that there is also variance in the number of offspring produced. We may further find that these two variables are correlated (as they are in Yanomamö). What can we conclude from this? As Chagnon points out, both variables may be causally related to some polymorphism in other characteristic such as strength, even though the most obvious measurements had not yielded such a result at the time of this study. In fact, such a separate causal factor is required by functional analysis, because otherwise there is no logical explanation for the persistence of variance in payoff: if killers have greater success than nonkillers, more men should turn aggressive until the correlation disappears. The absence of a third cause would go against the hypothesis that individuals choose the strategy that maximizes their own gains given the structure of the game. If all individuals have equal potential, they ought to have equal reproductive success. Since they do not, for our hypothesis to be true individuals must differ in some other property. They may be deploying their best individual option given their personal endowment.

As before, we are driven to the conclusion that evolutionary thinking is useful and perhaps indispensable in guiding the formulation of hypotheses about human behavior, but that it is in the failure to satisfy predictions (e.g., the persistence of variance in fitness) where it may be most useful. <u>Failure of predictions (when the predictions are sensible) guides further research into both the consequences of behavior and the mechanistic bases of behavioral control.</u>

Blurton Jones

Blurton Jones (see also Blurton Jones and Sibly 1978) presents a mathematical model of offspring recruitment, taking into account the costs caused by temporal overlap in the rearing period of successive infants. What made the case interesting from an evolutionist's point of view is a discrepancy between the simplest a priori expectation and the observed facts. A naive observer may have argued that if women maximize fitness they should be expected to conceive as frequently as possible, say, immediately after conception. Observed interbirth intervals of several years show that this is not the case and force some deeper thinking.

In this more elaborate model, Blurton Jones and Sibly hypothesized that the currency is something closely related to recruitment of offspring to age ten, that the strategy set is the set of all possible intervals between birth and conception, and that the feedback function is given by the hunter-gatherer lifestyle in a particular ecosystem. While rapid conception has the obvious advantage of increasing rate of birth, its main cost is transport of a large backload. If an infant contributes no foraging of its own and has to be carried on the mother's back, having two infants in carrying age makes life very difficult and reduces the gathering efficiency of the mother to the possible detriment of the whole family. The typical interbirth interval observed in !Kung women is close to (slightly shorter than) the interval that should maximize lifetime recruitment of offspring to age ten given the

feedback function assumed in the model. Once again, we do not wish to discuss the details of this model but use it instead to illustrate what is being tested by reference to field data.

What would it take to validate or reject the model? The model predicts an interbirth interval of four years. Statistically, the hypothesis is rejected if there is a high probability that the typical interbirth interval in the population is not in fact four years, but the reverse is not quite true because <u>lack of a significant difference is not very informative.</u> When we start collecting data the results will initially not show a significant difference to four years (nor to any other interval). As the data become more reliable as estimates of the true population parameters, lack of significant differences between observations and predictions become inferentially more valuable, but there is no discrete threshold beyond which we can establish that the model is true.

Let us revise the consequences of a potential failure of the predictions. Say, for instance, that the observed interbirth interval is reliably shorter than that predicted. That means that at least one component in the model is wrong. This could be the hypothesis about the surrogate currency (maximization of number of recruits to age ten is not actually a good estimate of inclusive fitness), that the strategy set is more constrained than it was thought (women may be unable to delay fertilization indefinitely because of some conflict with the interests of male partners), or the feedback function may be in error (if infants start gathering food earlier than previously assumed, their net cost would be smaller). None of these findings would be lethal to the overall conception; they would simply challenge the specific assumptions made in this instance.

We make these points to reinstate our claim about the ubiquity of hypotheses about mechanisms. Although Blurton Jones sees his effort as being connected to functional rather than mechanistic issues, empirical tests of the predictions may serve at least as much to investigate reproductive mechanisms as to confirm or test any evolutionary claim.

Hill and Hurtado

Hill and Hurtado examine menopause as a paradoxical feature of human life history. Given that menopause does occur, they construct their hypothesis by asking for the conditions under which this phenomenon may actually lead (or have led in the past) to higher inclusive fitness. Two main hypotheses are discussed: that current longevity is much greater now than it was in the environment under which female reproductive physiology evolved (so that what we are seeing as menopause is an epiphenomenon of other adaptations) and that the gains resulting when older women divert effort from their own reproduction to helping younger relatives may yield higher fitness gains than those accruing if they persisted reproducing themselves (the grandmother hypothesis). Notice that both are sensible evolutionary hypotheses, even though one of them (artifactual longevity) does not imply that menopause is an optimal behavior in today's conditions. Support for this hypothesis cannot be found by examining the reproductive consequences of menopause today but by testing the possibility that expected longevity was much shorter in the population's history. As it happens, their analysis of available evidence leads to the rejection of this possibility: there does not appear to have been a major lengthening of life span in the study population.

The grandmother hypothesis is suitable for empirical test. The details of what is required are spelled out by Hill and Hurtado. They are rather complex because it is necessary to evaluate the actual benefit provided by the grandmother to the grandchildren versus that of her potential offspring with appropriate devaluation according to relatedness. The currency is something close to cumulative fecundity of surviving grandchildren, the strategy set is the range of ages between menopause and general senescence, and the feedback function is a complex description of the variation in grandchildren's fitness as a consequence of grandmother's ability to help, together with the ability to raise offspring by the grandmother. The latter is a direct function of ecological circumstances.

In this case the study consists of examining whether the assumptions in the feedback function are met by a present-day nonindustrial population, the Ache Indians of Paraguay. According to the evidence, it would appear that the advantage conferred by grandmothers is not large enough to post-dict that menopause should occur at the age it does occur.

The failure of both available hypotheses is exciting because it exposes our lack of understanding. If we maintain the core hypothesis that human life history is the result of natural selection (and, as we said, there is no alternative to this), there must be something missing in our models since they fail to post-dict the observed life history. There could be a variety of scenarios under which the grandmother hypothesis might be correct in spite of its failure in the current Ache conditions. The Ache are unlikely to be living under the same circumstances as those under which menopause evolved. After all, given that menopause is a universal human feature, it has probably evolved once for all present human cultures, before the Americas were colonized and the Ache's lifestyle developed. Perhaps in the ecological circumstances under which current human life history evolved it was possible to benefit one's relatives to a greater extent than is possible for modern day Aches, or perhaps the marginal increase in mortality caused by pregnancy as a function of age was much steeper under different nutritional conditions. Naturally, if the grandmother hypothesis had been supported by evidence, research would also have continued. We would have concluded that this hypothesis is still tenable given what happens among the Ache, but we could hardly have claimed that there was strong evidence that grandmother benefits had been causally linked to the evolution of menopause, which occurred long before the Ache existed as a society.

Smith

Smith's study of group hunting in Inuits is based on a variety of models. His models contain a hypothesis about what is being maximized, another about what strategies are available (mostly joining groups of different sizes), and hypotheses about the local ecology (hunting payoffs as a function of group size). He starts by proposing that the currency is individual rate of gain, defined as the ratio of energy gain over the time of the hunting expedition, taking into account the distribution of gains among members of the group. Smith calculates the rate maximizing group sizes for different kinds of prey and compares them against the observed group sizes. As the observed group sizes do not match the predictions, he refines the currency hypothesis and proceeds to formulate new predictions, iterating the process several times. His strategy for modifying the models is based on questioning the unit of benefit, for instance, by taking into account relatedness of group members.

This strategy is certainly valid and interesting, but it is not the only possible path. It is possible to reexamine the specific currencies from a purely energetic perspective. For instance, in foraging theory the use of gain rate as a currency is grounded on the principle of lost opportunity, which is valid when foraging consists of repeated cycles so that the overall gains in the foraging time are limited by the time used per cycle: time employed in one cycle delays the forthcoming hunt. This logic applies well to a starling that makes three hundred daily hunting trips to feed its young, using 96 percent of its time foraging. It is less strongly justified for a pride of lions that may hunt for a large prey every few days and spend much of their time resting. There is no a priori reason why a pride of lions in a situation such as we describe should organize its hunting by discounting gains exactly in relation to the time involved in the hunt alone, without reference to digestion times and other activities. We suspect that the problems faced by Inuits may be closer to those of lions than to those of starlings. For instance, different hunting modes may require differential preparation times, and this would substantially modify the predictions.

The point, however, is that the optimality method serves, as usual, to discard some explanations and suggest others. In the process of testing successive models, a more complex picture of the social mechanisms and local circumstances that govern group hunting emerges. The output of the research is a mechanistic understanding of social dynamics among Inuits, which in turns allows for predictions of what they might decide to do under new circumstances and what consequences they might experience. We do not gain much further knowledge about human evolution, but we learn a lot about what current humans do.

Borgerhoff Mulder

Borgerhoff Mulder uses a human field study to examine wider theoretical ideas of mammalian breeding systems. She starts by realizing that humans provide longitudinal records of individual behavior that are more difficult to gather in other species. As a consequence, human field data may serve to test models based on lifetime reproductive success. The specific rationale for this study is approximately as follows.

There exists a theoretical model (the polygyny threshold model) that suggests how polygyny might evolve and be maintained through female choice. If each female starting reproduction settles with the male offering her the highest opportunities at the time of her choice and she is then committed to this partner, and if female performance declines with number of females sharing each male, then better-endowed males end up with more females than their competitors, and a system with variance in the number of females per male will be maintained through the mechanism of female choice whenever there is variance in male resource holding. If no other factors exert any influence, in the steady state there should be no variance in female reproductive performance. The model does not address the origin of variance among males, and the prediction of zero variance among female fitness does not apply to colonizing periods. Systems with variance in number of females per male do exist among vertebrates, including birds, humans, and other mammals. In many human systems rich men have more wives and a greater number of descendants than do their poorer competitors. What is not known is whether these systems could have evolved and/or been maintained through female choice. Female choice would be shown to be present (by definition) if females mated with those partners that maximize the females' expected inclusive fitness.

Borgerhoff Mulder uses the approach of evolutionarily optimal decision making to examine the marriage pattern among the Kipsigis of Kenya. Her specific optimality model can be characterized by: (1) a currency, given here by the expected number of offspring attained by postmenopausal women at the end of the period under study; (2) a strategy set, given by all the males available at the time of each female's marriage; and (3) a feedback function that postulates a relation between female offspring production and the parameters of male partners. Fitness is thought to be closely related to the ratio of amount of resources (land acreage) of a male divided by the number of females that male would have if he were to be chosen.

As always, the notion that female choice is evolutionarily optimal is not under test, inasmuch as it cannot be falsified in this study. Evolutionary optimality cannot be falsified because if one had found a lack of correlation between predictions and observed choice this would have been uninformative, as is the case with all negative results obtained from small samples (twenty-five families in this study). A statistically significant difference between predictions and observations would simply encourage the refinement of the elements of the model, not show that females are doing the wrong thing.

In fact, and according to the predictions of her model, Borgerhoff Mulder finds that males were preferred if they were offering a higher ratio of acreage of land owned per female. They were also preferred if, after controlling for land per female, they had fewer wives and had a successful record of previous breeding (chapter 11). Neither overall acreage owned nor male age had significant effects. Interestingly, Borgerhoff Mulder also found that females whose husbands had fewer cowives and a more successful breeding history had higher productivity. These results had not been predicted by the specific optimality model that triggered the inquiry, and provide encouragement for a refinement of the original model, including new factors in the feedback function. No doubt understanding marriage patterns among the Kipsigis requires a large number of additional elements, including historically determined local habits such as the existence of bridewealth and parent-offspring conflict among the bride and her own parents. As we said earlier, the fact that each individual may do her best given the social system does not explain why the social system exists in the first place. If there were no bridewealth custom, or females of neighboring males shared the land, then optimal female choice may or may not be different, but the difference in female behavior would not explain any of the cultural difference. Understanding marriage patterns involves both explaining why females do certain things given the present habits and attempting to account for the present habits. What this study successfully shows is

that an evolutionary framework is a useful guide in proposing specific hypotheses about mechanisms of family development.

In summary, ours is an allegation in favor of combining evolutionary with mechanistic hypotheses. We find untenable the resistance of some researchers to consider the evolutionary forces that shape human behavior, but we are also skeptical of evolutionary shortcuts—namely, we do not find it plausible that behavior of humans or other animals may be studied in depth, bypassing the processes by which individuals reach decisions or societies develop cultures. We do not believe that every bit of human psychology and physiology coincides with fitness maximization under all circumstances. This is not the case in other species either. In our own research on foraging decisions, evolutionary speculation normally leads to hypothetical mechanisms of choice, and experiments and observations mainly serve to test the exact nature of these mechanisms. Seen this way, evolutionary arguments are an aide to the study of mechanisms, but the opposite is also valid: evolutionary speculation about birth spacing cannot be made without reference to reproductive physiology (length of pregnancy, fecundity drop during lactation, infant growth rates, etc.), and there are many ways to go about investigating the latter. People interested in understanding humans from an evolutionary angle must incorporate what we know about their properties, and those interested in exposing these properties cannot ignore the selective forces that shape this—and all other—species.

Acknowledgement. Laura Betzig's invitation to write this commentary, her friendly response to our skepticism, and her patience with our delay in producing the present version are a definite proof of our claim that *Homo sapiens* does not behave optimally in all circumstances. We are very grateful to her for making us think about these issues and apologize both to authors whose ideas we used without detailed reference and to those whose ideas we may have misrepresented. Our intention is to promote understanding on the structure of the Darwinist research program, and to that objective we have to some extent played the devil's advocate.

$P(Behav|culture), P(culture)$

3

Cultural and Biological Success

WILLIAM IRONS

This paper proposes a research strategy for testing the proposition that human beings tend to behave in such a way as to maximize their genetic representation in future generations.[1] A general method for testing this theoretical principle is outlined, and then applied to data drawn from a particular population, the Turkmen of Persia. It is suggested that replication of this research procedure on data from a large number of human societies will provide a good test of the validity of this theoretical proposition.

CONSCIOUS GOALS AND REPRODUCTIVE SUCCESS

One of the more obvious features of human behavior is that it is goal-directed. Human beings set for themselves conscious goals and then choose courses of action which they believe will lead to the accomplishment of those goals. The specific goals involved vary widely from one society to another. For example, among the Yanomamö Indians of the Amazon basin, men strive to be fierce, that is, formidable in wielding violence against other men. Fierce men are able to acquire larger numbers of mates and male allies than less fierce men. These are aspirations that men consciously try to fulfill, and fulfilling them can be designated cultural success among the Yanomamö. Alternate terms might be emic success or perceived success. The Nuer value cattle and strive to increase the sizes of their herds, and a man with many cattle is judged successful. Tiwi men strive to acquire large numbers of wives, and, preferring a single quantitative measure of a man's success, measure it in terms of his wife list which includes all the living and deceased wives he has ever had, much as academics measure success in terms of the number of citations in an individual's bibliography. Middle-class Americans aim for a combination of interesting work, moderate economic prosperity (by the standards of their society), and financial security. Most of the examples offered here are of male goals. It is unfortunately the state of the ethnographic literature that female goals, which are analytically as important as those of males, are less frequently described.

Although some ethnographies tell us little about the common aspirations of the people they purport to describe, or local standards of success and failure, it is reasonable to assume that such things can be found in any human society. Conscious goals and generally agreed upon measures of success can be identified by participant observation, and quantitative tests can be applied to determine whether a particular goal is actually pursued in a particular society. It is possible that certain stated goals are merely verbal preferences which never affect behavior. It is only those which can be shown to motivate behavior which are important for the sort of analysis discussed here.

Reprinted, with permission from: N.A. Chagnon and W. Irons (eds.), *Evolutionary biology and human social behavior: An anthropological perspective*, pp. 257–272, North Scituate, Mass: Duxbury Press.

I suggest as a hypothesis that in most human societies cultural success consists in accomplishing those things which make biological success (that is, a high inclusive fitness) probable. While cultural success is by definition something people are conscious of, they may often be unaware of the biological consequences of their behavior. This paper does not inquire into the nature of the proximate psychological mechanisms which cause people to consciously strive for things which have evolutionary consequences beyond their recognition, although it is not difficult to suggest what some of these might be (see for example Dawkins 1976:60–64). As a result of environmental change, what has been defined in the past in a particular society as worth achieving may cease to make a high inclusive fitness probable. When this happens, I hypothesize, members of the society gradually redefine their goals to make them correspond with those things which will increase the probability of a high inclusive fitness. This hypothesis is derived from the following more general theoretical principle: Human beings track their environments and behave in ways which, given the specific environment in which they find themselves, maximize inclusive fitness; what is observed as culture and social structure is the outcome of this process (cf. Irons 1979b:5–10 and 34–37).

EMPIRICAL TESTING

The proposition that cultural, or emic, success makes a high inclusive fitness probable can be tested by collecting demographic data in combination with data on degrees of success by the standards defined by the population under study. One can then analyze the data to determine whether individuals who are emically successful have a higher inclusive fitness. This is a somewhat laborious procedure since it necessitates collecting large enough amounts of demographic data to estimate age-specific birth and death rates for different categories of individuals corresponding to different degrees of successfulness.[2] There is, however, much to recommend a procedure of this sort despite its difficulties, since predictions about the effect of social behavior on vital rates are central to sociobiology. Indeed, it can be said that it is a basic principle of sociobiology that the evolutionary significance of an individual is

completely contained in his or her effect on vital statistics (Williams 1966a:3–4). Direct measurement of these effects is, I suggest, a very effective way of testing sociobiological predictions. Testing for a positive association of cultural and biological success is a first step toward testing for causation. Often, given the association, the interpretation that cultural success increases the probability of biological success will be the most reasonable one in the ethnographic context in question. In other cases, an association may not justify such an inference, and additional tests may be necessary to permit a strong inference of cause. This issue is discussed in reference to a specific ethnographic context below.

Following is an illustration of the method proposed, using data I collected among the Turkmen of Persia in 1973–1974. These data are still being analyzed, so future papers will carry the analysis farther than this one and if they do not falsify the above hypothesis they will allow stronger inferential support (see Irons 1980, for some additional results). Nevertheless, the analysis presented here is a type of test which would falsify the hypothesis that striving for cultural success equates with striving for biological success, if the predicted relationship among variables did not emerge. It is suggested that replication of this type of test in many human societies would yield either strong support for the hypothesis, or would falsify it, depending on the outcome.

The most significant emic measure of success among the Turkmen is wealth. A large part of the daily activities of Turkmen is devoted to economic production, and participant observation suggests that their basic economic strategy approximates one of maximizing wealth (Irons 1975:155–170). The most reasonable alternative hypothesis is that the Turkmen have a sufficing strategy in which they strive to meet their needs for consumption, but once these needs are met prefer to refrain from further labor (cf. Sahlins 1972). Such strategies are common among populations which have no means of storage of produce beyond what is immediately required for consumption—that is, no dependable ways of saving. The Turkmen, like all other Middle Eastern and Central tribal peoples, have long been tied into a market economy that reaches beyond their tribal boundaries. A significant portion of production is for consumption by the producing household, but production for trade is something they have depended on for at least a millennium. Savings in the form of money, jewelry, and consumable goods such as cloth, are common. Acquisition of capital in agricultural land, and in livestock which provide produce and capital well beyond what is required for immediate consumption, is also common. Such savings and capital are valuable in many ways. They can be used for consumption in years of low rainfall, when crops fail and herds are decimated, to meet needs not met by current income. Bridewealth is necessary for marriage, and is exorbitant. In the community in which I resided in 1966 and 1967, it took a family of median wealth from two to four years to acquire enough capital to be ready to give the hundred sheep necessary to obtain a bride for a son. The number of years necessary in any specific case varied widely because crop yields and the increase of flocks varied widely from year to year. Increasing capital was also necessary to carry out the common practice of eventually setting up one's sons as independent heads of households. Extra wealth could also be used to enjoy a higher standard of living, including better food and medical care. Faced with a situation of this sort, the economically rational thing to do would be to try to increase income beyond immediate needs in terms of consumption and to accumulate capital beyond what is necessary for consumption alone.

If economic activities are governed by a sufficing strategy one would expect per capita wealth to be roughly equal among households, since consumptive needs are approximately equal from one individual to another. If strategies of increasing wealth beyond consumptive needs govern the economy, one would expect those who are more able to acquire wealth to in fact have more capital. One factor influencing the ability of a household to accumulate wealth is the number of able-bodied adults in the household. Wealth (measured in the form of the monetary value of all capital owned) and the number of able-bodied adults in a household show a Pearson correlation coefficient of .39 ($p < .001$, $n = 566$). The same statistic for per capita wealth and number of adult laborers is .21 ($p < .001$, $n = 566$). Future analysis will focus on diachronic trends in capital holdings for households with different labor resources, to control for the influence of such factors as

the initial patrimony with which a household starts and bridal payments (see Irons 1980).

The next step in the analysis is to demonstrate that vital rates vary with differences in wealth. The vital rates presented here were calculated from data collected in a survey of 566 Turkmen households. The relevant data include complete fertility records for all individuals in the households surveyed, complete survivorship records for all children born to these individuals, and a record of all capital in the form of land and livestock owned by each household. Since among the Turkmen all forms of wealth have a monetary value, the value of each household's capital can be expressed in terms of a single quantity. The households in the sample were ranked in terms of this quantity, which represents a good measure of the wealth enjoyed by all members of the household, and the sample population was then divided into wealthier and poorer halves.

Separate age-specific fertility rates were then calculated from the male and female birth records for each half of the population. The calculation of mortality records is somewhat more complex because the sample of deaths and person years at risk of death was large enough to yield a good estimate of mortality probabilities only for the earlier years of life. Mortality rates were computed for the first twenty years of life and the estimated survivorship curve yielded by these calculations was matched to model survivorship curves from Coale and Demeny (1966) using a chi-square goodness-of-fit test.

The p-values for differences in fertility rates were calculated from the chi-square values computed for the difference between actual numbers of births recorded during each age interval for each group and the expected number of births if the difference in number of births between the two groups were solely a result of the different number of person years recorded for each group in each interval. After I completed this paper, Clifford Clogg, acting as a statistical consultant, devised a more powerful test of difference in fertility (see Irons, in prep. b). The p-value for death rates in the age interval 0–20 was calculated by assuming that deaths have a Poisson distribution and assuming a South 12 age-sex structure from Coale and Demeny (1966). The estimated death rates and variance of death rates were age standardized and a z test was used to calculate the p-value

Table 3.1. Summary of Male Fertility Data

	Wealthier Half of Population			Poorer Half of Population		
Age	Person Years	Births	Age-Specific Birth Rate	Person Years	Births	Age-Specific Birth Rate
15–19	1,889	83	.044	2,189	49	.022
20–24	1,468	293	.200	1,842	228	.124
25–29	1,125	345	.307	1,516	335	.221
30–34	909	297	.327	1,265	337	.266
35–39	723	257	.356	1,008	275	.273
40–44	546	178	.326	735	178	.242
45–49	417	105	.252	528	123	.233
50–54	277	58	.209	338	51	.151
55–59	169	38	.225	223	18	.081
60–64	100	17	.170	156	11	.071
65–69	35	5	.143	86	4	.047
70–74	17	2	.118	39	1	.026

df = 12 χ^2 = 113.36   p < .001.

for a one-tailed alternative. The predictions tested are specific and directional, so that, in order to increase the power of my tests, one-sided p-values were calculated. These p-values are the probability of results equal to those reported or more extreme in the predicted direction than those reported if there were no difference between the two groups. The difference in fertility rates was significant only for males, but the difference in mortality rates was significant for both sexes. The data from which these rates are computed are presented in Tables 3.1 to 3.4. The empirical fertility rates are represented graphically in Figures 3.1 and 3.2, and the model survivorship curves yielding best fit to the empirical data are presented in Figures 3.3 and 3.4. Figures 3.1 and 3.2 present average births per year per hundred individuals in each

age interval. Figures 3.3 and 3.4 present percentages of individuals surviving from birth.

An estimate of the average Darwinian fitness of individuals of each sex in each half of the population can be made by combining these vital rates. Assuming that rates are uniform within five-year age intervals, the following relationship allows computation of the number of children produced during any five-year age interval.

Number of Children Born

$$= \left[1_i + \left(\frac{1_i + 1_{(i+5)}}{2} \right) \right] \cdot {}_5f_i \cdot 5 \qquad 1$$

In this relationship 1_i represents the proportion of individuals surviving from birth to the beginning of the interval which is equated with the

Table 3.2. Summary of Female Fertility Data

	Wealthier Half of Population			Poorer Half of Population		
Age	Person Years	Births	Age-Specific Birth Rate	Person Years	Births	Age-Specific Birth Rate
15–19	1,925	253	.131	2,254	292	.129
20–24	1,476	492	.333	1,868	547	.293
25–29	1,166	391	.335	1,366	428	.313
30–34	958	301	.314	1,032	303	.294
35–39	775	213	.275	804	218	.291
40–44	575	95	.165	587	92	.157
45–49	393	17	.048	395	16	.040
50–54	217	2	.009	202	0	.000

df = 12 χ^2 = 113.36   .3 < p < 5

Table 3.3. Summary of Male Mortality Data for the First Twenty Years of Life

Age	Wealthier Half of Population			Poorer Half of Population		
	Person Years	Deaths	Age-Specific Death Rate	Person Years	Deaths	Age-Specific Death Rate
Less than 1	981	131	.133	953	154	.162
1	781	43	.055	744	64	.086
2	703	31	.044	640	29	.045
3	634	9	.014	577	27	.047
4	598	9	.015	512	4	.008
5–9	2,116	14	.007	2,075	18	.009
10–14	1,695	5	.003	1,480	3	.002
15–19	1,071	1	.001	994	3	.003

$z = 2.223$ $p = .013$

Table 3.4. Summary of Female Mortality Data for the First Twenty Years of Life

Age	Wealthier Half of Population			Poorer Half of Population		
	Person Years	Deaths	Age-Specific Death Rate	Person Years	Deaths	Age-Specific Death Rate
Less than 1	850	117	.138	881	108	.123
1	694	28	.040	714	56	.078
2	639	26	.041	634	35	.055
3	568	15	.026	559	13	.023
4	516	0	.000	502	6	.012
5–9	2,360	8	.003	2,088	23	.011
10–14	1,473	1	.001	1,425	4	.003
15–19	946	2	.002	924	7	.008

$z = 2.548$ $p = .005$

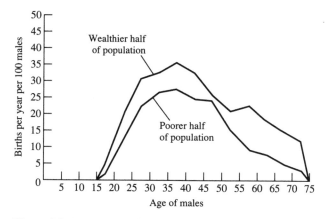

Figure 3.1. Male age-specific fertility rates.

point at which the individual has completed the ith year of life. l_{1+5} represents the proportion surviving at the end of the interval which is reached with completion of year $(i + 5)^{th}$ year of life. The symbol $\underline{5}f_1$ represents the average number of births per year to individuals in the age cohort which begins with age i. The total number of offspring produced by the end of any five-year interval can be calculated by summing those produced during each completed interval:

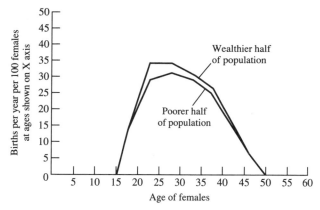

Figure 3.2. Female age-specific fertility rates. The empirical difference shown in this figure is not statistically significant. Fertility rates for women should be considered the same for both groups.

Total Children Born *using averages over 5 yr intervals*

$$= \sum_{i = 0}^{n = \text{max age}} \left[1_i - \left(\frac{1_i - 1_{(i+5)}}{2} \right) \right] \cdot 5f_i \cdot 5 \quad 2$$

These quantities for males and females in each half of the population are presented graphically in Figures 3.5 and 3.6. The number of children of each sex can also be computed by multiplying the total number of births by the proportion of births that are of each sex for each wealth stratum. When equation (2) is adjusted to give the

total female offspring of a female, then the quantity is the well known "net reproduction rate" developed by Fisher, Lotka, and others. Table 3.5 contains the total number of children of each sex that would be born in generation $n + 1$ by maximum reproductive age as a consequence of 100 hypothetical births in generation n, by using the vital rates above in combination with formula (2). The sex ratio at birth is different for the wealthier and poorer halves of the population, and empirical ratios drawn from the data were used in calculating the figures in Table 3.5.

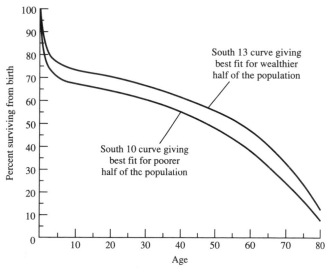

Figure 3.3. Male survivorship by wealth stratum.

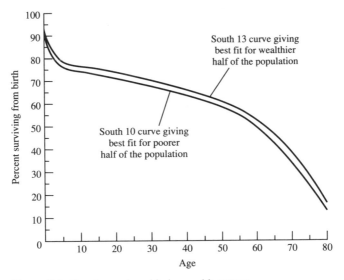

Figure 3.4. Female survivorship by wealth stratum.

money is culture !

The data in Table 3.5 indicate that on the average individuals of both sexes in the wealthier half of the population enjoy a higher Darwinian fitness than do individuals of the same sex in the poorer half of the population. Moreover, the variation in male fitness is greater than in female fitness. Males in the wealthier half of the population enjoy a higher average fitness than do females in the wealthier half. For the poorer half the situation is reversed. The higher variance in male reproductive success and the positive association of wealth and fitness support the theoretical model developed by Hartung (1976).

Some of the reasons for the variation in vital rates in response to variation in wealth can be seen in the descriptive ethnographic data on the Turkmen. Wealthier individuals of both sexes enjoy better diets and medical care and devote less time to forms of labor which are strenuous or involve high risks. This in turn affects survivorship rates. Wealthier males have higher fertility because their families can afford to acquire brides for them at an earlier-than-average age, because they remarry more quickly after a wife dies, and because they are more frequently polygynous. Polygyny among the Turkmen is a rich man's luxury. The bridewealth necessary to acquire a second or third wife is three times what one must pay for a first wife. This privilege of the upper stratum accounts for the wide divergence of male fertility rates in the later years of life visible in Figure 3.1. Wealthy women in contrast do not have an extensive advantage over their poorer sisters in fertility. Better health probably does lead to a small gain in fertility, but the data show only a small statistically insignificant trend in this direction. Lim-

Table 3.5. Numbers of Descendants in Generation Two of One Hundred Individuals in Generation One*

	Descendants of 100 Males in Generation One		Descendants of 100 Females in Generation One	
	Sons	**Daughters**	**Sons**	**Daughters**
Wealthier half of Population	442	371	305	256
Poorer half of Population	239	225	257	242

*Calculated using empirical fertility rates and model mortality tables.

itation of fertility through contraceptive techniques is extremely rare in this population and cannot explain the lack of a significant variation in female fertility with wealth.

One could suggest that the positive association of wealth and Darwinian fitness occurs because high accumulation of wealth is *purely* the effect of high survivorship and fertility. Given the ethnographic context, it is reasonable to assume that mortality—especially adult mortality—has a negative effect on household wealth, but it is improbable that this is the only relationship of cause and effect between these two variables. Better diet, better medical care, less need to perform heavy labor in the heat of a summer day, less need to sleep on the open steppe without a tent while tending sheep during the winter, more adequate shelter in general, and a number of other advantages conferred by wealth—I assume in this paper that all these have a positive effect on survivorship rates. I would not want to defend the assumption that they do not. The relationship between male fertility and wealth is also reasonably assumed to entail a similar two-way causation. High fertility does have a positive effect on wealth after a time lag of some fifteen to twenty years. (Child labor is not economically important in this society.) But it would be unreasonable to assume that earlier marriage, quicker remarriage after a wife's death, and more frequent polygyny do not have a positive effect on fertility—and only wealth makes them possible. The extent to which an association of emic success and high reproductive success allows inference in favor of the hypothesis explored in this paper depends on the form emic success assumes in a specific society. In the case discussed, I believe, an association of wealth and Darwinian fitness allows reasonably strong inferential support for the hypothesis. Future analysis of the Yomut material will use diachronic data to make more refined tests of the question of causation (see Irons 1980).

Generally it is reasonable to assume that an individual's behavior is biologically successful if it leads to a high Darwinian fitness. Such behavior can be maladaptive only if it has the side effect of lowering the Darwinian fitness of close relatives. In Yomut society, since adult women do not interact extensively with parents or siblings (cf. Irons 1979c), it is unlikely that female behavior has any such effect. Male behavior could be conceived of as having this effect only when men achieve wealth by cheating their brothers out of their patrimony. Since variance in male fitness is greater than variance in female fitness, this effect might be consequential. The crucial question is this: do the brothers of wealthy men tend to be wealthy also? It can be answered with the 1973–1974 survey data. They do indicate such a tendency: the brothers of wealthy men are often wealthy themselves.

During their early reproductive years brothers are usually members of the same patrilateral extended family. As such the products of their labor are pooled in a common household budget, and each draws on the household's resources according to his need as interpreted by the household head (Irons 1979c:200–203 discussed this aspect of Yomut social organization in greater depth). Normally the head of such an extended family is the father of the brothers in question, although it may be the oldest brother if the father is deceased. Thus during their early reproductive years brothers enjoy the same level of economic prosperity. As a rule, somewhere between the ages of thirty and forty, a man separates from his natal household and establishes an independent domestic household of his own. Brothers are supposed to separate according to their birth order, and each is supposed to receive an equal share of his natal household's capital as his patrimony. There appear to be only rare deviations from these expectations. After becoming the heads of separate households, brothers have different economic experiences. Nevertheless, the fact of starting with approximately equal patrimonies leads to a variance in wealth among economically independent brothers which is smaller than the variance in wealth among the population as a whole. The intraclass correlation coefficient for wealth of economically independent brothers is .17 with a significance level of .05 (for 65 sets of brothers ranging in size from 2 to 5 brothers).[3]

The effect of the reproductive success of sisters on their siblings has not yet been analyzed, but as noted above this source of variation in inclusive fitness should be small compared to that of brothers. Figures 3.5 and 3.6 give an indication of the relative contribution of brother and sister to variation in inclusive fitness. The analysis presented here supports the conclusion

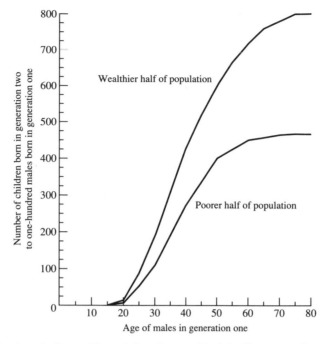

Figure 3.5. Variation in male fitness. Figure is based on empirical fertility rates and model mortality tables.

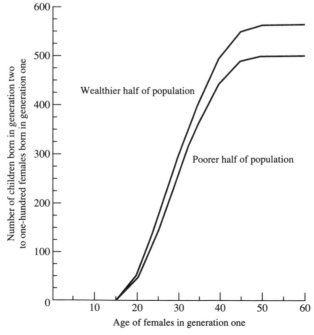

Figure 3.6. Variation in female fitness. Figure is based on empirical fertility rates and model mortality tables.

that emic success among the Turkmen makes a high inclusive fitness more probable.

APPLICATION TO OTHER POPULATIONS

The populations which are most likely to produce evidence falsifying the hypothesis explored in this paper are post-demographic-transition populations. It would not be surprising if the pattern found in the Turkmen data emerged in the analysis of data from other societies characterized by high fertility and high mortality. However, in modern industrial societies the pattern of higher fertility among more successful individuals tends not to occur because of modern contraceptive practices. Lower mortality among higher-status individuals, however, does occur. Whether or not lower fertility and lower mortality result in higher or lower fitness depends on the precise vital rates involved. It may turn out that the hypothesis above holds only for pre-industrial populations. If this should turn out to be the case, it may indicate that the novelty of modern social environments is such that the proximate behavioral mechanisms which were adaptive in pre-industrial societies are no longer adaptive (see Irons 1977 for further discussion of this). On the other hand, careful study of the connection between demography and social status in modern societies may indicate that the fertility limitation characteristic of industrial societies does contribute to a higher fitness. It is a common hypothesis that fertility limitation is part of a strategy either of upward social mobility or of the avoidance of downward mobility. This combined with lower mortality among individuals of higher social status could mean that maximum reproductive success in modern societies is achieved by limiting fertility. It is important to note that the more specific form of this hypothesis—that striving for wealth equates with striving for reproductive success—appropriate to the Yomut could have been falsified here in one of two ways: by showing that wealth has no effect on fitness, or by showing that Yomut do not, in fact, strive to increase wealth. In general, the research strategy suggested here consists of two broad steps: showing that people strive for a particular thing, and showing that this thing (whatever it may be) makes a high inclusive fitness more probable.

NOTES

1. The collection and analysis of data reported in this paper was supported by National Science Foundation Grant GS-37888 (1973–1974) and a grant from the Ford and Rockefeller Foundations Program in Support of Social Science and Legal Research on Population Policy (1974–1975). Continuing analysis is currently supported by National Science Foundation Grant BN576-11904 (1976–1978) and a grant from the Harry Frank Guggenheim Foundation (1976–1978). My wife, Marjorie Rogasner, accompanied me during the 1973–1974 field season and worked full time as a research assistant doing both participant observation and survey research. Following the field season, she assisted in the initial coding of field data. *Khoday shokr wa hileyime sogh bol diyen.* Richard Alexander, Napoleon Chagnon, Clifford Clogg, Mark Flinn, Nancy Howell, and Jeffrey Kurland read earlier drafts of this paper and made helpful suggestions. I alone am responsible for its flaws. The original title of this paper, now cited in some places, was "Emic and Reproductive Success."

2. It might be possible in some instances to utilize census data, but such data must be accurate (which often is not the case for the populations anthropologists study) and must allow for the association of variation in vital rates with variation in emic success.

3. This correlation coefficient was calculated on the basis of natural logarithms of wealth values, since the wealth values themselves violate the assumption of homogeneity of variance underlying the computation of the intraclass correlation coefficient. The analysis of variance was first performed on raw wealth scores, with sets of brothers constituting the groups in the one-way ANOVA, and it was found that the variances among groups were heteroscedastic, as judged by the Barlett test of homogeneity of variances. Taking log-wealth as the dependent variable, Clifford Clogg found that the variance among the groups was stable enough to warrant calculation of the intraclass correlation coefficient.

4
Looking Back Two Decades

WILLIAM IRONS

It may help readers to put "Cultural and Biological Success" in perspective if I recount some of the history of the article and the field project it grew out of. I do this with some trepidation because the experiences and thought processes leading to "Cultural and Biological Success" involve a number of twists and turns that are lacking in scientific rigor.

In 1972 I was an assistant professor in the Department of Social Relations at The Johns Hopkins University, and I was busy designing a research project to return to the Yomut Turkmen in Iran where I had already completed roughly eighteen months of field research. Defining a research goal at that time was difficult precisely because I had no testable theory to serve as a starting point for my research. My first eighteen months of research had been conducted without a testable theory using various existing ethnographies as vague models of what the end product of my research should look like. I also had notes and queries as a methodological guide. As I sat down to design a new research project, what I had as a guide was still some published studies I admired and wanted to emulate in some way. One of these studies was Rappaport's *Pigs for the Ancestors*, and another was Chagnon's *Yanomamo: The Fierce People*. Both of these appeared after I had begun my first stint of field research in December 1965, and both suggested new directions further research on the Yomut might take. I found Rappaport's idea of cultural institutions regulating an ecosystem very appealing and was somewhat irritated by the reviews that point out that his evidence did not strongly support his theoretical interpretation. I thought it would be "neat" to do a study that showed how

a cultural institution regulated some ecological variable and to have solid empirical support for the idea. The inspiration I took from Chagnon was vaguer in quality. It consisted of a conviction that careful collection and analysis of demographic data was an important way to gain new insights.

This, however, did not constitute a well-defined focus for a research project. I needed more. While looking for a better-defined focus for my research I happened across E. A. Wrigley's *Population and History* and found what I thought I needed. In this book Wrigley (1969, 40–43, 112–13) suggests that many customs of "primitive cultures" operated as "negative feedback systems" that prevent overpopulation and overexploitation of the society's resource base. This idea I translated into the hypothesis that, among the Yomut, their large and fixed bridewealth would act as a kind of feedback device, causing delays in marriage as the property needed for bridewealth became scarcer. This, in a Muslim population with no illegitimate births, would slow the birth rate as wealth became scarcer, keeping numbers and resources in balance. Wrigley's ideas were derived from the thinking of the biologist Wynne-Edwards, who believed that population-regulating mechanisms had evolved by group selection. As I read further I became aware that biologists, by and large, were skeptical of Wynne-Edwards, but like many anthropologists I was very comfortable with the notion that human beings, because of culture, would be different from other animals. I decided that I would design an empirical study of Yomut demography that would test the hypothesis that bridewealth in combination with certain other customs acted as a regulating mechanism preventing overpopulation (Irons 1975, 150–54). I justified the deviation from orthodox biological theory by suggesting that these beneficial customs had spread and were maintained by a process of cultural group selection (Irons 1975, 171–74).

In the spring of 1973 I set off with my wife, Marjorie Rogasner, for Iran to evaluate this hypothesis. Iran, like most third world countries, has a very high birth rate, and the idea that local customs among an Iranian tribal population would have the function of limiting population growth seemed counterintuitive. Strange as it may sound now, my belief was that if the Wynne-Edwards hypothesis could lead me to discover something counterintuitive it would indeed be a powerful theory. I turned this into a gamble. If this counterintuitive fact could be demonstrated, I would take it as evidence that the Wynne-Edwards hypothesis works for more traditional human populations that have stable cultures with long histories. Current rapid population growth might be seen as partly a result of a disruption of such stable systems of regulating fertility. In order to test this idea and look for this counterintuitive finding, I constructed a sample frame and took a random, stratified sample of Yomut households from two large descent groups. I was greatly aided in this work by the collaboration of my wife, Marjorie Rogasner, and Daniel Bates of Hunter College. The actual field research stretched from August 1973 to August 1974. We were in Iran from June 1973 to September 1974.

In the fall of 1974 I returned to the United States and to a new job at Pennsylvania State University, where I began, with extensive assistance from my wife, to code and analyze the survey data. The data disconfirmed my hypothesis! Two crucial tests were made. One was a comparison of the two descent groups surveyed. One descent group was wealthy on average and one was poor on average. I predicted that the poorer group would delay marriages because men would need more time to raise the bridewealth needed to marry, and that women would have to wait longer for husbands. This would follow because the descent groups were largely endogamous and women could, for the most part, not marry until a man of their descent group came up with the required bridewealth. It was important that the lower fertility of the poorer group result primarily from the social fact of delayed marriage, not from a higher infant death rate or lower fecundability that could be interpreted as a straightforward Malthusian check on population growth. The second test consisted of an attempt to estimate changes in fertility and ages at marriage over time. The Yomut had experienced dramatic improvement in their economic conditions in the period from the end of World War II to the time of our survey in 1974, and this I predicted would be associated with a trend toward a lowering of that age at marriage as wealth became more abundant. The earlier conditions revealed from life history data would reflect a time when wealth was scarcer and the social conventions of the Yomut had throttled down the rate of reproduction so as not to overtax resources. Neither prediction was borne out! The average age at marriage for the poorer group was not different from that of the wealthier group, and the temporal trend was slight and in the wrong direction. At earlier times, when wealth was scarcer, women married on average at a slightly earlier age (about fourteen instead of fifteen). These negative results are published, along with other findings, in my 1980 paper, "Is Yomut Social Organization Adaptive?" These negative results were clear by the spring of 1975. If nothing else at that point, I had provided a counterexample to the academic Left's common assertion that scientists never falsify their hypotheses.

In fairness, it should be noted that the disconfirmation of my population-regulation hypothesis has no implications for Rappaport's hypothesis to the effect that the rituals of the Tsembaga regulate their ecosystem. Although I took part of my initial inspiration from Rappaport's study, in the end I formulated a quite distinct hypothesis about a different society. My data disconfirmed my hypothesis, but as I see it they have no direct implication for Rappaport's hypothesis, which is quite distinct in its details.

After deciding to reject my population-regulation hypothesis, I came across Richard Alexander's 1974 paper, "The Evolution of Social Behavior." This paper inspired me to rethink my data in terms of adaptations for the reproductive success of individuals, which was more in line with accepted biological theory but far out of line with accepted thinking in anthropology. The idea came quickly to mind that Yomut striving for wealth was simply striving for reproductive success. This idea had actually occurred to me while I was with the Yomut in the winter of 1974, but I had rejected it for two reasons. First, it was out of line with the group-oriented thinking of most anthropologists (including myself at that time). Second, as I saw it then it painted a grim picture of winners and losers. Aesthetically, I preferred to view people as part of a homeostatically regulated system that served the population as a whole. Nevertheless, I never forgot the idea and, as I read Alexander's 1974 article, I began to think that—grim or not—it was worth testing. I re-analyzed my data to see whether there was a positive correlation between wealth and reproductive success, and the result was a paper entitled "Emic and Reproductive Success," presented at the 1976 meeting of the American Anthropological Association. The paper was given in a set of symposia I organized with my colleague and longtime friend Napoleon Chagnon. These symposia later became the 1979 volume Chagnon and I edited. The revised paper, entitled "Cultural and Reproductive Success," is the one reprinted here. It is not substantially different than the version given in 1976.

The decision to test the cultural success hypothesis was part of a larger change in my thinking. The disconfirmation of my special version of the Wynne-Edwards hypothesis was not the only factor moving me in this direction. As a result of a large amount of reading and thinking, my view of human behavior had changed. I had gradually moved from the orthodox anthropological position that one can analyze culture without much attention to the constants of human nature or the motivations of individuals to the heterodox position that individual human beings had robust propensities that were evolved adaptations. As a result, I became convinced that human behavior and culture could only be understood by taking these evolved propensities—human nature—into account.

If I had it to do over again, how would I make the paper different? Realistically, I find it hard to imagine doing a lot differently. I can, however, think of three things I would add to the paper. First, I would include a bit more of a discussion of proximate mechanism. It occurred to me while editing the Chagnon volume to point out that eventually neuroscience would probably tell something interesting about proximate mechanism, but lacking such information, I had at the moment to be agnostic on the subject. Some researchers have read into the paper an assumption that the Yomut (and all other human beings) have a generalized fitness mechanism in their heads. Had I been more specific about my agnosticism and my expectations for the future, this misunderstanding might have been avoided. Second, I would include some of the material later published in my 1980 paper that addresses the issue of whether wealth causes higher rates of reproduction or whether, owing to the value of child labor, the reverse is true. Third, I would include some discussion of the question of why cultural standards of success (wealth among the Yomut, fierceness among the Yanomamö, church rank among nineteenth-century Mormons) appear to be honest guides to adaptive behavior, rather than manipulative attempts to misdirect the strivings of competitors. The answer, I think, is twofold: (1) standards of success are primarily learned from parents, who have nothing to gain from deception, and (2) some deceptions are too transparently false to be useful as competitively manipulative tools. These changes would not have greatly changed the character of the paper but would have improved it. These are all additions to the paper that I contemplated making but did not make because of time constraints.

As a final capstone on my retrospective, let me point out the following. Near the end of "Cultural and Biological Success" I made two statements that are, I think, important. First, I suggested that replication of this study in other populations would be necessary before inferring the correctness of the hypothesis that standards of success tend to be guides to adaptive behavior. Second, I also suggested that because of environmental novelty, the hypothesis would probably not hold in societies that have passed through the demographic transition. Both of these facts are relevant to what has happened since the publication of "Cultural and Biological Success."

The study has been replicated many times in societies that have not completed the demographic transition (see chapter 1). These studies have overwhelmingly confirmed the hypothesis presented and tested in "Cultural and Biological Success." Currently I am doing a meta-analysis of these studies.

Second, the research of Paul Turke (1989) and Daniel Pérusse (1993) has greatly clarified what forms of novelty are responsible for the failure of the hypothesis to hold in modern populations. Specifically, human status striving (or striving for culturally defined success, or striving for prestige) evolved in environments that included polygyny and very limited attempts to limit the number of children raised through either infanticide or some form of contraception. These conditions can be described as the adaptively relevant environment of status striving. Given these conditions, it was not useful for people to ask whether status would confer greater reproductive success. It was far more efficient to simply strive for status or prestige and not question why. The results of the various replications of my 1979 paper suggest that as long as polygyny and, more importantly, limited contraception were the rule, striving for status paid off reproductively. However, once both conditions are gone, the result is the familiar inverse correlation of cultural success and the number of children reared. I take it as abundantly clear that, in modern societies, cultural success either lowers reproduction or has no effect on reproduction.

Of the two elements in the adaptively relevant environment of human status striving, contraception appears to be the most relevant. Even with socially imposed monogamy, the evidence suggests that cultural success makes reproductive success more probable as long as extensive fertility limitation is not practiced (see chapter 1). Modern low fertility (total fertility rates of less that four, and often less than two) is a very recent phenomenon. It is not something that appeared three-hundred-plus generations ago with the origin of agriculture. It began, for the most part, two to four generations ago and still has not been established in much of the so-called third world. That something this recent and this closely bound up with reproductive success should undo past adaptation is not, in my opinion, a far-fetched view. The phenomenon of a correlation of cultural and reproductive success is a robust one in societies that lack extensive contraception, and even more robust in those that also practice polygyny. If the hypothesis presented in "Cultural and Biological Success" is false, what explanation do we have for this robust phenomenon?

Why the adaptively relevant environment of status striving has disappeared in the modern urban world is a good question that I leave for future research. Answering a scientific question usually leads to the opening up of new questions. I suggest that the replications of the cultural success hypothesis have answered a basic question. Why do people always identify their own culture's standards of success and strive to achieve them? Because in the environments of human evolution such behavior led to greater reproductive success. Why does status striving now appear to confer a reproductive disadvantage? This is the new question opened up. Pointing to the absence of polygyny and extensive contraception is a beginning of an answer, but why do modern people prefer monogamy and very low fertility? These are questions for future research.

5

Inuit Foraging Groups: Some Simple Models Incorporating Conflicts of Interest, Relatedness, and Central Place Sharing

ERIC ALDEN SMITH

Current neo-Darwinian research on behavioral adaptation is guided by two major bodies of theory: evolutionary genetics, and evolutionary ecology. Although some versions of sociobiology provide a place for ecological theory, in general this approach (as exemplified in the work of Hamilton, Trivers, and the many who have applied their models and insights to various cases) draws primarily on theory from evolutionary genetics. At the same time, models in behavioral ecology, such as those of optimal foraging theory, have tended to develop rather independently of recent advances in natural selection theory (such as the inclusive fitness concept).

Because of their different theoretical sources, then, behavioral ecology and sociobiology often analyze the same set of phenomena from somewhat different perspectives. Models in behavioral ecology focus on the interaction of phenotypic traits with environmental parameters, viewing individuals as strategists who attempt to maximize the material returns on their investments of time and effort. In contrast, sociobiological models focus primarily on genetic and other genotypic factors structuring the fitness outcomes of behavioral interactions in Mendelian populations, and view individuals as the agents of gene replication who carry out the task of maximizing inclusive fitness.

In some cases, the independence of ecological and sociobiological theory and research is fully justifiable, given the different kinds of questions addressed by the two approaches. However, it should often be the case that sociobiology and behavioral ecology are of mutual relevance in analysis of particular theoretical issues of empirical phenomena. Furthermore, I suggest that although each approach can be pursued alone to a certain extent, both contain inherent limitations that favor a combined approach (Wrangham [1982] makes a similar argument). This is certainly not an original thesis, but it is one that bears repetition given the current state of affairs. I illustrate this general thesis with analysis of an empirical case—the adaptive significance of Inuit (Canadian Eskimo) hunting groups. I first approach the analysis of foraging group size using a simple model based on standard assumptions of optimal foraging theory. I then expand the analysis to consider factors of social interaction and genetic kinship, employing the basic logic of decision theory and evolutionary genetics.

OPTIMAL FORAGING THEORY

Optimal foraging theory is that branch of evolutionary ecology concerned with subsistence behavior. It represents an attempt to construct a set of models that specify a general (strategic) set of "decision rules for predators" (Krebs 1978). Foraging theory is based on economic

Reprinted with permission from *Ethology and Sociobiology* 6:27–47 (1985).

optimization arguments and the assumption that foragers have been designed by natural selection, learning processes, and/or enculturation (Pyke, Pulliam, and Charnov 1977) to make those choices that yield the greatest difference between foraging costs and benefits, and hence the greatest payoff for the individual forager's survival and reproductive success (Darwinian fitness). Since the costs and benefits of foraging options are difficult or impossible to quantify in increments of fitness, proximate currencies are employed in the models and in empirical tests. Typically, it is hypothesized that foragers seek to maximize the net rate of energy capture while foraging.

Optimal foraging theory breaks the foraging process into different decision categories, with a set of models devoted to analyzing each category. The most prominent categories include diet breadth (prey choice), time allocation and patch choice, movement rules, and group formation.

To the evolutionary theorist concerned with social behavior, several prominent features of optimal foraging theory stand out, and may indeed appear as deficiencies. First, foraging models hypothesize *phenotypic* (material) optimization, analyzing foraging decisions as if net rate of energy capture were a direct measure of individual fitness. Second, foraging theory deals with the decisions of individual foragers as if they were made in isolation from the behavior of conspecifics, ignoring the potential intricacies of social interaction. Third, when analysis of social processes in foraging is attempted, as in models of optimal group formation, the simplest case (equal abilities and needs, no competition or dominance, etc.) is usually assumed. Fourth, the possible role of population structure and genetic relatedness in altering the patterns favored by natural selection is ignored—hence the link of proximate currencies to individual, not inclusive, fitness.

Clearly the assumptions of decision making in isolation and foraging efficiency maximization ignore many potentially important factors. Is this simplification valid? I argue that it *is* valid as a first-order approximation, in that simple, parsimonious models are very useful for theory building and preliminary tests in a "young" field of inquiry. On the other hand, these simplifications become true deficiencies if and when they lead to repeated failures in ex-

plaining pertinent data. The data and analysis for Inuit foraging groups presented below will, I hope, illustrate both of these claims.

SOCIOBIOLOGY AND FORAGING STRATEGIES

The inclusive-fitness concept (Hamilton 1964) of evolutionary genetics, which played such a large role in instituting the discipline of sociobiology, could in principle remedy several of the limitations of optimal foraging theory just noted. Rather than view the decisions of individuals as affecting only their own fitness budgets, sociobiology considers that they may often affect the individual fitness of others, many of whom are relatives, reciprocators, or competitors (and perhaps all three at once!). As a consequence, the artificial notion of individuals pursuing their own best interests in blissful isolation from others, akin to the "Robinson Crusoe" fiction of classical economics, can be replaced by a socially dynamic view of adaptation, wherein the best strategy to pursue depends on what other actors are doing, and on their relatedness to each other.

However, focusing on the inclusive fitness outcomes of individual decisions brings its own limitations, of which two are most important here. First most sociobiological models pay little or no attention to how the "ultimate" cost-benefit currency of inclusive fitness should be operationalized in any empirical application. Thus, if we are concerned with conducting empirical tests, the apparently greater rigor and realism of the inclusive fitness currency often may be illusory. This is not to argue that proximate currencies cannot be found to substitute in tests of sociobiological hypotheses—in many cases they can—but rather that these substitutes are not necessarily going to be any better measures of inclusive fitness than currencies such as individual foraging efficiency.

The second major limitation of a narrowly sociobiological approach is that the theory of evolutionary genetics that is its basis is far too general, and hence empty of specific predictions, to be sufficient in itself for explaining differences between particular social systems (Smith 1979). It is not terribly useful to account for the difference between solitary foraging in one society and communal foraging in another by the demonstration that inclusive fitness is maximized in each case. We need to go on to ask how this state of affairs came to be, and thus to inquire into the <u>selective forces</u> acting on each of these systems (cf. Stephens and Charnov 1982:260). Since the forces of natural selection are to a large degree ecological, purely genetic models of adaptation are inherently incomplete (Slatkin and Maynard Smith 1979:233), and we are brought once again to the mutual relevance of sociobiology and evolutionary ecology.

THE ADAPTIVE SIGNIFICANCE OF FORAGING GROUPS

Cooperative foraging and resource distribution systems are conspicuous features of human evolutionary history. The adaptive significance of foraging groups is of concern in ecological and evolutionary theory. In general, at least three possible relations may pertain between foraging strategies and the adaptive value of group formation (Schoener 1971:392): (1) individuals foraging cooperatively may enjoy increased foraging success relative to solitary foragers; (2) individuals may simply aggregate in response to resource concentrations with no direct benefit arising from cooperative foraging per se; or (3) group formation may have a neutral or negative effect on individual foraging efficiency but bring compensating advantages (such as improved predator avoidance, resource defense, survival of dependents, maintenance of reciprocity networks, or reduction of risk or uncertainty involved in food harvest). The first case, where groups form because of <u>mutual advantages from group foraging</u>, may arise in several different ways (review in Smith 1981). Groups may increase per capita harvest rates by better location of prey, by division of labor in capturing prey, or by reducing the degree of foraging-area overlap. Groups may also allow foragers to reduce the *variance* in food capture rates, perhaps at a cost to individual foraging efficiency. Finally, groups foraging from a central place and exploiting unpredictable food patches may increase per capita foraging efficiency through passive or active information sharing.

This brief discussion indicates that foraging strategies can affect group formation in a variety of ways and can shape groups at (minimally) two levels—the foraging party, and the settlement system (Smith 1981). Because coopera-

tive foraging and settlement patterns are outcomes of individual strategies, and because they necessarily are shaped both by ecological factors (such as resource availability in space and time) and social factors (such as patterns of reciprocity and relatedness), the analysis of group formation would likely benefit from a combined ecological-sociobiological approach (see Brown [1982] and Vehrencamp [1983a] for parallel arguments).

Although many anthropologists and biologists have speculated on the selective factors structuring hunter-gatherer group formation, relatively few formal ecological or evolutionary models have been presented, and even less often have empirical tests of such models been attempted (Heffley 1981; Smith 1980, 1981; Beckerman 1983; Hill and Hawkes 1983). <u>In this article I focus on the adaptive significance of foraging group formation,</u> forgoing attention to the more complex case of settlement patterns (not to mention the strategic interactions between these two levels of group formation). First we consider a very simple optimal foraging model of group size. This model is then modified or reformulated in several ways, in order to incorporate factors ignored in the initial formulation—factors such as kinship and conflicts between individuals. In each case I test hypotheses derived from the model with data on Inuit (Canadian Eskimo) foragers, in an attempt to specify the importance of different factors in structuring foraging group formation in this society (see Appendix A for methods of data collection).

THE SIMPLE OPTIMAL GROUP SIZE MODEL

Given the basic assumptions of optimal foraging theory described above, we might expect foraging groups to form whenever cooperative foraging yields higher benefits *per forager* than does solitary foraging. More precisely, <u>foragers should seek to form groups that maximize the per capita rate of net energy capture.</u> For any particular foraging period, this per capita rate can be defined as

$$\bar{R} = \frac{\sum_{i}^{n} (E_a - E_e)}{t \cdot n} \tag{1}$$

where n is the foraging group size, t is the duration of the foraging period, and E_a and E_g label food energy acquired and metabolic energy expended, respectively, by each of the n members of the foraging group during period t. We thus predict that foragers will adjust group size (n) to changing ecological conditions, since the optimal size of n under one set of prey abundances or prey types will differ from that under another state of these (and other) variables. Note that I am assuming here—and in most models in this article—that there is an equal division of the harvest among members of a foraging group (this assumption is indeed met in most cases of Inuit foraging I have observed).

Elsewhere I have shown how one can derive a variety of hypotheses concerning foraging group size from the simple per capita maximization model (Smith 1980, 1981). In testing predictions from this model with data on Inuit hunting groups, I have constructed a classification of observed foraging trips into what I call "hunt types," defined by prey species, habitat characteristics, and foraging techniques (other than group size). I argued that for any particular hunt type, there will be at least one optimal group size (i.e., for any hunt of type j, the optimal group size $\hat{n}$ is the size for which mean per capita net return rate R_j is at maximum). One direct test of this prediction is to determine whether the modal group size for any hunt type is the one associated with the highest

per capita net capture rate (maximizes $\bar{R}_j$ varying n). A test of this prediction indicates that the modal group size is indeed the most efficient in four cases but is suboptimal in the four other hunt types, with two cases yielding indeterminate results (Table 5.1 and Figs. 5.1–5.10).

Clearly these results offer somewhat equivocal support for the simple model of per capita maximization. A statistical test of the rank order correlation between group size frequencies and per capita return rates yields the same ratios of supported, refuted, and indeterminate results (Smith 1981). Factors that might contribute to these mixed results without calling the basic logic of the model into question include small sample sizes in several of the negative cases (breathing hole, winter caribou, beluga), minor differences in return rates of modal versus optimal group sizes (spring goose, lead/floe edge), and the possibility that imperfect knowledge constrains Inuit to form groups that are of optimal size in the long term but may be suboptimal for a particular season. To leave it at that, however, is not very satisfactory. I prefer to view the simple per capita maximization model as a reasonable starting point, consistent with a fair share of the data, with the inconsistent results serving to suggest where further research and hypotheses are needed. For this reason, simple optimal foraging models are useful even when they fail to account for a substantial amount of the data used to test them, by virtue

Table 5.1. Inuit Foraging Groups: Data on Group Size and Foraging Efficiency for Ten Hunt Types

| Hunt Type | Sample Size (No. of Hunts) | Foraging Group Size | | | Maximum Per Capita Return Rates | |
		Mode	Mean	Range	Group Size	kcal/hr[a]
Lead/floe edge	54	1	2.7	1–10	2	2520
Breathing hole	19	4	3.9	1–8	3	4120
Beluga[b]	6	—	10.3	5–15	5–6	4760
Winter caribou[b]	10	3,5	4.0	1–7	6–7	12,710
Canoe seal	36	2	2.9	1–8	1	3980
Spring goose	55	1	2.4	1–7	1,3	3400,3410
Jig/goose	25	1	2.6	1–6	1	3290
Ptarmigan	27	1	1.5	1–6	1	1370
Lake jigging	60	1	2.8	1–10	1	1770
Ocean netting	69	1	1.6	1–5	1	21,350

[a]Net kilocalories per hunter per foraging hour, calculated as described in eq. (1) and accompanying text (see also Appendix A).
[b]No modal group size occurs in this sample of beluga hunts, while group size frequencies peak bimodally for winter caribou hunts. Maximum return rates averaged over two group sizes for both of these hunt types, in order to meet a sample criterion of ≥ 2 hunts.

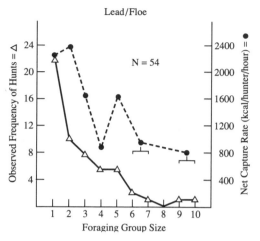

Figure 5.1. Return rates and observed frequencies, by group size, for Inujjuarmiut lead/floe edge hunts. Per capita net capture rates are averaged for each group size [see text, eq. (1)]; group sizes represented by a single case have been combined with data on an adjacent group size to calculate mean capture rates.

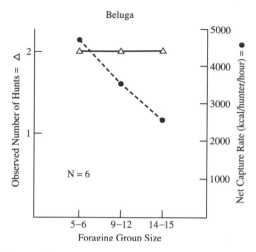

Figure 5.3. Beluga hunts (same format as Fig. 1).

of the role of precise predictions and clear refutations in stimulating further research.

In the present case, I think it instructive to note that all four of the hunt types where the hypothesis of per capita maximization is confirmed have an optimal (and modal) group size of 1, while only one of the negative or indeter-

minate cases has the optimum at $n = 1$. This suggests that while Inuit foragers are often quite capable of assessing the expected per capita return rate for different group sizes under various foraging conditions, they are more likely to behave so as to maximize this rate when the most efficient option is to forage alone, *unconstrained by social interactions*. It follows that we need to consider factors that might alter either the (proximate) currency individuals are attempting to maximize, or their ability to actu-

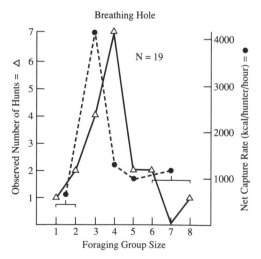

Figure 5.2. Breathing hole hunts (same format as Fig. 1).

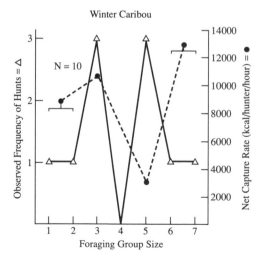

Figure 5.4. Winter caribou hunts (same format as Fig. 1).

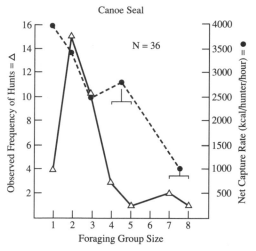

Figure 5.5. Canoe seal hunts (same format as Fig. 1).

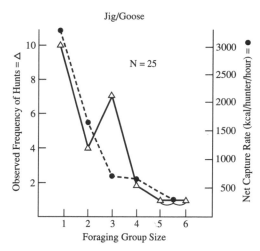

Figure 5.7. Jig/goose hunts (same format as Fig. 1).

ally maximize this currency, when we are dealing with foraging processes that involve social interactions. The following three sections present models that attempt, in various ways, to do just that.

CONFLICTS OF INTEREST BETWEEN MEMBERS AND JOINERS

In the best of all possible worlds, an individual would not only <u>know</u> what the optimal group

size was under each foraging condition but would also be under <u>no constraints in finding a place in such a group</u>. Obviously, in the real world there are many such constraints on the exercise of individual preferences. To maintain the analytical clarity provided by simple models, let us consider the effect just one such constraint might have on our basic per capita maximization model. Specifically, <u>what happens if a forager cannot always find precisely</u> $\hat{n} - 1$ <u>other foragers to team up with</u> (where $\hat{n}$ is the

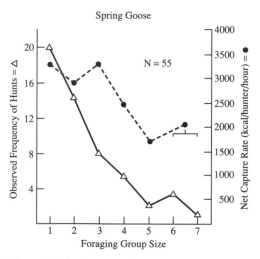

Figure 5.6. Spring goose hunts (same format as Fig. 1).

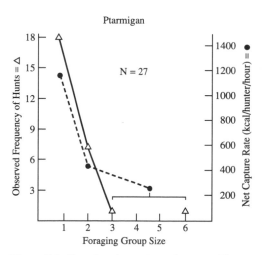

Figure 5.8. Ptarmigan hunts (same format as Fig. 1).

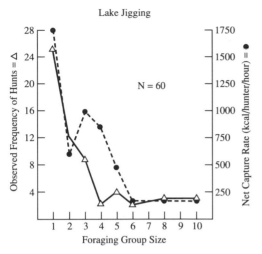

Figure 5.9. Lake jigging (same format as Fig. 1).

optimal group size as defined above)? In that case, while he or she may not be able to forage in a group of *optimal* size, the optimal forager should still try to join the group that yields the highest per capita return among the options available.

For simplicity, consider the case where there are only two options: to join a group of $n - 1$ foragers (and thus become the nth member), or to forage alone. In this case, the forager's preference is to join the group as long as

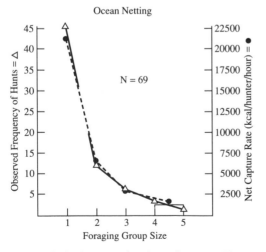

Figure 5.10. Ocean netting (same format as Fig. 1).

$$\bar{R}_n > \bar{R}_1 \qquad (2)$$

where $\bar{R}_n$ is the per capita return rate for a group of size n and the actual share for each member if equal sharing occurs. At the point where this inequality reverses, it will be preferable to forage alone. We can call this the "joiner's rule."

Once one is a member of a group, however, one's options are different, and hence one's preferences undergo a significant shift. In particular, the options are between maintaining the group size at $n - 1$ members or allowing another forager to join. With the same goal of per capita return rate maximization, a group member should favor the addition of an nth forager as long as

$$\bar{R}_n > \bar{R}_{n-1} \qquad (3)$$

The "member's rule" clearly differs from the "joiner's rule." It follows from the existence of two different rules or preference criteria that the rules, and hence the individuals holding those preferences, will sometimes be in conflict. Specifically, a conflict of interest between members and joiners will occur whenever

$$\bar{R}_{n-1} > \bar{R}_n > \bar{R}_1 \qquad (4)$$

that is, whenever the nth addition to a group could obtain a higher share from group foraging than from solitary foraging but by doing so would depress the total group harvest (and hence the shares the members would obtain without this additional member). A graphical version of this model (Fig. 5.11) makes this "zone of conflict" clear.

Under the assumptions of this model, conflicts of interest should be a quite common occurrence, especially when the expected returns from solitary foraging ($\bar{R}_1$) are low relative to the per capita returns from group foraging. As long as the expected share from group foraging is higher than that from solitary foraging, an individual will prefer to join the group—even if the resulting group size is not globally optimal. Once group size reaches the optimum, however, members should prefer to exclude additional foragers from joining.

Clearly, the predictions just derived depend on a number of assumptions that are less than exhaustive of the possibilities. In particular, the reduction of the decision problem to two choices—forage alone or join a group of size n—limits the realism, and complexity, consid-

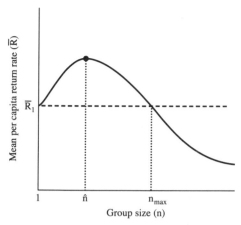

Figure 5.11. A graphical representation of the conflict between the "joiner's rule" and the "member's rule" [see text, eqs. (2)–(4)]. Per capita return rates peak at n, the size at which members will obtain the maximum share, but foragers faced with option of solitary foraging will improve their return rate by joining groups as large as n_{max} (the size where the per capita return rate R_n is equal to the solitary return rate R_1). This model can be generalized by substituting R_a—the expected return rate from *all* available alternatives open to a prospective joiner—for the solitary return rate (R_1); where the relevant data are available, this is the more robust hypothesis.

erably. A more realistic model would specify in some detail the initial frequency distribution of "seed groups" and potential joiners, the processes of group formation, the costs of and limits to obtaining information on these, and other aspects of the process of group formation. Furthermore, there are circumstances in which conflicts of interest between members and joiners will be avoided—whenever the highest returns come from solitary foraging, for example. Nevertheless, the present model clearly shows that the simple per capita maximization model is rather limited, since even when individuals share the same optimality criterion different opportunities may lead to different preferences. The occurrence of conflicts of interest considerably complicates the task of predicting the group sizes optimal foragers will form. For while the member/joiner model does clearly specify the preference rules for different circumstances, and pinpoints the conditions under which conflicts of interest will arise, it does not address the question of how such a conflict will

be resolved. To predict this, we would need to build an evolutionary or game theoretic model specifying the equilibrium outcome(s) (for important work along this line, but treating residential rather than foraging groups, see Vehrencamp 1983a and Pulliam and Caraco 1984).

Lacking a clear prediction of expected outcome, we can at least inquire what balance seems to have been achieved between member's and joiner's rules among Inuit foragers. Does the member/joiner model provide an improvement in accounting for variation in Inuit foraging group size? The relevant data are summarized in Table 5.2 (see also Figs. 5.1–5.10). Of the ten hunt types considered earlier, five can be ignored because the optimal size is $n = 1$, and we have already noted that in this case foragers will always maximize their own return rates by foraging alone. The remaining five hunt types do not fall into any neat pattern. In two or three cases (lead/floe edge, spring goose, and probably winter caribou), member's and joiner's rules lead to the same preferences, which do not differ much from that predicted by the simple per capita maximization model. Two suggestive cases remain. For the breathing hole hunt type, members should prefer to limit group size to that which maximizes per capita rates (R_{max}), which is $n = 3$, while the relatively low expected returns from solitary foraging mean that joiners will increase their expected returns by joining any group of up to eight members—which is in fact the maximum observed for this hunt type (see Fig. 5.2). It is conceivable that the reason modal group size exceeds the per capita optimum for this hunt type is that the observed range of group sizes

Table 5.2. Test of the Joiner's Rule and the Members' Rule for the Preferred Size of Inuit Foraging Groups

Hunt type[a]	Size	$\bar{R}_{max}$	$\bar{R}_n > \bar{R}_1$	$\bar{R}_n > \bar{R}_{n-1}$
Lead/floe edge	1	2	2	2
Breathing hole	4	3	8	3
Beluga	—	6	9	6
Winter caribou	3,5	6	7	6
Spring goose	1	3,1	3	3

[a]For each hunt type, the foraging group size that is associated with the highest mean per capita return rate, $\bar{R}_{max}$ (see eq. [1]), the largest group an individual should join if the alternative is solitary foraging (see eq. [2]), and the largest size that members should wish to see their group grow (see eq. [3]). All calculations derived from data presented in Smith (1980, Appendix H).

reflects various "compromises" between the interests of joiners and members. Testing this idea would require further information on the dynamics of group formation for breathing hole hunts. These hunts are organized a day or two in advance, and are highly structured and cooperative affairs, but I lack data on precisely how the size and composition of these hunting parties are determined.

The case of beluga hunting is less ambiguous. These hunts are relatively infrequent, since they are limited to the relatively short period when the whales are concentrated in the Nastapoka estuary, and require a long (ca. 210 km) journey from the village. I have quantitative time and energy data on six hunts, covering group sizes from 5 to 15 hunters and over 4100 hunter-hours of foraging. As can be seen from Figure 5.3, the per capita returns show a steady decline as group size increases. According to eq. (3), then, members should try to limit group size to six foragers. A joiner's preference depends on the expected returns from solitary foraging, and in this case we have no data on what these would be for beluga hunting. Informants' statements indicate that several canoes are usually required for successful beluga hunting, and my observations plus the absence of any solo kills support the assumption that the expected return for solo beluga hunters in the study locale is very low. Furthermore, since productive beluga hunting is limited to a particular time and place, it would rarely be possible for individuals to hunt beluga there on their own. However, individuals still have the option of solitary foraging involving other hunt types, and I have assumed that the mean return from all non-beluga hunting during July (the period when organized beluga hunts occur) which consists primarily of solo hunts, is the relevant value for R_1 that joiners following the rule formalized in eq. (3) would employ. Using this measure, the data indicate that joiners should prefer to join any group of beluga hunters to $n = 9$; interpolating missing values for $n = 10$ and $n = 11$ would suggest that even these group sizes yield per capita returns greater than R_1. This means that a conflict of interest between members and joiners exists between $n = 6$ and $n = 9$ or 11. Since beluga hunts are announced in advance, but foragers who wish to participate travel separately in small groups (two to three hunters per canoe), and all who show up

participate and share equally in the catch, we can predict that the joiner's rule will prevail over the member's rule. This would account for group sizes above the per capita maximum of $n = 5$, but not for groups above $n = 11$. I would suggest that lack of information about the number of foragers that will show up at the site (perhaps coupled with uncertainty concerning the density of whales) explains why some extremely large parties do form. In any case, the member/joiner model does seem to offer a better, if less than perfect, explanation for beluga hunting than does the simple per capita maximization model.

SOCIAL FORAGING AND INCLUSIVE FITNESS

In the preceding section, we modified the simple per capita maximization model by incorporating some constraints and options affecting individual decision makers but maintained the same currency of individual foraging efficiency. In seeking to understand foraging decisions in a social context, another possibility we might consider is that the currency that individuals seek to maximize should itself be modified. In sociobiology, the concept of inclusive fitness (Hamilton 1964) has fundamentally altered the way in which behavioral costs and benefits are assessed in evolutionary studies. The basic idea is that when actors are genetically related to each other, natural selection will favor those who take each other's interests into account and do *not* act purely in terms of "self-interest" (i.e., personal survival and reproduction). More precisely, inclusive fitness theory predicts that actors will weigh the costs and benefits absorbed by themselves and by other individuals *as a result of the actor's behavior* according to the closeness of genealogical relationship in each case—unity for costs and benefits absorbed by oneself, half that much for those of full siblings, etc.—and act so as to effect the maximum net benefits calculated in this way.

But what are the implications of this theory for analyses of optimal group size? There have been surprisingly few attempts to analyze this issue—a result no doubt of the lack of integration between behavioral ecology and sociobiology discussed in the introduction to this paper. Recently, however, several authors (Rodman

1981; Emlen 1982; Wrangham 1982; Vehrencamp 1983a) have presented models treating the effects of relatedness on group formation. Rodman's model considers the relation between group size and foraging efficiency, and hence is the most relevant to this article. He concludes that ". . . if individual fitness reaches a maximum at some group size, then inclusive fitness (of which individual fitness is a component; Hamilton 1964) will always peak at a larger group size (at which individual fitness is no longer maximized)" (Rodman 1981, p. 275). Rodman's model predicts this to be the case whenever there is some relatedness among group members, while there are large benefits to belonging in a group. That is, the model predicts that if group members have much higher individual fitness than those who are excluded from the group, then members should allow relatives to join or remain even if this lowers the members' own individual fitness, as long as the gain in relatives' fitness, devalued by the coefficient of relatedness, exceeds the loss in members' individual fitness.

Rodman uses this model to comment on data showing that groups of lions (Caraco and Wolf 1975) and wolves (Nudds 1977) often occur above the sizes that would be optimal for individual foraging efficiency, and he suggests that the model has very wide applicability. There are certain assumptions and simplifications in the model, however, that lead me to suggest that its predictions may not apply so broadly. First, Rodman does not distinguish between temporary groups, such as foraging parties, and more long-lasting social formations such as residential groups (e.g., lion prides, wolf packs, hunter-gatherer bands). The selective factors affecting foraging groups should often be rather different than those affecting residential units (cf. Smith 1981). Second, Rodman's model assumes that the fitness of solitary individuals is zero, an assumption that—and this relates to the point just raised—might be plausible in the case of exclusion from the coresidential unit but is unlikely to be true in the case of exclusion from a temporary hunting party.

A third and more general problem is in deciding how individual preferences will interact. Since each individual is likely to have a different set of genealogical ties to other foragers, the costs and benefits of admitting or excluding different individuals will also vary from one member to another. In addition, each potential joiner will also have a unique cost-benefit calculation dependent on particular coefficients of relatedness to group members. Thus, although one might suppose that a group composed of related individuals would be more likely to "altruistically" admit another related individual even though this decreased the net return per member, it also follows that the potential joiner should carefully weigh the benefits it receives from joining against the costs of decreasing the foraging profits of relatives. Again, since foraging alone should often have much less deleterious consequences than living alone, this tradeoff may often favor solitary foraging rather than depressing the foraging efficiency of the group. Furthermore, Rodman's specific predictions seem to depend on the assumption that a single dominant individual can exclude or include group members at will (Vehrencamp [1983a] makes the same assumption, while Sibly [1983] makes the opposite assumption that no member can exclude joiners). This problem of differential power of individuals to affect group size is one that we return to below.

Finally, among human foragers (as well as some social carnivores) the harvest from any hunt is generally shared widely beyond the confines of the foraging party itself. This sharing is reported to be kin-preferential in many hunter-gatherer societies (though often including affinal as well as consanguineal relatives). This means that foragers who are able to join foraging groups of sizes that maximize per capita harvest rates will make greater contributions to the time/energy budgets (and hence presumably fitness) of dependent kin.

In sum, the conclusion reached by Rodman that if there is any positive relatedness ($\bar{r} > 0$) kin selection will always favor groups above the individual selection optimum should apply generally. However, the *magnitude* of this effect may vary considerably. Only when costs and benefits to members versus (related) joiners are highly asymmetrical should we expect to find a marked effect of kin selection on group size. Although such asymmetry may be fairly common when considering membership in residential units, it should be less evident for membership in temporary foraging groups. (It may arise in the latter case, however—for example, when allowing young and inexperienced relatives to accompany a foraging party will provide them with valuable experience, even at the cost of some depression in the per capita harvest.) Furthermore, as shown above, individual selection alone can favor group sizes above the average per capita optimum (see also Sibly 1983; Pulliam and Caraco 1984). Hence observations of "above-optimal" group sizes are not clear evidence in favor of kin-selection effects.

A MODEL OF THE EFFECTS OF RELATEDNESS ON FORAGING GROUP SIZE

In order to empirically test the possible effect of relatedness on the size of Inuit foraging groups, we need a model that predicts individual preferences for this variable considering the effect of this preference on the individual's own benefits as well as on benefits that accrue to other (related) members of the foraging group.

By assuming that the inclusive fitness effect of different foraging group sizes can be directly calibrated in terms of energy capture rates, we can modify our previous inequalities for joiner's and member's rules, adding terms to express these effects. An individual deciding whether or not to become the nth member of a foraging group, at least some of whose members are close kin, should prefer to join if the sum of his share plus the share of the $n - 1$ members (devalued by $\bar{r}$, the mean coefficient of relatedness between the joiner and the members—see Appendix B) would exceed the sum of his harvest from solitary foraging plus the harvest the same group of foragers would obtain without him (again devalued by $(\bar{r})$ over the same period of time). That is, a joiner's preference rule should be to become the nth member of a group whenever

$$\bar{R}_n + [\bar{r}\bar{R}_n(n - 1)] > \bar{R}_1 + [\bar{r}\bar{R}_{n-1}(n - 1)] \quad (5)$$

(Again, I assume here that the harvest is equally divided among group members.) The second term on each side of this inequality express what we might call the "inclusive efficiency effect" of adding an nth forager to the group, *from this joiner's point of reference*.

It is clear from eq. (5) that the closer the degree of genealogical relationship between the joiner and the group members (the larger the value of $\bar{r}$), the greater the role we can expect the inclusive efficiency effect to play in determining a joiner's preferences. Specifically, the

larger $\bar{r}$ becomes (all else being equal), the more important the effect on members' shares of joining becomes to the joiner, and hence the less likely a joiner is to act selfishly in joining a group and depressing the per capita return rates simply because the joiner's share will be higher that way.[1] Note also that if there is no kinship recognized between the joiner and group members $(\bar{r} = 0)$, the inclusive efficiency terms go to zero, and this preference rule thus reduces to that given in eq. (2)—the special case for joiner's preference with no relatedness.

The cost-benefit criterion from a group member's point of view is of course different, and considerably more complex. In this case, the inclusive efficiency measure must take into account the effects of adding a new member on the shares of (1) the decision maker, (2) the joiner, and (3) other members, as well as the effect on (4) the members' shares if the prospective joiner is excluded and (5) the joiner's expected return from solitary foraging—all devalued by the appropriate coefficients of relatedness between the decision maker and the other affected parties. To construct appropriate preference rules, one must know which member one is considering as decision maker, since each member may have a unique set of genealogical ties to the joiner and to other members. In the empirical cases I consider below, it is not known which, if any, individual is the prime decision maker, nor which individual should be considered the "joiner" (the last to join the observed foraging group). Hence, I have employed a simplified version of the decision rules for members and joiners (see Appendix B for a detailed discussion of the various forms the rules can take). Specifically, I have assumed that all members of a foraging group have equal say in size limits, and that the mean coefficient of relatedness between all individuals, both "members" and "joiners" $(\bar{r}_n)$, is the appropriate weighting device. Under these assumptions, the preference rule for members is to add additional foragers to the group as long as

$$\bar{R}_n + [\bar{r}_n\bar{R}_n(n - 1)]$$
$$> \bar{R}_{n-1} + \bar{r}\bar{R}_1 + [\bar{r}\bar{R}_{n-1}(n - 2)] \quad (6)$$

This rule expresses the idea that each member will evaluate the effect of adding an additional member by assessing the changes in his or her own share ($\bar{R}_n$ vs. $\bar{R}_{n-1}$) as well as the effects on the other $n - 1$ members if the nth individual joins, or the effects on the excluded forager plus the $n - 2$ other members, devalued by the coefficient of relatedness. Since we are concerned with the average preference of all individuals, any one of whom could be the joiner, this coefficient is simply the mean relatedness between all the n individuals involved ($\bar{r}_n$).

As we might expect, eq. (6) predicts that the higher the coefficient of relatedness, the more likely members will be to prefer to admit another member (and the more likely members are to *agree* on this preference), even if this reduces all members' shares somewhat but markedly increases the share of the joiner. This result is clearly consistent with Rodman's (1981) model, discussed above. Note that, as was the case with the joiner's preference rule (eq. [5]), where relatedness is zero or unrecognized, all terms in eq. (6) except the first term on each side of the inequality go to zero, and eq. (6) thus reduces to the preference rule for members deduced prior to the consideration of inclusive efficiency (eq. [3]).[2]

Before considering the degree of fit between the inclusive efficiency predictions and the observed variation in Inuit group size, it is worth noting the gross patterns evident in the structuring of genealogical relationships within Inuit hunting groups. The population I studied spend much of the year concentrated in a single settlement (Inujjuaq) of over 600 residents, with approximately one fifth this number being individuals (primarily adult males) who engaged in at least a moderate amount of foraging during the study year. Thus, individual foragers could in theory choose from a large pool of potential hunting partners—a number without real historical precedent for this population, which until very recently lived in camps of 20–60 people.

Historically, Inuit camps were loosely amalgamated into regional groupings by extensive intermarriage and residential movement between camps, although boundaries of exogamy or territory were not clearly defined in the eastern Arctic. Hence, present residents of Inujjuaq (termed Inujjuarmiut) are linked by a web of kinship ties encompassing all but a few of the village residents. Nevertheless, individuals classify their relatives by genealogical closeness, and association into foraging groups does not approach randomness with respect to kinship for any but the largest beluga hunts. Since I have not completed a genealogical analysis of the entire village population, I cannot quantitatively demonstrate the degree to which positive assortment (by kinship) structures hunting groups in comparison to a random assortment model. However, 1 have analyzed the genealogical linkages between individuals in a sample of hunting groups, and can thus calculate the coefficient of relatedness specified in eqs. (5) and (6) (see Appendix B regarding methodology).

Data analyzed thus far cover 65 hunting groups representing 6 different hunt types, with groups ranging in size from 2 to 16 individuals (Table 5.3). These data indicate that average relatedness, even for small groups, is not terribly high. Specifically, r_n rarely averages more than 0.2, and usually falls below 0.1 (for comparison, a dyad consisting of full sibs has $r = 0.5$, while one of first cousins $= 0.125$). Given the large family size typical of Inujjuarmiut, it would certainly be feasible to assemble foraging groups of siblings, cousins, and other close relatives on a more consistent basis than is re-

Table 5.3. Genealogical Relatedness of Inuit Foraging Groups, by Group Size and Hunt Type

Hunt type	$\bar{r}_2$[a]	$\bar{r}_3$	$\bar{r}_4$	$\bar{r}_5$	$\bar{r}_6$	$\bar{r}_7$	$\bar{r}_9$	$\bar{r}_{10}$	$\bar{r}_{14}$	$\bar{r}_{16}$	$\bar{r}$
Lead/floe edge	0	0.021	0.021	0.063	—	—	—	—	—	—	0.013
Breathing hole	—	0.021	0.021	0.025	—	—	—	—	—	—	0.024
Beluga	—	—	—	0.006	0.070	0.065	—	0.017	0.032	0.013	0.046
Winter caribou	0.125	0	—	0.159	—	0.208	0.141	—	—	—	0.132
Spring goose	0.225	0.025	0.063	0.050	0.063	0.060	—	—	—	—	0.121
Ocean netting	0.203	0.167	0.165	—	—	—	—	—	—	—	0.185

[a]Relatedness coefficients are calculated as specified in Appendix B, and averaged for each group size for each hunt type. 0 indicates no known genealogical relationship between any members of the foraging group(s). A dash indicates lack of data on relatedness, or lack of occurrence of groups of that size in the sample for that hunt type. Overall $\bar{r}$ is weighted by the number of hunts per group size.

vealed in the present data. Thus, although genealogical kinship certainly plays some role in structuring Inujjuarmiut foraging groups, it does not appear to play a dominant one.

It is worth noting the contrast these data present to data on Yu'pik Eskimo whaling crews from St. Lawrence Island, Alaska reported by Morgan (1979). Whaling crews range from five to seven men, drawn from a village of 350 total population, and Morgan's sample documents an average coefficient of relatedness of 0.31 (weighted by number of hunts per crew). The reasons for this striking difference cannot be explored here, but I suspect the presence of corporate kin groups with well-defined property interests in the St. Lawrence case, and their absence in the Inuit case, may be crucial. The differences between these two related hunting societies might ultimately be ascribed to their differing ecological contexts, which presumably generate rather different selective pressures on patterns of social interaction, favoring unilineal kin groups with hereditary membership in the Yu'pik case (e.g., Hughes 1960) but an emphasis on bilateral kinship, widely extended social networks, partnerships, extensive adoption, and fictive kinship devices of several sorts that have been well documented in the Inuit case (e.g., Guemple 1976, 1979). These are differences for which the concepts of inclusive fitness and genetic relatedness are relevant but by no means analytically sufficient.

Reasons for the patterns of variation in foraging-group relatedness summarized in Table 5.3 cannot be analyzed in detail here and in many ways remain obscure. A few points may be noted, however. First, variation in group relatedness *between* hunt types does not seem to follow any simple pattern. Hunt types characterized by high degrees of cooperation and division of labor exhibit both relatively high (winter caribou) and low (breathing hole, beluga) coefficients of relatedness. Second, the genealogical and social relationships underlying similar $\bar{r}$ values are often quite different: thus, caribou hunts typically consist of a group of related men in their prime, age-mates with similar hunting abilities and experience, whereas the relatively high degree of relatedness observed for groups engaged in ocean netting usually represents teacher-pupil relationships (e.g., an adult and his adolescent nephew). Finally, I would stress that variation in $\bar{r}$ is often a poor

indicator of the inclusive fitness consequences of different associations. For example, while cases of brothers hunting together are fairly rare in my sample, teams of brothers-in-law are quite common (see Fig. 5.12 for a graphic but not atypical example). Yet the first dyad, with an $\bar{r}$ value of 0.5, may often be no better an avenue towards inclusive fitness enhancement than the latter, where r normally equals 0 in this rather exogamously inclined population.[3] Raymond Hames (1987) reports a similar case where the genetic relatedness of cooperators, such a seductively convenient measure, is a misleading index of the inclusive fitness consequences of social interaction (see also Smith 1979).

Imperfect as they are, do measures of genetic relatedness help us understand variation in the size of Inujjuarmiut foraging groups? The inequalities stated above predict the maximum or optimum group sizes that joiners (eq. [5]) and members (eq. [6]), respectively, will prefer when they are attempting to maximize their inclusive efficiency. As was the case before we considered relatedness, our main interest is in hunt types where individual efficiency is *not* maximized by solitary foraging, since otherwise the inclusion of a relatedness weighting has no effect on the optimum or preferred group size.

From Table 5.4, we see that joiners and members often have the same preference, which in these cases does not differ from the preferences predicted on the basis of individual foraging efficiency alone (see Table 5.2). In two cases, however, the inclusive efficiency rule for join-

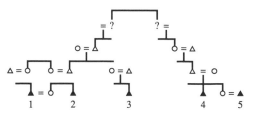

Figure 5.12. Genealogical composition of a single Inujjuarmiut breathing hole hunt. The five foragers, all males, are identified by darkened symbols. Note that three men (numbers 1, 2, and 5) have no known consanguineal links to each other or to any other group member, but are linked by affinal ties (in particular, the links between 1 and 2, and between 4 and 5, are those of "brothers-in-law").

Table 5.4. Inuit Foraging Group Size and Inclusive Efficiency Measures for Members and Joiners

Hunt Type	Modal Group Size	Group Size Satisfying Inclusive Efficiency Rule for	
		Joiners[a]	Members[b]
Lead/floe edge	1	2	2
Breathing hole	4	5	3
Beluga	—	10	6
Winter caribou	3.5	6	6
Spring goose	1	3[c]	3[c]

[a]The largest group size that a joiner seeking to maximize his or her inclusive efficiency would wish to join, if the alternative is solitary foraging (see eq. [5]).
[b]The group size that maximizes the inclusive efficiency of the average member (see eq. [6]).
[c]Because of the very small difference between $\bar{R}_1$ and $\bar{R}_3$ (see Table 5.1), joiners and members might be predicted to be indifferent between $n = 1$ and $n = 3$.

ers does lead to a conflict with that for members. For breathing hole hunts, individuals should prefer to join any group in the observed range if the only alternative is solitary foraging; the low degree of relatedness found among groups for this hunt type has no effect on the conclusion reached earlier that joiners and members are potentially in conflict when group size exceeds three hunters. For beluga hunting, members continue to prefer small groups ($n = 6$), whereas joiners should be willing to join parties as large as 10—almost identical to the predictions made without consideration of relatedness (Table 5.2). From these somewhat limited data, I conclude that genealogical ties and inclusive efficiency play little or no role in structuring the size of Inuit foraging groups, although kinship does play some role in shaping their *composition*.

COMMUNAL SHARING AT THE SETTLEMENT LEVEL

The models discussed above all assume that the catch of a foraging group is divided equally among the members of that group, these shares then being utilized as each group member sees fit. This sharing rule was not chosen at random, but because it matches the pattern I usually observed among Inuit foragers. Alternative sharing rules are conceivable, and this section models the consequences of adopting a different

rule. Specifically, I consider the case where all foragers coresident in a camp (often termed a "band" in the hunter-gatherer literature) pool their catch, whether obtained by solitary foragers or by groups. Such band-level sharing has been documented in detail for Ache Indians in Amazonia (Kaplan et al. 1984), and something like it occurs among Inuit in certain situations.

Let us assume that the sharing rule operates as follows: each day foragers leave camp and forage singly or in one or more groups, returning their catch to the camp, where it is pooled and then divided into equal shares for each resident. For simplicity, I will ignore differences between individuals in foraging effort and success, and will consider only the case where a single foraging group forms. The decision thus concerns how large this group will be and hence how many (if any) individuals will forage alone on any day. Note that at the end of each foraging period, every individual's share will equal

$$\frac{n\bar{R}_n + m\bar{R}_1}{N}$$

where n is the size of the foraging group, m is the number of solitary foragers, and N is the total membership of the band ($N \geq n + m$). The goal of each forager should then be to maximize this share, which is achieved by adding an nth forager to the foraging group, thus reducing the number of solitary foragers from m to $m - 1$, as long as

$$n\bar{R}_n + (m - 1)\bar{R}_1 > (n - 1)\bar{R}_{n-1} + m\bar{R}_1 \quad (7)$$

which simplifies to

$$n\bar{R}_n > (n - 1)\bar{R}_{n-1} + R_1 \quad (8)$$

(A similar model is presented in Hill and Hawkes [1983]; an earlier version of eq. [7] is given in Smith [1983].)

The interesting results of the band-sharing model concern the ways in which its predictions differ from those derived above under conditions of equal sharing within the foraging group. First, under settlement-wide sharing, eq. (8) expresses the optimal decision rule for *all* foragers in the sharing network since every individual's share is the same regardless of whether or not they are a member of a foraging group. Second, the decision rule given in eq. (8) holds true regardless of the coefficients of relatedness characterizing the foraging group or the band; indeed, these coefficients have no effect on optimal foraging group size or composition under this sharing rule. Third, because the model predicts that each forager should attempt to maximize the per capita share of band members, and hence the total band harvest, rather than their own personal catch, conflict of interest over group size per se should not occur. This last point assumes that each forager faithfully observes the sharing rule and is never tempted to cheat (e.g., to maximize their personal catch for prestige reasons, at the expense of the band harvest—see Hill and Hawkes [1983] for discussion of this point). Fourth, the optimal group size under the band-sharing rule will always be greater than or equal to the size that maximizes the per capita harvest of the foraging group, and less than or equal to the maximum size allowed by the joiner's preference rule.

This last point deserves emphasis. The optimal group size rule under band-wide sharing, as given in eq. (8), combines some elements of both joiner's and members' preference rules given earlier in eqs. (2) and (3), respectively. As in eq. (2), the preference for joining a particular group size depends on whether this will give a greater return than solitary foraging; but the precise criterion is not whether the per capita harvest rate of the group (R_n) is greater than the return rate for solitary foraging (R_1), but rather whether the *marginal gain in the group harvest rate* will exceed the solitary rate. This can easily be seen by transposing eq. (8) to read

$$n\overline{R}_n - (n - 1)\overline{R}_{n-1} > \overline{R}_1 \qquad (9)$$

The difference expressed by the left-hand side of this inequality is simply the marginal gain in the group harvest rate obtained by adding the nth member to the foraging group.

Indeed, under band-wide sharing, we can view the band as equivalent to a single production unit (a "firm") attempting to maximize overall foraging profits, and the group-size problem is thus the classical one of optimizing the input of each factor of production (in this case, labor allocation to group versus solitary foraging). The (neo)classical solution to this classical problem is, in the terminology of microeconomics, to add units of the production factor (group members) until marginal gains (in group harvest rate) equal marginal costs (R_1, the harvest rate for a solitary forager that is forgone

by taking one forager away from solo foraging and allocating his or her labor to group foraging).

Of course, hunter-gatherer bands (and wolf packs) do not operate like firms: there is no centralized management, or even usually much asymmetry in power (except by age and gender). My point is simply that where division of the harvest is even approximately on a settlement-wide basis, each individual forager will maximize his or her share by behaving *as if* the band is a unified production unit.[4] Evolutionary theory suggests that we then go on to ask why such a sharing rule might evolve, and how it might be maintained in the place of more individualistic strategies. This extremely interesting question cannot be explored here, but current research suggests that one answer might lie in ecological contexts favoring risk (variance) reduction via pooling of the catch among a large group of coresidents (Kaplan and Hill 1985a).

If the band-sharing rule often generates foraging group sizes above the optimum for individual foraging efficiency, then it may be an alternative explanation for the frequent occurrence of such groupings in human and nonhuman foragers. That is, in contrast to Rodman's (1981) arguments, individual-fitness enhancement rather than kin selection might be responsible for the evolution of these large foraging parties, if accompanied by a consistent tendency to pool the catch with other foragers at the home base. (Of course, the joiner's rule given in eq. [2] is another possible alternative explanation for such phenomena.)

In principle, then, the band-sharing rule can generate predictions concerning variation in foraging group size that differ systematically from those obtained using individual efficiency or inclusive efficiency rules, and lacking band-wide sharing of the harvest. In practice Hill and Hawkes (1983) have shown that a rule similar to eq. (8) predicts that Ache foragers will amalgamate into large parties for certain prey types, even though any individual's personal foraging efficiency would be maximized by solitary pursuit of the same prey. As it turns out, observed group sizes approach a random distribution, and evidence suggests that certain constraints on movement and communication prevent the band-maximizing strategy from prevailing in the Ache case.

The Inujjuarmiut data are even more ambiguous: for all ten hunt types, calculations using inequality (8) yield precisely the same predicted group sizes as are obtained using the simple per-capita maximization rule (eq. [1]), or the equivalent rule for members (eq. [3]). It should be noted that at present most Inujjuarmiut hunts do not end with a village-wide or camp-wide sharing of the harvest, and even in the past when settlement was in small economically integrated camps, sharing of the harvest was often more restrictive than is assumed under the band-sharing rule. But even for beluga and winter caribou hunt types, where actual sharing practices sometimes approximate settlement-wide sharing, eq. (8) does not predict group sizes over six, nor does it predict a different grouping pattern than if the catch were shared strictly within the foraging group.

In sum, for the Inujjuarmiut case, the band-sharing rule does not make predictions that can be distinguished from those of other rules, and like these other rules it fails to account for a substantial portion of the observed variation in foraging group size. Nevertheless, the band-sharing rule may well have explanatory value in other foraging societies where its assumptions are more closely met—among Amerindian bison hunters, or Subarctic caribou specialists for example.

CONCLUSIONS

A variety of simple models that illuminate aspects of the decision rules individuals might employ in structuring cooperative foraging have been presented here. Models of this sort should specify at least three elements: the currency individuals seek to maximize, the sharing rule governing the distribution of the harvest, and the relative power different individuals can exert when their preferences conflict. The models presented above have explored the implications of varying each of these elements to some degree, although many possibilities have been left uncharted, or even unstated.

Two currencies have been employed: individual (per capita) expected energy harvest rates, and inclusive (genealogically fractionated) energy harvest rates. The former is the standard currency in OFT, while the inclusive efficiency measure has been introduced here to model the nepotism (kin-directed altruism) that has become the cornerstone of sociobiological analysis. The results reported here suggest that the inclusion of a nepotistic weighting factor has very limited value in predicting variation in the size of Inujjuarmiut foraging groups, although this result should not be assumed to be general unless replicated among other foraging societies.

Two alternative sharing rules are incorporated in the present set of models: equal division of the harvest within the foraging group, and communal sharing with other groups and individuals who are members of the same settlement or band. The first sharing rule is capable of generating conflicts of interest over group size between potential "joiners" and existing "members" of foraging groups, whereas the second rule avoids this possibility. A communal sharing rule, where it prevails, may often act to increase the optimal foraging group size well above that which is optimal where sharing is restricted to foraging group members, although in the Inuit case examined above this does not occur.

The occurrence of conflicting individual interests is a fascinating problem that is still relatively unexplored. Here foraging models have the most to learn from sociobiology (as well as from microeconomics and game theory). My efforts in this direction are quite modest: the models presented here stress the difference between a joiner's preference and those of a group member but do not attempt to predict how these conflicting interests will be resolved when they arise. The prediction that joiners will frequently benefit from joining groups even when this will increase the size above the individual members' optima is a result that is probably quite robust. Inclusion of nepotistic considerations in the inclusive efficiency model greatly complicates the analysis of conflicting interests. Because each individual will generally have different genealogical ties to other foragers there might be not just two conflicting preferences (joiner's versus members'), but a variety of them.

The models presented in this article are all very simple ones. The primary justification for this is that simple models are easier to test, manipulate, and understand than are more complex models. Especially in the early stages of theory building, simple models allow us to isolate particular factors and to examine (theoretically and empirically) the effects of changes in these factors, one at a time. In the present case, it seemed wise to begin with simple models in order to explore the roles and relative importance of factors that have received little attention in previous models of cooperative foraging—that is, nepotism and individual conflicts of interest. Future models and tests will have to consider the role of additional factors and explore additional issues, as well as treating the above factors and problems in greater depth via more complex models. I am confident that this future research will demonstrate the mutual relevance of theory from evolutionary ecology, sociobiology, and the social sciences for analyzing strategies of cooperative foraging, and I hope that the present article has contributed toward such a demonstration.

APPENDIX A: DATA COLLECTION AND ANALYSIS

The data discussed in this article were collected over a 13-month period (July 1977 to August 1978) in and around the village of Inujjuaq (a.k.a. Port Harrison, Inoudjouac, etc.), on the east coast of Hudson Bay, arctic Quebec, Canada. A brief description of methods of data collection and analysis is given here; a detailed account can be found in my thesis (Smith 1980).

The 600-plus permanent residents of Inujjuaq, termed Inujjuarmiut ("people of Inujjuaq"), are all members of the Inuit (Canadian Eskimo) ethnolinguistic category. Although no Inujjuarmiut in the area have relied exclusively on foraging for their sustenance in the last two decades, comprehensive statistics collected by other researchers (NHRC 1979) demonstrate an annual harvest of approximately 180,600 kg (edible weight) of game, which amounts to an average daily harvest of 0.85 kg (1500 kcal) per capita. The foraging economy in this area is heavily marine-oriented in summer and fall, but terrestrial foraging in winter and spring accounts for the greater portion of the total annual harvest from the land. Virtually all foraging activities involve the use of mechanized transport (canoes with outboards, snowmobiles) and imported tools (rifles, fishnets, etc.). Fox trapping, commercial soapstone carving, wage labor, and government transfer payments are the main sources of cash income, allowing the

purchase of fuel and equipment for foraging, as well as store foods and other goods.

Inujjuarmiut harvest a wide range of species, ranging from fish and waterfowl to caribou and fairly large marine mammals (ringed seal, bearded seal, and beluga whale). The diversity of prey species, microhabitats and foraging conditions result in a fairly large number of hunt types, including traditional forms such as seal hunting at breathing holes. Inujjuarmiut foraging is often a solitary occupation, but cooperative foraging is also common, and extremely important in both economic and social dimensions.

Data on Inujjuarmiut foraging were collected in two principle ways: by direct observation, and via systematic interview. The first data set was generated by accompanying hunters on a total of 41 hunts covering approximately 400 hours of observation time. Interviews were conducted throughout the study period and utilized a self-recording "calendar" system to facilitate recall; interviews generated a sample of over 650 hunts and information on more than 25,500 hunter-hours of foraging effort. Neither observed nor interviewed foragers were selected at random, as this was not feasible in cases where informed consent was necessary and individuals varied in their willingness to be accompanied or interviewed. Nevertheless, the set of foragers included in my sample is quite large relative to the total number, and representative of Inujjuarmiut foragers in at least several respects (Smith 1980:223ff).

Observational data focused on the collection of detailed time-motion diaries. These were used in conjunction with published tables (Durnin and Passmore 1967; Godin and Shephard 1973) to estimate energy expenditure rates for each age-sex-class, by hunt type (see Smith 1980, Appendix B). Both observational and interview data include measures of time inputs, number and type of prey harvested, fuel consumption, trip itineraries and (for a fraction of hunts) identities of all members of the foraging group. Edible weights of prey species were calculated using a combination of field measurements and published and unpublished values; these were converted to caloric estimates in accordance with standard tables (where available) or unpublished laboratory measures (details in Smith 1980, Appendix A). These measurements or estimates of time expenditure, group size, energy expenditure, and energy harvest were then averaged over various categories of foraging trips to produce measures of mean net capture rates, as specified in the text (especially eq. [1]).

Genealogical information was collected from a number of informants, primarily older women, as part of a study of Inujjuarmiut demography. The genealogical charts published in Willmott (1961) were also consulted. The genealogical depth of the data extends to ancestors born in the late 1800s, about four generations. Genealogical data on the members of foraging groups were analyzed for 65 hunts; the method used to calculate coefficients of relatedness is described in Appendix B.

APPENDIX B: GENETIC RELATEDNESS AND INCLUSIVE EFFICIENCY

The measure of kinship employed in this article is the coefficient of genetic relatedness, r, given its modern sociobiological form and role in Hamilton's (1964) theory of kin selection and inclusive fitness maximization. Although I realize that there are some ambiguities associated with defining and measuring r (see Kurland and Gaulin 1979; Michod 1982; and Pamilo and Crozier 1982), I have followed standard practice and calculated this parameter by counting the genealogical pathways between each pair of individuals, ignoring any possible inbreeding that could not be traced genealogically. Thus, for any dyad, the coefficient of relatedness is given by

$$r = \left(\frac{1}{2}\right)^N \qquad (B1)$$

where N is the number of genealogical links between the two individuals. (If more than one common ancestor is involved, a more complicated formula needs to be used, but this was not encountered in my sample.)

To calculate the *average* coefficient of relatedness for a group of n individuals, one simply uses eq. (B1) to calculate r for each dyad included in the group, and then average these values. Specifically,

$$\bar{r}_n = \frac{\sum^d r}{d} \qquad (B2)$$

where $d = (n^2 - n)/2$, the number of dyadic pairs.

The manner in which r is used to construct cost-benefit criteria for foraging group size decision rules is discussed in the text. Here I expand on the discussion of alternative decision rules that can be generated for predicting members' preferences.

Consider first the problem of specifying the preference for a single member of a foraging group regarding whether or not to let another forager join the group. If we label the coefficient of relatedness between the ith member and the jth joiner as r_{ij}, and that between i and k other members ($k = n - 2$) as $\bar{r}_{ik}$; then member i should prefer to admit j as the nth member of the group as long as

$$\bar{R}_n + r_{ij}\bar{R}_n + [\bar{r}_{ik}\bar{R}_n(n-2)] > \bar{R}_{n-1}$$
$$+ r_{ij}\bar{R}_1 + [\bar{r}_{ik}\bar{R}_{n-1}(n-2)] \qquad (B3)$$

Note that the three terms on each side of this inequality are parallel expressions of the inclusive efficiency of a given group size from a focal member's point of view: the first expression is the return rate for ego (not devalued, since $r_{self} = 1$), the second expression is the return rate to the joiner, either if admitted ($\bar{R}_n$) or excluded ($\bar{R}_1$) and devalued by the degree of relatedness to the focal member (r_{ij}), and the third expression is the return rate for the $n - 2$ other members, devalued by the appropriate mean coefficient of relatedness to the focal member ($\bar{r}_{ik}$).

Although eq. (B3) gives the optimal preference rule for maximization of each member's inclusive efficiency, changing the identify of i will alter the various coefficients of relatedness (except in the special case where each member is identically related to all other members and to the joiner, as in a set of full siblings). Hence, each member will usually have differing inclusive efficiency values for aiding or excluding j, which may even result in different optimal group sizes for each i.

The actual decision-making process in such situations may be rather complex, but let us consider the case where all $n - 1$ members of the group have an equal voice in deciding whether to accept j as a member. Label the mean coefficient of relatedness between j and the members as $\bar{r}_{jm}$, and that between the group members themselves as $\bar{r}_m$. Then two of the three terms on each side of eq. (B3) can be collapsed, such that the average preference of the group members is to admit j as the nth member of the group as long as

$$\bar{R}_n + [\bar{r}_{jm}\bar{R}_n(n - 1)] > \bar{R}_{n-1}$$
$$+ r_{jm}\bar{R}_1 + [\bar{r}_m\bar{R}_{n-1}(n - 1)] \qquad \text{(B4)}$$

Note that this last expression specifies the *average* preference of group members as a function of their *average* relatedness to the joiner and to each other, and hence the outcome of following this rule might not be optimal for any one of them. That is, eq. (B4) is a compromise solution in the case of conflicting interests and assuming equal power among members (but not for the joiner) and equal sharing of the costs of excluding joiners. Although somewhat simpler than eq. (B3), it is hardly a rule of thumb that actual foragers might reasonably employ in reaching decisions about group size, but it does provide a precise and testable expectation of what the outcome of such decisions might look like.

Finally, what if the potential joiner has an equal say in the matter? Then we seek the expression that specifies the optimality criterion for all n individuals, *on average*. With equal division of the catch, each forager will attain a capture rate of R_n if the nth individual joins, or

$$\frac{(n - 1)\bar{R}_{n-1} + \bar{R}_1}{n}$$

if the group is limited to $n - 1$ members and the nth individual forages alone (note that this assumes that the solitary forager shares his catch with group members, or at least that the expected solitary return rate is a weighting factor in researching a group decision concerning

admission of the nth individual). The average relatedness between any individual and the $n - 1$ other individuals is labeled $\bar{r}_n$. Hence, *on average* any individual will benefit from increasing group size to n foragers as long as

$$\bar{R}_n + [\bar{r}_n\bar{R}_n(n - 1)] > \left[\frac{(n - 1)\bar{R}_{n-1} + \bar{R}_1}{n}\right]$$
$$+ \bar{r}_n\bar{R}_1 + [\bar{r}_n\bar{R}_{n-1}(n - 2)] \qquad \text{(B5)}$$

This is a more exact formulation than the similar inequality given in the text (eq. [6]), where five of the six parameters are identical to those in eq. (B5). An even more general and rigorous formulation might be possible using the matrix approach developed by Hughes (1983).

Acknowledgments. For comments on drafts of this article, and/or for sharing unpublished manuscripts, many thanks to John Atkins, Rob Boyd, Eric Charnov, Ray Hames, Kristen Hawkes, Henry Harpending, Kim Hill, Charlie Janson, Peter Nute, Ron Pulliam, Peter Rodman, Monty Slatkin, Sandra Vehrencamp, and Bruce Winterhalder. For assistance with fieldwork and data collections, I thank Carol Poliak, Lorraine Brooke, William Kemp, the Northheer Quebec Inuit Association, the Inukjuak Community Council, and the people of Innujuaq. Finally, I thank the National Institute of Mental Health and the Arctic Institute of North America for funding the field research, and the National Science Foundation for a postdoctoral fellowship that allowed me the time to formulate some preliminary versions of the models and analyses presented in this article.

NOTES

1. A worked example might make this clearer. Suppose there is a group of four members that would be increased to five if a prospective joiner were to be admitted ($n = 5$). Suppose further that the expected per capita return rate would decline from 1200 kcal/hr ($\bar{R}_{n-1}$) to 1000 kcal/hr ($\bar{R}_n$) if the fifth individual were to join, whereas the expected return from solitary foraging is 800 kcal/hr. Finally, suppose that all the individuals in question (members and joiner) are full siblings ($\bar{r} = 0.5$). Using eq. (5), we find that the inclusive efficiency of joining is 3000 kcal/hr, whereas that of solitary foraging (counting the effect on other members devalued by the coefficient of relatedness) is 3200 kcal/hr; hence, we predict that this joiner should prefer to forage alone, even though his or her personal return rate will be 200 kcal/hr *lower*. If the mean coefficient of relatedness between the joiner and the members were lowered to 0.1 (slightly less than that of first cousins), the joiner's inclusive efficiency would now be greater in the group (1400 kcal/hr) than alone (1280 kcal/hr), and the joiner's predicted preference would reverse. (At this point the predicted preferences of members and joiner would be in conflict, as calculated from eq. [6], below, whereas at the higher $\bar{r}$ of 0.5 they were not.)

2. All the expressions in this section (and in Appendix B) assume that selection favors increased inclusive fitness, and hence increased inclusive efficiency. However, recent theory demonstrates that selection does not maximize inclusive fitness under certain conditions of frequency dependence or strong selection (see Michod 1982 for a review). Nevertheless, given the rather hypothetical link between fitness and efficiency, a more rigorous derivation of predictions would be of little relevance here—hence, the simplifying assumption that selection favors traits that maximize inclusive fitness will be maintained.

3. It is possible to reformulate measures of inclusive fitness effects to take such factors into consideration (e.g., West-Eberhard 1975; Emlen 1982). Thus, the effect of foraging interactions on a brother-in-law's *offspring* (who, barring extramarital paternity, have a coefficient of relatedness to ego of 0.25) could be taken into account by knowing how much of the brother-in-law's harvest was allocated to those offspring. Given the present data, however, this modification cannot be made operational.

4. Technically, then, a foraging band is not a firm, but rather a *team*—a group of individuals cooperating to maximize a shared goal (see Marschak and Radner 1971). This correction, and the reference, was provided by Rob Boyd (personal communication).

6

Sex Is Not Enough

ERIC ALDEN SMITH

Almost all the chapters in this book are about sex—that is, mating and parenting. In contrast, mine is about food, and about the politics involved in obtaining and distributing that food. This tilt in the book's coverage is not the result of sampling bias on Laura Betzig's part: now even more than ten years ago, when my piece was written, evolutionary studies of human behavior focus heavily on sex. And that's fair enough, given that Darwinism makes differential replication the pivot of evolution. But the realities of thermodynamics have been around a long time—even longer than those of natural selection—and they continue to exercise a profound influence even in that upstart realm of the universe we call life. It worries me to think that my puny little chapter carries all the weight of bringing Darwinism to bear on human food-related behavior for this book.

My chapter focuses on collective action among foragers: cooperative foraging, group size, and food sharing. It links this topic to the more central concerns of human sociobiology via Hamilton's (1964) inclusive fitness concept. In 1983 (when I actually wrote my article), the theoretical literature on group formation and cooperative foraging was relatively sparse. That linking these topics to inclusive fitness was even sparser. Hence, I took the basic ideas of sociobiology and evolutionary ecology as I understood them and built my own models (with a lot of help from my friends). I had already published the main elements of what I called the "member-joiner model" (Smith 1983), advancing the intriguing notion that optimal group size was relative to one's position vis-à-vis group membership. My analysis of conflicts of interest between members and joiners thus co-

incided with Sibly's (1983) and Pulliam and Caraco's (1984) comparable work on group size. What I did not grasp so clearly was that where payoffs are frequency-dependent (as they are in group foraging and sharing), one needs to solve for evolutionarily stable strategies, not simple optima—even conflicting ones.

Since 1985, the theory of evolutionarily stable group size has grown significantly; reviews include Clark and Mangel (1986), Giraldeau (1988), Packer and Ruttan (1988), and Rannala and Brown (1994). While elaborating the insight that optimal group size is often unstable, these studies rarely consider that free access by joiners (e.g., Sibly 1983) is inherently no more likely than effective exclusion by members (e.g., Vehrencamp 1983b). Only recently has the pioneering work that Vehrencamp (1983b) and I did on member-controlled entry been given serious treatment, in papers by Giraldeau and Caraco (1993) and by Higashi and Yamamura (1993), which also consider the effect of relatedness.

I was relieved (after a few hours of algebraic labor) to determine that my "joiner's rule" is mathematically equivalent to the "free entry" or "outsider" case modeled by these authors. But the results of my "members' rule" differ from those derived by Giraldeau and Caraco, though they agree with those of Higashi and Yamamura. The former structure their model in terms of Hamilton's rule (Grafen 1984) that kin-directed behavior is favored only if $rB - C > 0$, where B = benefits conferred on others and C = costs incurred by ego. As Giraldeau and Caraco point out, the more general form of this rule is r(effect on relatives) + (effect on self) > 0. In this case of group members deciding whether to admit another member, (effect on self) consists of the difference between one's fitness (or its proxy, harvest share) if potential joiner X is admitted (increasing group size to n) or excluded (keeping group size to $n - 1$). In my model—and in Higashi and Yamamura's—the term (effect on others) includes two components, the effect on X's fitness, and the effect on the fitness of other $(n - 2)$ members of the group, both components devalued by the appropriate r. Surprisingly, Giraldeau and Caraco assume that "self is the entire group" (p. 434); in other words, they treat the set of $n - 1$ members as a single decision maker with $r = 1$. I believe my model (like Higashi and Yamamura's) makes more sense: Hamilton's rule requires that we devalue the effects of admitting a new member on the other members by the actual r that pertains.

Both of these papers show that relatedness acts to *decrease* stable group size under free access (joiner's rule) but *increase* it under controlled entry (members' rule), whereas I concluded (erroneously) that relatedness will increase the stable group size under both conditions. Higashi and Yamamura's article also provides an ESS solution to the conflict between joiner's and members' rules, something I raised in my article but could only wave my hands about. Unfortunately, their solution ignores the second-order collective action problem of the cost group members must pay to exclude a potential joiner; since such exclusion would benefit all members equally, but not necessarily require that all of them pay the cost, exclusion is a collective good with an opportunity for free riding that could undermine its provision.

Besides an exercise in model building and empirical testing, my paper was also an attempt to link behavioral ecology and sociobiology more explicitly than was then typical in human behavioral studies. One thing I concluded from this analysis was that, among the Inuit foragers I worked with, genetic kinship was not a very strong determinant of group composition or social cooperation (though it clearly played a role). This parallels similar results that have been published for a number of cases, including coalitions of male lions (Packer and Pusey 1982; Grinnell, Packer, and Pusey 1995), feeding groups of ravens (Parker et al. 1994), cliff swallows giving food calls (Brown, Brown, and

Schaffer 1991), and some instances of coalition formation in a variety of primate species (Silk 1987b:325ff). All this suggests that we need to be cautious about ascribing too much importance to kinship as a determinant of cooperation. Hamilton's formulation of inclusive fitness remains powerful and enchanting, but I think that too often analysts focus on r (relatedness), and forget that C and B (costs and benefits, socially and ecologically determined) are just as critical in structuring inclusive fitness effects.

When I published my first paper on hunter-gatherer group size (Smith 1981), there were no comparable data for other human foragers. Fifteen years later, the only other population with extensive quantitative data on foraging group size remains the Ache (Hill and Hawkes 1983; Hill and Hurtado 1996). I wonder why this is the case. Certainly my Inuit data are far too slender a reed on which to balance significant claims about human foraging groups (I still cringe when I look at the sample sizes for some of the hunt types!). If republication of my paper does nothing else, I hope it will stimulate others to gather the relevant data from other ethnographic settings and use these and other models in an attempt to explain the observed variation in group size and composition.

The other major concern of my article is food sharing. Here I am less happy with my accomplishments. For one thing, I had no real data on Inuit sharing, so was reduced to the level of pure theory. (Data on food sharing is damned hard to collect, and I continue to be amazed at what the Ache project accomplished in this regard [Kaplan, Hill, and Hurtado 1984, 1990; Kaplan and Hill, 1985a; see also Hames 1990 for Yanomamö data].) On the theoretical level, although I did highlight some ways in which different "sharing rules" affect individual strategies, I really had nothing to say about which sharing rules we might expect to predominate under which conditions. Continuing work on the causes and consequences of hunter-gatherer food sharing has failed to resolve matters.

There certainly are a variety of selective factors, models, and specific analyses concerning cooperation and resource transfer to choose from. These include *risk reduction* (Kaplan and Hill 1985a; Kaplan, Hill, and Hurtado 1990; Smith 1981; Winterhalder 1986, 1987, 1990), sometimes explicitly in a prisoner's dilemma framework (Smith 1988; Smith and Boyd 1990) or incorporating nepotism (Berté 1988; Hames 1990); *coercion* (Moore 1984) and its variant of *"tolerated theft"* (Blurton Jones 1987b; Hawkes 1992); *mating* strategies, including male risk seeking or "showing off" (Hawkes 1990, 1991, 1993); and *mutualistic* payoffs without reciprocity (Connor 1995; Mesterson-Gibbons and Dugatkin 1992). It is, of course, possible that there is no single best explanation for food sharing. One hopes that future research will provide some definitive answers.

By the way, my book on Inujjuamiut foraging strategies (Smith 1991) summarizes all I intend to say about foraging. These days I'm working on topics such as infanticide and sex ratio (e.g., Smith and Smith 1994). My reprint requests are way up, and for the first time ever, popular science magazines are calling me up for interviews. Clearly, food is passé and sex is in; who am I to buck a trend? But I still think the big questions have to do with how the two are linked (via politics, among other vectors). Maybe the 2005 edition of this book will prove me right.

7

Bushman Birth Spacing: A Test for Optimal Interbirth Intervals

NICHOLAS BLURTON JONES

The long interbirth intervals (IBIs), roughly four years, reported for the !Kung by Howell (1979) and Lee (1972, 1979) might seem to be a clear example of people failing to maximize reproductive success. Reproductive success would seem to be maximized by frequent births, particularly if offspring mortality is not taken into account. Yet it is widely accepted that in many human populations shorter interbirth intervals lead to higher mortality of infants and children (e.g., Hobcraft et al. 1983). If mortality is high enough when there are frequent, closely spaced births, then fewer, more widely spaced births may leave more descendants. In this paper I report a test, using reproductive histories collected by Howell from !Kung women, to see whether the 4-year interbirth interval leaves more surviving offspring than does either a shorter or a longer interval.

The proximate mechanism by which long intervals can be achieved without modern birth control seems to be no longer a puzzle. Frequent suckling apparently has quite direct effects on the mother's endocrine system (Konner and Worthman 1980; Howie and McNeilly 1982). However, in this paper I am not concerned with the nature of the mechanisms, only with their adaptiveness. I expect the mechanisms to be capable of giving flexible but adaptive outcomes, being able to produce intervals that vary from individual to individual and culture to culture, depending on where circumstances place the optimal interbirth interval.

Ultimate explanations that have been offered for such long intervals include the following: (1) children are not valued highly in !Kung society (this neglects to ask why these values are held and not others, and contradicts stated !Kung values); (2) restraint on population size in order to conserve resources and a leisurely life-style; and (3) Lee's (1972) clearer and more plausible suggestion that the work entailed by shorter interbirth intervals is simply too much. This nonetheless neglects the question of why that much work is too much work.

Blurton Jones and Sibly (1978) attempted to look at the adaptiveness of the long interbirth intervals, elaborating on Lee's proposition by including the weight of food carried by the mother in their calculations of mother's work, using other data gathered and published by Lee. Like Lee (1972), they showed that shorter intervals lead to greater workloads for the mother, specifically the weight of baby plus the food to be carried on foraging excursions (reprinted here as Figure 7.1). We suggested that exceeding these loads in the hot dry season could lead to risks of death or injury for the mother, perhaps from heat stresses. If, as seemed more likely, she took care to avoid such risks by limiting her load and her choice of days on which to forage, there might be a risk of nutritional shortage for the family. Undernutrition is widely regarded as increasing susceptibility to infection, and thus might influence child mortality. In addition it might be reasonable to expect an impairment of the mother's lactation at high levels of work, heat or water stress, and lowered

Reprinted with permission from *Ethology and Sociobiology* 7:91–105 (1986).

food intake. Though lactation seems to be a "protected" process, there is some evidence for such impairment presented by Jelliffe and Jelliffe (1978). Consequently unless mothers' work was somehow eased, shorter intervals might lead to much higher mortality of children or mothers, such that the reproductive success of a mother would actually be lower if she reproduced at short intervals than if she stayed in the range of 4 years. Much longer intervals would be less effective simply because fewer births could be fitted into the reproductive span. Thus we suggested that the work entailed for the mother had consequences that seemed very likely to render the 4-year intervals optimal reproductive intervals.

The direct test of Blurton Jones and Sibly's suggestion proceeds through three steps: from Howell's reproductive histories of !Kung women I (1) attempt to establish the relationship between mortality of children and interbirth interval and ask what curve of mortality against IBI is represented by the observations, (2) using this curve, I determine which intervals yield the greatest number of surviving offspring, and (3) I then match this to the observed number of women employing such intervals.

It should be clear that in this article I pursue the question of optimal birth spacing only from the mother's viewpoint. According to parent-offspring conflict theory optimal intervals for the baby would be rather longer.

Several studies of birth interval and mortality have indicated that mortality may cause short intervals as often as vice versa. There is much evidence that the death of a baby leads rapidly to a pregnancy in many populations. But my interest in this article is in the effects of interval length upon modality. For this reason I exclude from this analysis all "replacement" births when the first child died before the next pregnancy. I then assume that in the intervals used in this study (which are intervals when the next birth occurred while the previous child was still alive) any relationship between mortality and interval is a result of an influence of interval upon mortality.

METHODS

The Sample of Women

I use data on !Kung women whose reproductive lives were spent living predominantly in the bush and not at cattleposts. I chose this subsample because Lee (1972) showed that the long interbirth interval is primarily associated with dependence on bush foods, and because Blurton Jones and Sibly's model is entirely based on Lee's data on the bush food economy. Thus the total of 172 women were classified according to their subsistence economy as follows:

1. Lee provided me with the classifications used in his 1972 paper. He rated women on a scale of 1 to 4, from most exclusively dependent on bush foods to most dependent on cattlepost food sources, using a combination of his knowledge of the families during his fieldwork, the age of the women, and the place where they lived at the time of the observation. He emphasized that people changed their subsistence from time to time and so every woman may have used some of each kind of resource. Even the most cat-

tlepost-dependent women will have often used bush foods.

2. Because of these changeable subsistence histories, with Howell's help I categorized people by the locations at which they gave birth. Approximate dates are known for the arrival of cattle and pastoralists at most locations. This information is used to check the classification of people ranked as "2" and any about whom Lee had expressed doubt. The two approaches to classifying the women agree well. Nonetheless some cases remain difficult to classify with any confidence. These 37 are left out of the analyses.

I then take the classified women and combine the 1s and the 2s into a predominantly bush food group of 65 women and the 3s and 4s into a predominantly cattlepost group of 70 women. Only the 65 bush food women are used in this paper. ~⅛ of sample 172 !

The Sample of Interbirth Intervals

The methods by which the data were collected were described in detail by Howell (Howell 1979). This analysis was done from her data

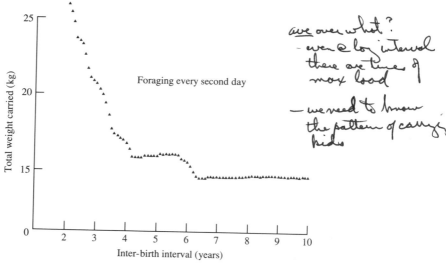

ave over what?
- even @ long interval
there are time of
max load

- we need to know
the pattern of carryg
kids

Figure 7.1. Graph of weight that the Blurton Jones and Sibly model calculates that a woman would carry if she maintained interbirth intervals shown (keeping other factors constant—described in Blurton Jones and Sibly [1978]) plotted against a range of possible IBI.

sheets. These contain a summary of each woman's reproductive history, and include reported season of birth, and calculated year of birth. From these I counted the length of interbirth interval with help, guidance, and some independent checks from Howell. These data sheets also show whether each child survived or died, and if it died when, and when was the last record of the child alive. From this I scored whether each child lived to 10 years of age or more (survivor), or died, and whether it died after the subsequent birth, or clearly before the next pregnancy (12 months or more before the next birth). Three cases were left out because they may have died just before or just after the next pregnancy began.

The outcome of an interval was categorized as "successful" if it added another surviving child to the family, or "failed" if either or both of the children died before reaching the age of 10. (I chose 10 years old because mortality was very low beyond that age, and taking a low age allows inclusion of more data, the births up to 10 years before Howell's last census.) The score that I refer to as "mortality" or "survivorship" is thus a slight underestimate of actual mortality because in 7 of the 96 intervals used in this paper, both of the children who delineate an interval died.

Each interval was designated as "replacement," "first," or "later." First interval in this case means the interval after the first child that a woman bears that survives at least until the next birth to that woman. Since the backload model predicts that first intervals will be under less constraint than later intervals (data that confirm this will be presented in another article), this article also only concerns intervals after the first interval.

"Replacement" intervals (when the first child dies before the next pregnancy) are also omitted from this analysis, because it seems clear that in these intervals mortality determines the interval and not vice versa. Thus I am examining a quite specific but major component of a set of adaptive strategies (the timing of about half the births).

The 65 bush food-dependent women provided data on 272 births. These provided 193 interbirth intervals, of which 57 were first intervals and 40 were "replacement" intervals. This leaves the 96 "later" intervals of bush-living women that are the subject of this paper.

All the analyses have used an interbirth interval as the basic unit. I have ignored two aspects of their independence from other units. First, I ignored their adjacency to other intervals (except in the definition of "replacement" intervals). This adjacency would introduce additional variation in the findings: a short interval following a long interval might have more success than if it followed another short interval (as shown by Hobcraft et al. 1983). In ignoring this distinction (a distinction that would improve our chance of finding what we expect), I err in the conservative direction. I also ignore the fact that some women contribute more intervals to the data than others. Sixty-five women provide us with 96 usable intervals. There is thus the question of whether our findings represent effects of women or of intervals. If my approach was an inductive one this would be a serious problem. It would still be a problem even if I used only one interval per woman. But my concern has been to make predictions about the data and test them.

Questions about Howell's original methods are relevant insofar as they argue for *bias* in birth dates rather than for extensive random variation. Note that Howell's methods do *not* depend on either Howell or the mother stating birth intervals. Such would have led to bias on the basis "he survived, so he must have been born long after his big sister." Howell describes in detail the way that date of birth of dead children was ascertained. This would appear to introduce noise and not bias.

The most important methodological question relating to Howell's data seems to me to concern the very long intervals (6 years and more). These appear to give a quite remarkable degree of protection to both children. Is this because a dead baby between the two births has been forgotten? In the field Howell paid special attention to such intervals, asking repeatedly and in different ways whether there was another child, or an abortion, and asking relatives and neighbors what they knew of this. Some of the intervals arise when a woman changed husbands. The intervening period of single life or marital discord and dispute, with lowered risk of pregnancy might account for these intervals but does not account for their low mortality.

Deriving and Testing the Hypotheses

Three steps in testing optimality of IBI are discussed in the sections that follow.

1. What is the relationship between mortality of children and interbirth interval? What curve of mortality against interbirth interval best fits the observations? This is the most important step in the study, for the answer determines where the calculated optimal interval will be. It is known that interbirth interval is strongly related to mortality under third world conditions in general (e.g., Hobcraft et al. 1983) but we can bring more specific expectations from Blurton Jones and Sibly's model. The Blurton Jones and Sibly backload model presupposes that mortality is somehow due to mother's workload. Specifically the model (Fig. 7.1) suggests that there should be an inflection in the curve of mortality against IBI, at around 4 years. At longer intervals, mortality (following backload) should be fairly level. Below 4 years, mortality should climb steeply to very high levels. To test this suggestion we examined the fit of a straight-line relationship between mortality and the backload implied by each IBI.

We might be skeptical about the data fitting every inflection of the calculated backload and therefore prefer to test the fit of a simple concave curve that would reach some asymptotic low level of mortality at long IBI. It seems unlikely that child and infant mortality ever gets very near zero under the conditions of !Kung life. It is therefore more realistic to suppose that

Table 7.1. The Raw Data (Grouped by IBI)

IBI (months)	Total (*N*)	Deaths	Survivors	Success %
24 (18–29)	6	5	1	16.7
36 (30–41)	23	14	9	39.1
48 (42–53)	29	13	16	55.2
60 (54–65)	16	7	9	56.2
72 (66–77)	6	0	6	100.0
84 (78–89)	7	0	7	100.0
96 (90–101)	2	0	2	100.0
108 (102–)	7	4	3	42.8
Totals	96	43	53	

Table 7.2. Comparison of Three Predictors of Success of an IBI: χ^2, Degrees of Freedom, and Probability for Four Tests[a]

	Backload	1/IBI	IBI
Improvement	15.47	15.76	10.23
df	1	1	1
p	<0.000	<0.000	0.001
Goodness of fit	33.22	35.03	38.85
df	28	32	31
p	0.228	0.326	0.157
Hosmer's	1.76	8.05	18.44
df	5	6	6
p	0.881	0.235	0.005
Brown's	1.05	0.75	9.59
df	5	6	6
p	0.592	0.687	−0.008

[a]High improvement chi-square with low p shows the independent variable contributes significantly to predicting the dependent variable. Low p for goodness of fit, and low p for Hosmer show poor fit of observed to predicted. Low p for Brown shows inappropriate model.

the data for long IBI would represent a steady, low mortality. An appropriate curve would be given by a reciprocal transformation, for example $Y = a + bx$ (1/IBI), or by a polynomial such as $Y = A + b'x + b''x^2$.

It is important to test whether these models really give any better account of the observations than would a simple straight-line relationship of success to interbirth interval. Thus a third model is tested: success predicted linearly by interbirth interval.

The relationships between mortality and predictor variables were investigated in two ways. One was by logistic regression (with the BMDP program [Dixon 1981]), using the original ungrouped data, with success (survival) or failure (death of a child) as a dichotomous dependent variable, making fuller use of the available information (Table 7.2, Fig. 7.2).

The other was by linear regression, using as dependent variable the percentage of interbirth intervals that were successes, having grouped the data into 12-month blocks, centered on year points. The data tend to cluster about the year point because of the way that IBI were determined. Blocks were 24 months (18–29), 36 months (30–41), 48 months (42–53), 60 months (54–65), 72 months (66–77), 84 months (78–89), 96 months (90–101), and 108 months (102–) (Tables 7.1, 7.3, and 7.4).

2. Which interbirth intervals yield most surviving offspring? If we know the mortality associated with each interval we can calculate the number of surviving offspring that its repeated use would give rise to. This can be calculated from the number of births (reproductive span/IBI) multiplied by the probability of survival at that IBI. I call this figure "Yield." It is the number of offspring expected to reach 10 years of age in a reproductive career that keeps to the IBI specified. The optimal IBI will be the one with the highest yield (Table 7.5, Figs. 7.3,

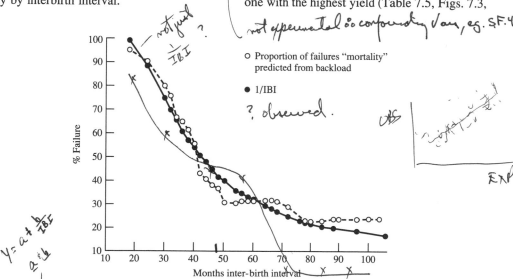

○ Proportion of failures "mortality" predicted from backload

● 1/IBI

Figure 7.2. Fitted curves of failure ("mortality") predicted by backload and by 1/IBI, shown plotted against IBI, for ungrouped data. Results obtained by logistic regression.

Table 7.3. Statistical Tests of Each Predictor of Mortality in Grouped Data

	Backload	1/IBI	IBI + (IBI)²	IBI
Overall F	7.61	7.08	7.40	3.37
P	0.033	0.037	0.032	>0.05
r^2	0.559	0.541	0.747	0.359

7.4). I assumed a constant reproductive span of 20 years, believing its duration to be independent of IBI, and determined by quite other factors.

3. How does the performance of !Kung women match up to the optimal performance? Given the premise that natural selection will have designed a reproductive system that is efficient, the simplest expectation is that the observed interbirth intervals will be normally distributed about the optimum interval. I seek to explain what most individuals in the population do by testing whether it is the course of action that appears to maximize reproductive success. Neglected factors in addition to mortality may render the apparent optimum misleading. These

cannot be investigated until, like first intervals and "replacement" intervals, their importance has been proposed.

To match up the actual performance of the women against the "ideal" performance the yield of each IBI is plotted in Figure 7.3 (for the ungrouped data) and Figure 7.4 for the grouped data, together with the number of times each IBI occurred.

The degree to which the women match the optimal interval can also be tested by the method used by Smith (1981). Using the *grouped* data we can correlate the yield of an IBI with the number of times that interval occurs, arguing that higher yielding intervals should be more often employed. A high positive correlation will indicate a close match (Table 7.5).

Another method would be to see what proportion of the intervals are intervals that yield within, say, 80% of the maximum yield (Table 7.6). This would be particularly useful if several intervals have very similar yields, so that suboptimal intervals nonetheless yield almost as high as the optimum interval.

Table 7.4. Predicted Percentage Success for Grouped Intervals

IBI (months)	Backload	1/IBI	IBI + (IBI)²	Observed
24 (18–29)	11.9	14.7	7.3	16.7
36 (30–41)	43.9	44.8	39.9	39.1
48 (42–53)	67.1	59.9	64.3	55.2
60 (54–65)	72.1	68.8	80.4	56.2
72 (66–77)	74.5	74.9	88.2	100.0
84 (78–89)	80.5	79.2	88.2	100.0
96 (90–101)	80.0	82.4	79.7	100.0
108 (102–)	79.8	85.0	63.1	42.8

Table 7.5. Yield of Surviving Offspring from Each Grouped Interval According to Each Predictor

IBI	N	Backload	1/IBI	IBI + (IBI)²	Observed
24	6	1.187	1.468	0.729	1.67
36	23	2.921	2.982	2.656	2.60
48	29	3.352	2.996	3.213	2.76
60	16	2.883	2.752	3.217	2.25
72	6	2.482	2.493	2.944	3.33
84	7	2.302	2.265	2.522	2.86
96	2	2.000	2.060	1.993	2.50
108	7	1.772	1.888	1.400	0.95
Correlation between N and yield:					
R		0.8102	0.8065	0.5817	0.2088

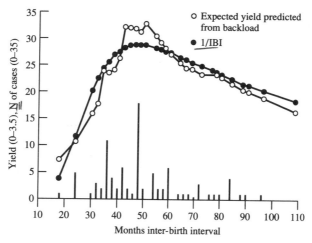

Figure 7.3. Graph of yield of surviving teenagers predicted by the best predictors (backload and 1/IBI), and bar chart of frequency of occurrence of each interbirth interval. Ungrouped data.

RESULTS

Relationship between Mortality and Interbirth Interval

Ungrouped data. We tested, using logistic regression, the goodness of fit of the data to curves predicted by 1/IBI, calculated backload, and IBI. Results are shown in Table 7.2 and Figure 7.2.

It can be seen that the best fit is obtained from Load and from 1/IBI. In Table 7.2 we see that not only does IBI give us a substantially lower chi-square to enter the model but it fails the tests for the significance and reliability of predictor variables.

Grouped data. Linear regression using the grouped data gave similar results (Tables 7.3, 7.4). IBI as the only predictor failed to pass any

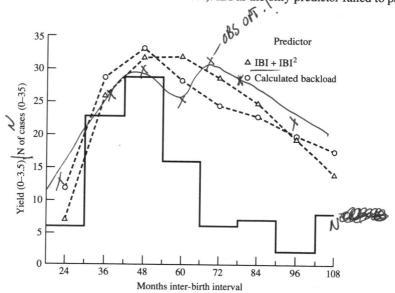

Figure 7.4. Graph of yield of surviving teenagers predicted by the best predictors (backload and 1/IBI), and histogram of frequency of occurrence of each interbirth interval. Grouped data.

statistical tests and did not give a significant model (*F* test). Calculated backload, 1/IBI, and the polynomial all gave significant models, predicting curved relationships between IBI and success.

Thus as hypothesized, a concave curve seems to be the best fit to the observations, with mortality never declining to zero.

Optimal Interbirth Intervals

Ungrouped data. The yield of each IBI predicted by the best two predictors (backload and 1/IBI) is shown in Figure 7.3. This indicates that maximum yields derive from the intervals around 50 months.

Grouped data. For the grouped data, Table 7.5 and Figure 7.4 show that the best predictors (backload and 1/IBI again) give the highest yield from the 36-, 48-, and 60-month groups. The observed raw data (column six in Table 7.5) suggest that yet longer intervals yield better. This is discussed below.

Is Performance Optimal?

Ungrouped data. The match with optima predicted from concave curves (1/IBI and backload) is remarkably close (see Fig. 7.3). For yield predicted by backload the optimum IBI was 50 months. For yield predicted by 1/IBI equal yields arose from 46, 48, and 50 months. Interbirth intervals from 42 to 54 months yielded almost as highly. Intervals of 20 and 30 months are predicted to yield poorly, and intervals of 80, 90, and 100 months yield poorly. These very short intervals are markedly less abundant than the 40 to 60 range.

The frequency distribution of IBI has a mean value of 55 months. The mode and median is 48 months.

Grouped data. The highest yield predicted by backload and 1/IBI is from the 48-month group: prediction from the polynomial gives 60 months, closely followed by 48 months (Table 7.5, Fig. 7.4).

The block with most cases is the 48 (42–53) month block, followed by the 36 (30–41) month block, and then the 60 (54–65) month block. All other blocks contain only a handful of cases.

The correlation method, applicable to the grouped data, suggests that the performance of

the women fits very closely with the optimum when yield is calculated from the predictions of backload, 1/IBI, and the polynomial $r = 0.8102, 0.8065,$ and $0.5817,$ respectively. Yield predicted by the raw data gives a surprisingly low correlation $r = 0.2088$ (Table 7.5).

Table 7.6 shows what proportion of intervals yield at 80% or more of the maximum yield. This again suggests that performance matches optimal yield rather well.

Are Even Longer Intervals Really Better?

If any of the fitted curves (1/IBI, backload, two-term regression) is the right summary of the data, then the !Kung optimize with remarkable precision. But the raw observations suggest that the 72-month interval is optimal, and IBIs of this length are very rare. If 72 months is optimal, the !Kung fail to optimize. They would fail in an unexpected direction: most of the time they do not wait long enough between births. They cluster around the second best region, 48 months. Do the six cases at 66–77 month intervals give a reliable estimate of mortality?

Several arguments enable us to decide the meaningfulness of the 72-month observation:

1. The 72-month observation is not significantly different from the 60-month observation. This is perhaps an unfairly harsh test, for if 72 and 84 are combined they are significantly different from 48 and 60 months (Fisher's exact test, $p = 0.006$).
2. It is hard to believe that mortality ever falls to zero, or even near it, under the circumstances of !Kung life.

Table 7.6. Percentage of Intervals That Yield More Than 80% or 70% of Maximum Yield[a]

Percent of	Yield Predicted by		
Maximum Attained	**Backload**	**1/IBI**	**IBI + (IBI)²**
Predictions from Grouped Data			
80%	71%	77%	77%
70%	74%	84%	84%
Predictions from Ungrouped Data			
80%		46%	73%
70%		70%	85%

[a]Example: the top leftmost figure, 71%, means that 71% of all 96 intervals were of a length that yields more than 80% of the highest yield of any interval. The highest yield was 3.35: 80% of this is 2.68. Intervals in the following groups yield higher than 2.68: 36, 48, and 60. These groups contain 68 of the 96 intervals which is 71% of the 96 intervals.

3. Deaths at the 72-month interval occurred in cattlepost people and in first intervals (to be reported elsewhere). Overall mortality would be expected to be lower in cattlepost people and yet we have a death at 72-month IBI.
4. Mortality would have to fall below 17% at 72 months (less than 17% failing to survive from birth to 10 years of age) for this interval to yield more descendants than 48 months.
5. An observation of just one death at 72-month interval would give a mortality of 16.7%, which renders 72 months no better than 48 months.

Thus perhaps we should not take 72 months too seriously as a candidate for optimal IBI.

DISCUSSION

The common-sense hypothesis about !Kung birth spacing reproductive success will be maximized by short interbirth intervals, therefore long intervals are not optimal and the !Kung do not maximize reproductive success— is not supported by the data. Each analysis shows that short intervals leave fewer descendants than do long intervals. It is clear that the !Kung do not show maladaptively long interbirth intervals, nor do they show a random scatter of intervals. The !Kung interbirth intervals have a slightly skewed but nearly normal distribution about the most likely optimum interval.

All the potential errors and problems in my analysis combine to suggest that if the performance is not actually optimal then it errs in the direction of too many short intervals and not enough long ones. For example, in all models the 60-month intervals yield as well as do the 36-month intervals. Yet there are more intervals in the 36-month group than in the 60-month group. If we discard all the very long intervals (of greater than 90 months) than the calculated optimum is 72 months. There are very few intervals of this length. I have already discussed reasons for regarding the observed zero mortality at this interval as unrepresentative. But that the errors go in this direction strengthens our disproof of the "common-sense" hypothesis. Again, if the bush-living !Kung women fail to optimize it is because their interbirth intervals are too short, not because they are too long.

In this analysis I have ignored variation in length of reproductive career. Yet Howell's data show that this is clearly a major determinant of lifetime reproductive success. This in turn should make us ask why anyone stops reproducing earlier than anyone else. A number of questions and predictions can be derived from the backload model and from the proposition that investment in grandchildren may rapidly outweigh the value of investment in further children. But at present the issue of variation in length of reproductive career is better explained by ideas such as "target fertility" and "replacement," which postulate that reproduction is aimed not at the maximum possible but at a target family size, or at attaining at least some adult descendants.

Several other topics for discussion arise from this article but can only receive brief mention here:

1. How good a measure of fitness is the number of children raised to 10 years of age? I was unable to examine reproductive success of the children of the intervals, or the risks of maternal death associated with different interbirth intervals.
2. Does theory really lead us to expect performance to be normally distributed about the optimum? Are the individuals who produce intervals that are far from the optimum failing to be adaptive or are they doing the best that they can under circumstances that actually differ from those of the majority?
3. Only if mortality reaches very high levels at short IBIs, the graph of mortality against IBI having at some point a very steep slope, will selection favor lengthening IBI. A comment in Hobcraft et al. (1983, p. 606) suggests that this was not the case for the societies from which their data came.
4. The "gee whiz" aspect of testing optimization is probably less important than the original modeling exercise of Blurton Jones and Sibly. The direct reproductive data show it was not entirely fanciful to suggest that 4-year interbirth intervals were optimal for the !Kung. But this is mainly important for the encouragement that it gives to efforts to find out whether the !Kung could somehow rearrange their lives to leave more descendants, and if not, why not. These efforts could lead us to a detailed and precise

knowledge of the practical constraints on !Kung life.

5. Why does the backload model make such good predictions? The backload model succeeds in producing a remarkably close fit to the curve of mortality against IBI (and in making several other correct predictions to be reported elsewhere). Backload as a predictor accounts for an amazing 55% of the variance in mortality of children under 10 years old born of intervals selected for this sample. It may thus be that mother's load really is an important influence. But we may wonder by what causal route it influences mortality, and time to next conception, and what are the significant correlates of backload? Is some other measure of mother's work really the crucial variable, such as the amount of time or energy her work leaves for other fitness enhancing activities? Can other costs of parenting substitute for backload? The crucial issue may be the shape and dimension of the curve of costs of parenting against age of child, rather than the particular nature of the parental behavior and its particular costs. Although weight of food seems to be an important component of the Blurton Jones and Sibly model, considering a wider taxonomic spectrum accentuates this question. Chimpanzees have longer IBIs than do humans (Tutin 1980). Since chimpanzees do not provision their families, mother's work as a provider cannot be the explanation of the long IBI, although her work at carrying her offspring might be. However, to try to cover too wide a taxonomic sample might lead us to ignore the extreme variation in IBI within and between human populations. This seems to be an extremely labile characteristic, and clearly of great potential adaptive significance.

One way to approach these questions is to examine mother's work and IBI in other populations. It is often claimed that all hunter-gatherers have such long IBIs. The Blurton Jones and Sibly backload model is very specific to !Kung ecology and geography, but if it applies at all to other hunter-gatherer cultures it predicts shorter IBIs whenever women do not have to carry so much food for so far as do the !Kung women. At present there are no quantitative data published on the IBI of other hunter-gatherers.

Acknowledgments. This investigation was made possible by Nancy Howell's generous spirit of scientific cooperation. She shared her data and her advice for an investigation from a perspective quite foreign to her own. Faults of interpretation are mine and not hers. The existence of the data is entirely her responsibility. I shared none of the endurance, persuasiveness, and meticulousness that it takes for the kind of fieldwork that Howell did and to build up the data base that she did. Richard Lee kindly helped with rating the level of dependence of the women on bush foods and cattlepost foods.

I also wish to thank for helpful discussions on statistics, optimization, and hunter-gatherer ecology Drs. Lynne Fairbanks, Alan Forsyth, K. Hawkes, K. Hill, M. Hurtado, H. Kaplan, Richard M. Sibly, and Ronald M. Weigel.

8

Too Good to Be True? Is There Really a Trade-off between Number and Care of Offspring in Human Reproduction?

NICHOLAS BLURTON JONES

In science we often learn more when things don't work out the way we expected. But sometimes they do turn out as expected, and then we get suspicious! Despite an obsessive amount of care and attention to detail, my paper may look like just too good a confirmation of the expectations derived from Sibly and my model of bushwomen's work. Two attempts to replicate it seem to have failed. What are we to think?

The failure of Pennington and Harpending's (1988) attempt seems to mainly stem from the inclusion in their study of bushwomen who were not living in the ecology from which we drew our predictions. This and a number of detailed problems were discussed by Harpending (1994) and Blurton Jones (1994): migration, diseases of the reproductive tract, age estimation, nonindependent intervals, right censoring. Here I wish to attend to broader issues: the glaring absence of overt discussion of "phenotypic correlation," pointed out by Borgerhoff Mulder (1992a); and alternative ideas about fertility and human life history developed by Hill and Hurtado when they tried to look for a trade-off between interbirth interval and offspring survival in their study of the Ache in Paraguay.

"PHENOTYPIC CORRELATION": DID I TEST THE RIGHT PREDICTION?

Behavioral ecologists have found that trade-offs seldom show up directly in nonexperimental studies. If individuals respond adaptively, a short interbirth interval may indicate an individual who is in better than usual condition, or with better access to resources, and who is also better able to raise her offspring. A poorly endowed individual may also respond adaptively, with a longer interbirth interval, and since this individual has poor access to resources, the survival of her offspring may be no better than the survival of the well-endowed mother's offspring. In my paper, in contrast, I made the naive prediction that short intervals will be accompanied by more offspring deaths, which presupposes that short intervals were mostly maladaptive "mistakes."

Thus contemporary behavioral ecologists would not make the same prediction as I made. A !Kung woman who was in especially good condition at a good time would be expected, if her reproductive system responds adaptively, to have another birth sooner than a woman in poor condition, and to be roughly as successful at keeping the child alive. If her reproductive system responds adaptively she should make few "mistakes"—short intervals at a time when she could not support the resulting offspring. Thus it is surprising that short intervals were associated with higher mortality. In expecting to see greater mortality at shorter interbirth intervals I made a hidden assumption that short interbirth intervals are mostly "mistakes"—errors by the reproductive system—that, although they increase the number of births, might be too costly in offspring survival. I gave readers no clear reason to think mistakes were more numerous than adaptive shortening of intervals by a mother in good condition, or with better access to resources.

I can offer some defense. The more we control for differences in access to resources or helpers, the bigger the proportion of extreme interbirth intervals that may be "mistakes"—maladaptive responses by the reproductive system that show us something of their cost. I did control for some of the variation in access to resources that the Blurton Jones and Sibly (1978) model suggested was most important (further discussion in Blurton Jones 1994). Women who had settled with herders were excluded, first intervals were excluded, and an assumption of the model was that helpers provided more food as intervals shortened (they continued to provide the same proportion of the food needed to feed the family). This implies that supporting short interbirth intervals would require not only a mother in better condition than most but also much more productive helpers than most. Thus obtaining the result that I apparently did, may not be so surprising.

Nonetheless, we should continue to worry about the small sample (96 intervals), and whether Howell's original data should have been expected to withstand analyses for which they were never designed. Hill (1993) suggests that Howell could have unconsciously biased her estimates of birth years and seasons by her expectation of a relationship between interval and offspring mortality. Howell reports (1979, 28) that children who had died, and thus were not present to fit themselves into her ranking of relative ages, "were placed by asking a close relative to place them." If dead children were fitted into the age ranking between living contemporaries (not just between their siblings), the error would be neither great, nor systematic (Blurton Jones 1994).

In the hypothetico-deductive method a testable hypothesis is derived explicitly and rigorously from theory. Most human behavioral disciplines fall short of this ideal, merely drawing their predictions from observations reported in prior literature or from suggestions by well-known authors, neither with any demonstrable link to theory. Our field claims to do better. Thus whenever we can show that a prediction did *not* follow necessarily from the theory, we show a weakened use of our paradigm. Thus,

within the limits discussed here, my paper falls short of our hypothetico-deductive ideal. It must also follow that I failed to show whether !Kung reproductive systems perform in accord with expectations from natural selection theory because I did not show whether theory really predicts what I found. I think I can claim that I did more to set out the route from theory to prediction than many other authors have. But just to do better than others is not necessarily our goal.

Did I neglect other aspects of theory? Theory suggests that early births enhance fitness more than later births in an increasing population. In preparing Blurton Jones and Sibly (1978) we considered this and decided that the very slow rate of increase of the !Kung population entitled us to ignore it. What about costs to mother's survival from early reproduction, or risks of her failing to survive long enough to have an otherwise optimally timed next birth? I explicitly ignored maternal mortality. What about the expectation that reproductive effort should increase with age and the careless assumption that this would lead to greater fertility late in the career, or more care of the last offspring? If postweaning care is a significant feature of human life histories, then it is by no means clear that increasing effort will show as increased fertility; the effort may all be employed caring for the accumulating number of previous offspring (Altmann 1981). How would we expect all these considerations to balance out? Existing life history theory (Stearns 1992; Roff 1992; Charnov 1993) appears not to consider postweaning care, which must be one of the most notable things about human reproduction. Blurton Jones and Sibly tried to take it into account in what was undoubtedly too simple a model. We need more theory for animals with protracted and costly postweaning care, and meanwhile we should be careful about borrowing from established theory. Theory must discriminate between "depreciable" or individual care, like providing food, which requires more effort for each added offspring, and "nondepreciable" or "umbrella" care in which little extra effort is needed to shelter or guard one more offspring (Clutton-Brock 1991 and other). Fairbanks (1996) points out how a high-ranking vervet monkey matriarch benefits several offspring and grandoffspring at once by working to maintain her rank position. The effort required for this will be no greater if she has three live offspring than if she has one (it may even be easier). Her situation would be very different if, like many human mothers and grandmothers, she was trying to feed them all.

A NUMBER VERSUS CARE TRADE-OFF IN HUMAN REPRODUCTION?

Is there any better evidence about a number versus care trade-off having an influence on human reproduction? Many studies report associations between short interbirth intervals and mortality (Hobcraft et al. 1983), some even after accounting for "replacement" births. Others report observations clearly compatible with a trade-off between number and care of offspring in people (e.g., Turke 1988; Hrdy 1992). But Pennington and Harpending (1988, 1993) report that data from a wider !Kung population fail to fit predictions they drew from Blurton Jones and Sibly. Blurton Jones (1994) argues that these predictions did not follow from our model. The closest replication is by Hill and Hurtado (1996) on the Ache. They point out that the "phenotypic correlation" might be overcome by statistically controlling for each woman's access to resources. But even then Hill and Hurtado find little indication of cost of short interbirth interval to offspring survival, certainly not enough to explain the observed nearly three-year interval between births. They favor other explanations of fertility, especially centering around the "production function" that Charnov (1993) sets at the root of life history theory. Biological productivity increases with size; at maturity (in determinate growers) productivity is switched from growth to reproduction. Hill and Hurtado find that larger Ache women have more frequent births. Perhaps greater productivity allows faster growth of the baby to weaning and faster recovery of the mother to breeding condition. Their suggestion offers a simple explanation for differences between !Kung, Hadza, and Ache fertility (adult women weigh 40, 48, an 53 kg, respectively, and bear 4.7–5.0, 6.2, and 7.8–8.3 babies per career).

The idea has many attractions and raises the interesting possibility that the cost of post-weaning care is negligible. But enlarging the sample slightly by taking fertilities from Hewlett (1991) and finding adult female body weights in other publications gives a very small and nonsignificant correlation between fertility and body weight (Pearson correlation coefficient $= .061$, $P = .897$, $n = 7$). But variations in infant mortality levels (if there really are any) could confuse the picture. When an infant dies, a new birth follows quickly; thus as infant mortality increases, fertility also increases.

But I do not want to count the ecology of women's work as caretakers out of the fertility picture yet. The data on Ache interbirth interval look just like the data on settled !Kung. Settled !Kung women are freed at least to some extent from the constraints of foraging, and the association between interbirth interval and child mortality was not found among them (Blurton Jones 1986a). This draws attention to Ache women's work. Much of Hill and Hurtado's analysis is on women living in settlements. But even in the forest Ache women provided only 13 percent of the calories (Hill, cited in Hewlett 1991). Would this lead us to expect a very harsh trade-off between number of offspring and care of offspring? Ache woman carry children of greater weight, if fewer hours, than !Kung women. But if time needed to provide food is the important constraint and not weight carried (see Blurton Jones et al. 1989), perhaps the Ache mother is less handicapped by increased numbers of children than the !Kung mother. Nonetheless, Hurtado and colleagues (1985) have shown that among Ache women child care conflicts with food acquisition. Hewlett (1991) shows data on total fertility rate, and on the percentage of calories provided by women. If we put these together (and add subsistence estimates for Nunamuit, Kutchin, Tiwi, and !Gwi from other literature), we find that where women provide more of the food they are less fertile ($r = -.656$, $P = .028$, $n = 11$). The correlation was calculated without the !Kung (up to 10 percent primary sterility) and the Efe (even higher primary sterility), whose inclusion would have strengthened the association. Now this may mean that when women work so much, everyone eats worse. But it is also quite suggestive of a care-versus-number trade-off, and supports the suggestions we have made about Hadza fertility (Blurton Jones et al. 1989, 1992,

1994, 1996). It may be that under some ecological conditions (when women provide a substantial proportion of the food), an increase in
the number of children could threaten their survival, and the mechanisms that link suckling,
and mother's energy budget to fecundability
can adjust fertility in an adaptive direction. The
issue is still undecided.

9

Life Histories, Blood Revenge, and Warfare in a Tribal Population

NAPOLEON CHAGNON

In this article I show how several forms of violence in a tribal society are interrelated and describe my theory of violent conflict among primitive peoples in which homicide, blood revenge, and warfare are manifestations of individual conflicts of interest over material and reproductive resources. Violence is a potent force in human society and may be the principal driving force behind the evolution of culture.[1] For two reasons, anthropologists find it difficult to explain many aspects of human violence. First, although ethnographic reports are numerous, data on how much violence occurs and the variables that relate to it are available from only a few primitive societies. Second, many anthropologists tend to treat warfare as a phenomenon that occurs independently of other forms of violence in the same group. However, duels may lead to deaths which, in turn, may lead to community fissioning and then to retaliatory killings by members of the two now-independent communities. As a result many restrict the search for the causes of the war to issues over which whole groups might contest—such as access to rich land, productive hunting regions, and scarce resources—and, hence, view primitive warfare as being reducible solely to contests over scarce or dwindling material resources.[2] Such views fail to take into account the developmental sequences of conflicts and the multiplicity of causes, especially sexual jealousy, accusations of sorcery, and revenge killings, in each step of conflict escalation.

[margin annotations: ult, PROX]

My theory synthesizes components drawn from two more general bodies of theory. One is the approach of political anthropology in which conflict development is analyzed in terms of the goals for which individuals strive, individual strategies for achieving these goals, and the developmental histories of specific conflicts.[3] The second draws on several key insights from modern evolutionary thought.[4] Specifically, (i) the mechanisms that constitute organisms were designed by selection to promote survival and reproduction in the environments of evolutionary adaptedness. This implies that organisms living in such environments can be generally expected to act in ways that promote survival and reproduction or, as many biologists now state it, their inclusive fitnesses.[5] For humans, these mechanisms include learning and mimicking successful social strategies. (ii) Because no two organisms are genetically identical (save for identical twins and cloning species) and many of life's resources are finite, conflicts of interest between individuals are inevitable because the nature of some of life's resources ensures that individuals can achieve certain goals only at the expense of other individuals.[6] (iii) Organisms expend two kinds of effort during their lifetimes: somatic effort, relevant to their survival, and reproductive effort in the interests of inclusive fitness. Such life effort often entails competition for both material resources (for example, food, water, and territory) and reproductive resources (for example, mates, alliances with those who can provide mates, and favor of those who can aid one's offspring).[6,7] (iv) It is to be expected that individuals (or groups of closely related individuals) will attempt to appropriate both material and reproductive resources from neighbors whenever the probable costs are less than the benefits. While

Reprinted with permission from *Science* 239:985–92 (1988).

conflicts thus initiated need not take violent forms, they might be expected to do so when violence on average advances individual interests. I do not assume that humans consciously strive to increase or maximize their inclusive fitness, but I do assume that humans strive for goals that their cultural traditions deem as valued and esteemed. In many societies, achieving cultural success appears to lead to biological (genetic) success.[8]

In this article I focus on revenge killing, using data collected among the Yanomamö Indians of southern Venezuela and adjacent portions of northern Brazil.[9-11] Blood revenge is one of the most commonly cited causes of violence and warfare in primitive societies,[12] and it has persisted in many state-organized societies as well.[13]

I am using the terms revenge and blood revenge here to mean a retaliatory killing in which the initial victim's close kinsmen conduct a revenge raid on the members of the current community of the initial killer.[14] Although Yanomamö raiders always hope to dispatch the original killer, almost any member of the attacked community is a suitable target.

YANOMAMÖ CONFLICTS: HOMICIDE, REVENGE, AND WARFARE

The Yanomamö have no written language, precise number system, formal laws, or institutionalized adjudicators such as chiefs or judges.[15] Although there are customs and general rules about proper behavior, individuals violate them regularly when it seems in their interests to do so.[16] When conflicts emerge each individual must rely on his own skills and coercive abilities and the support of his close kin. Most fights begin over sexual issues: infidelity and suspicion of infidelity, attempts to seduce another man's wife, sexual jealousy, forcible appropriation of women from visiting groups, failure to give a promised girl in marriage, and (rarely) rape.[9,10,17]

Yanomamö conflicts constitute a graded sequence of increasing seriousness and potential lethality: shouting matches, chest pounding duels, side slapping duels, club fights, fights with axes and machetes, and shooting with bows and arrows with the intent to kill.[10] In all but the last case, fights are not intended to and generally do not lead to mortalities. Nevertheless, many fights lead to killings both within and between villages. If killing occurs within the village, the village fissions and the principals of the two new groups then begin raiding each other.[17,18] The most common explanation given for raids (warfare) is revenge (no yuwo) for a previous killing, and the most common explanation for the initial cause of the fighting is "women" (suwä tä nowä ha).[9,10,17,19]

At first glance, raids motivated by revenge seem counterproductive. Raiders may inflict deaths on their enemies, but by so doing make themselves and kin prime targets for retaliation. But ethnographic evidence suggests that revenge has an underlying rationality: swift retaliation in kind serves as a deterrent over the long run. War motivated by revenge seems to be a tit-for-tat strategy[20] in which the participants' score might best be measured in terms of minimizing losses rather than in terms of maximizing gains.

If gain (benefit) is associated with revenge killing in the primitive world, what is gained and precisely who gains? Casting these questions into evolutionary terms, where gain (benefit) is discussed in terms of individual differences in inclusive fitness, might shed new light on the problem. Losing a close genetic relative (for example, a parent, sibling, or child) potentially constitutes a significant loss to one's inclusive fitness. Anything that counterbalances these losses would be advantageous. Yanomamö data suggest two possibilities. First, kinship groups that retaliate swiftly and demonstrate their resolve to avenge deaths acquire reputations for ferocity that deter the violent designs of their neighbors. The Yanomamö explain that a group with a reputation for swift retaliation is attacked less frequently and thus suffers a lower rate of mortality. They also note that other forms of predation, such as the abduction of women, are thwarted by adopting an aggressive stance. Aggressive groups coerce nubile females from less aggressive groups whenever the opportunity arises. Many appear to calculate the costs and benefits of forcibly appropriating or coercing females from groups that are perceived to be weak.[10,17] Second, men who demonstrate their willingness to act violently and to exact revenge for the deaths of kin may have higher marital and reproductive success.

THE YANOMAMÖ POPULATION

The Yanomamö number some 15,000 individuals and are subdivided into approximately 200 politically independent communities. During the past 23 years I have visited 60 villages on 13 field trips and have spent 50 months living among the Yanomamö. Warfare has recently diminished in most regions due to the increasing influence of missionaries and government agents and is almost nonexistent in some villages. Here I summarize the roles that killing and revenge play in the lives of the members of some dozen villages in one area of the tribe who were actively engaged in warfare during the course of my continuing field research.[21] The current descendants of these communities (and their immediate historical antecedents) were studied more intensely than others between 1964 and 1987.[9] The population was distributed among 12 villages and numbered 1394 as of April 1987. Approximately 30% of deaths among adult males in this region of the Yanomamö tribe is due to violence.[9,22] This level of warfare mortality among adult males is similar to rates from the few other anthropological studies that report such data. Warfare mortality among adult males is reported as 28.5% for the Mae Enga, 19.5% for the Huli, and 28.5% for the Dugum Dani, all of Highland New Guinea.[23,24]

LIFE HISTORIES, KILLERS, KINSHIP, AND REVENGE MOTIVES

In order to understand why avenging the death of a kinsman is such a commonly reported cause of warfare in primitive societies, one needs to document the vital events in the lifetimes of all or most individuals, recording marriages, abductions, genealogical connections, births, deaths, and causes of death.[9] These data must then be put into the historical context of specific wars whose origins and development are described by multiple information. Finally, native views, explanations, and attitudes have to be taken into consideration, particularly on topics such as vengeance, legitimacy of violent actions in particular circumstances, and societal rules and values regarding principals of justice.

The Yanomamö are frank about vengeance as a legitimate motive for killing. Their very notion of bereavement implies violence: they describe the feelings of the bereaved as *hushuwo*, a word that can be translated as anger verging on violence. It is dangerous to provoke a grieving person no matter what the cause of death of the lost kin. It is common to hear statements such as, "If my sick mother dies, I will kill some people."

Vengeance motivation persists for many years. In January 1965, for example, the headman of one of the smaller villages (about 75 people) was killed by raiders in retaliation for an earlier killing. His ashes were carefully stored in several dry gourds, small quantities being consumed by the women of the village on the eve of each revenge raid against the village that killed him. According to the Yanomamö, women alone drink the ashes of the slain to make raiders *hushuwo* and fill them with resolve.[25] In 1975, 10 years after his death, several gourds of his ashes remained, and the villagers were still raiding the group that killed him, who by then lived nearly 4 days' walk away.

This case is telling in another way as well. When the headman was killed, his death so demoralized the group that for about a year its members refused to conduct revenge raids, thereby acquiring the reputation of cowardice. They sought refuge and protection among several neighboring groups whose men grew bolder in direct proportion to the visitors' cowardice. These neighbors openly seduced the visitors' women and appropriated a number of them by force, predicting, correctly, that the visiting men would not retaliate. The group later regained its dignity and independence after embarking on an ambitious schedule of revenge raids.[10]

Revenge is also sought for the deaths of individuals who are alleged to have died as a consequence of harmful magic practiced by shamans in enemy villages. As is widely found in other primitive societies, an astonishingly large fraction of deaths are considered to have been the result of human malevolence: sorcery in the form of stealing souls, blowing lethal charms, stealing someone's footprint, or directing one's personal spirit associates (*hekura*) to cause a snake to bite someone fatally or a tree to fall on him. Few deaths are considered to be natural. Infant mortality is high and invariably attributed to enemy shamans. Long, bitter wars can be initiated when a visitor from a suspected village is killed by the bereaved of the dead infant.[10] None of the deaths attributed to magic are considered in this article as violent deaths caused by human malevolence.

Unokais: *Those who have killed.* When a Yanomamö man kills he must perform a ritual purification called unokaimou, one purpose of which is to avert any supernatural harm that might be inflicted on him by the soul of his victim, a belief similar to that found among the headhunting Jivaro of Peru.[26] Men who have performed the unokaimou ceremony are referred to as unokai, and it is widely known within the village and in most neighboring villages who the unokais are and who their victims were. Recruitment to the unokai status is on a self-selective basis, although boys are encouraged to be valiant and are rewarded for showing aggressive tendencies.[10]

Most victims are males killed during revenge raids against enemy groups, but a number of killings were within the groups.[9,22,27] Most of the latter have to do with sexual jealousy, an extremely common cause of violence among the Yanomamö, other tribal groups, and our own population.[28]

Raiding parties usually include 10 to 20 men, but not all men go on all raids and some men never go on raids. An enemy village might be as far as 4 or 5 days' march away. Many raiding parties run back before reaching their destination, either because someone has a dream that portends disaster, or because the enemy group is not where it was believed to be. In all but the most determined raiding parties, a few men drop out for reasons such as being "sick" or "stepping on a thorn." Some of these dropouts privately admitted to me that they were simply frightened. Chronic dropouts acquire a reputation for cowardice (*têhe*) and often become the subject of frequent insult and ridicule, and their wives become targets of increased sexual attention from other men.

The number of victims per raid is usually small—one or two individuals—but occasionally a "massacre" takes place resulting in the deaths of ten or more people.[6,29] On the eve of a raid the warriors make an effigy (*no owä*) of the person they most want to kill; but in fact, they usually kill the first man they encounter. When a raiding party strikes, usually at dawn, as many raiders as possible (but almost never

all members of the raiding party) shoot the victim or victims from ambush with their arrows and hastily retreat, hoping to put as much distance as possible between themselves and the enemy before the victim is discovered. Everyone who has shot an arrow into the victim must undergo the *unokaimuou* ceremony on reaching home. Most victims are shot by just one or two raiders, but one victim was shot by 15 members of the raiding party.

The number of (living) *unokais* in the current population is 137, 132 of whom are estimated to be 25 or older, and represent 44% of the men age 25 or older.[15] A retrospective perusal of the data indicates that this has generally been the case in those villages whose *unokais* have not killed someone during the past 5 years. I have recorded 282 violent deaths during 23 years of studies of villages in the region under consideration,[21] deaths that occurred sometime during the past 50 to 60 years.[15] These include victims who were residents of villages in this area or victims from immediately adjacent areas killed by residents or now-deceased former residents of the groups considered here. Of these 282 violent deaths, the number of victims of living *unokais* is 153. These victims were killed during approximately the past 35 years.[9] All the *unokais* come from the village under discussion, but not all of the victims do; some are from villages in adjacent areas beyond the focus of my field studies.

Individual capacities of unokais. Most killers have unokaied once. Some, however, have a deserved reputation for being waiteri (fierce) and have participated in many killings (Fig. 9.1). One man has unokaied 16 times. The village from which he comes is considered to be, by its neighbors, a particularly waiteri group: 8 of the 11 men who have unokaied ten or more times come from this one village. In this village, 97% of the 164 members are related in at least one way to 75% or more of the other residents of the village (Table 9.1). The "village" in this case is almost synonymous with "kinship group."

Unit of analysis: Village or kin group? It is customary for anthropologists to use the community as the natural unit of analysis in their studies of primitive warfare because war, by most definitions, is lethal conflict between members of politically distinct groups. The

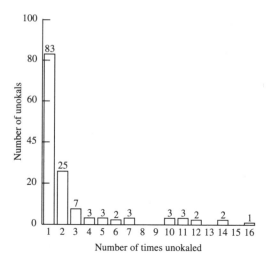

Figure 9.1. Number of victims for which living killers *unokaied*. Sixty percent (83 of 137) of Yanomamö *unokais* have participated in only one killing; one man participated in 16 different killings.

Yanomamö village, however, is a transient community whose membership changes by migration, emigration, and fissioning.[10] As a result, unokais who now live in different villages, and may be mortal enemies, may once have been residents of the same village and collaborators in raids. It cannot be assumed that their

violent activities can be understood as actions taken on behalf of a village since any given *unokai* is likely, at some point in time, to be attacking members of a village among whom he once lived. It is more accurate to view Yanomamö revenge raids as actions promoted by prominent men to benefit themselves or close kin and to view the village as a set of kin groups that form around individual leaders, each with selfish interests.

In order to understand why blood revenge is such a powerful motive among the Yanomamö and other tribal groups organized by kinship, one must first understand how complex and pervasive kinship relationships are in such communities and that the major fount of the individual's political status, economic support, marriage possibilities, and protection from aggressors derives from kinsmen. One of the most important functions of kin groups is to pool resources and reallocate them to needy members. In the context of threats or coercion by others or of potentially violent encounters, group members cooperate for mutual protection and use their collective skills and abilities to this end, including the capacities of group members to act violently if necessary.[30]

All Yanomamö villages have several (unnamed) patrilineal descent groups: males and females of all ages who are related to each other through the male line of descent. Members of

Table 9.1. Measures of Kinship Relatedness among Members of 12 Villages Studied

Village	Population (1987)	Fg(ALL)*	Fg(CON)†	Quartiles‡ 1	2	3	4
5	188	0.057987	0.085104	0.04	0.09	0.05	0.81
6	121	0.063239	0.084429	0.03	0.13	0.07	0.77
7	105	0.089063	0.116243	0.03	0.15	0.00	0.82
50	63	0.084405	0.139225	0.13	0.02	0.11	0.75
51	164	0.103778	0.109175	0.02	0.01	0.01	0.97
52	94	0.080369	0.106137	0.03	0.05	0.02	0.89
53	136	0.063444	0.102216	0.10	0.04	0.01	0.85
54	109	0.078648	0.123159	0.11	0.00	0.10	0.79
84	66	0.117921	0.128590	0.03	0.00	0.00	0.97
90	55	0.111806	0.136574	0.02	0.04	0.25	0.69
92	188	0.095861	0.110016	0.04	0.00	0.03	0.93
93	105	0.080615	0.093202	0.04	0.00	0.09	0.88
Average		0.0860	0.1112	0.05	0.04	0.06	0.84

*Fg (ALL), average of each individual's average relatedness to all members of the village, including unrelated individuals (34). †Fg(CON), average of each individual's average relatedness to just genetic kin in the village. ‡Quartiles: 1, fraction of the village members related in at least one way to 25% or fewer of the village members; 2, fraction of the village members related in at least one way to 26 to 50% of the village members; 3, fraction of the village members related in at least one way to 51 to 75% of the village members; 4, fraction of the village members related in at least one way to 75% or more of the village members. The data in Tables 9.2 and 9.3 are additive to arrive at the figures presented in this table for current village sizes.

these groups must find their spouses in some other patrilineal descent group, preferably within the village. Reciprocal marriage exchanges between such groups over several generations mean that the members of any one descent group have close relatives in other descent groups.

Each descent group has one or more *patas* ("big ones") who are the political leaders of that group.[10] The leader of the largest descent group is invariably the headman of the village, but if the village has two descent groups of approximately equal size it will have two (or more) leaders who, because of past marriages between their groups, are often first (cross) cousins and married to each other's sisters. Political leaders, therefore, usually have, on average, many more kinsmen in the village than do other men of comparable age.

Headmen are usually polygynous, and over a lifetime a successful man may have had up to a dozen or more different wives, but rarely more than six wives simultaneously. One result is that some men have many children. In the sample considered here, one man (now deceased) had 43 children by 11 wives. Needless to say, nuclear and extended families cannot only become very large but their respective members, because of repetitive intermarriage, are related to each other in many ways.

The village, then, is composed of large kin groups: people who are related to members of their own lineal descent group through male links and related to members of other lineal descent groups through consanguineal marriages and matrilateral ties. If someone in the village is killed, the probability is very high that he or she will have many bereaved close kin, including the village leader or leaders who have more kin than others; the leaders are the very individuals who decide whether killings are revenged. All headmen in this study are *unokai*. If, as Clausewitz suggested, (modern) warfare is the conduct of politics by other means,[31] in the tribal world warfare is ipso facto the extension of kinship obligations by violence because the political system is organized by kinship.

With the passing of time and generations, adult male members in each village become more remotely related to each other. Their fathers may have been brothers and first cousins, but they themselves are divided into sets of brothers and sets of second parallel cousins or second cross cousins. The sons of these men, in turn, will be even more remotely related, third cousins. Fission produces two new villages in which the coefficients of relatedness among members is higher in the two new groups than what it was when both were members of the same, larger, village.[9,16,32]

Not all individuals are able to remain with the closest of kin at fission, usually because they are married to a person whose kin group elects to leave, and they have to go along or dissolve their marriage. A war between their new group and the old one puts such individuals in an ambiguous position. Such men often refuse to participate in raids against the group whence they fissioned, pointing out that they wish their close kin no harm. No stigma is associated with this, nor is such a man considered a legitimate target of vengeance by members of his current residential group. If one of his close kin in the original group is killed on a revenge raid by members of his current residential group a man may be moved by grief to the point of deserting his wife and rejoining his original group with the intent to retaliate. Or, he might remain in his current group, filled with smoldering resentment and a concealed hatred of those co-residents who participated in the killing of his kinsman. In the next village club fight, he would most likely support those who are contending with his kinsman's killers. This underscores the difficulty of interpreting Yanomamö warfare as a phenomenon that pits all the members of one political community against all the members of a different political community and makes clear why the village is not the most useful unit with which to analyze warfare in many tribes.

KINSHIP RELATEDNESS AND LOSS OF KIN BY VIOLENCE

Number of relatives. Few published anthropological accounts give statistics on kinship relatedness among all individuals in tribal organized communities, which may in part explain the anthropological tendency to ignore blood revenge as a cause of warfare in the tribal world.[2] Table 9.1 provides statistics on relatedness among members of each of the villages. A person is considered to be related to another if at least one genealogical connection between them exists. Most individuals, however, are related to their kin in multiple ways. In most villages well over 80% of the members are related to more than 75% of the village (see fourth quartile).

Closeness of kinship relationship. Table 9.1 presents statistics on closeness of relationship among village members.[33] These data show that in most villages, members are related to each other more closely than half-cousinship (relatedness to a half cousin is 0.0625), and, to just their actual genetic kin, approximately as first cousins (relatedness to a first cousin is 0.1250).[34]

Kinship Density and the Will for Revenge. The quantitative dimensions of kinship relatedness in Yanomamö communities can be referred to as kinship density, which is a combination of the numbers of kin each individual has, how closely related the individual is to these kin, and the obligations and expectations that are associated with particular kinds of kinship relatedness.

A kinship density factor appears to be involved in revenge raids. It is difficult for a small or heterogeneous Yanomamö group to put together a raiding party. The risks are high and men are willing to take them in proportion to the amount of mutual support they receive from comrades and where unwillingness to do so is condemned and ridiculed. Lone raiders do not exist. The higher the kinship density in a local community, the greater is the likelihood that a large number of mutual supportive individuals will take such life-threatening risks and that retaliation will occur if one of the members of the group is killed. Included is the support of the women, who alone consume the ashes of the slain in order to put the raiders in a state of frenzy and strengthen their resolve. The existence of a tradition of revenge killing promotes kinship density by encouraging individuals to remain with close kin when new communities are formed by fissioning. High levels of relatedness also make it likely that almost every violent death will trigger revenge killing, for most of the members of the victim's community will be close genetic kin.

Measuring levels of societal Violence: Numbers and kinds of kinsmen lost by individuals. Anthropology has no generally accepted measure for describing and comparing levels of violence and warfare cross culturally. With few exceptions,[23,24] much, if not most, of our knowledge about tribal warfare is based on fragmentary reports by untrained observers or on information collected long after the tribes studied had been decimated by introduced diseases and their political sovereignty taken from them by colonial powers. If the data contain numbers, one never knows the universe from which the sample is taken.

This presents a problem in interpreting Yanomamö violence and placing it into a comparative framework. Are the Yanomamö more or less violent than other tribesmen of the past or present? What should be measured or counted to compare levels of violence in different societies? I suspect that the amount of violence in Yanomamö culture would not be atypical if we had comparative measures of precontact violence in other similar tribes while still independent of colonial nation states.[24]

One potentially useful measure of the amount or level of violence in tribal societies (or even modern nations) is the fraction of the population that has participated in the deliberate killing of one or more members of his own or some other community. Another useful measure might be the extent to which violence affects the lives of all (or a significant sample) of society's members in terms of the numbers and kinds of close kinsmen each person has lost through violence.[24,35] As individuals age, more and more of them lose a close genetic kin due to violence (Fig. 9.2). Nearly 70% of all individuals (males and females) age 40 or older have lost at least one close genetic kin due to violence, and most (57%) have lost two or more.

REPRODUCTIVE SUCCESS AND *UNOKAIS*

The deterrent effect of vengeance killing might not be the only factor driving and maintaining Yanomamö warfare. Men who are killers may gain marital and reproductive benefits.

A preliminary analysis of data on reproductive success among *unokais* and non-*unokais* of the same age categories indicates that the former are more successful (Table 9.2). The higher reproductive success of *unokais* is mainly due to their greater success in finding mates (Table 9.3), either by appropriating them forcibly from

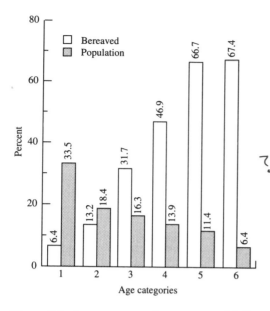

Figure 9.2. Age structure and percentage of individuals losing close genetic kin in each 10-year age category. Age categories: 1, birth to 10 years; 2, 11 to 20 years; 3, 21 to 30 years; 4, 31 to 40 years; 5, 41 to 50 years; and 6, 51+ years. Hachured bars represent the percentage of the 1987 living population (male and female) in each age category. Open bars represent the percentage of individuals (male and female) in each age category who had lost a parent, sibling or half-sibling, or child. Approximately 34% of the population falls in age category 1; approximately 6% of these individuals had lost a close kin due to violence. Since individuals in this age category are children, the kinsmen they lost are primarily parents and elder siblings. Two-thirds of the individuals age 40 or older (age categories 5 and 6) have lost one or more close kin due to violence.

others, or by customary marriage alliance arrangements in which they seem to be more attractive as mates than non-*unokais*.[36]

DISCUSSION

A number of problems are presented by these data. First, high reproductive success among *unokais* is probably caused by a number of factors, and it is not clear what portion might be due to their motivation to seek violent retribution when a kinsman is killed. I can only speculate about the mechanisms that link a high reproductive success with *unokai* status, but I can cast doubt on some logical possibilities. For ex-

ample, it is known that high male reproductive success among the Yanomamö correlates with membership in large descent groups.[32] If *unokais* come disproportionately from these groups, that might explain the data: both could be caused by a third variable. But *unokais* do not come disproportionately from larger descent groups. The three largest patrilineal descent groups among the Yanomamö considered here include 49.4% of the population, but only 48.9% of the *unokais*. The four largest descent groups include 55.9% of the population but only 55.5% of the *unokais*.

Second, it is possible that many men strive to be *unokais* but die trying and that the apparent higher fertility of those who survive may be achieved at an extraordinarily high mortality rate. In other words, men who do not engage in violence might have a lower risk of mortality due to violence and produce more offspring on average than men who tried to be *unokais*. This explanation would be supported by data indicating that a disproportionate fraction of the victims of violence were *unokais*. The data do not appear to lend support to this possibility. Of 15 recent killings, four of the victims were females: there are no female *unokais*. Nine of the males were under 30 years of age, of whom four were under an estimated 25 years of age. Although I do not have the *unokai* histories of these individuals, their ages at death and the political histories of their respective villages at the time they were killed suggest that few, if any, of them, were *unokais*. Also, recent wars in two other regions of the study area resulted in the deaths of approximately 15 additional individuals, many of whom were very young men who were unlikely to have been *unokais*.

Third, additional variables not fully investigated might help account for the correlations in Tables 9.2 and 9.3. For example, there might be biometric attributes of *unokais* and non-*unokais* not readily apparent to the outside observer, such as differential skills at concealment, agility in moving through dense forest on raids, athletic ability, or other favors. Personal, long-term familiarity with all the adult males in this study does not encourage me to conclude at this point that they could easily be sorted into two distinct groups on the basis of obvious biometric characteristics, nor have detailed anthropometric studies of large numbers of Yanomamö males suggested this as a very likely possibility.[37]

Table 9.2. Reproductive Success of *Unokais* and Non-*unokais* of 1987. In Each Age Category There are Individuals who have Sired No Children. However, 88% of the 137 *Unokais* have Reproduced Compared to 49% of the 243 Non-*unokais*. This Table is not Additive with the Data in Table 9.3 to arrive at the Village Sizes given in Table 9.1. Some of the offspring Listed Here are Dead. Living Children whose Fathers are Dead or whose Fathers Live outside the Village in the Study Area are not Included in this Table; Some Older Adult Males have Adult Sons who are Listed Both as Offspring and as either *Unokais* or Non-*unokais*.

		Unokais			Non-unokais	
Ages	n	Number of offspring	Average number of offspring	n	Number of offspring	Average number of offspring
20–24	5	5	1.00	78	14	0.18
25–30	14	22	1.57	58	50	0.86
31–40	43	122	2.83	61	123	2.02
>41	75	524	6.99	46	193	4.19
Total	137	673	4.91	243	380	1.59

Fourth, there is the issue of the deterrent effects of swift, lethal, retaliation and whether or not it can be measured. A logical assumption would be that if *unokais* deter the violence of enemies, they would lose fewer close kin than non-*unokais*. In actual fact, they lose about as many close kin due to violence as non-*unokais* do. Two factors complicate the measurement of the deterrent effect. One is that village membership changes chronically and fissioning redistributes individuals in such a way that *unokais* will have some close kin living in distant villages. An *unokai* in one village cannot, by his actions, have much effect on the safety of a close kinsman in another village. Another is the fact that if *unokais* deter the violent designs of

others, all members of their kin group benefit, including the non-*unokais* and their dependents.

The last problem suggests that the argument that cultural success leads to biological success[8] among the Yanomamö might be the most promising avenue of investigation to account for the high reproductive success of *unokais*. Indeed, the Yanomamö frequently say that some men are valuable (*a nowä dodihiwä*) and give, among the several reasons, that they are *unokai*, avenge deaths, or are fierce (*waiteri*) on behalf of kin. In short, military achievements are valued and associated with high esteem, as they are in many other cultures, including our own.[38] Until recently in human history, successful warriors were traditionally rewarded

Table 9.3. Marital Success of *Unokais* and Non-*unokais* of 1987. In each age Category there are Individuals who have no Wives in 1987. However, 88% of the 137 *Unokais* are Married compared to 51% of the 243 Non-*unokais*. The Data in this Table are not Additive with the Data in Table 9.2 to arrive at Village Sizes given in Table 9.1. Currently Unmarried Women are not included in this Table.

		Unokais			Non-unokais	
Ages	n	Number of offspring	Average number of offspring	n	Number of offspring	Average number of offspring
20–24	5	4	0.80	78	10	0.13
25–30	14	13	0.93	58	31	0.53
31–40	43	49	1.14	61	59	0.97
>41	75	157	2.09	46	54	1.17
Total	137	223	1.63	243	154	0.63

with public offices and political power which, in turn, was used for reproductive advantage.[39] Among the Yanomamö, non-*unokais* might be willing to concede more reproductive opportunities to *unokais* in exchange for a life with fewer moral risks and fewer reproductive advantages.[40]

Some Yanomamö men are in general more responsible, ambitious, economically industrious, aggressive, concerned about the welfare of their kin, and willing to take risks. Becoming an *unokai* is simply one of a number of male characteristics valued by the Yanomamö and an integral component in a more general complex of goals for which ambitious men strive. All the characteristics just mentioned make some males more attractive as mates in arranged marriages and dispose some of them to take the risks involved in appropriating additional females by force. Both paths lead to higher reproductive success.

Jacoby's[13] study of revenge in modern societies makes a compelling case that the desire for *lex talionis* is widespread even in societies with law and formal judicial systems and that justice everywhere has an undeniable element of retribution. It is difficult for us to imagine the terror that might characterize our own social lives in the absence of laws prohibiting individuals from seeking lethal retribution when a close kinsman dies at the hands of another human, be it premeditated murder or the consequence of an irresponsible accidental act, such as a drunk driver causing the deaths of innocent people. A particularly acute insight into the power of law to thwart killing for revenge was provided to me by a young Yanomamö man in 1987. He had been taught Spanish by missionaries and sent to the territorial capital for training in practical nursing. There he discovered police and laws. He excitedly told me that he had visited the town's largest *pata* (the territorial governor) and urged him to make law and police available to his people so that they would not have to engage any longer in their wars of revenge and have to live in constant fear. Many of his close kinsmen had died violently and had, in turn, exacted lethal revenge; he worried about being a potential target of retaliations and made it known to all that he would have nothing to do with raiding.[41]

Acknowledgments. Field research was sponsored by NSF and the Harry Frank Guggenheim Foundation and data analysis by the Harry Frank Guggenheim Foundation. I would like to thank R. Alexander, R. Axelrod, D. Brown, R. Carneiro, R. Hames, M. Daly, T. Harding, M. Harrell, W. Irons, M. Meggitt, S. Plattner, D. Symons, R. Thornhill, and P. Van den Berghe, for critical comments on the manuscript. I thank M. de la Luz Ibarra E. Kargard for assistance with library research, manuscript preparation, graphics, and computer analyses. I thank A. Spaulding for assistance on the statistical tests.

NOTES

1. Alexander (1979); Carneiro (1970).

2. Gross (1975); Harris (1979a, 1979b, 1984); Johnson and Earle (1987); Ross (1978); Sponsel (1983). For counterarguments, see: Chagnon (1980a); Hames and Vickers (1983).

3. Barth (1966, 1967); Swartz, Turner, and Tuden (1966); Bailey (1969); Nicholas (1965)

4. Alexander (1987); Barash (1977); Chagnon and Irons (1979); Daly and Wilson (1983); Dawkins (1976); King's College Sociobiology Group (1982); Lumsden and Wilson (1982); Maynard Smith (1964); Van den Berghe (1979); Tiger and Fox (1966); Trivers (1971); Williams (1966a); E. Wilson (1975, 1978).

5. Hamilton (1964); Alexander and Borgia (1978).

6. Alexander (1985); Chagnon (1990).

7. Darwin's second major work, *The Descent of Man, and Selection in Relation to Sex* (1871), focused on "sexual" selection and those attributes of organisms that appear to have evolved because they conferred an advantage in mate competition. By distinguishing between competition for material resources and reproductive resources I wish to emphasize the importance of sexual competition as a cause of violence. See also Campbell (1972).

8. Irons (1979a); Borgerhoff Mulder (1987a).

9. Chagnon (1974).

10. Chagnon (1992).

11. Lizot (1984, 1985).

12. Davie (1929); Turney-High (1971); Wright (1965); Daly and Wilson (1988a); Otterbein (1970).

13. Boehm (1984); Jacoby (1983); Hasluck (1954); Kelsen (1946).

14. Blood revenge in many other societies entails elaborate rules that specify who is obligated to avenge a death and, sometimes, the range of kinsmen (brother, cousin, and so forth) of the killer that is an appropriate target for retaliation. Yanomamö revenge customs are not this specific.

15. Yanomamö lack a written language and precise notions of time and distance. Therefore, all ages are based on my estimates, which are more accurate for those groups I have been re-censusing since 1964, but less accurate for groups I contacted more recently. However, their language contains words that describe the state of maturity of individuals, making it possible to distinguish between broad categories such as infants, juveniles and adults (reproductively mature and post-reproductive individuals). While I witnessed many violent and near-lethal conflicts, in none of these incidents did the participants die while I was present. I did not accompany raiding parties and did not witness the killings that occurred while I lived there. News of killings travels fast and is widely known. All the data on violent deaths are therefore based on assertions of multiple informants whose accounts were cross-checked. There was remarkable consistency in their reports on violent deaths. The weakest category of data is that dealing with infant and child mortality, due mainly to the Yanomamö taboo on discussing deceased close kin and the horror and anger this provokes when one inquires about it from close relatives. Estimates of fertility should therefore be taken as underestimates due to underreporting. Blood group studies of possible paternity exclusion indicate that informant-provided genealogical data are probably quite accurate (see Neel and Weiss 1975). For a detailed discussion of my data collecting methods and possible levels of error, see (9).

16. Chagnon (1982, 1988b).

17. Chagnon (1966, 1968b).

18. The members of the villages reported here (and their recently deceased kin) have made approximately 200 garden-village sites in the region under consideration during approximately the past 50 years (see Chagnon 1968a and [9] and [17] for further discussion of some of these settlement sites). Nearly half these sites were established during my 23-year study. Approximately 50 fissions took place at these locations, followed in many cases by fusion. About ten within-group killings occurred during the time of my studies, half involving male victims. In all cases involving males, the group fissioned as a consequence of the killing. Fission did not follow the killings of three abducted females who had no co-resident close kin in the group.

19. In 1986, a Ye'kwana Indian, totally unaware of the theoretical debates in anthropology about tribal warfare, described to me a conference in Caracas in which various anthropologists presented theories about customs and phenomena they had studied among Venezuelan native peoples. After one presentation on Yanomamö warfare he said he stood up and told the audience the following: "Even though I am Ye'kwana, I have also lived with the Yanomamö many years. I speak their language fluently and I know their warfare. While the last speaker used many words and elaborate arguments I do not understand, he missed the most fundamental fact about Yanomamö warfare. What he does not seem to understand is that their wars always start over women."

20. Axelrod and Hamilton (1981); Axelrod (1984).

21. This region has been occupied by the same core Yanomamö populations for at least 70 to 80 years, but population growth and village fissions and fusions have been such that the actual number of discrete villages changes from year to year. The area of focus includes the drainages of the Mavaca and Bocon Rivers, both tributaries of the upper Orinoco River, and immediately adjacent portions of the Siapa River, a large affluent of the Casiquiare River, in southern Venezuela. Fissions, abductions, marriage alliances, and migrations among the villages in this area since the mid-1970's have blurred not only the distinctions between the two clusters of historically distinct villages (9), but the identities of specific villages as well.

22. Chagnon (1972).

23. Meggitt (1977); Glasse (1968); Heider (1970); see also Lee (1979); Steadman (1971); Koch (1974).

24. Knauft (1987b) has compiled or estimated mortality rates for a number of modern cities, nations, and primitive societies in terms of violent deaths per 100,000 people. Sample rates from his study are: Britain, 1959 data, 0.50; Detroit, Michigan, 1958 data, 58.2; Yanomamö, 1972–74 data, 165.9; Australian aborigines (Murngin), 1906–26 data, 330.0; Hewa of New Guinea, 1971 data, 778.0. The homicide rates for tribesman are staggeringly high compared to rates for modern cities and nations wherever adequate data has been collected by anthropologists, despite the fact that deaths in tribal societies due to diseases occur at very high rates. However, a major difficulty in characterizing rates of violence in tribal societies with this kind of statistic is the fact that violence waxes and wanes radically over relatively short periods of time in most tribal societies, and grossly different estimates of homicide rates for the same population can be obtained from studies done of the same local group at two different periods of time, or neighboring groups at the same point in time. Knauft's estimate for the Yanomamö is based on an analysis of a relatively small portion of my data for the brief period 1972–74 (Melancon 1982). Radically different estimates could be calculated for the Yanomamö

from a different set of villages or different time periods. For example, Lizot's accounts (11) of events in one small Yanomamö village (approximately 70 people) between 1968 and 1976 indicates that mortality due to violence was very low to almost nonexistent during that time period. But, in 1982, a very large fraction of the adult males, as well as several women and children of that village, were killed in a war with a neighboring Yanomamö village (see Chagnon in [6]).

25. The role of female grief in Yanomamö warfare is an important fact in perpetuating revenge killings. One *unokai* organized and led a raid on a distant village whose members had done him or his kin no personal harm. He killed the headman of that village on this raid. But this *unokai* had married into his current village recently and had lost no genetic kin to raiders of the enemy village. He explained that his wife grieved so intensely for a sister who had been killed by members of the village that he raided that he felt compelled to avenge her death. He said that his wife was very pleased with his actions. Intensity of grief appears to follow patterns predicted from kin selection theory: female kin grieve more intensely than male kin, and genetically close kin more than less closely related kin (see Littlefield and Rushton (1986).

26. Harner (1962). The Jivaro also believe that killing confers immunity from the retaliatory designs of others, since the killer accumulates power from his victim. The power wanes with time and Jivaro men must therefore periodically kill in order to maintain a proper level of immunity.

27. Approximately 6% of the violent deaths are presently classified as "within group," but some may be found to be "between group." These incidents involved violent conflicts between factions that were in the process of fissioning into two new villages and became new villages at approximately the time of these killings.

28. Symons (1979); Daly, Wilson, and Weghorst (1982).

29. Valero (1984); Biocca (1970).

30. Irons (1981).

31. K. von Clauzewitz (1968).

32. Chagnon (1979a, 1981); Chagnon and Bugos (1979).

33. Wright (1922).

34. Values in Table 9.1 were calculated as follows. Each individual was compared to all members of his or her village to determine the identities of any common ancestors. The genealogies are from three to five generations deep, depending on the ages of the individuals compared. Genealogical connections between pairs of related individuals were established for every identifiable common ancestor and the coefficient of relatedness for each connection was calculated and summed. The quartiles in Table 9.1 are based on the definition that a person is related to another if at least one genealogical connection between them has been established in the computer search for common ancestors. Closeness of relatedness among individuals was calculated in two ways, with a variant of Wright's formula for coefficient of relatedness (inbreeding coefficients of remote ancestors were not considered). For relatives, Fg[CON], the values of the coefficients of relatedness through all separate loops between Ego and all relatives were added and then divided by the number of relatives to get each Ego's average relatedness to demonstrable relatives. Each Ego's average values were then averaged to give the village average. For all residents, Fg[ALL], the sum of all coefficients of relatedness between Ego and all demonstrable relatives were added and then divided by the total number of residents in the village, including nonrelated residents. These values were then averaged to give the village average.

35. Taken by itself this measure might "inflate" the amount of a society's violence: if all members of a society were related, then a few deaths would result in a statistic showing that a large fraction of people have lost close kin. A standard sociological measure, number of victims per 100,000 population per annum, would be very difficult to estimate in tribal populations where violence waxes and wanes radically over short time spans and where communities are small and scattered. Meaningful comparable statistics using this measure would require long-term residence by several fieldworkers in many separate villages (24).

36. In each of the four age categories, the *unokais* were characterized by both more children and more wives non-*unokais*. For Table 9.2, all age categories yielded chi-square values statistically significant at at least the 0.05 level. For Table 9.3 the chi-square values were not statistically significant for age categories 25 to 30 and 31 to 40 but were at the 0.05 level for the other two age categories. For both Tables 9.2 and 9.3, the pooled data (tools) were significant ($P < 0.00001$). In both tables the differences between expected and observed values were in the same direction for all age categories and pooled.

37. R. Spielman, thesis, University of Michigan, Ann Arbor (1971, 1973); Spielman *et al.* (1972). During the anthropomorphic field studies the biomedical personnel, unfamiliar with the life histories of the individuals, informally attempted to guess whether or not particular men being measured were among the *waiteri* (fierce ones), were political leaders, or were otherwise prominent in the group; comparison of their predictions against my life history data on these same individuals showed uniformly poor results.

38. Many U.S. congressmen are and traditionally have been officers in the U.S. Army (Hoebel 1968).

39. Betzig (1986).

40. C. Lévi-Strauss (1944), in an article on "chieftainship" in a South American tribal society, the Nambikwara of Brazil, argued that tribal communities might profitably be viewed as clusters of people who form around prominent men whose only compensation for the onerous tasks of leadership was the concession the group made to the leaders in the form of multiple wives.

41. Ironically, this man was married polyandrously. His duties as a practical nurse did not allow him time to garden so he had to compromise and share his wife with another man who had a garden.

10

Sticks and Stones

NAPOLEON CHAGNON

My 1988 *Science* article summarized approximately twenty-five years of data on selected demographic patterns among residents of the cluster of Yanomamö villages whose residents and their life histories I knew well. It reflected a specific slice in time and captured the mortality patterns, marriage and reproductive variations, and the perpetrators of violent deaths that were characteristic of that time and of the immediate past. The focus of the study was on males who were alive in 1985 and their life histories.

It is important to note that Yanomamö mortality patterns were beginning to change radically in the 1980s due to increasing contact with the outside world, and it would today be difficult to write a similar paper in view of these accelerating changes, especially because of the epidemiological effects of a massive gold rush into the Brazilian Yanomamö area in 1987. Were this paper written after 1988, the fraction of adult male deaths due to violence would appear to be smaller than those I reported in 1988 principally because the fraction of deaths due to diseases was increasing radically by that date. On the other hand, had I published this paper ten years earlier, the fraction of adult male deaths due to violence would probably have been higher and, I suspect, so also would the correlations between *unokai* status, polygyny, and higher reproductive success of *unokais*. Introduced diseases probably contaminated the "aboriginal" mortality patterns to some degree in the data on which my 1988 article was based and probably resulted in an underestimate of the rates of violent death in the populations studied.

As I have reported in many earlier publications, warfare intensity and conflict vary markedly from one region of the Yanomamö area to another, and vary over time within each region. It would be useful to have similar data from other Yanomamö areas where other anthropologists have worked for many years, but for reasons unclear to me they either did not collect these data or, if they did, have not published them. I know from private conversations with French anthropologist Jacques Lizot that the warfare patterns and rates of mortality due to violence are similar in some of the areas he has worked, and French anthropologist Catherine Ales's initial publications on Yanomamö groups in the Parima B area confirmed earlier published accounts by a New Tribes missionary, Margaret Jank, that warfare in that area was comparable in intensity to that found in the areas on which I reported (Ales 1984; Jank 1977); they also confirmed the impressions I developed during a brief visit I made to the Parima B area in the late 1960s. In addition, my own partial data on villages immediately south of the Siapa River headwaters in or near Brazil indicate that the pattern is similar there as well, but French anthropologist Bruce Albert is not only silent on this topic but suggests that warfare is rare or inconsequential there (Albert 1989). Protestant missionaries working there say that warfare is still quite intense (as of 1994), and my own recent (unpublished) data on villages in the adjacent Siapa basin reveal significant numbers of individuals who have been killed recently by raiders from this area of Brazil. In brief, while we do not have comparable data from other regions of the Yanomamö tribe, my hunch is that what I reported in my *Science* article is probably not peculiar to the areas I studied.

An important question regarding my article is the consequence of two problems specific to the Yanomamö as a population. The issue, which I discussed, is determining if *unokais* are at greater risk of being killed by raiders than non-*unokais*, that is, do they gain their reproductive advantages at high mortality costs compared to non-*unokais*? To establish this one must know causes of death and the ages of people at the time of their death, as well as their *unokai* status.

The first problem is the Yanomamö's reluctance to speak about deceased kin and ancestors, so individuals who failed to reproduce might not even appear in my data. If they reproduced, it is unlikely they escaped my attention. The second is the fact that they do not have a numbering system and cannot accurately specify absolute ages of people. This is a particularly serious handicap in cases of people who died before I could meet them and estimate their ages by inspection. The only reasonable way to deal with this is to either estimate the age of the deceased by extrapolating from the estimated ages of their oldest living offspring, or, if they produced no offspring, resort to "age estimates" based on Yanomamö categories of human ontology (maturation), such as *huya* or *pata*—"younger man" and "older, more mature, politically significant man," respectively. This is unsatisfactory for some maturation categories. For example, a *huya* can be an adolescent of fifteen years or a young man up to thirty years of age. Their categories are more reliable for other age groups, such as *pata*—if the informant adds additional information like *rohote* (old). A consideration of these kinds of maturation data does <u>not</u> suggest that *unokais* are at greater risk of being killed or as a function of age, but it would be a more robust conclusion if accurate ages could be established, especially for men whose *unokai* status at the time of their violent death was not known to my informants. For example, it is unlikely that an eighteen-year old who was killed by raiders was himself an *unokai*, but it is more likely that a "really old man" may have been.

Finally, the publication of this article in 1988 provoked extremely intense reaction and anger from a number of anthropologists and led to several denunciations and vigorous criticisms in various anthropological and other journals (Carneiro da Cunha 1989; Ferguson 1989; Albert 1989; Lizot 1989; Moore 1990). These reactions began immediately and continue to the present (e.g., Lizot 1994; cf. Chagnon 1995), coming initially from Brazilian and French anthropologists who, along with many others, were deeply involved in admirable efforts to keep the plight of the Yanomamö at the hands of the illegal gold miners in the international news. The reactions seemed to stem from a number of considerations. The first was justifiable outrage at how a handful of journalists sensationalized and misrepresented the findings in my *Science* article and irresponsibly added twists and extensions they felt would be of interest to the public at large.[1] One journalist began his story with an argument to the effect that "when the Yanomamö are not out peacefully collecting wild honey and gathering berries, they are murdering each other." A second reason for so much criticism is more complex and murky. Part of it stems from opposition to scientific approaches, especially biological approaches, to the study of human behavior—violent behavior in particular. A final component might be due to professional jealousy on the part of other anthropologists who have worked among the Yanomamö, some of whom resent the fact that may work is more widely known and more frequently cited than theirs. One of them seriously suggested to me in 1973 at the annual meetings of the American Anthropological Association that we change the name of the tribe so that his work would stand out more and not be subsumed into or be confused with mine. Largely for reasons of professional jealousy and, perhaps, nationalism, between 1975 and 1984 Venezuelan anthropologists succeeded in preventing me from continuing my field studies and appear to have been very annoyed that shortly after I was able to resume field studies in the mid-1980s I published an article that attracted so much attention in the academic community and in the international press.

Their reaction was to rescind my already awarded field research permit in 1989. My field trips after that date were made possible only because people very high in the Venezuelan government, including two presidents of Venezuela, personally authorized my returns.

The dismal conclusion is that the Yanomamö might be the last relatively unacculturated tribal people on earth where anthropological field research on the relationships between violence, warrior status, marriage, and reproductive variables can be meaningfully studied. Opposing this are many cultural anthropologists from France, Brazil, Venezuela and now, some in the United States, the Salesian Missions of Venezuela, and a variety of academics and politicians from several countries representing political correctness or varieties of postmodernism (Chagnon 1996). A whole lot of people, especially anthropologists, seem to not want others to know about these things, and what I reported in *Science* might simply become an isolated and therefore problematic instance because no comparative anthropological studies exist and none are likely to appear in the future.

NOTE

1. I was not aware that lead articles in all issues of *Science* are automatically sent to members of the press and notable science writers. The fact that my article dealt with primitive warfare, violence, sex, and abduction led to some astonishing misrepresentations in some newspaper stories, a few of the more garish of which soon appeared in Spanish and Portuguese in Venezuelan and Brazilian newspapers, which at the time were also carrying stories portraying the Yanomamö as an innocent, beleaguered, peaceful Amazon Indian society. The contrast was stark and incongruent.

11

Kipsigis Women's Preferences for Wealthy Men: Evidence for Female Choice in Mammals?

MONIQUE BORGERHOFF MULDER

Where resources critical to female breeding success can be monopolized by males, polygynous mating is commonly attributed to the differential resource holding power of males (Emlen and Oring 1977). Female choice for males with high quality resources may contribute to the evolution of polygyny, if the differences in quality between resources held by males are great enough that females raise as many or more offspring by mating with already-paired males on superior territories than with bachelors on inferior territories (Orians 1969). This difference in territory quality is called the "polygyny threshold" (Verner 1964; Verner and Willson 1966), and female decisions can be characterized as following an "ideal free" distribution (Fretwell 1972). The classic test of the polygyny threshold model is that the fitness of monogamously and polygynously mated females should be equal but, because this prediction is based on a number of assumptions that are difficult to substantiate (Davies 1989; Searcy and Yakusawa 1989; see Discussion), such evidence is weak support that females assort themselves as predicted by the model.

A more robust prediction from the model is that the quality of resources held by a male will influence his breeding success through enhanced access to females attracted to his territory. Studies of passerine birds provide consistent evidence that the number of females settling on a male territory is influenced by features favored by females; these include shaded nest sites in lark buntings *Calamospiza melanocorys* (Pleszczynska 1978), cattail density in redwinged blackbirds *Agelaius phoeniceus* (Lenington 1980; see also Searcy 1979) and elevated nest sites in pied flycatchers *Ficedula hypoleuca* (Alatalo et al. 1986).

Correlational evidence, however, is always open to alternative explanations. The most conclusive demonstration (bar experimental manipulation) that females do actively choose males for the territories they hold is to examine whether females chose the best breeding option available to them at the time of their settlement (Lenington 1980; Davies 1989; Searcy and Yakusawa 1989); this can be done through the analysis of settlement sequences. "MICROCAL

In mammals resource-defense polygyny is far rarer than in birds; consequently female preference for males defending large territories or valued resources is not prominent, even in territorial species (Owen-Smith 1977). However, among the Kipsigis people of Kenya, strong correlations between resource ownership and the number of a man's wives are found (Borgerhoff Mulder 1987a). Resource access is also a primary determinant of women's breeding success (Borgerhoff Mulder 1987b), so polygyny may be a consequence of the preferences of females (or their kin) for wealthy males.

Reprinted with permission from *Behavioral Ecology and Sociobiology* 27:255–64 (1990).

This paper has two aims: to test whether Kipsigis women prefer wealthy men, by examining the sequence of marriages among a group of Kipsigis pioneers who, in the 1930s and 1940s, settled different sized plots of land in the territory of their neighbors and enemies, the Masai. Second, to determine whether women in the full demographic sample of post-menopausal women (Borgerhoff Mulder 1988e) suffer reproductively as a result of polygynous marriage choices. In short, can the marriages that occurred during a period of pioneer settlement be characterized as resource-defense polygyny mediated by adaptive female choice for men with large plots of land?

ETHNOGRAPHIC BACKGROUND

Resources and Reproduction

The Kipsigis are a Southern Nilotic pastoralist group, now settled as agro-pastoralists in southwestern Kenya, between latitudes 0°9″ and 1° south and longitude 35° and 35°30″ east. Families derive their entire subsistence from the cultivation of maize and the herding of domestic stock. The primary capital resources for these activities are land and cattle which are owned exclusively by men. Men marry up to 12 wives, who almost invariably reside on their husband's property and are entirely dependent on his land and stock. Some men hold single land plots, others more than one in different locations. Ownership of land persists through life as plots are largely inalienable. Competition among men over land is prominent, and pervades all accounts of the Kipsigis during the Colonial period (Manners 1967; Saltman 1977), stimulating the incursions of Kipsigis into Masai-land (see below). The bitterness of disputes over land among related and unrelated men in semi-sedentary East African pastoralists is vividly depicted by many ethnographers (e.g., Goldschmidt [1986] for the Sebei and Gulliver [1963] for the Arusha Masai, with accounts of physical violence and lifelong feuds).

Land is shared on an equal basis among a man's wives (Peristiany 1939; Orchardson 1961). Land access is correlated with women's reproductive success, and may be an important causal factor contributing to reproductive differentials, given the greater availability of food in the homes of "richer" women and the lower incidence of illness among them and their offspring (Borgerhoff Mulder 1987b).

Divorce is not formally recognized, but a severely maltreated wife can desert her husband for several years or even permanently and produce children fathered by other men.

Marriage

A Kipsigis girl spends several months in seclusion after reaching menarche. During this time the father of each of her prospective suitors visits her parents and makes a proposal of marriage, entailing a bridewealth offer (see Peristiany 1939:57; Orchardson 1961:69; Borgerhoff Mulder 1988c for details). Such payments are required at marriage and are high, constituting almost one third of an average man's wealth. The parents of the young woman choose from among competing suitors a potential son-in-law, by ascertaining the man's character, wealth and social connections; usually this information will already be known to them, or to neighbors or relatives. The final bridewealth is negotiated with the suitor's father. The wishes of bride and groom are not formally taken into consideration (Peristiany 1939:57), except in so far as they can influence their parents. Finally, certain relatives and associates are banned from marrying one another, such as members of the same patriclan (see Peristiany 1939:107), but these prohibitions do not appear severely to restrict the number of potential marriage partners (pers. obs. at marriage negotiations where up to 11 suitors may be considered).

Given parental involvement in the marriage process, Kipsigis women are not technically "free" to choose their own mates. The role of a girl's parents in choosing a son-in-law suggests that the unwieldy term "bride's parents' choice" is more appropriate. Does this undermine the assumption of free female choice? In societies where women are coerced into marriages that are in their *parents'* political interests, and possibly against their own personal reproductive interests (e.g., Dickemann 1979a, 1982), the female choice model is clearly inappropriate (Daly and Wilson 1983; Gray 1985; Flinn and Low 1986). However Kipsigis daughters are rarely forced into marriages with which they do not concur (for exceptions see Discussion), because a discontented wife will desert her husband, return to her natal home and continue to produce offspring who must be fed from the produce of the parental land plot; this can place severe economic stress on the rest of the family, particularly if the deserting bride had brothers who are already married. Consequently, a primary concern of Kipsigis parents in selecting a son-in-law is to find a man with whom they expect their daughter will remain contented. Scope for parental manipulation in this particular ethnographic context is therefore limited, and the term female choice is retained on the assumption that the interests of parents and daughters are largely coincident, at least with respect to the parameters measured in this study.

Settlement of the Abosi area

Two events occurred soon after the arrival (1906–1907) of the first Europeans in Kericho District (south-western Kenya) that led to a pioneer group of Kipsigis families settling in the vicinity of Abosi, part of the traditional land of the Masai (Fig. 11.1). First, almost 50% of the Kipsigis' traditional territory was forcibly alienated, for both the founding of European dairy farms and the commercial production of tea and flax. This precipitated the establishment of Native Reserves in the central and south-eastern areas of the District. Second the Kipsigis, traditionally semi-nomadic pastoralists, were encouraged through market incentives to cultivate maize, leading to the development of individual rights over land (Saltman 1977). As a result of changed land use patterns in the geographically circumscribed Reserve, land shortages escalated and a number of families emigrated into the territory of the Masai, their traditional enemies. These events led to a number of migratory waves southwards in which individual Kipsigis men, pairs or trios broke away from their fathers and established new farms, rather than settling on small inherited plots in the Reserve (Manners 1967, pp. 274–282). Abosi (see Fig. 11.1) was settled by 25 such pioneers between 1930 and 1949. Most of these men arrived with 1 (32%) or more (44%) wives but continued to marry young women who came largely from the overpopulated Reserve.

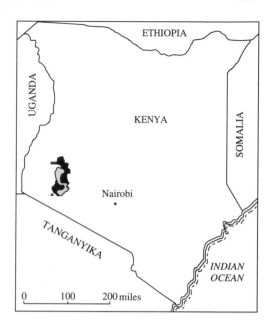

Figure 11.1. Kenya, with its capital Nairobi, in 1960, after Manners (1967), showing the location of Kericho District; alienated land shown in black and the Kipsigis Reserve cross-hatched. The triangle indicates the location of the settlement at Abosi.

At Abosi, each pioneer staked out a plot of land, guided by the concept of individual ownership that predominated in the Reserve, forcing later-arriving men to settle smaller plots deeper in Masai country. In interviews men stated that the size of the plot settled was influenced by the number of cattle and small stock requiring pasture. Land plots were fenced by laying cut thorn shrub branches on the ground. Skirmishes with Masai occurred quite frequently, but conflicts over land with other Kipsigis were normally arbitrated in favor of the contender who was first to arrive in the area, although some brawls were reported.

METHODS

Fieldwork. Between June 1982 and December 1983 a study area of 35 sq. km was established on the border of Kericho and Narok Districts, Rift Valley Province, Kenya, incorporating a portion of the Native Reserve, the Abosi settlement area (see above) and other settlement areas. Interviews with men and women conducted in Kipsigis were used to determine land plot size, livestock holdings and marital histories; past events were dated to the year through the use of a calendar of local events such as circumcision ceremonies, droughts and administrative changes (see Borgerhoff Mulder 1987a for details).

Pioneer settlement study: variables, sample and analysis. Year of arrival in Abosi was determined for each pioneer. The ranking was then cross-checked with two of the earliest settlers, and no inconsistencies were found. The size of the plot settled was determined from the results of a land survey conducted by the Government Land Office in 1982 and 1983, the purpose of which was to register the current plots owned by different individuals which very closely reflect the original plots settled. After 1949 there was such an influx of families that it became difficult to determine a clear ranking of arrivals, so analyses were limited to the "Pioneer period" (1930–1949) during which 25 men settled. Age and marital history were available from reproductive interviews (Borgerhoff Mulder 1987a). The number of a man's surviving offspring was divided by the sum of the number of years he had spent married to each of his various wives (during the latters' reproductive years) to produce the measure "man's reproductive history."

Wives already married to pioneers at arrival were termed "previous wives," those married during the Pioneer period "pioneer wives," and those married after 1949 "subsequent wives;" these sum to a measure termed "total wives." Six men arrived at Abosi as bachelors, that is with no previous wives. The "breeding opportunity" offered by a pioneer at any one time was measured as the number of acres divided by the total number of his wives *plus 1*, so as to capture the resources potentially available to a *new wife.*

To examine whether men are chosen as husbands with respect to resources the rank order in which women chose men should be compared to the rank order of breeding opportunities on offer (cf. Lenington 1980). However because some Kipsigis women chose mates before other men had arrived, comparisons of such rankings across years is inappropriate. Facing the same analytical difficulty Alatalo et al. (1984) resorted to within year comparisons, yielding small sample sizes with little potential for multivariate analysis.

In the present study a stratified Cox (1972) regression analysis was used to determine the effects of breeding opportunity on the probability of a man being selected. Cox's model offers two important features. First, it allows the risk set to vary between years, thus accommodating both the changing breeding opportunities on offer each year as a result of pioneers' marriages in a preceding year, and the arrival of new pioneers each year. Second, it permits assessment of the effects of a number of covariates on the probability of a man being selected, using a method analogous to multiple regression (BMDP 1985a). Where two or more men were chosen in one year, they were considered as ties, as month of marriage had not been recorded. The regression was run using a stepwise function; for each independently significant covariate the ratio of the beta coefficient to the standard error and its associated significance level is reported, together with the likelihood ratio chi-square improvement statistic. For all other variables tested the raw chi-square statistics are given. The analysis here is identical with Luce's choice model (Maddala 1983), except for the handling of ties; a similar type of survival analysis is presented in BMDP (1985b). Cox's model is particularly appropriate to the study of female settlement patterns in which some males are chosen before others have arrived and where male mating status changes over time, as occurs in Kipsigis and several passerines.

Demographic study: variables, samples and analysis. All women of reproductive age in the study area were interviewed yielding reproductive histories that could be related to the economic and marital circumstances of their husbands. The analyses in this paper are based on two cohorts of women ("Maina" and "Chuma") who had entirely terminated their reproductive careers by 1983 and for whom lifetime reproductive success could be measured as numbers of surviving offspring (Borgerhoff Mulder 1988e).

Using information from men's marital interviews, two measures of polygyny could be calculated for each woman: the number of women married to her husband ("number of cowives") and her marital status (monogamous, primary polygynous, secondary polygynous, etc.; for further details, see Borgerhoff Mulder 1989c).

Husband's plot size ("husband's acres") was determined through interviews with men (Borgerhoff Mulder 1987a) in conjunction with the use of Land Office maps. The demographic sample is slightly smaller than that presented in Borgerhoff Mulder (1989c) because adequate wealth data were not available for the husbands of all women.

Analyses of variance, incorporating tests for deviation from linearity, were used to determine whether the number of surviving offspring produced by a woman is affected by polygyny; the effect of husband's acres was controlled using the Options subcommands available in SPSSx (1983). The effect of polygyny on number of surviving offspring was also examined within wealth categories.

RESULTS

Settlement, Wealth, Age and Mating Success during the Pioneer Period

For each of the pioneers his year of arrival, the size of the land plot he settled, and the number of his previous wives, pioneer wives and total wives are shown in Table 11.1. Pioneer's year

of arrival in Abosi was negatively associated with size of land plot he settled ($r = 0.66$, $n = 25$ and thereafter this paragraph, $p < 0.001$); earlier arriving men established larger plots, as the Kipsigis themselves recognized. Plot size was strongly correlated with number of pioneer wives ($r = 0.79$, $p < 0.001$) and total wives ($r = 0.81$, $p < 0.001$), but not with number of previous wives ($r = -0.15$, NS), suggesting that the size of a man's plot was more a cause than a consequence of his marital history (Borgerhoff Mulder 1989b).

Some other correlated but unmeasured quality of the land, such as terrain, location or drainage, might be more important than the size of a man's plot in attracting a large number of wives; if such favorable plots were settled first, the number of pioneer and total wives would be more strongly correlated with a man's arrival date than with the size of the plot he settled. As anticipated, year of arrival was negatively associated with the number of pioneer and total wives ($r = 0.50$, $r = -0.57$, $n = 25$, $p < 0.01$), but partial correlations showed that both were still strongly correlated with plot size when the

Table 11.1. Arrival Date, Wealth and Number of Wives of the 25 Pioneers

Year of arrival	Husband	Size of plot settled	Previous wives	Pioneer wives	Husband's total wives
1930	O	150	3	1	4
1932	D	100	2	2	4
	A	160	3	1	4
1933	C	100	0	2	4
	B	300	0	6	8
1935	F	50	2	1	3
1936	E	30	0	2	3
1937	I	70	2	1	4
1938	S	100	4	0	4
1939	H	60	1	1	2
	G	120	0	3	3
1940	P	60	1	1	3
1942	L	40	1	1	4
1943	J	180	0	2	4
	K	32	2	1	3
1944	M	40	1	1	3
	T	20	2	0	3
1945	U	20	2	0	3
1946	V	8	1	0	2
	N	36	1	1	2
1947	W	20	4	0	4
	X	20	2	0	3
1949	Q	29	0	1	2
	R	20	1	1	3
	Y	10	1	0	1

effects of arrival date were controlled ("pioneer wives" partial $r = 0.71$, "total wives" partial $r = 0.70$, both $n = 22$, $p < 0.001$); neither pioneer nor total wives were correlated with arrival date when plot size was controlled (partial $r = 0.05$, partial $r = 0.09$, both $n = 22$, NS). These results suggest that acreage (rather than other aspects of a man's plot) is a potentially important factor influencing polygyny.

There was no association between pioneer's age at arrival and the year of his arrival ($r = 0.22$, $n = 25$, NS), but men who were older unsurprisingly had more wives at settlement ($r = 0.69$, $p < 0.001$) and obtained fewer pioneer ($r = -0.58$, $p < 0.01$) or subsequent wives ($r = -0.57$, $p < 0.01$). Older settlers also established rather smaller land plots ($r = 0.43$, $p < 0.05$). Despite these age effects, the associations between plot size and the number of both pioneer and total wives were independent of the effects of arrival age (partial $r = 0.74$, partial $r = 0.80$, both $n = 22$, $p < 0.001$).

Female Choice of Breeding Opportunities during the Pioneer Period

Men of 1st or 2nd rank with respect to breeding opportunities in acres were selected as husbands in 43% of the 29 marriages occurring during the Pioneer period (Fig. 11.2): a sign test (Siegel 1956) shows that marriages were preferentially made with men offering above the median ranked breeding opportunity ($X = 2.16$, non-tied observations $= 27$, $p = 0.05$).

Results of the Cox stepwise regression analysis showed independent effects of two covariates on the probability of being chosen: men were preferred if they were offering larger breeding opportunities (beta coefficient/standard error 2.7046, $p = 0.01$); they were also more likely to be chosen if married to fewer wives (-2.2095, $p < 0.01$). The model yielded likelihood ratio chi-square improvement values that were significant for both covariates (breeding opportunity [step # 1]: $X^2 = 14.94$, $p < 0.001$; number of wives [step #2]: $X^2 = 4.35$, $p < 0.05$). The effects of three further variables were examined. Men were more likely to be chosen if they had a high rate of production of surviving offspring with the women to whom they were already married ($X^2 = 7.71$, $p < 0.001$), whereas neither the overall size of the plot a man settled ($X^2 = 3.36$, $0.05 < p < 0.10$)

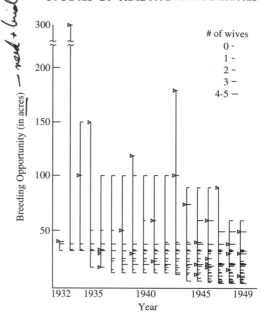

Figure 11.2. Breeding opportunities selected by females arriving in the Abosi area between 1932 and 1949. Each horizontal bar indicates a breeding opportunity, with triangles denoting the breeding opportunities selected each year. The length of the horizontal bar shows the man's marital status (see key). Thus in 1934 (years denoted as vertical bars) five men had already settled in Abosi. In that year one marriage occurred; the bachelor offering a breeding opportunity of 100 acres was chosen, in preference to the other four men offering 150 (monogamist), 37.5 (trigamist), 33 (bigamist) and 32 (tetragamist) acres. In 1935 the situation had changed: the bachelor who married in the preceding year has become a monogamist offering a breeding opportunity of 50 acres; in addition, a new pioneer bigamist arrives, with a breeding opportunity of 16.7 acres; the monogamist offering 150 acres obtains a second wife. Settlers were considered as offering a breeding opportunity the year they arrived and every subsequent year until 1949 (end of sampled period): settlers are therefore multiply represented in the Figure, although the breeding opportunity on offer and their marital status might change over the sampled period; for statistics, see text.

nor his age ($X^2 = 2.02$, NS) was significantly associated with his probability of being selected. None of these three variables entered into the stepwise regression analysis reported above, for which tolerance levels for entry were set at $p < 0.10$.

To tackle the problem that the 232 breeding opportunities are not independent of each other (being offered by the same 25 men), each man was coded as a dummy variable, none of which entered into the stepwise regression at $p < 0.10$. It was not possible to enter the 25 dummy variables together with the covariates into a single simultaneous regression analysis, because of the small sample size.

Costs of Polygyny

The number of surviving offspring produced by post-menopausal women is negatively affected by the number of cowives in 3 of the 4 wealth categories (Table 11.2) when the sample is split into lower, lower middle, upper middle and upper wealth divisions according to husband's ownership of land; note however that later few women join large polygynous households in the poorest wealth categories.

The polygyny threshold model essentially predicts that women with perfect information and foresight (see Discussion) should minimize fitness differences by marrying judiciously. However number of cowives negatively affects lifetime reproductive success, even after husband's acres are controlled in an analysis of variance ($F_{3,253} = 8.72, p < 0.001$), suggesting that in this population there are costs associated with polygyny for which careful marriage choices do not entirely compensate. This may

account for women's preferences for monogamous and bachelor pioneers even when breeding opportunity is controlled (see above).

Marital status, by contrast, has no overall statistically significant effect on lifetime reproductive success (Table 11.3), even after the effects of husband's acres are controlled ($F_{3,253} = 1.79$, NS; and see Borgerhoff Mulder 1989c). Nevertheless weak depressing effects of marital status are found in the poorer wealth categories where the lifetime reproductive success of secondary and tertiary wives is low.

DISCUSSION

Resource-Defense Polygyny

In several respects Kipsigis polygyny can be characterized as "resource defense" (Emlen and Oring 1977), resulting from both intra- and intersexual selection. First, early arriving men established larger plots, and compete over retaining access to these plots. Second, men with larger plots were able to attract more wives, both during the Pioneer period and over their entire reproductive lifespans up to the present.

Acquisition of wives was more closely associated with a man's land plot size than his arrival date, suggesting that acreage itself is an important aspect of resource quality. The importance of plot size per se is also suggested by its correlation with the availability of food

Table 11.2. The Effect of Numbers of Cowives on Numbers of Surviving Offspring in 2 Cohorts of Post-reproductive Women

Marital status	Full sample[a]	Husband's acres[b]				
		0–14*	15–29	30–58*	59–300	Total N
0 cowife	7.05	7.27	6.75	7.86	7.33	
	(60)	(33)	(12)	(7)	(3)	(55)
1 cowife	6.82	5.96	6.54	8.00	8.80	
	(102)	(27)	(24)	(31)	(10)	(92)
2 cowives	5.58	3.00	5.18	5.24	6.46	
	(60)	(4)	(11)	(25)	(15)	(55)
3 cowives or more	5.81	4.00	5.00	5.25	6.32	
	(58)	(2)	(1)	(16)	(37)	(56)
Total N	(280)	(66)	(48)	(79)	(65)	(258)

[a]The effects of numbers of cowives on the numbers of surviving offspring per woman. Difference between groups $F_{3,276} = 4.37, p = 0.005$; deviation from linearity $F_{1,276} = 10.10$, P < 0.002.
[b]Husband's acres broken into four percentile ranges 0%–25%, 26%–50% etc. A slightly smaller sample ($n = 258$) of women with husband's ownership of acres known was available for these analyses. Within each of these wealth categories the effects of marital status on number of surviving offspring were tested with analyses of variance. 0–14 acres: $F_{3,62} = 5.00, p < 0.005$; 15–29 acres: $F_{3,44} = 0.93$, NS; 30–58 acres: $F_{3,75} = 6.54, p < 0.001$; 59–300 acres: $F_{3,61} = 2.16, 0.05 < p < 010$. Where F-values are P < 0.10, deviations from linearity tests are also significant and indicated with * in the Table. 1–14 acres: $F_{1,162} = 13.24, p < 0.001$; 30–58 acres $F_{1,175} = 14.57, p < 0.001$; 59–300 acres: $F_{1,161} = 4.00, p < 0.05$

Table 11.3. The Effect of Marital Status on Numbers of Surviving Offspring in 2 Cohorts of Post-reproductive Women

Marital status	Full sample[a]	Husband's acres[b]					
		0–14*	15–29	30–58	59–300	Total N
Monogamous	7.05	7.27	6.75	7.86	7.33	
	(60)	(33)	(12)	(7)	(3)	(55)
Polygynous (1st)	6.29	5.58	6.58	6.20	6.74	
	(122)	(24)	(24)	(46)	(23)	(117)
Polygynous (2nd)	6.02	5.14	6.13	6.58	6.77	
	(56)	(7)	(8)	(19)	(13)	(47)
Polygynous (>2nd)	6.29	5.50	3.00	7.57	6.77	
	(42)	(2)	(4)	(7)	(26)	(39)
Total N	(280)	(66)	(48)	(79)	(65)	(258)

[a]The effects of marital status on number of surviving offspring per woman. Difference between groups $F_{3,276} = 1.45$, NS; deviation from linearity $F_{1,276} = 2.28$, NS.
[b]Statistics as in Table 11.2, note[b]. 1–14 acres: $F_{3,62} = 2.79$, $p < 0.05$; 15–29 acres: $F_{3,44} = 2.58$, $0.05 < p < 0.10$; 30–58 acres: $F_{3,75} = 0.92$, NS; 59–300 acres: $F_{3,61} = 0.04$, NS. Where F-values are $p < 0.10$, deviations from linearity are also significant and indicated with * in the Table. 1–14 acres: $F_{1,62} = 6.65$, $p = 0.01$; 15–29 acres: $F_{1,44} = 4.91$, $p = 0.03$.

stuffs and milk in households (Borgerhoff Mulder 1987b). The significance of correlated factors such as drainage, terrain or location that might improve the productivity of land and livestock cannot be excluded as influences on female preference as they were not measured in this study. However, Kipsigis' parallel settlement patterns along hillsides ensure that plots are rather homogenous, with each family using well drained slopes for cultivation, lower-lying river flats for grazing cattle, and the stony hilltops for cattle and smallstock; in Abosi semipermanent water is no further than a mile from any farm plot. For these reasons, then, size of plot itself, particularly the area suited to grazing and cultivation, is likely to be the critical component of territory quality. Small amounts of cash (up to $150 per annum, not measured in this study), obtained by men through the sale of maize and expended largely in the restocking of herds, is also likely to enhance a man's chances of becoming polygynous, particularly through the purchase of cattle for bridewealth. This suggestion is supported by the very large number of wives married to men of the "Maina" cohort, many of whom as young men in the 1930s benefited from employment opportunities on the farms of Colonial European settlers (Borgerhoff Mulder 1988e).

Consistent with this view of Kipsigis polygyny as "resource-defense" is the intense competition observed over land: this was the driving force behind the emigration of men to Abosi (see Ethnographic Background), and is a constant factor in hostilities and feuds within Kipsigis communities over, for example, incursions of livestock into a neighbor's property. There was one case during the 1982–83 field study when young men of one family attempted to "move" a neighbor's fence surreptitiously, and then argued that it got accidentally dragged in the tails of their cattle; this took over a year to arbitrate, using a traditional council of elders (Peristiany 1939). Finally, intense competition over resources, both within and between pastoralist groups, is key to the migration and expansion that characterizes East African history (Waller 1986), hence this Kipsigis pioneer settlement cannot be considered as an isolated or unusual incident.

Men who control vast sources of wealth often acquire large numbers of mates in human societies (e.g., Betzig 1986; reviewed Flinn and Low 1986). Furthermore, in 63% of societies in Murdock's *Ethnographic Atlas* (Standard Half Sample $n = 93$) property of economic value is exclusively or predominantly inherited by men (Whyte 1978). In addition, with increasing land limitation (as in the Kipsigis and many contemporary populations) the potential for men to control the resources critical to female productive activities (agriculture and husbandry) becomes critical (cf. White 1988, 1989; Borgerhoff Mulder 1989b). Therefore the potential for resource-defense polygyny may be widespread across human societies, both traditional and those in transition.

Female Choice

The fact that men who control vast sources of wealth often acquire large numbers of mates has led to the suggestion that female preferences for wealthy men may be an important factor in the evolution and current incidence of polygyny in humans (Dickemann 1979b; Hartung 1982; Irons 1983). Earlier interview data showing that Kipsigis parents place considerable emphasis on the wealth of a potential son-in-law pointed to the possible importance of such patterns of choice in contributing to polygyny in the Kipsigis (Borgerhoff Mulder 1988e). Several questions nevertheless remained unanswered.

First, are potential sons-in-law favored for their overall wealth or for the resources they can offer an incoming wife? The finding that the size of the breeding opportunity on offer predicts whether or not a man would be chosen in any year whereas his total acreage does not suggests that parents are selecting a husband for their daughter on the basis of the specific resources he can provide for her and her offspring. This is the best documented and theoretically most straightforward form of female choice (Partridge and Halliday 1984), and provides some evidence for the importance of epigamic vis-à-vis intrasexual selection in this study.

Second, are men chosen as mates for the breeding opportunity they offer, or for genetic qualities or other phenotypic traits that might be correlated with (and hence masked by) breeding opportunity? This question has been tackled both experimentally (Alatalo et al. 1986) and analytically (Catchpole et al. 1985; Eckert and Weatherhead 1987) in non-human studies, and can only be addressed indirectly here. First, older men were not favored over younger men, providing some evidence against the "good genes" argument, namely that females use prolonged survivorship as an indicator of genetic viability. Second, although men with successful reproductive histories (maintenance of a high rate of production of surviving offspring with their wives over their reproductive careers to date) were favored over men with less distinguished reproductive histories, this was not an independently significant factor affecting female choice. Such an effect would however be much more precisely investigated with data on *fertility* rather than surviving offspring (itself correlated with wealth, Borgerhoff Mulder 1987b); unfortunately retrospectively

dated livebirth records were not reliable for this early period. Third, it is plausible that, given the violent relations between Masai and Kipsigis (Orchardson 1961), brave, risk-taking Kipsigis men may have been the first to settle in pioneer communities such as Abosi, and may have been favored for these traits. Partial correlations showing that the effects of plot size on polygyny were independent of arrival order provide some evidence against this hypothesis, at least insofar as these traits are uncorrelated with plot size. Furthermore, as mentioned above, men were chosen on the basis of their breeding opportunity on offer that year, not their overall plot size. what about underwealth

In sum, the importance of male qualities other than the resources they offer females cannot be discounted, as they were not directly measured in this study. Nevertheless to demonstrate choice that has evolved solely because of *genetic* consequences it is necessary to rule out non-genetic benefits contingent on the choice (Partridge and Halliday 1984), benefits that are clearly in evidence in the Kipsigis.

Female Settlement Sequences

Only two other studies have determined female choice through an examination of settlement sequences. In redwinged blackbirds females arrive after all the males have established territories, allowing a comparison of the rank order in which females choose territories to the rank-ordered anticipated reproductive success from such nests (Lenington 1980). The correlation coefficient was rather low ($r_S = 0.15$, NS), although higher when only the number of young fledged from successful nests was considered ($r_S = 0.57$, $p < 0.01$). In pied flycatchers, where females begin choosing before all males have arrived (as in the Kipsigis settlement of Abosi), only comparisons within days could be conducted (Alatalo et al. 1984); females preferred early arriving males (paired $t = 3.71$, $n = 19, p < 0.01$), who offered better nest sites. In both studies, however, the tests reported give no indication of the number of incidences where females fail to choose the very best breeding opportunity. Thus, returning to the Kipsigis, although the breeding opportunity selected by women is not always the highest on offer, the strength of support for such preferences is similar to that shown in studies of passerines.

Factors that might contribute to the exceptions in this population include: (1) Negative consequences of polygyny other than reduced access to land. There is ample ethnographic evidence that polygynous (particularly junior status) cowives can suffer sexual neglect, reduced assistance from their husbands, increased exposure to venereal disease and tense family circumstances (e.g., Curley 1973; Brabin 1984; Borgerhoff Mulder 1989c). (2) The importance of the suitor's reputation. Sixty-one percent of parents interviewed (n = 94) said " good reputation" was an important consideration in selecting a son-in-law (Borgerhoff Mulder 1988b). Because rich men can be notoriously unreliable and arrogant, a poor man with a good reputation is seen by some parents as a safer matrimonial option than a wealthy man with an unpredictable nature; this may represent some sort of bet hedging with respect to marriage choice. (3) Socioeconomic ties. Marriage in many traditional populations, including Kipsigis, entails not just a mating relationship between two individuals, but social and economic ties between two sets of kin, such as acquiring access to political office (Comaroff and Comaroff 1981), settling disputes over land or cattle (Evans-Pritchard 1940) or reestablishing bonds of kinship (Stenning 1959). These considerations may in some circumstances override the importance of wealth. (4) Bridewealth. A suitor's wealth does not correlate with his bridewealth payment (Borgerhoff Mulder 1988c). Three anecdotal cases (3%) arose in my interviews (n = 94) where parents reported having given their daughters to men who were patently poor because, they said, "the bridewealth offer was so good." These constitute cases where daughters' reproductive interests may have been sacrificed to parental manipulative interests (see Introduction), and indicate the potential for parent/offspring conflict in marriage systems such as this.

On account of these factors the size of breeding opportunity is unlikely to be the single determinant of the settlement sequence. The value of the present study is its application of a statistical technique that permits assessment of a number of independent covariates on patterns of female choice. Clearly for a Kipsigis woman, marital status is an important consideration *in addition to* the availability of land on which to raise her offspring; many other important considerations, such as status, reputation and long-term enduring friendships between families that may be consolidated through marriage alliances, remain unmeasured.

Polygyny and Reproductive Consequences

In proposing the polygyny threshold model, Orians (1969) predicted that the fitness of monogamously and polygynously mated females should be at least equal, because females will assort themselves optimally with respect to their fitness interests. Despite some supportive data (reviewed by Wittenberger 1981b; Garson et al. 1981) there are problems with this prediction. First, it ignores the possibility that a female's mating status during her reproductive period may be different from that she originally *chose*, because of subsequent females who may settle on the territory (Altmann et al. 1977). Second, it fails to consider factors (such as arrival or egg-laying dates) that may be responsible for differences among females in breeding success that are independent of mating status (Garson et al. 1981). Third, it assumes females have access to reliable information on territory quality and male mating status (but see Alatalo et al. 1982 and Catchpole et al. 1985 for evidence of deception). Fourth, it assumes that the costs of assessing and choosing a mate are small (as questioned by Slagsvold et al. 1988; see also Christie 1983). Fifth, the model assumes that females do not cooperate, that they cannot gain benefits from the presence of other females, and other specific patterns of cost-sharing among polygynously mated females (cf. Altmann et al. 1977; Davies 1989). Sixth, it assumes that female preferences are never thwarted by aggression from other females; detailed studies suggest female competition cannot be disregarded (e.g., redwinged blackbirds, Lenington 1980). Seventh, the model completely ignores the possibility that male and female interests may conflict (Davies and Houston 1986; Davies 1989), a situation which may prevent females from following their optimal strategy. Finally, it assumes females face identical options at settlement, rarely the case when arrival is not simultaneous, or at least that male territories are continuously distributed such that later-arriving females can make compensatory choices (Searcy and Yakusawa 1989). Because the equal fitness prediction is based on a number of assumptions that are difficult to substantiate, evidence that the reproductive success of monogamous, primary polygynous, secondary polygynous and tertiary (plus) polygynous women is equal in six different cohorts (Borgerhoff Mulder 1989c) provides only very weak evidence that women assort themselves at marriage as predicted by the polygyny threshold model.

A more appropriate investigation of the reproductive costs of polygyny entails considering the original Verner-Willson-Orians model as one of a suite of alternative models that might explain the incidence of polygyny across mammals and birds (Searcy and Yakusawa 1989). They propose a hierarchical series of considerations that should be used to differentiate between alternative models: male coercion, whether polygyny is costly and whether these costs are compensated for, sex ratio biases, search costs, and possibilities for deception. The analyses presented above, in addition to the ethnographic background, suggest that polygynous marriage among Kipsigis women is not a result of coercion; furthermore coercion might be implicated if the reproductive costs were particularly high among women married to the wealthiest (most influential, and potentially most coercive) men in the sample, but this was not the case (Tables 11.2 and 11.3). Polygyny nevertheless entails a cost to women, a cost that is not entirely compensated for by women's preferences for large breeding opportunities, and which may result from lower rates of sexual intercourse, reduced direct paternal care or other male contributions unrelated to plot size. What may account for this tolerance of cost? Women are highly unlikely to be deceived as to the marital status of a suitor (marriage is a formal public event and always entails coresidence); indeed some women favor polygyny for the opportunity it gives them to assess what kind of a *husband* a man is. Search costs are likely to be low (in so far as grooms look for brides, whereas brides and their families assess the suitors' suitability using information from friends, neighbors and acquaintances). The default alternative, that females are behaving maladaptively seems unlikely given the marital choices reported in this paper. What seems most likely is that *partial* compensation (cf. Searcy and Yakusawa 1989) is occurring; either some women make compensatory choices and others

do not, or adequate compensation can rarely be attained by any woman. For example, it is possible that compensatory factors, such as cowife cooperation or marriage to a high status polygynous man, may have had positive fitness consequences for Kipsigis women living as pastoralists, but not nowadays; variations of Searcy and Yakusawa's models are now being tested with pure pastoralists (Borgerhoff Mulder 1992b). It is also possible that a form of delayed compensation through a sexy son effect is entailed.

Finally, although the sex ratio at independence is not skewed towards females (unpubl. data), competition over land leads to delayed marriage for men and to unsuccessful competitors leaving the area for tea plantations and other forms of wage labor in the vicinity of Kericho and Sotik (Borgerhoff Mulder 1988e); this presents women with the choice of also leaving the Kipsigis area for a plantation (an option not favored by many) or marrying polygynously. Although Searcy and Yakusawa would not classify this as a model based on sex-biased availability of mates, the discontinuous distribution of viable-sized territories among men is an important ecological factor underlying polygyny in the Kipsigis and perhaps many other persistently polygynous agricultural populations in Kenya, given the intense land shortages that exist in the highland areas.

Resource-Defense Polygyny and Female Choice in Mammals

In contrast to birds, there is no clear evidence that polygyny has evolved through female choice for males with high quality resources in non-human mammals. The classic mammalian example of resource-defense polygyny mediated by female choice, yellow-bellied marmots *Marmota flaviventris* (Emlen and Oring 1977; Krebs and Davies 1987), is now more accurately characterized as male defense of harems (Armitage 1986). More generally, evidence from ungulates that males tend to hold territories in areas favored by females (e.g., waterbuck *Kobus defassa*, Spinage 1969) and that the number of females in a male's territory correlates with its forage quality (e.g., pronghorn *Antilocapra americana*, Kitchen 1974, and topi *Damiliscus korrigum*, Duncan 1975) is suggestive, but it provides no conclusive demonstration of female preferences for males with high quality territories; furthermore, the sequence of arrival of males and females in a particular area is often unknown and the extent of male coercion is often ambivalent. Without detailed longitudinal studies of known females, the settling options available to them, and their reproductive performance, the importance of female preferences for males with high quality resources is difficult to determine in non-human mammals. Studies of human societies such as the Kipsigis, where longitudinal data can be obtained retrospectively, are therefore of potential value to the study of mammalian breeding systems.

Acknowledgments. Critical comments and helpful suggestions on the manuscript were made by Richard Alexander, Nick Davies, Tim Caro, Warren Holmes, Magdalena Hurtado, Arne Lundberg, Alison Rosser, Dan Sellen, Daniela Sieff and Margo Wilson. John Warner offered generous statistical guidance; John Pepper and Andy Kerr drew the figures. The project was funded by the National Geographic Society, and permission to conduct research in Kenya granted by the Office of the President, Nairobi. Special thanks to the Kipsigis families for their friendship and cheerful cooperation throughout the study.

12

Marrying a Married Man: A Postscript

MONIQUE BORGERHOFF MULDER

In some senses I still think of this as the best piece of analysis from my Ph.D. research conducted among the Kipsigis in 1982–83. In those heady early days of human sociobiology (as it was then unashamedly named), I was lucky to be part of a cohort of graduate students who were being enthusiastically encouraged by Richard Alexander, Napoleon Chagnon, and William Irons to go out and expose our ideas and hypotheses to rigorous field testing. Orians' polygyny threshold model appealed to me, both for its elegance and for its appropriateness to highland land-limited Kenyan populations. Before the 1980s, and indeed until the end of that decade, most of the empirical tests of the polygyny threshold model (restricted, of course, to nonhumans) had focused on fitness outcomes for females, as had my own earlier work (e.g., Borgerhoff Mulder 1988b). An equally important test of the model, however, is the question of whether and how females select breeding opportunities (Searcy and Yasukawa 1989; Davies 1989). Fortuitously, as part of an attempt to reconstruct the history of the Kipsigis community at Abosi, I had collected settlement histories of all the families, which, together with detailed demographic records, enabled me to conduct the necessary tests pertaining to the sequence of marriages in the community. Fortuitous it was for, to be honest, the settlement histories were compiled primarily to ingratiate myself with the elders, who maintained (as coincidentally would have my undergraduate mentors in sociocultural anthropology) that without a grasp of tradition and history, my ethnography would be rotten. Despite their having been generated in part by accident, I still feel that for 1990 the analyses in this paper were timely and appro-

priate. But how does this work look now, in the hard-nosed days of 1996?

First, the analysis. The weakest part of this paper lies in its exploration of the fitness consequences of different marital statuses. These were based only on postmenopausal women. In addition, by grouping women according to their marital status, the analyses took no account of the mother's actual marital status at the birth/raising of the offspring; this can be a problem, as some men only marry second wives after their first wife has neared menopause. Also, by looking only at numbers of *surviving* offspring, the analyses confounded the effects of marital status on fertility and offspring survival. Each of these issues was superficially dealt with in a narrowly focused demographic paper (Borgerhoff Mulder 1988). Here I report a more sensitive investigation of the effects of marital status on reproductive performance. It examines *independently* the interbirth interval (Table 12.1A) and the probability of offspring mortality (Table 12.1B), categorizing each *birth* in terms of the marital status (number of cowives) of the mother in the year of the birth. The results confirm the general finding that the impact of polygynous marriage on women varies with their husband's wealth. Interestingly, however, poor cowives suffer in terms of (long) birth intervals, whereas rich cowives benefit in terms of the mortality chances of their offspring. These new analyses point to the complex mechanisms that underlie the relationships between polygyny, wealth, and women's fitness in this population.

Second, and much more broadly, how does this study show how evolutionary thinking can help sociocultural anthropology, the discipline

Table 12.1. A. Cox Regression On Interbirth Interval ($n = 518$ intervals, 122 women)[a,b]

| | Model if Term Removed | | | |
Term Removed	− 2 Log LR	df	Significance of Log LR	Partial Correl. Coeffic (R)
Mother's age	3.11	1	.0780	.0138
Year of birth	23.35	1	.0000	−.0609
#Cowives *Wealth[c]	3.22	1	.0729 NS	.0144

[a]Removal criteria based on the ratio of the likelihood for the reduced model divided by the likelihood for the full model (−2 Log LR, see Norusis 1993).
[b]Births where precedng child died before 24 months dropped.
[c]Poor versus medium/rich wealth rank of father (for methods see Borgerhoff Mulder 1995). Poor with 0 cowives, 30.18 months; poor with >0 cowives, 34.17 months; medium/rich with 0 cowives, 30.48 months; medium rich with >0 cowives, 31.01 months.

B. Logistic regression on mortality between first and fifth birhtday[a]

| | Model if Term Removed | | | |
Term Removed	−2 Log LR	df	Significance of Log LR	Partial Correl. Coeffic (R)
Birth year	10.441	1	.0012	.1647
Wealth[b]	2.602	1	.1067	.0509
#Cowives x *Wealth[c]	2.179	1	.1399 NS	−.0297

[a]Measuring mothers' number of cowives in the first to fourth years subsequent to birth has no substantial effects on signficance levels.
[b]Wealth is coded as a dummy variable (poor = 1, Medium/rich = 2), with the reference category being the last. Children born to poor parents have a higher probability of experiencing mortality than children born to medium/rich parents, since (1, poor) has a higher value than the reference category (2, medium/rich, which is set to 0).
[c]Poor with 0 cowives, .09 mortality; poor with >0 cowives, .08 mortality; medium/rich with 0 cowives, .08 mortality; medium rich with >0 cowives, .03 mortality.

to which I have always wanted to contribute? As I look at it today, not very much! Of course, it does add empirical bricks to the growing wall of evidence that we can predict human behavior in contemporary (and past) populations using simple reductionist fitness-maximizing models. But it becomes increasingly clear to me, as I design new projects for myself and with students, that we still have both a very poor understanding of the *social and ecological constraints* that shape behavioral options and, more worryingly, almost no methodology for characterizing these constraints. In other words, while this paper showed that Kipsigis women appear to make the "right" choice, it provided only a very poor analysis of the particular social, ecological, and even institutional factors that lead to the marital rules that we observe in Abosi. Clearly, one important factor is the pressing shortage of land in highland Kenya; another is the institutional prohibition on women owning capital resources. The first of these, namely, the availability, distribution, and elasticity of the principal resource (land), affords a whole gamut of predictions about how we would expect populations with increasingly diminished capital resources to differ with respect to things like the distribution of polygyny, the costs of polygyny, and the marital discrimination of women—predictions I am now trying to test using coded ethnographic data on a regional African sample. The second constraint, the obligate dependence of women on resources held exclusively by men, may result in part from the monopolizability of land, but it begs a whole suite of questions that point us to new theoretical developments within behavioral ecology, in particular models for intersexual conflict (Parker 1979; Smuts 1992; Gowaty 1995). In sum, though this paper may identify cues in Kipsigis women's marital choices, it fails to tackle seriously the question of why different marriage systems emerge. *As always, we trade comparative breadth for intrasocietal depth.*

Let us now look at the subsequent fate of the suite of polygyny threshold hypotheses, as defined by Searcy and Yasukawa (1989). As regards nonhumans, most studies still show polygyny to be a costly option to females; however, the costs are lower than had originally been anticipated, they are highly variable both between and within species, and exceptions are rife. The hypothesis that polygyny will occur primarily in species where paternal care has only small effects on offspring survival receives little support (Webster 1991). Rather, with growing appreciation of the frequency of extra-pair copulations, the male's decision of whether to engage in a polygynous breeding situation is now viewed primarily as resulting from a trade-off between seeking extra-pair copulations, on the one hand, and securing a secondary breeding partner (variably entailing territorial defense or display, paternal care, and mate guarding), on the other (Westneat, Sherman, and Morton 1990). Despite these modifications in the way that behavioral ecologists now think about mating systems (e.g., Dew, Spoon, and Towner 1994), environmental heterogeneity (or differences in territory size) still remains a crucial condition favoring resource-defense polygyny. So, given that I still believe that extramarital sexual relations are rare among Kipsigis (because of the extraordinary high costs to women), the resource-defense polygyny model remains the most appropriate for this system.

As regards humans, there have been surprisingly few further empirical tests, reflecting, I suspect, the tremendous swing among evolutionary social scientists toward working on psychological issues in Western populations. Important advances that can be detected in recent ethnographic studies are (1) investigation of compensatory second-generation effects (Josephson 1993); (2) evidence that polygynously married women may enjoy compensatory benefits resulting from their husband's political (as opposed to economic) status (Hames 1996); and (3) the suggestion that women use sororal polygyny as a counterstrategy to the "coerced" polygyny that we see, for example, among Australian aborigines (Chisholm and Burbank 1991).

Finally, though this paper falls in a section entitled "Studies of Traditional Societies," the Kipsigis are experiencing rapid social and economic change, as everywhere else on the globe. A restudy in 1991 shows that although polygyny persists in Abosi at near its traditional level, the circumstances in which men attract second wives are changing. In some respects the threshold is blurring; in other respects the criteria on which women are basing their choices are altered (Luttbeg, Borgerhoff Mulder, and Mangel 1996). Men, too, seem to be adjusting their martial preferences, insofar as they pay heavily for very different kinds of women in the 1990s than they did previously (Borgerhoff Mulder 1995); these shifts in the covariates of bridewealth track changes in the reproductive and economic roles of Kipsigis women over the last four decades in a way that is consistent with a deductively derived optimality model (Borgerhoff Mulder 1996). This new evidence of facultative flexibility in marriage strategy among Kipsigis women and men provides important evidence of the *sensitivity* of peoples' mating strategies to even relatively subtle socioeconomic changes. It also points to a potentially valuable area of congruence between behavioral ecology and evolutionary psychology by highlighting the need to investigate decision-making rules that, on account of their sensitivity to features of the social and ecological environment, might shape cultural change (e.g., Borgerhoff Mulder et al. 1996; Cosmides and Tooby 1992).

13

The Evolution of ~~Premature~~ Reproductive Senescence and Menopause in Human Females: An Evaluation of the "Grandmother Hypothesis"

KIM HILL
A. MAGDALENA HURTADO

Human females are characterized by a life-history profile rarely found in mammals and probably unique to primates (see Lancaster and King 1985). Despite the fact that human females enjoy a long lifespan, reproductive function is completely terminated well before other physiological signs of senescence are significantly pronounced (Figure 13.1). This pattern has long been noted by evolutionary biologists who have speculated that, as women age, greater fitness benefits may be gained through investing time and resources in already existing offspring and potential grandchildren than could be expected from continuing to invest in the production of additional offspring (e.g., Alexander 1974; Gaulin 1980; Hamilton 1966; Hawkes et al. 1989; Trivers 1972; Williams 1957). We refer to this suggestion as the "grandmother hypothesis" of reproductive senescence. The most widely cited competing evolutionary hypothesis holds that premature reproductive senescence is essentially an artifact of a very recent increase in the lifespan (e.g., Washburn 1981; Weiss 1981). Finally, some (e.g., Wood 1990) have simply argued that premature reproductive senescence is just another form of general senescence whose timing does not coincide with the senescence of other body functions for reasons that are unclear or unspecified. *JUST BECAUSE*

Lancaster and King (1985) provide a general overview of the evolutionary significance of human female reproductive senescence and menopause. These authors conclude that females in most recent traditional populations *did* live long enough to experience menopause. They also find human parental investment patterns that are sufficiently unusual to lend preliminary support for the "grandmother hypothesis."

Recent theoretical advances in mammalian life history (see Charnov 1991; Harvey and Nee 1991; Promislow and Harvey 1990) and careful evaluation of hominid life histories in particular (e.g., B. Smith 1991) should lead to renewed interest in the problem of the evolution and functional significance of premature reproductive senescence and menopause in human females. In addition, the trend in modern society for women to delay reproduction means that understanding why reproductive senescence occurs has practical implications. The availability of high-quality behavioral and demographic data on hunter-gatherers and isolated traditional subsistence societies should enable a detailed evaluation of explicitly functional hypotheses. In particular, although data relevant to the *origin* of female reproductive senescence may be difficult to obtain, data relevant to the current *maintenance* of reproductive senescence in human populations that practice natural fertility and have not undergone rapid demographic transition are more easily available. In this paper we use demographic data collected from Ache hunter-gatherers of Paraguay (see Hill and Hurtado 1989) to evaluate two hypotheses of reproductive senescence and to stimulate further investigation by other researchers with appropriate demographic data.

FERTILITY DECLINE AND MENOPAUSE

Age-specific fertility decline among primate and mammalian females is probably universal (e.g., Biggers et al. 1962; Dunbar 1987; Fowler and Smith 1981; Marsh and Kasuya 1986; cf. Mizrooh 1981). Among mammals, female reproductive function appears to decline at approximately the same rate and point in time that other body functions senesce (Smith and Polacheck 1981:108–110; van Wagenen 1972). The life expectancy *at age of first reproduction* is generally no longer (and is often shorter) than the maximum reproductive span. Even when mammalian females live to an advanced age, their postreproductive phase is generally only about 10% of the total lifespan (Jones 1975; Nishida et al. 1990).

Humans and a few other mammals (e.g., toothed whales [Marsh and Kasuya 1986]; certain strains of laboratory mice [Festing and Blackmore1971]) show termination of female reproductive function well before the end of the typical lifespan. Other large mammals show no termination of female reproductive function even though they may enjoy long lifespans. For example, around 5% of all elephants reach 55 years of age, yet at that age female fertility is still approximately 50% of the maximum observed age-specific fertility (Croze et al. 1981:306).

A comparison with our nearest phylogenetic relative highlights the premature nature of human female fertility decline. Female common chimpanzees begin reproduction at 14–15 years of age. At that time, mean life expectancy is an additional 13 years, but the maximum chimpanzee reproductive span is about 20 years.[1] Thus, the reproductive span is expected in most cases to last through the lifespan. This is not the case for humans. Ache and !Kung hunter-gatherers show a mean additional life expectancy at sexual maturity of just over 40 years, but maximum reproductive span is only

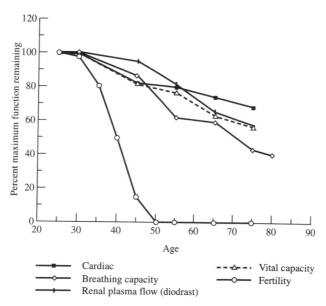

Figure 13.1. Physiologic function in humans by age. Data from Mildvan and Strehler (1960) and fertility data from Wood (1990:Fig. 2). Most body functions senesce at about the same time late in life, but female reproductive function is completely terminated by age 50.

about 30 years (Figure 13.2).[2] More striking is the fact that when reproduction is completely terminated in human females, life expectancy is still high. For example, among Ache hunter-gatherers prior to first peaceful outside contact, the mean age at last reproduction for females was 42 years, yet the mean life expectancy at age 42 (e_{42}) was an additional 23 years!

It is also important to note that the short reproductive span relative to expected adult lifespan is only characteristic of human *females.* Male fertility remains high in some traditional societies until the men reach their late fifties or early sixties (e.g., El-Faedy and Bean 1987; Hill and Hurtado 1991; Irons 1979a), and reproductive function does not show significant decrease until other body functions also begin to senesce (Comfort 1956; Deslypere and Vermeulen 1984; Goldman and Montgomery 1989).

Human female reproductive senescence is expressed as decreasing fertility with increasing age. Females in societies without contraception typically show maximum fertility around 20–30 years of age and decreasing fertility until probability of live birth approaches zero (between age 45 and 50; Ravenholt and Chao 1974; Wood 1990). Menstrual cycling becomes irregular and eventually ceases altogether (vom Saal and Finch 1988). The observed age-specific fertility decline generally

precedes menopause by several years; thus, menopause (cessation of menstruation) is simply the last step in a process of ever-decreasing fertility. Because this paper examines the evolutionary significance of reproductive senescence, we will concentrate mainly on the observed age-specific fertility decline, which directly affects the fitness of the individual women who experience it.

Undoubtedly, menopause itself is related to the observed fertility decline. Age-specific fertility decline, reproductive cessation, and subsequent menopause appear to be primarily due to the ever-decreasing number of viable oocytes, which are necessary to maintain the hormonal cycle of normal female reproduction (Block 1952; Gosden 1987; Richardson et al. 1987; van Wagenen and Simpson 1973). Other mechanisms, such as deterioration of uterine environment and increasing embryonic inviability, also play a part (see Kline et al. 1989). Women start life with a large number of viable oocytes, and that number decreases through time until reproduction becomes impossible either because no *viable* oocytes can be fertilized or because there are no longer enough *viable* oocytes to regulate reproductive hormonal cycling. Regardless of the precise mechanism, an evolutionary dilemma is apparent. If natural selection favors those individuals who leave the highest numbers of viable offspring (and close

ACHE

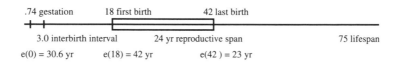

.74 gestation   18 first birth   42 last birth

    3.0 interbirth interval   24 yr reproductive span   75 lifespan

e(0) = 30.6 yr   e(18) = 42 yr   e(42) = 23 yr

PAN TROGLODYTES

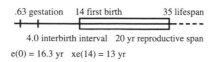

.63 gestation   14 first birth   35 lifespan

    4.0 interbirth interval   20 yr reproductive span

e(0) = 16.3 yr   xe(14) = 13 yr

Figure 13.2. Comparison of some important life-history variables for a group of human hunter-gatherers (Ache) and *Pan troglodytes*. Points along the bar mark gestation period, interbirth interval (completed), age at first birth, reproductive span, age at last birth, and lifespan (age at which approximately 5% of the individuals ever born are still alive). Below the bar are calculated life expectancy (e_x) at birth, at first reproduction, and at last reproduction for Ache women and chimpanzees.

kin), why does selection not simply favor higher numbers of initial oocytes, or a slower rate of oocyte degradation, or some other mechanism that would prolong fertility? It seems almost certain that some types of genetic variation could affect either of these two parameters (see Jones 1975). Why were these genes not favored in our evolutionary past, and why have they not been favored recently?

Several risk factors during reproduction are associated with maternal age in humans. These factors include an increasing probability with maternal age that the fetus will be aborted, have a low birth weight, be genetically aberrant, or experience perinatal mortality (Kline et al. 1989). In addition is the increase in difficult deliveries and maternal mortality rates as a function of maternal age (Llewellyn-Jones 1974; George Washington University 1975). For example, in the Netherlands in 1936–1937, maternal mortality was 70 deaths per 10,000 births among women who gave birth after age 40 but only 10 deaths per 10,000 births for women who gave birth at age 20. All these factors may be considered potential forces selecting against continued reproduction among older human females; however, it is also important to note that each of these factors may be the *result* of reproductive senescence rather than a contributing cause. Once women have evolved a pattern of reproductive termination around 45 years of age there may be very little selective pressure against deleterious mutations that express themselves late in the reproductive span. These factors may be quite relevant to maintenance of reproductive senescence in modern populations, however.

EVOLUTIONARY EXPLANATIONS FOR REPRODUCTIVE SENESCENCE

The functional significance of decline in fertility well before the decline of other body functions is an intriguing problem. It should be noted, however, that characters affecting survivorship and characters affecting fertility may not necessarily senesce at the same rate. Charlesworth (1980) has shown that selection for genes that might increase fertility at a specific age or decrease mortality at the same age is not dependent on exactly the same parameters. In fact, under many conditions, physiological traits that affect lifespan are expected to

senesce at an earlier age than traits that determine reproductive function (Charlesworth 1980). This lack of contemporaneity may be one reason why most mammals show significant fertility right up to the end of the lifespan. Thus, premature reproductive senescence among human females presents a dilemma.

One adaptive hypothesis has been strongly favored as the explanation for female reproductive senescence. This hypothesis proposes that, at some age, the increase in fitness that can be attained through investment in grandchildren (and possibly other kin) is greater than that expected by continuous direct reproduction. Thus, investment in kin rather than in reproduction is favored by natural selection (Alexander 1974; Gaulin 1980; Hamilton 1966; Hawkes et al. 1989; Trivers 1972; Williams 1957). The most frequently cited alternative proposes that reproductive senescence has not evolved at all, but is simply an artifact of a recent increase in the lifespan. This essentially nonfunctional hypothesis has received wide support (e.g., Jones 1975; Washburn 1981; Weiss 1981). Additional hypotheses will be considered in the discussion section.

The "lifespan-artifact hypothesis" has several weaknesses that make it unappealing. First, it fails to clarify what types of conditions might have recently changed in human environments to promote much lower rates of senescence for other body functions than that characteristic of female reproductive function. If nutrition or health care, for example, is responsible for the currently observed longer lifespan, why have they not affected reproductive function in a similar way? Indeed, if lifespan has only recently become longer, why do body functions senesce *as if* humans were designed to live well into their seventies? What selective forces could have favored efficient body function at age 55 if no human populations lived beyond 45–50 years until very recently? If enough time has elapsed to allow for selection to favor traits that are expressed later in the currently observed lifespan, why have the genes responsible for lengthening female reproductive spans not also been favored by selection? Equally puzzling is the issue of why male reproductive function shows no early senescence. If human lifespan has been short until very recently, why does male reproductive function not senesce at age 45?

The second problem with the lifespan-artifact hypothesis is that empirical evidence of a significantly shorter human lifespan until the recent past is derived entirely from paleodemographic studies. These studies use small samples, assume unbiased recovery of skeletal remains, often confound fertility and mortality effects on age structure, and assert an ability to age adult skeletal remains that has never been independently verified (Buikstra and Konigsberg 1985). Populations characterized by the extremely high mortality rates reported in paleodemographic studies would have to show exceptionally high fertility rates and juvenile survivorship rates, or extremely rapid growth and reproductive maturation, in order to be maintained at a stable size.

Since the values of most of these parameters are limited in traditional human populations by the availability of food, paleodemographic populations would also be required to show exceptionally good nutrition relative to most modern subsistence-level human groups. In addition to these problems, paleodemographic studies have also been criticized as implying an age structure and societal composition that are extremely unlikely for humans or any other social primate (e.g., Howell 1982).

Finally the results of paleodemographic studies contradict generalizations derived from all observed modern populations. Most notably, available data from hunter-gatherers or isolated technologically primitive populations studied by anthropological demographers suggest that about 20% of all individuals survive to age 60, and about 10% survive to age 70 (Figure 13.3; cf. Blurton Jones et al. 1991; Early and Peters 1990; Hill and Hurtado 1991; Howell 1979; Melancon 1982). No human population ever observed directly anywhere in the world shows a survivorship curve like that proposed by paleodemographers.

Although we consider the lifespan-artifact hypothesis quite unlikely, it should ultimately be testable using the fossil record. Measures of maximum lifespan (maximum observed age of an individual in captivity) or expected adult lifespan (life expectancy at maturity, e_m) in mammals and primates have been shown to correlate quite well with a variety of parameters, such as body size, brain size, and age at first reproduction (Charnov 1991; Millar and Zammuto 1983; Sacher 1975; B. Smith 1991). The strongest predictor of *expected* adult lifespan (e_m) discovered thus far is age at sexual maturity ($R^2 = .94$; Millar and Zammuto 1983), which unfortunately cannot be easily determined from the fossil record (but perhaps someday can be).

Brain size correlates well with maximum lifespan and can be determined from the fossil

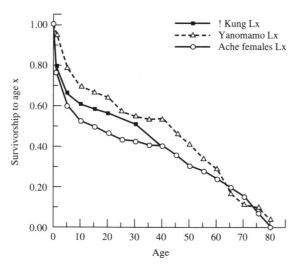

Figure 13.3. Survivorship from birth for the !Kung (Howell 1979:81), the Yanomamö (Melancon 1982:65), and Ache women (see Table 13.1). Most studies on technologically primitive human populations show similar survivorship curves during adulthood. None show survivorship curves like those reported in many paleodemographic studies in which all adults are dead by age 50 to 55.

record. Since hominid brain size has not changed much during the past 100,000 years, it is unlikely that maximum lifespan significantly changed during that same time period.[3] Unfortunately, a regression analysis of maximum lifespan and brain size for primates results in a wide confidence interval (R^2 of $\log_{10}$ plots = 0.62; B. Smith 1991) and therefore we cannot completely rule out the possibility that until recently humans had only a 45-year lifespan.

The "grandmother hypothesis" is consistent with modern evolutionary theory and has logical appeal. If, with a given amount of time and resources, females can make a greater contribution to the population gene pool by investing in kin (particularly grandchildren) than they could by producing their own offspring, natural selection might favor mechanisms that turn off female reproductive function at a particular age. This hypothesis is attractive since it makes intuitive sense that older females help their offspring to reproduce, and since altruistic grandmother behaviors directed at kin have been reported for nonhuman primates (e.g., Cheney and Seyfarth 1990; Fairbanks and McGuire 1986) as well as hunter-gatherers (e.g., Hawkes et al. 1989; Hurtado and Hill 1990). According to Hamilton's rule (Hamilton 1964), whenever the fitness benefits that can be derived by investment in kin (B) times the probability of sharing a rare allele with those kin (r) is greater than the fitness costs to self or other kin incurred by this investment (C), a heritable tendency to invest in kin will be favored by natural selection. According to the grandmother model of reproductive senescence, if time (or the resources that can be produced with time) is invested in a mutually exclusive manner (a woman can only invest time either in helping her relatives or in producing offspring herself), termination of reproduction should evolve whenever

$$-2 \sum Br > C \tag{1}$$

where B is the increase in the number of surviving kin that will result from the time a woman invests helping each relative to reproduce, r is the genetic coefficient of relatedness of each of the kin being helped, and C is the number of offspring that she could produce if she did not invest time in helping her kin to reproduce and raise their offspring. When the benefits of helping grandchildren offspring are

calculated, for example, r will be $1/4$. For women of any age, ΣB can be estimated by measuring the effect of a mother's presence on her adult daughters's and sons's reproductive success (or that of any other relative of interest), multiplying this effect times the probability of the mother having a child to help, and then summing for all children (or other relatives) of reproductive age that an older woman can expect to be able to help during the period of analyses. C can be estimated by assuming that if women did not terminate reproduction, their fertility would continue to decline throughout the lifespan in a manner similar to that seen in other primates.

In at least two situations the inequality in equation 1 is likely to favor the benefits side of the equation. First, if an older woman has a high probability of death in some time interval and if her offspring are unlikely to survive if she dies during their juvenile period, the cost side of the equation might be expected to be small, since few offspring that an older woman produces will be expected to survive. Data from Ache foragers do suggest that offspring survivorship is low when mothers die in the first 5 years of the child's life (Figure 13.4); however, the probability of older women dying within the first 5 years after a child has been born appears to be quite low until women reach a very old age (Table 13.1).

Second, age-specific fertility differentials could favor reproductive senescence. Imagine that older women are characterized by very low inherent fertility and that some increment of investment by them results in a low probability of producing a live birth. If their offspring are characterized by high inherent fertility (and the same amount of investment would produce a large increase in the fertility of the offspring), older women may gain higher fitness by investment designed to increase their offspring's fertility rather than by investing in their own fertility. Again, demographic data do suggest that older women have very low fertility relative to their younger offspring (Table 13.1), but we must be cautious about interpreting this difference, since the drop in age-specific fertility *is the factor we are attempting to explain*. It makes no sense to invoke fertility decline in older women as the explanation for fertility decline in older women, unless it can be shown that a relatively small reduction in fertility with

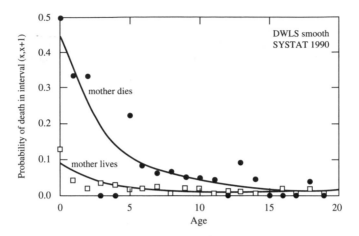

Figure 13.4. Probability of mortality in each 1-year interval (q_x) for children whose mothers either survive to the end of that interval (squares) or die before it is complete (circles). A curve was plotted for each set of points using a distance-weighted least-squares regression at tension 0.1. See note 4 for statistical significance of the difference in q_x by age.

age would ultimately favor a complete termination of female reproductive function.

A TEST OF THE "GRANDMOTHER HYPOTHESIS"

Between 1980 and 1990 we collected demographic data on the Ache foragers of eastern Paraguay. The Ache were isolated, nomadic hunter-gatherers until 1971, when they began

to be peaceably settled by missionaries and the Paraguayan government. Previous publications have described the economy and time allocation patterns of Ache foragers, food-sharing patterns, reproduction, and a variety of other aspects of their behavioral ecology (see Hill and Hurtado 1989 for a review). Demographic data from retrospective interviews were specifically collected with the intention of addressing a variety of topics related to life-history theory and

Table 13.1. Demographic Parameters of the Northern Ache prior to 1971

Interval $[x,y)$	$P[x,y)$ Female	Person-years at Risk	$f[x,y)$ Female	Person-years at Risk	$P[0,y)$ Female 1.000	$P[0,y)$ Male 1.000
0,1	0.760	480	0.000	—	0.760	0.858
1,5	0.795	195	0.000	—	0.604	0.767
5,10	0.868	835	0.000	—	0.525	0.712
10,15	0.944	630	0.043	814	0.496	0.664
15,20	0.939	495	0.750	720	0.466	0.621
20,25	0.928	345	1.411	581	0.432	0.558
25,30	0.988	415	1.522	437	0.427	0.521
30,35	0.954	325	1.533	336	0.407	0.482
35,40	0.983	290	1.320	284	0.400	0.448
40,45	0.898	245	0.975	241	0.359	0.412
45,50	0.850	200	0.311	161	0.305	0.364
50,55	0.906	160	0.000	—	0.277	0.291
55,60	0.880	125	0.000	—	0.243	0.221
60,65	0.824	85	0.000	—	0.200	0.158
65,70	0.750	40	0.000	—	0.150	0.110

P = probability of survivorship through specified interval.
f = probability of producing a live birth during specified interval.

variations in fertility and mortality rates across individuals in the population. Methods of aging the population were developed that use a relative age list for all individuals and informant assessments of absolute age differences between a subset of well-acquainted individuals in the population who saw each other during childhood. A fifth-order polynomial of "known ages" vs. age rank in the relative age list was then used to assign years of birth for all individuals in the population. This method provides age estimates that are independent of any assumptions about population age structure, fertility, or mortality patterns in the population. The precontact sample consists of 955 individuals born between 1890 and 1970. Further details of the methods, the sample, and a description of fertility and mortality patterns are described in a forthcoming monograph (Hill and Hurtado 1996).

During reproductive history interviews each Ache adult was asked to list all offspring, all siblings ever born, parents, and all siblings ever born of both parents, and to recount the reproductive histories and year of death of each individual mentioned. Year of death was determined by matching deaths to years in which particular individuals were born. These data were extensively cross-checked over a 10-year period and are quite reliable (with some qualifications not relevant to this study—e.g, children who died young were systematically underrepresented in cohorts that were born before 1945). The data base enables calculations concerning age-specific reproductive success (abbreviated RS, and defined here as number of surviving offspring who survived to some specified age) for a large number of men and women. Unlike most other anthropological demographic studies, which only collect data on the reproductive histories of living adults, the Ache sample enables an estimate to be made of the effects of maternal or paternal death on subsequent offspring survivorship and reproductive success in the next generation. All data reported in this paper refer only to demographic parameters in the precontact Ache society (i.e., before 1971). These data allow for the first direct test of the "grandmother hypothesis" for the maintenance of female reproductive senescence in a population. Although the study seems contextually appropriate, it should be noted that the Ache have experienced rapid population growth during the twentieth century, and the mortality and fertility rates that we report here could not have characterized the population during most of its history. The implications for testing the "grandmother hypothesis" of menopause are unclear, but many other human populations must also have experienced rapid growth periods during human evolution.

According to equation 1, reproductive senescence will be favored by natural selection whenever a woman's effect on her offspring's (and other kin's) RS, discounted by the more distant genetic relationship of the additional kin produced, is greater than the number of offspring she could successfully rear during some interval of time. Both ΣB and C can be estimated using Ache data and by making some assumptions about the fertility and survivorship of older women if they continued to reproduce. In order to assess whether or not women should cease to reproduce, a demographic model is developed in which the expected benefits and costs of reproductive senescence are estimated over standard 5-year intervals. The model allows us to predict the age at which women should cease to be fertile in order to maximize fitness if all energy and time are diverted from reproduction to helping close kin to reproduce. The model does not predict how much women should invest in existing offspring or how they might divert resources from younger to older offspring after they cease direct reproduction.

We begin by considering the case in which older women invest only in helping their sons and daughters to reproduce; thus, $r = \frac{1}{4}$ and B is measured in additional grandchildren produced who are expected to survive to age 10. First consider the fitness benefits ($2\Sigma Br$) that can be expected in each interval if a woman survives to the beginning of the interval. For simplicity we assume that a woman provides no help to her offspring unless she survives the entire interval, and that the probability of survival for children from age 5 to age 10 is determined by whether their mother is alive during that period. The additional surviving grandchildren that the woman can expect to have during the interval x to $x' + 5$ years by helping her sons and daughters who are within a specified age interval (x' to $x' + 5$) is

$$\sum B_{x,x+5} = \{(P_{x,x+5} \sum (S_{x'x'+5}) (a_{x'x'+5})\}$$
$$\times (\hat{P}_{5,10}) \quad (2)$$

where $\Sigma B_{x,x+5}$ is the expected increase in number of grandchildren who survive to age 10 produced by all sons and daughters owing to ego's aid during a 5-year interval beginning at age x, $P_{x,x+5}$ is the probability that ego survives the interval $s_{x'x'+5}$ is the expected number of offspring of specified age and sex who are alive to receive her help throughout the interval, and $\alpha_{x'x'+5}$ is the increase in number of grandchildren who survive to age 5 owing to ego's help during the interval when her son or daughter is of specified age. The probability that children who survive to age 5 will survive to age 10 is $\hat{P}_{5,10}$. This probability is estimated as follows:

$$\hat{P}_{5,10} = [(P_{5,10}|x'd \geq 10)(P_{x+5,x+10})] + [(P_{5,10}|x'd < 10)(1 - P_{x+5,x+10})] \quad (3)$$

where $x'd$ is the age of a child when its mother dies.

Figure 13.4 (above) shows the probability of death in a 1-year interval $(q_{x,x+1})$ for Ache children whose mothers lived to the end of the interval or had died before it ended. The difference in survivorship through 5-year intervals is significant until 15 years of age.[4] The values for offspring survivorship from age 5 to 10 years when the mother lives to the end of this interval $(P_{5,10}|x'd \geq 10)$ or dies before the interval ends $d(P_{5,10}|x'd < 10)$ can be calculated as the product of $(1 - q_{x,x+1}|x'd)$ in the appropriate child's age at mother's death $(x'd)$ category. If the mother dies at the midpoint of the interval, and the child is 5 years old, $P_{5,10}|x'd \geq 10$ is 0.908, and $P_{5,10}|x'd < 10$ is 0.796.

The total number of expected offspring of specified sex in each 5-year interval in equation 2 is

$$s_{x',x'+5} = f_{(x-[x'+5],x-x')}\Omega'P_{0,x'+5} \quad (4)$$

where $f_{(x-[x'+5],x-x')}$ is the number of children to whom a woman can expect to give birth during the age interval specified in the subscript (i.e., it is an age-specific fertility rate), Ω' is the proportion of all offspring born of a specified sex (males = Ω = .52, and therefore females = $1 - \Omega$ = .48), and $P_{0,x'+5}$ is the probability that an offspring of a specified sex will survive to age $x' + 5$.

Equations 2 through 4 state that the total benefits a woman can expect in a 5-year interval by helping her adult offspring to reproduce are equal to her survivorship through that interval times the sum of all the children she has of dif-

ferent ages and sexes multiplied by the increase in numbers of surviving grandchildren that she can produce by helping each of her offspring and finally multiplied by the probability that they will survive to age 10 given the survivorship of their mother. The "mother effect" $\alpha_{x'x'+5}$ can be measured directly (see below), and the probability of having a child to help in any particular age sex category, $s_{x'+5}$, is simply a function of a woman's fertility at the appropriate time in the past when the child would have been born multiplied by the proportion of children born who are of the specified sex, times the probability of the child's survivorship to age $x' + 5$. Note that all the parameters needed to calculate $s_{x'+5}$ (age-specific fertility and mortality, and sex ratio) come from standard demographic analyses and are available for a wide variety of human societies.

The "mother effect" on any particular child's age-specific reproductive success (RS) can be estimated by comparing the reproductive success of men and women at different ages whose mothers are still alive to the RS of those whose mothers have died. This effect was estimated using the Ache data in a multiple regression with number of ego's offspring greater than or equal to age 5 as the dependent variable (y) and age of ego (z_1), number of years during ego's reproductive span that his/her mother was alive (z_2),[5] and age difference between ego and his/her mother (z_3) as independent variables. Because we expected the relationship between z_2 and y to be altered by the value of z_1 we included the interaction term z_1z_2 in the regression. The sample in this regression contains 108 women and 146 men who were at least 15 years old before 1971 and whose mothers were at least 25 years older than they were.[6] The dependent variable was transformed ($ty = \log_{10} y + 1$), and the z_1 variable was similarly transformed ($tz_1 = \log_{10} z_1 + 1$). These transformations successfully linearized the relationship between the y and z_1 variables. Regression residuals were normally distributed and did not increase with the transformed z_1 variables (Durbin-Watson test for autocorrelation). The remaining independent variables were included in the model without transformation, and none of the independent variables showed significant collinearity.

In order to estimate $\alpha_{x'x'+5}$, we examined the effects of z_2 and the interaction term that includes z_2 on the dependent variable. The multiple regressions for both sexes are significant at the $p = .0001$ level, and the regressions explain about 50% of the total variance in y ($R^2 = 0.53$ for sons, 0.51 for daughters). The multiple regression for sons showed age as the only significant predictor of the dependent variable.[7] For daughters, the relationships between the dependent variable (ty) and three independent variables (tz_1, z_2, and $z_2^* \ tz_1$) are significant. Difference in age between mother-daughter[7] pairs is not significant in the regression. The "mother effect" on sons and daughters in each 1-year interval can thus be estimated as $y(z_1|z_2 = 1) - y(z_1|z_2 = 0)$ using the β coefficients from the following regressions:

$$ty = -2.67 + 1.89tz_1 + 0.01375z_2$$
$$+ \ 0.0005z_3 - 0.005969z_2tz_1 \quad (5)$$

for sons, and

$$ty = -3.10 + 2.27tz_1 + 0.09642z_2$$
$$+ \ 0.0009z_3 + 0.055723z_2tz_1 \quad (6)$$

for daughters.

The negative slopes associated with the interaction terms mean that as offspring become older, the "mother effect" decreases. Figure 13.5 shows $y(z_1|z_2 = 1) - y(z_1|z_2 = 1)$ for each age x by the sex of the offspring being helped.

It displays the "mother effect" during a 1-year interval, or the number of additional children ≥ 5 years of age that an Ache son or daughter can expect to have at the end of the interval if his or her mother lives to the end of the interval compared to the number of children ≥ 5 years of age they could expect to have at the end of the interval if their mother dies before the end of the interval. The age of ego and his/her mother can be used to calculate directly how many more offspring who survive to age 5 can be expected at any age if ego's mother survives (and presumably helps him/her) for one more year. The effect at age 25, for example, when ego's mother survives an additional year ($a_{25,26}$), is approximately 0.041 more offspring ≥ 5 years of age than would be expected if ego's mother were not alive during the interval.

As seen in Figure 13.5, the number of years that a mother is alive during a son's reproductive span is not a significant predictor of the number of children ≥ 5 years of age that he has fathered at a specific age. This result may be due to a small sample size, to high variance owing to independent variables that have not been measured, or to a real lack of any effect. In order to provide a test of the "grandmother hypothesis" that is most favorable to that hypoth-

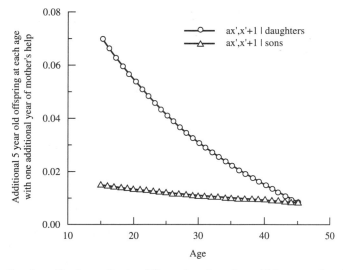

Figure 13.5. The "mother effect" on offspring RS as a function of age. Values are plotted using the regression equations 5 and 6 derived from the Ache data. Values on the vertical axis are measured in units of additional offspring $\geq$age 5 produced by an adult son or daughter of age x each additional year that the parent's mother survives.

esis, we can use the slope of y as a function of z_2 to estimate the "mother effect" for sons if it exists among the Ache. The same procedure described above is used to estimate that the effect $(a_{25,26})$ for sons is 0.012 additional offspring ≥ 5 years of age. For simplicity, the "mother effect" for sons and daughters during a 5-year interval $(\alpha_{x',x'+5})$ is estimated as 5 times the effect at the mid-interval age.

The measured parameters of $P_{x,x+5}$ and $f_{x,x+5}$ for females and the sex-specific $P_{0,x+5}$ for the Ache population are shown in Table 13.1. The Ache demographic parameters are apparently quite similar to those often experienced by rapidly growing traditional populations. For example, the Ache survivorship curve is very similar to that reported for the !Kung or Yanomamö, whereas age-specific fertility and sex ratio at birth are higher than the !Kung but similar to that of the Yanomamö (Early and Peters 1990; Howell 1979; Melancon 1982).

The fitness cost experienced during some 5-year interval $(C_{x,x+5})$ associated with terminating reproduction at the beginning of that interval can be expressed as follows:

$$C_{x,x+5} = (P^*_{x,x+5})(f^*_{x,x+5})(P_{0,5})(\hat{P}_{5,10}) \quad (7)$$

where $C_{x,x+5}$ is the number of children that a woman expects to produce in the specified interval who are expected to survive to age 10 given her own future survivorship, $P^*_{x,x+5}$ is her expected survivorship in the interval if she continues to reproduce, and $f^*_{x,x+5}$ is her expected fertility in the interval.

Estimating $P^*_{x,y}$ and $f^*_{x,y}$ for older women is complicated since few living human females continue to reproduce beyond age 45–50. As a first approximation we assume that continued reproduction will have a negligible effect (relative to what it would be if she did not reproduce) on a woman's probability of survivorship through a given interval. Death in childbirth is rare among the Ache, representing only about 3% of all deaths of reproductive-aged women. Even the assumption that childbirth for older Ache women would result in a tenfold higher risk of maternal death would only decrease the probability of surviving the 50–55 age interval from 0.879 to 0.846.[8] This mortality rate due to childbirth (about 363/10,000 births) is about five times higher than the highest rates ever observed in developing countries (George Washington University 1975). Nevertheless, even

this high rate of maternal mortality has only a minor effect on the survivorship of older women. It is also possible that reproduction at an older age would be associated with additional mortality (not just that caused during childbirth) that is higher than the rate observed among currently postreproductive Ache females. It has been shown, for example, that lactation and other forms of parental care can depress subsequent adult survivorship in birds and some mammals (see Clutton-Brock 1991:31 47). Nevertheless, the probable magnitude of this effect among older Ache women is difficult to estimate. This problem will be considered again in the discussion section, but in order to test the "grandmother hypothesis" we begin by assuming that $P_{x,y}$ is a close approximation of $P^*_{x,y}$.

The most difficult parameter to estimate is the age-specific fertility of older women if they did not experience menopause or premature reproductive senescence. In our test we would like to employ a fertility curve that declines toward the end of the lifespan in a manner similar to that for other mammals and, in particular, for primates. Thus, for example, if chimpanzee females show a peak fertility at age 20 and a decline such that when they reach 80% of their maximum lifespan they still exhibit 40% of the maximum age-specific fertility, we might simply assume that human females, if they did not undergo premature reproductive senescence, would also show about 40% of their maximum age-specific fertility when they reached 80% of their maximum lifespan. Although no chimpanzee data are available that can be used for this calculation, good data do exist on the age-specific fertility decline of macaques throughout their lifespan (Sade et al. 1976, cited in Dunbar 1987). We have used these data to estimate hypothetical age-specific fertility rates for Ache females if they continued to reproduce throughout their lifespan and showed a fertility decline similar to that measured in macaques (see Appendix). Use of the macaque data results in an expected fertility reduction to 43% of maximum fertility by age 65 in Ache women who are assumed not to experience reproductive senescence and enables us to test whether a fertility reduction to 0% by age 50 would be favored by natural selection. Use of comparative data that would allow for any greater drop in fertility through time would essentially be allowing fertility decline to "explain itself."[9]

Since all parameters that determine the potential benefits to reproductive senescence (equations 2, 3, and 4) and costs of reproductive senescence (equation 7) at specific ages have been measured in the Ache or estimated as described in the text, it is a simple matter to substitute in the relevant values and plot the values of $2\Sigma Br$ and C for each 5-year age interval during a woman's adult lifespan. These values are plotted in Figure 13.6, and the calculations are detailed in spreadsheet form in the Appendix. It is readily apparent that reproductive senescence will not be favored by natural selection under the conditions specified, since the potential cost outweighs the sum of the benefits (discounted by r) over the entire span of adult ages from 40 to 65 years. Expected benefits do rise with age, but they generally remain low because the grandmother effect is small and because most women can expect to have few living adult offspring who could benefit from their help. Expected costs also fall with age, but they generally remain high because women over age 40 have a very good chance of surviving each additional 5-year interval.

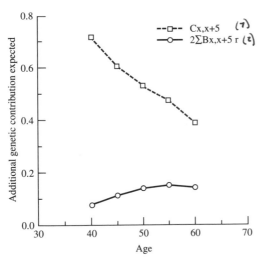

Figure 13.6. Fitness benefits and costs expected after cessation of reproduction in each 5-year interval for Ache women according to calculations specified in equations 2–7 and parameters described in the text. The calculations are shown in the appendix.

The estimates used to test the "grandmother hypothesis" are very rough, and they rest on some important assumptions about the values of unmeasured parameters. It is therefore useful to consider whether reasonable changes in parameter estimates might significantly alter the conclusion that the costs of reproductive senescence outweigh the benefits for Ache women in the kin selection model. Several demographic variables (e.g., age-specific fertility and mortality rates) show up in both sides of the equation and are therefore unlikely to affect the conclusion if they are allowed to vary for the entire population. Instead we focus on factors that would increase only the benefits of reproductive senescence (e.g., additional kin; increased $a_{x,x+5}$), or decrease the costs of reproductive senescence (lower $P^*_{x,y}$; lower $P_{5,10}x'd < 10$). These factors are considered one at a time. Fertility in older age is not allowed to vary, because, as mentioned above, fertility decline is precisely what we are trying to explain, and we have already allowed for a considerable decline with maternal age.

First we consider the possibility that the model has underestimated the number of adult offspring for older women or the possibility that older women could help their younger siblings as well as their own offspring. Living adult offspring might be underestimated by population fertility and mortality parameters if, for example, those women who survive to age 45 have higher fertility and lower offspring mortality than is the case for the population in general. Table 13.2 shows the average number of kin of several different categories for women of ages 45, 50, and 55.[10] It can be seen that the actual number of adult offspring is very close to the estimates $s_{x',x'+5}$ calculated from equation 4 using values specified in the Appendix. The number of younger brothers and sisters that might be helped by older women is generally quite low, and even if we allow older sisters to have the same effect on the reproduction of the younger siblings that we measured for mother and offspring pairs, the ratio of $2\Sigma Br$ and C is still not favorable to reproductive senescence.

Next we consider the possibility that a woman could also help her nieces and nephews to reproduce. The mean number of nieces and nephews observed for older Ache women before 1971 is shown in Table 13.2. Note that the number shows high variance relative to the

Table 13.2. Number of Genetic Relatives (Aged 15–40) of Ache Women Aged 45, 50, and 55

Age 45 ID#	Year of birth	Number of Children		Number of Siblings		Number of Nieces/Nephews	
		M	F	M	F	M	F
4006	1918	0	1	0	1	1	3
4097	1919	2	1	0	0	0	1
4120	1920	1	1	?	?	?	?
3047	1920	0	0	0	1	5	4
3048	1921	3	0	0	0	0	2
3088	1922	2	3	0	2	1	2
4022	1922	2	1	0	0	0	1
4021	1922	1	2	3	0	0	1
4023	1923	1	1	1	0	1	1
3058	1924	1	2	3	3	5	3
3061	1925	1	0	1	3	4	2
3064	1925	0	3	?	?	?	?
4019	1925	1	1	0	0	0	0
4044	1925	2	2	0	0	0	0
3994	1925	0	3	0	0	0	2
3066	1926	2	0	0	0	0	1
3067	1926	1	2	1	1	0	0
Average		1.176	1.353	0.600	0.733	1.333	1.800
"mother effect"		0.057	0.168	0.057	0.168	0.057	0.168
ΣB		0.054	0.183	0.027	0.099	0.061	0.243
$2r$		0.500	0.500	0.500	0.500	0.250	0.250
$2r\Sigma B$, each kin type		0.027	0.091	0.014	0.050	0.015	0.061
$2r\Sigma B$, all kin		0.258					
2064	1909	0	0	0	0	12	5
4323	1910	3	0	0	0	0	0
2058	1910	3	1	0	0	0	0
3021	1913	2	1	0	0	3	2
3019	1913	3	1	0	0	3	0
3020	1913	1	1	0	1	0	3
4053	1914	2	1	?	?	?	?
3025	1915	2	1	0	0	18	7
3030	1916	3	2	0	1	2	1
3031	1916	3	1	0	0	3	1
4297	1916	1	1	1	0	3	1
3033	1917	3	1	1	3	1	0
3035	1917	0	2	2	1	2	0
3032	1917	3	0	0	2	4	9
4120	1920	0	2	?	?	?	?
3047	1920	1	1	0	0	6	4
3048	1921	4	1	0	0	1	1
Average		2.000	1.000	0.267	0.533	3.867	2.267
"mother effect"		0.057	0.168	0.057	0.168	0.057	0.168
ΣB		0.091	0.134	0.012	0.072	0.176	0.304
$2r$		0.500	0.500	0.500	0.500	0.250	0.250
$2r\Sigma B$, each kin type		0.045	0.067	0.006	0.036	0.044	0.076
$2r\Sigma B$, all kin		0.274					
2086	1891	2	1	?	?	?	?
2091	1891	0	2	0	0	3	0
2073	1895	3	0	0	0	0	0
2095	1895	2	1	0	0	5	4
4402	1895	0	0	?	?	?	?
2028	1897	2	1	?	?	?	?
2032	1900	3	2	2	0	3	0
2031	1900	0	4	1	1	0	2
2030	1901	1	2	0	0	3	0
2035	1902	3	0	0	0	0	0
2034	1903	1	0	1	0	6	3
2042	1905	3	3	0	0	1	1
2085	1905	2	2	0	0	14	6

Table 13.2. (continued)

Age 45 ID#	Year of birth	Number of Children		Number of Siblings		Number of Nieces/Nephews	
		M	F	M	F	M	F
2090	1905	3	0	0	0	0	0
2092	1905	1	0	0	0	6	7
2046	1906	4	0	0	0	2	2
3001	1907	3	1	0	0	8	3
Average		1.941	1.118	0.286	0.071	3.643	2.000
"mother effect"		0.057	0.168	0.057	0.168	0.057	0.168
ΣB		0.087	0.148	0.013	0.009	0.164	0.265
$2r$		0.500	0.500	0.500	0.500	0.250	0.250
$2r\Sigma B$, each kin type		0.044	0.074	0.006	0.005	0.041	0.066
$2r\Sigma B$, all kin		0.236					

number of adult offspring, mainly because it includes the reproductive output of brothers who show much higher variance in RS than do their sisters. Although it is impossible for a woman to reside closely with *all* her nieces and nephews (the way she might with her own children), we have assumed that the effect of helping these kin is also the same as that measured for mother-offspring pairs. The total $2\Sigma Br$ that a woman might obtain helping all kin (offspring, siblings, nieces and nephews) between the ages of 15 and 40 is shown in Table 13.2 and plotted in Figure 13.7a relative to the cost function already calculated. Even when we include the hypothetical benefits from helping younger siblings, nieces, and nephews to reproduce, selection will not favor reproductive senescence in Ache women.

A second calculation of $2\Sigma Br$ is shown in Figure 13.7b. In this case we have allowed the value for $a_{x,x+5}$ to be determined by the upper 95% confidence interval for the slope, β_2, in equations 5 and 6. Under these conditions a mother's help would increase her daughter's RS by about 0.098 offspring who survive to age 5 per year when the daughter is 25 years old. This new estimate of $a_{x,y}$ implies an increase of 2.88 offspring who survive to age 5 over the daughter's entire reproductive span.[11] These values of $a_{x,x+5}$ are probably about as high as can be expected for any traditional human group given the limitations to population growth these groups experience. Under these conditions reproductive senescence is favored at approximately 53 years of age.

The parameters that affect the *cost* of premature reproductive senescence seem to have

less of an effect on the likelihood that menopause might evolve as a result of kin selection. Figure 13.7c shows how the cost of reproductive senescence changes if the probability of death in an interval ($q_{x,x+5}$) is tripled for women after age 40, owing to continued reproduction. In this simulation either women can cease to reproduce and experience Ache-like survivorship or they can continue to reproduce and experience much higher mortality ($P*_{x,x+5} = 1 - 3q_{x,x+5}$). The latter option would lead to a serious reduction of the lifespan for women, with only about 10% of the females ever born surviving to age 52, whereas in the current Ache population 10% of females survive to age 72. Nevertheless, this dramatic increase in mortality still does not favor reproductive senescence in Ache women. Finally, Figure 13.7d shows that 100% offspring mortality when a mother dies before her child reaches 10 years of age will not lead to conditions that favor the evolution of reproductive senescence.

DISCUSSION

Data collected from Ache foragers enable a test of the "grandmother hypothesis" under some very specific conditions. The test described is not necessarily relevant to the origin of human menopause, but it is relevant to its maintenance in the Ache population and possibly to its maintenance through much of human history when members of our species lived in small foraging groups. The data do not support the proposition that reproductive senescence in the Ache population has been *maintained* via natural selec-

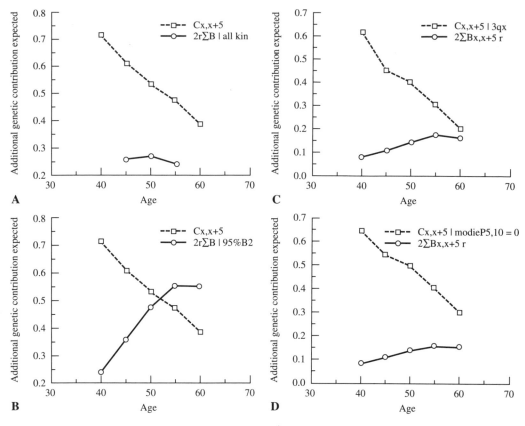

Figure 13.7. Fitness benefits and costs expected after reproductive termination in each 5-year interval for Ache women if (*a*) women help offspring, siblings, and nieces and nephews, as described in the text; (*b*) the highest slope within the 95% confidence interval in equations 5 and 6 is used to estimate the value for $a_{x,y}$; (*c*) the probability of dying in an interval (q_x) is triple that observed for Ache women between 40 and 65 years; and (*d*) all offspring die when their mother dies before they reach age 10.

tion favoring women who ceased to reproduce in order to invest in their grandchildren. When the highest slope within the 95% confidence interval in equations 5 and 6 is used to estimate the "mother effect," however, the result indicates that reproductive senescence might be favored at an age near that at which menopause occurs in the population. Thus, the data that we present do not allow us to firmly reject the "grandmother hypothesis" either. Future analyses may allow us to obtain a more precise estimate of $a_{x,y}$ for a variety of potential recipients of an older woman's aid. Improved estimates are especially possible in the Ache case since the current sample is small and other important joint effects on age-specific reproductive suc-

cess produced by additional independent or interacting variables have not been measured. A multivariate model including other factors known to affect reproductive success should enable a more precise measurement of the "mother effect" on adult sons and daughters. Measurement of this effect in several additional societies is crucial to the assessment of the "grandmother hypothesis." The most important contribution of this study, however, is that it attempts to specify what conditions would need to be met for the "grandmother hypothesis" to be correct, and how to estimate the appropriate parameters.

For example, *if* older women could significantly affect the reproductive success of a wide array of collateral and descendent kin, and *if* their effect was somewhat greater than that measured among the Ache, and *if* mortality rates associated with continued childbirth after age 40 were significantly higher than those reported to date, natural selection could indeed favor premature reproductive senescence. Whether or not these conditions are met in other human populations, or were met at some point in human evolutionary history, is a difficult empirical question, but one that can probably ultimately be ascertained.

Further adjustments of model parameters are also possible. It might be argued, for example, that the "mother effect" we estimate for the Ache is small because the population was rapidly growing throughout the twentieth century. Under these conditions perhaps all sons and daughters are easily able to reproduce at a high rate. Under zero-growth conditions the "mother effect" might be much larger relative to the expected reproductive performance without the mother's help, and therefore only offspring who received their mother's help during their reproductive years would produce significant numbers of surviving offspring. This argument seems plausible, but it will have to be verified empirically in some modern zero-growth population in order to be persuasive.

Other complications of our measure of $a_{x,y}$ may need to be considered. First, potential confounding variables have not yet been included in the regression. Perhaps mothers who live to a greater age are likely to have daughters with higher-than-average RS regardless of their help. Perhaps "father effects" are correlated with "mother effects" on offspring RS. These issues need to be examined. In addition, the "mother effect" may not remain constant when summed across potential kin recipients. It may be the case, for example, that women with few younger kin make a larger difference to the RS of each of those kin than do women with more kin. Sons and daughters in our sample who reproduced without their mother's help (i.e., whose mother had died) may have received help from other kin; thus we may have underestimated the "mother effect." Although these concerns are valid, it must be remembered that older women operate within a statistically determined social context. Our measures of $a_{x,y}$ should be correct on average because most women have neither few nor many kin, and

most women who help their offspring to reproduce do so in a context in which those offspring have other kin to help them if the mother does not.

Some adjustments of the model's parameters simply introduce new questions of functional significance. For example, if we have underestimated maternal mortality resulting from reproduction after age 45, the question of functional significance is simply shifted to that trait. Undoubtedly women should stop reproducing at some age if reproduction will lead to their death, but why should selection favor a phenotype that includes high mortality from continued reproduction long before other body systems begin to fail? High maternal mortality therefore would not provide the answer to the dilemma, it would just shift the focus of the question.

Even if the conditions for the evolution of reproductive senescence through kin investment are met in some circumstances, we must wonder why reproductive cessation is not a facultative response. For example, the number of close kin between the ages of 15 and 40 for Ache women at age 50 varies from 3 to 28 (Table 13.2). Thus, some Ache women have enough close kin by the age of 50 that shifting their investment to kin would probably be favored by selection. Other women have few living kin to help at age 50. Women who live near many close kin as they approach middle age and live in circumstances where they can make a large difference in the reproductive success of those kin should perhaps facultatively terminate their own reproduction. Women who do not find themselves in these circumstances should continue to reproduce. A cultural rule that mimics this strategy is indeed found in some human societies. Among the Nyakyusa a woman is required by taboo to cease reproduction when she becomes a grandmother (Wilson 1957:137). Thus, reproductive termination is facultatively dependent on the presence of grandchildren.

Such conditions as postmarital residence pattern and avoidable causes of child mortality should also exert a strong effect on the $a_{x,y}$ parameter in the model. It seems unlikely that the conditions necessary to favor menopause through kin selection are met in all societies. Nevertheless, reproductive senescence appears to be under strong genetic determination and universal, with very little variation in age of onset across populations or through time (Jones 1975). This uniformity suggests that it must be a response to almost universally experienced conditions.

Another weakness of the "grandmother hypothesis" is its inability to account for age-specific fertility decline prior to menopause. The "grandmother hypothesis" is essentially a threshold hypothesis; it predicts a constant or even an increasing investment by females in their own reproduction until the point at which the cost-benefit curves cross (Peter Ellison, personal communication). Instead, reproductive function in humans begins to decline significantly well before the age of menopause.

Thus, we are still left with the puzzling question, what forces have been maintaining premature reproductive senescence in the Ache population or other human populations over the past few thousand years? Have we simply misestimated an important parameter in the model, or is there another explanation for the maintenance of premature reproduc-tive senescence?

This examination of reproductive senescence in light of an explicit model and concrete data measured on a real human population should provoke more intensive investigation of the "grandmother hypothesis" and perhaps lead to the development of alternatives. For example, it may be physiologically impossible for human females to continue reproducing into old age if they experience high levels of fertility early in life. This general idea has been around for at least two centuries. As John Hunter, the father of experimental medicine, stated in 1787:

You will observe that when a woman begins to breed at an early period, as at fifteen, and has her children fast, that she seldom breeds longer than age thirty to thirty-five. Therefore we may suppose either that the parts are then worn out, or the breeding constitution is over. If a woman begins later, as at 20 or 25, she may continue to breed to the age of forty or more. (in Kline et al. 1989:260)

Despite Hunter's observation, there is no evidence that age at menarche correlates with age at menopause in modern human populations.[12] Age at menarche and age at last birth also show no association in at least one natural-fertility population (Borgerhoff Mulder 1989a), but whether early, high age-specific fertility is correlated with early age at last birth when a fe-

male's overall physical condition is taken into consideration is unknown at this time.

Nevertheless, in theory a trade-off may exist: rapid early reproduction followed by menopause, or a slower reproductive rate with reproductive function lasting later into the lifespan. Studies of genetic correlation between life-history traits suggest that high early fertility does lead to lowered later fertility through either negative pleiotropy or the costs of early reproduction (Bell and Koufopanou 1986). For example, mice selected for high fecundity early in life show lower fecundity later in life (Wallinga and Baker 1978).

Human female fertility does appear exceptionally high during the early part of the lifespan, given human body size, juvenile survivorship, and expected adult survivorship. For example, human interbirth intervals are shorter than those of chimpanzees and gorillas (which tend to be around 5 years) despite the fact that human juvenile survivorship is higher (see Goodall 1986; Nishida et al. 1990), parental investment continues longer, and lifespan is significantly longer. Perhaps this "racing" of the female reproductive machinery and required parental investment lead to parity-related depletion of physical condition (e.g., Tracer 1991) and reproductive physiology that ultimately will not support further successful reproduction. Increased susceptibility to skeletal fractures in females at around the age of menopause may, for example, be related to rapid reproduction and ultimately results in a five- to tenfold increase in fracture rate by age 60 (Utian 1980). Once successful reproduction is unlikely, menopause may indeed be favored through kin selection, as envisioned in the "grandmother hypothesis." This hypothesis, which includes both negative pleiotropy and subsequent kin selection, is appealing because it would account for both age-specific fertility decline and subsequent reproductive senescence. In fact, it allows for significant fertility decline to be the crucial factor that favors complete reproductive termination. For these observations to constitute an explanation of menopause, however, a trade-off between rapid early reproduction and slower reproduction over a longer time period is necessarily implied. Whether or not this trade-off is inevitable is unknown.

Another similar trade-off model between early and late reproduction has been suggested by Peter Ellison (personal communication). Ellison points out that because of high investment per offspring, women, unlike men, cannot make up reproductive losses early in life by reproducing at a high rate later in life. Thus selection might favor any mechanism that improved the quality and quantity of early reproduction in females even if these mechanisms led to detrimental effects later in the reproductive span. Ellison suggests that the arrested metaphase experienced by human oocytes minimizes early deleterious mutations (because total mutations are partially a function of the number of cell divisions experienced), and that this same mechanism is ultimately responsible for the rapid exponentially increasing rate of oocyte deterioration later in life that results in menopause. This explanation, however, seems relevant to the life history of all female mammals. Why do female elephants and whales continue to reproduce at ages beyond that of any human females (although they do eventually experience reproductive senescence; Marsh and Kasuya 1986; Smuts 1977)?

Other aspects of the mechanism of menopause are also puzzling and should be addressed in any evolutionary model. For example, the recent finding that age at menopause is positively correlated with subsequent lifespan (Snowdon et al. 1989) is intriguing. Is this correlation due to a genetic link between reproductive senescence and the senescence of other body functions, or is it simply due to environmental factors that affect general overall health and lead to subsequent changes in both age at menopause and lifespan? These issues await further exploration.

At the present, we believe that very little evidence supports the hypothesis that the human lifespan only recently increased beyond the age of female reproductive senescence. Almost certainly this extension of the lifespan is not the case for toothed whales, and yet they too seem to undergo menopause and reproductive senescence well before the end of the typical adult female lifespan (Figure 13.8; Marsh and Kasuya 1986). Simply accepting menopause as an inevitable feature of the reproductive system also seems unwarranted. The suggestion that oocytes simply deteriorate at a constant rate,

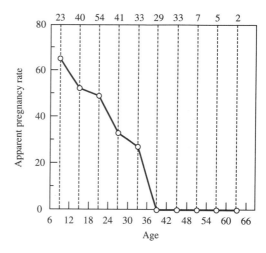

Figure 13.8. Age-specific pregnancy rate of harvest pilot whale females. Adapted from Marsh and Kasuya 1986:Fig. 3. The numbers along the top show the sample size in each age category. None of the 76 females older than age 36 were pregnant. Age estimates are based on tooth ring counts.

which ultimately leads to menopause, is no explanation at all. Other mammals, such as elephants and baleen whales, reproduce at ages well beyond that of human females even though their lifespan is no longer. Certainly selection should be able to affect the initial number of viable oocytes in the human female, or the rate of their deterioration, enabling reproductive senescence to be postponed if it resulted in higher fitness. Indeed, reproductive senescence in human females appears an adaptive design feature of the organism that demands a functional explanation consistent with our current understanding of how complex phenotypes evolve.

Acknowledgments. We would like to thank Monique Borgerhoff Mulder, Ray Hames, Henry Harpending, Eric Smith, Holly Smith, and three anonymous reviewers for useful written comments on the first draft of this paper. Discussions with Peter Ellison, Kristen Hawkes, and Alan Rogers were especially valuable throughout. This research was supported by NSF grant BNS8613186 and grants from the Rackham Graduate School and the L. S. B. Leakey Foundation.

NOTES

1. Chimpanzee demographic parameters are estimated from Goodall 1986:112 and Nishida et al. 1990.

2. Data from Howell 1979:81 and Hill and Hurtado 1991.

3. In order to develop a measure of maximum lifespan that is independent of sample size, we should designate an arbitrarily low value on the cumulative survivorship curve ($P_{0,x}$) as "maximum lifespan." If for example we define maximum lifespan as the age to which 1% of the population survives, then for Ache hunter-gatherers maximum lifespan would be between 75 and 80 years (Hill and Hurtado 1991).

4. To determine the effect of a woman's death on the survivorship of her offspring up to age 20, we ran a Cochran-Mantel-Haenszel test on each of four 5-year intervals (0–4, 5–9, 10–14, 15–19) (PROC FREQ: SAS Institute 1986). For example, the interval between 0 and 5 years includes data on the mortality status of mother and offspring in the 0–1, 1–2, 2–3, 3–4, and 4–5 intervals. This test pools information on each interval to determine if differences between the two mortality curves (offspring whose mothers live vs. offspring whose mothers die) are statistically significant. Differences are statistically significant in the first three 5-year intervals (based on the chi-square value for general association, $p < 0.05$) The relative increase in the probability of modality due to mother's death is considerable in these three intervals. In our sample, children between birth and 5 years of age whose mothers die are 6.7 times more likely to die than children whose mothers live (logit odds ratio 9.5% C.I. = 2–22, $n = 2359$). In later years, mortality risks decrease slightly for children whose mothers die before the end of the interval. From 5 to 9 and from 10 to 14 years, Ache children whose mothers die are approximately five times more likely to die within this interval than are children whose mothers live (logit odds ratio 95% C.I. = 2.2–14.2, $n = 2881$ and C.I. = 1.8–14.7, $n = 1534$). Finally, from 15 to 20 years of age, mother's death has no effect on offspring survivorship in our sample (logit odds ratio 95% C.I. = 0.167–2, $n = 1198$).

5. The variable z_2 in this model is defined as year of mother's death or 1970 (whichever came first) minus year of ego's birth plus 15 years (beginning of reproductive age).

6. Mothers who are close in age to their own offspring and are likely to continue to reproduce after their offspring begin reproducing will theoretically not help as much as mothers who have terminated their own reproduction before their offspring start to reproduce. Previous empirical support for this prediction has been found in humans (Turke 1988), and a multivariate model using all mother-offspring pairs in our data also supports this expectation. Since the cost-benefit model discussed here requires help from *nonreproducing mothers* on the benefits side of the equation, we used only mother-offspring pairs with an age difference greater than 25 years in the multiple regression.

7. Multiple regression analyses were conducted separately using data on sons ($n = 146$) and daughters ($n = 108$; PROC FREQ: SAS Institute 1986). Variance inflation factors, correlation matrices, and analyses of reduced models indicate that collinearity between the independent variables does not bias the magnitude or direction of the regression parameters. Not surprisingly, for both sexes, the effect of age (tz_1) on number of children ≥5 years of age (ty) is highly significant (daughters: $\beta_1 = 2.27 \pm 0.3$, T-test, p[two-tailed] = 0.0001 sons: $\beta_1 = 1.89 \pm 0.3$, T-test, p[two-tailed] = 0.0001). In the daughters sample, the number of years helped by mother (z_2) is highly significant ($\beta_2 = 0.096 \pm 0.03$, T-test, p[two-tailed] = 0.0003), but not in the sons sample ($\beta_2 = 0.013 \pm 0.03$, T-test, p[two-tailed] = 0.6316). The estimator describing interaction effects between age and number of years helped (tz_1z_2) is also significant for daughters ($\beta_{12} = -0.056 \pm 0.01$, T-test, p[two-tailed] = 0.0003), but not for sons ($\beta_{12} = -0.006 \pm 0.02$, T-test p[two tailed] = 0.7234).

8. Assuming that the number of deaths due to childbirth would be 10 times higher than the observed rate of deaths due to childbirth we can calculate the increase in probability of death in the 50–55 year interval as follows. Expected deaths per 100 women who enter the interval is 12.1 (Table 13.1). Only 3% of these would be due to childbirth, or about 0.363 deaths. This number multiplied by 10 equals an expected number of deaths in childbirth of about 3.63; thus the total number of deaths expected in the interval is 12.1 + 3.63 − 0.363 or about 15.367. Probability of survivorship would be about .846, and if we assume that f_x is approximately 0.2, the probability of death in childbirth would be about 363/10,000.

9. It might be expected, however, that an initial small decline in fertility could favor an additional fertility decline, and that positive feedback between initial decline and subsequent decline might ultimately drive selection to favor reproductive senescence (Alan Rogers, personal communication).

10. In order to keep sample sizes equal, the first 17 women in the database who meet the criteria (e.g., reach age x before 1971) are used in each sample.

11. The new slopes are calculated by adding the standard error of the β_2 given in note 8. The slope at the upper 95% confidence interval is $ty = .04237z_2$ for sons and $ty = .12188z_2$ for daughters. The interaction effect was held constant in this simulation.

12. Personal communication from Stanley Garn, Center for Human Growth and Development, University of Michigan, based on analyses from national databases TSNS, NHANES I and II, and Tecumseh Community Study.

Appendix. Calculations of the Benefits and Costs of Reproductive Senescence as Defined in Equations 2–4 and 7

Benefits Expected		Ego Age	Offspring Age	Ego Survival		Ego-Offspring Age Difference	Prob. Offspr. born	Proportion Offspring		Offspring Survival		"Mother Effect"	
Sons $B[x,x+5]$	Daughters $B[x,x+5]$	x	x'	$P[x,x+5]$	$P[x+5,x+10]$	$x-x'$	$f[x-(x'+5), x-x']$	Male Ω	Female $1-\Omega$	Male $P[0,x'+5]$	Female $P[0,x'+5]$	Male $a[x',x'+5]$	Female $a[x',x'+5]$
0.0275	0.0813	40	15	0.940	0.885	25	1.411	0.52	0.48	0.6207	0.4656	0.0718	0.3602
0.0118	0.0309	40	20	0.940	0.885	20	0.750	0.52	0.48	0.5579	0.4319	0.0645	0.2359
0.0006	0.0013	40	25	0.940	0.885	15	0.043	0.52	0.48	0.5207	0.4267	0.0587	0.1799
0.0000	0.0000	40	30	0.940	0.885	10	0.000	0.52	0.48	0.4822	0.4070	0.0538	0.1335
0.0000	0.0000	40	35	0.940	0.885	5	0.000	0.52	0.48	0.4477	0.4000	0.0496	0.0939
0.0000	0.0000	40	40	0.940	0.885	0	0.000	0.52	0.48	0.4414	0.3760	0.0459	0.0593

$\Sigma B(x,x+5)$ 0.1533

Benefits Expected		Ego Age	Offspring Age	Ego Survival		Ego-Offspring Age Difference	Prob. Offspr. born	Proportion Offspring		Offspring Survival		"Mother Effect"	
Sons $B[x,x+5]$	Daughters $B[x,x+5]$	x	x'	$P[x,x+5]$	$P[x+5,x+10]$	$x-x'$	$f[x-(x'+5), x-x']$	Male Ω	Female $1-\Omega$	Male $P[0,x'+5]$	Female $P[0,x'+5]$	Male $a[x',x'+5]$	Female $a[x',x'+5]$
0.0279	0.0824	45	15	0.885	0.879	30	1.522	0.52	0.48	0.6207	0.4656	0.0718	0.3602
0.0209	0.0546	45	20	0.885	0.879	25	1.411	0.52	0.48	0.5579	0.4319	0.0645	0.2359
0.0094	0.0219	45	25	0.885	0.879	20	0.750	0.52	0.48	0.5207	0.4267	0.0587	0.1799
0.0005	0.0009	45	30	0.885	0.879	15	0.043	0.52	0.48	0.4822	0.4070	0.0538	0.1335
0.0000	0.0000	45	35	0.885	0.879	10	0.000	0.52	0.48	0.4477	0.4000	0.0496	0.0939
0.0000	0.0000	45	40	0.885	0.879	5	0.000	0.52	0.48	0.4414	0.3760	0.0459	0.0593

$\Sigma B(x,x+5)$ 0.2185

Benefits Expected		Ego Age	Offspring Age	Ego Survival		Ego-Offspring Age Difference	Prob. Offspr. born	Proportion Offspring		Offspring Survival		"Mother Effect"	
Sons $B[x,x+5]$	Daughters $B[x,x+5]$	x	x'	$P[x,x+5]$	$P[x+5,x+10]$	$x-x'$	$f[x-(x'+5), x-x']$	Male Ω	Female $1-\Omega$	Male $P[0,x'+5]$	Female $P[0,x'+5]$	Male $a[x',x'+5]$	Female $a[x',x'+5]$
0.0279	0.0823	50	15	0.879	0.870	35	1.533	0.52	0.48	0.6207	0.4656	0.0718	0.3602
0.0224	0.0584	50	20	0.879	0.870	30	1.522	0.52	0.48	0.5579	0.4319	0.0645	0.2359
0.0176	0.0408	50	25	0.879	0.870	25	1.411	0.52	0.48	0.5207	0.4267	0.0587	0.1799
0.0079	0.0154	50	30	0.879	0.870	20	0.750	0.52	0.48	0.4822	0.4070	0.0538	0.1335
0.0004	0.0006	50	35	0.879	0.870	15	0.043	0.52	0.48	0.4477	0.4000	0.0496	0.0939
0.0000	0.0000	50	40	0.879	0.870	10	0.000	0.52	0.48	0.4414	0.3760	0.0459	0.0593

$\Sigma B(x,x+5)$ 0.2738

Benefits Expected (Ego Age 55)

Benefits Expected		Ego Age	Offspring Age	Ego Survival		Ego-Offspring Age Difference	Prob. Offspr. born	Proportion Offspring		Offspring Survival		"Mother Effect"	
Sons $B[x,x+5]$	Daughters $B[x,x+5]$	x	x'	$P[x,x+5]$	$P[x+5, x+10]$	$x-x'$	$f[x-(x'+5), x-x']$	Male Ω	Female $1-\Omega$	Male $P[0,x'+5]$	Female $P[0,x'+5]$	Male $a[x',x'+5]$	Female $a[x',x'+5]$
0.0236	0.0698	55	15	0.870	0.818	40	1.320	0.52	0.48	0.6207	0.4656	0.0718	0.3602
0.0222	0.0579	55	20	0.870	0.818	35	1.533	0.52	0.48	0.5579	0.4319	0.0645	0.2359
0.0187	0.0433	55	25	0.870	0.818	30	1.522	0.52	0.48	0.5207	0.4267	0.0587	0.1799
0.0147	0.0284	55	30	0.870	0.818	25	1.411	0.52	0.48	0.4822	0.4070	0.0538	0.1335
0.0067	0.0104	55	35	0.870	0.818	20	0.750	0.52	0.48	0.4477	0.4000	0.0496	0.0939
0.0004	0.0004	55	40	0.870	0.818	15	0.043	0.52	0.48	0.4414	0.3760	0.0459	0.0593

$\Sigma B(x,x+5)$ 0.2964

Benefits Expected (Ego Age 60)

Benefits Expected		Ego Age	Offspring Age	Ego Survival		Ego-Offspring Age Difference	Prob. Offspr. born	Proportion Offspring		Offspring Survival		"Mother Effect"	
Sons $B[x,x+5]$	Daughters $B[x,x+5]$	x	x'	$P[x,x+5]$	$P[x+5, x+10]$	$x-x'$	$f[x-(x'+5), x-x']$	Male Ω	Female $1-\Omega$	Male $P[0,x'+5]$	Female $P[0,x'+5]$	Male $a[x',x'+5]$	Female $a[x',x'+5]$
0.0163	0.0480	60	15	0.818	0.750	45	0.975	0.52	0.48	0.6207	0.4656	0.0718	0.3602
0.0178	0.0465	60	20	0.818	0.750	40	1.320	0.52	0.48	0.5579	0.4319	0.0645	0.2359
0.0175	0.0407	60	25	0.818	0.750	35	1.533	0.52	0.48	0.5207	0.4267	0.0587	0.1799
0.0148	0.0286	60	30	0.818	0.750	30	1.522	0.52	0.48	0.4822	0.4070	0.0538	0.1335
0.0117	0.0183	60	35	0.818	0.750	25	1.411	0.52	0.48	0.4477	0.4000	0.0496	0.0939
0.0057	0.0058	60	40	0.818	0.750	20	0.750	0.52	0.48	0.4414	0.3760	0.0459	0.0593

$\Sigma B(x,x+5)$ 0.2716

Cost $C[x,x+5]$	Age x	Expected Mortality		Fertility $f[x+5]$	% Maximum Fertility Macaques	Offspring Survivorship $P[0,5]$
		$P*[x,x+5]$	$P*[x+5,x+10]$			
0.717	40	0.940	0.885	1.196	0.780	0.713
0.0605	45	0.885	0.879	1.073	0.700	0.713
0.532	50	0.879	0.870	0.950	0.620	0.713
0.473	55	0.870	0.818	0.858	0.560	0.713
0.385	60	0.818	0.750	0.751	0.490	0.713

14

How Much Does Grandma Help?

KIM HILL
ANA MAGDALENA HURTADO

Our paper on the evolution of menopause in human females addresses an important functional question about human life history. Since our initial publication, several articles by other authors have been published, or are in press, that further explore this issue (see Pavelka and Fedigan 1991; Austad 1993; Rogers 1993; Caro et al. 1994; Peccei 1994a, 1994b; Turke 1996b). We, too, recently published a new analysis of Ache data attempting to test the "grandmother hypothesis" of menopause, in a monograph that contains much more detail about the methods of data collection as well as new statistical techniques (Hill and Hurtado 1996).

In the target article we attempted to test one hypothesis of female reproductive senescence using one of many possible appropriate data sets (humans living under conditions similar to those experienced by our ancestors). The paper, however, is characterized by some weaknesses in the mathematical model and the statistical isolation of the parameters that need to be measured for use in that model. Many of these weaknesses were corrected in subsequent analyses of the same problem (Hill and Hurtado 1996, chap. 13), but our ability to truly measure relevant parameters in the model remains problematic and cannot be easily corrected with currently available data. Finally, we have recently become more concerned that our main conclusion (that menopause is not maintained by kin selection) could be erroneous given the implications of the fact that human female adult lifespans are at least as long on average as those of human males. This is discussed more below.

The question, as we identify it in the original article, is why did human females evolve the cessation of reproduction function well before the probable end of the adult lifespan and well before most other body functions senesce? We recognized (unlike some other authors) that the causes of the *origin* of menopause might be difficult to assess with data on modern human groups. However, we can ask what has maintained early female reproductive senescence as a trait in modern human populations. Good demographic data from a variety of human groups (see Hill and Hurtado 1996, chaps. 6 and 14) show that modern human groups experiencing conditions similar to those in the past ten thousand years of human history have *mean adult life expectancies* well beyond the age of female menopause. The period of human history living under such conditions is probably long enough to have evolved a longer female reproductive span if such a trait were favored by natural selection. Why is the human female reproductive span so short relative to expected lifespan? This trait is extremely rare among other mammals or primates.

A prominent evolutionary explanation of menopause has been based on the idea that older women might be able to attain a greater genetic contribution to the gene pool through providing assistance to existing kin rather than producing new offspring. The most commonly discussed reason that offspring production might lead to little genetic contribution for *older* women was the possibility that older women experience higher mortality than younger women, and that infants whose mothers die might also be expected to perish. Thus reproduction might be wasteful in old age and resources might be better expended on existing kin. Demographic data analyses in our target article correctly point out that while infants (and children) do often perish when their mother dies, older women still die at rates so low (about 3 percent mortality per year for an Ache woman of age fifty years) that very few infants produced by women at the age of menopause would be expected to experience maternal death. Even allowing for increases in maternal death with age, as observed in modern populations, the impact on infant survival would be almost negligible (because death in childbirth rarely occurs to women of any age). Thus, we should seek alternative explanations for the short human female reproductive span.

THE MODEL AND STATISTICS

In our article a mathematical life history model is developed that allows women to either continue reproducing or to divert all time, energy, and resources that would have been used in reproduction into helping close kin (mainly offspring and grandoffspring). Whichever of these two alternatives would lead to the greatest number of genetic equivalents added to the population during any specified interval is considered to be the alternative that would be favored by natural selection.

In the target article the *cost* of menopause is estimated as the number of children that could have been produced by an older woman if she were to have continued reproduction. Since older women do not produce children in modern human populations, we can simply substitute some reasonable fertility rate that might characterize such women if they did not experience menopause. In the target article we simply allow for a fertility decline typical of other mammals or primates in order to guess at the expected fertility rate of older human women if they did not undergo menopause. We also modify this number appropriately to take into account the likelihood that most young children will not survive if their mother dies. We found that the reproductive potential of older women who did not experience menopause in a five-year interval would be considerable under these conditions, and not too much lower than that of younger women.

The *benefits* of menopause are estimated in the target article as the genetic contribution of older women in a five-year interval through

helping kin. The helping effect of older women is estimated by comparing the reproductive success of men and women whose mothers are present (i.e., alive) or not present through a particular interval. It is thus assumed that older women who are alive help their kin and those who are dead do not, and that all energy and time that would have been devoted to reproduction by postmenopausal women are instead invested in helping kin. The difference in the number of grandoffspring of age five or more between older women who survive through a five-year interval compared with those who do not is assumed to be a measure of the genetic contribution that results from kin helping after reproductive cessation. The genetic contribution through grandmaternal kin helping is estimated in the target article using a linear regression on transformed data of numbers of surviving offspring for men and women, and the number of years during the reproductive span that the mothers of those individuals were alive (to provide help to them). This means that the slope of the partial regression "years with mother alive" by "offspring at least five years old" for reproducing adults (once age is controlled) forms the basis for measuring the impact of older women on their children's fertility and grandchildren's survival.

The model in the target article is unfortunate in that it does not isolate the female impact on grandoffspring survival independently from the impact on offspring fertility, and the measure of kin help is cumulative rather than measured over a yearly interval. The model presented also calculates benefits of kin help in units of surviving ten-year-old descendants as a method of achieving parity in the value of children produced or the increase in surviving close kin, and it assumes that all children who survive to age five experience average survival to age ten regardless of grandparental input. These shortcomings are all corrected in our new analysis (Hill and Hurtado 1996, chap. 13). In that analyses we weight all genetic contributions of different-aged individuals by the reproductive value of those individuals (see Rogers 1993) and we analyze the difference in survival and fertility of grandoffspring and offspring through each yearly interval of a woman's life by using a discrete time logistic regression hazard model. Logistic regression provides a method to directly measure the impact of a time-varying covariate (e.g., mother alive versus dead) on the rate of an event happening through time (e.g., live birth) and is discussed in detail in Hill and Hurtado (1996 chaps. 6, 8, 10). Logistic regression allows us to examine fertility and mortality independently and ask in each case whether the presence or absence of a surviving mother or grandmother has an impact on the vital rate. This statistical technique is ideal for measuring the impact of older women on their children's fertility or their grandchildren's survival. The new analysis again assumes that the difference in vital rates between individuals who do or do not have an older surviving mother/grandmother to help them is a measure of the helping effect provided by postreproductive women. The sum of all effects on all likely kin for a woman of any particular age can be calculated to estimate the potential benefits of reproductive cessation and a diversion of time and resources to help kin.

Our new analyses show that men and women with a living mother do experience marginally higher fertility, and that children do experience slightly higher survival if they have a living grandmother. All these effects are small, however, and none is statistically significant in the Ache database. The sum total of all increases in kin produced or surviving relative to that experienced when no mother or grandmother is available suggests that fifty-year-old women produce only about 0.05 newborn offspring genetic equivalents (reproductive value = 1) per year by helping their daughters, sons, and grandoffspring. Among the Ache, most of this effect is due to an increase in sons' fertility and the infant survival of grandoffspring when a fifty-year-old mother/grandmother is alive. The effect is small partially because fifty-year-old women have few surviving close kin to help on average. Thus older women who could invest time and resources to achieve an annual fertility rate above about 0.05 would be expected to achieve higher fitness if they continued direct reproduction rather than experience menopause in order to focus on helping close kin. This means that female age-specific fertility would have to drop to about one-sixth its maximum value in Ache women before natural selection would favor the complete cessation of reproductive function in order to divert time and resources to close kin. The female age-specific fertility rate does indeed drop that low by about

age forty-five, but *that drop is precisely the trait we wish to explain.*

MEASURING THE "GRANDMOTHER EFFECT"

Several considerations suggest that the measures described previously fail to adequately capture the true impact of grandmothers on the survival of their grandoffspring or the fertility of their adult children. First, the Ache data represent a period of relative resource abundance and high population growth. Some life history studies suggest that the costs of underinvestment in a life history component are primarily expressed (and detected by fieldworkers) during periods of resource stress or population decline (e.g., Tatar and Carey 1994). It is thus possible that grandmothers have a very pronounced effect on the survival or fertility of their descendant kin during times of stress, and that such an effect, if frequent enough through evolutionary history, could favor a female life history that included menopause long prior to death. This is a concern in our study since the Ache did experience a severe population decline in the 1970s, but we culled those data from the analyses because newly introduced disease epidemics were the cause of the crash.

Second, the impact of postmenopausal women on the vital rates of their descendant kin may not be accurately estimated by observing what happens to adult children whose mother dies or juvenile children whose grandmother dies. If other kin recognize that a mother/grandmother has been providing significant support for her offspring and grandoffspring, they may partially substitute for her in the event of her death. Thus, for example, an aunt may begin to provide supplementary food and help to raise a child after its grandmother dies, mitigating the negative effects of such a loss. Such adjustments by other kin will result in an underestimate of the demographic impact of grandmaternal help, when comparisons are made between individuals who do or do not have a surviving mother/grandmother. In order to assess the importance of this problem we need good data on the time and resources provided by various kin categories as well as the ultimate demographic consequences of that investment. Such data would allow us to determine whether resources being provided by a mother/grandmother were later provided by other close kin in the event of her death. A statistical calibration of the impact of different forms of help on survival and fertility of close kin would allow us to indirectly assess the fitness value of kin help by postmenopausal women regardless of the observed demographic consequences of their removal.

WHY DO POSTMENOPAUSAL WOMEN LIVE AS LONG AS MEN?

Our target article suggested that women produce very few genetic descendants through kin helping after they experience menopause. For this reason we suggested that direct reproduction would always be favored by natural selection if it were possible. We therefore concluded that female reproductive senescence might be the consequence of other evolved traits of female reproductive physiology that resulted in favorable early reproduction but decreasing efficiency for later reproduction. In the previous section we mentioned that perhaps we have underestimated the genetic contribution due to the efforts of postreproductive women. The fact that women live as long as (or longer than) men further supports the position that genetic con-

tribution must be significant in postmenopausal women (and about the same, on average, as that characterizing same-aged "reproductive" males). Population genetic models of senescence have shown that the selection pressure on survival is directly a function of reproductive value at any particular age (see Charlesworth 1980; Rose 1991). With no reproductive value, there is no selection pressure to counteract deleterious alleles that would result in rapid senescence and death. Thus, although postmenopausal women do not produce offspring, they must indeed be characterized by a "genetic reproductive value" not too different from that of males. Ache males produce an average of about 0.15 offspring per year at age fifty, when Ache women have all experienced menopause (Hill and Hurtado 1996, chap. 9). Unless we can explain why women do not senesce more rapidly than men, we should probably assume that their true genetic contribution due to the help they provide by not reproducing is about the same (i.e., about 0.15 offspring genetic equivalents per year). Thus, human evolutionary biologists must work in the future to obtain a better fit between our imperfect data sets and mathematically convincing but untested theory.

II
STUDIES OF MODERN SOCIETIES

15

Forward and Backward: Alternative Approaches to Studying Human Social Evolution

PAUL W. SHERMAN
HUDSON KERN REEVE

The six papers in this section sample a rapidly developing new field: evolutionary psychology. Evolutionary psychologists are Darwinians. They believe that since humans, like other organisms, evolved by natural selection, our bodies and our brains "consist of a set of adaptations, designed to solve the long-standing adaptive problems humans encountered as hunter-gatherers" (Cosmides and Tooby, chapter 26). The studies in this section illustrate how evolutionary psychologists have investigated (1) social behaviors, such as child abuse (Daly and Wilson, chapter 16) and rules of social exchange (Cosmides and Tooby, chapter 26); (2) differences between men and women, for example, in mate choice criteria (Buss, chapter 18; Kenrick et al., chapter 22) and sexual fantasies (Ellis and Symons, chapter 20); and (3) emotions, such as the mental anguish of rape victims (Thornhill and Thornhill, chapter 24).

The general approach of these studies is controversial. Attempts to infuse Darwinism into psychology have encountered resistance from social scientists, especially traditionalists who adhere to nonevolutionary models of human behavior (e.g., see the many responses to Buss [1989b] in *Behavioral and Brain Sciences* 12:14–39, and to Buss [1995a] in *Psychological Inquiry* 6:31–81). We will not address this controversy, except to say that we also believe serious progress in understanding human social behavior cannot be achieved without a Darwinian perspective (see Alexander 1979, 1987, 1989).

This essay addresses two main issues that were raised by the papers in this section. First, what is the correct methodology for testing evolutionary hypotheses about human behavior? Should we measure how behaviors currently affect fitness, or infer adaptive design features that result in the behaviors from the circumstances in which they are performed today? Second, what do evolutionary investigations tell us about the nature of the psychological mechanisms that generate behavior? Are our brains composed of a few generalized learning rules leading to local adaptation or of many specialized, possibly innate, algorithms that interlock to form a unitary human nature? These issues have created a major rift among scholars investigating human social evolution, which took up an entire issue of *Ethology and Sociobiology* (11:241–463, 1990; see also Symons 1987b; Smuts 1991; Crawford 1993). This contention is unfortunate and, for reasons that will soon become clear, unnecessary. We hope to speed a resolution of this debate and to encourage both "sides" to accept a more pluralistic approach to hypothesis development and testing.

TESTING EVOLUTIONARY HYPOTHESES

Let us begin by reviewing the general logic of testing hypotheses linking natural selection to phenotypic traits. As pointed out by Antonovics (1987) and Reeve and Sherman (1993), there are two types of questions evolutionary biologists ask and attempt to answer: those dealing with *phenotype existence* (i.e., why we observe certain traits rather than others today) and those dealing with *phenotype history* (i.e., the origins of traits and how they were modified through time). Competition among alternative hypotheses appropriately occurs only within and not between these two "levels of analysis" (Sherman 1988; Holekamp and Sherman 1989). Indeed, logical muddles and unresolvable debates result when hypotheses about phenotype history are pitted against hypotheses about phenotype existence (for examples, see Sherman 1988, 1989a). Accepting that there are multiple types of answerable questions helps identify which hypotheses legitimately compete as alternatives and limits the conflicts among explanations to those occurring within a given level of analysis.

At the level of phenotype existence, the hypothesis that a behavior occurs because natural selection has acted in a certain way is usually pitted against hypotheses that selection acted in alternative ways or, less commonly, that nonselective mechanisms explain the occurrence of the behavior. Tests of phenotype existence hypotheses always involve three elements (see Reeve and Sherman 1993). First, they explicitly or implicitly assume a set of alternative competing behavioral phenotypes, which we denote $\{B_1, B_2, \ldots B_i\}$. The phenotype set can be continuous or discontinuous, and may involve overt behaviors or their underlying psychological mechanisms. Second, these tests associate with each phenotype B_i a measure of fitness, $F(B_i)$. On the one hand, F may refer narrowly to immediate reproductive benefits arising from solutions to a particular, well-defined "problem," such as foraging efficiently or finding a high-quality mate (see Williams 1992). On the other hand, F may refer broadly to lifetime reproductive success. Of course, in order for narrow fitness criteria to be useful in evolutionary investigations, they must ultimately be connected to lifetime reproductive success (appropriately adjusted for changing population sizes). Third, tests must specify the environmental context (E) within which reproductive competition occurs (or occurred) and fitness is measured. E may encompass both the abiotic and biotic environments, even including the relative frequency of the variant itself (e.g., when there is frequency-dependent selection).

Once a set of alternative phenotypes, a fitness criterion, and a selective context have been specified, the hypothesis that natural selection maintains any trait can be tested. The core prediction of this hypothesis is that the trait's frequency is determined by its relative fitness value in E. More formally and precisely,

$$F_E,(B_i) \rightarrow P(B_i) \qquad (1)$$

which means that the probability $P(B_i)$ of seeing trait B_i increases with the relative fitness $F(B_i)$ of trait B_i in environment E. When this prediction is true, the particular hypothesis under scrutiny is supported; when it is false, the hypothesis is weakened and (possibly) falsified.

There are two main ways to test prediction 1. In what we term the *forward approach* (with reference to the arrow in expression 1), the investigator postulates the relevant features of environment E, deduces the relative fitnesses $F(B_i) \ldots F(B_n)$ of observed or assumed variants $B_i \ldots B_n$ in E, and then checks to see if the most frequently observed behaviors are the ones postulated to have the highest fitnesses (Fig. 15.1). In the *backward approach* (again with reference to the arrow in expression 1), the investigator first determines the frequencies of the alternative behaviors in E, then measures their relative fitnesses in the same E, and finally checks to see if the most frequently observed behaviors indeed are the ones with the highest fitnesses (Fig. 15.1). An important "submethod" of the backward approach involves measuring different components of fitness separately to determine if the component accounting for the principal advantage of the favored behavioral strategy is the one predicted by the specific selectionist hypothesis being tested.

To see the differences between the forward and backward approaches more clearly, let's try a thought experiment. Imagine that the question of interest is why so many people use tobacco. Applying the forward approach, we might hypothesize that our brains were designed by selection to detect successful risk takers who, it may be supposed, were more attractive to members of the opposite sex than were cautious individuals in the selective environments of the Pleistocene (perhaps because successful risk taking was an honest indicator of genetic quality). To assess this possibility we might observe whether people (especially men) are more likely to smoke when members of the opposite

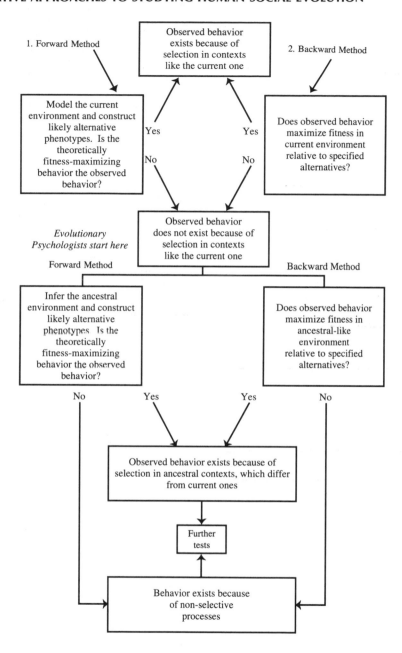

Figure 15.1. An idealized methodological flow-chart for answering phenotype-existence questions of the form "why do we observe certain traits rather than others today?" Either (1) or (2) are appropriate starting points for evolutionary analyses. Investigations that begin at (1) follow what we term the forward approach (with respect to the arrow in text expression [1]), and those that begin at (2) follow the backward approach (again with respect to text expression [1]). All studies in this section of the book use, essentially, the forward approach to analyze human social evolution, starting at the indicated (middle) box. Many of the studies in the other two sections use the backward approach. The forward and backward methods are complementary, and neither supersedes the other; indeed, each approach is useful under different circumstances (see the text). Application of both approaches results in maximal use of available information, and yields the most comprehensive understanding.

sex are nearby, or we might give them questionnaires designed to reveal the circumstances in which they are likely to smoke.

Using the backward approach, we would investigate tobacco use in a different way. First we might look for correlations between the frequency and type of tobacco use (cigarettes, pipes, snuff, etc.) and lifetime reproductive success across cultures; or we might compare the reproductive success of the same individuals (or some correlate of it) as smokers and nonsmokers. Positive correlations would imply that smoking is adaptive, and would encourage further studies to determine why. As one possibility, perhaps smoking is favored by sexual selection, either because the habit drives away rivals of the same sex or because it increases individuals' attractiveness to members of the opposite sex (e.g., by showing that they can successfully take health risks, or making them appear older, more sophisticated, etc.).

Negative correlations with fitness would imply that smoking is maladaptive. In this case the frequency of the behavior must be due to some nonselective cause—such as recent proliferation in the availability of smoking materials and physiological susceptibility to addiction, the underlying mechanisms of which evolved in another context. Indeed, Bailey (1985, cited in Symons 1990) blamed the recent introduction of tobacco and cannabis into the environment of Efe Pygmies for the negative correlation he found between the frequency of smoking by men and their numbers of wives.

This example reveals that the forward and backward methods are compatible, indeed complementary, ways of evaluating prediction 1. Both assume a phenotype set and an environmental context, and both employ some kind of fitness criterion, at least implicitly. They differ primarily in whether the test concludes with measuring fitnesses (backward method) or with observing behaviors (forward method). If a test of a particular selectionist hypothesis fails using either the forward or backward approach, the frequency of the behavior must be due to selection in a context different from the present one (e.g., if the environment recently changed), or to some nonselective process such as migration, drift, or lack of genetic variation.

THE FORWARD APPROACH IN EVOLUTIONARY PSYCHOLOGY

All six studies in this section employed the forward method of hypothesis testing (Fig. 15.1), and they illustrate its potential and power. For example, Daly and Wilson (chapter 16) predicted that child abuse, or the psychological mechanism(s) underlying "discriminative parental solicitude," is likely to have been adaptive (or least likely to have been maladaptive) in ancestral human societies when victims were unrelated to the abuser. Daly and Wilson searched the records of children's aid societies in Hamilton, Ontario, and discovered that abuse is significantly more common in households with one stepparent (particularly a male stepparent) than would be expected if abuse were random with respect to family composition. Daly and Wilson argued that this is consistent with their Darwinian hypothesis (but see Alexander 1988).

Also employing the forward method, Ellis and Symons (chapter 20), Buss (chapter 18), and Kenrick et al. (chapter 22), respectively, hypothesized differences between men and women in sex-related fantasies and mate choice criteria that they presumed would have been adaptive in Pleistocene environments, and used data obtained from questionnaires to argue that the fantasies and preferences of the sexes today accord with sexual selection theory. Likewise, Thornhill and Thornhill (chapter 24) hypothesized that "in human evolutionary history raped females had increased fitness as a result of mental pain, because the pain forced them to focus attention on the fitness-reducing circumstances surrounding rape." These investigators analyzed victims' reports and found that married and reproductive-aged women were most severely traumatized. They argued that since rape has especially negative effects on the inclusive fitnesses of such women, "our analysis of the psychological pain of rape victims . . . is pointing to some design features of the psychological adaptation regulating mental pain" (228).

Finally, Cosmides and Tooby (chapter 26) used reciprocal altruism theory (e.g., Axelrod and Hamilton 1981) to predict that our ancestors should have evolved to detect violations of social conventions when those violations were interpretable as cheating on a social contract.

They used cleverly constructed questionnaires about social scenarios that differed subtly one from another to explore the sensitivity of undergraduates to hypothetical violations of certain conditional rules. The results led Cosmides and Tooby to conclude that "the algorithms governing reasoning about social contracts include inference procedures specialized for cheater detection . . . [but] they do not include altruist detection procedures" (276).

PROBLEMS IN EVOLUTIONARY PSYCHOLOGY

The forward approach to hypothesis testing has obviously yielded many interesting insights, but is it the best (or only) way to investigate human social evolution? In what follows we will explore this question.

Is the Forward Method Superior to the Backward Method?

The authors of all six studies in this section interpreted their results from a Darwinian perspective, yet none actually measured the reproductive successes of any of the behavioral variants they studied. Failure to address fitness consequences is obviously not sufficient reason to dismiss the authors' conclusions, however; as we have argued, the forward approach is a legitimate method of evolutionary inquiry. A more subtle issue is whether the successes of these forward-method studies raise doubts about the usefulness of the converse (backward) method for investigating human behavior. In our opinion they do not. Indeed, the many studies in the other two sections of this volume that employed the backward method illustrate the power of that approach. There has been a failure by some practitioners of each method to recognize the value of the other. The resulting *methodology controversy* (e.g., Turke 1990a, 1990b versus Symons 1990; Tooby and Cosmides 1990b versus Smuts 1991) has had the unfortunate consequence of decoupling the forward and backward approaches (see Crawford 1993).

We are behavioral ecologists, one interested primarily in social rodents and the other in social wasps. We, and most of our colleagues, routinely evaluate selectionist hypotheses (i.e.,

prediction 1) using both forward and backward approaches. For example, Sherman and Holmes (1985) and Gamboa et al. (1986) used the forward method in their investigations of kin recognition in Belding's ground squirrels *(Spermophilus beldingi)* and various paper wasps *(Polistes* spp.), respectively. When animals regularly encounter individuals that differ in relatedness, theories of kin selection and optimal outbreeding predict that behavioral mechanisms for identifying relatives should evolve (see Pfennig and Sherman 1995). We, along with many others, have tested this by looking for kin discrimination in the predicted contexts and, based on the results, have developed hypotheses about the cognitive mechanisms that are involved in the recognition process (e.g., Waldman et al. 1988; Reeve 1989).

We both also frequently use the backward method to investigate the adaptive significance of alternative behaviors in nature. The backward approach has helped us to understand, for example, the reproductive advantages and disadvantages of alarm calling and territorial behavior by female Belding's ground squirrels (Sherman 1977 and 1981, respectively), of mate guarding by male Idaho ground squirrels *(Spermophilus brunneus:* Sherman 1989b), and of joint nest founding in paper wasps *(Polistes dominulus:* Nonacs and Reeve 1995).

Sometimes the forward approach is more useful than the backward, or vice versa, depending on the study organism and its circumstances. For example, if the costs of measuring fitnesses are prohibitive, or alternative phenotypes do not exist naturally and would be difficult to simulate experimentally, the forward approach is favored. In contrast, if the critical fitness components within an environmental context are unclear, but alternative behavioral variants exist and their fitnesses are measurable, the backward approach is more useful. Fortunately, neither the forward nor the backward approach is precluded for humans, and the papers in this volume illustrate the value of each method.

Unfortunately, however, the methodology controversy does not totally dissolve once the complementarity of the forward and backward approaches is appreciated. This is because Symons (1990:428–30) and Tooby and Cosmides (1990b:398–99) argued that we are essentially forced to use the forward approach because the "environment of evolutionary adaptedness (EEA)" (Symons 1990:429; E in expression [1]), in which our psychological mechanisms were last in selective competition with alternative "Darwinian algorithms," largely disappeared sometime during the past 1.8 million years (i.e., between the Pleistocene and the present). From this perspective, time, technological innovation, and cultural evolution have eliminated enough of the EEA that, according to Tooby and Cosmides (1989:35), "there is no *a priori* reason to suppose that any specific modern cultural practice is adaptive." If the value of quantifying reproductive success in contemporary environments is questionable, and measuring fitnesses in the EEA is impossible, the best we can do is to infer what the EEA was like and then look for cognitive structures that presumably would have been advantageous in it. By this reasoning, we are essentially constrained to use only the forward approach to study human behavioral evolution.

There are several problems with this line of argument, however. First, it assumes that there is only one EEA to be inferred. But during the past 1.8 million years there likely has been a series of EEAs, changing as human social groups grew in size and developed languages, means of symbolic communication, technologies, and so on. How can we pinpoint the EEA in which any particular cognitive structure was favored? Second, if it were true, then our power to understand the adaptive significance of human behaviors or cognitive structures using *any* approach would be diminished. The conclusiveness of tests of prediction 1 using the forward method depends critically on our ability to reconstruct key features of the appropriate EEA. If this EEA is largely gone, and there are only fragmentary fossil or artifact records with which to reconstruct it, it will be difficult both to specify alternative phenotypes and to assign relative fitnesses to them with any confidence. This would be less of a problem if we were only interested in clearly defined, plausible alternative behaviors with fitnesses that were easily ordered in a wide range of environments. To the extent this is true, however, the selectively important features of the EEA should not differ much from those of today's environments— which, in turn, makes the backward method a potentially useful procedure again.

It might be argued that we actually do know a lot about EEAs, based on extensive field studies of traditional societies (e.g., the first section of this volume; also K. Hill et al. 1987; Hill and Hurtado 1996), since these probably resemble the ancestral social groups in which our psychological tendencies were naturally selected. If this is true, then it would also be appropriate to employ the backward method to analyze fitness consequences of behavioral differences in, say, various hunter-gatherer societies. Thus, to the extent that we grasp the relevant EEA, we likely can learn about human social evolution using both forward and backward approaches. And to the extent that we do not grasp the relevant EEA, neither method will prove very satisfactory.

Symons (1990) and Cosmides and Tooby (1987, 1989) began by assuming that "there is no reason to suppose" current human behaviors are adaptive. Others, such as Alexander (1979) and Flinn and Alexander (1982), began by hypothesizing precisely the opposite, citing human learning abilities and the frequency with which we imitate successful behaviors and do not imitate failures. The most direct way to evaluate these alternatives, obviously, is to apply the backward method—that is, to *measure* the relative reproductive successes of behavioral variants in modern societies. Suppose performance of a particular, prevalent behavior does result in higher reproductive success than any alternative behavior. This outcome would imply that (1) the differential reproduction of genes (or memes) led to the high frequency of the behavior because only selection theory predicts this outcome (Reeve and Sherman, 1993); or (2) those aspects of Pleistocene and modern social environments in which the behavior functions are less different than might be supposed; or (3) some generalized learning mechanism likely exists that enables individuals to track changing reproductive consequences of behaviors (Flinn and Alexander 1982).

Symons (1992:155) and Tooby and Cosmides (1990b:399) claimed, as have some others (e.g., Armstrong 1991), that explanations of behaviors based on their present consequences for survival and reproduction mix up current fitness effects with functions in the past. Dewsbury (1992:97) agreed, stating the undeniable point that "events cannot cause events that precede them." Therefore, "it is illogical for evolutionary biologists to appeal to present advantages as an explanation for present adaptations," as Tooby and Cosmides (1990b:420) put it. The problem with these arguments is that they fail to appreciate the power of the backward approach for testing selective hypotheses. Finding that the prevalent behavioral variant maximizes current fitness strongly supports the hypothesis that this variant persists due to selection in environments like the current one. There is no implication from this logic that events precede causes (for further discussion see Betzig 1989b; Alcock and Sherman 1994).

Symons (1990:431) further argued, "To conclude that the measurement of differential reproduction illuminates adaptations from the premise that adaptations were produced in the past by differential reproduction is simply a *non sequitur*." We agree that just because a behavior was favored by natural selection in antecedent environments does not necessarily imply that it will improve its bearers' fitness today, but this obviously does not mean that measuring present-day reproductive differentials cannot in principle illuminate adaptations (see Reeve and Sherman 1993).

There is another way in which the backward approach can be illuminating. Howard (1979, 1988) suggested that current fitness can be partitioned into components that differ in their "proximity" to the bottom-line currency of lifetime reproductive success. Among men, for example, fitness components that become increasingly distal to numbers of children sired in a lifetime are (1) number of different sex partners and copulatory frequency with each, (2) ability to attract women and maintain relationships with them, (3) ability to control resources attractive to women, and so on. Even if an observed behavior does not enhance lifetime reproductive success today, it would be useful to know which of these increasingly distal fitness measures is no longer maximized by the behavior. The point at which the behavior becomes "disconnected" from offspring production may yield information both on the recency of the decoupling and on how the two became decoupled. Knowing the most proximal fitness measure at which reproductive success is apparently maximized for one behavior also opens the door to using the same measure as a probe to test selective hypotheses for other behaviors, again by applying the backward method.

For example, Pérusse (1993) reported a strong positive correlation between social status (based on income, education, and occupational prestige) and mating success among contemporary Canadian men. However, he found no association between status and the number of children the men acknowledged siring. Pérusse argued that the number of potential conceptions (estimated from the copulatory frequencies and numbers of sex partners the men reported) is the best measure of fitness under the novel social conditions imposed by monogamy and widespread contraception. Pérusse's results imply that status-seeking behavior was selectively favored among men (and, for that matter, it still may be, depending upon respondents' veracity about numbers of sex partners and knowledge of paternity). The point at which status seeking apparently becomes disconnected from offspring production is just proximal to copulatory frequency. This suggests that status-seeking behavior was favored among Canadian men until recent cultural forces uncoupled copulation from conception. Male status-seeking behavior was (Low and Clarke 1992) and still is (e.g., Turke and Betzig 1985) favored by sexual selection in some societies in which polygyny is sanctioned and contraceptives are not widely available.

As another example of how the backward approach could be useful, consider a hypothetical extension of Thornhill and Thornhill's (1990a) study. One prediction might be that a positive or concave relationship should exist between the intensity of rape victims' psychological pain and their lifetime reproductive success, controlling for age and marital status when the assault occurred. Confirmation of this prediction would strongly support Thornhill and Thornhill's hypothesis; disconfirmation would mean either (1) that the hypothesis is wrong or (2) that the fitness measure is no longer appropriate because of a changed environment. The second possibility could be assessed by using several increasingly "distal" fitness measures (e.g., male parental solicitude toward spouse's offspring before and after rape). Alternatively, the intensity of rape-induced psychological pain could be correlated with lifetime reproductive success in present-day traditional societies.

In sum, the forward approach alone cannot answer all interesting questions about human social evolution. Attempts to support the use of the forward approach to the exclusion of the backward are therefore misguided. The most powerful tests of evolutionary hypotheses will probably result when both approaches arc applied.

Can We Correctly Identify Selective Contexts and Predict What Behaviors Will Be Adaptive in Them?

A critical step in applying the forward approach is ranking the relative fitnesses of all known or assumed behavioral variants (see Figure 15.1). The correctness of any such ranking depends on identifying the appropriate selective context. Forward-method tests of selective hypotheses frequently must deal with difficulties in specifying selective environments, especially if these environments have changed (see Reeve and Sherman 1993). Two special problems confront applications of the forward approach to humans. These were at the heart of some severe attacks on human sociobiology (e.g., Gould 1980; Kitcher 1985)—ample reason for taking them seriously. First, if the relevant ancestral environment no longer exists, how can we know if we have correctly derived the relative fitness rankings? Second, since all investigators who apply the forward method to humans are members of the study species, they "already know" how humans behave and what underlying feelings they possess. The danger is that this knowledge might conceivably (and unconsciously) lead to descriptions of the selective context *(E)* which guarantee that the "right" behaviors are "predicted".

Consider, for example, Ellis and Symons's (chapter 20) study. They used basic sexual selection theory (e.g., Trivers 1972) to derive several predictions about sex-related differences in erotic fantasies. In particular, they hypothesized that females should emphasize partner quality more than males and partner variety less, based on reasoning that "in ancestral populations, a female's reproductive success probably depended in large part on her mate's quality," as determined by "physical and psychological characteristics indicative of good genes, by signs of current or future political and economic success, and by signs of sincere interest in the particular female who was doing the choosing" (chapter 20:197). To our knowledge, there is no evidence for "good genes" mate preferences in humans, nor that women's reproductive success

was or is determined by any of the factors highlighted by Ellis and Symons. However, it is certainly plausible that females should emphasize mate quality and males mate quantity, based on what we know about the mating systems of most mammals, including humans in current and ancient times (e.g., Betzig et al. 1988; Betzig 1992c).

Less compelling is Ellis and Symons's prediction that visual images will be the primary foci of men's sexual fantasies. As justification, they state that "female mate value is more reliably correlated with (and thus more readily detected by) specific visible characteristics than male mate value is" (chapter 20:198). No evidence is provided to support this claim, however. The validity of Ellis and Symons's tests, and the validity of the forward method in general, depends on evidence about the critical features of selective environments that yield different fitness rankings (in this case, for the roles of visible characteristics of men versus women).

The solution to these problems is straightforward, albeit difficult: independent evidence must be obtained that the assumed selective environment *(E)* is the correct one, and procedures for ranking the relative fitnesses of behavioral variants in *E* must be clearly stated and justified. Fortunately, there are several ways to proceed. First, independent data sets that support predictions of multiple forward tests involving different phenotypic sets in a common *E* can provide reinforcing evidence that the selective environment has been correctly identified. For example, finding that during courtship women invest more in improving their physical appearance than do men, together with Ellis and Symons's evidence that men fantasize more about their partner's physical characteristics than do women, would increase our confidence in the assumption that use of visual cues is more beneficial to males than to females.

A second and more powerful way of verifying the critical features of the assumed selective environment involves predicting—and confirming—the occurrence of different behaviors by individuals in contexts differing in the hypothetically important feature. Several nice examples appear in this section. The studies of Ellis and Symons (chapter 20), Buss (chapter 18), and Kenrick et al. (chapter 22) in effect tested for predicted differences in sexual fantasies and mate choice, respectively, according to the context of sex (male or female); Thornhill and Thornhill (chapter 24) predicted and found differences in psychological pain following rape among nonreproductive-aged versus reproductive-aged women and married versus unmarried women; Daly and Wilson (chapter 16) examined child abuse in stepparent versus single-parent households; and Cosmides and Tooby (chapter 26) found differences in abilities to detect violations of conditional rules in logically abstract versus social exchange contexts. In general, the greater the number of contexts that generate unambiguously different predictions about a set of behaviors, and the more finely resolved those predictions, the more powerful will be forward tests of the selective significance of those behaviors.

Do the Predicted Behaviors Actually Occur?

The final step in the forward method of testing evolutionary hypotheses involves checking to see if the most frequently observed behaviors are the ones postulated to have the highest fitnesses (see Figure 15.1). For most nonhuman organisms, this involves field observations and manipulative experiments. Humans obviously present special challenges. In most societies, directly observing behaviors associated with mate choice and mating is difficult or impossible. Such behaviors generally are performed surreptitiously, and attempts to observe and quantify them are likely to be met with hostility.

Among the studies in this section, only Daly and Wilson (chapter 16) assessed the actual performance of the behavior (child abuse) predicted by the hypothesis under test. In the other five cases, investigators relied on oral or written responses to questionnaires. Thus they studied behaviors that may or may not be strongly coupled to the real behaviors of interest. In order to accept the results of these analyses, one must assume that subjects' responses reflect actual behavior in the context posed by the investigator. Buss (chapter 18) tested this assumption and found that verbally reported preferences about ages of potential mates did correlate with actual population-wide age differences between spouses. For the other studies, the link between verbal reports and actual behaviors was merely assumed.

Why should anyone question the existence of such a link? The reason is that verbal behavior is itself a phenotypic attribute subject to selection, not a transparent window into the mind. Whenever someone perceives him- or herself to be interacting with other humans, there is a chance that his or her verbal behavior, however seemingly introspective, is consciously or unconsciously designed to deceive or otherwise manipulate the behavior of receivers, rather than to communicate accurately the person's behavioral predispositions. The evolutionary reasons for viewing communication in this way were set forth by Dawkins and Krebs (1978) and by Harper (1991). Alexander (1987:117–29) and Trivers (1991) have further proposed that <u>selection can favor self-deception</u>, raising the possibility that even "earnest" verbal introspections may not reflect actual behaviors.

If deceit and self-deception are rampant among humans, it is crucial that investigators using the forward method provide, in the manner of Buss (chapter 18), evidential connections between verbal self-reports and the behaviors that are predicted. Indeed, this would seem to be a methodological *requirement* for all research involving questionnaires. These considerations also suggest an interesting and potentially useful research avenue: determining the extent to which the verbal reports of individuals from contemporary traditional societies, which presumably afford more nearly "natural" selective contexts, are reflective of actual behaviors.

What Can We Learn about Brain <u>Mechanisms</u> from Studies in Evolutionary Psychology?

Many evolutionary psychologists regard contemporary human behaviors primarily as indicators of functional design in neural architecture, revealing the potentially adaptive nature of the proximate psychological mechanisms underlying behaviors. According to Symons (1989:135 and 143) "the study of adaptation is the study of phenotypic design" and "design is usually manifested at the psychological rather than the behavioral level." Yet, as many evolutionary biologists have pointed out (e.g., Turke 1990b; Palmer 1992), behavior is what we observe and what directly influences reproductive success. Therefore, Alexander (1990:253) argued, Symons's assertion "is precisely backward: adaptive design is always manifested at the behavioral (or other ultimate phenotypic) level, even if verification or explanation requires (or benefits from) exploration of other epigenetic features, such as underlying psychological, physiological, morphological, and developmental phenomena" (italics in original). Turke (1990a:307) agreed, noting that "behaviors can be adaptations every bit as much as the morphological, physiological, and psychological mechanisms comprising behaviors."

This mechanism controversy revolves around the question of what exactly constitutes a "psychological mechanism." On the one hand, Cosmides and Tooby (1989:93) believe their studies have revealed numerous "highly structured information processing algorithms," the "innate mechanisms" underlying the expression of culture. Many evolutionary psychologists, among them Tooby and Cosmides (1989) and Symons (1989), have agreed with this assessment (see Crawford 1993). On the other hand, Alexander (1990:252) asserted that "Symons (1989) describes not a single physiological or psychological mechanism underlying any adaptive performance by humans, and his insistence that it is not necessary to identify neurophysiological structures to study such mechanisms in humans (as opposed, he says, to grasshoppers!) causes even the identity of such mechanisms to become mysterious."

Five of the six papers in this section appeared after Symons's and Alexander's papers were written. Two of these (i.e., chapters 24 and 26) attempted to link their results to specific psychological mechanisms, but neither identified or described any physiological structures or neural circuitry. Such mechanisms were revealed only in the sense that the range of observed responses imposes a lower limit on the capabilities of the human mind. In fact, we know of no study by an evolutionary psychologist that deals with the physiological substrates or neural hardware underlying particular behaviors or questionnaire responses.

Thus Darwinian algorithms are hypothetical constructs—unseen mental features that are postulated to exist in order to clarify and simplify understanding of the factors controlling

behavior. Hypothetical constructs are just convenient metaphors for organizing knowledge about complex problem-solving behaviors, which may or may not bear any simple correspondence to actual neurophysiological mechanisms. "Darwinian algorithms" and "mental modules" are to evolutionary psychologists what "information-processing mechanisms" are to cognitive psychologists and "kin recognition mechanisms" are to behavioral ecologists.

There is one potential problem with using hypothetical constructs to describe mental mechanisms, however: the temptation to take them too literally. For example, Cosmides and Tooby (chapter 26:288) believe that their research "supports the contention that human reasoning is governed by a diverse collection of evolved mechanisms, many of which are functionally specialized, domain-specific, content-imbued, and content-imparting" and that "the human mind imposes contentful structure on the social world, derived from specialized functional design inherent in its evolved cognitive architecture." Their treatment leaves unclear, however, exactly what constitutes a mental mechanism—or what is lacking when one is absent. Also unclear is how these "modules" are to be individuated; that is, to what extent and in what ways they are hypothesized to be distinct from each other.

How can we be certain that we have discovered a "genuine" brain module? Behaviors that may be described as "highly patterned reasoning performances" are evident in numerous aspects of daily life, but how can we determine if they represent "adaptive design features" or "dedicated brain circuitry"? For example, does the ability of most people to quickly square integers up to about 15^2 in their head indicate a special Darwinian algorithm (e.g., corresponding to the magnitude of the numbers our ancestors dealt with, such as the size of Pleistocene game herds) or memorization of the squared numbers used frequently in daily life? Is it possible that the students sampled by Cosmides and Tooby (chapter 26) were good at detecting cheaters not because they possessed a "cheater detection module" but because in their own lives they had encountered cheaters frequently, had practiced exposing them, and were rewarded for doing so? (One of us was also a Stanford undergraduate, so this suggestion is not totally hypothetical!) It might be interesting to test this by giving the same questionnaires to people who grew up in an egalitarian society where altruism was rampant and cheating rare. Would eighteen- to twenty-two-year-old Hutterites exhibit greater abilities to detect altruists than cheaters? In general, how many different types of social contract scenarios must be examined, how many different age, sex, and cultural groups must be sampled, and how large a sample must be obtained from each to be certain that a particular brain module does or does not exist?

Although Tooby and Cosmides (1989:38), and some others (e.g., Symons 1990; Ellis and Symons chapter 20), apparently believe that they have discovered and modeled the "innate human psychological mechanisms" underlying observable behaviors, in reality any number of different *actual* mechanisms are capable of generating a finite set of behavioral outputs. Indeed, as Alexander (1987:15) noted, "Quite different sets of proximate mechanisms may lead to what appears to be the same goal in different individuals, or to different goals in the same individual at different times and in different circumstances."

It is important to realize that evolutionary analyses can be applied as directly to learned, locally adaptive behaviors, as to unlearned, species-specific behaviors, because natural selection should modify when and how learning occurs just as powerfully as it shapes other aspects of phenotypes (see Lehrman 1970; Alexander 1979). It is unnecessary, therefore, to assume that there is a "universal" human nature or to justify the need for evolutionary analyses by forcing behaviors into the "hardwired" category. Moreover, Wilson (1994) has recently rejected the notion that human brains are wired similarly, citing evidence of adaptive genetic polymorphisms and individual psychological differences in many creatures, including humans. Successful application of the forward method requires no assumptions about any of these issues because the phenotype set can accommodate behaviors that are learned or unlearned, simple or complicated, and panhuman or individually variable.

In sum, the forward approach exemplified by the papers in this section neither assumes nor reveals anything special about the nature or development of brain mechanisms underlying adaptive behaviors. Thus the mechanistic pictures in which Cosmides and Tooby and Symons imbedded their results should not be taken too literally. Studies of the ontogeny of brain mechanisms underlying adaptive behaviors are undoubtedly just over the horizon, but they will almost certainly involve research techniques quite different from those currently employed by evolutionary psychologists.

SUMMARY

The six papers in this section sample a rapidly developing new field known as evolutionary psychology. These papers illustrate the usefulness of what we term the "forward method" of evaluating selectionist hypotheses about human behavior (see Figure 15.1). Many papers in the other sections (see also Low and Clarke 1992; Pérusse 1993) illustrate the converse or "backward method" and how it can yield complementary assessments of the same kinds of hypotheses. The forward and backward methods are broadly applicable, fundamentally equivalent approaches, not mutually exclusive alternatives. The possibility that some human behaviors may currently be maladaptive does not force us to rely solely on the forward approach.

Evolutionary psychologists have made some impressive advances in understanding human social behaviors and their probable adaptive significance. As this field matures, investigators should (1) provide strong, independent evidence that they have identified the correct selective environment and properly ordered the fitnesses of behavioral variants considered in tests of their adaptationist hypotheses; (2) show that verbal or written responses to questionnaires are accurate predictors of actual behavior across cultures; and (3) determine how the behaviors they are studying developed in their subjects, and how they vary with age, socioeconomic status, and other environmental variables before identifying those behaviors as revealing "innate human psychological mechanisms." Evolutionary psychologists would also benefit by adding the backward method of hypothesis development and testing to their methodological toolbox, in view of our arguments and the many advances made by colleagues using that approach, some of which are showcased in this volume.

Acknowledgments. We thank Laura Betzig for inviting our commentary. Richard D. Alexander, Laura Betzig, David M. Buss, Martin Daly, Jennifer Davis-Walton, Randy Thornhill, Paul W. Turke, David S. Wilson, and Margo Wilson and her students commented on a preliminary draft. We thank all these people for helping us to clarify, sharpen, and focus our commentary.

16

Child Abuse and Other Risks of Not Living with Both Parents

MARTIN DALY
MARGO WILSON

N.S. → DISCRIM.

Child-rearing is a costly, prolonged undertaking. A parental psychology shaped by natural selection is therefore unlikely to be indiscriminate. Rather, we should expect parental feeling to vary as a function of the prospective fitness value of the child in question to the parent. One obvious determinant of that value is the certainty or reality of the link of biological parenthood: we thus expect parental feeling to be more readily and more profoundly established with own offspring than in cases where the parent-offspring relationship is artificial. When people are called upon to fill parental roles toward unrelated children, we may anticipate an elevated risk of lapses of parental solicitude. This has been our rationale for investigating the risk of child maltreatment by stepparents.

Wilson, Daly, and Weghorst (1980) reported an elevated risk of child abuse in stepparent homes in the United States. For children under 3 years of age, the risk in a stepparent-plus-natural-parent household was estimated to be 6.9 times that in a two-natural-parent household. This ratio of risks declined with the child's age, but stepparent households were still estimated to be more than twice as risky as natural-parent households for the oldest children.

Several problems attended these analyses, however. The U.S. census bureau does not discriminate natural and substitute parents, so that the prevalence of various household types in the population-at-large had first to be estimated. These estimations required several assumptions (which were made conservatively so as not to underestimate the incidence of step-relationships and thereby overestimate their risk; see Wilson, Daly, and Weghorst 1980; Daly and Wilson 1981a). The abuse sample itself consisted of validated case reports to the American Humane Association from 29 states with a variety of reporting practices, so that the definition of the criterion variable was imprecise. We were furthermore concerned whether the effect might be due in part to a confound with socioeconomic status, a concern since laid to rest by Bachrach's (1983) finding that there is no appreciable confound between step-relationships and income.

Other research approaches have verified the phenomenon of stepparental violence by direct comparisons between criterion groups. Fergusson, Fleming, and O'Neill (1972), for example, compared two groups of children treated in New Zealand hospitals—those with injuries appearing to have been inflicted intentionally versus those whose injuries were apparently accidental. The former children proved more than twice as likely to reside with a stepparent as the latter. Daly and Wilson (1981b) analyzed data from a sample of 177 Canadian households to which police had been called to quell a disturbance involving a juvenile. A stepparent resided in 48% of those households in which there was evidence of physical abuse of the juvenile, compared to 21% of those in which there was not. In a study of identified abusive families in Pennsylvania, Lightcap, Kurland, and Burgess (1982) found that abusive stepfathers typically spared their natural children within the same household. All these studies clearly implicate stepparenthood in child abuse, but do not, of course, address the epidemiological question of relative rates of victimization in step- vs. natural-parent households.

To characterize the stepparent risk effect better, more intensive, local study seems necessary. One can select a sample of relatively severe abuse cases known to the local child welfare agencies, and one can conduct the requisite survey of household compositions in the appropriate base population served by those agencies. One can furthermore assess whether abuse cases and stepparent households are both unusually prevalent in low-income districts within the reporting area, and thus deal directly with the hypothesis that high abuse risk in stepparent households might be an incidental consequence of an economic confound.

In an intensive study it is possible, moreover, to assess the relationship between household composition and *other* negative outcomes for children. This should be of interest for at least two reasons. In the first place, physical abuse is only one extreme manifestation of the relative maltreatment of nonbiological children that we expect on theoretical grounds. Subtler evidences of disadvantage might be widely manifested in measures of children's performance and welfare. In the second place, we have suggested that the statistical association between stepparenting and child abuse is attributable to stresses engendered by the stepparent-stepchild relationship per se, but it remains possible that the high risk in stepparent households merely reflects a general syndrome of broken homes, bad rearing environments, and bad outcomes. Were that so, we might expect that various household types would exhibit consistent ranking with respect to risks of various negative outcomes. If, on the other hand, abuse risk is higher in stepparent households than in single-parent households whereas the reverse holds for other risks, the argument would be strengthened that step-relationships per se constitute a threat to children rather than being incidentally correlated with some syndrome of disadvantage. The study reported here represents a first such effort to quantify various risks to children as a function of the identity of the person(s) *in loco parentis*.

The present study also permits analysis of abuse risk as a function of maternal age. Parents are expected to value and invest in dependent offspring increasingly as their own reproductive value declines (e.g., Pugesek 1981). In keeping with this expectation, the probability of infanticide declines with the age of Canadian (Daly and Wilson 1984) and Ayoreo (Bugos and McCarthy 1984) mothers. If the risk of child abuse is decreased by factors associated with increased maternal solicitude, then abuse, like infanticide, should be observed to decline with maternal age.

METHODS

Study Locale

The regional municipality of Hamilton-Wentworth is a predominantly urban, heavily industrialized area of 1113 sq km, with a population of 411,445 in 1981 (Statistics Canada 1982), situated at the western end of Lake Ontario.

Regional Population-at-Large Survey

In order to estimate the household compositions of children in the population-at-large, we conducted a telephone survey between August and November, 1983. Telephone interview was chosen as a survey method on the basis of its economy and its superior response rate (Groves and Kahn 1979). Only about 2% of urban Canadian households lack telephones (personal communication from R. T. Ryan, Special surveys, Statistics Canada).

A sample of 2000 telephone numbers was generated as follows. Three-digit exchanges in the region were selected in proportion to their representation in regional telephone listings. The final four digits were then generated at random, a technique designed to make unlisted and listed numbers equally likely to be sampled. The 2000 numbers were called in random order. Each number was called back until either it had been reached or eight unsuccessful calls had been made; the eight calls always included at least one weekday morning, one weekday afternoon, one weekday evening, and one Saturday call, and were spaced over an interval of at least 1 week. If a child answered, the interviewer asked to speak to a resident adult.

When the telephone was answered, the interviewer said,

Hello. This is Dr. Martin Daly (or Dr. Margo Wilson), calling from the Psychology Department at McMaster University. We're conducting a study of the living arrangements of children in the Hamilton-Wentworth region, under sponsorship of Health & Welfare Canada, and I'm calling a random sample of households in the region. Your number was generated by a computer, so I don't know who I'm talking to, but if anyone 17 years old or younger lives in your home, then I'd like to ask you just a couple of anonymous questions if I might.

If the respondent concurred, the interviewer continued,

Thank you. What we're trying to find out is what proportion of children in the region live with what sorts of relatives and nonrelatives. For example, no one knows what proportion of children of a given age live with a substitute parent such as a stepparent. You'd think you could find out from the census, but the census bureau doesn't ask the detailed relationships of children to the people they live with. So that's what we're trying to find out and the information is entirely anonymous. I don't want to know anyone's name. Okay?

The interviewer then asked the number of persons living in the home, their ages, sexes, and relationships to one another, verifying the latter explicitly (e.g., "So the two children are the natural offspring of your husband and yourself? Is that correct?"). Finally the interviewer said,

One last question. We try to place our respondents by the general area in which they live. I wonder if you could tell me either your postal code or a nearby street intersection.

The interviewer then thanked the informant and rang off. The typical interview lasted 2–3 minutes. Those few respondents who wished to verify the interviewer's identity were directed to call the psychology department through the university switchboard.

Hamilton-Wentworth is divided into 115 census tracts. Canadian postal codes specify addresses within a block or less, so that the request for a postal code or nearby intersection enabled us to place respondents by census tract. The median family income for a respondent's census tract, according to the 1981 census, was then used as an index of socioeconomic status. Census tracts were categorized as "high income" (mean family income above the median census tract) or "low income" (below the median).

Child-Abuse Sample

The two children's aid societies of Hamilton-Wentworth (CAS and Catholic CAS) each provided us with data on the living arrangements of abused children, recording on a form the age, sex, relationship to the focal child and the duration of dwelling with the focal child, for each person dwelling in the same household with the focal child. The sample of children consisted of all those active cases that had been designated "abuse" cases for purposes of the Ontario Child Abuse Registry, during a 12-month period ending in mid-1983. All the cases were well known to society workers from repeated calls, and most of the children had been taken into protective care, at least temporarily, at one time or another. Altogether the sample comprised 99 abused children, aged 0–17, living in the region in households of known composition—53 boys, 45 girls, and 1 child of unspecified sex, 46 on the case list of the Children's Aid Society and 53 on that of the Catholic agency.

Police Sample

During the 3-month period of August to October, 1983, Youth Branch officers of the Hamilton-Wentworth Regional Police collected data for the project, recording demographic and household composition information, as above, for each apprehended juvenile. Reports, including the reason for police apprehension, were filed on 542 children residing in the region. Ninety-three were runaways (52 boys, 41 girls); the other 449 (362 boys, 87 girls) were apprehended for a variety of criminal offenses.

RESULTS

Population-at-Large Survey

The sample consisted of 2000 telephone numbers, of which 599 proved to be either business addresses or numbers not in service, leaving 1401 possible households. Of these, 56 (4.0%) were not reached after eight calls, leaving 1345 households contacted. In 17 of these, no English- or French-speaking respondent was available, leaving 1328 potential respondents, of

Table 16.1. Hamilton-Wentworth Population-at-Large Survey, 1983: Responding Households by the Number of Children 17 Years of Age or Younger

Number of Children in Household	0	1	2	3	4	5	6
Number of households	840	168	194	59	19	4	2
Proportion of children		0.200	0.461	0.210	0.090	0.024	0.014

whom 1286 (96.8%) participated in the survey, while 42 (3.2%) refused. The 1286 responding households included 841 children 17 years of age or younger (Table 16.1).

The household types of these 841 children are categorized in Table 16.2 according to the relationship of the person(s) *in loco parentis* to each focal child. The category "stepparent" includes both legally married and common-law spouses of the natural parent. Ages are collapsed into three categories in order that the overall pattern may be discernible without distraction by chance fluctuations.

The distributions of household types did not differ between the sexes: 81.3% of girls and 80.5% of boys lived with two natural parents; 9.6% of girls and 10.3% of boys with a single parent; and 5.7% of girls and 5.8% of boys with one natural and one stepparent.

Telephone survey respondents were classified as living in "high-income" or "low-income" districts according to the mean census tract income. Household circumstances of the two income classes are compared in Table 16.3. Single-parent households are significantly more prevalent in low- than in high-income districts ($X^2_{1\ df} = 14.7$, $p < 0.001$), but there is no evidence that the prevalence of stepparent situations is associated with socioeconomic status.

Child-Abuse Sample

The household circumstances of the 99 abused children on active case lists of the local children's aid societies are summarized in Table 16.4. Comparing these results with those for the population-at-large (Table 16.2), it is evident that abused children lived in circumstances other than with two natural parents far more often than would be expected by chance. In particular, when population-at-large estimates are used to generate expected proportions of household types, single-parent households and stepparent households are both significantly overrepresented in the abuse sample relative to two-natural-parent households, within each of

Table 16.2. Persons *in loco parentis* to Children in Hamilton-Wentworth in 1983, According to Telephone Survey[a]

	Child's Age (Years)		
	0–4	**5–10**	**11–17**
Two natural parents	214 (89.5)	210 (79.5)	263 (77.8)
One natural parent	15 (6.3)	28 (10.6)	39 (11.5)
Mother alone	13	25	31
Father alone	2	3	8
Natural + stepparent	2 (0.8)	17 (6.4)	29 (8.6)
Mother + steppfather	2	16	19
Father + stepmother	0	1	10
Other substitute	8 (3.3)	9 (3.4)	7 (2.1)
Other biological relative	3	2	2
Nonrelative adoptive	5	4	4
Other nonrelative	0	3	1

[a]Entries are numbers of children. Parentheses enclose percentages of children within each age class.

Table 16.3. Persons *in loco parentis* to Children Residing in Census Tracts with Mean Family Incomes Below vs. Above the Median[a]

	Low-Income Districts	High-Income Districts
Two natural parents	303 (77.5)	286 (84.9)
One natural parent	56 (14.3)	19 (5.6)
Natural + stepparent	25 (6.4)	18 (5.3)
Other substitute	7 (1.8)	14 (4.2)

[a]Entries are numbers of children. Parentheses enclose percentages within income-district categories.

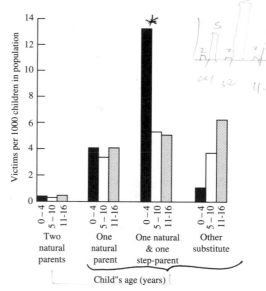

Figure 16.1. Child abuse victimization rates in Hamilton-Wentworth by age and household type. "Victims" are abused children on active case lists of the local children's aid societies.

the three age classes ($p < 0.001$ by binomial test, for each of six comparisons).

The household compositions in Tables 16.2 and 16.4 are combined with census information on the numbers of persons in each age class to produce the victimization rates in Figure 16.1. All household types other than two-natural-parents are high-risk environments for becoming a children's aid society abuse case, especially stepparent households. It is also of interest to express the degree of risk in the various household types relative to risk in a two-natural-parent household (Table 16.5); thus, for example, preschoolers living with a single natural parent are 12.5 times as likely to become registered abuse victims as like-aged children living with two natural parents (first entry in Table 16.5). It is noteworthy that the elevation of risk in stepparent households is maximal for the youngest children.

Census tract information was available for 87 of the 99 abuse cases. Eighty-one (93%) resided

in "low-income" and only six in "high-income" census tracts (whereas only 54% of children in the population-at-large survey resided in "low-income" tracts, according to Table 16.3).

Police Samples

Youth Branch of the Hamilton-Wentworth Regional Police filed data forms on 542 apprehended juveniles residing in households (as op-

Table 16.4. Numbers of Abuse Victims by Age and Household Type[a]

	Child's Age (Years)		
	0–4	5–10	11–17
Two natural parents	8 (42.1)	7 (21.2)	13 (27.7)
One natural parent	7 (36.8)	11 (33.3)	16 (34.0)
Mother alone	7	11	15
Father alone	0	0	1
Natural + stepparent	3 (15.8)	11 (33.3)	14 (29.8)
Mother + steppfather	2	8	11
Father + stepmother	1	3	3
Other substitute	1 (5.3)	4 (12.1)	4 (8.5)
Biological relative	1	1	1
Nonrelative adoptive	0	1	0
Other nonrelative	0	2	3

[a]Parentheses enclose percentages within each age class.

Table 16.5. Risk of Appearing in the Child Abuse Sample by Age and Household Type, Relative to a Child Living with Two Natural Parents.

	Child's Age (Years)		
	0–4	5–10	11–17
One natural parent	12.5	11.8	8.3
Natural + stepparent	40.1	19.4	9.8
Other substitute	3.3	13.3	11.6

posed to institutions) in the region. Ninety-three of these were runaways not accused of any criminal offense. The remaining 449 were accused of a variety of offenses, the most common of which (186 cases) was "theft or possession of stolen goods valued at less than $200" (Canadian Criminal code s.294; i.e., shoplifting). Rates of apprehension of adolescents aged 11–16, relative to their numbers in the regional population, are presented in Figure 16.2.

Household types of apprehended juveniles are compared in Table 16.6 with the distributions expected from the population-at-large survey. The majority of apprehended juveniles were 14 or 15 years of age; the youngest were two 4-year-olds (one accused of shoplifting, one of breaking and entering). Since household compositions vary by age (Table 16.2), expected frequencies for the apprehended juveniles are computed by weighting age-specific household composition distributions in proportion to the observed age distribution of the criterion group. (Four runaways from institutions and four criminal offenders residing with no one *in loco parentis* are excluded from the analyses in Figure 16.2 and Table 16.6.)

Children from two-natural-parent homes are far less likely to be apprehended as runaways than children from any other household type. Similarly, there is an elevated risk of arrest for criminal offenses for all other household types in comparison to two-natural-parent households, but this elevation is much greater for single-parent households than for substitute-parent households, a reversal of the pattern with abuse risk (Table 16.5). Cases of violence towards persons (44 "assaults," including 8 sexual assaults) show a pattern of risk by household type that is not different from that for other criminal offenses.

Census tract information was available for 83 runaways and 420 criminal offenders. Sixty-

four (77%) of the runaways and 296 (70%) of the criminal offenders lived in "low-income" tracts.

Average Relatedness of Focal Child to Cohabitants

The categorization of household types according to the persons *in loco parentis* ignores such complications as the possible presence of grandparents, distant relatives, or nonrelatives not *in loco parentis*. On theoretical grounds, we might anticipate greater conflict between, say, half-siblings than full-siblings (Holmes and Sherman 1982) or greater risks to children in households containing unrelated stepsiblings. As an index of such capacity for conflict, we computed the average degree of relatedness of each focal child to all other members of its household. Results are presented in Figure 16.3. The criminal-arrest group shows an average relatedness to household members similar to that of children in the population at large. Abuse victims and runaways, however, are substantially less closely related to other household members. The reduced average relatedness of the latter two groups is not due to a greater presence of relatives of degree less than 0.5 (i.e.,

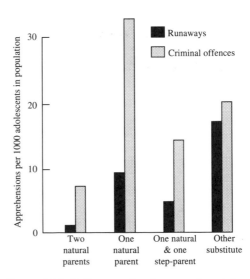

Figure 16.2. Police apprehension rates for adolescents (ages 11–16 years) in Hamilton-Wentworth by household type.

Table 16.6. Observed Household Circumstances of Juveniles Apprehended by Police in Comparison to the Expected Distributions of Household Circumstances Given Those of Like-aged Juveniles in the Population at Large

	Observed	Expected	Risk relative to two-natural parent home
Runaways			
Two natural parents	29	72.0	
One natural parent	36	10.1	8.9
Natural + stepparent	13	4.4	7.4
Other substitute	11	2.5	10.9
$\chi^2_{3\,df} = 138.4\ p < 0.0001$			
Criminal Offenses			
Two natural parents	225	358.2	
One natural parent	162	46.2	5.6
Natural + stepparent	45	29.8	2.4
Other substitute	13	10.8	1.9
$\chi^2_{3\,df} = 331.8\ p < 0.0001$			
Assaults (a subset of criminal offsenses)			
Two natural parents	23	35.4	
One natural parent	15	4.6	5.0
One natural + one stepparent	5	2.9	2.7
Other substitute	1	1.1	1.4

relatives other than parents and full siblings), but rather to a greater presence of persons of no blood relation whatever. Of the abuse victims, 36.4% lived with one or more nonrelatives compared to an age-weighted expected value (i.e., for like-aged children in the population-at-large) of 10.6%. Of the runaways, 25.8% lived with one or more nonrelatives compared to an age-weighted expected value of 12.2%.

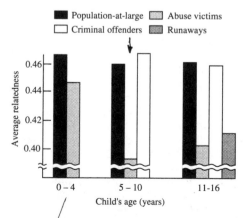

Figure 16.3. Average relatedness of focal child to all household cohabitants.

Effect of Maternal Age

The distribution of maternal ages at the child's birth (MACB) for the population surveyed by telephone is presented in Figure 16.4 (top). It approximates the distribution expected from 1981 census data (Statistics Canada 1982). For the abuse, runaway, and criminal-offense samples, risk was calculated as a function of MACB by comparing the observed frequencies with those expected on the basis of the population-at-large distribution (Fig. 16.4, bottom). In all four data sets (population at large, abuse, runaways, criminal offenders), only children still residing with their natural mothers are included, since natural mothers' ages were not otherwise recorded.

Risk of abuse is maximal for children born to young mothers and declines monotonically with MACB. The risk of appearing in the police samples is also maximal for children born to young mothers, but unlike abuse risk, the risk of apprehension declined and then rose again for children born to women in their late 30s and 40s (Fig. 16.4, bottom).

The abuse data for this analysis are based on just 36 cases for which maternal ages were available. (This datum was not recorded by one of the two reporting agencies.) Nevertheless,

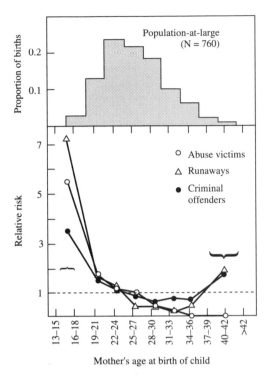

Figure 16.4. Maternal age at birth of child (MACB). Top: frequency distribution of MACB for 760 children according to telephone survey. Bottom: Risks of abuse and police apprehension of children as a function of MACB. "Relative risk" is the ratio of the MACB-specific victimization rate to the average victimization rate overall.

the departure from an expected distribution of maternal ages is highly significant (combining adjacent MACB categories in order to maintain expected values greater than five, $X^2_{4\,df} = 19.7$, $p < 0.001$). The runaways ($N = 73$) and criminal offenders ($N = 425$) each exhibited MACB distributions departing from chance expectation at $p < 0.00001$ (X^2 tests).

In the population at large, children living with two natural parents were born at a mean maternal age of 26.7 years whereas those living with natural mother and stepfather were born at a mean maternal age of 23.6. Since children born to young mothers are both likelier to be abused and likelier to acquire a stepfather, one should test whether the elevation of abuse risk in stepparent households could be an artifact of a causally prior MACB variable. To test

this hypothesis, "expected" distributions of household types were computed for abused children living with their natural mothers, with and without consideration of the MACB variable (Table 16.7). When MACB is used as a predictor, the expected number of stepfather households indeed increases, but only 13% of the observed excess of stepfather households in the abuse sample is accounted for, indicating that the stepparent risk factor is largely independent of the maternal age risk factor.

DISCUSSION

Stepparents and Abuse Risk

The present study provides the most direct evidence to date of a substantial elevation in the risk of child abuse for children living in households other than with the two natural parents, and especially for children living with a stepparent. We are not talking about a small effect: preschoolers in stepparent-natural-parent homes, for example, are estimated to be *40 times* as likely to become abuse statistics as like-aged children living with two natural parents (i.e., about 40 chances in 3000 vs. 1 in 3000; Figure 16.1).

One might hypothesize that abuse in stepparent households is not really more prevalent than in natural-parent households, but is just more often detected or reported. Wilson and Daly (1987) examine this hypothesis and reject it; their most telling argument is that detection and reporting biases should be least influential with the most severe forms of abuse, and yet that is where stepparent overrepresentation is maximal.

Homes other than those with two natural parents are high-risk environments for all the problems investigated here (abuse, running away, and criminal arrest). But more than this, the presence of a stepparent is shown to be a specific risk factor for child abuse. In this study, children from stepparent homes were actually slightly less likely than those from single-parent homes to run away (cf. Rankin 1983) or to be arrested for a criminal offense, but they were much more likely to be abused.

The present study also strengthens the argument that the stepparent effect is not an artifact of a correlated socioeconomic variable. Giles-Sims and Finkelhor (1984) suggest such a con-

Table 16.7. Household Compositions of Abused Children Living with their Natural Mothers, Compared to Two Model "Expected" Distributions

	Observed	Expected$_1$[a]	Expected$_2$[b]
Two natural parents	28	70.8	66.9
Natural mother alone	33	7.3	8.9
Natural mother + stepfather	21	3.9	6.2

Observed vs. Expected$_1$: $\chi^2_{2\,df} = 192, p < 0.00001$
Observed vs. Expected$_2$: $\chi^2_{2\,df} = 124, p < 0.00001$

[a]Expected$_1$ is proportional to the frequencies of the three household types in the population at large.
[b]Expected$_2$ incorporates effects of maternal-age-at-child's-birth (MACB), by weighting MACB-specific household composition distributions in proportion to the MACB distribution of the abuse sample.

found as an explanation for the stepparent-abuse association, pointing to the negative relationship between divorce rate and income as suggestive evidence that step-relationships may be associated with poverty. Bachrach (1983), however, has shown that step- vs . natural- parent relationship was virtually unrelated to family income in the United States in 1976, coincidentally the same year for which Wilson, Daly, and Weghorst (1980) analyzed abuse data. Similarly, in the present study, step-relationships in the Hamilton-Wentworth region proved not to be exceptionally prevalent in lower socioeconomic strata (Table 16.3). Low income *is* associated with abuse in the present study, as in previous ones (e.g., Pelton 1978), but the stepparent effect is not an incidental consequence of this fact.

It remains possible that step-relationships are correlates of some noneconomic sort of "disadvantage" which is the real cause of elevated abuse rates. For example, there is some evidence that abusive parents were themselves abused as children (e.g., Egeland 1987), and such experience might also be associated with high rates of marital breakup and reconstitution. In a related argument, Giles-Sims and Finkelhor (1984) propose that there may be a higher proportion of people with violent dispositions among remarried people than among first-marrieds, and that the stepparent-abuse connection might be a spurious result of this confound. But this hypothesis, and indeed any other that invokes cross-situational personality characteristics of abusers, cannot account for the fact that abusive stepparents are discriminative. Lightcap, Kurland, and Burgess (1982) found that only the stepchildren were abused in each of ten Pennsylvania cases where there were also children of the present marriage. Similarly, in the present study, the abuse sample included ten households in which children of the present marriage and stepchildren resided together. Only the stepchildren were abused in nine of the ten, while in the exceptional case, a stepchild and a child of the present marriage were both victims. In neither study was any child of the present marriage abused while a stepchild was spared, which should be equally likely under a null hypothesis that the step-relationship per se is irrelevant.

Yet another possible confound is family size. Abuse rates for children with either no cohabitant siblings or with three or more were higher in the present study than the rates for children with exactly one or two. However, the distribution of family sizes did not differ between stepparent and natural-parent households, so that this factor cannot account for the stepparent effect either. Moreover, the analysis presented in Table 16.7 demonstrates that the stepparent effect is not an incidental consequence of the higher abuse risk for children born to young mothers, although this factor may contribute slightly to stepparent household over-representation among the abused. The essentially negative results with all of these possible confounds reinforce the conclusion that stepparenthood per se is a risk factor for child abuse, as theory leads one to expect.

The present results replicate another feature of our earlier American study: the ratio of abuse risk in a stepparent household to that in a natural-parent household declines with the child's age. We have suggested that this phenomenon reflects the greater costliness of assuming a parental role, and hence a greater resentment of the obligation, the younger the child (Daly and Wilson 1981b). Alternatively, stepparents of older children may simply have had longer to establish positive relationships with them. We should like to make the same comparison while confining the sample of step-relationships to newly established ones; we predict that a declining ratio of risk would still be evident, but the data for such an analysis will not be easily gathered. One argument against the familiarity alternative deserves note: in the case of infants, neither natural nor stepparents have had much time to establish positive bonds, and yet it is with this age group that the probability of abuse is most different between the two types of caretakers.

The "Other Substitute" Category

The label "other substitute" encompasses a variety of household types, each too rare to be treated separately. Lumping them all together may have obscured some important distinctions that would warrant analysis in a larger survey.

Nonrelative adoptions (as opposed to adoptions by blood relative or by natural parent plus stepparent) compose most of the "other substitutes" for the population at large (13 of 24), but only one of nine "other substitutes" among the abused children. Thus, if adoptive parents were removed to a separate category, the computed risk of abuse in the remaining "other substitute" households would double. There are many reasons why adoptive parents would be expected to be low-risk "substitutes." Nonrelative adoptions are primarily the recourse of childless couples who are strongly motivated to simulate a natural family experience; rather than having their position *in loco parentis* thrust upon them, they have actively sought it. Applicants to adopt are screened by agencies, and many are rejected as unsuitable. Adoptive households are much wealthier on average than either stepparent or two-natural-parent households (Bachrach 1983). Finally, if the adoption (or the marriage) fails, the couple can return the child, which happens more often than is generally realized (e.g., Kadushin and Seidl 1971).

At the opposite extreme are substitute parents left in charge of children they may never have wanted in the first place. Four of the "other substitute" children in the abuse sample (Table 16.4) resided with a single stepfather, a circumstance that was never encountered among the 841 children in the population-at-large survey. We cannot, of course, compute an abuse rate for this rare household type, but even these few data are sufficient to show that stepfather alone was riskier than natural mother plus stepfather: the natural mother was absent for 4 of 25 abuse victims living with a stepfather vs. 0 of 37 for the population-at-large ($p = 0.023$ Fisher exact test).

The Nature of "Abuse"

A recurring problem for students of child maltreatment is that of definition. Our criterion was the Children's Aid Society's decision that a case warranted inclusion in the provincial registry.

Twenty-eight of the 99 cases were entirely or in part matters of "sexual abuse"—22 of 46 from the Children's Aid Society and 6 of 53 from the Catholic agency. Victims were 23 girls (ages 3–16), 4 boys (ages 7–16) and one 10-year-old of unspecified sex. The Children's Aid Society identified perpetrators in 21 cases; all were men, including three putative fathers and six stepfathers.

It is important to note that the high risk of abuse in stepparent households (Table 16.5 and Fig. 16.1) is not solely or even mainly a matter of sexual abuse. Among preschoolers (in whom the elevation of abuse risk in step-households was maximal) the only two sexual abuse cases resided with a single mother and maternal relatives, respectively. In the 5-10-year-old group, step-households comprised an identical proportion (0.33) of sexual and nonsexual cases. Only among adolescent victims (ages 11–16) was the proportion of natural parent plus stepparent homes higher among sexual abuse victims (0.43) than for nonsexual abuse (0.26). These facts suggest that the decline in "relative risk" from step-parents as a function of the child's age (Table 16.5) might be still more pronounced if attention were confined to nonsexual forms of maltreatment.

"Abuse" as here defined encompasses various acts, and a larger study might usefully distinguish them (cf. Wilson, Daly, and Weghorst 1983). For our present purposes, however, the

Abuse Registry criterion has the virtue of capturing diverse cases with this common denominator: the care being provided by those *in loco parentis* is, in the opinion of child welfare professionals, so poor or unreliable as to imperil the child. We consider such a criterion particularly apt, because psychological constructs such as "child-specific parental solicitude" afford the best level of abstraction for evolutionary theoretical analyses (see Barkow 1984; Daly and Wilson 1987; Symons 1987). What, after all, can most usefully be considered to have evolved by natural selection? Certainly not "child abuse" ! Lenington (1981) erects a straw man when she writes,

although it is possible to present very plausible arguments for the adaptive significance of child abuse, it has not been possible, and would be extraordinarily difficult, to show that individuals who abuse their children are, in fact, increasing their reproductive success. The entire sociobiological argument, in this case, rests on plausibility.

Abusive parents commonly persist in inflicting damage upon their wards, while continuing to invest in them. This is hardly an efficient strategy of parental effort allocation, as Giles-Sims and Finkelhor (1984) correctly note, but they are wrong to conclude that such considerations invalidate a sociobiological approach to stepparental abuse. We agree entirely that chronic abuse lacks the "design features" (Williams 1966a) of an evolved adaptation; it is therefore most unlikely that "individuals who abuse their children are, in fact, increasing their reproductive success." We propose, however, that discriminative parental solicitude (Daly and Wilson 1980, 1981a) *is* an evolved adaptation, exhibiting predictable relationships to several independent variables that were historically predictive of the child's expected contribution to parental fitness, and to several dependent variables including the risk of child maltreatment.

Lapses of parental solicitude include, but are not confined to, direct violence. Neglecting a child and deliberately inflicting injury are certainly different, but both betray a failure of parental love. The caretaker who is truly concerned for a child's welfare will furthermore not normally use that child as a sexual object. There is thus a certain motivational commonality to these diverse acts. Lapses of parental solicitude may also be manifested in reduced protection of the child from third parties; perpetrators of sexual abuse in Hamilton, for example, included neighbors, a stepfather's male friend, and other such nonrelatives (indeed the majority of perpetrators of sexual abuse were not themselves *in loco parentis* to the child).

Variation in the quality of parental protection from third parties raises another point: failures of parental solicitude might in principle be separated into failures of parental inclination (which we have emphasized thus far) and failures of parental capability. This distinction seems especially relevant to the risk of abuse in single-parent households, where money and other parental resources may be in short supply. In the present study, 13 children living with single mothers were abused (seven of them sexually) by identified persons. Men were involved in 11 of these cases, and only 2 were putative fathers of their victims. Thus the threat to children with single mothers appears to be much the same threat as confronts stepchildren: men other than their fathers.

Maternal Age

The decline in abuse risk as a function of maternal age (Fig. 16.4) we interpret as reflecting a tendency for women to value their children more highly as their own reproductive value declines. This is also the interpretation offered by Daly and Wilson (1984) and by Bugos and McCarthy (1984) for a similar decline in the probability of maternally instigated infanticide as a function of maternal age in Canadian and Ayoreo women, respectively. Unfortunately, the analysis of maternal age omitted those cases in which children were no longer residing with their mothers. It seems probable that such cases might also include a disproportionate representation of younger mothers. The somewhat different pattern with respect to the police samples (Fig. 16.4) invites further speculation. Whereas the high risk for children of young mothers may reflect poor supervision and care, the high risk for children of older mothers might also be due to a declining capacity for supervision or alternatively to overindulgence of late-borns.

Population-at-Large Estimates

Several possible sources of error in the estimates derived from the telephone survey warrant consideration. Our advisers at Statistics Canada suggested that only 2% of urban Canadian households lack telephones, and it seems likely that many of these will be childless, but some bias due to this factor is conceivable. The 17 households not included due to language difficulties comprised just 1.2% of contacted households, and we know of no reason to suspect that their exclusion seriously affects any of the estimates. The 56 numbers not reached, comprising just 4% of possible households, are also unlikely to be an important source of error. Some were surely not households; telephone booths are one possibility. Moreover, the proportion of contacted households that contained children declined the more calls it took to reach the number: 37% of households reached on the first call included children, compared to 33% of those requiring two to four calls, and 28% of those requiring five or more. The implication is that relatively few households requiring more than eight calls would include children.

More problematic are the 42 refusals. Although the refusal rate of 3.2% was remarkably low for a survey of this sort, it is certainly possible that refusers differ systematically from respondents. A few people interrupted the introductory remarks to refuse, but almost all refusals came only after "living arrangements of children" had been mentioned. In 16 cases, the conversation before refusal was such as to indicate that there were indeed children in the home, but most refusals were brusque and uninformative. A single respondent was verbally abusive to the interviewer. We have no basis for surmising whether refusals might include a disproportionate number of one household type or another.

Some people may have "refused" deceptively, by falsely stating that no children resided at the number and quickly terminating the interview. The census provides some indirect evidence on the probable frequency of such deceptions. According to the 1981 census (Statistics Canada 1982), the average household in Hamilton-Wentworth contained 0.709 children. For our responding households in 1983, the corresponding figure is 0.654, an apparent 8% shortfall. However, the discrepancy between obtained and expected numbers of children per household must actually have declined between 1981 and 1983, for two reasons. One

has to do with the population's age structure: four people turned 18 (and thus left the "children" category) for every three that were born each year. If the number of persons per household had remained constant from 1981 to 1983, this factor alone should have reduced the average number of children from 0.709 to 0.698. But the second reason why children per household will have declined is that household size itself has been on the decline, a trend that accelerated over several decades prior to 1981. Between 1971 and 1981, the average Canadian household shrank from 3.5 persons to 2.9, mainly because of the increased number of people residing alone (Pryor 1983). If, as seems likely, these trends have continued, then the number of children per household will have fallen still lower. Furthermore, if half of the overtly refusing households contained children, as seems a conservative guess, and if we assume the same 1.89 children per household as for those who reported children, then the estimated number of children per household rises to 0.663. We conclude that deceptive denials of the presence of children were probably few. And as in the case of overt refusals, one can only speculate whether the probability of such a deception might vary according to household type.

Finally, it is of course possible that some of the people interviewed gave false information. The interviewers were especially concerned that substitute parents be correctly identified as such, and always checked relationships by rephrasing the respondent's reply, asking in particular whether these relationships described as parent-to-offspring involved "natural" parents. Inadvertent misinformation therefore seems unlikely, but some respondents may have been deceptive. If some interviewees indeed misrepresented step-relationships as biological, we will have underestimated their incidence and hence overestimated attendant risks. But there is no particular reason to suppose that this occurred, and there could as readily be error leading us to *under*estimate the risks in step-households. One such source of error would arise if mothers living common-law with new mates represented themselves as single in order to retain welfare benefits. The Children's Aid workers doubted that this was a serious problem, stressing their familiarity with the mothers and household circumstances. The police, on the other hand, suggested that some of the women in their sample might have been concealing live-in boyfriends, on the basis of having seen unidentified men at some single mothers' homes. If such men were really residents, then the tendency for single-parent households to be riskier than stepparent households with respect to arrest could be spurious. But again, there is no compelling reason to imagine that women should have been deceptive in this direction.

For the present, our estimated incidences of household types are as good as available for risk estimation. We hope that official agencies, particularly census bureaus, will soon recognize the importance of the distinction between natural and substitute parenthood.

Step-Relationships in Darwinian Perspective

There is a substantial literature on "reconstituted families," ranging from empirical surveys through anecdotes and autobiographical tips to exhortative pop psychology. The prevalent theme is *coping*, and the literature abounds with acknowledgments that step-relationships are stressful. A Darwinian view of the organism suggests that the reason *why* they are stressful is because they demand that all parties overcome their usual inclinations toward nepotistic discrimination. The stepparent has, after all, usually entered into the relationship out of an attraction to the new mate; the stepchild must frequently enter into the remarriage decision as a cost, not a benefit. Whereas satisfying relationships with nonrelatives ordinarily involve careful reciprocity, parental investment is exceptional: parents tolerate a cumulative imbalance in the flow of resources. With all the good will in the world, stepparents may strive to feel the altruism of a natural parent, but they do not always—perhaps do not often—succeed (e.g., Duberman 1975). It is thus not surprising that many professionals have concluded that the

common attempt to simulate a natural parent-offspring relationship is misguided (e.g., Perkins and Kahan 1979; Johnson 1980; Einstein 1982; Turnbull and Turnbull 1983; Mills 1984; Clingempeel, Brand, and Ievoli 1984).

Most writers on step-relationships do not, of course, take a Darwinian view of the organism. The dominant framework is instead to speak of step-parenthood as a "role" and to attribute its problems to ambiguity and "newness" (e.g., Cherlin 1978; Kompara 1980; Giles-Sims 1984): stress is said to result from uncertain and conflicting expectations about what a stepparent can and should do, and will continue until "society" defines the role more clearly. This view must be challenged. Its proponents have not shown that there is greater uncertainty or conflict about roles and duties in stepparent households than in natural-parent households, nor that there is any lesser degree of societal consensus about what duties stepfathers ought to assume than about what duties fathers ought to assume. Neither have they criticized (or apparently even considered) the common-sense alternative view that "well-defined," easy roles differ from "ambiguous," difficult ones in that the former match our inclinations while the latter defy them. Why situate role ambiguity in "society" rather than within the ambivalences of the actors themselves? Finally, the "ill-defined new role" theory evidently predicts that the difficulty attending step-relationships will fade as they become more common and receive more media attention. We are not aware of any evidence that this is happening.

Acknowledgments. We thank Health and Welfare Canada for financial support, R. T. Ryan of Statistics Canada for advice, Susan Abell and staff of the Children's Aid Society of Hamilton-Wentworth, Georgina Gibbons and staff of the Catholic Children's Aid Society of Hamilton-Wentworth, and Staff Sergeants James Galloway and Larry Dawson and the officers of Youth Branch of the Hamilton-Wentworth Regional Police.

17

Cinderella Revisited

MARTIN DALY
MARGO WILSON

Wilson, Daly, and Weghorst (1980) provided the first quantitative evidence that stepchildren are disproportionately mistreated, using American Humane Association data. But we were not confident of the quality of those data. That was our major reason for conducting a more localized study in the city where we live, with better information on the relevant population-at-large and a more severe and consistent abuse criterion. It is this more localized study that is reprinted in this volume.

Even with this improved focus on relatively severe cases of child abuse, our conclusions remained vulnerable to the possibility that the data are not so much a reflection of the differential perpetration of "abuse" in one versus another sort of family as a reflection of differential allegations, detection, or reportage. For this reason, we subsequently turned our attention to the most severe and unequivocal cases: the lethal ones. What we have found, in Canada, in the United States, and in Great Britain, is that the overrepresentation of stepchildren as homicide victims is even more extreme than their considerable overrepresentation as victims of nonfatal child abuse (Daly and Wilson, 1988a, 1988b, 1994b; Wilson and Daly 1987).

A question that is often raised about this differential risk is whether it might be a consequence of the stepparent's late arrival on the scene. This is generally offered as an "alternative" to the Darwinian account. But it would not necessarily challenge that account even if it were true, since it is a hypothesis about the process by which the antipathy or lesser solicitude of stepparents comes to be, rather than an alternative account of the adaptive organization of discriminative parental solicitude. In any event, the limited available evidence indicates that it is probably not true. The first hint can be seen in Figure 16.1 of the reprinted article: the excess risk to stepchildren as compared to genetic children was maximal for the youngest children, and this has proven to be true of homicide risk, too (Daly and Wilson 1988b). Some more direct evidence on this point is provided by Flinn's (1988c) observational study of parent-child interactions in a Caribbean village: stepfathers' interactions with children were more antagonistic than those of genetic fathers, and this was especially true in the rare cases in which the stepfather had dwelt with the child from the time of its birth.

Two published studies have been portrayed by their authors as failures to replicate the finding of elevated rates of abuse of stepchildren. Gelles and Harrop (1991) found that stepparents surveyed by telephone were no more likely to profess to having assaulted their children than were genetic parents, and concluded that reports of differential abuse must be artifactual; we suggest that there is another, more plausible, interpretation. Malkin and Lamb (1994) analyzed the same sort of American Humane Association data as Wilson, Daly, and Weghorst (1980:129) had done and concluded that "biological parents were more rather than less likely than nonbiological parents to abuse severely and to kill rather than cause major physical injuries to their children," but they did not compute per capita rates at all, confining their analysis to log-linear analyses of cross-tabulations within the sample of abuse victims; in fact, the overrepresentation of stepchildren was even greater in the 1984 data set that they analyzed than in the 1976 data analyzed by Wilson, Daly, and Weghorst (1980).

Another possibly contrary result is that of Figueredo and McCloskey (1993), who interviewed a sample of Tucson women, most of whom were victims of domestic violence, and their children, almost half of whom dwelt with stepfathers. Path analysis of "latent variables" produced by a factor analysis of the correlations among a large sample of response items led Figueredo and McCloskey to conclude that "direct effects" of genetic versus step-paternity on child maltreatment were not statistically significant, the association between the two being mediated by nonpaternity's direct effects on violence against the wives, and that this result was contrary to the evolutionary psychological theory of discriminative parental solicitude. It is impossible to discern, however, whether or to what extent stepchildren and genetic children may have been differentially victimized in this study, and an association between stepfatherhood and violence against the wife as well as the child is entirely to be expected from the evolutionary psychological argument (Daly and Wilson 1995).

It is increasingly clear that children have been and are disproportionately exploited and assaulted in a wide range of human societies. Since our Hamilton study was conducted, data from child welfare agency records, homicide cases, hospital admissions, historical archives, cohort studies, ethnographic fieldwork, and victimization surveys have been brought to bear on this issue, showing that stepchildren incur excess sexual abuse, homicide victimization, physical assaults, neglect, illness, injuries both accidental and nonaccidental, and gross mortality (e.g., Creighton 1985; Creighton and Noyes 1989; Daly and Wilson 1988a, 1988b, 1994b; Ferri 1984; Flinn 1988c; Gordon 1989; Gordon and Creighton 1988; Hill and Kaplan 1988; Kim and Ko 1990; Russell 1986; Voland 1988; Wallace 1986).

These results have reinforced our claim that the concept of "abuse," while encompassing many distinct phenomena, was appropriate to the purposes of the reprinted study. Diverse mistreatments share at least one major causal determinant: if parents lack concern for an in-

dividual child's well-being, then all manner of risks to that child are likely to increase. And as we argued in the reprinted study, parents clearly do not cherish stepchildren as their own. There is now a wealth of evidence that step-relationships are not as affectionate or supportive as genetic parent-child relationships and that children of former unions detract from the remarriageability of custodial parents (reviews by Wilson and Daly 1987; Daly and Wilson 1994c). However, we also argued in the reprinted study that stepchildren are not just generically disadvantaged but incur a special risk of violent assault. Recent analyses of the means of killing in filicides by stepfathers versus genetic fathers underline this point. Those killed by stepfathers are especially likely to have been beaten to death, whereas the victims of genetic fathers are relatively likely to have been killed in ways seemingly less indicative of hostility (e.g., by suffocation) and in the context of a paternal suicide (Daly and Wilson 1994b; Wilson and Daly 1995).

The mistreated stepchild is a folkloric staple, the world round (Thompson 1955), but those child abuse researchers who lacked a Darwinian imagination never thought to investigate the issue. It has turned out that the presence of a stepparent in the home is the most powerful statistical predictor of severe child abuse and child homicide yet discovered. The possibility that the presence of stepchildren might be a source of marital conflict and therefore of relevance to the risk of violence against wives was similarly neglected until Daly, Singh, and Wilson (1993) reported that women with children sired by previous partners sought refuge from assaultive male partners at a shelter at much higher rates than those whose children were all sired by the present partner. Again, one might imagine that ordinary human experience would have suggested this hypothesis without the necessity of assistance from a Darwinian perspective. But it did not.

Ten years after our 1985 paper, we still often find it necessary to explain that we are not proposing that abusing or killing a stepchild is or ever was an adaptation. As we noted in the reprinted article, chronic abuse lacks the "design features" of an evolved adaptation, and killing is often, albeit not always, an overreaction that is likely to elicit costly reprisals, even in a nonstate society. What we do maintain is that the complex psychology of discriminative parental solicitude (Daly and Wilson 1988c, 1994a), and more specifically a lesser valuation of one's predecessor's children than one's own, are almost certainly adaptations created by a history of Darwinian selection.

Acknowledgments. We wish to thank the Natural Sciences and Engineering Research Council of Canada, the Social Sciences and Humanities Research Council of Canada, and the Harry Frank Guggenheim Foundation for financial support. We also thank Jennifer Davis-Walton, Nicholas Pound, Catherine Salmon, and Joanna Scheib for valuable comments and criticisms of the 1985 reprinted paper.

18

Sex Differences in Human Mate Preferences: Evolutionary Hypotheses Tested in 37 Cultures

DAVID M. BUSS

Mate preferences acquire importance in at least three scientific contexts. First, they can affect the *current direction* of sexual selection by influencing who is differentially excluded from and included in mating (Darwin 1871). Favored mate characteristics that show some heritability will typically be represented more frequently in subsequent generations. Individuals lacking favored characteristics tend to become no one's ancestors (Thornhill and Thornhill 1983). Second, current mate preferences may reflect *prior* selection pressures, thus providing important clues to a species' reproductive history. Third, mate preferences can exert selective pressures on other components of the mating system. In the context of intrasexual competition, for example, tactics used to attract and retain mates should be strongly influenced by the mate preferences expressed by members of the opposite sex (Buss 1988a). Because of the powerful reproductive consequences of preferential mating, it is reasonable to assume that mate preferences will depart from randomness and evolve through sexual selection (Darwin 1859, 1871; Fisher 1958). This assumption, first advanced by Darwin, has been documented empirically for a variety of nonhuman species (e.g., Bateson 1983; Majerus 1986).

In spite of the importance of mate preferences, little is known about precisely which characteristics in potential mates are valued by human males and females (Buss 1985; Thiessen and Gregg 1980). Particularly lacking are good cross-cultural data. Cross-cultural studies become crucial for testing evolution-based hypotheses that posit species-typical or sex-typical mate preferences. Recent theoretical work by Trivers (1972), Williams (1975), Symons (1979), and Buss (1987) provides a foundation from which specific evolutionary hypotheses about mate preferences can be derived. (See also multiple book review of Symons's *Evolution of Human Sexuality*, BBS 3[2] 1980 and Hartung's "Matrilineal Inheritance" BBS 8[4] 1985.)

Predictions from Parental Investment and Sexual Selection Theory

Trivers (1972) posits that sexual selection is driven in part by different levels of investment by males and females in their offspring (Bateman 1948). In humans and other mammals, male parental investment tends to be less than female parental investment (Fisher 1958; Trivers 1972; Williams 1975). Mammalian fertilization occurs internally within females, as does gestation. A copulation that requires minimal male investment can produce a 9-month investment by the female that is substantial in terms of time, energy, resources, and foreclosed alternatives.

Investment, of course, does not begin with fertilization, nor does it end with parturition. Trivers describes several forms of male invest-

Reprinted with permission from *Behavioral and Brain Sciences* 12:1–14 (1989).

ment. Males may provide mates with food, find or defend territories, defend the female against aggressors, and feed and protect the young. Human males may also provide opportunities for learning, they may transfer status, power, or resources, and they may aid their offspring in forming reciprocal alliances. These forms of male investment, when provided, tend to decrease the investment disparities between males and females (Trivers 1972:142).

Trivers's theory proposes that the sex investing more in offspring (typically the female) will be selected to exert stronger preferences about mating partners. This greater choosiness by the more heavily investing sex exists because greater reproductive costs are associated with indiscriminate mating and greater benefits are associated with exerting a choice. The costs of less discriminating mating will be lower for the sex investing less and the benefits will be greater. In species where investment in offspring by males and females is equivalent, the sexes are expected to be equally discriminating in their choice of mating partners (Trivers 1985).

What mate characteristics might be predicted on theoretical grounds in the selection preferences of females? In species with male parental investment, such as *Homo sapiens* (Alexander and Noonan 1979), females should seek to mate with males who have the ability and willingness to provide resources related to parental investment such as food, shelter, territory, and protection. Trivers's prediction should apply only in contexts where resources can be accrued, monopolized, and defended, where males tend to control such resources, and where male variance in resource acquisition is sufficiently high (Emlen and Oring 1977; Trivers 1972). The hypothesis that females will mate preferentially with males bearing greater gifts, holding better territories, or displaying higher rank has been confirmed empirically in many nonhuman species (Calder 1967; Lack 1940; Trivers 1985; see also Betzig et al. 1988).

These resources can provide (a) immediate material advantage to the female and her offspring, (b) enhanced reproductive advantage for offspring through acquired social and economic benefits, and (c) genetic reproductive advantage for the female and her offspring if variation in the qualities that lead to resource acquisition is partly heritable.

Among humans, resources typically translate into earning capacity. This suggests that females will value characteristics in potential mates that are associated with increased earning capacity, such as ambition and industriousness (Barron 1963; Willerman 1979). These premises, combined with conditions of resource defensibility and high variance in male resource acquisition, produce a specific prediction: Females, more than males, should value attributes in potential mates such as ambition, industriousness, and earning capacity that signal the possession or likely acquisition of resources.

Predictions Based on Fertility and Reproductive Value

For males more than for females, reproduction is limited by access to reproductively valuable or fertile mates (Symons 1979; Trivers 1972; Williams 1975). *Reproductive value* is defined actuarially in units of expected future reproduction—the extent to which persons of a given age and sex will contribute, on average, to the ancestry of future generations (Fisher 1958). *Fertility* is defined as the probability of present reproduction. In human females, reproductive value typically peaks in the mid-teens and declines monotonically thereafter with age. Fertility typically peaks in the early 20s and shows a similar decrement with age (Thornhill and Thornhill 1983). The difference between fertility and reproductive value may be illustrated by contrasting two females, aged 13 and 23. The younger female would have higher reproductive value than the older one because, actuarially, her future reproduction is expected to be higher. In contrast, the 23-year-old female would be more fertile than the 13-year-old because the current probability of reproduction is higher for the 23-year-old.

Both fertility and reproductive value differ across cultures and are affected by factors such as cultural norms, contraceptive practices, and differences in age-specific mortality. In all cultures, however, female fertility and reproductive value are strongly age-dependent (Williams 1975). Thus, age provides a powerful cue to female reproductive capacity—a cue that can be inferred through physical and behavioral attributes or with veridical use of accounting systems.

Males should prefer attributes in potential mates associated with reproductive value *or* fertility, depending on whether males in human evolutionary history have tended to seek long-term or short-term mating partners (Buss 1987; Symons 1979; Williams 1975). Specifically, if males in our evolutionary past have tended to seek short-term mating partners, selection should have favored male preferences for females in their early 20s who show cues that are positively correlated with fertility. If males in our evolutionary past have tended to seek long-term mating partners, selection should have favored preferences for females in their mid-teens who show cues indicative of high reproductive value. Evolutionary theorists differ on which of these hypotheses they judge to be most likely. Symons (1979) argues that males have been selected to find most attractive those females of high reproductive value. Williams (1975), in contrast, predicts a compromise preference between reproductive value and fertility due to the existence of both long-term mating bonds *and* some possibility of divorce and extrapair matings.

Features of physical appearance associated with youth—such as smooth skin, good muscle tone, lustrous hair, and full lips—and behavioral indicators of youth—such as high energy level and sprightly gait—have been hypothesized to provide the strongest cues to female reproductive capacity (Symons 1979; Williams 1975). Sexual attraction and standards of beauty are hypothesized to have evolved to correspond to these features. On this account, males *failing* to prefer females possessing attributes that signal high reproductive capacity would, on average, leave fewer offspring than would males who do prefer to mate with females displaying these attributes.

Female reproductive success, in contrast to male reproductive success, is not as closely linked with obtaining fertile mates. Male fertility, to the degree that it is valued by females, is less steeply age-graded from puberty on than is female fertility and therefore cannot be assessed as accurately from physical appearance. Physical appearance, therefore, should be less central to female mate preferences than to male mate preferences. These premises lead to specific predictions: Males, more than females, will value relative *youth* and *physical attractiveness* in potential mates because of their links with fertility and reproductive value.

DIRECT ?

Predicting that males will value physical attractiveness in females because of its association with reproductive capacity does not negate or deny the existence of cultural and other determinants of standards for attractiveness. Ford and Beach (1951) have documented cultural variability in standards for female attractiveness along the dimensions of plump versus slim body build, light versus dark skin, and emphasis on particular features such as the eyes, ears, or genitals. Symons (1979) suggested that regularity of features, proximity to the population average, and association with status might also have an important influence on attractiveness standards (see also Buss 1987).

The predicted sex differences in mate preferences for youth and physical attractiveness, however, are expected to transcend cultural variations and other determinants of beauty standards. The physical and behavioral cues that signal youth and health and are regarded as attractive should be linked with reproductive capacity among human females in all cultures. These sex differences are predicted to be species-typical among *Homo sapiens*, despite cross-cultural variations in absolute age preferences, the presence or absence of counting systems to mark age, or culture-specific criteria for female attractiveness that are not linked with reproductive capacity.

Prediction Based on Paternity Probability

In mating systems where males invest parentally, selection should favor males who act to insure that their investment is directed toward their own offspring and not the offspring of another male. Sexual jealousy is one mechanism that has been proposed to increase paternity probability (Daly et al. 1982). Male sexual jealousy presumably functions to guard a mate and to dissuade intrasexual competitors, thus lowering the likelihood of alien insemination. Daly et al. (1982) and Daly and Wilson (1988b) present compelling evidence that many homicides and much male violence stem from male sexual jealousy.

Another possible paternity probability mechanism is valuation of *chastity* in a potential mate (Dickemann 1981). Males who preferred chaste females in our environment of evolutionary EEA adaptedness, *ceteris paribus,* presumably enjoyed greater reproductive success than males who were indifferent to the sexual contact that a potential mate had with other males. Prior to the use of modern contraceptive devices, chastity of a potential mate would provide a cue to paternity confidence. Assuming some temporal stability to behavioral proclivities, chastity would also provide a cue to the *future* fidelity of a selected mate. A male failing to express such a preference would risk wasting the time and effort involved in courtship and would risk investing in offspring that were not his (Daly and Wilson 1983; Dickemann 1981).

The association between chastity and probability of parenthood, however, shows a sexual asymmetry. In our environment of evolutionary adaptedness, maternity was never in doubt. A female could be sure that her putative children were her own, regardless of the prior sexual experiences of her mate. This sexual asymmetry yields a specific prediction: Males will value chastity in a potential mate more than will females. Evidence limited to a few cultures exists regarding the importance of a mate's lack of prior sexual experience in mate preferences (Borgerhoff Mulder 1988c; Dickemann 1981a).

It should be noted that this predicted sex difference would be compromised if prior sexual experience by a male provided a cue that signaled diversion of resources away from the female and her offspring (Buss 1988a). To the degree that prior sexual experience by males provides this cue, females should also value chastity in a potential mate.

In sum, three clusters of sex differences in mate preferences were predicted, based on an evolutionary account of differing male and female reproductive strategies. A woman's "mate value" (Symons 1987a) should be determined more by her reproductive capacity. Youth and physical appearance, as powerful cues to this capacity, should be more highly valued by men. Chastity should also be valued because it functions to increase a male's probability of paternity. A man's "mate value" is determined less by fertility and more by the external resources he can provide. Characteristics indicative of one's potential to provide resources, such as earning capacity, ambition, and industriousness, should receive more emphasis in female mate preferences. The following study was designed to test these hypotheses in 37 cultures differing widely in ecology, location, racial and ethnic composi-

tion, religious orientation, political inclination, and nature of mating system.

METHODS

Samples

Thirty-seven samples were obtained from 33 countries located on six continents and five islands, with a total N of 10,047 (see Table 18.1). The samples range in mean age from 16.96 (New Zealand) to 28.71 (West Germany), with an overall unit-weighted mean of 23.05. Sample sizes vary from a low of 55 (Iran) to highs of 500 (mainland China), 566 (Taiwan, Republic of China), 630 (Brazil), 1,083 (West Germany), and 1,491 (mainland United States). All samples but one have Ns exceeding 100. The mean sample size for the 37 samples is 272. Obviously, greater confidence can be placed in the results from the large samples; results from all samples are presented for completeness.

The samples obtained cannot be viewed as representative of the populations in each country. In general, rural, less-educated, and lower levels of socioeconomic status are underrepresented, although there are many exceptions, such as the Soviet Estonian, Gujarati Indian, South African Zulu, Venezuelan, and Santa Catarina Brazilian samples. The 37 samples do represent a tremendous diversity of geographic, cultural, political, ethnic, religious, racial, and economic groups; combined, they are the largest ever obtained on mate preferences.

Sampling techniques varied widely across countries. In Estonia, for example, one subsample consisted of all couples applying for a marriage license at a certain location within a given time span, whereas another Estonian subsample consisted of 200 high school students. The Venezuelan sample was obtained by contacting every fifth house within each of a series of neighborhoods that varied in socioeconomic class. The South African Zulu sample was rural, and questions were read aloud to some subjects. The West German sample was obtained by mail through newspaper advertisements. The New Zealand samples were drawn from three public high schools, two urban and one rural, with subjects differing widely in socioeconomic level. Many were samples of convenience (e.g., university students) and cannot be viewed as representative. The wide variety of sampling tech-

Table 18.1. Sample Sizes and Mean Ages

	Sample Size			Age of males		Age of females	
Sample	Total	Male	Female	Mean	SD	Mean	SD
African							
Nigeria	172	117	55	23.36	3.39	21.13	1.38
S. Africa (whites)	128	47	81	20.88	2.17	19.44	1.28
S. Africa (Zulu)	100	52	48	25.30	9.40	23.53	6.18
Zambia	119	70	49	25.67	7.42	22.60	4.17
Asian							
China	500	265	235	23.37	4.87	22.46	5.29
India	247	103	144	30.46	12.46	24.90	10.92
Indonesia	143	88	55	23.52	3.16	22.76	3.19
Iran	55	28	27	24.14	5.14	22.74	5.70
Israel (Jewish)	473	205	268	25.52	4.26	23.29	3.65
Israel (Palestinian)	109	54	55	23.51	3.79	21.50	3.23
Japan	259	106	153	20.05	1.50	19.37	0.88
Taiwan	566	288	278	21.13	1.85	20.54	1.63
European-Eastern							
Bulgaria	269	127	142	22.28	6.16	23.06	7.04
Estonian S.S.R.	303	153	150	19.12	3.50	18.32	2.64
Poland	240	122	118	21.98	1.97	21.44	1.51
Yugoslavia	140	66	74	21.53	1.55	20.72	1.33
European-Western							
Belgium	145	55	90	23.80	6.23	21.38	5.49
France	191	100	91	25.27	7.29	25.83	7.95
Finland	204	55	149	23.87	4.58	24.60	5.29
Germany-West	1083	530	553	28.29	10.81	29.14	12.40
Great Britain	130	46	84	20.87	3.92	21.09	5.38
Greece	132	67	65	20.72	2.50	18.71	1.46
Ireland	122	55	67	19.60	1.50	19.27	1.31
Italy	101	46	55	27.83	5.32	25.96	5.39
Netherlands	417	177	240	22.74	3.86	21.65	3.31
Norway	134	67	67	22.25	4.10	22.46	4.46
Spain	124	44	80	22.89	2.58	22.75	3.59
Sweden	172	89	83	29.79	9.88	26.70	8.20
North American							
Canada (English)	101	56	45	20.89	2.98	23.05	6.84
Canada (French)	105	34	71	26.00	6.32	25.17	8.16
USA (Mainland)	1491	639	852	19.98	3.45	20.37	4.63
USA (Hawaii)	179	66	113	23.79	7.23	22.76	6.20
Oceanian							
Australia	280	78	202	25.06	8.50	23.12	8.38
New Zealand	151	75	76	17.00	0.79	16.92	0.81
South American							
Brazil	630	275	355	22.84	4.59	21.72	4.47
Colombia	139	61	78	25.89	6.76	24.34	6.03
Venezuela	193	95	98	28.07	7.19	28.52	7.19
Summary	10,047	4,601	5,446	23.49	3.01	22.52	2.67

Note: SD = standard deviation.

niques used tends to increase the generality of consistent results that do emerge by minimizing biasing effects of any particular sampling procedure.

Problems were encountered, and data collection proved difficult and time consuming. In Sweden, many couples do not get married, but instead live together without the official mar-

riage certificate. The instruments had to be modified to reflect this cultural difference. In Nigeria, polygyny is practiced, and so questions had to be added to reflect the possibility of multiple wives. In South Africa, data collection was described as "a rather frightening experience" due to the political turmoil and its violent ramifications. In several countries, mailing the data was delayed for many months, pending approval of central government committees. In one country, after data collection was nearly completed, the study had to be terminated because of a failure to obtain official sanction. Data from this country were never received.

In most cases, data were collected by native residents within each country and mailed to the United States for statistical analysis. The original protocols were requested, and in most cases these were sent. In a few cases it proved impossible to send the original protocols. In these cases, the raw data were transcribed onto coding sheets and sent to the United States. Research collaborators were blind with respect to the central hypotheses.

Measures

Factors in choosing a mate. This instrument consisted of three parts. The first part requested biographical data, including age, sex, religion, marital status, number of brothers, and number of sisters. The second section requested information on the age at which the respondent preferred to marry, the age difference the respondent preferred to have between self and spouse, who the respondent preferred to be older (self or spouse), and how many children were desired.

The third section requested subjects to rate each of 18 characteristics (e.g., dependable character, sociability, chastity, intelligence) on how important or desirable it would be in choosing a mate. A four-point scale was used, ranging from "3" (indispensable) to "0" (irrelevant or unimportant). The 18 characteristics were drawn from a previously developed instrument used widely within the United States over the past 50 years (Hill 1945; Hudson and Henze 1969; McGinnis 1958). Interspersed among the 18 characteristics were the target variables "good financial prospect," "good looks," "chastity: no previous sexual intercourse," and "ambition and industriousness."

Preferences concerning potential mates. The second instrument was developed from the factor analysis (Buss and Barnes 1986) of an expanded 76-item instrument (Gough 1973). The highest loading items from this factor analysis were included (e.g., religious, kind and understanding, exciting personality), along with several items to test the specific hypotheses about

sex differences in mate preferences. Interspersed among the 13 characteristics were the target variables "good earning capacity" and "physically attractive."

In contrast to the rating procedure used in the first instrument, subjects were requested to rank each characteristic on its desirability in a mate. The instructional set was as follows:

Below are listed a set of characteristics. Please rank them on their desirability in someone you might marry. Give a "1" to the most desirable characteristic in a potential mate, a "2" to the second most desirable characteristic in a potential mate, a "3" to the third most desirable characteristic, and so on down to a "13" for the 13th most desirable characteristic in a potential mate.

In sum, two instruments were used, each containing target variables to test the key predictions. They differed in context (presence of other items) and scaling procedure (rating vs. ranking), permitting a partial test of the generality of the findings across methods.

Translations. Instructions were provided to each research collaborator for translating the two instruments into the appropriate language for their sample. These included the use of three bilingual speakers who, respectively, (a) translated from English to the native language, (b) back-translated from the native language to English, and (c) resolved discrepancies between the first two translators. Instructions were provided to make all terms "sex neutral" in the sense of being equally applicable to males and females. The phrase "physically attractive, " for example, could be applied to either sex, whereas "handsome" and "beautiful" were considered sex-linked and were therefore not used.

RESULTS

Earning Potential and Ambition-Industriousness

To conserve space, only data from the *rated* variables are presented in tabular form. Discrepancies between parallel tests using the rating and ranking instruments are noted in the text and with asterisks in the tables. Tables presenting the full parallel analyses for the ranking instrument are available from the author on request.

Table 18.2 shows the means, standard deviations, *t*-tests for sex differences, and significance levels for valuation of the rated variable "good financial prospect" for each of the 37 samples. Samples vary considerably in how much this mate characteristic is valued, ranging from quite high (Indonesia, Nigeria, Zambia) to quite low (South African Zulu, Netherlands, Great Britain). In general, South American, North American, Asian, and African samples valued earning capacity more than did Western European samples, although there are important variations among samples within each continent.

In 36 of 37 samples, the predicted sex difference emerged—females valued "good financial prospect" in a potential mate more highly than males did. The sole exception was the sample from Spain, which showed the predicted direction of the sex difference, but not signifi-

Table 18.2. Good Financial Prospect

	Males		Females			
Sample	**Mean**	**SD**	**Mean**	**SD**	*t*-test	Sig.
African						
Nigeria	1.37	0.82	2.30	0.76	−7.00	.000
S. Africa (whites)	0.94	0.78	1.73	0.78	−5.58	.000
S. Africa (Zulu)	0.70	0.87	1.14	0.80	−2.61	.006
Zambia	1.46	0.90	2.33	0.62	−6.35	.000
Asian						
China	1.10	0.98	1.56	0.94	−5.34	.000
India	1.60	0.96	2.00	0.69	3.63	.000
Indonesia	1.42	0.87	2.55	0.57	−9.46	.000
Iran	1.25	1.04	2.04	0.85	−3.06	.002
Israel (Jewish)	1.31	1.01	1.82	0.87	−5.58	.000
Israel (Palestinian)	1.28	1.05	1.67	0.92	−2.05	.023
Japan	0.92	0.75	2.29	0.58	−15.97	.000
Taiwan	1.25	0.81	2.21	0.70	−15.16	.000
European-Eastern						
Bulgaria	1.16	0.94	1.64	0.91	−4.29	.000
Estonian S.S.R.	1.31	0.86	1.51	0.85	−2.06	.025
Poland	1.09	0.82	1.74	0.80	−6.18	.000
Yugoslavia	1.27	0.76	1.66	0.75	−3.07	.002
European-Western						
Belgium	0.95	0.87	1.36	0.88	−2.74	.004
France	1.22	0.97	1.68	0.92	−3.35	.001
Finland	0.65	0.76	1.18	0.84	−4.10	.000
Germany-West	1.14	0.88	1.81	0.93	−10.19	.000
Great Britain	0.67	0.63	1.16	0.78	−3.65	.000
Greece	1.16	0.95	1.92	0.78	−4.97	.000
Ireland	0.82	0.95	1.67	0.77	−5.51	.000
Italy	0.87	0.69	1.33	0.80	−3.06	.002
Netherlands	0.69	0.81	0.94	0.84	−3.00	.002
Norway	1.10	0.84	1.42	0.97	−2.03	.023
Spain	1.25	0.94	1.39	0.89	−0.80	ns
Sweden	1.18	0.90	1.75	0.75	−4.44	.000
North American						
Canada (English)	1.02	0.82	1.91	0.76	−5.61	.000
Canada (French)	1.47	0.83	1.94	0.63	−3.25	.001
USA (Mainland)	1.08	0.88	1.96	0.82	−20.00	.000
USA (Hawaii)	1.50	0.81	2.10	0.72	−5.10	.000
Oceanian						
Australia	0.69	0.73	1.54	0.80	−8.47	.000
New Zealand	1.35	0.97	1.63	0.75	−2.03	.022
South American						
Brazil	1.24	0.89	1.91	0.78	−9.91	.000
Colombia	1.72	0.90	2.21	0.75	−3.47	.001
Venezuela	1.66	0.96	2.26	0.78	−4.72	.000

Note: Potential mean values can range from 0 (unimportant) to 3 (indispensable). Sig. = significance; ns = not significant.

cantly so. The ranked variable "good earning capacity" similarly did not show a significant sex difference for the Spanish sample. Whether this lack of significant sex difference is due to particulars of the Spanish mating system, features of the broader socioecology, or chance sample fluctuation must await replication. In sum, with the exception of the Spanish sample, the predicted sex difference in preferences for mates with good earning potential was found

across widely varying cultures, typically at a high level of statistical significance.

Table 18.3 shows analogous results for valuation of "ambition and industriousness." Across both sexes, the Nigerian, Zulu, Chinese, Taiwanese, Estonian, Palestinian, Colombian, and Venezuelan samples placed particularly high value on this mate characteristic. In no sample was ambition industriousness rated low. Samples from the Netherlands, Great Britain,

Table 18.3. Ambition and Industriousness

| Sample | Males | | Females | | | |
	Mean	SD	Mean	SD	t-test	Sig.
African						
Nigeria	2.25	0.68	2.61	0.56	−3.49	.001
S. Africa (whites)	1.73	0.84	2.16	0.70	−3.14	.001
S. Africa (Zulu)✷	2.41	0.81	2.10	0.73	2.02	.023
Zambia	1.97	0.92	2.14	0.75	−1.06	ns
Asian						
China	2.22	0.85	2.63	0.59	−6.41	.000
India	1.79	0.86	2.44	0.76	−6.31	.000
Indonesia	1.97	0.73	2.29	0.62	−2.70	.004
Iran	2.68	0.55	2.81	0.48	−0.98	ns
Israel (Jewish)	1.78	0.99	2.43	0.71	−7.66	.000
Israel (Palestinian)	2.28	0.76	2.58	0.71	−2.15	.017
Japan	1.92	0.71	2.37	0.62	−5.53	.000
Taiwan	2.24	0.73	2.81	0.42	−11.31	.000
European-Eastern						
Bulgaria	1.67	0.91	2.15	0.81	−4.63	.000
Estonian S.S.R.	2.31	0.68	2.46	0.64	−2.06	.020
Poland	1.93	0.84	2.29	0.72	−3.49	.001
Yugoslavia	1.82	0.72	2.24	0.74	−3.44	.001
European-Western						
Belgium	1.67	0.82	1.97	0.87	−2.01	.023
France	1.75	1.02	2.00	0.90	−1.79	.037
Finland	1.44	0.83	1.56	0.73	−1.07	ns
Germany-West	1.40	0.81	1.66	0.87	−4.23	.000
Great Britain	1.15	0.70	1.59	0.90	−2.84	.003
Greece	1.96	0.94	2.25	0.90	−1.81	.037
Ireland	1.44	0.88	1.76	0.81	−2.10	.019
Italy	1.63	0.85	2.07	0.94	−2.46	.008
Netherlands	1.28	0.97	1.41	0.93	−1.35	ns
Norway	1.60	0.80	1.70	0.87	−0.72	ns
Spain	1.73	0.90	1.69	0.98	0.22	ns
Sweden	1.97	0.78	2.04	0.76	−0.60	ns
North American						
Canada (English)	1.82	0.69	2.32	0.71	−3.53	.001
Canada (French)	1.79	0.85	2.08	0.75	−1.78	.039
USA (Mainland)	1.84	0.76	2.45	0.61	−16.66	.000
USA (Hawaii)	1.95	0.76	2.24	0.65	−2.66	.005
Oceanian						
Australia	1.38	0.92	1.82	0.77	−3.69	.000
New Zealand	1.57	0.76	1.86	0.53	−2.64	.005
South American						
Brazil	1.70	0.90	2.21	0.82	−7.25	.000
Colombia	2.36	0.80	2.24	0.90	0.80	ns
Venezuela	2.18	0.89	2.42	0.75	−2.03	.022

Note: Potential mean values can range from 0 (unimportant) to 3 (indispensable).

[handwritten margin notes: "in consistency across cultures due to similar genes or similar environments?" and "note: heritability of universal trait (e.g. 4 limbs – tetrapods) is ∅"]

West Germany, and Finland, however, expressed less preference for this mate characteristic than did other samples.

Thirty-four of the 37 samples (92%) for ambition-industriousness were in the predicted direction, with females expressing a higher valuation than males. In 29 samples (78%), the sex difference was statistically significant beyond the .05 level. Three samples—Colombian, Spanish, and South African Zulu—show the opposite sex difference, significant only in the Zulu sample. According to the research collaborator who collected the Zulu data, it is considered women's work to build the house, fetch water, and perform other arduous physical tasks, whereas men often travel from their rural homes to urban centers for work. This local division of labor might account for the sex difference reversal among the Zulu. In sum, moderate support was found for the hypothesized sex difference in this cue to resource acquisition, although this difference cannot be considered universal.

Age Differences

Table 18.4 shows the age differences preferred between self and mate. In each of the 37 samples, males prefer mates who are younger, which is consistent with the hypothesis that males value mates with higher reproductive capacity. These sex differences are the largest ones found in this study, showing statistical significance beyond the .0001 level in each of the 37 samples. Do the age preferences males express for females correspond more closely to peak reproductive value (mid-teens) or to peak fertility (early 20s)? By subtracting the mean age difference preferred between males and their mates (2.66 years) from the age at which males prefer to marry (27.49 years), it can be inferred that males in these samples prefer to marry females who are approximately 24.83 years old. This age preference is closer to peak female fertility than to peak reproductive value.

Not specifically predicted, but also consistent across all countries, females prefer mates who are older than they are. Indeed, females appear to prefer a larger age difference (3.42 years older) than do males (2.66 years younger). Adding the mean age difference preferred by females to the age at which females prefer to marry (25.39 years) yields a preferred mate age of 28.81 years.

The samples vary strikingly in age difference preferences. Nigeria and Zambia are the two countries in which males prefer the largest age difference between self and mate, 6.45 and 7.38 years younger, respectively. These are the only two countries in this study that practice substantial polygyny. In polygynous mating systems, males are typically older when they acquire wives than is the case in monogamous mating systems (Hart and Pilling 1960; Murdock 1967).

Actual Age Difference at Marriage—A Validity Check

Two crucial questions can be posed about the validity of the methods and the reality of the preferences indicated by this study: Are self-reported preferences accurate indices of actual preferences? Are mate preferences reflected in actual mating decisions? To begin to address these questions, data were obtained from the most recent *Demographic Yearbook* (United Nations 1988) and the *Demographic Fact Book* (Republic of China 1987) on actual age at marriage. Demographic statistics were obtained for 27 of the 33 countries sampled in this study.

Actual age at marriage is not the same variable as preferred age at marriage or preferred mate age. Actual age at marriage is undoubtedly determined by many factors, including personal preferences, parental preferences, preferences exerted by members of the opposite sex, sex ratio, local availability of mates, and perhaps current resource holdings. Nonetheless, personal preferences, if they are to bear the conceptual importance ascribed to them in this study, should be reflected to some degree in actual mating decisions.

Actual age at marriage was estimated from the data presented for each country in the *Demographic Yearbook* and the *Demographic Fact Book*. Data in the *Yearbook* are broken down by age of bride and age of groom within each of a series of 5-year age brackets (e.g., 15–19; 20–24; 25–29). An estimated mean age of marriage was obtained by taking the midpoint of each of these age ranges and weighting this by the actual number of brides or grooms falling within the range. This must be regarded as an estimate or approximation of actual marriage age.

Table 18.4. Age Difference Preferred Between Self and Spouse

Sample	Males		Females				Actual
	Mean	SD	Mean	SD	t-test	Sig.	Age difference
African							
Nigeria	−6.45	5.04	4.90	2.17	21.99	.000	—
S. Africa (whites)	−2.30	2.19	3.50	2.23	13.38	.000	3.13
S. Africa (Zulu)	−3.33	2.31	3.76	3.68	10.80	.000	2.38
Zambia	−7.38	6.39	4.14	1.99	12.22	.000	—
Asian							
China	−2.05	2.47	3.45	1.73	29.06	.000	—
India	−3.06	2.55	3.29	1.96	19.07	.000	—
Indonesia	−2.72	4.41	4.69	1.87	13.29	.000	—
Iran	−4.02	1.62	5.10	1.79	17.98	.000	—
Israel (Jewish)	−2.88	3.82	3.95	4.90	14.13	.000	3.57
Israel (Palestinian)	−3.75	1.99	3.71	1.86	6.66	.000	3.57
Japan	−2.37	2.29	3.05	1.62	20.98	.000	2.92
Taiwan	−3.13	2.29	3.78	1.98	36.76	.000	3.50
European-Eastern							
Bulgaria	−3.13	2.87	4.18	2.61	21.35	.000	3.54
Estonian S.S.R.	−2.19	2.58	2.85	1.52	22.69	.000	2.49
Poland	−2.85	2.94	3.38	3.02	14.66	.000	2.10
Yugoslavia	−2.47	2.29	3.61	1.98	16.29	.000	3.55
European-Western							
Belgium	−2.53	5.15	2.46	2.49	5.49	.000	2.37
France	−1.94	2.47	4.00	3.17	12.97	.000	2.28
Finland	−0.38	3.22	2.83	2.35	5.57	.000	2.30
Germany-West	−2.52	3.87	3.70	3.67	20.18	.000	3.19
Great Britain	−1.92	3.78	2.26	2.58	6.02	.000	2.61
Greece	−3.36	3.20	4.54	2.55	14.98	.000	4.92
Ireland	−2.07	1.93	2.78	1.91	12.79	.000	2.17
Italy	−2.76	2.77	3.24	2.41	10.85	.000	3.68
Netherlands	−1.01	2.51	2.72	3.01	9.82	.000	2.58
Norway	−1.91	4.14	3.12	2.36	7.80	.000	2.87
Spain	−1.46	2.43	2.60	4.25	5.92	.000	2.45
Sweden	−2.34	4.87	2.91	2.79	8.08	.000	2.97
North American							
Canada (English)	−1.53	1.93	2.72	2.01	10.15	.000	2.51
Canada (French)	−1.22	1.69	1.82	1.83	7.43	.000	2.51
USA (Mainland)	−1.65	2.62	2.54	1.90	31.76	.000	2.71
USA (Hawaii)	−1.92	2.46	3.30	3.25	11.57	.000	—
Oceanian							
Australia	−1.77	2.34	2.86	2.72	12.16	.000	2.73
New Zealand	−1.59	2.47	2.91	1.85	11.66	.000	2.78
South American							
Brazil	−2.94	3.35	3.94	3.23	22.06	.000	3.52
Colombia	−4.45	3.01	4.51	2.85	16.88	.000	4.53
Venezuela	−2.99	3.05	3.62	3.25	13.63	.000	3.47
Mean	−2.66		3.42				2.99

Note: Negative values signify preference for a *younger* mate; positive values signify preference for an *older* mate.

Several validity checks can be conducted by comparing these data with the preferred age at marriage, the age difference desired between self and mate, and the preferred mate age derived from these variables. Perhaps most central to this article are the comparisons between the age difference desired between self and mate and the actual age difference between marriage partners. These data are shown in Table 18.4 along with data on preferred age differences.

Across the 27 countries, the actual age differences between men and women at marriage range from 2.17 years (Ireland) to 4.92 years (Greece), all showing the wives to be younger on average than their husbands. The unit-weighted average age difference between husbands and wives across countries is 2.99 years. The present study found that males prefer their marriage partners to be 2.66 years younger on average, whereas females prefer mates to be 3.42 years older. Averaging across the sexes yields a mean preferred age difference of 3.04 years, which corresponds closely to the actual age difference of 2.99 years between spouses. Thus, preferred age differences between spouses are indeed reflected in actual age differences at marriage. Cause or effect (rationalization)?

A second validity check can be made by comparing the absolute values of actual age at marriage with (a) preferred age at marriage and (b) preferred mate age. Males in this study indicate an average preferred marriage age of 27.5 years, with a preferred spouse age of 24.8 years. Females express a preference to marry at 25.4, and a spouse preferred to be 28.8 years old. Both preferred age of marriage and preferred mate age correspond closely in absolute value to the actual mean ages of grooms (28.2) and brides (25.3).

A third and perhaps more subtle validity check may be made across countries by correlating the magnitude of the preferred age difference with the magnitude of the actual age difference. This cross-country correlation is +.68 ($p < .001$, $n = 28$) for males and +.71 ($p < .001$, $n = 28$) for females. Samples preferring larger age differences indeed reside in countries where actual marriages show larger age differences. Samples from countries preferring smaller age differences inhabit countries where actual marriages show smaller age differences.

Several conclusions may be drawn from these validity checks. First, they provide strong validation for the self-report method used to obtain age preferences, and by implication, circumstantial validation for the other self-report measures used in this study. Second, they yield evidence that stated preferences are reflected in actual mating decisions. Third, they provide further support for the evolution-based hypothesis that males both prefer *and* choose females displaying cues to high reproductive capacity.

Physical Attractiveness

Table 18.5 shows the results for the rated variable "good looks." All 37 samples show sex differences in the predicted direction, with 34 significant beyond the .05 level. For those three countries (India, Poland, and Sweden) in which the difference was not significant for "good looks," the sex difference was significant in the predicted direction for the ranked variable "physically attractive." Thus, the hypothesis that males value physical attractiveness in potential mates more than females do is strongly supported by these cross-cultural data.

Chastity: No Previous Sexual Intercourse

Table 18.6 shows the results for the variable of "chastity: no previous experience in sexual intercourse." Cultures in this study vary tremendously in the value placed on this mate characteristic. The samples from China, India, Indonesia, Iran, Taiwan, and Israel (Palestinian Arabs only) attach high value to chastity in a potential mate. At the opposite extreme, samples from Sweden, Norway, Finland, the Netherlands, West Germany, and France indicate that prior sexual experience is irrelevant or unimportant in a potential mate. A few subjects even indicated in writing that chastity was *undesirable* in a potential mate. The Irish sample departs from the other Western European samples in placing moderate emphasis on chastity. Also showing moderate valuation of chastity are samples from Africa, Japan, Poland, and the Soviet republic of Estonia. It is noteworthy that chastity shows greater cross-cultural variability than any other rated variable in this study.

In contrast to the strong cross-cultural consistency of sex differences found with the previous four variables, only 23 (62%) of the samples show significant sex differences in the predicted direction. The remaining 14 samples (38%) show no significant sex differences in valuation of chastity. These results provide only moderate support for the evolution-based paternity probability hypothesis. They also yield equally powerful evidence of proximate cultural influences on the degree of importance placed on lack of prior sexual intercourse in a potential mate.

CONCLUSIONS

Each of the five evolution-based predictions received some empirical support from these data. Females value the financial capacity of poten-

Table 18.5. Good Looks

Sample	Males		Females		t-test	Sig.
	Mean	**SD**	**Mean**	**SD**		
African						
Nigeria	2.24	0.67	1.82	0.72	3.65	.000
S. Africa (whites)	1.58	0.65	1.22	0.65	3.05	.002
S. Africa (Zulu)	1.17	0.80	0.88	0.68	1.94	.027
Zambia	2.23	0.85	1.65	0.84	3.72	.000
Asian						
China	2.06	0.62	1.59	0.68	8.17	.000
India	2.03	0.73	1.97	0.75	0.59	ns*
Indonesia	1.81	0.81	1.36	0.62	3.76	.000
Iran	2.07	0.73	1.69	0.68	1.97	.027
Israel (Jewish)	1.77	0.93	1.56	0.75	2.52	.006
Israel (Palestinian)	2.38	0.60	1.47	0.81	6.72	.000
Japan	1.50	0.75	1.09	0.74	4.36	.000
Taiwan	1.76	0.77	1.28	0.66	8.07	.000
European-Eastern						
Bulgaria	2.39	0.68	1.95	0.84	4.70	.000
Estonian S.S.R.	2.27	0.69	1.63	0.70	8.10	.000
Poland	1.93	0.83	1.77	0.76	1.57	ns*
Yugoslavia	2.20	0.66	1.74	0.72	3.86	.000
European-Western						
Belgium	1.78	0.84	1.28	0.79	3.58	.000
France	2.08	0.81	1.76	0.77	2.78	.003
Finland	1.56	0.81	0.99	0.73	4.79	.000
Germany-West	1.92	0.74	1.32	0.72	11.37	.000
Great Britain	1.96	0.60	1.36	0.72	4.76	.003
Greece	2.22	0.69	1.94	0.77	2.14	.018
Ireland	1.87	0.64	1.22	0.69	5.33	.000
Italy	2.00	0.70	1.64	0.83	2.36	.010
Netherlands	1.76	0.72	1.21	0.72	7.81	.000
Norway	1.87	0.83	1.32	0.83	3.85	.000
Spain	1.91	0.68	1.24	0.82	4.65	.000
Sweden	1.65	0.77	1.46	0.83	1.55	ns*
North American						
Canada (English)	1.96	0.50	1.64	0.71	2.55	.007
Canada (French)	1.68	0.64	1.41	0.65	2.00	.024
USA (Mainland)	2.11	0.69	1.67	0.69	12.19	.000
USA (Hawaii)	2.06	0.75	1.49	0.81	4.67	.000
Oceanian						
Australia	1.65	0.74	1.24	0.73	4.20	.000
New Zealand	1.99	0.69	1.29	0.73	5.98	.000
South American						
Brazil	1.89	0.75	1.68	0.86	3.25	.001
Colombia	1.56	0.79	1.22	0.75	2.63	.005
Venezuela	1.76	0.90	1.27	0.98	3.64	.000

Note: * indicates significant in predicted direction on the ranking procedure for variable "physically attractive."

tial mates more than males do. Ambition and industriousness, cues to resource acquisition, also tend to be valued more heavily by females than by males across cultures. Support was strong for the financial capacity prediction (36 of 37 samples), and moderate for the ambition-industriousness prediction (29 of 37 samples).

Although these results give powerful support to the evolution-based hypothesis about female preference for males with high providing ca-pacity, the precise functions of this preference remain obscure. By way of comparison, the male arctic tern's ability to bring food to the female during courtship is a good predictor of his ability to feed chicks (Nisbet 1973). Does earn-ing potential provide a similar cue in humans? Or does it provide a cue to increased status, pro-tection, and perhaps even "good genes" (Trivers 1972) that pass to the female's offspring? Fu-ture research is needed to identify these functions and to examine characteristics that signal not just the capacity to acquire resources, but the male's *willingness* to devote those resources to a female and her offspring.

Males value physical attractiveness and relative youth in potential mates more than do females—sex differences that show remarkable generality across cultures. Our demographic data corroborate the preference data, showing that females are younger than males at actual age of marriage. The greater male preference

for relative youth and physical attractiveness supports the evolution-based hypothesis about male preference for females showing cues to high reproductive capacity. These findings are especially noteworthy in that they reverse a general trend in these data suggesting that females in a majority of cultures tend to be more exacting in mate preferences across many characteristics. Although cultural variations exist with respect to standards of beauty, these variations apparently do not override sex differ-

Table 18.6. Chastity: No Previous Experience in Sexual Intercourse

[handwritten: Bonferroni correction for mult. tests / sign test?]

	Males		Females			
Sample	**Mean**	**SD**	**Mean**	**SD**	*t*-test	Sig.
African						
Nigeria	1.22	1.10	0.51	0.72	4.97	.000
S. Africa (whites)	1.06	1.05	0.84	1.12	1.13	ns
S. Africa (Zulu)	1.17	1.06	0.31	0.62	4.82	.000
Zambia	1.66	1.03	0.98	1.03	3.29	.001
Asian						
China	2.54	0.82	2.61	0.77	−1.03	ns
India	2.44	0.98	2.17	1.11	1.95	.027
Indonesia	2.06	1.10	1.98	1.18	0.39	ns
Iran	2.67	0.88	2.23	0.99	1.70	.049
Israel (Jewish)	0.93	1.12	0.58	0.97	3.46	.001
Israel (Palestinian)	2.24	1.10	0.96	1.18	5.81	.000
Japan	1.42	1.09	0.78	0.86	5.17	.000
Taiwan	2.32	0.85	2.20	0.91	1.71	.040
European-Eastern						
Bulgaria	0.69	0.90	0.44	0.86	2.31	.011
Estonian S.S.R.	1.25	1.04	0.84	0.98	3.51	.001
Poland	1.23	1.03	0.99	1.03	1.80	.031
Yugoslavia	0.47	0.81	0.08	0.36	3.60	.001
European-Western						
Belgium	0.67	1.02	0.38	0.72	1.89	.031
France	0.45	0.88	0.41	0.81	0.30	ns
Finland	0.27	0.59	0.29	0.67	−0.17	ns
Germany-West	0.34	0.73	0.17	0.52	3.61	.000
Great Britain	0.46	0.75	0.49	0.93	−0.20	ns
Greece	0.48	0.85	0.40	0.88	0.51	ns
Ireland	1.49	1.03	1.47	1.08	0.11	ns
Italy	0.65	0.92	0.27	0.53	2.47	.008
Netherlands	0.29	0.69	0.29	0.69	−0.01	ns
Norway	0.31	0.72	0.30	0.74	0.08	ns
Spain	0.66	0.96	0.36	0.73	1.92	.029
Sweden	0.25	0.53	0.28	0.67	−0.32	ns
North American						
Canada (English)	0.55	0.76	0.33	0.80	1.41	ns
Canada (French)	0.62	0.95	0.33	0.68	1.58	ns
USA (Mainland)	0.85	0.96	0.52	0.85	6.58	.000
USA (Hawaii)	0.91	0.94	0.58	0.87	2.33	.011
Oceanian						
Australia	0.73	0.93	0.45	0.86	2.40	.009
New Zealand	0.88	1.07	0.72	1.04	0.91	ns
South American						
Brazil	0.93	1.08	0.36	0.78	7.32	.000
Colombia	1.27	1.06	0.30	0.61	6.33	.000
Venezuela	0.93	1.07	0.59	0.97	2.35	.010

ences in the importance attached to physical attractiveness.

The male age preference for females of just under 25 years implies that *fertility* has been a stronger ultimate cause of mate preferences than reproductive value. The fact that this age preference appears to be several years beyond peak fertility, however, suggests that other variables such as similarity (Rushton et al. 1984), compatability (Murstein 1986), and perhaps maturity might also affect these age preferences. Recent data suggest that fertility may peak later in females than previously thought, perhaps in the mid-twenties (Anderson 1986; Short 1976a). If these recent estimates are confirmed, then male age preferences may turn out to be closely calibrated with female fertility.

Although these data seem to falsify Symons's (1979) hypothesis that males prefer females of high reproductive value rather than of high fertility, a cautionary note must be added. These findings are based on the inference that subtracting the preferred age difference between self and mate from the age at which one prefers to marry accurately represents the true age preferred in mates. It is possible that this inference is unwarranted, and that when males actually reach the age at which they decide to marry, they may prefer females who are younger. Nonetheless, the validity check on actual age at marriage corroborates the finding on preferred age differences between self and mates as well as the finding that females tend to marry on average at approximately 25 years of age. Future research could profitably explore this issue in greater detail by examining mate age preferences and actual ages within both short-term and long-term mating relationships.

Not specifically predicted was the finding that *females prefer somewhat older mates* in all 37 cultures. This finding, in conjunction with the known positive correlation between age and income among males (Jencks 1979; Willerman 1979), provides additional circumstantial evidence for the hypothesis that females prefer mates who show characteristics associated with having a high providing capacity. Older male age also could provide a cue to longevity, maturity, prowess, confidence, judgement, or experience (cf. Ellis 1992 ; Symons 1979). Further research is needed to uncover the functions of this cross-culturally robust female preference for older males.

The fifth evolution-based prediction, that males would value *chastity* in potential mates more than would females, was supported in 23 out of the 37 samples. In the remaining 14 samples, no significant sex differences emerged. Samples from Africa, the Middle East, South America, and Eastern Europe generally show the predicted sex differences in preferences for chastity in a potential mate. Many of the samples indicating no sex differences were concentrated in Western Europe, Canada, New Zealand, China, and Indonesia. These results provide modest support for the evolutionary hypothesis based on paternity probability. The wide variation in preference for chastity suggests that cultural differences, ecological differences, or mating system differences exert powerful effects on the value attached to chastity.

A speculation is warranted regarding the cross-cultural variability of sex differences in chastity valuation, when contrasted with the more pervasive sex differences found in mate preferences for earning power, relative age, and physical attractiveness. Chastity differs from these other variables in that it is less directly observable. Even physical tests of female virginity are unreliable due to variations in the morphology of the hymen, rupture due to nonsexual causes, and deliberate alteration (Dickemann 1981a). Sexual selection should favor preference mechanisms for cues that are reliably associated with characteristics that have fitness advantage for the mate selection. Where cues are not directly observable or cannot be reliably assessed as in the case of chastity, it is difficult to imagine how *specific* preference mechanisms could have been fashioned by sexual selection. These considerations, of course, do not preclude selection for a more *general* mechanism such as sexual jealousy (Daly et al. 1982) that promotes a heightened concern about females having sexual contact with other males, either prior to or after mate choice. These speculations highlight our profound lack of knowledge about basic psychological mechanisms involved in human mating decisions (Symons 1987b).

In sum, three of the five predictions—those involving mate preferences for earning potential, relative youth, and physical attractiveness—were strongly confirmed across cultures. The prediction regarding ambition-industriousness was confirmed only in 29 samples, and showed a significant reversal among the Zulu. The chastity prediction received still less empirical support, with only 23 of the 37 samples showing significant sex differences.

Qualifications and Limitations

Several important qualifications must attend the interpretation of these findings. First, the samples cannot be viewed as representative of the populations of each country; rural and less-educated individuals are underrepresented, although the samples of such individuals in this study indicate no departure from the primary predicted sex differences. Second, male and female preference distributions overlap considerably, in spite of mean differences. Third, neither earning potential nor physical appearance emerged as the highest rated or ranked characteristic for either sex, even though these characteristics showed large sex differences. Both sexes ranked the characteristics "kind-understanding" and "intelligent" higher than earning power and attractiveness in all samples, suggesting that species-typical mate preferences may be more potent than sex-linked preferences.

Other limitations surround the instruments, data sources, and operationalizations of the key constructs. Self-report contains obvious limitations and should be supplemented by alternative data sources in future studies. The close correspondence between the demographic data showing actual age at marriage data and the expressed mate preference data, however, suggests that we need not be pessimistic about the capacity of individuals to report preferences that are reflected in their actual mating decisions. Another limitation is that the single items used here may underestimate the magnitudes of the present sex differences, as they tend to be less reliable than composite clusters of items (Nunally 1978). And the set of characteristics representing each construct could be expanded to assess other mate characteristics such as the willingness of a male to invest resources, the willingness of a female to devote reproductive capacity to a given male, and behavioral cues associated with both proclivities.

A potential limitation involves the particular cultures selected for study. These samples are biased toward urbanized, cash-economy cultures. Less urbanized, non-cash cultures obviously must be studied to circumvent this bias. The tremendous cultural variability with respect to chastity, however, belies the notion that these 37 samples might somehow be culturally homogeneous and gives greater credibility to the empirical sex differences that transcend this cultural diversity.

Arranged marriages in some cultures pose another potential problem. If parents and other kin arrange marriages, how could mate preferences evolve or be expressed? We lack knowledge about the prevalence of arranged marriages in our environment of evolutionary adaptedness. Nonetheless, two factors mitigate this potential problem. First, if parents do arrange the marriages of their children, there is no reason to assume that they would not express preferences reflecting the reproductive considerations on which the central hypotheses here have been based. Research on parents' preferences for the mates of their sons and daughters is needed to confirm or falsify this speculation. Second, even in societies with arranged marriages, sons and daughters do exert choice. Offspring influence their parents' choices, carry on clandestine affairs, defy their parents' wishes, make threats of various sorts, and sometimes simply elope with a preferred mate (O'Kelly and Carney 1986). Personal preferences appear to be expressed even under socially constrained conditions.

Finally, these results yield little information about the proximate (social, psychological, physiological, ontogenetic) mechanisms directly responsible for their existence. Possible candidates include genetic differences between the sexes, sensory preferences analogous to food preferences, socialization differences during development, and structural effects at a societal level such as those that limit female access to economic resources (Buss and Barnes 1986). Although the evolutionary hypotheses presented here are largely supported by the results, research on proximate mechanisms is needed to develop a more complete explanatory account of observed sex differences in mate preferences.

Implications

This is the first study to examine human mate preferences across cultures on a broad scale (cf.

Kurian 1979). It exceeds prior studies in geographic, cultural, political, economic, ethnic, religious, and racial diversity. However, many questions remain unanswered. Currently unknown are the cultural and ecological causes of variation from country to country in (1) the magnitudes of obtained sex differences, and (2) the absolute levels of valuing reproductively relevant mate characteristics. The internationally consistent sex differences in mate preferences found here, however, yield insight into human reproductive history, provide hypotheses about current sexual selection, and are among the most robust psychological sex differences of any kind ever documented across cultures (cf. Maccoby and Jacklin 1974; Willerman 1979).

What do these results reveal about human reproductive history? They support the hypothesis that males and females have faced different constraints on reproductive success in our evolutionary past. Females appear to have been limited in reproductive success by access to resources for self and offspring. Males appear to have been limited by access to fertile females. These different selection pressures have presumably produced different male and female reproductive strategies. The greater female preference for mates displaying cues to high resource potential and the greater male preference for mates displaying cues to high reproductive capacity appear to represent adaptations to sex-differentiated reproductive constraints in our evolutionary past.

What do these results reveal about current sexual selection? No definitive answer can be provided, as we lack data on reproductive differences associated with the expression of mate preferences. The findings, however, have strong implications for human intrasexual competition—a key component of Darwin's theory of sexual selection. Mate preferences should influence intrasexual competition such that males compete with each other to display the resources that females desire in mates; females should compete with each other to display the reproductively linked cues that males desire in mates (Buss 1988b). Furthermore, mate preferences should affect opposite sex intrasexual maneuvers, such as tactics used to guard or retain mates (Buss 1988a; Flinn 1987), tactics used for mate poaching, and perhaps tactics used to derogate intrasexual competitors (Buss and Dedden 1990). These now established sex differences in mate preferences across 37 cul-

tures provide a foundation for testing hypotheses about human intrasexual competition on an international scale.

Most generally, these results suggest that selective preferences in mating are not the sole province of females (Anderson 1986; Bernstain and Wade 1983; Robinson 1982; Smuts 1987), as is implied by some evolutionary accounts that stress female choosiness. Human males and females both express preferences, and it is clear that there are powerful selective advantages for doing so. These results also implicate cultural systems in determining sex differences or the absence of sex differences. The cross-cultural variability in chastity valuation serves as a strong reminder that even mechanisms closely linked with reproduction are not "genetically determined" in the sense of being inevitable or intractable. Finally, these results support the broad hypothesis that human males and females differ in reproductive strategies, and the specific hypothesis that mate preferences represent important components of these strategies.

Acknowledgments. Special thanks go to research collaborators of the International Mate Selection Project: M. Abbott, A. Angleitner, A. Asherian, A. Biaggio, A. Blanco, H-Y. Ch'u, B. Ekehammar, J. Czapinski, B. DeRaad, M. Fioravanti, J. Georgas, P. Gjerde, R. Guttman, F. Hazan, S. Iwawaki, N. Janakiramaiah, F. Khosroshahi, S. Kreitler, L. Lachenicht, M. Lee, K. Liik, S. Makim, S. Mika, M. Moadel-Shahidi, G. Moane, A. Mundy-Castle, B. Little, M. Montero, E. Nsenduluka, T. Niit, R. Pienkowski, A. Pirttila-Backman, J. Ponce de Leon, J. Rousseau, M. Runco, M. Safir, C. Samuels, R. Sanitioso, B. Schweitzer, R. Serpell, N. Smid, C. Spencer, M. Tadinac, E. Todorova, K. Troland, L. Van den Brande, G. Van Heck, L. Van Langenhove, and K. S. Yang.

This article has benefited from insightful suggestions on earlier drafts by John Alcock, Richard D. Alexander, Monique Borgerhoff Mulder, Linnda Caporael, Bruce Ellis, Elizabeth Hill, Katharine Hoyenga, Carolyn Phinney, Donald Symons, Barb Smuts, Bob Smuts, Debra Umberson, and Lee Willerman. Lisa Chiodo, Lisa Dedden, and Karen Kleinsmith deserve special thanks for meticulous processing of this enormous data set. This research could not have been completed without the insight and effort of Armen Asherian in all phases of the project.

19

Just Another Brick in the Wall: Building the Foundation of <u>Evolutionary Psychology</u>

DAVID M. BUSS

When I began the study of mate preferences in thirty-seven cultures back in the early 1980s, the empirical foundation for evolutionary psychology could be charitably described as tenuous. Powerful theories had been advanced, starting with inclusive fitness theory (Hamilton 1964) and proceeding to parental investment theory (Trivers 1972), the theory of parent-offspring conflict (Trivers 1974), and the parasite theory of the origins of sexual reproduction (Hamilton and Zuk 1982). But practically no empirical research had been conducted to test the applicability of these theories to our own species.

It was in this context that I launched the International Mate Selection Project (IMSP). When data from local populations *within* the United States first came in and confirmed the hypothesized sex differences, my social science colleagues assured me that such sex differences would *only* be found within the United States, or perhaps only in Western capitalist cultures. The social sciences at the time were characterized by extreme environmentalism and a widely shared assumption of the mind as a blank slate, or at best a domain-general information processor. The possibility that our minds might contain specialized psychological mechanisms, evolved in response to adaptive problems such as mate selection, was ridiculed and met with outright hostility. Such a proposition contradicted what every social scientist "knew"—that culture, socialization, and "rationality" molded the human mind into whatever shape desired. In part for these reasons, I sought to collect data as I could—from different ethnic groups, racial groups, geographic locations, political systems, mating systems, ages, cultures, and subcultures.

The results from thirty-seven cultures contradicted the fundamental assumptions of mainstream social scientists in showing <u>adaptively patterned universal design of the mating mind</u>. They showed that men and women differed in their desires in a mate in a manner that precisely corresponded to the a priori predictions of evolutionary psychologists. Men universally placed a greater premium than women on physical attractiveness and youth—two powerful cues to fertility. Women universally placed a greater premium on financial resources, as well as on the qualities known to lead to such resources, such as ambition-industriousness, older age, and social status. This provided one of the first empirical bricks in the foundation of evolutionary psychology. This brick has weathered well the attempted assaults by other scientists. Despite the outrage the study provoked, and repeated attempts to find exceptions to my claims for the universality of sex differences in desire, subsequent studies have only confirmed what I found in the thirty-seven cultures. No one has discovered a single exception.

But one brick does not a foundation make. Our evolved psychology of mating turned out to be far more complex that I had imagined when I began studying human desires. I had vastly underestimated the number of different sorts of adaptive problems that our ancestors recurrently faced, and hence vastly underestimated the complexity of our evolved sexual strategies. In subsequent work my colleagues and I have attempted to address some of these complexities. I'll discuss a few of them here; interested readers are referred to a more extensive treatment in *The Evolution of Desire: Strategies of Human Mating* (Buss 1994).

PSYCHOLOGICAL MECHANISMS SENSITIVE TO CONTEXT

Several critics noted that my study of thirty-seven cultures had ignored context. They were right. In subsequent studies we have focused on psychological mechanisms sensitive to important contextual shifts in the nature of the adaptive mating problem. One is temporal context—whether the mateship is expected to be *short-term* (e.g., a one-night stand) or *long-term* (e.g., an enduring marriage). It turns out that mate preferences shift in predictable ways according to this temporal context (Buss and Schmitt 1993). For example, in the short-term context, as contrasted with the long-term context, women place more importance on physical attractiveness (perhaps as a cue to "sexy son" genes) and immediate resources (e.g., "spends a lot of money on me right away"). Men in the short-term context place more importance on physical attractiveness and sex appeal, and also prefer women who seem easily sexually accessible and who will not inflict the costs of entangling commitments. These context shifts also emerge in the strategies that each sex uses to attract mates—strategies that are designed to embody the characteristics desired by the opposite sex in the relevant context (Buss 1994).

Another critical context is that of the individual's "mate value" or desirability on the mating market. Men higher in mate value elevate their standards for qualities such as attractiveness and also pursue on average more short-term matings. Women higher in mate value also elevate their standards for qualities such as financial resources, but in contrast to men they do not pursue short-term matings any more than do women who are lower in mate value.

Many other contexts have been shown to importantly affect mating decisions, including whether the mating system is polygynous or presumptively monogamous; whether it is a first marriage or second, third, or fourth marriage; whether the mating constitutes an extramarital affair or not, and if so, whether it is a one-night stand or a more enduring affair (e.g.,

Greiling and Buss 1996), and so on (see Buss 1994). In sum, our psychology of mating is far more complex, and far more sensitive to social context, than I had envisioned when conducting the study of thirty-seven cultures.

LINKS TO ACTUAL MATING BEHAVIOR

Another criticism is that expressed desires are not the same as actual mating behavior. There are two forms of response to this criticism. First, on conceptual grounds, desires represent only one class of causes of behavior, and there are many reasons why we would not expect a one-to-one correspondence between mating desires and behavior: (1) you can't always get what you want; (2) parents and other kin exert an influence on actual mating decision, regardless of the individuals' desires; (3) desirable mates are in rare supply compared with the large numbers that desire them, rendering only those high in mate value able to achieve their desires; and so on.

Despite these real conceptual complexities, subsequent research has shown strong links between mating desires and actual mating behavior: (1) Men desire younger women, women desire older men, and actual marriages confirm the universality of the age difference between brides and grooms; (2) large-scale sociological studies show that the single best predictor of the occupational status of the man a woman marries is her physical attractiveness (e.g., Udry and Eckland 1984); (3) the single best predictor of the physical attractiveness of the woman a man actually marries is his occupational status; (4) men in a position to get what they want, such as emperors and despots, routinely stock their harems with young, attractive women who embody the desires discovered in the thirty-seven-culture study (Betzig 1992c); (5) there are sex-linked causes of conjugal dissolution, such as a man's failure to provide economic resources and a woman's older age (Betzig 1989a); (6) behavioral data on tactics used to attract partners mirror the desires of the opposite sex (e.g., Greer and Buss 1994); (7) behavioral data on deception in mate attraction show that each sex attempts to exaggerate precisely those dimensions desired by the opposite sex (Tooke and Camire 1991); and (8) behavioral data show that the most effective mate retention tactics are those that embody the desires of the opposite sex (e.g., Buss 1988b, 1994). Clearly, the findings on desires in a mate do a good job of predicting many different facets of human mating behavior.

THE FUTURE FOUNDATION OF EVOLUTIONARY PSYCHOLOGY

Future studies, perhaps conducted by readers of this book, will undoubtedly show that human mating is more complex than I have depicted—that we have evolved psychological mechanisms sensitive to contexts as yet not envisioned, and that the links between desire and behavior will prove even more circuitous than depicted. For these reasons, I hope that readers will be inspired to discover these complexities and challenge the links I've proposed. In so doing, we will collectively build a stronger foundation for evolutionary psychology.

20

Sex Differences in Sexual Fantasy: An Evolutionary Psychological Approach

BRUCE J. ELLIS
DONALD SYMONS

Sexual fantasies—surely the most common form of human sexual experience—are private and potentially unconstrained by real-life exigencies. Thus they probably provide more insight than sexual activities do into the psychological mechanisms (i.e., the information processing rules or algorithms) that underpin sexual feeling, thought, and action. And if, as we argue, men and women differ in their innate sexual psychologies, sexually dimorphic psychological mechanisms should be revealed more sharply and dramatically in sexual fantasies than in sexual activities, since real-life heterosexual interactions must inevitably compromise, and hence blur, male and female desires and dispositions (Symons 1979). Our approach to the study of sexual fantasy is that of "evolutionary psychology," which Daly and Wilson (1988b:7) define as "psychological theorizing informed by modern evolutionary theory." This approach is proving to be a powerful heuristic in the study of many aspects of human psychology, e.g., attachment (Bowlby 1982), mate choice (Buss 1989b), social exchange (Cosmides 1989), homicide (Daly and Wilson 1988b), and sexuality (Symons 1979).

Sex Differences in Sexual Fantasies: A Review of the Literature

Empirical studies that have directly compared the frequency and content of male and female sexual fantasies have documented striking sex differences. Men are more likely than women to have sexual fantasies and to be physically aroused by their sexual thoughts (Hessellund 1976; Kinsey et al. 1948, 1953; Knoth, Boyd, and Singer 1988). American teenage boys are nearly twice as likely as teenage girls to fantasize about sex once a day or more (Knoth, Boyd, and Singer 1988). Studies in Japan, the United States, and Great Britain indicate that in each country men have about twice as many sexual fantasies as women do (Iwawaki and Wilson 1983; Jones and Barlow 1987; Wilson and Lang 1981; but compare Knafo and Jaffee 1984, and Sue 1979, who do not find overall sex differences in fantasy rates). Men are also more likely to have specifically sexual dreams while they sleep (Kinsey et al. 1948, 1953; Van de Castle 1971; Wilson 1975; Winget, Kramer, and Whitman 1972).

Female sexual fantasies are more likely than male fantasies to contain familiar partners and to include descriptions of the context, setting, and feelings associated with the sexual encounter (Barclay 1973; Gagnon and Simon 1973; Hass 1979; Wilson and Lang 1981; Wilson 1987). Women are much more likely than men to be only emotionally, rather than physically, aroused by their sexual fantasies (Knoth,

Reprinted with permission from *Journal of Sex Research* 27:527–55 (1990).

note all this literature on diffs before this study so the "hypotheses" already known
- a posteriori
- designed to confirm

Boyd, and Singer 1988). Furthermore, women's sexual fantasies have been found to contain more affection and commitment (Kelley 1984–1985; Pryzbyla, Byrne, and Kelley 1983), and are more likely to emphasize themes of tenderness and emotionality (Hessellund 1976). Female sexual fantasies also contain greater implicit sexual content, embedding or only implying sexual details in a general context, while male fantasies contain greater explicit content, stressing overt sexual details rather than general context (Brickman 1978). Females are more likely than males to imagine themselves as recipients of sexual activity from fantasized partners; males are more likely to imagine sexual partners as recipients of their activities (Barclay 1973; Iwawaki and Wilson 1983; Knafo and Jaffe 1984; Mednick 1977; Wilson and Lang 1981). This sex difference implies that men are more likely to view others as the objects of their sexual desires, whereas women are more likely to view themselves as the objects of sexual desire. Thoughts of being forced or overpowered into a sexual act are fairly common among both sexes, but probably more so among females (Knafo and Jaffe 1984; Sue 1979).

Male sexual fantasies specify many more sexual acts, more sexual organs, and a greater variety of visual content than female sexual fantasies do (Follingstad and Kimbrell 1986; also see Hass 1979). Male fantasies are more likely to contain visual imagery (Gottlieb 1985) and are much more likely to focus on minute details of the partners' physical appearance and to involve strangers, multiple partners, or anonymous partners (Arndt et al. 1985; Barclay 1973; Gagnon and Simon 1973; Hessellund 1976; Hunt 1974; Iwawaki and Wilson 1983; Knafo and Jaffe 1984; Pryzbyla, Byrne, and Kelley 1983; Wilson and Lang 1981; Wilson 1987). Males and females also differ in the stimulative source of their sexual fantasies. Jones and Barlow (1987) report that, whereas men and women do not differ in the frequency of internally generated sexual imagery, men are more than twice as likely as women to experience externally provoked sexual fantasies (i.e., fantasies in response to something heard, read, or seen in the environment). In brief, male sexual fantasies tend to be more ubiquitous, frequent, visual, specifically sexual, promiscuous, and active. Female sexual fantasies tend to be more contextual, emotive, intimate, and passive.

Despite this accumulation of data on the frequency and content of male and female sexual fantasies, many of the basic psychological processes underlying sex differences in sexual fantasy remain unexplored or inadequately examined. As noted above, Barclay (1973) and Hass (1979) found that the context, setting, and feelings associated with imagined sexual encounters are very important aspects of female sexual fantasies. These authors may come closest to providing rich psychological descriptions of fantasy experiences. However, both researchers conducted qualitative studies in which experimenters analyzed the content of written sexual fantasies. Quantitative data on the psychological phenomena described by Barclay and Hass are lacking, and many questions remain unanswered: Toward whom are sexual fantasies directed? Do fantasizing people concentrate more on themselves or on their partners? What are the important contextual and interpersonal factors associated with male and female fantasies? How important is the emotional setting, the physical setting, touching, partner variety, partner specificity, partner response, nurturance, foreplay, visual imagery, and seduction in men's and women's sexual fantasies?

The present study represents an exploratory attempt to investigate sex differences in these areas. Information about positive and negative affect associated with sexual fantasy and arousal was also collected. An adaptationist perspective on human psychology (i.e., mindfulness of the fact that our brain/mind mechanisms are ultimately the products of natural selection) provides both an integrative explanatory framework, which has been largely lacking in previous studies, and a heuristic for hypothesis formation. We do not propose that specific sexual fantasies represent adaptations (although some may), but rather that a comparison of male and female sexual fantasies may shed light on species-typical sex differences in sexual psychologies, and that these psychological differences are necessarily the consequences of different selective pressures that operated on males and females during the course of human evolutionary history.

It is important to emphasize that neither the present study nor other evolutionary psychological investigations "test" Darwin's theory of evolution by natural selection: this theory is not

JUST SO
JUST
MAYBE

on trial. Rather, "selectional thinking" guides the generation of psychological hypotheses, and it is these hypotheses that are being tested. Evolution-inspired hypotheses can be considered to vary along a continuum of confidence. At one end of the continuum are firm predictions in which all Darwinians are likely to concur; for example, selectional thinking clearly and unambiguously implies that the human brain/mind will be found to be sexually dimorphic (for reasons discussed below). As one moves along the continuum, however, "prediction" grades insensibly into "expectation" and thence into "an interesting question" or "hunch," and different Darwinians can and do have different expectations and hunches. For example, one of our questions asks about the importance of the physical setting in sexual fantasies. One of us expected that the physical setting would be more important in female than in male fantasies because of the greater importance of context to females; the other author, however, expected that any such effect would be washed out by the male tendency to visualize; hence he predicted no sex difference on this question.

Since the psychological mechanisms that constitute the human brain/mind were designed by natural selection in ancient Pleistocene environments, these mechanisms must be described solely in terms of phenomena that existed in such environments. For example, the phrase "romance novel" obviously cannot be used properly in the description of any human adaptation—psychological or otherwise—since romance novels have existed for an evolutionarily insignificant amount of time. The kinds of data that can be used to evaluate evolutionary psychological hypotheses, however, are potentially limitless, and evolutionarily recent phenomena (such as romance novels) can be just as informative as phenomena that existed in the Pleistocene, or more so.

This line of reasoning has implications for evaluating the data described in this article. On the one hand, since the California college students who were our subjects cannot be construed by any stretch of the imagination to constitute a random sample of humanity, much less of ancestral Pleistocene peoples, the present study can only be regarded as exploratory, and its results as tentative. On the other hand, however, nonrepresentative samples may sometimes provide especially clear insight into hu-

man psychological adaptations. The study of modern fast food cuisine probably reveals more about the basic human machinery of appetite than do studies of hunter-gatherer cuisine or archeological data on the diets of our Pleistocene ancestors. The former highlights clearly and dramatically the fundamental human appetites for sugar, salt, and fat. By analogy, a study of sexual fantasy among modern college students, who tend to be more sexually progressive and experienced than the general population (cf. Abramson and Handschumacher 1978), who often use modern contraceptive technology (which dramatically reduces the male-female disparity in the consequences of sexual intercourse), who are generally free to choose their own sexual partners, and who often adhere to the ideology that male and female psychologies are intrinsically identical, may be an especially interesting population to study if one's goal is to illuminate innate sex differences in sexual psychology. It is in just such a population that one might expect male and female sexualities to be most alike.

¿o. CONSERVATIVE bIAS ?

Hypothesized Sex Differences

All psychological theories, environmentalist and nativist alike, imply a human nature; that is, they imply that the brain/mind comprises mechanisms typical of *Homo sapiens* as a species, in the sense that arms and lips rather than wings and beaks are typical of our species. Theories differ, however, in the extent to which these species-typical brain/mind mechanisms are conceived of as generalized and few, on the one hand, or specialized and many, on the other. Because Darwinians focus on function, they typically favor the latter. Specifically, Darwinians are mindful of the fact that organisms have been designed by natural selection to solve many different kinds of problems. There is no more reason to imagine that one or a few generalized brain/mind mechanisms could solve all behavioral problems than there is to imagine that one or a few generalized organs could solve all physiological problems (Symons 1987b; Cosmides and Tooby 1987). A corollary of the basic Darwinian prediction that the human brain/mind comprises many specialized mechanisms is the prediction that the human brain/mind is sexually dimorphic: the nature of mammalian reproduction ensures that throughout the course of evolutionary history, ancestral males and females encountered very different reproductive opportunities and constraints, hence selection can be expected to have designed males and females to solve somewhat different problems (Daly and Wilson 1983, 1988b; Singer 1985a, 1985b; Symons 1979; Symons and Ellis 1989).

Selectional thinking can be a useful guide to forming specific hypotheses about the nature of sexually dimorphic psychological mechanisms. What follows are (1) a series of selectionist arguments for expected contrasts between male and female sexual psychologies and (2) specific hypotheses, derived from these contrasts, about sexual fantasies.

The Desire for Sexual Variety. Whatever the *typical* parental investments[1] might have been during the course of our evolutionary history, ancestral males and females necessarily differed enormously in the *minimum possible* investment. Ancestral males could potentially have benefited reproductively from copulating with any fertile female (close kin excepted) as long as the risks were low enough; hence it is reasonable to hypothesize that selection favored males who had low thresholds for sexual arousal and who found new females—in Byron's words, "fresh features"—especially sexually attractive. Ancestral females, on the other hand, would have had little to gain reproductively and a great deal to lose from random copulations with new males; hence selection is unlikely to have favored females who were sexually attracted to males on the basis of variety per se or simply because the males were there (Symons 1979, 1987a). This does not imply that ancestral females never benefited from engaging in sexual relations with more than one male (see R. L. Smith 1984), but rather that males had much more to gain by desiring and enjoying sexual variety for its own sake. The following hypothesis set derives from these male-female contrasts.

HYPOTHESIS SET 1. Partner variety will be a more central aspect of male than of female sexual fantasies. Men will have imagined sexual encounters with a greater variety of partners in the course of a given day and will be more likely than women to have had fantasized encounters with over 1,000 different partners in the course of their lives. Men will be more

likely to substitute or switch one imagined partner for another during the course of a single sexual fantasy. Men will have sexual fantasies more frequently than women do. And men will be more likely than women to fantasize about someone they simply want to have sex with (but do not necessarily want to become involved with in any other way).

Visual versus Tactile Arousal: the Importance of Context and Personal Characteristics. In ancestral populations, a female's reproductive success probably depended in large part on her mate's quality. Quality included good genes but, more importantly, in a species like ours, in which males typically invest substantially in their offspring, quality also included male ability and willingness to make such investments (Ellis 1992; Trivers 1972). The "best" males almost certainly were men of high-status and exceptional competitive abilities who were willing to invest their resources in a given female and her offspring. A male's "mate value" thus was determined by physical and psychological characteristics indicative of good genes, by signs of current or future political and economic success, and by signs of sincere interest in the particular female who was doing the choosing (perhaps evidenced by the male's willingness to woo, to pay real and symbolic costs—including the cost implicit in the phrase "to pay attention"). Selection thus favored females who were discriminating and slow to arouse sexually, since reflex-like sexual arousal on the basis of visual stimuli would have tended to undermine female choice. Female sexual arousal usually results from tactile stimulation by a favored male (Faust 1980; Symons 1979). Female experiences of sexual attraction and desire should incorporate a wide range of information about male quality and the quality of the specific male/female relationship in question.

Nonhuman primate females generally advertise ovulation, but human females do not; hence, selection favored human males who were sexually aroused by other indices of female "mate value." Since human beings, like all higher primates, are fundamentally visual creatures, and since female mate value was closely associated with health and youth (Symons 1979), ancestral males were selected to become sexually aroused by visually detected characteristics that were reliable indica-

'CHEAP TALK'?

tors of health and youth (e.g., clear eyes, unwrinkled skin). Cues to male mate value, on the other hand, are more complex and more dependent on psychosocial characteristics, which are not normally detected by stereotyped visual cues.

In short, female mate value is more reliably correlated with (and thus more readily detected by) specific visible characteristics than male mate value is; hence, selection favored in males, more than in females, a tendency to become sexually aroused by specific visual cues (Symons 1979, 1987a). And since males can inseminate females at almost no cost to themselves, males should also have been selected to become easily aroused by the sight or thought of females (especially novel females). It follows, therefore, that males have been designed by selection to experience sexual arousal largely on the basis of visually detected cosmetic qualities and to focus outward on their sexual partners as objects of desire. Because ancestral females were normally the objects of male sexual desire, females were selected to imagine themselves in this role, so as to manage and manipulate male sexual desire and assess the quality and significance of male sexual attention (Symons 1979). Females were selected to evaluate male sexual attractiveness (and thus become sexually interested) largely on the basis of noncosmetic cues to male quality and to experience sexual arousal primarily on the basis of tactile stimulation by favored males.[2] The following hypothesis set derives from these male/female contrasts.

HYPOTHESIS SET 2. Visual images will be the primary focus of men's sexual fantasies, whereas women's fantasies will emphasize touching, feelings, and partner response. Women will tend to focus inward on the self as the object of the imagined partner's desire; men will tend to focus outward on the partner as a sexual object. Women will focus more on their own physical and emotional responses, men on visual images of their fantasized partners. Caressing and nongenital touching will be a more important aspect of women's than of men's sexual fantasies. Women's sexual fantasies will be more likely to focus on a specific, special sexual partner. Women will be more likely than men to fantasize about someone they are or would like to become romantically involved with. The buildup, enticement, and interplay

that may precede a sexual encounter will be a more important aspect of women's than of men's sexual fantasies. The sexual scene will unfold more slowly and unhurriedly in women's sexual fantasies; men's sexual fantasies will move more quickly to explicitly sexual activity. Women's sexual fantasies will include more details about the nonphysical characteristics (such as the profession or specific character traits) of imagined partners. Women will have a clearer image of the facial features of their imagined partners; men will have a clearer image of the genital features of their imagined partners. The emotional setting (such as mood and ambiance) will be a more important aspect of women's than of men's sexual fantasies. Finally, as discussed above, the authors had divergent expectations about the importance of the physical setting in men's and women's sexual fantasies.

METHODS

The subjects were 307 students (182 females, 125 males) enrolled in introductory-level general education courses (General Psychology or Cultural Anthropology) at a California state university or at a California junior college. Approximately half of the subjects came from each school. Introductory-level general education courses were chosen for study because the students enrolled in such courses represent a broad cross-section of academic majors at both schools. The subjects were 111 females and 56 males in the 17–21-year age range, 59 females and 60 males in the 22–29-year age range, and 9 females and 12 males in the 30-year and above age range; 74.2% of the subjects were Caucasian, 13.1% were Asian, 5.9% were Hispanic, 3.9% were black, and 2.9% were "other." The overwhelming majority (88.6%) had never been married.

The questionnaire was an anonymous paper-and-pencil survey consisting of multiple-choice questions about sexual fantasy and arousal, along with demographic questions. The following description appeared at the head of the survey:

We are doing an independent study in the field of human sexuality. All questions refer to *you* and *your* sexual thoughts and fantasies. Please be as honest as possible. Remember this is not a test, and there are no trick questions.

evol. psych of punk or blue?

Description: Sexual fantasies may be externally provoked or internally generated. That is, sexual fantasies may be stimulated by something you see, read, or hear in the environment, or they may occur spontaneously.

The survey was given to entire class sections without prior warning in order to obtain as large a response rate as possible. To engage the subjects' interest in the study, they were told, before the questionnaires were distributed, that the experimenter would return to their class at a later date to explain the purpose of the survey and to discuss the results (which he did). Responses were recorded on a scantron-like sheet designed to minimize the visibility of answers and ensure confidentiality.

Of the 421 students who took the survey, 307 returned usable questionnaires. The other 114 surveys (27%) were discarded because of incompleteness, internal inconsistencies, or admitted dishonesty. As a control for internal consistency, Question 17 appeared twice in the questionnaire. Subjects who recorded two different answers to this question were eliminated. The final question in the survey asked students directly whether or not they had answered the questionnaire honestly.

RESULTS

A t test for sex differences, using pooled variance estimates, was performed on the twelve questions that employed rating scales. A one-tailed test was used because the theory generated directional predictions.

Questions 1 and 2 used a 0 to 7 rating scale with the alternative answers: Never, Once a week, Once a day or less, About once a day, 2 or 3 times a day, 4 to 6 times a day, 7 to 10 times a day, or More than 10 times a day. Question 1 asked, "Approximately how often do you have sexual fantasies?" and resulted in means of 1.97 (SD = 1.16) for females and 3.22 (SD = 1.46) for males ($t = -8.33$, $df = 304$, $p < .001$). Question 2 asked, "Approximately how often do you get sexually aroused?" and resulted in means of 2.17 (SD = 1.12) for females and 3.27 (SD = 1.35) for males ($t = -7.74$, $df = 302$, $p < .001$). Question 3 used a 0 to 6 scale with the alternative answers: None, One, Two, Three to four, Five to six, Seven to eight, and More than eight. Question 3 asked, "On the average, how many

different imagined partners do you have sexual fantasies about in a single day?" and resulted in means of 1.08 (SD = .87) for females and 1.96 (SD = 1.20) for males ($t = -7.46$, $df = 305$, $p < .001$).

Questions 4–6 used a 0 to 3 rating scale with the alternative answers: Very important, Somewhat important, Not very important, or Not at all important. Question 4 asked, "How important is the physical setting (such as the look, textures, sounds, and smells of a place) in your sexual fantasies?" and resulted in means of .91 (SD = .75) for females and 1.08 (SD = .78) for males ($t = -1.917$, $df = 304$, $p < .03$). Question 5 asked, "How important is caressing and non-genital touching in your sexual fantasies?" and resulted in means of .49 (SD = .81) for females and 1.04 (SD = .83) for males ($t = -5.29$, $df = 305$, $p < .001$). Question 6 asked, "How important is the emotional setting (such as the mood and ambiance) in your sexual fantasies?" and resulted in means of .61 (SD = .68) for females and .96 (SD = .81) for males ($t = -4.09$, $df = 302$, $p < .001$).

Questions 7–10 used a 0 to 4 scale with the alternative answers: Always, Usually, Sometimes, Rarely, or Never. Question 7 asked, "In your sexual fantasies do you have a clear image of the genital features of your imagined partner?" and resulted in means of 2.29 (SD = 1.11) for females and 1.29 (SD = .89) for males ($t = 8.37$, $df = 303$, $p < .001$). Question 8 asked, "In your sexual fantasies do you have a clear image of the facial features of your imagined partner?" and resulted in means of 1.09 (SD = 1.19) for females and .95 (SD = .99) for males ($t = 1.08$, $df = 304$, p = n.s.). Question 9 asked, "Do your fantasies include many details about the nonphysical characteristics (such as the profession or specific character traits) of your fantasized partner?" and resulted in means of 2.14 (SD = 1.12) for females and 2.51 (SD = 1.08) for males ($t = -2.89$, $df = 304$, $p < .002$). Question 10 asked, "Is the buildup, enticement, and interplay that sometimes precedes a sexual encounter an important part of your sexual fantasies?" and resulted in means of .85 (SD = .93) for females and 1.15 (SD = .98) for males ($t = -2.70$, $df = 305$, $p < .004$)

Questions 11 and 12 used a 0 to 4 scale with the alternative answers: Regularly, Often, Sometimes, Rarely, or Never. Question 11 asked, "How often do you substitute or switch one imagined partner for another during the course of a single sexual fantasy?" and resulted in means of 3.08 ($SD = .97$) for females and 2.30 ($SD = 1.10$) for males ($t = 6.54$, $df = 303$, $p < .001$). Question 12 stated, "Some people regularly experience sexual desire for people with whom it would be taboo to have sex. For example, they may experience desire for a relative or in-law, or for their best friend's lover, or they may experience strong extramarital urges. These desires are real, often lead to sexual fantasies, and may occur whether one wants them to or not. How often do you experience these kinds of desires?" This question resulted in means of 2.75 ($SD = 1.11$) for females and 2.60 ($SD = 1.21$) for males ($t = 1.11$, $df = 298$, $p =$ n.s.).

The remainder of the questions and responses are cross-tabulated by sex. These results, and the chi-square values for sex differences, are presented in Table 20.1.

Within the two basic hypothesis sets, the 26 survey questions can be grouped into seven categories, with some overlap (i.e., some questions are relevant to more than one category).

Hypothesis set 1: the desire for sexual variety. First, we expected a preference for partner variety to be evidenced in men's fantasies, a preference which entails discriminating—presumably visually—one imagined partner from another. The large number of fantasized partners that men reported may be one manifestation of a distinctly male preference for sexual variety. Men were more than twice as likely as women to report having sexual fantasies at least once a day (Question 1), and men were twice as likely as women to report becoming sexually aroused at least once a day (Question 2). Thus it is not surprising that men reported fantasizing about a greater number of different partners during the course of an average day than women

Table 20.1. Responses of Males and Females to Questionnaire Items

13. If you answered "Regularly," "Often," or "Sometimes" to Question 12: How do you generally feel about these kinds of desires? ($x^2 = .276$, $df = 3$, $p =$ n.s.)

	I wish that I didn't experience them	I find myself unable to control them	Both A and B	None of the Above
Females	21%	23%	20%	36%
Males	19%	25%	23%	33%

14. If you answered "Regularly," "Often," or "Sometimes" to Question 12: When you experience these kinds of desires, do you: ($x^2 = .845$, $df = 4$, $p =$ n.s.)

	Find them bothersome	Feel bad about them	Both and A and B	Enjoy them without feeling bad or guilty	None of the above
Females	10%	19%	13%	41%	17%
Males	14%	18%	16%	37%	16%

15. Considering your sexual fantasies throughout the course of your life, do you think that in your imagination you have had sexual encounters with over 1,000 different people? ($x^2 = 27.96$, $df = 1$, $p < .001$).

	Yes	No
Females	8%	92%
Males	32%	68%

16. Are your sexual fantasies typically about: ($x^2 = 34.33$, $df = 3$, $p < .001$)

	Someone who you are, or have been, romantically/sexually involved with	Someone (even if he or she is made up) who you would like to become romantically involved with	Someone (even if he or she is made up) who you would simply like to have sex with	None of the above
Females	59%	25%	9%	7%
Males	28%	38%	29%	5%

17. Which is a more important part of your sexual fantasies? ($x^2 = 23.34$, $df = 2$, $p < .001$)

	Visual Images	Touching	Neither one is an important part of my sexual fantasies
Females	39%	55%	6%
Males	66%	28%	6%

Table 20.1. (continued)

18. During sexual fantasy, do you focus more on: ($x^2 = 43.47$, $df = 1$, $p < .001$)

	Visual images	Feelings
Females	43%	57%
Males	81%	19%

19. Which is more important in your sexual fantasies? ($x^2 = 9.56$, $df = 1$, $p < .003$)

	Visual images of your fantasized partner	How your fantasized partner responds to you
Females	36%	64%
Males	54%	46%

20. During sexual fantasy, do you focus more on: ($x^2 = 66.64$, $df = 3$, $p < .001$).

	The sexual act itself	The physical characteristics of your fantasized partner	The personal or emotional characteristics of your fantasized partner	Your own physical or emotional responses within the fantasy
Females	12%	13%	41%	34%
Males	20%	50%	16%	13%

21. Which statement most accurately describes your sexual fantasies? ($x^2 = 43.35$, $df = 3$, $p < .001$)

	My imagined partner has the power to stir my emotions and excite me physically as no one else can	Other imagined partners would be just as exciting as long as they were equally attractive
Females	75%	25%
Males	38%	62%

22. Which of the following best describes your typical sexual fantasies? ($x^2 = 37.85$, $df = 2$, $p < .001$)

	The situation unfolds slowly and unhurriedly, so that a good deal of time passes before explicitly sexual activity	The situation quickly includes explicitly sexual activity	The situation doesn't include explicitly sexual activity at all
Females	72%	17%	11%
Males	50%	48%	2%

23. For you, what kind of feelings generally accompany your sexual thoughts and fantasies? (Choose only your strongest feeling) ($x^2 = 5.88$, $df = 6$, $p =$ n.s.)

	Good/ Happy	Frustration	Guilt/ Shame	Elation	Fear/ Anxiety	Excitement/ Involvement	Disgust
Females	46%	3%	4%	2%	3%	43%	0%
Males	41%	4%	2%	5%	1%	47%	0%

24. For you, what kind of feelings generally accompany your physical sexual arousal? (Choose only your strongest feeling) ($x^2 = 5.14$, $df = 6$, $p =$ n.s.)

	Good/ Happy	Frustration	Guilt/ Shame	Elation	Fear/ Anxiety	Excitement/ Involvement	Disgust
Females	42%	3%	3%	4%	3%	44%	0%
Males	42%	6%	2%	7%	2%	40%	1%

25. When you get sexually aroused, do you usually: ($x^2 = .27$, $df = 1$, $p =$ n.s.)

	Enjoy the feeling	Try to repress the feeling
Females	85%	15%
Males	82%	18%

26. When you have sexual fantasies, do you usually: ($x^2 = .78$, $df = 1$, $p =$ n.s.)

	Enjoy the feeling	Try to repress the feeling
Females	89%	11%
Males	92%	8%

did (Question 3) or that men were much more likely than women to report having had sexual fantasies about more than 1,000 different people in the course of their lives (Question 15). There was no sex difference, however, in the frequency of reported sexual desires for tabooed partners (Question 12), although neither sex admitted to having such desires very often. Men were, however, much more likely than women to report that their sexual fantasies are typically about someone they simply would like to have sex with, as opposed to someone they are or have been sexually or romantically involved with (Question 16). Perhaps most directly relevant to the issue of sexual variety is the fact that only 12% of the men, but 43% of the women, reported that they never substitute or switch partners during the course of a single sexual fantasy (Question 11).

Hypothesis set 2: visual versus tactile arousal; the importance of context and personal characteristics. Second, we expected visual images to dominate men's fantasies more than women's, and this expectation was confirmed by responses to several survey questions. Men reported that during sexual fantasy, visual images are more important than touching (Question 17), feelings (Question 18), or the responses of their fantasized partners (Question 19), while in each case the reverse was true for women. Sex differences along all three of these dimensions were very significant. Men were also much more likely than women to report having a clear image of the genital features of their fantasized partners (Question 7) and to report focusing on the physical rather than on the personal or emotional characteristics of their fantasized partners (Question 20).

Third, the male tendency to emphasize visual images in sexual fantasy implies an outward focus on the fantasized partner as an object of desire; we expected to find a complementary female tendency to focus inward on the self as the object of the imagined partner's desire. This hypothesis received some support. Women were two and a half times as likely as men to report focusing on their own physical or emotional responses during sexual fantasy (Question 20); women were much more likely than men to report that how their fantasized partner responds to them is more important than visual images of that partner (Question 19); and

women were far more likely than men to report that touching is a very important part of their sexual fantasies (Questions 5 and 17).

Fourth, we expected women's sexual fantasies to be more personal than men's fantasies, and this expectation was confirmed in a number of different ways. Women were far more likely than men to report that their imagined partners are uniquely able to arouse them physically and emotionally, whereas men were far more likely than women to report that they can substitute different imagined partners without compromising sexual excitement (Question 21). Women were two and a half times as likely as men to report focusing on the personal or emotional characteristics of their fantasized partners (Question 20); women were far less likely than men to switch partners in mid-fantasy (Question 11); and women were twice as likely as men to report that their fantasies are typically about someone they are, or have been, romantically or sexually involved with (Question 16). Women were also significantly more likely than men to report that their sexual fantasies include details about the nonphysical characteristics of their fantasized partners (Question 9), though this sex difference was not as dramatic as we had anticipated. There was no sex difference in the tendency to have a clear image of the facial features of the imagined partner: a majority of both sexes reported that they always or often have such images during their sexual fantasies (Question 8).

Fifth, we expected that the emotional context would be more important in women's than in men's sexual fantasies. This expectation was confirmed. The mood and ambiance (Question 6) and caressing and nongenital touching (Question 17) are more important in women's than in men's fantasies. Women's fantasies are much more likely than men's to slowly build to explicitly sexual activity; conversely, men's fantasies are much more likely than women's to move quickly to explicitly sexual acts (Question 22). Finally, women were two and a half times as likely as men to report focusing on the personal or emotional characteristics of their imagined partners (Question 20).

Sixth, we disagreed in our expectations about the importance of the physical setting: One of us anticipated that the physical setting would be more prominent in women's than in men's fantasies because of the greater salience of context to women; the other author anticipated that any such difference would be washed out by the male tendency to visualize. In fact, a small but significant sex difference was found (Question 4), suggesting that the physical setting is more important in women's than in men's sexual fantasies.

Affect. Seventh, several questions were designed to determine whether men and women differ in the feelings or attitudes that accompany sexual arousal and fantasy. On none of these questions did a sex difference emerge: On the contrary, men's and women's responses to these questions were astonishingly similar, particularly in light of the large sex differences in responses to the questions that probed the nature of sexual fantasies themselves. Overwhelmingly, both sexes reported that positive feelings accompany sexual arousal and fantasy (Questions 23, 24, 25, 26), and although some of the subjects who experienced sexual desires for tabooed partners (Question 12) found these desires bothersome, there were no sex differences in feelings about, or attitudes toward, these desires (Questions 13 and 14).

— yes but - ontogeny ? phylogeny ?
- single pop.

DISCUSSION

This study provides evidence of substantial sex differences in sexual fantasy. Women's fantasies were less frequent and less dominated by visual images than men's fantasies were; women, more than men, emphasized touching, feelings, partner response, their own physical and emotional responses, and emotional states, such as mood and ambiance. Women's fantasies were more personal than men's fantasies: women were more likely to fantasize about someone they were, or had been, involved with, to focus on personal or emotional characteristics of their imagined partner, to include nonphysical details about their imagined partner, and to report that their imagined partner was uniquely able to arouse them emotionally and physically. Women's fantasies unfolded more slowly than men's fantasies and included more caressing and nongenital touching, and this buildup and interplay was more important to women than to men. Women's tendencies to focus on their own responses and on how their imagined partners respond to them implies that women are more likely than men to see them-

selves as the objects of their partner's sexual desire. By contrast, men's fantasies were more frequent, featured more imagined partners, were more impersonal, were more dominated by visual images, particularly genital images, moved more quickly to explicitly sexual acts, tended to focus outward on the imagined partner as a sexual object, were more likely to be about someone the fantasizer merely wanted to have sex with, and were more likely to emphasize partner variety.

The one predictive failure in our study concerned the clarity of facial images in sexual fantasy (Question 8). In accordance with the greater female emphasis on partner specificity, we expected women, more than men, to focus clearly on the facial characteristics of their imagined partners. No such difference was found. Perhaps men were as likely as women to have a clear image of their imagined partner's face because men use facial features to discriminate between different females (a preference for sexual variety implies an ability to recognize individual differences, a partiality toward novelty, and a prejudice against familiarity [Symons 1979]).

Male and Female Literatures of Erotic Fantasy

The sex differences highlighted in this study are consistent with previous research on sexual fantasy (reviewed above); moreover, these sex differences are clearly mirrored in the contrasts between male and female literatures of erotic fantasy: male-oriented pornography and female-oriented romance novels. There is little overlap in the readership (or viewership) of these two genres, presumably because male-oriented pornography combines all the elements that appeal particularly to men, while erotic romances combine all the elements that appeal particularly to women. Pornotopia—the fantasy realm portrayed in male-oriented pornography (Marcus 1966)—varies little through time and space (Smith 1976). Whether written or pictorial, pornotopia overwhelmingly depicts or evokes visual images of female bodies (or male bodies, in the case of male homosexual pornography), particularly the genitals. The most striking feature of male-oriented pornography is that sex is sheer lust and physical gratification, devoid of encumbering relationships, emotional elaboration, complicated plot lines, flirtation, courtship, and extended foreplay; in pornotopia, women, like men, are easily aroused and willing.

Erotic romance novels, which are almost exclusively written by and for women, and which are so popular that a single title often sells millions of copies, differ profoundly from male-oriented pornography. Many modern romances portray sexual activity far more graphically than their historical predecessors did, and a modern romance heroine may have a career as interesting as that of the hero; but the basic fictional world of the romance—like the vastly different realm of pornotopia—has remained remarkably stable over the centuries (Mussel 1984). In her study of Japanese romance novels Mulhern (1989:55) remarks: "It may be that the romance form best suits the female psyche, because its formula reflects women's universal reality better than any other formulaic type." The following brief summary of the romance novel's nature is distilled from Faust (1980), Mussell (1984), and Radway (1984) (also see Hazen 1983).

Romances are fundamentally about mate selection, and they vary widely in the degree to which sexual activity is graphically depicted (if it is depicted at all). "In all romances, the love story is the central action and the most significant motivating force. . . . [Romances] assert and reinforce a woman's desire to identify and marry the one right man who will remain hers for the rest of her life" (Mussel 1984:11). Sex in the romance novel serves the plot without dominating it; the emotional focus of the romance is on love, commitment, domesticity, and nurturing. "Where masculinity porn emphasizes physical encounters," writes Faust (1980:152), "romance novels elaborate on the relationships in which the encounters take place. Male writers exploit every orifice, every position, every combination of organs, gender, number and kinship. . . . When women write sexually explicit novels, they explore all the emotional nuances that transform the simple conjunction of bodies." Satisfying sexual encounters in erotic romances identify partners who share a commitment to fidelity: "Unlike pornography, erotic romances do not portray variety as a sexual goal for women. Although erotic heroines do not preserve their virginity, they nevertheless demonstrate emotional—or

serial—monogamy" (Mussel 1984:43). The romance readers Radway (1984) studied were angry about the human male's taste for sexual variety, and they didn't want to adopt male standards; they wanted men to adopt their standards.

In a romance novel, the hero discovers in the heroine a fulfilling focus for his passion, which ensures his future sexual fidelity; he becomes dependent on the heroine: ". . . sex scenes offer a model not for [female] sexual submission but for [female] sexual control" (Mussel 1984:21). As Mulhern (1989:66) remarks, "One of the basic assumptions of romance is the primacy of love, but it by no means implies an abject emotional dependency on the woman's part." Sexual activity in romances is described primarily through the heroine's emotions rather than through descriptions of her physical responses or through visual imagery. The heroine is aroused through touch rather than sight (Faust 1980). The hero is not sexually objectified (although he may be viewed as a success object—Farrell 1986); rather, the reader subjectively identifies with the heroine as the object of male passion and solicitude.

Although the raison d'être of erotic romances, unlike male-oriented pornography, presumably is not masturbation-enhancement, romance readers may derive significant sexual satisfaction from their reading. Coles and Shamp (1984) found no personality or demographic differences between female readers and nonreaders of erotic romances except with respect to sexuality: readers engaged in sexual intercourse much more frequently than nonreaders did, and readers were much more likely to use fantasy to enhance the experience of sexual intercourse. Coles and Shamp conclude "that erotic romances provide a form of sexual stimulation for their readers similar to that provided by sexual fantasies and that they are a form of "soft core" pornography that women find socially acceptable and nonthreatening" (1984:187); women do not buy male-oriented pornography because it tends to be "written by and for men and emphasizes situations in which the female characters are impersonalized and objectified . . ." (1984:207). In short, the romance novel is an erotic, utopian, female counterfantasy to pornotopia. Just as the women depicted in pornotopia exhibit a suspiciously male-like sexuality, romances "are exercises in the imaginative transformation of masculinity to conform with female standards" (Radway 1984:147).

Causes of Sex Differences

Social scientists usually attribute sex differences in sexual fantasy to sex differences in life experiences (e.g., Barclay 1973; Fisher et al. 1988; Follingstad and Kimbrell 1986; Hass 1979; Knafo and Jaffe 1984). We do not, of course, deny that various life experiences are likely to affect people's sexual fantasies (see Chick and Gold 1987–1988 for a review of social variables affecting fantasy production); indeed, variation in life experiences may underlie much of the intrasex variation in responses to our survey questions. Nor do we deny that males and females may typically differ in some life experiences that are likely to affect various aspects of sexuality, including sexual fantasy. Since sexual intercourse exposes males and females to very different risks, one might expect most parents to attempt in various subtle and unsubtle ways to circumscribe their daughters' sexual activities more than their sons'. An evolutionary perspective on our species, however, should arouse suspicion of any hypothesis that purports to account for sex differences in sexual fantasy solely in terms of differential life experiences. The reason is this: all such hypotheses imply that males and females possess essentially the same (i.e., sexually monomorphic) innate brain/mind mechanisms; but to a Darwinian, it would be astonishing if selection had failed to produce sexually dimorphic mechanisms underlying human sexual feeling and action.

Throughout our evolutionary history, males and females necessarily encountered dramatically different reproductive opportunities and constraints. The minimal parental investment (Trivers 1972) that ancestral females had to make in each successful offspring (including nine months of gestation and several years of nursing) was enormous; thus the careful choice of mates and other sexual partners and attention to the circumstances surrounding sexual intercourse must always have been crucial determinants of female fitness. A tendency to become sexually aroused merely on the basis of cosmetic, visually detected qualities, or a taste for sexual variety for its own sake, surely

would have promoted random copulations, undermined female choice of partners and the circumstances of conception, reduced the likelihood of acquiring male parental investment, increased the likelihood of being beaten, abandoned, or killed by a jealous husband (and also by angry brothers), and drastically impaired female fitness.

The minimal (as opposed to typical) male parental investment, on the other hand, was virtually nil throughout our evolutionary history, and successful men were normally able to obtain multiple wives. Thus, if the risks were low enough, it presumably would have been adaptive for an ancestral male to copulate with almost any fertile woman (close kin excepted) and to desire new women simply because they were new. If even one sexual impulse in a thousand was consummated, the reproductive payoff for ancestral males was potentially enormous; hence males would have benefited from relatively fast and frequent sexual arousal (Knoth, Boyd, and Singer 1988) that varied in intensity directly with visually detected cues of female "mate value" (see Daly and Wilson 1983; and Symons 1979, 1987a for further discussion).

In conclusion, the contrasting male and female sexual psychologies implied by the data presented here, the scientific literature on sexual fantasy, and the male and female literatures of erotic fantasy do not represent capricious or arbitrary amalgams of traits; on the contrary, they appear to reflect precisely the *coherent*, *integrated*, *sexually differentiated* systems that an adaptationist perspective on our species leads us to expect. Some social scientists have attributed sex differences in sexual fantasy to such generalized phenomena as erotophobia-erotophilia (Fisher et al. 1988), the tendency to like or dislike sexuality, or to sex guilt (Follingstad and Kimbrell 1986), the tendency toward self-mediated punishment for violating standards of proper sexual conduct (Mosher and Cross 1971). If phenomena such as sex guilt or erotophobia are to affect experiences of sexual arousal and fantasy, they presumably must do so via their effects on the feelings that accompany these experiences (Knoth, Boyd, and Singer 1988). But we found no sex differences in accompanying feelings: women were as likely as men to report enjoying and feeling excited by their sexual fantasies; men were as likely as women to report feeling guilty about and trying to repress their fantasies.[3] Overwhelmingly both women and men felt positive about sexual arousal and fantasy. Most striking, women were as likely as men to report having sexual desires for tabooed partners, such as relatives or in-laws. Thus, even though men and women differed strongly in many dimensions of sexual fantasy, they were equally likely to violate social conventions by experiencing (or admitting experiencing) forbidden desires. Moreover, women were as likely as men to report enjoying tabooed sexual desires without feeling bad or guilty about them, and men were as likely as women to report feeling bothered by these desires and unable to control them. These findings concur with those of Carlson and Coleman (1977) and Knoth, Boyd, and Singer (1988), who found that women and men report equally high levels of positive affect during sexual fantasy, despite large sex differences in fantasy rates and complexity.

Although specific neuroanatomical data relevant to the question of sex differences in sexual fantasy are lacking, the frequency of sexual fantasy does appear to be associated with androgen levels. Udry et al. (1985 1986) have recently shown that the increase in "the frequency of thinking about sex" around puberty is directly related to rising androgen levels in both males and females and is *not* secondary to accompanying physical or psychosocial changes. Further, "the androgens of puberty provide a more powerful jolt to male than to female libido. Before puberty, male and female testosterone levels are not much different. At maturity, these levels have increased by a factor of ten or twenty in males, while they only double in females" (Udry et al. 1986:226). The most convincing evidence of androgen effects on adult male sexuality comes from placebo-controlled studies of hypogonadal men on androgen replacement therapy. "Frequency of sexual thoughts" declines sharply in hypogonadal men about three weeks after the cessation of treatment, but then shows a rapid increase within two weeks of resuming treatment (Bancroft 1984). Similar effects have been documented in young, surgically menopausal women who have been administered exogenous androgens: subjective reports of desire, arousal, and frequency of sexual fan-

tasy increase markedly in most subjects (Sherwin, Gelfand, and Brender 1985). These data constitute a challenge to any hypothesis that attempts to explain sexual fantasy purely in terms of "social influences."

Furthermore, it is surely a mistake to assume, as many writers seem to do, that social influences necessarily foster rather than reduce sex differences in sexuality. In fact, a distinct ideology about sex differences is widespread among educated people in the Western world: male and female psychologies are held to be identical by nature, and differences between the sexes are assumed to result entirely from "social influences" (the rise of this ideology is discussed in Durden-Smith and DeSimone 1983). Most college students—in fact most middle-class people—are exposed to and often espouse this belief system. Liberated women may be encouraged to act as men do; at male strip shows, for example, many women enthusiastically whoop it up as they mistakenly believe men do in such settings (see Symons 1987a). Conversely, male indulgence in pornography and sexual variety is often characterized in the popular and scientific media as immature, adolescent, and evidencing sexual insecurity; "real men" are loving fathers and faithful husbands. Indeed, it would be surprising if messages of this sort were *not* promulgated: whether I myself am a philanderer or a faithful husband, it is surely in my interest (however defined) to convince *other men* that it is better to be the latter. It is entirely conceivable—and in our opinion likely—that many "social influences" mitigate, rather than amplify, some sex differences in sexual expression.

Summary of Sex Differences

The data on sexual fantasy reported here, the scientific literature on sexual fantasy (reviewed above), the consumer-driven selective forces of a free market (which have shaped the historically stable contrasts between male-oriented pornography and female-oriented romance novels), the ethnographic record on human sexuality (Symons 1979), and the ineluctable implications of an evolutionary perspective on our species, taken together, imply the existence of profound sex differences in sexual psychology. These differences can be summarized as follows.

1. Both sexes can experience both lust and limerence (the experience of being in love—Tennov 1979); however, lust tends to be an autonomous, appetitive desire in men but not in women, whereas limerence tends to be an autonomous, appetitive desire in women but not in men (Weinrich 1988). Male sexual fantasies and pornotopia reflect the autonomy of lust, while female sexual fantasies and erotic romances reflect the autonomy of limerence. Thus, women rarely seek out depictions of pornotopia, although they are capable of becoming sexually aroused by them (see Symons 1979, 1987a), and men rarely read romance novels, although they are capable of falling in love. Furthermore, there is evidently no market for a female-oriented version of pornotopia (in which men are portrayed as anonymous sex objects) or for male-oriented romance novels. In women's fantasies, lust is the servant of limerence and is intimately bound up with mate choice; in men's fantasies the goal is the satiation of lust.

2. Because the goal of limerence is mate choice, the "limerent object" (Weinrich 1988) in women's fantasies is personalized, hence the importance of nonphysical partner characteristics, context, and feelings. Because the goal of lust is sexual satisfaction, the lusty object (Weinrich 1988) in men's fantasies tends to be objectified rather than personalized, hence the focus on sexual organs, sexual acts, and physical attributes, and (compared with women's fantasies) the lesser importance of nonphysical partner characteristics, context, and feelings.

3. Men tend to become sexually aroused by visual stimulation; hence men's sexual fantasies are overwhelmingly likely to focus on visual images of the imagined partner. Women's fantasies are also visual, of course, since *Homo sapiens*, like other higher primates, is a fundamentally visual species, but women become sexually aroused (as opposed to sexually interested) primarily via tactile stimulation by favored males; hence women's fantasies tend to emphasize the touch of an imagined partner who has passed a (partly visual) test of desirability. The ethnographic record strongly implies that the sex difference in the tendency to become sexually aroused by visual stimuli is a human universal (Symons 1979). (Though we neglected to do so, it would be interesting to investigate the relative importance of touching versus being touched in sexual fantasies; we predict that men will emphasize the former and women the latter.)

4. Women tend to imagine themselves as objects of male passion and solicitude, while men tend to imagine women as responsive, lusty objects. As Money and Ehrhardt (1972) note, when men and women become sexually aroused by viewing pictures or films of explicit sexual activity, they do so via fundamentally different psychological processes: to a man, the female in the scene is a sexual object, and he imagines taking her out of the scene and having sex with her; but a woman, viewing the same scene, subjectively identifies with the female and imagines herself as the lusty object of male passion. This type of sex difference has also emerged in studies of projective sexual fantasies in response to masturbation stimuli (Abramson and Mosher 1979; Mosher and Abramson 1977).

5. In contrast to women, men tend to experience an autonomous predilection for a variety of sexual partners (Symons 1979), and their fantasies reflect this, though both sexes may usually experience maximal sexual excitement at the beginning of a new relationship (Symons 1987a).

Limitations and Implications

PREFERENCES vs. ACTIONS

Since sexual fantasies are not constrained by most real-life exigencies, the study of sexual fantasy probably provides a clearer picture of male and female sexual natures than does the study of sexual action. Our goal has been to characterize, approximately and provisionally, some of the sexually dimorphic brain/mind mechanisms underlying human sexuality by analyzing sex differences in patterns of sexual fantasy. Our understanding of these patterns could be greatly augmented and refined by giving the present questionnaire to other samples that vary in age, social class, culture, and so forth. One limitation of the present study is the relative youth and inexperience of its subjects; it will be interesting to compare their responses with those of older, more experienced men and women. Another limitation of the present study is that the survey questions were developed by two men. No doubt female sexual psychology would have been more fully and subtly probed had women collaborated in designing the questionnaire.

It is probably impossible to fully or adequately characterize a sexually dimorphic human psyche using a unisex language (there are English words for distinctively male and female body parts, but none for distinctively male and female experiences). Nevertheless, one way to increase our understanding of psychological sex differences would be to progressively alter questionnaire items with the intent of *maximizing* sex differences in response. By comparing questions that elicited a sex difference with variants that did not, and questions that elicited minor sex differences with variants that elicited major differences, we might eventually expand and refine our conceptions of male and female sexual natures.

Our data have implications for future research on sexual fantasy. We found touching, partner response, and emotional responses to be important aspects of women's fantasies—more important than visual images of sexual acts or partners. Yet most research on sexual fantasy has focused on content themes, either using fantasy checklists (e.g., Iwawaki and Wilson 1983; Knafo and Jaffe 1984; Wilson and Lang 1981) or content analysis of written fantasies (e.g., Barclay 1973; Follingstad and Kimbrell 1986; Hass 1979). Checklists offer a compendium of visualized sexual acts, but they neglect the affective dimensions of fantasy that seem to be so important to women. Content analyses circumvent some of these problems by allowing

for the expression of emotions; however, recording sexual fantasies on paper may tend to bias them in a graphic, visual direction. In a study of sexual fantasies among female prostitutes, Diana (1985) found that the women fantasized predominantly about romance, falling in love, marriage, and being desired for their physical and inner beauty. Diana writes: "So in a real sense the fantasies are not sexual at all. Primarily, they seem to reflect the deep desire to be loved, appreciated and cared for materially and emotionally. Yet, when asked to write out one of their fantasies, most of [the prostitutes] described fantasies with explicit sexual themes" (1985:134). The explanation may be that sexual acts and body parts are simply easier to describe than are romantic nuances and emotions. The nonvisual dimensions of female sexual fantasies are richly evoked by professional writers of erotic romances, but such expression is probably much more difficult for the average person. Furthermore, to many people sexual fantasy may connote a visual image of a sexual act; hence many women may not consider their erotic fantasies to be sexual per se, and thus may not think it appropriate to record them. Future research should strive to encompass the manifold dimensions of imagined erotic experiences.

Acknowledgments. We thank Don Brown, David Buss, and Kelly Hardesty-Ellis for helpful comments on earlier drafts of this article, Marc Kodack and Herb Maschner for assistance on data analysis and presentation, and Pat McKim for help in data collection.

NOTES

1. Trivers (1972) defines parental investment as "any investment by the parent in an individual offspring that increases the offspring's chance of surviving (and hence reproductive success) at the cost of the parent's ability to invest in other offspring" (p. 139). Investments can take the form of time, energy, and risk.

2. The important distinction here is between *sexual interest*, an evaluative process that is based largely on vision in both sexes, and *sexual arousal*, which occurs on the basis of sight as well as touch in men, but primarily on the basis of touch in women.

3. Given the availability of a valid sex guilt measure—the Mosher Sex-Guilt Inventory (MSGI)—one might ask why we did not use this measure. There are two reasons. First, while the MSGI has been shown to predict a variety of sexual behaviors, *no* clear relationship has been found between scores on the MSGI and most measures of sexual arousal (Morokoff 1985) or sexual fantasy (Follingstad and Kimbrell 1986). Second, almost none of the questions in the MSGI are actually about either sexual fantasy or arousal. As an alternative to the MSGI, we constructed a series of questions designed to measure the types of affect associated with sexual fantasy and arousal. While the construct validity of these questions is unknown, they do have face validity for the topic at hand.

21

Unobtrusive Measures of Human Sexuality

DONALD SYMONS
CATHERINE SALMON
BRUCE J. ELLIS

Many kinds of data can illuminate male and female sexual psychologies, and different research methods have different strengths and weaknesses. Webb et al. (1966) argue, "Interviews and questionnaires intrude as a foreign element into the social setting they would describe, they create as well as measure attitudes, they elicit atypical roles and responses, they are limited to those who are accessible and will cooperate, and the responses obtained are produced in part by dimensions of individual differences irrelevant to the topic at hand" (1). One way of mitigating these weaknesses, according to Webb et al., is to supplement and cross-validate interviews and questionnaires by using methods with *different* weaknesses, in particular by using *unobtrusive measures*, which are measures that do not require the cooperation of a respondent and do not themselves contaminate the response.

Some evolution-minded researchers have employed unobtrusive measures to excellent effect. For example, Daly and Wilson (1988b) used police homicide statistics to illuminate the psychology of male sexual proprietariness; Borgerhoff Mulder (1988c) used variation in brideprice to elucidate the determinants of female "mate value"; and Orians (1980) used variation in real estate prices to shed light on the psychology of human landscape preferences. As the last two examples illustrate, free markets are potential gold mines of information about human psychology, which we believe have been greatly underutilized.

Male-oriented pornography and female-oriented romance novels are multi-billion-dollar global industries, whose products have been shaped in free markets by consumer preferences. A strength of conducting research on these products is that the design features of mass-market erotica constitute unobtrusive measures of male and female sexual psychologies, just as the design features of food served in popular fast-food restaurants constitute unobtrusive measures of human gustatory psychology. A weakness of such research, however, is that the characteristics of mass-market erotica are determined by factors in addition to consumer preferences, including the skills and imagination of the producers, legal constraints, available technologies, and costs of production. For example, many aspects of commercially successful pornographic videos with low production values clearly do not represent the unconstrained ideal from the standpoint of maximizing male sexual arousal but rather the cost-effective ideal from the standpoint of maximizing pornographers' profits. Mass-market erotica thus may fail to manifest certain features of male and female sexual psychologies that are of theoretical interest. In contrast, a strength of conducting experimental and questionnaire research is that these methods allow for a broader range of hypothesis testing and can be used to probe dimensions of male and female sexual psychologies that are not manifest in mass-market erotica. In short, data derived from mass-market erotica and data derived from experiments and questionnaires can complement and cross-fertilize each other, because the weaknesses of one are often the strengths of the other.

Consider, for example, research on human female waist-to-hip ratio (WHR). A number of evolutionists (e.g., Buss 1994; Ellis and Symons, chapter 20; Symons 1979) have posited that in ancestral human populations selection favored males who were sexually aroused by visually detected characteristics of female bodies that reliably indexed high "mate value." Among human females, WHR provides reliable information about health, age, hormonal status, parity, and fecundity; hence, human males can be expected to have evolved psychological mechanisms specialized to extract and process this information (Singh 1993). Because female mate value varies inversely with WHR, other things being equal, female sexual attractiveness also can be expected to vary inversely with WHR. Singh (1993, 1994) tested this hypothesis using both unobtrusive measures and experimental data.

Based on analyses of the measurements of *Playboy* centerfold models and Miss America contest winners over the last thirty to sixty years, Singh concluded that "a narrow waist set against full hips [a WHR in the .68–.72 range] has been a consistent feature for female attractiveness, whereas other bodily features, such as bustline, overall body weight, or physique, have been assigned varying degrees of importance over the years" (Singh 1993:296). Unobtrusive measures thus support the hypothesis that a low female WHR is perceived as attractive, but these measures do not fully illuminate the parameters of the psychological mechanisms that extract and process WHR information. Specifically, the *Playboy* centerfold and Miss America data do not reveal the relationship between attractiveness and WHR over the normal range of variation or allow one to separate the effects of WHR on female attractiveness from the effects of other physical attributes.

To address these limitations, Singh supplemented his unobtrusive measures with experimental data. Using line drawings or photographs of female figures, he varied WHR while holding other physical attributes constant. Subjects then rank-ordered the stimulus figures from most to least attractive. WHR systematically affected judgments of attractiveness over the normal female range of variation: from .60 to 1.00, WHR and attractiveness ratings were inversely related (Singh 1993, 1994).

Unobtrusive measures of erotica can be used to illuminate sexual psychologies in a number of ways. One approach is to use analyses of erotica as a means of generating or clarifying hypotheses about human sexuality. For example, the only predictive failure in the preceding study by Ellis and Symons was their hypothesis that women would report having clearer images of their imagined partners' faces during sexual fantasy than men would. In fact, both men and women reported that they usually have clear images of their imagined partners' faces, and there was no significant sex difference. The adaptationist logic behind this prediction was that in ancestral human populations the particular person with whom a female had sexual intercourse was extremely important, whereas for an ancestral male sexual intercourse with any fertile female (close kin excepted) would have been potentially adaptive, as long as the risks were low enough. However, had we analyzed male-oriented pornographic videos before making this prediction, we would have noticed that close-up shots of women's faces are an essential ingredient of the genre. Even the crudest, most impoverished videos, with the lowest production values, include such close-ups. This would have motivated us to think more carefully about facial imagery as a source of male sexual arousal and to realize that there are a number of selectionally sound reasons for expecting men to fantasize about women's faces. Images of faces probably promote male sexual arousal by establishing individual identity (and hence potential novelty), by displaying real or simulated sexual arousal and pleasure, and by displaying physical attractiveness (in most cases). In sum, more careful consideration of pornography probably would have prevented us from making the prediction in the first place.

Another way to use unobtrusive measures of erotica is to compare commercially successful products with less successful ones. Indeed, in a recent collection of trenchant essays on the nature of the romance novel by the professionals who write them (Kretz 1992), many of the romance authors note that sales figures and royalty checks provide important insights into female psychology. The best-selling romance novels, for example, almost never feature gentle, sensitive heroes, because women readers prefer to fantasize about "a strong, dominant, aggressive male brought to the point of surren-

here: promote current work rather than review preceding study

der by a woman" (Malek 1992:74), and because "winning against a wimp is no triumph" (1992:75). (One of these essays [Donald 1992] actually contains a brief evolutionary psychological account of the romance novel.)

Yet another approach is to identify the essential ingredients of erotic genres; that is, to distill their essences (as Ellis and Symons attempted to do in the preceding article). For example, a common characteristic of pornographic videos is humor (or, at least, attempted humor), but humor is *not* an essential ingredient: thousands of humorless porn videos are commercially successful.

all this is elaborate fallen not process

A final use of unobtrusive measures of erotica is to analyze smaller, more esoteric genres and to compare them to the mainstream forms, because (apparent) exceptions can prove (i.e., *test*) the rules. Comparing smaller erotic genres with mainstream forms can highlight the essential ingredients in male and female eroticas and also can suggest hypotheses about the causes of within-sex variation in erotic preferences. This approach is currently being pursued by Salmon and Symons in their ongoing study of male/male romances, including slash fiction.

The term "slash" has nothing to do with violence; it refers to erotic romances, written almost exclusively by and for heterosexual women, in which both protagonists are expropriated *male* media characters, costars of various American and British police, detective, adventure, spy, and science fiction television series or literary works (e.g., Sherlock Holmes and Dr. Watson). The first major slash protagonists were Captain Kirk and Mr. Spock from the 1960s *Star Trek* television series, and the term "slash" originally referred to the punctuation mark in "Kirk/Spock" or "K/S." Although the protagonists in slash fall in love and have sex with each other, they usually are depicted as heterosexual in orientation (however improbable this may seem to those unfamiliar with the genre); less often they are bisexual; and only occasionally are they both homosexual. Slash fiction and mainstream romances obviously differ in certain respects, yet in many ways they are surprisingly similar. Both the differences and the similarities are instructive.

For example, as emphasized in a number of the essays in Krentz (1992), romance novel heroes are "warriors"; in slash, however, *both* protagonists are "warriors" in the sense that they

are long-term partners in a dangerous and honorable profession who have risked their lives for one another in the past and will likely do so again in the future. The relationships between slash protagonists are often characterized by students of the genre as being more "egalitarian" than the relationships between heroes and heroines in mainstream romances (or, for that matter, than most relationships between men and women in real life). And it is indeed true that slash does not overtly dramatize the battle of the sexes (at least this element is muted compared with mainstream romances). This suggests the following hypothesis: although the heroine's taming of the hero, by virtue of his passionate attachment to her, is a staple theme of mainstream romances, it nonetheless is not an essential ingredient of women's erotic fantasies.

Academic studies of slash (e.g., Bacon-Smith 1992; Jenkins 1992; Lamb and Veith 1986; Penley 1992a; Russ 1985), although insightful in many respects, have in our view tended to underestimate the similarities between slash fiction and mainstream romances. For example, many of these studies emphasize the graphic portrayal of sexual activities in slash; but, in fact, sexual activities in slash sometimes are described at length and in vivid detail, sometimes are sketched briefly and obliquely, and sometimes occur entirely offstage. In other words, although graphic sex is a common feature of slash, it is not an essential ingredient, just as it is not an essential ingredient of mainstream romances. Furthermore, many features of the hero/heroine relationship portrayed in mainstream romances are also to be found in slash. For example, although slash protagonists are ostensibly male, wherever possible the point-of-view character is depicted as the smaller of the two, lighter in coloring, less hairy, physically weaker, more flirty and seductive, more psychologically insightful, quicker to detect the existence of mutual love, and more responsible for the developing love relationship. The similarities to mainstream romances in these respects may provide clues to the nature of female psychosexuality.

Because the essential ingredients of slash fiction and mainstream romances appear to be so similar, Salmon and Symons hypothesized that slash readers and mainstream romance readers do not differ significantly in their fundamental psychosexualities and, therefore, that given the opportunity, most women who enjoy reading mainstream romances would also enjoy reading high-quality male/male romances. As a preliminary test of this prediction, we asked members of a (mainstream) romance readers' group in Hamilton, Ontario—none of whom had previously read a male/male romance—to read a male/male romance novel and then to complete anonymously a length questionnaire designed to elicit their reactions to the novel, their views on romances, and various kinds of personal and demographic information. On average, these women reported enjoying the test novel as much as they enjoy most mainstream romances. By studying male/male romance fiction and women's responses to it, Salmon and Symons hope to home in on the essential ingredients of women's erotica and, by extension, on the essence of female psychosexuality.

Acknowledgments. We thank Paul Abramson, Sunni Baran, Don Brown, Peggy La Cerra, Joanna Scheib, and Margo Wilson for helpful comments on previous drafts of this essay.

22

[handwritten marginalia: ie. on' evol. perspective': max. repro. success but even opp. typical gender diffs may result from some contingency rule (norm.) but opp. typ. diffs in gender env. com.]

Evolution, Traits, and the <u>Stages of Human</u> <u>Courtship</u>: Qualifying the Parental Investment Model

DOUGLAS T. KENRICK
EDWARD K. SADALLA
GARY GROTH
MELANIE R. TROST

[handwritten marginalia: note the leap from differences to evolution nothing about prox. mechanism or ontogeny or phylogeny.]

One hears much talk these days about the need for a rapprochement between <u>personality</u> and <u>social psychology</u> (e.g., Blass 1984; Kenrick 1986). The December 1987 issue of the *Journal of Personality and Social Psychology* was dedicated to articles integrating the two areas. When the two subdisciplines were emerging at the turn of the century, both were influenced by the same intellectual tradition—Darwinian evolutionary theory. Sigmund Freud, whom many regard as the originator of the modern field of personality, took his ideas about life instincts and the primal horde directly from Darwin. The first psychology text with the title *Social Psychology*, written in 1908 by William McDougall, took an even more explicitly Darwinian approach.

This common birthplace may be the ideal ground for a reunion between personality and social psychology. We have argued elsewhere that <u>a biosocial model can connect the proximate processes</u> of social cognition and social learning with <u>the ultimate framework of sociobiology</u> (Kenrick 1987; Kenrick, Montello, and MacFarlane 1985). We have also argued that there are two areas where this framework is particularly relevant: <u>(a)</u> in explaining <u>gender differences</u> in personality and social behavior (Kenrick 1987); and <u>(b)</u> in explaining how those gender differences are intimately connected to different <u>mating strategies</u> (Kenrick and Trost 1987, 1989; Sadalla, Kenrick, and Vershure 1987). In this article, we discuss research that uses an evolutionary perspective to connect gender differences in personality to the social-psychological process of mate selection.

Sexual Selection

From its inception, Darwinian theory assumed an intimate association between social processes and gender differences in traits. Darwin connected the two via the process of *sexual selection*, first discussed in *The Origin of Species*:

... I believe, that when the males and females of any animal have the same general habits of life, but differ in structure, color, or ornament, such differences have been mainly caused by sexual selection: that is, by individual males having had, in successive generations, some slight advantage over other males, in their weapons, means of defense, or charms, which they have transmitted to their male offspring alone. (Darwin 1859:95)

In humans, individual differences in "charms" are <u>more likely</u> to be expressed in social be-

[handwritten marginalia: a priori !?!?]

Reprinted with permission from *Journal of Personality* 58:97–116 (1990).

[handwritten annotations: "really going out on a limb here, predicting humans unlikely to have antlers!"; "CARS"; "Very portmann"; "atypical diff."; "FISHER: total invest is 6:9:9; also by relevance"]

havior than in physical ornaments like antlers. Given that humans interact with familiar others over long time periods, human traits related to social dominance may be at least as important as physical weapons of defense are to other animals. Darwin further divided sexual selection into *intrasexual selection*, which results from competition between members of the same sex, and *epigamic selection*, which results from the fact that the members of one sex make choices about which members of the opposite sex they prefer to mate with:

> The rock-thrush of Guiana, birds of paradise, and some others, congregate; and successive males display with the most elaborate care, and show off in the best manner, their gorgeous plumage: they likewise perform strange antics before the females, which standing by as spectators, at last choose the most attractive partner. (Darwin 1859:94)

The fact that males and females across the spectrum of human cultures differ reliably in certain personality traits (Williams and Best 1982) may be due, in part, to sexual selection. It is assumed that our male and female ancestors fancied slightly different traits in one another. Presumably, males were chosen for traits related to dominance and social status, which signaled their capacity to contribute external resources to offspring. Because of their special mammalian abilities to contribute direct biological resources to potential offspring, females were chosen for traits signaling reproductive value and potential nurturance toward offspring (Buss and Barnes 1986). Traits such as male dominance and female nurturance may have their evolutionary roots in natural selection (tangible advantages are conferred on individuals who manifest such behavior), intrasexual selection (males who compete effectively with other males have more access to both resources and mates), and epigamic selection (individuals engaging in such behavior are more desirable as mating partners).

Differential Parental Investment by Males and Females

Darwin saw sexual selection as more relevant to males' than to females' characteristics. He believed that males are more likely to compete amongst themselves for access to females, and that females are more likely to exercise selectivity in their choice of mates. Modern evolutionary theorists follow Darwin in assuming that females are choosier about a mate's traits than are males. This difference is generally explained in terms of *differential parental investment* (Trivers 1972; Williams 1966a). Parental investment is typically defined (e.g., Trivers 1985) as the contributions a parent makes to one offspring's reproductive success at a cost to its own ability to invest in other offspring. In mammals, females typically make a greater investment in each offspring because the female carries the fetus, nurses the infant, and is, compared with the male, limited in the number of offspring she can produce. Because of their different levels of investment in each offspring, females and males should engage in different mating strategies. Females should attempt to maximize the viability and reproductive potential of each offspring, while males should attempt to maximize the number of offspring. In terms of the criteria for a sexual partner, females should be more selective. Males, conversely, are presumed to have less to lose from an ill-chosen mating.

The human sexuality literature provides ample evidence to suggest that humans fit the typical mammalian pattern of differential parental investment, with greater consequent female selectivity (Daly and Wilson 1983). Men are generally more eager and less discriminating with regard to sexuality (Hinde 1984; Kenrick and Trost 1987, 1989; Symons 1979). For instance, Kenrick, Stringfield, Wagenhals, Dahl, and Ransdell (1980) found men more likely to volunteer for experiments on erotica than were women, and there is abundant evidence that men seek more experience with erotica outside the laboratory (Kinsey, Pomeroy, and Martin 1948; Kinsey, Pomeroy, Martin, and Gebhard 1953; Shepher and Reisman 1985). Likewise, men are overrepresented in virtually every category of sexual deviation (Davison and Neale 1982).

We applied the differential parental investment model to humans in a series of studies on dominance and heterosexual attraction (Sadalla et al. 1987). In line with the above discussion, the model predicts that females will be attracted to males who show characteristics associated with social dominance. Males, who have less to lose from an ill-chosen mating, should be less discriminating about those characteristics in potential female partners. In support of the model, we found that males who expressed nonverbal dominance were, compared with less dominant males, rated as more sexually attractive by female subjects. Male subjects did not discriminate between dominant and nondominant female targets, but rated both as equally attractive. The effect was robust, appearing in four studies with three distinct manipulations of dominance. Sadalla and Fausal (1980) replicated the pattern across several different age samples of employees at a local manufacturing plant, and Buss (1989b) found that characteristics related to dominance and social status were associated with male attractiveness across a wide range of different cultures.

Pair Bonding Increases Male Parental Investment *quality vs quantity*

The parental investment model implies that the sex investing more (most commonly the female) will be most choosy; whereas the sex investing least (most commonly the male) should be most competitive. Compared to most mammalian species, however, human males make a substantial parental investment in their progeny. In our own society there is a well-established pattern of parental bonding. Approximately 95% of all Americans get married at least once, and Daly and Wilson (1983) note that there is some form of marriage in every known society. While the specific details of courtship vary within and across cultures, mate bonding is a universal feature of human society. It is important to keep in mind that high male parental investment in humans contrasts with most other mammalian species.

For the above reasons, one must take care in applying ideas about differential parental investment from other mammals (in which low-investing males are often indiscriminate in mate choice) to humans (in which males may be quite discriminating). Consider a study by Buss and Barnes (1986). These authors asked students to rank the characteristics they preferred in a mate and found some sex differences. Females ranked "earning potential" and "college graduate" higher than did males, whereas males ranked physical attractiveness higher than did females. Those gender differences are consistent with an evolutionary model: Males have historically contributed indirect resources (like food and protection) to the offspring, which in-

crease with education and socioeconomic status, whereas females have contributed direct physical resources via gestation and nurturing. Since physical attractiveness judgments are partially dependent on a female's youthfulness, those judgments correlate with her remaining reproductive potential (Buss and Barnes 1986; Kenrick and Keefe 1989; Symons 1979). The most relevant feature of Buss and Barnes's data, however, is the striking similarity between male and female preferences. Of the top 10 preferences, 7 were the same for the two sexes. Consistent with our discussion above, Buss and Barnes note that gender differences in mate criteria are diminished in monogamous species.

What accounts for the fact that Sadalla et al. (1987) found strong sex differences supporting an unqualified parental investment model, whereas Buss and Barnes found fewer sex differences? Symons (1979) suggests that it is necessary to distinguish between sex differences in *typical* parental investment, and sex differences in *minimum possible* parental investment. Humans are like other mammals in that a male's minimum possible parental investment is very small, but different from other mammals in that a male's typical parental investment is very large.

Qualifying the Parental Investment Model

The distinction between typical and minimum possible parental investment may allow us to specify the circumstances under which humans will show the strong gender differences found in most other mammals, and distinguish those from the circumstances under which humans will show the lack of gender differences found in many monogamous species. Note that Sadalla et al. (1987) focused on the sexual attractiveness of a stranger. Sexual liaisons between strangers have the potential for very low investment by males, and these authors found sex differences similar to those found in other mammalian species. Buss and Barnes, on the other hand, examined the characteristics desired in a long-term mate (associated with high parental investment by both sexes), and they found many gender similarities. The difference between these studies suggests a central qualification on the parental investment model in its application to human courtship. In line with a *relationship-qualified parental investment model,* we hypothesize that anticipated investment in the relationship is a crucial moderator of the variations in gender differences found in earlier studies.

In the present study, we examine the degree to which preferences in a partner are associated with the level of anticipated investment in the relationship. At the level of casual dating, there is relatively little investment by either sex, so few male/female differences in selectivity should be observed. As the relationship moves to the level of sexual involvement, potential female investment increases greatly, so a corresponding increase in female selectivity would be predicted. Since sexual involvement does not involve a similar increase in investment for males, no concomitant increase in male selectivity would be expected at that level. At the level of exclusive dating, investment increases substantially for males and should be accompanied by parallel increases in selectivity. At the marriage level, both males and females make sizable investments, so both sexes should be highly selective.

A second difference between the Sadalla et al. (1987) and the Buss and Barnes (1986) studies also suggests a limiting condition on when gender differences do and do not occur. Sadalla et al. examined only dominance-related characteristics, whereas Buss and Barnes examined a wide range of characteristics. In line with the earlier findings, and with the classical Darwinian view that females preferentially mate with males who show signals that indicate their relative dominance over other males, we expect that characteristics related to dominance will be differentially valued by the two sexes.

METHOD

Subjects

Ninety-three undergraduate students (29 males, 64 females) participated in the study during class time. Participation was voluntary and students were given extra course credit.

Procedure

Students were asked to consider the criteria that they would use in choosing a partner for involvement in (a) a single date, (b) sexual relations, (c) steady dating, and (d) marriage. For each level of involvement, they were asked to

rate the importance of 24 criteria. Thirteen of these criteria were from Buss and Barnes (1986, Study 2): kind and understanding, religious, exciting personality, creative and artistic, good housekeeper, intelligent, good earning capacity, wants children, easygoing, good heredity, college graduate, physically attractive, and healthy. Eleven additional descriptors were also added: aggressive, emotionally stable, friendly, popular, powerful, sexy, wealthy, ambitious, good sense of humor, high social status, and dominant. Participants were asked to give the minimum and maximum percentiles of each characteristic that they would find acceptable in a partner at each level of involvement. Several examples were given to clarify any questions about the percentile concept, e.g., "A person at the 50th percentile would be above 50% of other people on kind and understanding, and below 49% of the people on this dimension." For ease of description, subjects were simply told to use 100 to indicate someone who was above the rest of the population, and 0 to indicate someone below the rest of the population.

RESULTS

The minimum acceptable criteria are of most relevance to our present hypotheses.[1] Using gender as a between-subjects factor, and level of involvement as a within-subjects factor, we conducted a repeated measures analysis of variance using the MANOVA approach (O'Brien and Kaiser 1985) on an aggregate composed of the mean minimum values (averaged across all dependent variables). In line with the general parental investment hypothesis, this analysis indicated that females were generally more selective, F (1,86) = 10.99, $p < .001$. Consistent with the qualified parental investment hypothesis, there was also a significant interaction of Gender × Level of Involvement, F (3,84) = 5.57, $p < .002$. As shown in Table 22.1, the

Table 22.1. Aggregate Minimum Value for Each Sex at Each Level of Involvement

| Sex of Subject | Involvement Level | | | |
	Date	Sexual relations	Date exclusively	Marry
Female	39.1	45.6	52.7	56.9
Male	35.0	35.1	45.1	48.9

data supported the expectation that gender differences would be most pronounced at the level of sexual relations. Females showed a steady increase in criteria, whereas males' criteria did not increase between the level of date and sexual relations, but paralleled the female pattern after that. There was also a main effect of level of involvement, F (3,84) = 80.0, $p < .001$. As shown in Table 22.1, the main effect is accounted for by the general increase in criteria with increasing level of involvement (qualified by the interaction discussed above).

Fine-grained analyses. Given that earlier findings have indicated that males and females select one another based on different criteria, it was of interest to examine the individual variables. Univariate analyses indicated significant Gender × Level of Involvement interactions on 11 of the variables: intelligent, friendly, kind, exciting, healthy, easygoing, creative, emotionally stable, sense of humor, college graduate, and social status. In line with the overall analysis, the general tendency on these variables was

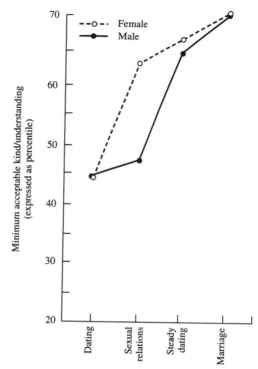

Figure 22.2. Minimum acceptable values on "kind and understanding" at each level of involvement.

for gender differences to be strongest at the level of sexual relations. Figure 22.1 presents the results for intelligence.

As shown in Figure 22.1, males were actually willing to accept a slightly lower standard for intelligence in a sexual partner than in a date. The analysis of variance for the intelligence variable was F (3,90) = 44.2, $p < .001$, for level of involvement; $F < 1$ for gender; and F (3,90) = 7.3, $p < .01$, for the interaction. (F values for simple gender comparisons at each level of involvement will be presented in more detail below.)

For several of the other variables showing an interaction, males failed to increase their demands from the dating level to the sexual relations level. Figure 22.2 shows the results for the variable "kind and understanding." The analysis of variance for this variable yielded F (3,90) = 73.4, $p < .001$, for level of involvement; F (1,92) = 2.4, *ns* for gender; and F (3,90) = 9.6, $p < .01$, for the interaction. Once again, the figure (and detailed analyses we pre-

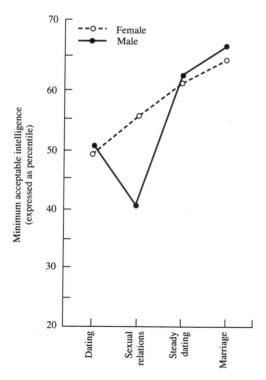

Figure 22.1. Minimum acceptable values of intelligence at each level of involvement.

sent below) indicates that the largest sex differences are found at the level of sexual relations.

For 13 of the variables, females were more selective at all levels of involvement. Figure 22.3 shows the results for "earning capacity." Note again that males and females differ most at the level of sexual relations. However, these data show a main effect of subject sex, F $(1,90) = 44.52$, $p < .001$, that is somewhat larger than the interaction, F $(3,88) = 2.4$, ns. Once again there was a main effect of level of involvement, F $(3,88) = 31.22$, $p < .001$. Variations in denominator degrees of freedom for univariate analyses are due to some subjects' failure to complete all items.

In addition to earning capacity, females also were generally more selective for the following variables: powerful, wealthy, high social status, dominant, ambitious, popular, wants children, good heredity, good housekeeper, religious, and emotionally stable. The only reversal of this tendency occurred for physical attractiveness.

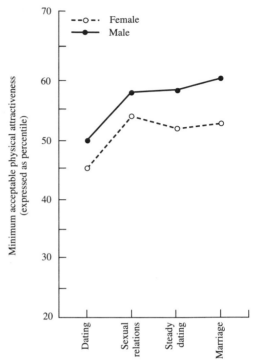

Figure 22.4. Minimum acceptable physical attractiveness at each level of involvement.

In fact, males were more selective about physical attractiveness at every level of involvement, but only significantly so at the level of marriage, F $(1,92) = 3.99$, $p < .05$. Figure 22.4 plots the results for this variable.

Factor analysis. In order to empirically organize any further examination of the 24 separate variables, we performed a principal components analysis using the average score for each variable across all levels of involvement (with varimax rotation to orthogonal factors). The factor structure is displayed in Table 22.2.

Analyses of variance were performed on composite scores (derived by averaging scores across all variables within each of the five factors). Table 22.3 plots the means for each of those composite scores (bold face) along with results for each of the constituent variables (listed below each composite). As indicated, the different factors resulted in different patterns of results. For the aggregate status (I) variable (Table 22.3, Row 1), for instance, the analysis for main effect of gender, F $(1,86) = 18.5$, $p <$

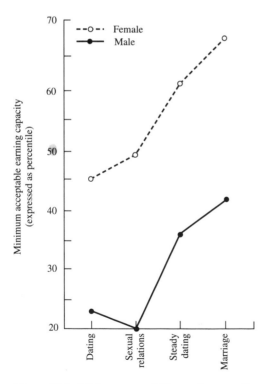

Figure 22.3. Minimum acceptable earning capacity at each level of involvement.

.001, indicated a larger effect than did the analysis for a Gender × Level of Involvement interaction, $F (3,84) = 3.8$, $p < .05$. (The F value for involvement level was $F [3,84] = 45.7, p < .001$.) An examination of the mean values for variables listed under the status (I) factor in Table 22.3 indicates that females generally have higher status requirements than do males at each level of involvement. For variables related to attractiveness (II) and friendliness (III), on the other hand, significant gender effects occurred mainly at the level of sexual relations. Variables related to health (IV) and family orientation (V) also showed relatively greater gender differences at the level of sexual relations.

As indicated in Table 22.3, minimum standards for a mate tended to increase for both sexes as the level of involvement increased. From these analyses, it appears that two things account for most of the sex differences. First, the gender difference tends to occur at the level of sexual relations regardless of the factor being considered. Second, the variables related to status show a sex difference regardless of the level of involvement being considered. The importance of these two distinctions was shown in a final analysis. We repeated the initial aggregate analysis of variance, removing the level of sexual relations, and including all variables *except* those related to status. Although this analysis left a significant effect of level of involvement, $F (2,88) = 125.04, p < .001$, it indicated neither a main effect of gender, $F (1,89) = 1.78$, *ns*, nor a Gender × Level of Involvement interaction, $F (2,88) = 1.31$, *ns*. Thus, by removing the effects of status variables and the sexual relations level, gender differences in selectivity were erased.

DISCUSSION

In general, the results of the present study supported the modified parental investment model. We found larger gender differences in trait requirements for a sexual partner than for a partner at other levels of courtship. At the level of a single date, neither sex is highly invested, whereas at the level of serious commitment, both sexes are highly invested. When considering sexual relations, however, females risk a much larger investment than males do, and are consequently more demanding about a partner's characteristics at this level of involvement.

Studies of nonhuman species support the value of a distinction between low and high levels of relationship commitment. Monogamous species typically have lengthy courtship periods, during which both members of the pair appraise one another (Barash 1977). Polygynous species, on the other hand, have very brief courtships in which multiple females mate with males who are demonstrably superior to their competitors (as indicated by dominance rankings and/or physical characteristics).

Regarding particular traits, we found support for the hypothesis that the sexes would differ most on criteria related to status and dominance. This follows the typical mam-

Table 22.2. Orthogonal Factor Structure from Factor Analysis of All Dependent Variables

Factor I: Status		Factor III: Friendliness	
Powerful	.88	Sense of humor	.83
Status	.86	Friendliness	.72
Popular	.82	Easygoing	.55
Wealthy	.78		
Good heredity	.72	Factor IV: Health	
Earning capacity	.63	Emotionally stable	.69
Dominance	.62	Healthy	.63
Good housekeeper	.57		
College degree	.56	Factor V: Family Orientation	
Factor II: Attractiveness		Wants children	.75
Attractiveness	.80	Religious	.64
Intelligence	.69	Kind and understanding	.54
Sexy	.64		
Exciting	.60		
Creative	.53		

Note: Only variables having loadings >50 are shown.

Table 22.3. Gender Comparison by Level: Means and Significance Levels for Factors and Individual Variables

	Sex	Date	Sexual relations	Date exclusively	Marry
I. Status	F	**33.84**	**38.25**	**47.89**	**52.27**
	M	**24.09**	**23.35**	**33.27**	**36.24**
		***	***	***	***
1. Powerful	F	33.38	34.63	42.12	44.80
	M	21.15	20.07	26.67	28.15
		**	**	***	***
2. High social status	F	32.23	35.98	43.80	47.57
	M	26.50	24.58	32.85	34.00
		ns	**	*	**
3. Popular	F	37.45	38.85	42.65	44.49
	M	28.11	26.67	34.78	34.22
		*	**	ns	**
4. Wealthy	F	34.38	36.08	44.95	48.94
	M	22.48	19.04	30.33	33.67
		**	***	***	**
5. Good heredity	F	30.82	41.46	52.80	58.63
	M	22.29	26.37	38.48	44.04
		ns	**	**	**
6. Good earning capacity	F	44.58	49.01	61.08	67.17
	M	23.79	19.93	36.86	42.21
		***	***	***	***
7. Dominant	F	30.80	38.02	41.75	43.03
	M	28.20	30.04	35.80	36.00
		ns	ns	ns	ns
8. Good housekeeper	F	24.77	31.58	46.11	53.35
	M	21.93	21.07	38.25	45.43
		ns	*	ns	ns
9. College graduate	F	37.31	40.34	59.12	66.82
	M	24.79	21.29	31.89	37.71
		*	***	***	***
II. Attractiveness	F	**43.97**	**53.55**	**56.32**	**60.61**
	M	**46.05**	**47.65**	**57.83**	**60.99**
		ns	ns	ns	ns
1. Physically attractive	F	45.45	54.98	51.59	52.73
	M	50.18	57.14	57.57	59.96
		ns	ns	ns	*
2. Intelligent	F	49.39	55.23	62.88	66.36
	M	50.93	43.21	63.21	67.32
		ns	**	ns	ns
3. Sexy	F	43.17	57.25	56.46	58.69
	M	44.07	53.52	54.44	56.69
		ns	ns	ns	ns
4. Exciting personality	F	42.03	54.52	59.06	70.26
	M	46.25	46.61	62.68	67.14
		ns	ns	ns	ns
5. Creative	F	38.94	45.45	51.36	54.77
	M	39.32	37.43	52.68	57.68
		ns	ns	ns	ns
III. Friendliness	F	**49.14**	**52.13**	**59.73**	**62.42**
	M	**46.07**	**43.23**	**54.95**	**59.08**
		ns	**	ns	ns
1. Good sense of humor	F	52.37	53.83	62.49	64.37
	M	52.59	46.29	59.07	61.67
		ns	*	ns	ns
2. Friendly	F	55.23	58.85	63.08	64.92
	M	47.32	48.86	58.57	66.43
		*	**	ns	ns
3. Easygoing	F	44.09	48.56	54.47	57.12
	M	44.46	38.79	53.21	55.04
		ns	**	ns	ns

Table 22.3. (continued)

	Sex	Date	Sexual relations	Date exclusively	Marry
4. Ambitious	F	43.95	47.05	58.64	63.26
	M	39.26	38.52	49.63	54.26
		ns	*	**	**
IV. Health	F	**50.52**	**60.81**	**64.96**	**67.85**
	M	**46.71**	**48.93**	**57.50**	**62.36**
		ns	***	**	*ns*
1. Emotionally stable	F	52.57	60.00	67.23	70.62
	M	43.07	43.39	56.61	62.32
		**	***	***	*
2. Healthy	F	47.88	61.44	62.50	64.85
	M	50.36	54.46	58.39	62.39
		ns	*ns*	*ns*	*ns*
V. Family orientation	F	**31.32**	**41.29**	**50.94**	**57.75**
	M	**28.11**	**28.24**	**42.07**	**49.68**
		ns	***	**	*
1. Wants children	F	21.12	27.15	45.03	55.48
	M	16.43	17.14	31.04	43.82
		ns	*ns*	*	*ns*
2. Religious	F	27.31	32.94	40.03	45.71
	M	22.54	19.71	30.14	34.00
		ns	*	*ns*	*ns*
3. Kind and	F	45.29	63.32	67.41	71.71
understanding	M	45.36	47.86	65.04	71.21
		ns	***	*ns*	*ns*
VI. Aggressiveness	F	**26.12**	**31.40**	**33.63**	**35.77**
	M	**28.50**	**30.61**	**34.86**	**36.82**
		ns	*ns*	*ns*	*ns*
Average of all	F	**39.09**	**45.60**	**52.71**	**56.89**
variables	M	**35.00**	**35.06**	**45.09**	**48.87**
		ns	***	***	**

Note: The means for each main factor (indicated by Roman numerals) are presented in bold face. Below each main factor, we present the means for each variable that constituted a given factor (numbered with Arabic numerals within a given factor). Significance levels refer to comparisons of male and female means within a given level of involvement.
*p < .05.
**p < .01.
***p < .001.

not really

malian pattern, in which a female selects a dominant male who, even if he contributes few direct resources, will contribute desirable genes. Our findings on the particular variables replicated the findings of both Buss and Barnes (1986) and Sadalla et al. (1987). In line with Buss and Barnes's results, males were generally more selective regarding physical attractiveness, whereas females were more selective regarding traits related to resource allocation. In line with Sadalla et al., dominance was also found to be more important to women as a minimum criterion for mate selection. At the same time, these results extend those earlier findings and put them in a larger interactional context.

so far, nothing about evol.

Connecting Personality with Social Psychology

Our decision to examine sex differences in mate criteria at the different stages of relationships was instigated by our involvement with social-psychological models of relationship formation (Kenrick and Trost 1987, 1989). Social-psychological models commonly distinguish between different levels of involvement in a relationship, and this distinction is crucial to understanding how the parental investment model should be qualified when applied to humans. Social-psychological approaches to relationships, however, have two important limitations. First, they have almost completely ignored the crucial importance of reproduction in heterosexual relationships. Social psychologists have instead focused on immediate cognitive variables and explained relationships in terms of unexamined assumptions about cultural norms. We have argued elsewhere (Kenrick 1987; Kenrick and Trost 1987, 1989) that such a focus has led to difficulties in explaining a number of findings, including: (*a*) gender differences in courtship that are inconsistent with a cultural model; (*b*) cross-cultural universalities in human mating patterns (e.g., Buss 1989b); and (*c*) hormonal influences on human courtship. An evolutionary perspective can address these findings and can also incorporate the proximate findings from social-psychological studies into the most powerful explanatory theory in the life sciences.

An evolutionary perspective can also connect the social-psychological enterprise with research on personality assessment. A central postulate of Darwinian theory is that there is an inherent connection between individual differences and reproduction. Other theorists have pointed out that by attending to the central dimensions of personality, our ancestors may have improved their chances of survival (Goldberg 1981; Hogan 1982). To survive in a hominid group, it may well have been essential for our progenitors to recognize dominance, agreeableness, conscientiousness, emotional stability, and intellect in other group members (Goldberg 1981). However, survival is only the first half of evolutionary success. Reproduction, the primary payoff for survival, is the other half. From the biosocial view, we are sensitive to personality traits partly because those traits reflect adaptive characteristics of potential mates. To mate carelessly after successful survival would be like squandering a hard-earned life savings.

NOTE

1. Since the criteria were generally positive characteristics, analyses of maximum acceptable levels resulted in ceiling effects. From an evolutionary perspective, the interesting differences will show up in the minimum criteria people are willing to settle for (Symons 1979), not in the maximum benefits they are willing to accept.

23

Where and When Are Women More Selective Than Men?

DOUGLAS T. KENRICK
EDWARD R. SADALLA
GARY GROTH
MELANIE R. TROST

How low will a person go in selecting a mating partner? Actual mate choices are constrained by the standards of the opposite sex, by one's own attractiveness, and so on. Those "market-based" constraints usually lead men and women to end up with actual partners very similar to themselves (see, e.g., Kenrick et al. 1993). As we argue in the paper, an evolutionary perspective leads to an expectation of greatest sex differences in what people would settle for in a sexual partner. Self-reports allow us to investigate such minimum standards in a way that actual mate choice (which always involves negotiation between two partners) does not. Although self-report data thus buy some insights, they come with costs.

CAN SELF-REPORTS BE TRUSTED?

Foremost is the problem often encountered in studies of attitude-behavior relationships—that people do not always act as they say they would. Perhaps, for instance, the sex difference is only found in what people say and does not show up in what they do. There are ethical problems with conducting experiments in which people's actual copulatory behaviors are recorded after they are presented with opportunities to have sex with partners varying in desirability. However, indirect corroboration comes from a vast nomological network of findings on mate choice. For instance, experimental subjects presented with the choice of either viewing erotica or judging geometric forms showed similar sex-differentiated choices to those that would be expected from the findings presented here (Kenrick et al. 1980). Also, males are more likely to advertise for sexual partners in singles advertisements, to engage in promiscuous behavior when unconstrained by the choices of the other sex (as in homosexual relationships), to pay money to have sex with complete strangers, to engage in diverse sexual variations, and so on (see, e.g., Symons 1979; Buss and Schmitt 1992; Daly and Wilson 1983; Wiederman 1993). Clark and Hatfield (1989) actually conducted a field experiment in which students were approached by an opposite-sex experimenter and invited to either "go out tonight," "come over to my apartment," or "go to bed with me." Approximately 50 percent of men and women responded affirmatively to the invitation to go out. Men were even more responsive to the invitation to "go to bed" (75 percent yes), whereas the comparable acceptance rate by female subjects was 0.

DO THE SEXES DEFINE "SEXUAL RELATIONS" DIFFERENTLY?

Another limitation of our paper is that, although we emphasized the difference between casual and long-term mating, we asked subjects about partners for "sexual relations," leaving this term vaguely defined. The two sexes could have made different assumptions about how committed they would be before having sexual relations. In a later study, we asked explicitly about a partner for a "one-night stand," making it clear that the person would never be seen again. Under these circumstances the sex differences were, consistent with the model, greatly enhanced (Kenrick et al. 1993). In the later research we also examined the relationship between minimum standards and self-evaluations. Consistent with economic models of mate selection, both men and women demanded more in a mate when they thought more of themselves. The only exception to this general principle occurred for one-night stands. Whereas women showed the same high correlation between self-ratings and minimum standards here, men considering a one-night stand seemed to turn off their "comparison shopping" mechanisms.

DO THESE DATA REFLECT THE NORMS OF AMERICAN SOCIETY?

Although these self-reports are consistent with "harder" behavioral data, it could nevertheless be argued that they reflect acculturation to sex-typed norms of American culture. In later research we included a standard measure of subjects' commitment to standard sex roles, but it had no effect on the pattern found here (Kenrick et al. 1993). Nevertheless, it would be interesting to examine the cross-cultural robustness of these sex differences (as in e.g., Buss 1989b). Are they as clear in a sexually liberal society such as the Netherlands or the Trobriand Islands? We presume these differences are based on fundamental gender differences in mating strategies, as are the cross-cultural universals in homicide patterns (Daly and Wilson 1988b) and in age preferences for mates (Kenrick and Keefe 1992). Given the substantial theoretical and empirical evidence for gender differences in minimum parental investment, we think that parsimony favors an evolutionary ex-

planation of these results, but the pattern might vary in interesting ways with mating arrangements in different societies.

ARE THERE EXCEPTIONS TO THIS PATTERN?

General principles are often proven by the telling exception (as in the behaviors of species in which males invest more in the offspring). We think the universal difference we found in age preferences for mates (Kenrick and Keefe 1992) would actually be minimized in the context of a one-night stand. The reason is that women seek older men because they can generally provide more resources. However, a woman who had a one-night stand would benefit very little from the male's resources and should seek a male of maximum attractiveness, as an index of viable genetic characteristics. Unlike wines and older men's bank accounts, genes gain nothing from aging, and a young partner, if attractive, should be desirable. We have two reservations about this prediction, though. First, affairs intended as one-night stands often grow into longer relationships. Second, an older man who has managed to stay attractive may give more evidence of superior genetic characteristics than an attractive younger man.

THE PUNCH LINES OF THIS RESEARCH

Although we believe there are many questions remaining here, two "punch lines" are important. First, social psychologists had long erred in ignoring the role of reproduction in human courtship. Second, evolutionary psychologists had been muddling the distinction between high- and low-investment relationships, discussing human males as if they were Ugandan kob on a lek. For eminently sensible Darwinian reasons, human mating sometimes looks like a singles bar in Los Angeles, but it also sometimes looks like those television families from 1959.

24

An Evolutionary Analysis of Psychological Pain Following Rape: I. The Effects of Victim's Age and Marital Status

NANCY WILMSEN THORNHILL
RANDY THORNHILL

In this paper we use the adaptationist approach to evaluate the psychological trauma experienced by rape victims which often accompanies the immediate postrape period. In an earlier paper (R. Thornhill and N . W. Thornhill 1989) we detailed a hypothesis for the evolutionary significance of mental pain and outlined the hypothesis's predictions about the circumstances that are expected to bring about psychological pain (e.g., rape, loss of social status, loss of a child or mate) and predictions about variation in the magnitude of psychological pain in each important circumstance. Here we will discuss briefly the adaptationist approach, reiterate briefly the hypothesis for the evolutionary meaning of psychological pain, and then report some results of our study of psychological trauma following rape that address patterns predicted by the hypothesis.

ADAPTATIONIST APPROACH

There remains some negativism toward the application of adaptationism in the study of human behavior and the mental adaptations that guide human behavior. This negativism and the resulting controversy stem to an important extent from misunderstanding of the modern adaptationist approach (e.g., Scarr's [1989] view of evolutionary psychology; but see Crawford et al. 1991). In this section we discuss some fundamentals in hope that our work will not be misunderstood by the many scholars who conduct research on rape victims, most of whom are not evolutionary biologists.

There are both proximate and ultimate causes and thus explanations for adaptations, the complexly integrated, purposeful traits of individual organisms. Proximate explanations for the existence of adaptations focus on genetic, biochemical, physiological, developmental, social, and *all other immediate causes* leading to the expression of adaptations. Ultimate explanations of adaptation have their theoretical foundation in causes that operated during evolutionary history to lead to adaptation. Because selection is the *only* agent of evolution that can produce phenotypic design/adaptation, the ultimate approach's theoretical foundation is the relationship between adaptation and the nature of the selection that produced adaptation—that is, how an adaptation of interest allowed its bearers to out-reproduce others in the environments of EBA evolutionary history. The ultimate causal theo-

Reprinted with permission from *Ethology and Sociobiology* 11:155–76 (1990).

retical framework can be used productively to study proximate causation. We should emphasize that in no way do proximate and evolutionary explanations of causation conflict. Both proximate and ultimate explanations are needed for complete understanding of adaptations, and by understanding the evolutionary purpose of an adaptation one should be able to predict and understand, successfully, the proximate causes that affect the expression of the adaptation.

Biologists study adaptations as long-term products of nonrandom differential reproduction of individuals, *individual* selection, rather than selection at the level of groups (e.g., Hamilton 1964; Alexander 1975, 1979, 1987; Dawkins 1976, 1982, 1986; Daly and Wilson 1983; Mayr 1983; Thornhill and Alcock 1983; Alcock 1984; Trivers 1985; Williams 1985; Rubenstein and Wrangham 1986). This theory of organisms has been adopted, in part, because nonrandom differential reproduction of individuals is a much more powerful agent of evolution than is group selection. Another reason for viewing adaptations as designed by individual selection is that individuals but not groups possess phenotypic design. The final reason that the adaptations of organisms are viewed as long-term outcomes of individual selection is that this perspective has proven very productive in the sense that matters in science; i.e., useful for gaining new information about life via successful prediction of the unknown.

The general theory is to view organisms' adaptations as long-term consequences of selection that is only effective at the level of individuals. This theory argues that organisms will show adaptations that are designed ultimately for perpetuation of *their own genes*— because selection is always for Hamiltonian inclusive fitness. It is at the level of inclusive fitness differentials among individuals where selection is most effective in bringing about evolutionary change (Hamilton 1964; Grafen 1984). Natural selection cannot distinguish between a gene that increases its representation in subsequent generations via its effect on its own bearer and a gene that increases its representation via its effect on relatives (descendent and nondescendent) of the gene's bearer.

From this general theory of biology, hypotheses are derived by investigators in an attempt to understand the evolutionary purpose of an adaptation of interest. The hypotheses so derived are then tested against nature in a specific way. A prediction is a logical consequence of a hypothesis. Thus predictions serve as a means of testing hypotheses by attempts to falsify them. A prediction of a hypothesis must be true if a hypothesis is valid, and when a hypothesis predicts something that turns out to be false, the hypothesis must be false. The adaptationist uses the same basic scientific approach used in all sciences: the hypothetico-deductive method. Adaptations are long-term outcomes of selection, and thus an adaptation's functional design or evolutionary function identifies the type of selection that designed it (e.g., selection in the context of avoiding a type of predator). The predictions of adaptationist hypotheses pertain to the functional design of adaptations.

Hypotheses can sometimes be evaluated by tests of their assumptions. However, evolutionists studying adaptations using hypotheses derived from the theory that adaptations of organisms are products of individual selection focus on evaluation of predictions. An assumption of a hypothesis is something required to get a result or consequence. Assumptions of hypotheses about adaptation pertain to evolutionary history, and even if an assumption is valid in ecological time (i.e., now), it does not follow that the assumption held historically in evolutionary time. Thus the most straightforward way to test a hypothesis about the evolutionary function of an adaptation (i.e., an adaptation's selective history) is to examine its predictions about functional design. If the hypothesis identifies relevant selective history, design features should be predictably revealed. (The study of adaptation is discussed in detail by R. Thornhill 1990.)

PSYCHOLOGICAL PAIN

From the perspective outlined above we derived a hypothesis in an attempt to understand psychological pain within the adaptationist framework. The hypothesis is that mental pain is a manifestation of psychological adaptation by which individuals deal with social circumstances that would have reduced inclusive fitness in human evolutionary history (R. Thornhill and N. W. Thornhill 1989; also R. Thornhill and N. W. Thornhill 1983, 1987; R. Thornhill, N. W. Thornhill, and Dizinno 1986; Alexander 1986). This hypothesis views the evolutionary *if pr(rape) → 0; then x doing bar door after ....*

significance of mental pain as analogous to the evolutionary importance of physical pain. Physical pain serves to draw an individual's attention to some aspect of anatomy that needs tending and *can be fixed* by the individual's attention. Mental pain seems to focus an individual's attention on the significant social events surrounding the pain and promotes correction of the events causing the pain and avoidance of these events in the future. As Alexander (1986) put it,

Typically we suffer pain when we incur an injury that, prior to medical technology, was *reparable* provided certain actions were taken and others avoided (as in protecting an injured part). We typically do not suffer pain when injuries irreparable prior to medical technology occur (e.g. object thrust into the brain, damage to the spinal cord). I assume that *mental* pain and pleasure analogues serve similar functions in the social scene—e.g. that the only way, in the end, to deal with frustration and distress is to solve the problem that is causing it. In other words, I see frustration and distress as mechanisms serving some function, not as either incidental or pathological conditions to be relieved per se, without connection to other difficulties ... (p. 108, emphases in original)

Mental pain, like physical pain, may be associated with social display of need. Social displays of feelings are what are typically called emotions by psychologists (see Plutchik and Kellerman 1980). Psychological pain is distinguished from emotion in that it does not itself involve display.

Our (and Alexander's) emphasis on fitness-reducing *social* circumstances in the hypothesis derives from the current general hypothesis for the evolution of the human mind. It appears that the main context for the evolution of the human psyche was social competition among individuals, as opposed to selection from the physical environment or from biotic factors other than conspecific humans (Humphrey 1976, 1980, 1981; Alexander 1987, 1989).

Psychological adaptations are information-processing mechanisms that are phenotypic solutions to information-processing problems that influenced inclusive fitness during evolutionary history. A psychological adaptation's evolutionary purpose is precisely identified by the kind of information that the adaptation is designed to process (see Cosmides and Tooby 1987b, 1989; Symons 1987b, 1989; Tooby and

Cosmides 1989 for detailed discussion of modern adaptationism applied to psychological analysis). If, as we have hypothesized, psychological pain reflects a psychological adaptation that is designed for the purpose of examining, correcting, and preventing problems stemming from social interactions, mental pain will show patterns indicative of this purposive design. The hypothesis of psychological pain makes the following two *general* predictions about the kinds of environmental information that will result in psychological pain: First, it predicts that the proximate ecological causes of mental pain will be circumstances that affected inclusive fitness of individuals under social competition. Second, the hypothesis predicts that the more an event potentially or actually negatively affects the evolved social tendencies, desires, and aspirations of humans, the more psychological pain will occur surrounding the event. Furthermore, the hypothesis makes many *specific* predictions about social events that are expected to lead to psychological distress. These predictions are explained in detail elsewhere (R. Thornhill and N. W. Thornhill 1989). Here we deal only with certain predictions pertaining to the psychological pain associated with rape victimization.

RAPE VICTIMIZATION IN EVOLUTIONARY CONTEXT

Copulation without implicit or explicit consent distinguishes rape from other copulatory behavior. Why has selection favored females that do not consent to and may resist copulation under certain circumstances? The general answer is probably that rape was disadvantageous to our female ancestors—that is, in evolutionary terms, rape reduced the inclusive fitness or potential for genetic propagation of human females during evolutionary history (R. Thornhill and N. W. Thornhill 1983).

In human evolutionary history, rape may have resulted in a reduction in female fitness in the following four ways. (1) Rape may lead to the victim's injury. (2) Rape may reduce a woman's ability to choose the timing and circumstances for reproduction, as well as the man who fathers her offspring. When rape leads to conception and gestation of a zygote, women may expend their limited reproductive effort in the wrong (for successful reproduction) circumstances and with the wrong male. (3) Rape also circumvents a woman's ability to use copulation as a means of securing material benefits from men for herself or her genetic relatives. The second and third ways in which rape may reduce female fitness are related to female mate choice. (4) Rape of a pair-bonded woman may adversely influence her pair-bond mate's protection of her or the quantity and quality of parental care she receives. Human males are one of the most parentally investing of male mammals and parental care from both sexes has been critical to the fitness of each sex during our evolutionary history (see Alexander and Noonan 1979; Benshoof and Thornhill 1979). Human paternal care is discriminative in terms of genetic overlap between men and offspring; men care more for their genetic offspring (Daly and Wilson 1988b). Actual or suspected rape would reduce reliability of male parentage. In human evolutionary history this could have negatively influenced a male's behavior toward a female and the offspring she produced and thereby decreased a raped female's potential reproduction. Even attempted rape may have been of great concern to our male ancestors from the standpoint of paternity reliability. In the male mind, a woman placing herself in a situation conducive to a rape attempt may fail to avoid similar situations in the future.

We feel that rape from the woman's perspective can best be understood by considering the negative influences of rape on female fitness as outlined above, especially factors 2–4, which may have reduced a woman's options for future reproduction in the evolutionary environment of human adaptation. If rape was a fitness-reducing social event for women in human evolutionary history, our evolutionary perspective on mental pain should apply to psychological changes experienced by rape victims. The mental pain hypothesis applied to rape victims assumes that in human evolutionary history raped females had increased fitness as a result of mental pain, because the pain forced them to focus attention on the evaluation of the above outlined fitness-reducing circumstances surrounding rape, including the evaluation of the social circumstances that resulted in the sexual assault. Just as physical pain prompts an individual to avoid situations that may lead to similar injury, mental pain may cause individuals to more carefully consider circumstances that resulted in the pain and to avoid them in the future.

The evolutionary perspective on psychological pain requires that in general mental pain will be manifested in women who are victims of rape. Indeed, social scientists have documented, especially in work in the last 10–15 years, that rape victims do experience psychological distress following rape that is caused by the rape and circumstances precipitated by the rape (references in R. Thornhill and N. W. Thornhill 1989). This perspective makes certain specific predictions about the characteristics of rape victims that will influence the degree of mental pain experienced by victims. Two of these predictions pertaining to age and marital status of victims are discussed and empirically supported in the following.

THE DATA SET

The data used in all analyses to follow were obtained from the Joseph Peters Institute in Philadelphia (USA). These data comprise a set of 265 variables that were coded for 790 rape victims. The victims were females of all ages who reported to authorities an attempted or actual sexual assault (primarily rape) and who were examined at the Philadelphia General Hospital between April 1, 1973 and June 30, 1974; victims 12 years old or less were included through June 30, 1975. The total number of rape victims examined during this time period was 1,401. Seven hundred and ninety of these agreed to participate in the Peters Institute study (headed by T. W. McCahill, L. C. Meyer, and A. M. Fischman) and were interviewed by social workers within five days following the rape. These 790 victims comprise the basic data set. Some victims answered only some interview questions, and some victims were not asked some interview questions or were not always included in the data set for other reasons unknown to us. Because of this, the data set contains many missing values. As a result the sample of victims available for analyses rarely includes all 790 victims. In cases of child victims (see later), the child's caretaker sometimes helped the child respond to interview questions, or with very young victims, the caretaker gave the responses to the questions based on his/her perception of the effect of the sexual assault on the child (see McCahill et al. 1979).

We received the data in hard-copy computer printout form. We also obtained the original interview schedules, coding documentation, and summary statistics for each variable. The data were copied onto our computer system and proofed for errors before analysis. The analyses were done using SAS-PC.

The data include 13 psychological pain variables for the majority of the victims. These were used by the Peters Institute researchers to measure psychological adjustment of the victims by recording each victim's own verbal assessment of her return to the prerape state for each variable. We used these variables as a measure of the magnitude of psychological trauma experienced by each victim. These 13 variables are fear of being out on the street alone, fear of being home alone, change in social activities, change in eating habits, change in sleeping habits, frequency of nightmares, change in heterosexual relationships (i.e. nonsexual relations with men), change in negative feelings toward known men, change in negative feelings toward unknown men, change in relations with husband or boyfriend, change in sexual relations with partner, insecurities concerning sexual attractiveness, and change in relations with family (other than husband). The variables are meant to measure the impact of rape on each victim's own feelings of her ability to cope psychologically with each of the 13 circumstances. These variables were coded for each victim by a social worker during an interview on a scale of −4 to +4 with a score of 0 indicating no change and deviation from 0 in either direction indicating a change but not necessarily a negative or positive change based on sign alone. For example, for the variable change in sexual relations with partner, a negative number means a negative change in the relationship. But, for example, for the variable negative change in feelings toward known men, a negative number means less negative feelings (i.e. a positive change).

The data also include each victim's age and marital status, whether she had received psychiatric assistance prior to the rape, whether or not she felt the rape would affect her future, and whether or not she considered keeping the rape a secret. All of the variables mentioned are relevant to this paper.

Before proceeding to the predictions and analyses of the data, we provide some general demographic information about this population of victims. In the sample of 790 victims the ages of victims ranged from 2 months to 88 years with the mean age being 19.6 years and the mode 16 years; 19% were children (0–11 years old). Relative to most victim data sets, this is a fairly young group of rape victims (see R. Thornhill and N. W. Thornhill 1983 and Russell 1984 for summaries of victim age data sets). The relatively large number of child victims is the result of an attempt by the Peters Institute researchers to include a reasonable sample of child victims in the study; victims 12 years old or less were included for an additional year after adults were no longer included (see McCahill et al. 1979 for details). Rape victim populations are characterized by young, reproductive-aged women (R. Thornhill and N. W. Thornhill 1983). The mean age for most data sets is around 24 years.

Eighty-one percent of the victims were unmarried (either by widowhood, divorce, or never having been married) at the time of the rape incident. Approximately one-half of the victims were receiving some form of public financial assistance at the time of the rape and almost all (725 of the 790) victims had an annual income of $12,000 or less. For 80% of the victims, this rape was the first sexual assault ever experienced. Of the remaining 20%, 64% had experienced one previous sexual assault. The remainder had experienced two or more.

Although the sample of 790 victims is by far the largest sample of rape victims ever studied in terms of psychological trauma following rape, the sample is not representative of US females. It is biased in terms of young and unmarried females of low socioeconomic standing. However, our analysis of psychological pain is focused on a species-typical adaptation and how it regulates females' feelings surrounding rape victimization. There is no reason to believe that the sample of victims is atypical in regard to the psychology of interest here.

PREDICTIONS AND TESTS

The first prediction we will discuss is that young women (i.e. women of reproductive ages) will experience greater psychological distress than will girls (nonreproductive) or older women (women of nonreproductive ages) as a result of rape (R. Thornhill and N. W. Thorn-

[handwritten annotation at top: failure to reject; follows Popper in the concep...]

hill 1983). We predict that age of victim will be a proximate cause of psychological pain because the negative fitness effects in the event of rape that we described earlier (reduction in optimal timing and circumstances for reproduction, inability to choose the father of the offspring, etc.) would have fallen most heavily on reproductive-aged women during human evolutionary history. Remember that the psychological pain hypothesis predicts psychological pain will be experienced in direct relation to the effects that the pain causing social incident would have had on individual fitness in the human evolutionary environment.

We first categorized age into (1) nonreproductive, 0–11 and 45–88 years old and (2) reproductive, 12–44 years old. We categorized age this way because girls between 0–11 years of age and women over 45 years of age have a very limited fertility in the US (R. Thornhill and N. W. Thornhill 1983). Fertility refers to age-specific birth rate and thus the probability that any given copulation will lead to pregnancy, gestation, and live birth.

The results of chi-square analyses for the first prediction are summarized in Table 24.1 (data in Appendix I). Eight of the 13 variables show significant differences between reproductive-aged and nonreproductive-aged victims in magnitude of the psychological pain associated with rape. Reproductive-aged victims were significantly more psychologically traumatized than nonreproductive-aged rape victims.

Three of the five variables showing no significant difference require brief comment. For the two variables change in sexual relationships and change in relationships with husband/boyfriend the sample sizes of the nonreproductive victims are 10 and 14, respectively (see Appendix I). This results from only women over the age of 12 years being asked to respond to these questions. Thus our nonreproductive age category for these two variables includes only women aged 45 and over. Given that young women (particularly those between 15 and 29, in most victim samples) are far more likely to be raped than older women or girls (R. Thornhill and N. W. Thornhill 1983; Russell 1984)

Table 24.1. Psychological Trauma of Reproductive- and Nonreproductive-Aged Victims

Variables	Chi-square Analysis
Change in eating (eat)	$X^2 = 59.8$, n = 595, df = 4 p = 0.000
Change in sleeping (sleep)	$X^2 = 31.6$, n = 596, df = 3 p = 0.000
Change in nightmares (night)	$X^2 = 11.95$, n = 590, df = 3 p = 0.000
Change in fear of being out in the street (street)	$X^2 = 18.1$, n = 483, df = 2 p = 0.000
Change in fear of known men (known)	$X^2 = 9.3$, n = 494, df = 2 p = 0.01
Change in fear of unknown men (unknown)	$X^2 = 20.0$, n = 487, df = 2 p = 0.000
Change in fear of being home alone (home alone)	$X^2 = 3.3$, n = 478, df = 2 p = 0.25
Change in family relationships (family)	$X^2 = 1.6$, n = 481, df = 4 p = 0.80
Change in insecurities about sexual attractiveness (sexual attractiveness)	$X^2 = 1.3$, n = 463, df = 1 p = 0.25
Change in heterosexual relationships (heterosexual)	$X^2 = 15.3$, n = 487, df = 2 p = 0.000
Change in social activities (social)	$X^2 = 10.8$, n = 488, df = 3 p = 0.01
Change in husband/boyfriend relationship (husband/boyfriend)	$X^2 = 2.3$, n = 291, df = 2 p = 0.31
Change in sexual relations with partner (sexual relations)	$X^2 = .6$, n = 232, df = 1 p = 0.43

these small samples do not surprise us, but they do make statistical analyses questionable. One other variable that showed no significant difference between age categories was change in family relationships. This result remains consistent throughout all the analyses in this paper and elsewhere (N. W. Thornhill and R. Thornhill 1990b). Family relationships appear to be little affected by rape and may even be positively affected in some cases (e.g., gang rape, N. W. Thornhill and R. Thornhill 1991).

We wanted to know if the significant differences between reproductive-aged women and nonreproductive-aged females in psychological pain were a result of either prereproductive-aged girls or post-reproductive-aged women having little psychological trauma compared to reproductive-aged women. We recategorized age into prereproductive (0–11), reproductive (12–44), and post-reproductive (45+) ages and reran the 13 psychological trauma variables. The variables were all analyzed by nonparametric analysis of variance (Kruskal-Wallis) tests, except the two variables change in eating and change in sleeping patterns. These were analyzed by chi-square because there is no directionality implied by a negative or positive score. We were only interested in change (more or less eating or sleeping) for these two variables. Thus, to rank a negative score as less than a positive score would be inappropriate.

Table 24.2 shows that for 10 of the 11 relevant variables there are significant differences between prereproductive, reproductive, and post-reproductive victims. The variables change in husband/boyfriend relationship and change in sexual relations with partner were not relevant here because, as noted, only women over the age of 12 were asked to respond to these questions. In all but two cases (the variables known and heterosexual) the statistical significance is most influenced by the magnitude of difference between prereproductive girls and reproductive-aged women. That is, in general prereproductive-aged girls are far *less* likely to be psychologically traumatized by rape and reproductive-aged women are far *more* likely to be so than expected under the null hypothesis. That prereproductive-aged girls are relatively nontraumatized by sexual abuse has been suggested by findings from other studies (Finkelhor 1984; Mannarino and Cohen 1987). For the most part post-reproductive-aged

women conform to expectations under the null hypothesis. The victims' family relationships showed no significant difference on the basis of the three victim-age classes.

Next we predicted that rape would adversely influence the victims' relations with husband or boyfriend, but especially the former; and the negative effect of rape on mateships, especially marriages, will be a proximate cause of psychological pain in victims (R. Thornhill and N. W. Thornhill 1983). This prediction stems from the negative effect of rape on reliability of paternity and the consequent lowered potential of successful reproduction by a pair-bonded man via his mate. Mates for rape victims are expected often to reduce or withdraw entirely their material support of the woman and her children.

Victims' marital status was broken into five categories in the original data: unmarried, married, widowed, separated, and divorced. We reduced these five marital categories to two categories and only included women (i.e. not prereproductive victims) for the following analysis. One marital category we called unmarried and it included all single women (unmarried, widowed, and divorced). The other category we called married and it included married and separated women. We did this by reasoning that unmarried women (for whatever reason they are unmarried) are often without investing men. Married women, on the other hand, even if they are separated, are more likely to have investing men in their lives. It was impossible to check the accuracy of this reasoning in any satisfactory way because the data do not include whether or not the victim lived with the husband (or boyfriend). The social workers collecting the data asked the victims about several possible living partners (e.g. father, mother, sister, brother) or if the victim lived alone, but failed to record if the victim lived with her husband (or boyfriend).

We did check the accuracy of our reasoning in a far from satisfactory (but the only available) manner. Forty-five victims said that they lived alone. If a given victim scored that she lived alone we checked her marital status. Of the 45 only one also scored that she was married and 5 scored their marital status as separated. The remaining 39 were either unmarried (24), divorced (8), or widowed (7). This check gives us no feeling for married women who live with someone other than husband, nor does it

Table 24.2. Psychological Trauma of Prereproductive-, Reproductive- and Post-reproductive-Aged Victims

	Variables Eat‡ Sleep		Chi-square Analysis $X^2 = 75.3$, n = 599, df = 6 p = 0.000 $X^2 = 47.6$, n = 600, df = 6 p = 0.000	
Variables	Age	N	Mean Ranks	(2-tailed) Significance
Night**	1 (pre)	123	267.37a†	
	2 (repro)	445	306.17a	p = 0.02
	3 (post)	26	291.44	
Street**	1	39	146.78a,b	
	2	431	258.63a	p = 0.0001
	3	27	242.80b	
Known**	1	40	219.17	
	2	430	255.11a	p = 0.01
	3	27	195.79a	
Unknown**	1	38	160.73a	
	2	426	254.91a	p = 0.0001
	3	27	225.35	
Home Alone**	1	32	179.92a,b	
	2	424	245.37a	p = 0.01
	3	27	262.55b	
Family*	1	39	231.84	
	2	424	243.12	p = 0.65
	3	22	260.40	
Sexual Attractiveness**	1	25	192.00a	
	2	419	236.37a	p = 0.05
	3	23	243.15a	
Heterosexual*	1	36	308.75a	
	2	428	237.47a,b	p = 0.0003
	3	27	297.48b	
Social Activities*	1	39	330.19a,b	
	2	426	239.60a	p = 0.0002
	3	27	234.37b	

‡Data for variable eat (see text for method of coding psychological trauma):

	−4,−3	−2,−1	0	1,2,3,4
Prereproductive	3	9	108	5
Reproductive	60	83	168	49
Post-reproductive	5	3	9	0
Data for variable sleep:				
Prereproductive	10	12	94	9
Reproductive	64	101	169	24
Post-reproductive	8	2	6	1

†Numbers followed by same letter are significantly different, p ≤ 0.05; ** Higher mean = greatest negative effect; * Higher mean = least negative effect

for unmarried women who live with someone who is something like a husband, but it does give us some confidence that our reasoning (and subsequent division of women victims into unmarried and married categories) may be accurate.

The analysis bearing on the prediction is shown in Table 24.3 (data in Appendix II). Six of the 13 variables show that married women are more significantly psychologically trauma-tized by rape than are unmarried women as measured by the chi-square statistic. Four other variables are in the predicted direction but fail to reach statistical significance. Married women are nonsignificantly more likely than unmarried women to have worsened heterosexual relationships with men, worsened sexual relationships, to become more insecure about their sexual attractiveness, and to suffer worsened relationships with their husbands and boy-

Table 24.3. Psychological Trauma of Married Victims Compared to Unmarried Women Victims

Variables	Chi-square Analysis
Eat	$X^2 = 16.6$, n = 490, df = 3 p = 0.001
Sleep	$X^2 = 15.3$, n = 491, df = 3 p = 0.002
Night	$X^2 = 7.8$, n = 487, df = 2 p = 0.020
Street	$X^2 = 25.7$, n = 495, df = 2 r, = 0.000
Unknown	$X^2 = 9.7$, n = 489, df = 2 p = 0.008
Home Alone	$X^2 = 27.4$, n = 481, df = 2 p = 0.000

friends. These trends are interesting. We predict that a more thorough study—one in which pair-bond relationships were clearly defined—would sharpen the differences between unmarried and married victims with respect to these variables.

Given that there apparently is an effect of marriage on psychological trauma following rape and that married women are likely to be of reproductive ages, we wanted to remove the married victims from the two relevant age categories, reproductive-aged and post-reproductive-aged women, to see if there still was an effect of age on postrape psychological pain. The prediction is that the significant differences between reproductive and nonreproductive-aged women in psychological pain will hold.

Six variables showed significant differences between women both in the analysis of age categories and in the analysis of marital status. These are shown in Table 24.4 (data in Appendix III). The differences between reproductive- and post-reproductive-aged women remain significant for all but one variable, nightmares, when marital status is controlled by removing married victims from the analyses (Table 24.4).

The results of these analyses clearly suggest that age itself is a proximate cause of psychological trauma following rape. Perhaps there is a proximate explanation for this result which some readers would find sufficient. It has been suggested to us that perhaps young (reproductive-aged) women are more prone to mental distress

("more emotional") than older (post-reproductive) women or than girls (prereproductive).

One of the variables codes a yes/no answer to the question "Have you received psychiatric assistance prior to the rape?" The question implies (at least as discernible from the interview schedules) no time limit, thus we assume this means psychiatric assistance received at any time in the victim's life. We analyzed this variable by our age categories (both the reproductive and nonreproductive-age comparison and the prereproductive, reproductive, and post-reproductive comparison) and found that indeed young, reproductive-aged women in this population were significantly more likely to have replied yes to the question about prior psychiatric assistance (Table 24.5). Thus, if one accepts that the older women in this data set were equally likely to answer yes to such a question if, in fact, they have received psychiatric assistance, and if one accepts that psychiatric assistance is a good measure of psychological instability, then this group of young, reproductive-aged women appear to be more psychologically unstable than either older women (post-reproductive) or girls (prereproductive). However, Frank et al. (1981) found that previous psychiatric assistance had no effect on the severity of psychological trauma following rape when they compared young (X age = 23) rape victims who had received psychiatric assistance with those who had not.

Table 24.4. Psychological Trauma of Unmarried Reproductive-Aged and Post-reproductive-Aged Women

Variables	Chi-square Analysis
Eat	$X^2 = 20.1$, n = 393, df = 3 p = 0.000
Sleep	$X^2 = 8.6$, n = 394, df = 3 p = 0.036
Night	$X^2 = 0.425$, n = 393, df = 2 p = 0.809
Street	$X^2 = 18.1$, n = 399, df = 2 r, = 0.000
Unknown	$X^2 = 9.7$, n = 393, df = 2 p = 0.001
Home Alone	$X^2 = 27.4$, n = 392, df = 2 p = 0.001

Table 24.5. Psychiatric Assistance *by* Age and Marital Status

	No Psychiatric Assistance		Psychiatric Assistance		
Nonreproductive	n = 168	d = 33	n = 17	d = −33	n = 781
	e = 135	c = 8	e = 50	c = 22	df = 1
Reproductive	n = 402	d = −33	n = 194	d = 33	X² = 37.9
	e = 435	c = 3	e = 161	c = 7	p = 0.000
Prereproductive	n = 138	d = 27	n = 9	d = −27	n = 781
	e = 107	c = 7	e = 40	c = 20	df = 2
Reproductive	n = 402	d = −29	n = 194	d = 29	X² = 42.5
	e = 435	c = 2	e = 161	c = 7	p = 0.000
Post-reproductive	n = 30	d = 2	n = 8	d = − 2	
	e = 28	c = 0.1	e = 10	c = 4	
Unmarried	n = 391	d = 11.8	n = 151	d = −11.8	n = 669
	e = 379	c = 0.4	e = 163	c = 0.9	df = 1
Married	n = 77	d = −11.8	n = 50	d = 11.8	X² = 5.95
	e = 89	c = 2	e = 38	c = 4	p = 0.015
Unmarried reproductive	n = 340	d = 16	n = 140	d = −16	n = 592
	e = 324	c = 0.3	e = 154	c = 0.5	df = 1
Married reproductive	n = 70	d = − 9	n = 42	d = 9	X² = 3.8
	e = 81	c = 1	e = 33	c = 2	p = 0.05

n = number of victims; e = expected frequency; d = deviation of n from e; c = contribution of cell to X^2 (rounded to the nearest tenth).

When we analyzed the psychiatric assistance variable by marital status, we found that the married women *were significantly more likely* than were the unmarried females (prereproductive, reproductive-aged, and post-reproductive-aged) to have sought psychiatric assistance (Table 24.5). This suggests that the married women in this data set are more psychologically unstable than are the unmarried females. Furthermore, the married reproductive-aged women were significantly more likely than were the unmarried reproductive-aged women to have sought psychiatric assistance (Table 24.5). So, if the explanation suggested to us (that our results about age having a great effect on psychological trauma following rape reflects *only* the general psychological instability of reproductive-aged women) were entirely sufficient we would not expect married victims to show the same effect. It appears that young women in this population are more psychologically unstable (as measured by psychiatric assistance) but so may be married women. We suspect that the explanation that young women are more psychologically unstable is right, but incomplete. The pattern raises the question of why. We suggest that the social lives of young married women are often more complex than those of prereproductive girls or post-reproductive women, because young married women are expending more reproductive effort as mating effort. However, under some circumstances the psychological pain hypothesis discussed above predicts *older* women to be more "emotional" than younger women. For example, an older mother who loses her only child is expected be more grief-stricken than a younger mother who loses her only child. (See R. Thornhill and N. W. Thornhill 1989, for discussion and other predictions pertaining to psychological pain in relation to age outside the context of rape.)

Next we predicted that reproductive-aged victims should be more likely than should nonreproductive-aged victims to consider keeping the rape a secret. This prediction stems from our view that reproductive-aged victims, compared to nonreproductive-aged victims, will have evolved to perceive that their rape victimization, if widely known, will have more devastating social consequences for them. Table 24.6 shows the results of the analyses for this prediction for both breakdowns of age category. The differences are not statistically significant but are in the predicted direction. Nonreproductive-aged victims were less likely than expected to consider keeping the rape a secret and reproductive-aged women were more likely to so consider.

The same prediction would seem to apply to married rape victims. Compared to unmarried women, married women may have more to lose as a result of rape and thus might be more likely than unmarried women to consider keeping it a

Table 24.6. Consider Keeping Rape a Secret by Age and Marital Status

	Considered Keeping Rape a Secret				Did Not Consider Keeping Rape a Secret					
Nonreproductive	n = 30	d = −8			n = 97	d = 8			n = 659	
	e = 38	c = 2			e = 89	c = 0.7			df = 1	
Reproductive	n = 166	d = 8			n = 366	d = 8			X^2 = 2.5	
	e = 158	c = 0.4			e = 374	c = 0.2			p = 0.116	
Prereproductive	n = 18	d = 1			n = 46	d = 1				
	e = 19	c = 0.1			e = 45	c = 0			n = 659	
Reproductive	n = 166	d = 8			n = 366	d = −8			df = 2	
	e = 158	c = 0.4			e = 374	c = 0.2			X^2 = 4.1	
Post-reproductive	n = 12	d = −7			n = 51	d = 7			p = 0.131	
	e = 19	c = 2			e = 44	c = 1				
Unmarried women	n = 165	d = 5			n = 372	d = −5			n = 659	
	e = 160	c = 0.2			e = 377	c = 0.1			df = 1	
Married women	n = 31	d = −5			n = 91	J = 5			X^2 = 1.1	
	e = 36	c = 0.8			e = 86	c = 0.3			p = 0.294	

n = numbers of victims; e = expected frequency; d = deviation of n from e; c = contribution of cell to X^2 (rounded to the nearest tenth).

secret. R. Alexander has suggested to us that unmarried women may be better able than married women to keep rape a secret and that this might lead unmarried women more frequently to consider keeping rape a secret. If so, the opposite pattern than the one we just suggested would be found. However, there is no significant difference between married and unmarried women in the consideration to keep the rape a secret (Table 24.6).

Finally, we predicted that reproductive-aged women would feel that their futures would be affected by the rape more than would nonreproductive-aged victims. The analyses for the variable show that there is a significant difference between reproductive-aged women and nonreproductive-aged victims, as well as between prereproductive girls, reproductive-aged and post-reproductive-aged women (Table 24.7). For the analysis between reproductive

Table 24.7. Feelings of Rape Effect on Victim's Future by Age and Marital Status

	Future Affected			Uncertain		Future Not Affected			
Nonreproductive	n = 16	c = 2		n = 71	c = 6	n = 41	c = 2		
	e = 23			e = 53		e = 52			n = 669
	d = −7			d = 18		d = −11			df = 2
Reproductive	n = 105	c = 0.5		n = 207	c = 1	n = 229	c = 0.5		X^2 = 12.8
	e = 98			e = 225		e = 21			p = 0.002
	d = 7			d = −18		d = 11			
Prereproductive	n = 5	c = 4		n = 44	c = 10	n = 17	c = 3		
	e = 12			e = 27		e = 27			
	d = −7			d = 17		d = −10			n = 669
Reproductive	n = 105	c = 0.5		n = 207	c = 1	n = 218	c = 0.5		df = 4
	e = 98			e = 225		e = 229			X^2 = 20.0
	d = 7			d = −18		d = −11			p = 0.000
Post-reproductive	n = 11	c = 0		n = 27	c = 0	n = 24	c = 0		
	e = 11			e = 26		e = 25			
	d = 0			d = 1.2		d = − 1			
Unmarried Women	n = 89	c = 1		n = 229	c = 0	n = 228	c = 0.3		
	e = 99			e = 227		e = 220			n = 669
	d = −10			d = 2.1		d = 8			df = 22
Married Women	n = 32	c = 4		n = 49	c = 0.1	n = 42	c = 1		X^2 = 6.8
	e = 22			e = 51		e = 50			p = 0.03
	d = 10			d = −2		d = − 8			

n = number of victims; e = expected frequency; d = deviation n from e; c = contribution of cell to X^2 (rounded to nearest tenth).

and nonreproductive ages, nonreproductive-aged victims were more likely to feel uncertain about the effects of the rape on their futures and reproductive-aged victims were less likely to be uncertain. When the age categories are divided into three, the analysis shows that reproductive-aged victims were more likely to feel that their futures were affected by the rape and more likely not to be uncertain about the rape's effect than were either prereproductive or post-reproductive-aged victims.

We also predicted that married victims would feel that their futures were more profoundly affected by the rape than would unmarried women victims. Married victims were significantly more likely to feel that their futures were affected than were unmarried women victims (Table 24.7).

CONCLUSIONS

Our analyses indicate that, as predicted, age and marital status are proximate causes of the magnitude of psychological pain following rape. Young girls (<12) and older women (>44) appear to be less severely psychologically traumatized by rape than do reproductive-aged women (12–44). Married women seem to be more psychologically traumatized by rape than do unmarried women. When the effect of marital status is removed, age is still a significant predictor of the magnitude of psychological pain following rape.

We also expected that the age and marital status of each victim would affect the likelihood that she would consider keeping the rape a secret. The results indicate that reproductive-aged women and married women were not significantly more likely to consider keeping the rape a secret. However, as predicted, reproductive-aged women and married women were significantly more likely to feel that their futures had been affected by the rape than were nonreproductive women and girls and unmarried women. For this variable, age and marital status seem interactive with both resulting in the feeling by the victim that her future has been affected.

Interestingly, we discovered that a victim's relationship with family members (all members of her family except her husband) is virtually unaffected by rape. This is true regardless of her age or marital status (or whether the rape was perpetrated by a stranger, friend, or family

member—N. W. Thornhill and R. Thornhill 1990b). Given this finding, we feel that change in family relationship is a poor measure of psychological pain. If family relationships change for the worse, our guess is it would cause (rather than measure) psychological pain (see R. Thornhill and N. W. Thornhill 1989).

The results presented in this paper suggest that the psychology that regulates mental pain processes information about age and mateship status in the event of a woman's rape. If age and mateship status are shown to be actual causes of the mental pain of rape victims then these two factors identify design features, evolved information-processing procedures of the psychological adaptation involved. The approach we outline in this paper has great promise for elucidating the evolved nature of the psychological adaptation regulating mental pain. Only when the evolved design of the psychology of mental pain is understood, i.e. the precise environmental information that causes mental pain is known, will humans have the knowledge that is needed to reduce psychological pain.

This is the first in a series of papers resulting from our study of the psychological pain of rape victims using the data set described. The second paper in this series assesses the effect of stranger, friend, or family-member rape on victim psychological pain; it shows that rape-offender type does not confound the effects of age and mateship status identified herein (N. W. Thornhill and R. Thornhill 1990b). Future papers will assess in further detail the effects of type of rape and circumstances surrounding rape on the victims's psychological pain. Some examples of these are the extent of nonphysical and physical force used to accomplish the rape (N. W. Thornhill and R. Thornhill 1990c), group/gang rape compared to single-offender rape, whether the rape is associated with other crime (e.g., robbery), and the nature of the sexual acts during rape.

We suspect that one possible reason for our failure to find any consistent effects of age or marital status on the change in husband/boyfriend relationship or change in sexual relationship is that all the analyses in this paper reflect data gathered within five days following the rape. It would not be surprising that a victim would have little change in these areas (or at least be unable to assess them) in such a short time. It seems that marital and sexual relations do continuously deteriorate long after the rape (Miller et al. 1982). We are anxious to assess this.

Our analysis of the psychological pain of rape victims has uncovered some patterns that have not been discovered in previous rape studies, and it is pointing to some design features of the psychological adaptation regulating mental pain. Our conviction is that insights into the human mind can best be generated by the scientific use of the modern evolutionary approach as it is typically used by biologists to study adaptations.

Acknowledgments. For assistance in data entry we thank Robert Coven and Dave Keller. Financial support was provided by the Harry Frank Guggenheim Foundation and by Paul Risser, Vice President for Research, UNM. Richard Alexander, Michael McGuire, and an anonymous reviewer provided useful suggestions on how to improve the manuscript. Pleasant distractions were provided by Patrick and Aubri Thornhill. Steve Andrews' help with library work and other tasks is appreciated. We thank Irene Farmer for professionally typing the manuscript.

Appendix I. Psychological Trauma of Reproductive- and Nonreproductive-Aged Victims. See Text for Discussion of the Coding of Trauma

†1. Eat	−4, −3	−2, −1	0	1,2	3,4
Nonreproductive	9	16	120	4	2
Reproductive	86	110	192	30	26
†2. Sleep	−4, −3	−2, −1	0	1,2,3,4	
Nonreproductive	20	17	105	9	
Reproductive	96	119	194	36	
†3. Night	−4, −3	−2, −1	0	1,2	3,4
Nonreproductive	4	112	22	10	
Reproductive	32	269	87	54	
†4. Street	−4, −3, −2, −1		0	1, 2, 3, 4	
Nonreproductive	37		12	16	
Reproductive	130		107	191	
†5. Known	−4, −3, −2, −1		0	1, 2, 3, 4	
Nonreproductive	54		7	6	
Reproductive	262		88	77	
†6. Unknown	−4, −3, −2, −1		0	1, 2, 3, 4	
Nonreproductive	44		8	12	
Reproductive	166		124	133	
†7. Home Alone	−4, −3, −2, −1		0	1, 2, 3, 4	
Nonreproductive	39		8	11	
Reproductive	232		66	122	
†8. Family	−3, −4	−2, −1	0	1,2	3,4
Nonreproductive	4	7	42	5	2
Reproductive	47	46	274	32	22
†9. Sexual Attractiveness	−4, −3, −2, −1		0	1,2,3,4	
Nonreproductive	42			5	
Reproductive	339			77	
*10. Heterosexual	−4, −3	−2, −1	0, 1, 2, 3, 4		
Nonreproductive	2	9	51		
Reproductive	59	126	240		
*11. Social	−4, −3	−2, −1	0	1, 2, 3, 4	
Nonreproductive	9	12	42	2	
Reproductive	109	114	182	18	
*12. Husband/ Boyfriend	−4, −3, −2, −1		0	1, 2, 3, 4	
Nonreproductive	2		10	2	
Reproductive	73		140	64	
*13. Sexual Relations	−4, −3, −2, −1,		0	1, 2, 3, 4	
Nonreproductive	3			7	
Reproductive	106			116	

†Positive numbers = greater negative effect; negative numbers = less negative effect.
*Negative numbers = greater negative effect; positive numbers = less negative effect

Appendix II. Psychological Trauma of Married Compared to Unmarried Women Victims. See Text for Discussion of the Coding of Trauma.

†1. Eat	−4, −3	−2, −1	0	1, 2, 3, 4
Unmarried	64	86	196	47
Married	27	32	30	8
†2. Sleep	−4, −3	−2, −1	0	1, 2, 3, 4
Unmarried	73	103	191	27
Married	34	23	31	9
†3. Night	−4, −3, −2, −1, 0		1,2	3,4
Unmarried	270		80	43
Married	52		23	19
†4. Street	−4, −3, −2, −1, 0		1, 2	3, 4
Unmarried	152		101	146
Married	17		17	62
†5. Unknown	−4, −3, −2, −1, 0		1,2	3, 4
Unmarried	182		105	106
Married	29		28	39
†6. Home Alone	−4, −3, −2, 1,0		1,2	3,4
Unmarried	240		55	89
Married	33		19	45

†Positive numbers = greater negative effect; negative numbers = less negative effect.

Appendix III. Psychological Trauma of Unmarried Reproductive and Post-reproductive-Aged Victims. See Text for Discussion of the Coding of Trauma.

†1. Eat	−4, −3	−2, −1	0	1, 2, 3, 4
Post-reproductive	5	7	44	1
Reproductive	59	79	152	46
†2. Sleep	−4, −3	−2, −1	0	1, 2, 3, 4
Post-reproductive	10	8	37	2
Reproductive	63	95	154	25
†3. Night	−4, −3, −2, −1, 0		1, 2	3, 4
Post-reproductive	41		11	5
Reproductive	229		69	38
†4. Street	−4, −3, −2, −1, 0		1, 2	3, 4
Post-reproductive	35		10	10
Reproductive	117		91	136
†5. Unknown	−4, −3, −2, 1, 0		1, 2	3, 4
Post-reproductive	38		6	10
Reproductive	144		99	96
†6. Home Alone	−4, −3, −2, −1, 0		1, 2	3, 4
Post-reproductive	1		8	43
Reproductive	44		102	194

†Positive numbers = greater negative effect; negative numbers = less negative effect.

25

Rape-Victim Psychological Pain Revisited

RANDY THORNHILL

Thornhill and Thornhill (1989) hypothesized that human mental pain is an adaptation that is designed to guide cognition, feelings, and behavior toward solutions to personal social problems that reduced inclusive fitness in human evolutionary history, and to provide inferences for avoiding such problems later in life. That paper derives the hypothesis's general predictions about the social circumstances that are expected to generate psychological pain (e.g., rape, loss of social status, death of a relative, desertion by a mate) as well as specific predictions about the variation in magnitude of psychological pain with each type of social loss (e.g., death of high-reproductive-value relative more painful than death of a low-reproductive-value relative; more psychological pain for young women than for either girls or postreproductive women in the event of their rape).

The target paper is one of four papers published in 1990 and 1991 (Thornhill and Thornhill 1990a, 1990b, 1990c, 1991) that attempted to test the application of the hypothesis of psychological pain to rape victims' post-rape mental pain. The study was based on five-day-post-rape interviews with a large sample of U.S. (Philadelphia) females of all ages who reported to authorities an attempted or actual sexual assault (primarily rape). Researchers at the Joseph Peters Institute conducted the interviews (McCahill et al. 1979). The data included thirteen psychological pain variables (e.g., change in feelings toward unknown men) that were used by the researchers to measure post-rape psychological change in the victims. The data also included each victim's age and the various circumstances surrounding the rape (e.g., the de-

gree of violence other than the rape itself, the nature of the sex act[s] involved).

Our approach was to examine the extent to which variation in mental pain was predictable from the mental pain hypothesis. The four papers mentioned earlier examined different predictions. This progression of four papers controlled significant variables predicting post-rape mental trauma as they were identified, thus strengthening the inferences about proximal causation of the pain. Overall, the results indicated that the psychology that regulates mental pain processes information that it should if mental pain is designed according to the hypothesis: (1) *victim age* (prereproductive, reproductive, postreproductive): reproductive-aged victims experience the most psychological pain, which was predicted because only reproductive-aged females can become pregnant as a result of rape; (2) *mateship status* (married versus unmarried): married victims had more psychological pain, which was predicted because married victims face husbands whose paternity may be questioned as a result of the rape; (3) *rape credibility*: victims of less violent rapes unmarked by physical injury have more mental pain, which was predicted because more violent rapes marked by physical injury are less likely to be interpreted as consensual sexual intercourse by victims' mates, and thus pose less of a paternity threat; and (4) *the nature of the sex act during rape*: vaginal intercourse constituted the most psychologically devastating form of sexual assault for reproductive-aged women but not for nonreproductive-aged victims, which was predicted because there is a risk of pregnancy only with rape of reproductive-aged females.

These results suggest that women have a special-purpose psychological adaptation designed for recognizing the circumstances that, in human evolutionary history, would have resulted in reduced fitness of an adult female who experienced forced sexual assault by a male. However, more research is needed to demonstrate the specificity of certain information processing in the event of rape versus other crimes perpetrated against women. In the event of property theft without physical contact or threat of physical contact, if young women are more psychologically traumatized than older women, the greater psychological trauma of young women rape victims would not be specific to rape. I predict that women's psychological trauma in the event of these forms of theft will correlate positively with the value of the property and not with age per se.

In the last several years adaptationist research on negative human emotions has increased, and there is growing evidence that mental pain is an adaptation that defends against the losses experienced by human ancestors (for introduction and partial review, see Nesse and Williams 1994). However, to my knowledge, there has been no subsequent research that has examined psychological pain of rape victims from the adaptationist perspective.

Any future studies in the area of rape victim psychological pain could be improved by collecting data that is relevant to strong tests of the predictions. For example, the original data on rape victims did not allow distinguishing between unmarried women with and without boyfriends. Unmarried victims with investing boyfriends may respond more like married victims. In both cases there is cuckoldry potential with rape. Also, it may be possible to derive from the hypothesis of mental pain predictions about the mix of the various negative emotions expressed (anger, anxiety, fear, sadness) by reproductive-aged women versus other age categories of victims as time elapses after the rape and in different settings (e.g., pair-bonded versus not). Future research might also examine the behavior of rape victims that is expected under the mental pain hypothesis. For example, victims paired to investing mates are predicted to emphasize to their mate the force required,

especially in the absence of physical evidence of it. In addition, the nature of social activity changes after rape should be predictably based on circumstances such as victim age and mateship status. Finally, victims who are prescribed and take psychotropic drugs to alleviate psychological pain after being raped could be compared with victims who don't use these drugs in order to determine if the drug users experience disadvantages in coping with rape-related problems.

Research on rape victim mental pain is grounded in the relatively recent ideas about coevolutionary contests between males and females. Theoretical models of sexual conflicts over mating decisions predict the evolution of female counteradaptations to male traits that increase male mating success at a significant cost to females (e.g., Parker 1979, 1984; Eberhard 1985). These antirape adaptations of females can be psychological features or morphological features not based in the nervous system. The target paper and the other three empirical papers on psychological pain of rape victims provide evidence for a female adaptation that is designed to cope with historical fitness-reducing problems in the event of rape, rather than to prevent rape from occurring. It is reasonable to hypothesize that women will have psychological adaptation that is specifically designed to detect risk of rape and motivate departure from and avoidance of situations of significant risk. This hypothetical adaptation is predicted to process cues of female vulnerability to rape (e.g., female age, settings that provide low costs to males who rape) and adjust female anxiety and fear accordingly. The best evidence of a female adaptation designed to prevent rape is in the water strider (*Gerris incognitis*). Arnqvist and Rowe (1996) have experimentally demonstrated that the abdominal spines on the female strider function to thwart mating attempts of harassing males. See Smuts and Smuts (1993) for discussion of some candidate antirape behavioral adaptations of female nonhuman primates.

Acknowledgments. For financial support of research on sexual coercion, I thank the Harry Frank Guggenheim Foundation. Laura Betzig provided useful suggestions on the manuscript.

26

Cognitive Adaptations for Social Exchange

LEDA COSMIDES
JOHN TOOBY

*Is it not reasonable to anticipate that our understanding of the human mind would
be aided greatly by knowing the purpose for which it was designed?*

—George C. Williams

Research Background

The human mind is the most complex natural
phenomenon humans have yet encountered,
and Darwin's gift to those who wish to understand it is a knowledge of the process that created it and gave it its distinctive organization:
evolution. Because we know that the human
mind is the product of the evolutionary process,
we know something vitally illuminating: that,
aside from those properties acquired by chance,
the mind consists of a set of adaptations, designed to solve the long-standing adaptive
problems humans encountered as hunter-gatherers. Such a view is uncontroversial to most
behavioral scientists when applied to topics
such as vision or balance. Yet adaptationist approaches to human psychology are considered
radical—or even transparently false—when
applied to most other areas of human thought
and action, especially social behavior. Nevertheless, the logic of the adaptationist position
is completely general, and a dispassionate evaluation of its implications leads to the expectation that humans should have evolved a constellation of cognitive adaptations to social life.
Our ancestors have been members of social
groups and engaging in social interactions for
millions and probably tens of millions of years.
To behave adaptively, they not only needed to
construct a spatial map of the objects disclosed
to them by their retinas, but a social map of the
persons, relationships, motives, interactions,
emotions, and intentions that made up their social world.

Our view, then, is that humans have a faculty of social cognition consisting of a rich collection of dedicated, functionally specialized,
interrelated modules (i.e., functional isolable
subunits, mechanisms, mental organs, etc.), organized to collectively guide thought and behavior with respect to the evolutionarily recurrent adaptive problems posed by the social
world. Nonetheless, if such a view has merit, it
not only must be argued for on theoretical
grounds—however compelling—but also must
be substantiated by experimental evidence, as
well as by converging lines of empirical support drawn from related fields such as neuroscience, linguistics, and anthropology. The
eventual goal is to recover out of carefully designed experimental studies "high-resolution"
maps of the intricate mechanisms involved.
Such an approach is intended to exploit the signal virtue of cognitive psychology: With its emphasis on mechanisms, cognitive approaches allow causal pathways to be precisely specified
through reference to explicitly described algorithms and representations.

Toward this end, we have conducted an experimental research program over the last eight
years, exploring the hypothesis that the human
mind contains algorithms (specialized mechanisms) designed for reasoning about social exchange. The topic of reasoning about social exchange was selected for several reasons. In the

Reprinted with permission from Barkow et al. (eds.). *The Adapted Mind*, pp. 163–228, New York: Oxford University Press
(1992).

first place, as we will discuss, many aspects of the evolutionary theory of social exchange (also sometimes called cooperation, reciprocal altruism, or reciprocation) are relatively well developed and unambiguous. Consequently, certain features of the functional logic of social exchange can be confidently relied on in constructing hypotheses about the structure of the information-processing procedures that this activity requires.

In the second place, complex adaptations are constructed in response to evolutionarily long-enduring problems, and it is likely that our ancestors have engaged in social exchange for at least several million years. Several converging lines of evidence support this view. Social exchange behavior is both universal and highly elaborated across all human cultures—including hunter-gatherer cultures (e.g., Cashdan 1989; Lee and DeVore 1968; Sharp 1952; Weissner 1982)—as would be expected if it were an ancient and central part of human social life. If social exchange were merely a recent invention, like writing or rice cultivation, one would expect to find evidence of its having one or several points of origin, of its having spread by contact, and of its being extremely elaborated in some cultures and absent in others. Moreover, the nearest relatives to the hominid line, the chimpanzees, also engage in certain types of sophisticated reciprocation (de Waal 1982; de Waal and Luttrell 1988), which implies that some cognitive adaptations to social exchange were present in the hominid lineage at least as far back as the common ancestors that we share with the chimpanzees, five to ten million years ago. Finally, paleoanthropological evidence also supports the view that exchange behavior is extremely ancient (e.g., Isaac 1978; McGrew and Feistner 1992; Tooby and DeVore 1987). These facts, plus the existence of reciprocation among members of primate species that are even more distantly related to us than chimpanzees—such as macaques and baboons (Packer 1977; de Waal and Luttrell 1988)—strongly support the view that situations involving social exchange have constituted a long-enduring selection pressure on hominids.

The third reason we selected reasoning about social exchange as the focus of this experimental series was that theories about reasoning and rationality have played a central role in both

cognitive science and the social sciences. Research in this area can, as a result, function as a powerful test of certain traditional social science postulates. An adaptationist approach to human psychology is often viewed as radical or false not because of gaps in its logic or any comparative lack of evidence for its hypotheses, but because it violates certain privileged tenets of this century's dominant behavioral and social science paradigm—what we have called elsewhere the Standard Social Science Model (see Tooby and Cosmides 1992). According to this view, all of the specific content of the human mind originally derives from the "outside"—from the environment and the social world—and the evolved architecture of the mind consists solely or predominantly of a small number of general-purpose mechanisms that are content-independent, and which sail under names such as "learning," "induction," "intelligence," "imitation," "rationality," "the capacity for culture," or, simply, "culture." On this view, the same mechanisms are thought to govern how one acquires a language and how one acquires a gender identity. This is because the mechanisms that govern reasoning, learning, and memory are assumed to operate uniformly across all domains: They do not impart content, they are not imbued with content, and they have no features specialized for processing particular kinds of content. Hypotheses that are inconsistent with this content-free view of the mind are, a priori, not considered credible, and the data that support them are usually explained away by invoking as alternatives the operation of general-purpose processes of an unspecified nature. Strong results indicating the involvement of domain-specific adaptations in areas such as perception, language, and emotion have sometimes—though grudgingly—been accepted as genuine, but have been ghettoized as exceptional cases, not characteristic of the great majority of mental processes.

In this dialogue, reasoning has served as the paradigm case of the "general-purpose" psychological process: It has been viewed as preeminently characteristic of those processes that are purportedly the central engine of the human mind. Even vigorous advocates of modularity have held so-called central processes, such as reasoning, to be general-purpose and content-independent (e.g., Fodor 1983). Consequently, we felt that reasoning about social exchange offered an excellent opportunity to cut to the quick of the controversy. If even human reasoning, the doctrinal "citadel" of the advocates of content-free, general-purpose processes, turns out to include a large number of content-dependent cognitive adaptations, then the presumption that psychological mechanisms are characteristically domain-general and originally content-free can no longer be accorded privileged status. Such results would jeopardize the assumption that whenever content-dependent psychological phenomena are found, they necessarily imply the prior action of cultural or environmental shaping. Instead, such results would add credibility to the contrary view that the mind is richly textured with content-specialized psychological adaptations.

Evolutionary biologists have developed useful criteria for establishing the existence of adaptations (e.g., Dawkins 1982, 1986; Symons 1992; R. Thornhill 1991; Tooby and Cosmides 1990b; Williams 1966a, 1985), and these criteria are helpful in evaluating experimental evidence that bears on these two positions. Adaptations can be recognized by "evidence of special design" (Williams 1966a)—that is, by recognizing that features of the evolved species-typical design of an organism are "components of some special problem-solving machinery" that solves an evolutionarily long-standing problem (Williams 1985:1). Standards for recognizing special design include factors such as economy, efficiency, complexity, precision, specialization, and reliability, which—like a key fitting a lock—render the design too good a solution to an adaptive problem to have arisen by chance (Williams 1966a). For example, the eye is extremely well suited for the detection and extraction of information presented by ambient light, and poorly designed as an orifice for ingesting food or as armor to protect the vulnerable brain from sharp objects. It displays many properties that are only plausibly interpreted as design features for solving the problem of vision. Moreover, the properties of an adaptation can be used to identify the class of problems, at the correct level of specificity or generality, that the adaptation was designed to solve. The eye allows humans to see hyenas, but that does not mean it is an adaptation that evolved particularly for hyena detection: There are no features that render it better designed for seeing hyenas than for seeing any of a far larger class of comparable objects. These principles governing adaptations can be developed into a series of methods for empirically arbitrating the dispute between traditional and domain-specific views of the mind. The Standard Social Science Model and evolutionary psychological approaches differ most strongly on the grounds of functional specialization, of content-specificity, and of evolutionary appropriateness (Tooby and Cosmides 1992).

According to the evolutionary psychological approach to social cognition outlined here and elsewhere (Cosmides 1985, 1989; Cosmides and Tooby 1987, 1989; Tooby 1985; Tooby and Cosmides 1989, 1990b), the mind should contain organized systems of inference that are specialized for solving various families of problem, such as social exchange, threat, coalitional relations, and mate choice. Advocates of evolutionary views do not deny that humans learn, reason, develop, or acquire a culture; however, they do argue that these functions are accomplished at least in part through the operation of cognitive mechanisms that are content-specialized—mechanisms that are activated by particular content domains and that are designed to process information from those domains. Each cognitive specialization is expected to contain design features targeted to mesh with the recurrent structure of its characteristic problem type, as encountered under Pleistocene conditions. Consequently, one expects cognitive adaptations specialized for reasoning about social exchange to have some design features that are particular and appropriate to social exchange, but that are not activated by or applied to other content domains.

In contrast, the Standard Social Science Model predicts that the reasoning procedures applied to situations of social exchange should be the same reasoning procedures that are applied to other kinds of content. On this view, reasoning is viewed as the operation of content-independent procedures, such as formal logic, applied impartially and uniformly to every problem, regardless of the nature of the content involved. There should be nothing in the evolved structure of the mind—no content-sensitive procedures, no special representational format—that is more appropriate for reasoning about social exchange than about hat racks, rutabagas, warfare, Hinayana scripture, turbulence, or sexuality. In other words, the standard view is that the faculty of reasoning consists of a small number of processes that are designed to solve the most inclusive and general class of reasoning problems possible—a class not defined in terms of its content, as the class includes all potential contents equally. On this view, any variability in reasoning due to content must be the product of experiential variables such as familiarity or explicit instruction.

For these reasons, the questions of interest for this experimental program include the following: Do patterns of performance on problems that require reasoning about social exchange reflect content-general rules of logic? Do patterns of performance on social exchange content, as compared with other contents, show systematic differences? If so, can these differences be explained through invoking general-purpose variables such as familiarity? Does the complexly articulated performance of subjects on social exchange problems have the detailed properties predicted in advance by an evolutionary analysis of the design features required for a cognitive adaptation to social exchange? By answering these and related questions, building from one experimental result to the next, the functional structure of human cognitive adaptations for reasoning about social exchange can begin to be delineated, and the adequacy of the Standard Social Science Model can be assessed.

Standard Analyses of the Evolution of Altruism

Natural selection is a feedback process that is driven by the differential reproduction of alternative designs. If a change in an organism's design allows it to outreproduce the alternative designs in the population, then that design change will become more common—it will be *selected for*. If this reproductive advantage continues, then over many generations that design change will spread through the population until all members of the species have it. Design changes that enhance reproduction are selected for; those that hinder reproduction relative to others are selected against and, therefore, tend to disappear. This ongoing process leads over time to the accumulation of designs organized for reproduction.

Consider, then, a design change that appears to *decrease* the reproduction of an individual who has it while simultaneously increasing the reproduction of other individuals. How could such a design change possibly spread through the population? At first glance, it would seem that a design feature that had this property would be selected against.

Yet many organisms do engage in behaviors that decrease their own reproduction while enhancing that of others. One chimpanzee will endanger itself to help another in a fight (de Waal 1982). A vampire bat will feed blood that it has collected from its prey to a hungry conspecific (Wilkinson 1988, 1990). A ground squirrel will warn others of the presence of a predator by emitting an alarm call that can draw the predator's attention to itself (Sherman 1977). Among many species of social insects, workers forgo reproduction entirely in order to help raise their sisters (Wilson 1971). People sometimes put themselves at great peril to help their fellow human beings, and carry out innumerable acts on a daily basis whose purpose is to help others. If a psychological mechanism generates such behavior on a regular basis, how could it possibly have been selected for?

Evolutionary biologists call this the "problem of altruism." An "altruistic" design feature is an aspect of the phenotype that is designed to produce some effect that enhances the reproduction of other individuals even though it may cause the individual who has it to reproduce less. The question is, how can designs that generate such behavior spread through a population until they become universal and species-typical?

So far, evolutionary biologists have provided two answers to the problem of altruism. The first, kin selection theory (or inclusive fitness theory), was proposed by W. D. Hamilton in 1964 (see also Maynard Smith 1964; Williams and Williams 1957). Imagine a design change that causes an individual to increase the reproduction of that individual's relatives, but that decreases the individual's own reproduction. There is some probability, r that the kin member who receives the help has inherited that very same design change from a common ancestor. Therefore, the design change—through helping the relative to reproduce—may be spreading new copies of itself in the population, even though it is simultaneously decreasing the rate at which it creates new copies of itself through the individual it is in, by slowing the reproduction of that particular individual. Whenever a design change affects both direct reproduction and kin reproduction, there is a trade-off between these two different avenues by which a design change can be reproduced. The fate of the design change will be determined by how much it helps (or harms) the relative, how much it harms (or helps) the helper, and the probability the relative shares the design change by virtue of their sharing common ancestors. By using what was, in effect, mathematical game theory, Hamilton showed that a "helping design" can spread through the population if it causes an organism to help a kin member whenever the cost to the organism's own reproduction is offset by the benefit to the reproduction of its kin member, discounted by the probability, r, that the kin member has inherited the same helping design. Although helping under these circumstances decreases the helper's *personal* reproduction, through its effect on other individuals it causes a net increase in the reproduction of the helping design itself in the population.

Consequently, if C_i and B_i refer to costs and benefits to an individual's own reproduction, then an altruistic design change can be selected for if it causes i to help j whenever $C_i < r_{ij}B_j$. Any design change that causes an individual to help more than this—or less than this—would be selected against. This constraint is completely general and falls out of the logic of natural selection theory: It should be true of any species on any planet at any time. A species may be solitary, and individuals may have no social interactions with their relatives; but if members of a species consistently interact socially with their relatives in ways that affect their reproduction, then they will be selected to evolve information-processing mechanisms that produce behavior that respects this constraint.

Because it suggested a rich set of hypotheses about phenotypic design, kin selection theory allowed animal behavior researchers to discover a flood of new phenomena. They began to find that the altruistic behavior of many species shows the design features that one would expect if their information-processing mechanisms had been shaped by kin selection. For example, ground squirrels are far more likely to give an alarm call if a close relative lives nearby (Sherman 1977), and they have psychological mechanisms that allow them to discriminate full siblings from half siblings from unrelated individuals (Hanken and Sherman 1981; Holmes and Sherman 1982). Similarly, kinship is a major predictor of whether a vampire bat will share its food with a particular individual (Wilkinson 1988, 1990). Most strikingly, kin selection theory (e.g., Hamilton 1964; Williams and Williams 1957) finally explained the existence of the sterile worker castes in the eusocial insects that had so troubled Darwin, providing an elegant set of hypotheses concerning how eusocial insects should allocate their reproductive effort among sisters, half-sisters, brothers and offspring, which have since been tested and confirmed (e.g., Frumhoff and Baker 1988; Frumhoff and Schneider 1987; Trivers and Hare 1976).

The realization that a design feature can make copies of itself not only by affecting the reproductive success of its bearer, but also by affecting the reproductive success of its bearers' kin, led to a new definition of the concept of fitness. Previously, evolutionary biologists spoke of a design's "Darwinian fitness": its effect on the number of offspring produced by an individual who has the design. But since Hamilton, one speaks of a design's "inclusive fitness": its effect on the number of offspring produced by an individual who has the design *plus* its effects on the number of offspring produced by others who may have the same design—that individual's relatives—with each effect discounted by the appropriate measure of relatedness, often designated by r (Dawkins 1982; Hamilton 1964). Above, we used C_i and B_i to refer to effects on a design's Darwinian fitness; henceforth, we will use these variables to refer to effects on a design's inclusive fitness.

Kin-directed helping behavior is common in the animal kingdom. But on occasion, one finds a species in which individuals help nonrelatives as well. How can a design feature that decreases one's own inclusive fitness while simultaneously increasing that of nonrelatives be selected for? Although rare compared to kin-directed helping, such behavior does exist. For example, although kinship is a major predictor of food sharing in vampire bats, they share food with certain nonrelatives as well. Male baboons sometimes protect offspring not their own (Smuts 1986). Unrelated chimpanzees will come to each other's aid when threatened (de Waal and Luttrell 1988).

Williams (1966a), Trivers (1971), Axelrod and Hamilton (1981), and Axelrod (1984) provided a second approach to the problem of altruism, reciprocal altruism theory, which in effect draws on the economist's concept of trade. Selection may act to create physiological or psychological mechanisms designed to deliver benefits even to nonrelatives, provided that the delivery of such benefits acts, with sufficient probability, to cause reciprocal benefits to be delivered in return. Such social exchange is easily understood as advantageous whenever there exist what economists call "gains in trade"— that is, whenever what each party receives is worth more than what it cost to deliver the reciprocal benefit to the other party. Ecologically realistic conditions, however, seldom provide opportunities in which two parties simultaneously have value to offer each other. For this reason, biologists have tended to focus on situations of deferred implicit exchange, where one party helps another at one point in time, in order to increase the probability that when their situations are reversed at some (usually) unspecified time in the future, the act will be reciprocated (hence the terms reciprocal altruism, reciprocation, or, as we prefer for the general class, social exchange).

If the reproductive benefit one receives in return is larger than the cost one incurred in rendering help, then individuals who engage in this kind of reciprocal helping behavior will outreproduce those who do not, causing this kind of helping design to spread. For example, if a vampire bat fails to find food for two nights in a row it will die, and there is high variance in food-gathering success. Sharing food allows the bats to cope with this variance, and the major predictor of whether a bat will share food with a nonrelative is whether the nonrelative has shared with that individual in the past (Wilkinson 1988, 1990). Reciprocal altruism is simply cooperation between two or more individuals for mutual benefit, and it is variously known in the literature as social exchange, cooperation, or reciprocation. Design features that allow one to engage in reciprocal altruism can be selected for because they result in a net increase in one's own reproduction or that of one's relatives and, consequently, in the reproduction of the design features that produce this particular kind of cooperative behavior.

For example, according to reciprocal altruism theory, cognitive programs that generate food sharing among nonrelatives can be selected for only if they exhibit certain design features. By cataloging these design features, Wilkinson (1988, 1990) was able to look for— and discover—heretofore unknown aspects of the psychology and behavior of female vampire bats. Reciprocal altruism theory guided his research program:

I needed to demonstrate that five criteria were being met: that females associate for long periods, so that each one has a large but unpredictable number of opportunities to engage in blood sharing; that the likelihood of an individual regurgitating to a roostmate can be predicted on the basis of their past association; that the roles of donor and recipient frequently reverse; that the short-term benefits to the recipient are greater than the costs to the donor; and that donors are able to recognize and expel cheaters from the system. (Wilkinson 1990:77)

Like kin selection theory, reciprocal altruism theory suggested a host of hypotheses about phenotypic design, which allowed animal behavior researchers to discover many previously unsuspected phenomena. Recently, it has done the same for those who study social exchange in humans. Reciprocal altruism theory has allowed researchers to derive a rich set of hypotheses about the design features of the cognitive programs that generate cooperative behavior in humans. We will examine some of these hypotheses and the evidence for them.

This chapter is divided into three parts. In the first part (Selection Pressures) we explore some of the constraints reciprocal altruism theory places on the class of designs that can evolve in humans. These "evolvability constraints" (see Tooby and Cosmides 1992) led us to develop a set of hypotheses about the design features of the cognitive programs that are responsible for reasoning about social exchange. In the second part (Cognitive Processes) we review research that we and others have conducted to test these hypotheses and show that the cognitive programs that govern reasoning about social exchange in humans have many of the design features one would expect if they were adaptations sculpted by the selection pressures discussed in the first part. In the third part (Implications for Culture) we discuss the implications of this work for understanding cross-cultural uniformities and variability in cooperative behavior.

SELECTION PRESSURES

Natural selection permits the evolution of only certain strategies for engaging social exchange. To be selected for, a design governing reasoning about social exchange must embody one of these strategies—in other words, it must meet an "evolvability criterion" (see Tooby and Cosmides 1992). By studying the nature of these strategies, one can deduce many properties that human algorithms regulating social exchange must have, as well as much about the associated capabilities such algorithms require to function properly. Using this framework, one can then make empirical predictions about human performance in areas that are the traditional concern of cognitive psychologists: attention, communication, reasoning, the organization of memory, and learning. One can also make specific predictions about human performance on reasoning tests, such as the ones we will discuss in Cognitive Processes (following).

In this part, we explore the nature of the selection pressures on social exchange during hominid evolution—the relevant evolvability constraints—and see what these allow one to infer about the psychological basis for social exchange in humans.

Game-Theoretic Constraints on the Evolution of Social Exchange

The critical act in formulating computational theories turns out to be the discovery of valid constraints on the way the world is structured. (Marr and Nishihara 1978:41)

In *Evolution and the Theory of Games*, John Maynard Smith (1982) pointed out that natural selection has a game-theoretic structure. Alternative designs are selected for or not because of the different effects they have on their "own" reproduction—that is, on the reproduction of all identical designs in the population. Some designs will outreproduce others until they become universal in the population; others will be selected out. Using game theory, one can mathematically model this process with some precision. This is true whether one is describing the alternative designs anatomically, physiologi-

cally, or cognitively. For example, it is irrelevant to the analysis whether one describes a design change in a particular region of the brain anatomically—as an increase in the density of serotonin receptors in that region—physiologically—as an increase in the rate of serotonin uptake (which was caused by the increased receptor density)—or cognitively—as a difference in how the individual who has the increased receptor density processes information. All that matters to the analysis is what effect the design change—however described—has on its own reproduction. Because our concern in this chapter is the evolution of the information-processing mechanisms that generate cooperative behavior, we will describe alternative designs cognitively, by specifying the different rules that they embody and the representations that those rules act upon.

To see how a game-theoretic analysis works, consider how one can use it to understand the ramifications of reciprocal altruism theory for the evolution of social exchange between unrelated individuals.

Designs reproduce themselves through the reproduction of the individuals who embody them. Given an individual, i, define a *benefit to i* (B_i) as the extent to which any act, entity, or state of affairs increases the inclusive fitness of that individual. Similarly, define a *cost to i* (C_i) as the extent to which any act, entity, or state of affairs decreases the inclusive fitness of individual i. Let 0_i refer to any act, entity, or state of affairs that has no effect on i's inclusive fitness. A cognitive program that causes a decrease in its own inclusive fitness while increasing that of an unrelated individual can evolve only if it has design features that embody the evolvability constraints of reciprocal altruism theory. A game-theoretic analysis allows one to explore what these constraints are. For ease of explication, the two interactants in a hypothetical social exchange will be designated "you" and "I," with appropriate possessive pronouns.

Reciprocal altruism, or social exchange, typically involves two acts: what "you" do for "me" (act 1), and what "I" do for "you" (act 2). For example, you might help me out by babysitting my child (act 1), and I might help you by taking care of your vegetable garden when you are out of town (act 2). Imagine the following situation: Baby-sitting my child inconveniences you a bit, but this inconvenience is more than compensated for by my watering your garden when you are out of town. Similarly, watering your garden inconveniences me a bit, but this is outweighed by the benefit to me of your baby-sitting my child. Formally put:

1. Your doing act 1 for me benefits me (B_{me}) at some cost to yourself (C_{you}).
2. My doing act 2 for you benefits you (B_{you}) at some cost to myself (C_{me}).
3. The benefit to you of receiving my act 2 is greater than the cost to you of doing act 1 for me (B_{you} of act 2 > C_{you} of act 1).
4. The benefit to me of receiving act 1 from you is greater than the cost to me of doing act 2 for you (B_{me} of act 1 > C_{me} of act 2).

If these four conditions are met—if acts 1 and 2 have this cost/benefit structure—then we would both get a net benefit by exchanging acts 1 and 2. Social exchange, or reciprocal altruism, is an interaction that has this mutually beneficial cost/benefit structure (see Table 26.1).

At first glance, one might think that natural selection would favor the emergence of cognitive programs with decision rules that cause organisms to participate in social exchange whenever the above conditions hold. After all, participation would result, by definition, in a net increase in the replication of such designs, as compared with alternative designs that cause one to not participate.

But there is a hitch: You can benefit *even more* by cheating me. If I take care of your garden, but you do not baby-sit my child—i.e., if I cooperate by doing act 2 for you, but you defect on the agreement by not doing act 1 for me—then you benefit more than if we both cooperate. This is because your payoff for cheating when I have cooperated (B_{you}) is greater than your payoff for mutual cooperation ($B_{you} - C_{you}$)—you have benefited from my taking care of your garden without having inconvenienced yourself by baby-sitting for me. Moreover, the same set of incentives applies to me. This single fact constitutes a barrier to the evolution of social exchange, a problem that is structurally identical to one of the most famous situations in game theory: the one-move Prisoner's Dilemma (e.g., Axelrod 1984; Axelrod and Hamilton 1981; Boyd 1988; Trivers 1971).[2]

Mathematicians and economists use game theory to determine which decision rules will maximize an individual's monetary profits or subjective utility. Consequently, they express payoffs in dollars or "utils." Such currencies are inappropriate to an evolutionary analysis, however, because the goal of an evolutionary analysis is different. Evolutionary biologists use game theory to explore evolvability constraints. The goal is to determine which decision rules can, in principle, be selected for—which will, over generations, promote their own inclusive fitness. For this purpose, units of inclusive fitness are the only relevant payoff currency. Other assumptions are minimal. The organism

Table 26.1. Sincere Social Contracts: Cost/Benefit Relations When One Party Is Sincere, and That Party Believes the Other Party Is Also Sincere[a]

	My offer: "If you do Act 1 for me then I'll do Act 2 for you.			
	Sincere offer I believe:		Sincere acceptance You believe:	
You do Act 1	B_{me}	C_{you}	B_{me}	C_{you}
You do not do Act 1	0_{me}	0_{you}	0_{me}	0_{you}
I do Act 2	C_{me}	B_{you}	C_{me}	B_{you}
I do not do Act 2	0_{me}	0_{you}	0_{me}	0_{you}
Profit margin	positive: $B_{me} > C_{me}$	positive: $B_{you} > C_{you}$	positive: $B_{me} > C_{me}$	positive: $B_{you} > C_{you}$
Translation of the offer into the value systems of the participants:				
My terms	"If B_{me} then C_{me}"		"If B_{me} then C_{me}"	
Your terms	"If C_{you} then B_{you}"		"If C_{you} then B_{you}"	

[a]B_x = benefit to x; C_x = cost to x; 0_x = no change in x's zero-level utility baseline. The zero-level utility baseline is the individual's level of well-being (including expectations about the future) at the time the offer is made, but independent of it. Benefits and costs are increases and decreases in one's utility, relative to one's zero-level utility baseline.

need not "know," either consciously or unconsciously, *why* the decision rule it executes is better or worse than others, or even *that* the rule it executes is better or worse than others. To be selected for, a decision rule must promote its inclusive fitness better than alternative rules—and that's all. It doesn't need to make one happy, it doesn't need to maximize subjective utility, it doesn't need to promote the survival of the species, it doesn't need to promote social welfare. To be selected for, it need only promote its own replication better than alternative designs.

Mathematicians and economists have used the Prisoner's Dilemma to understand how cooperation can arise in the absence of a "Leviathan," that is, a powerful state or agency that enforces contracts. Evolutionary biologists have used it to understand the conditions under which design features that allow individuals to cooperate can be selected for. It is a game in which mutual cooperation would benefit both players, but it is in the interest of each player, individually, to defect, cheat, or inform on the other. It is frequently conceptualized as a situation in which two people who have collaborated in committing a crime are prevented from communicating with each other, while a district attorney offers each individual a lighter sentence if he will snitch on his partner. But the payoffs can represent anything for which both players have a similar preference ranking: money, prestige, points in a game—even inclusive fitness. A possible payoff matrix and the relationship that must exist between variables is shown in Figure 26.1.

Looking at this payoff matrix, one might ask: "What's the dilemma? I will be better off,

and so will you, if we both cooperate—you will surely recognize this and cooperate with me." If there is only one move in the game, however, it is always in the interest of each party to defect (Luce and Raiffa 1957). That is what creates the dilemma, as we will show below.

Figure 26.2 shows that the cost/benefit structure of a social exchange creates the same payoff matrix as a Prisoner's Dilemma: $(B_i) > (B_i - C_i) < 0 > C_i$ (i.e., $T > R > P > S$); and $(B_i - C_i) > (B_i - C_i)/2$ (i.e., $R > T + S/2$). In other words, if I cooperate on our agreement, you get B_{you} for defecting, which is greater than the $B_{you} - C_{you}$ you would get for cooperating (i.e., $T > R$). If I defect on our agreement, you get nothing for defecting (this is equivalent to our not interacting at all; thus $P = O$ and $R > P$), which is better than the C_{you} loss you would incur by cooperating (i.e., $P > S$). The payoffs are in inclusive fitness units—the numbers listed are included simply to reinforce the analogy with Figure 26.1. In actuality, there is no reason why C_{me} must equal C_{you} (or $B_{me} = B_{you}$); an exchange will have the structure of a Prisoner's Dilemma as long as mutual cooperation would produce a net benefit for both of us.

Now that we have defined the situation, consider two alternative decision rules:

Decision rule 1: *Always cooperate.*

Decision rule 2: Always defect.

An individual with cognitive programs that embody decision rule 1 would be an indiscriminate cooperator; an individual with cognitive programs that embody decision rule 2 would be an indiscriminate cheater.

		you	
C - Cooperate		C	D
D - Defect			
R - Reward for mutual cooperation			
T - Temptation to defect	40	me: R = +3 you:R = +3	me: S = −2 you:T = +5
S - Sucker's payoff			
P - Punishment for mutual defection	**me**		
	D	me: T = +5 you:S = −2	me: P = 0 you:P = 0

Constraints: $T > R > P > S$; $R > (T+S)/2$*

*For an interated game, $R > (T+S)/2$. This is to prevent players from "cooperating" to maximize their utility by alternately defecting on one another.

Figure 26.1. Payoff schedule for the prisoner's dilemma situation in game theory.

you

		C	D
me	C	me: $R = B_{me} - C_{me} = +3$ you:$R = B_{you} - C_{you} = +3$	me: $S = C_{me} = -2$ you:$T = B_{you} = +5$
	D	me: $T = B_{me} = +5$ you:$S = C_{you} = -2$	me: $P = 0_{me} = 0$ you:$P = 0_{you} = 0$

Figure 26.2. Social exchange sets up a prisoner's dilemma. B_i = Benefit to i, C_i = Cost to i, 0_i = i's inclusive fitness is unchanged.

Now imagine a population of organisms, most of whom have cognitive programs that embody decision rule 1, but a few of whom have cognitive programs that embody decision rule 2.[3] Then imagine a tournament that pits the reproduction of decision rule 1 against that of decision rule 2.

In this tournament, both sets of individuals face similar environments. For example, one might specify that both types of organisms are subject to the same payoff matrix, that each organism participates in three interactions per "generation," and that these three interactions must be with three different individuals, randomly chosen from the population. After every organism has completed its three interactions, each organism "reproduces" and then "dies." "Offspring" carry the same decision rule as the "parent," and the number of offspring produced by an individual is proportional to the payoffs it gained in the three interactions it participated in in that generation. This process repeats itself every generation.

Using this tournament, one can ask, After one generation, how many replicas of rule 1 versus rule 2 exist in the population? How many replicas of each rule exist after n generations? If one were to run a computer model of this tournament, one would find that after a few generations individuals who operate according to rule 2 ("Always defect") would, on average, be leaving more offspring than individuals operating according to rule 1 ("Always cooperate"); the magnitude of the difference between them is rule 2's "selective advantage" over rule 1. This magnitude will depend on what payoff and opportunity parameters were specified in the program used, as well as the population composition.

After a larger number of "generations," rule 1—"Always cooperate"—would be selected out. For every interaction with a cheater, rule 1 would lose two inclusive fitness points, and rule 2 would gain five. Consequently, indiscriminate cooperators would eventually be selected out, and indiscriminate cheaters would spread through the population; the number of generations this would take is a function of how many cheaters versus indiscriminate cooperators were in the initial population. In practice, a population of "cheaters" is a population of individuals who never participate in social exchange; if you "cheat" by not doing act 1 for me, and I "cheat" by not doing act 2 for you, then, in effect, we have exchanged nothing. And an indiscriminate cooperator in the midst of defectors is, in practice, always an "altruist" or victim, continually incurring costs in the course of helping others, but receiving no benefits in return.

So, after n generations, where n is a function of the magnitude of rule 2's selective advantage in the tournament's "environment" and other population parameters, one would find that rule 2 had "gone to fixation": Virtually all individuals would have rule 2, and, regardless of the population's absolute size, a vanishingly small proportion of the individuals in it would have rule 1.[4]

By using this kind of logic, one can show that if a new design coding for rule 2—"Always defect"—were to appear in a population that is dominated by individuals with rule 1—"Always cooperate"—it would spread through the population until it became fixed, and it would not be vulnerable to invasion by rule 1 (see, e.g., Axelrod 1984). In a tournament pitting indiscriminate altruists against indiscriminate cheaters, the cheaters will come to dominate the population.

One might object that real life is not like a Prisoner's Dilemma, because real-life exchanges are simultaneous, face-to-face interactions. You can directly recognize whether I am about to cheat you or not (provided you are equipped with cognitive equipment that guides you into making this discrimination). If I show up without the item I promised, then you simply do not give me what I want. This is often true in a twentieth-century market economy, where money is used as a medium of exchange. But no species that engages in social exchange, including our own, evolved the information-processing mechanisms that enable this behavior in the context of a market economy with a medium of exchange.

Virtually any nonsimultaneous exchange increases the opportunity for defection, and in nature, most opportunities for exchange are not simultaneous. For example, a drowning man needs immediate assistance, but while he is being pulled from the water, he is in no position to help his benefactor. Opportunities for simultaneous mutual aid—and therefore for the withdrawal of benefits in the face of cheating—are rare in nature for several reasons:

The "items" of exchange are frequently acts that, once done, cannot be undone (e.g., protection from an attack and alerting others to the presence of a food source).

The needs and abilities of organisms are rarely exactly and simultaneously complementary. For example, a female baboon is not fertile when her infant needs protection, yet this is when the male's ability to protect is of most value to her.

On those occasions when repayment is made in the same currency, simultaneous exchange is senseless. If two hunters both make kills on the same day, they gain nothing from sharing their kills with each other: They would be swapping identical goods. In contrast, repayment in the same currency can be advantageous when exchange is not simultaneous, because of declining marginal utilities: The value of a piece of meat is larger to a hungry individual than to a sated one.

Thus, in the absence of a widely accepted medium of exchange, most exchanges are not simultaneous and therefore do provide opportunities for defection. You must decide whether to benefit me or not without any guarantee that I will return the favor in the future. This is why

Trivers (1971) describes social exchange in nature as "reciprocal altruism." I behave "altruistically" (i.e., I incur a cost in order to benefit you) at one point in time, on the possibility that you will reciprocate my altruistic act in the future. If you do, in fact, reciprocate, then our "reciprocally altruistic" interaction is properly described as an instance of delayed mutual benefit: Neither of us has incurred a net cost; both of us have gained a net benefit.

A system of mutual cooperation cannot emerge in a one-move Prisoner's Dilemma because it is always in the interest of each player to defect. In fact, the argument is general to any known, fixed number of games (Luce and Raiffa 1957). But selection pressures change radically when individuals play a series of Prisoner's Dilemma games. Mutual cooperation—and therefore social exchange—can emerge between two players when (a) there is a high probability that they will meet again, (b) neither knows for sure exactly how many times they will meet,[5] and (c) they do not value later payoffs by too much less than earlier payoffs (Axelrod 1984; Axelrod and Hamilton 1981). If the parties are making a series of moves rather than just one, then one party's behavior on a move can influence the other's behavior on future moves. If I defect when you cooperated, then you can retaliate by defecting; on the next move if I cooperate, then you can reward me by cooperating on the next move. In an iterated Prisoner's Dilemma game, a system can emerge that has incentives for cooperation and disincentives for defection.

The work of Trivers (1971), Axelrod and Hamilton (1981), and Axelrod (1984) has shown that indiscriminate cooperation (Decision rule 1) cannot be selected for when the opportunity for cheating exists. But *selective* cooperation can be selected for. Decision rules that cause one to cooperate with other cooperators and defect on cheaters can invade a population of noncooperators.

Consider, for example, Decision rule 3:

Decision rule 3: *Cooperate on the first move; on subsequent moves, do whatever your partner did on the previous move.*

This decision rule is known in the literature as *tit for tat* (Axelrod and Hamilton 1981). If rule 3's partner cooperates on a move, rule 3 will cooperate on the next move with that partner.

If rule 3's partner defects on a move, rule 3 will defect on the next move with that partner. It has been shown that rule 3 can invade a population dominated by indiscriminate cheaters (individuals who behave according to decision rule 2: "Always defect"). Using the payoff matrix in Figure 26.2, it is clear that rule 3 would outreproduce rule 2: Mutual cooperators (pairs of individuals who behave according to rule 3) would get strings of $+3$ inclusive fitness points, peppered with a few -2s from a first trial with a rule 2 cheater (after which the cooperator would cease to cooperate with that individual). In contrast, mutual defectors (pairs of individuals who behave according to rule 2) would get strings of 0s, peppered with a few $+5$s from an occasional first trial with a rule 3 cooperator (after which the cooperator would never cooperate with that individual again).

Game-theoretic analyses have shown that a decision rule embodying a cooperative strategy can invade a population of noncooperators if, and only if, it cooperates with other cooperators and excludes (or retaliates against) cheaters. If a decision rule regulating when one should cooperate and when one should cheat violates this constraint, then it will be selected against.

Axelrod (1984) has shown that there are many decision rules that do embody this constraint. All else equal (an important caveat), any of these could, in theory, have been selected for in humans. Which decision rule, out of this constrained set, is embodied in the cognitive programs that actually evolved in the human lineage is an empirical question. But note that to embody any of this class of decision rules, the cognitive programs involved would have to incorporate a number of specific design features:

1. They must include algorithms that are sensitive to cues that indicate when an exchange is being offered and when reciprocation is expected.
2. They must include algorithms that estimate the costs and benefits of various actions, entities, or states of affairs to oneself.[6]
3. They must include algorithms that estimate the costs and benefits of various actions, entities, or states of affairs to others (in order to know when to initiate an exchange).
4. They must include algorithms that estimate the probability that these actions, entities,

or states of affairs will come about in the absence of an exchange.
5. They must include algorithms that compare these estimates to one another (in order to determine whether $B_i > C_i$).
6. They must include decision rules that cause i to reject an exchange offer when $B_i < C_i$.
7. They must include decision rules that cause i to accept (or initiate) an exchange when $B_i > C_i$ (and other conditions are met).
8. They must include algorithms with inference procedures that capture the intercontingent nature of exchange (see Cosmides and Tooby 1989:81–84).
9. They must include algorithms that can translate the exchange into the value assignments appropriate to each participant.
10. They must include algorithms that can detect cheaters (these must define cheating as an illicitly taken benefit).
11. They must include algorithms that cause one to punish cheating under the appropriate circumstances.
12. They must include algorithms that store information about the history of one's past exchanges with other individuals (in order to know when to cooperate, when to defect, and when to punish defection).
13. They must include algorithms that can recognize different individuals (in order to do any of the above).
14. They need not include algorithms for detecting indiscriminate altruists, because there shouldn't be any.

Not all of these algorithms need to be part of the same "mental organ." For example, because algorithms that can do 2, 3, 4, 5, and 13 are necessary to engage in social interactions other than exchange—such as aggressive threat—these might be activated even when the algorithms that are specific to social exchange are not.

Design features 1 to 14 are just a partial listing, based on some very general constraints on the evolution of social exchange that fall out of an examination of the iterated Prisoner's Dilemma. These constraints are general in the sense that they apply to the evolution of reciprocal altruism in almost any species—from reciprocal egg trading in hermaphroditic fish (Fischer 1988) to food sharing in humans. Other, species-specific constraints on the design of social exchange algorithms can be derived by considering how these general selection pressures would have manifested themselves in the ecological context of hominid evolution.

For example, the sharing rules that are applied to high-variance resources, such as hunted meat, should differ in some ways from those that are applied to low-variance resources, such as gathered plant foods (Kaplan and Hill 1985a; see also Implications for Culture, this chapter). This raises the possibility that human exchange algorithms have two alternative, context-specific modes of activation. Both modes would have to satisfy the general constraints listed above, but they might differ considerably in various details, such as whether one expects to be repaid in the same currency (e.g., meat for meat), whether one requires reciprocation before one is willing to help a second time, or whether one is quick to punish suspected cheaters. Another example of how ecological context can place species-specific constraints on design concerns the kind of representations that exchange algorithms can be expected to operate on. For example, exchange algorithms in humans should operate on more abstract representations than exchange algorithms in vampire bats. The reciprocation algorithms of vampire bats could, in principle, operate on representations of regurgitated blood, because this is the only item that they exchange. But item-specific representations of this kind would not make sense for the exchange algorithms of humans. Because our ancestors evolved the ability to make and use tools and to communicate information verbally, exchange algorithms that could accept a wide and ever-changing variety of goods, services, and information as input would enjoy a selective advantage over ones that were limited to only a few items of exchange. To accommodate an almost limitless variety of inputs—stone axes, meat, help in fights, sexual access, information about one's enemies, access to one's water hole, necklaces, blow guns, and so forth—representations of particular items of exchange would have to be translated into an abstract "lingua franca" that the various exchange algorithms could operate on. This constraint led us to hypothesize that an item-specific representation of an exchange would be translated into more abstract cost-benefit representations (like those in the last two lines of Table 26.1) at a relatively early

stage in processing, and that many of the algorithms listed earlier would operate on these cost-benefit representations (Cosmides and Tooby 1989). Because some of these species-specific constraints on the evolution of social exchange in humans have interesting implications for cultural variation, we will defer a discussion of them to the third part of this chapter (Implications for Culture), where we discuss social exchange and culture.

David Marr argued that "an algorithm is likely to be understood more readily by understanding the nature of the problem being solved than by examining the mechanism (and the hardware) in which it is embodied" (1982:27). This is because the literature of the problem places constraints on the class of designs capable of solving it. The iterated Prisoner's Dilemma is an abstract description of the problem of altruism between nonrelatives. By studying it, one can derive a set of general constraints that the cognitive problems of virtually any species must satisfy to be selected for under these circumstances. By studying the ecological context in which this problem manifested itself for our Pleistocene ancestors, one can derive additional constraints. All these constraints on the evolution of social exchange—those that apply across species and those that apply just to humans—allow one to develop a task analysis or, to use Marr's term, a "computational theory" of the adaptive problem of social exchange. Cosmides and Tooby (1989) used some of these constraints to develop the beginnings of a computational theory of social exchange, which we call "social contract theory." So as not to repeat ourselves here, we refer the reader to that article for details. By constraining the class of possible designs, this theory allowed us and others to make some predictions about the design features of the algorithms and representations that evolved to solve the problem of social exchange in humans. Design features 1–14 listed earlier are a small subset of those predictions.

The computational theory we developed has guided our research program on human reasoning. We have been conducting experiments to see whether people have cognitive processes that are specialized for reasoning about social exchange. The experiments we will review in the following part were designed to test for design features 1, 9, 10, and 14, as well as some other predictions derived from the computational theory. We have been particularly interested in testing the hypothesis that humans have algorithms that are specialized for detecting cheaters in situations of social exchange.

COGNITIVE PROCESSES

Differential reproduction of alternative designs is the engine that drives natural selection: If having a particular mental structure, such as a rule of inference, allows a design to outreproduce other designs that exist in the species, then that mental structure will be selected for. Over many generations it will spread through the population until it becomes a universal, species-typical trait.

Traditionally, cognitive psychologists have assumed that the human mind includes only general-purpose rules of reasoning and that these rules are few in number and content-free. But a cognitive perspective that is informed by evolutionary biology casts doubt on these assumptions. This is because natural selection is also likely to have produced many mental rules that are specialized for reasoning about various evolutionarily important domains, such as cooperation, aggressive threat, parenting, disease avoidance, predator avoidance, object permanence, and object movement. Different adaptive problems frequently have different optimal solutions, and can therefore be solved more efficiently by the application of different problem-solving procedures. When two adaptive problems have different optimal solutions, a single general solution will be inferior to two specialized solutions. In such cases, a jack-of-all-trades necessarily be a master of none, because generality can be achieved only by sacrificing efficiency. Indeed, it is usually more than efficiency that is lost by being limited to a general-purpose method—generality may often sacrifice the very possibility of successfully solving a problem, as, for example, when the solution requires supplemental information that cannot be sensorily derived (this is known as the "frame problem" in artificial intelligence research).

The same principle applies to adaptive problems that require reasoning: There are cases where the rules for reasoning adaptively about one domain will lead one into serious error if applied to a different domain. Such problems cannot, in principle, be solved by a single general-purpose reasoning procedure. They are best solved by different special-purpose reasoning procedures.

For example, the rules of inference of the propositional calculus (formal logic) are general-purpose rules of inference: They can be applied regardless of what subject matter one is reasoning about. Yet the consistent application of these rules of logical reasoning will not allow one to detect cheaters in situations of social exchange, because what counts as cheating does not map onto the definition of violation imposed by the propositional calculus. Suppose you and I agree to the following exchange: "If you give me your watch then I'll give you $20." You would have violated our agreement—you would have cheated me—if you had taken my $20 but not given me your watch. But according to the rules of inference of the propositional calculus, the only way this rule can be violated is by your giving me your watch but my not giving you $20.[7] If the only mental rules my mind contained were the rules of inference of the propositional calculus, then I would not be able to tell when you had cheated me. Similarly, rules of inference for detecting cheaters on social contracts will not allow one to detect bluffs or double crosses in situations of aggressive threat (Cosmides and Tooby in prep., b). What counts as a violation differs for a social contract, a threat, a rule describing the state of the world, and so on. Because of this difference, the same reasoning procedure cannot be successfully applied to all of these situations. As a result, there cannot be a general-purpose reasoning procedure that works for all of them. If these problems are to be solved at all, they must be solved by different specialized reasoning procedures.

Given the selection pressures discussed earlier, we can define a social contract as a situation in which an individual is obligated to satisfy a requirement of some kind, usually at some cost to him- or herself, in order to be entitled to receive a benefit from another individual (or group). The requirement is imposed because its satisfaction creates a situation that benefits the party that imposed it. Thus, a well-formed social contract expresses an intercontingent situation of mutual benefit: To receive a benefit, an individual (or group) is required to provide a benefit. Usually (but not always) one incurs a cost by satisfying the requirement. But that cost is outweighed by the benefit one receives in return.

Cheating is a violation of a social contract. A cheater is an individual who illicitly benefits himself or herself by taking a benefit without having satisfied the requirement that the other party to the contract made the provision of that benefit contingent on. In this section, we review evidence that people have cognitive adaptations that are specialized for reasoning about social contracts. We will pay particular attention to the hypothesis that people have inference procedures specialized for cheater detection.

Adaptations are aspects of the phenotype that were designed by natural selection. To show that an aspect of the phenotype is an adaptation, one must produce evidence that it is well designed for solving an adaptive problem. Contrary to popular belief, developmental evidence is not criterial: Adaptations need not be present from birth (e.g., breasts), they need not develop in the absence of learning or experience (e.g., vision, language—see Pinker and Bloom 1992),[8] and they need not be heritable (Tooby and Cosmides 1990a). In fact, although the developmental processes that create adaptations are inherited, adaptations will usually exhibit low heritability. Differences between individuals will not be due to differences in their genes because adaptations are, in most cases, universal and species-typical—everyone has the genes that guide their development. The filter of natural selection does not sift designs on the basis of their developmental trajectory per se:[9] It doesn't matter how a design was built, only *that* it was built, and to the proper specifications.

To say that an organism has cognitive procedures that are adaptations for detecting cheaters, one must show that these procedures are well designed for detecting cheaters on social contracts. One must also show that their design features are not more parsimoniously explained as by-products of cognitive processes that evolved to solve some other kind of problem, or a more general class of problems. We approached this question by studying human reasoning. A large literature already existed that showed that people are not very good at detecting violations of conditional rules, even when these rules deal with familiar content drawn from everyday life. To show that people who ordinarily cannot detect violations of conditional rules can do so when that violation represents cheating on a social contract would constitute evidence that people have reasoning procedures that are specially designed for detecting cheaters in situations of social exchange.

The Wason Selection Task

One of the most intriguing and widely used experimental paradigms for exploring people's ability to detect violations of conditional rules has been the Wason selection task (Wason 1966: see Figure 26.3, panel a). Peter Wason was interested in Karl Popper's view that the structure of science was hypothetico-deductive. He wondered if everyday learning was really hypothesis testing—i.e., the search for evidence that contradicts a hypothesis. Wason devised his selection task because he wanted to see whether people are well equipped to test hypotheses by looking for evidence that could potentially falsify them. In the Wason selection task, a subject is asked to see whether a conditional hypothesis of the form *If P then Q* has been violated by any one of four instances represented by cards.

A hypothesis of the form *If P then Q* is violated only when *P* is true but *Q* is false: The rule in Figure 26.3, panel a, for example, can be violated only by a card that has a D on one side and a number other than 3 on the other side. Thus, one would have to turn over the *P* card (to see if it has a *not-Q* on the back) and the *not-Q* card (to see if it has a *P* on the back)— D and 7, respectively, for the rule in Figure 26.3, panel a. Consequently, the logically correct response for a rule of the form *If P then Q* is always *P* and *not-Q*.

Wason expected that people would be good at detecting violations of conditional rules. Nevertheless, over the past 25 years, he and many other psychologists have found that few people actually give this logically correct answer (less than 25% for rules expressing unfamiliar relations). Most people choose either the *P* card alone or *P & Q*. Few people choose the *not-Q* card, even though a *P* on the other side of it would falsify the rule.

A wide variety of conditional rules that describe some aspect of the world ("descriptive rules") have been tested; some of these have expressed relatively familiar relations, such as "If a person goes to Boston, then he takes the sub-

A. Abstract problem

Part of your new clerical job at the local high school is to make sure that the student documents have been processed correctly. Your job is to make sure the documents conform to the following alphanumeric rule:

> "If a person has a 'D' rating, then his documents must be marked code '3'."
> *(If   P   then   Q   )**

You suspect the secretary you replaced did not categorize the students' documents correctly. The cards below have information about the documents of four people who are enrolled at this high school. Each card represents one person. One side of a card tells a person's letter rating and the other side of the card tells that person's number code.

Indicate only those card(s) you definitely need to turn over to see if the documents of any of these people violate this rule.

D	F	3	7
(P)	*(not - P)*	*(Q)*	*(not - Q)*

B. Drinking age problem (adapted from Griggs & Cox, 1982)

In its crackdown against drunk drivers, Massachusetts law enforcement officials are revoking liquor licenses left and right. You are a bouncer in a Boston bar, and you'll lose your job unless you enforce the following law:

> "If a person is drinking beer, then he must be over 20 years old."
> *(If   P   then   Q   )*

The cards below have information about four people sitting at a table in your bar. Each card represents one person. One side of a card tells what a person is drinking and the other side of the card tells that person's age.

Indicate only those card(s) you definitely need to turn over to see if any of these people are breaking this law.

drinking beer	drinking coke	25 years old	16 years old
(P)	*(not - P)*	*(Q)*	*(not - Q)*

C. Structure of social contract problems

It is your job to enforce the following law:

> ***Rule 1*** - Standard Social Contract: "If you take the benefit, then you pay the cost."
> *(If   P   then   Q)*
> ***Rule 2*** - Switched Social Contract: "If you take the cost, then you take the benefit."
> *(If   P   then   Q)*

The cards below have information about four people. Each card represents one person. One side of a card tells whether a person accepted the benefit and the other side of the card tells whether that person paid the cost.

Indicate only those card(s) you definitely need to turn over to see if of any of these people are breaking this law.

	benefit accepted	benefit *not accepted*	cost paid	cost *not paid*
Rule 1	*(P)*	*(not - P)*	*(Q)*	*(not - Q)*
Rule 2	*(Q)*	*(not - Q)*	*(P)*	*(not - P)*

*The logical categories (Ps and Qs) marked on the rules and cards here are only for the reader's benefit: they never appear on problems given to subjects.

way" or "If a person eats hot chili peppers, then he will drink a cold beer." Others have expressed unfamiliar relations, such as "If you eat duiker meat, then you have found an ostrich eggshell" or "If there is an 'A' on one side of a card, then there is a '3' on the other side." In many experiments, performance on familiar descriptive rules is just as low as on unfamiliar ones. For example, rules relating food to drink, such as the hot chili pepper rule above, have never elicited logical performance higher than that elicited by unfamiliar rules, even though the typical sophomore in such experiments has had about 22,000 experiences in which he or she has had both food and drink, and even though recurrent relations between certain foods and certain drinks are common—cereal with orange juice at breakfast, red wine with red meat, coffee with dessert, and so on. Sometimes familiar rules do elicit a higher percentage of logically correct responses than unfamiliar ones, but even when they do, they typically elicit the logically correct response from fewer than half of the people tested. For example, in the Wason selection task literature, the transportation problem—"If a person goes to Boston, then he takes the subway"—is the familiar descriptive rule that has the best record for eliciting logically correct responses and performance on this rule was consistently higher in Cosmides's (1989) experiments than in most others. Even so, it elicited the logically correct *P & not-Q* response from only 48% of the 96 subjects tested. Recently, Stone and Cosmides (in prep.) tested rules expressing causal relations; the pattern of results is essentially the same as for descriptive rules. Humans do not appear to be naturally equipped to seek out violations of descriptive or causal rules.

When subjects are asked to look for violations of conditional rules that express social contracts, however, their performance changes radically. Consider the drinking age problem in Figure 26.3, panel b. It expresses a social contract in which one is entitled to receive a benefit (beer) only if one has satisfied a requirement (being a certain age).[10] The drinking age problem elicits the logically correct response, *P & not-Q*, from about 75% of subjects (e.g., Griggs and Cox 1982; Cosmides 1985). On this rule, it is very easy to see why one needs to check what the 16-year-old is drinking (the *not-Q* card) and the age of the person drinking beer (*P*), and it is equally obvious why the 25-year-old (*Q*) and the coke drinker (*not-P*) need not be checked. Experiments with the drinking age problem and other familiar social contracts show that human reasoning changes dramatically depending on the subject matter one is reasoning about. Such changes are known as "content effects."

Figure 26.3, panel c, shows the abstract structure of a social contract problem. To detect cheaters on a social contract one would always want to choose the "benefit accepted" card and the "cost not paid" card regardless of what logical category these cards happen to correspond to. For the drinking age problem, these cards happen to correspond to the logical categories *P* and *not-Q*. Consequently, a subject who was looking for cheaters on a social contract would by coincidence choose the logically correct answer. But, as this figure also shows, there are situations in which the correct answer if one is looking for cheaters is not the logically correct answer. This point is important and we will return to it later.

When we began this research in 1983, the literature on the Wason selection task was full of reports of a wide variety of content effects, and there was no satisfying theory or empirical generalization that could account for these content effects. When we categorized these content effects according to whether they conformed to

---

Figure 26.3. Content effects on the Wason selection task. The logical structures of these three Wason selection tasks are identical: They differ only in propositional content. Regardless of content, the logical solution to all three problems is the same: *P & not-Q*. Although <25% of college students choose both these cards for the abstract problem in panel a, about 75% do for the drinking age problem (panel b)—a familiar standard social contract. Panel c shows the abstract structure of a social contract problem. Cheater detection algorithms should cause subjects to choose the "benefit accepted" card and the "cost not paid" card, regardless of which logical categories they represent. These cards correspond to the logical categories *P & not-Q* for the "standard" form in rule 1, but to the logical categories *not-P & Q* for the "switched" form in rule 2.

social contracts, a striking pattern emerged. Robust and replicable content effects were found only for rules that related terms that are recognizable as benefits and cost/requirements in the format of a standard social contract—i.e., in the format of Rule 1 in Figure 26.3, panel c (see Cosmides 1985 for a review). No thematic rule that was not a social contract had ever produced a content effect that was both robust and replicable. Moreover, most of the content effects reported for non–social contract rules were either weak, clouded by procedural difficulties, or had some earmarks of a social contract problem. All told, for non–social contract thematic problems, 3 experiments had produced a substantial content effect, 2 had produced a weak content effect, and 14 had produced no content effect at all. The few effects that were found did not replicate. In contrast, 16 out of 16 experiments that fit the criteria for standard social contracts—i.e., 100%—elicited substantial content effects. (Since that time, additional types of content have been tested; evolutionarily salient contents have elicited new highly patterned content effects that are indicative of additional cognitive specializations in reasoning.)[11]

Special design is the hallmark of adaptation. As promising as these initial results were, they were not sufficient to demonstrate the existence of an adaptation for social exchange. First, although the familiar rules that were social contracts always elicited a robust effect, and the familiar rules that were not social contracts failed to elicit a robust and replicable effect, this was true *across* experiments; individual experiments usually pitted performance on a familiar social contract against performance on an unfamiliar descriptive rule. Because they confounded familiarity with whether a rule was a social contract or not, these experiments could not decide the issue.[12] Familiarity could still be causing the differences in performance in complex ways that varied across different subject populations. Second, even if it were shown that familiarity could not account for the result, these experiments could not rule out the hypothesis that social contract content simply facilitates *logical* reasoning. This is because the adaptively correct answer, if one is looking for cheaters on the social contracts tested, happened to also be the logically correct answer. To show that the results were caused by rules of inference that are specialized for reasoning

about social exchange, one would have to test social contract rules in which the correct "look for cheaters" answer is *different* from the logically correct answer.

Below, we review evidence addressing these, and other, hypotheses. Our goal will be twofold: (a) to show that the reasoning procedures involved show the features of special design that one would expect if they were adaptations for social exchange, and (b) to show that the results cannot be explained as by-products of other, more general-purpose reasoning procedures.

Did the social contract problems elicit superior performance because they were familiar? Familiar social contracts elicited high levels of apparently logical performance. Could this result be a by-product of the familiarity of the social contract rules tested? Suppose we have general-purpose reasoning procedures whose design makes us more likely to produce logically correct answers for familiar or thematic rules. Then high levels of *P & not-Q* responses to familiar social contract rules could be a by-product of the operation of these general-purpose mechanisms, rather than the result of algorithms specialized for reasoning about social exchange.

The first family of hypotheses that we tested against was the availability theories of reasoning, which are sophisticated and detailed versions of this "by-product" hypothesis (Griggs and Cox 1982; Johnson-Laird 1982; Manktelow and Evans 1979; Pollard 1982; Wason 1983; for a detailed review, see Cosmides 1985). These theories come in a variety of forms with some important theoretical differences, but common to all is the notion that the subject's actual past experiences create associational links between terms mentioned in the selection task. These theories sought to explain the "now you see it, now you don't" results common for certain familiar descriptive rules, such as the transportation problem. Sometimes these rules elicited a small content effect; other times they elicited none at all. This was in spite of the fact that the *relations* tested—between, for example, destinations and means of transportation or between eating certain foods in conjunction with certain drinks—were perfectly familiar to subjects. This meant that a general familiarity with the relation itself was not sufficient to explain the results. The proposal, therefore, was that subjects who had, for example, gone to Boston more often by cab than by subway would be more likely to pick "Boston" and "cab"—i.e., *P & not-Q*—for the rule "If one goes to Boston, then one takes the subway" than those who had gone to Boston more often by subway (*Q*). According to the availability theories, the more exposures a subject has had to the co-occurrence of *P* and *Q*, the stronger that association will become, and the easier it will come to mind, i.e., become "available" as a response. A subject is more likely to have actually experienced the co-occurrence of *P* and *not-Q* for a familiar rule, therefore familiar rules are more likely to elicit logically correct responses than unfamiliar rules. But whether a given rule elicits a content effect or not will depend on the actual, concrete experiences of the subject population tested.

Despite their differences, the various availability theories make the same prediction about unfamiliar rules. If all the terms in a task are unfamiliar, the only associational link available will be that created between *P* and *Q* by the conditional rule itself, because no previous link will exist among any of the terms. Thus *P & Q* will be the most common response for unfamiliar rules. *P & not-Q* responses will be rare for all unfamiliar rules, whether they are social contracts or not. The fact that a social-contract-type *relation* might be familiar to subjects is irrelevant: Previous results had already shown that the familiarity of a relation could not, by itself, enhance performance.

We can test against this family of hypotheses because social contract theory makes very different predictions. If people do have inference procedures that are specialized for reasoning about social contracts, then they ought to function, in part, as frame or schema builders, which structure new experiences. This means they should operate in *unfamiliar* situations. No matter how unfamiliar the relation or terms of a rule, if the subject perceives the terms as representing a rationed benefit and a cost/requirement in the implicational arrangement appropriate to a social contract, then a cheater detection procedure should be activated. Social contract algorithms need to be able to operate in new contexts if one is to be able to take advantage of new exchange opportunities. Therefore, the ability to operate on social contracts even when they are unfamiliar is a design feature that algorithms specialized for reasoning

about social exchange should have. Social contract theory predicts a high level of *P & not-Q* responses on all "standard" social contract problems, whether they are familiar or not. It is silent on whether availability exerts an independent effect on non–social contract problems. A standard social contract is one that has the abstract form, *If you take the benefit, then you pay the cost* (see Rule 1, Figure 26.3, panel c).

In the first set of experiments, we pitted social contract theory against the availability family of theories by testing performance on an *unfamiliar* standard social contract—a problem for which the two hypotheses make diametrically opposite predictions (for details, see Cosmides 1989, Experiments 1 and 2). Each subject was given four Wason selection tasks to solve: an unfamiliar social contract, an unfamiliar descriptive rule, a familiar descriptive rule (the transportation problem), and an abstract problem (as in Figure 26.3, panel a). Problem order was counterbalanced across subjects. The abstract problem was included because it is the usual standard for assessing the presence of a content effect in the Wason selection task literature; the transportation problem was included as a standard against which to judge the size of any social contract effect that might occur.

Rules such as, "If you eat duiker meat, then you have found an ostrich eggshell," or, "If a man eats cassava root, then he must have a tattoo on his face," were used for the unfamiliar problems; we felt it was safe to assume that our subjects would not have associative links between terms such as "cassava root" and "no tattoo" stored in long-term memory. An unfamiliar rule was made into a social contract or a descriptive rule by manipulating the surrounding story context. For example, a social contract version of the cassava root rule might say that in this (fictitious) culture, cassava root (*P*) is a much prized aphrodisiac whereas molo nuts (*not-P*) are considered nasty and bitter, thereby conveying that eating cassava root is considered a benefit compared to eating molo nuts, which are the alternative food. Having a tattoo on one's face (*Q*) means one is married; not having a tattoo (*not-Q*) means one is unmarried. As subjects know that marriage is a contract in which certain obligations are incurred to secure certain benefits (many of which involve sexual access), being married in this story is the cost/requirement. Finally, the story explains that because the people of this culture are concerned about sexual mores, they have created the rule, "If a man eats cassava root, then he must have a tattoo on his face." The four cards, each representing one man, would read "eats cassava root," "eats molo nuts," "tattoo," and "no tattoo." Other story contexts were invented for other rules.

The descriptive version of the unfamiliar rule would also give meaning to the terms and suggest a meaningful relation between them, but the surrounding story would not give the rule the cost/benefit structure of a social contract. For example, it might explain that cassava root and molo nuts are both staple foods eaten by the people of the fictitious culture (i.e., there is no differential benefit to eating one over the other), but that cassava root grows only at one end of the island they live on, whereas molo nuts grow only at the other end. Having a tattoo on your face or not again indicates whether a man is married, and it so happens that married men live on the side of the island where the cassava root grows, whereas unmarried men live on the side where the molo nuts grow. Note that in this version, being married has no significance as a cost/requirement; it is merely a correlate of where one lives. The story then provides a meaningful relation to link the terms of the rule, "If a man eats cassava root, then he must have a tattoo on his face," by suggesting that it simply describes the fact that men are eating the foods that are most available to them.

Subjects who were given a cassava root version of the social contract rule were given a duiker meat version of the descriptive rule, and vice versa, so that no subject encountered two versions of the exact same unfamiliar rule. The availability theories predict low levels of P & not-Q responses on both unfamiliar rules, whether they are portrayed as social contracts or not. Social contract theory predicts high levels of P & not-Q responses for the unfamiliar social contract, but not for the unfamiliar descriptive rule. The predictions of the two theories, and the results of two different sets of experiments, are shown in Figure 26.4.

The results clearly favor social contract theory. Even though they were unfamiliar and culturally alien, the social contract problems elicited a high percentage of P & not-Q responses. In fact, both we and Gigerenzer and Hug (in press) found that the performance level for unfamiliar social contracts is just as high as it usually is for familiar social contracts such as the drinking age problem—around 75% correct in our experiments. Unfamiliar social contracts elicited levels of P & not-Q responses that were even higher than those elicited by the familiar descriptive transporation problem. From our various experiments, we estimated the size of the social contract effect to be about 1.49 times larger than the size of the effect that availability has on familiar descriptive problems.

Familiarity, therefore, cannot account for the pattern of reasoning elicited by social contract problems. Social contract performance is not a by-product of familiarity.

Does social contract content simply facilitate logical reasoning? In the experiments just described, the adaptively correct answer if one is looking for cheaters happens to be the same as the logically correct answer—P & not-Q. Therefore, they cannot tell one whether performance on social contracts problems is governed by rules of inference that are specialized for reasoning about social exchange or by the rules of inference of the propositional calculus. Although we can think of no reason why this would be the case, perhaps social contract content simply facilitates logical reasoning. If so, then social contract performance could be a by-product of a logic faculty.

Two different sets of experiments show that this is not the case. The first involves "switched" social contracts (Cosmides 1989, Experiments 3 and 4), and the second involves perspective change (Gigerenzer and Hug, in press).

SWITCHED SOCIAL CONTRACTS. The propositional calculus is content-independent: The combination of P & not-Q violates any conditional rule of the form *If P then Q*, no matter what "P" and "Q" stand for. The proposed social contract algorithms are not content-independent: Cheating is defined as accepting a benefit without paying the required cost. It does not matter what logical category these values happen to correspond to. For example, although the same social contract is expressed by both of the following statements, the proposition "you give me your watch" corresponds to the logical category P in the first rule and to Q in the second one.

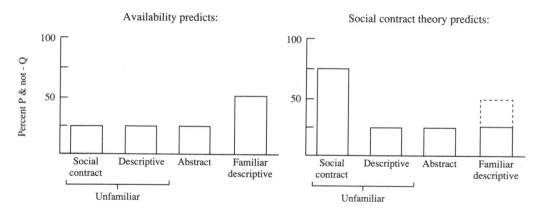

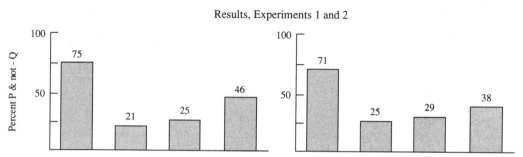

Figure 26.4. Social contract theory versus availability theory: Predictions and results for standard social contracts (from Cosmides, 1989, Experiments 1 and 2).

Rule 1: "If you give me your watch, I'll give you $20" (standard form).

Rule 2: "If I give you $20, you give me your watch" (switched form).

No matter how the contract is expressed, I will have cheated you if I accept your watch but do not offer you the $20, that is, if I accept a benefit from you without paying the required cost. If you are looking for cheaters, you should therefore choose the "benefit accepted" card (I took your watch) and the "cost not paid" card (I did not give you the $20) no matter what logical category they correspond to. In the case of Rule 1, my taking your watch without paying you the $20 would correspond to the logical categories P and $not\text{-}Q$, which happens to be the logically correct answer. But in the case of Rule 2, my taking your watch without giving you the $20 corresponds to the logical categories Q and $not\text{-}P$. This is not the logically correct response. In this case, choosing the logically correct an-

swer, P & $not\text{-}Q$, would constitute an adaptive error: If I gave you the $20 ($P$) but did not take your watch ($not\text{-}Q$), I have paid the cost but not accepted the benefit. This makes me an altruist or a fool, but not a cheater.

The general principle is illustrated in Figure 26.3, panel c, which shows the cost-benefit structure of a social contract. Rule 1 ("If you take the benefit, then you pay the cost") expresses the same social contract as Rule 2 ("If you pay the cost, then you take the benefit"). A person looking for cheaters should always pick the "benefit accepted" card and the "cost not paid" card. But for Rule 1, a "standard" social contract, these cards correspond to the logical categories P and $not\text{-}Q$, whereas for Rule 2, a "switched" social contract, they correspond to the logical categories Q and $not\text{-}P$. Because the correct social contract answer is different from the correct logical answer for switched social contracts, by testing such rules we can see whether social contracts activate inference procedures of the propositional calculus, such as modus ponens and modus tollens, or inference procedures that are specialized for detecting cheaters on social contracts.

The design of the following experiments was similar to that just described. Each subject solved four Wason selection tasks, prevented in counterbalanced order: an unfamiliar social contract, an unfamiliar deceptive problem, a familiar descriptive problem, and an abstract problem. The only difference was that in this case the terms of the two unfamiliar rules were "switched" within the "If-then" structure of the rule. For example, instead of reading, "If you eat duiker meat, then you have found an ostrich eggshell," the rule would read, "If you have found an ostrich eggshell, then you eat duiker meat." This was true for both the unfamiliar social contract and the unfamiliar descriptive rule. For the social contract rules, this switch in the order of the terms had the effect of putting the cost term in the "If" clause, and the benefit term

in the "then" clause, giving the rule the structure of the switched social contract shown in Rule 2 of Figure 26.3, panel c.

The predictions of social contract theory and the availability theories are shown in Figure 26.5, along with the results of two experiments. *Not-P & Q* is an extremely rare response on the Wason selection task, but social contract theory predicts that it will be very common on switched social contracts. That is exactly what happened. In fact, as many people chose *not-P & Q* on the unfamiliar switched social contracts as chose *P & not-Q* on the standard social contract problems described above.

If social contract content merely facilitates logical reasoning, then subjects should have chosen *P & not-Q* on these switched social contract problems. The fact that they chose *not-P & Q*—a logically incorrect response—shows that social contract performance is not caused by the activation of a logic faculty. This is, however, the response one would expect if humans

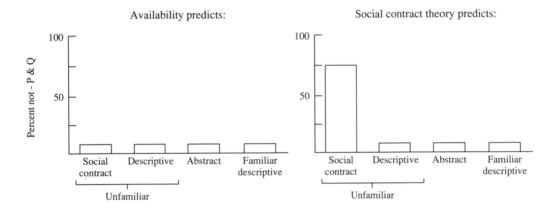

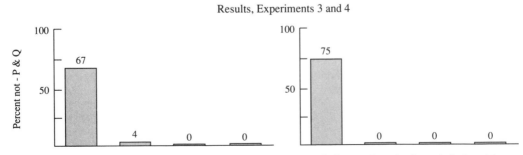

Figure 26.5. Social contract theory versus availability theory: Predictions and results for switched social contracts (from Cosmides, 1989, Experiments 3 and 4).

have rules of inference that are specialized for cheater detection.

Table 26.2 shows individual card choices for matching sets of experiments with standard versus switched social contracts sorted by logical category and by social contract category. The results for non–social contract problems replicate beautifully when sorted by logical category. But not the results for the social contract problems. These results replicate when sorted by social contract category, not by logical category. This shows that the content-dependent social contract categories, not the logical categories, are psychologically real for subjects solving social contract problems. This confirms another predicted design feature of the social contract algorithms: They define cheating in terms of cost-benefit categories not in terms of logical categories.

Manktelow and Over (1987) have pointed out that even when words such as "must" or "may" are left out of a social contract, one tends to interpret a standard social contract as meaning, "If you take the benefit then you (must) pay the cost," whereas one tends to interpret a switched social contract as meaning "If you pay the cost, then you (may) take the benefit." This is, in fact, a prediction of social contract theory: A cost is something one is obligated to pay when one has accepted a benefit, whereas a benefit is something that one is entitled to take (but need not) when one has paid the required cost. Thus, the interpretive component of the social contract algorithms should cause subjects to

"read in" the appropriate "musts" and "mays," even when they are not actually present in the problem (three out of four of the standard social contracts had no "must," and none of the switched social contracts had a "may"). Could it be that subjects are in fact reasoning with the propositional calculus, but applying it to these reinterpretations of the social contract rules?

No. In the propositional calculus, "may" and "must" refer to possibility and necessity, not to entitlement and obligation. On the Wason selection task, the logically correct answer for the rule, "If you pay the cost, then it is possible for you to take the benefit," is to choose no cards at all. Because this rule admits only of possibility, not of necessity, no combination of values can falsify it. The fact that most subjects chose *not-P & Q*, rather than no cards at all, shows that they were not applying the propositional calculus to a rule reinterpreted in this way.[13] To choose *not-P & Q*, one would have to be following the implicational structure of social exchange specified in Cosmides and Tooby (1989).

PERSPECTIVE CHANGE. Gigerenzer and Hug (in press) have conducted an elegant series of experiments that test another design feature of the proposed social contract algorithms, while simultaneously showing that the results cannot be explained by the propositional calculus or by permission schema theory, which is discussed later. They gave two groups of subjects Wason selection tasks in which they were to look for violations of social contract rules such as, "If

Table 26.2. Selection Frequencies for Individual Cards, Sorted by Logical Category and by Social Contract Category[a]

| | Unfamiliar Descriptive | | Abstract Problem | | Familiar Descriptive | | Unfamiliar Social Contract | |
| | | | | | | | Standard | Standard |
Logical category	Exp. 1&2	Exp. 3&4	Exp. 1&2	Exp. 3&4	Exp. 1&2	Exp 3&4	Exp. 1&2	Exp. 3&4
P	43	40	46	46	46	45	43	3
not-P	9	11	10	11	1	2	3	36
Q	20	23	15	23	8	6	0	44
not-Q	18	20	21	25	23	32	39	3
Social Contract Category:								
Benefit accepted							43	44
Benefit not accepted							3	3
Cost paid							0	3
Cost not paid							39	36

[a]Experiments 1 and 2 tested standard versions of the two unfamiliar rules, whereas Experiments 3 and 4 tested switched versions of these rules

an employee gets a pension, then that employee must have worked for the firm for at least 10 years." The only difference between the two groups was that one group was told "You are the employer" whereas the other group was told "You are the employee."

In social contract theory, what counts as cheating depends on one's perspective. Providing a pension is a cost that the employer incurs to benefit the employee, whereas working 10 or more years is a cost that the employee incurs to benefit the employer. Whether the event "the employee gets a pension" is considered a cost or a benefit therefore depends on whether one is taking the perspective of the employer (=cost) or the employee (=benefit). The definition of cheating as taking a benefit without paying the cost is invariant across perspectives, but the theory predicts that which events count as benefit and cost will differ across actors. From the employer's perspective, cheating is when an employee gets a pension (the employee has taken the benefit), but has not worked for the firm for at least 10 years (the employee has not paid the cost). These cards correspond to the logical categories P & not-Q. From the employee's perspective, cheating is when an employee has worked for at least 10 years (the employer has taken the benefit), but has not been given the pension that he or she is therefore entitled to (the employer has not paid the cost). These cards correspond to the logical categories not-P & Q.

In other words, there are two different states of affairs that count as cheating in this situation, which correspond to the perspectives of the two parties to the exchange. What counts as cheating depends on what role one occupies; cheating is a well-defined concept but its definition is preeminently content- and context-dependent.

In contrast, whether one is cued into the role of employer or employee is irrelevant to the content-independent propositional calculus. The correct answer on such a problem is P & not-Q (employee got the pension but did not work 10 years), regardless of whether the subject is assigned the role of the employer or the employee.

Gigerenzer and Hug conducted four experiments using different social contract rules to test the perspective change hypothesis. The predictions of both social contract theory and the

propositional calculus are shown in Figure 26.6 along with the results. The results are as social contract theory predicts: Even though it is logically incorrect, subjects answer not-P & Q when these values correspond to the adaptively correct "look for cheaters" response. The hypothesis that social contract content simply facilitates logical reasoning cannot explain this result. The perspective change results and the switched social contract results show that social contract performance is not a by-product of the activation of a logic faculty.

In light of these results it is interesting to note that although schizophrenic individuals often perform more poorly than normals on problems requiring logical reasoning, deliberation, or seriation, Maljkovic found that their reasoning about social contracts is unimpaired (Maljkovic 1987). She argues that this result makes sense if one assumes that the brain centers that govern reasoning about social contracts are different from those that govern logical reasoning.

To show adaptation one must both eliminate by-product hypotheses *and* show evidence of special design for accomplishing an adaptive function. Algorithms specialized for reasoning about social exchange should have certain specific design features, and the switched social contract and perspective change experiments confirm three more predictions about those design features:

1. The definition of cheating embodied in the social contract algorithms should depend on one's perspective. The perspective change experiments confirm the existence of this design feature.

2. Computing a cost-benefit representation of a social contract from one party's perspective should be just as easy as computing it from the other party's perspective. There are two reasons for this prediction: First, to successfully negotiate with others, one must be able to compute the conditions under which others would feel that you had cheated them, as well as the conditions under which they had cheated you. Second, being able to understand what counts as cheating from both perspectives facilitates social learning; by watching other people's exchanges one can gather information about the values, and perhaps about the trustworthiness, of people one may interact with in the future. If peo-

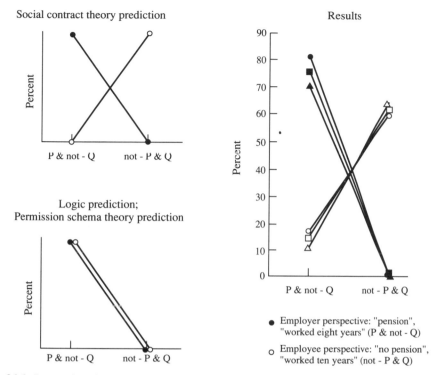

Social contract theory prediction

Results

Logic prediction;
Permission schema theory prediction

● Employer perspective: "pension",
"worked eight years" (P & not - Q)

○ Employee perspective: "no pension",
"worked ten years" (not - P & Q)

Figure 26.6. Perspective change experiments. Social contract theory versus logic facilitation hypothesis and permission schema theory: Predictions and results. Three separate experiments were conducted, testing the predictions of the theories against one another. The results of the three experiments are indicated by circles, squares, and triangles. Filled versus unfilled represents versions otherwise identical, except that the perspective (e.g., employer versus employee) is reversed (from Gigerenzer and Hug, in press).

ple are just as good at translating a social contract into the values of one party as the other, then they should be just as good at detecting cheaters from one perspective as the other. There should be just as many *P & not-Q* responses to the "employer" version as there are *not-P and Q* responses to the "employee" version. This was, in fact, the case.

3. The implicational structure of social contract theory mandates that the statement "If an employee gets a pension, then that employee must have worked for the firm for at least 10 years" be taken to imply "If the employee has worked for 10 years, then the employer must give that employee a pension." This is because when the employee has fulfilled his obligation to benefit the employer, the employer is obligated to benefit the employee in return. If subjects draw this implication, then they should choose *not-P & Q* in both

the switched social contract experiments and in the employee version of the perspective change experiments. The fact that they did confirms this design feature of the proposed social contract algorithms.

Is there a cheater detection procedure, or are people simply good at reasoning about social contracts? Social contract theory posits that the mind contains inference procedures specialized for detecting cheaters and that this explains the high percentage of correct social contract answers that these problems elicit. But maybe social contract problems simply "afford" clear thinking. Perhaps they are interesting or motivationally compelling in a way that other problems are not. Rather than having inference procedures specialized for detecting cheaters, perhaps we form a more complete mental model of a problem space for social contract problems, and this allows us to correctly answer any question that we might be asked about them, whether it is about cheating or not (for descriptions of mental model theories of reasoning, see Evans 1984; Johnson-Laird 1983; Manktelow and Over 1987). Although it would be difficult to reconcile the perspective change data with this hypothesis, it is still worth considering.

No one has presented any independent criteria for judging what kinds of problems ought to be "interesting," "motivationally compelling," or "easy to understand," which makes this hypothesis nebulous. Nevertheless, it can be tested by studying performance on reasoning problems in which the rule is portrayed as a social contract, but in which the subject is *not* asked to look for cheaters.

Two sets of experiments did just that. One set asked subjects to look for altruists in a situation of social exchange; the other asked subjects to look for violations of a social contract rule in a context in which looking for violations did not correspond to looking for cheaters. If people are good at detecting cheaters merely because social contract problems are easy to understand, then performance on such problems should be just as good as performance on cheater detection problems.[14] But if people are good at detecting cheaters because they have inference procedures specialized for doing so, then such problems should elicit lower levels of performance than social contract problems that require cheater detection.

ARE PEOPLE GOOD AT LOOKING FOR ALTRUISTS? The game-theoretic models for the evolution of cooperation that could be reasonably applied to the range of population structures that typified hominid hunter-gatherers require the existence of some mechanism for detecting cheaters or otherwise excluding them from the benefits of cooperation. This is because the capacity to engage in social exchange could not have evolved in the first place unless the individuals involved could avoid being continually exploited by cheaters. But most models do not require the existence of a mechanism for detecting "altruists"—individuals who follow the strategy of paying the required cost (thereby benefiting the other party), but not accepting from the other party the benefit to which this act entitles them.[15] Indeed, because individuals who were consistently altru-

istic would incur costs but receive no compensating benefits, under most plausible scenarios they would be selected out. Because they would not be a long-enduring feature of the adaptive landscape, there would be no selection pressure for "altruist detection" mechanisms. Thus, while we did expect the existence of inference procedures specialized for detecting cheaters, we did not expect the existence of inference procedures specialized for detecting altruists.

In contrast, if people are good at detecting cheaters merely because social contract problems afford clear thinking, then performance on altruist detection problems should be just as good as performance on cheater detection problems. The mental model of the social contract would be the same in either case; one would simply search the problem space for altruists rather than for cheaters.

To see whether this was so, we tested 75 Stanford students on some of the same social contract problems that were used by Cosmides (1985, 1989), but instead of asking them to look for cheaters, they were asked to look for altruists (the procedure was the same as that described in Cosmides 1989 for Experiments 5 through 9). Each subject was given one social contract problem and this problem required altruist detection. There were three conditions with 25 subjects each; a different social contract problem was tested in each condition. The first two conditions tested problems that portrayed a private exchange between "Big Kiku" (a headman in a fictitious culture) and four hungry men from another band; the third condition tested a problem about a social law. The first group's problem was identical to the cheater detection problem tested by Cosmides (1989) in Experiment 2, except for the instruction to look for altruists (see Figure 26.7 for a comparison between the cheater detection version and the altruist detection version). The problem in the second condition was essentially the same, but instead of portraying Big Kiku (the potential altruist) as a ruthless character, he was portrayed as having a generous personality. The third condition tested the social law, "If you eat duiker meat, then you have found an ostrich eggshell" (see Cosmides 1989, Experiment 1). The instructions on this problem were suitably modified to ask subjects to look for altruists rather than cheaters.[16]

Because altruists are individuals who have paid the cost but have not accepted the benefit, subjects should choose the "benefit not accepted" card (*not-P*) and the "cost paid" card (*Q*) on these problems. These values would correspond to the "no tattoo" card and the "Big Kiku gave him cassava root" card for the first two problems, and to the "does not eat any duiker meat" card and the "has found an ostrich eggshell" card for the social law problem. Table 26.3 shows that the percentage of subjects who made this response was quite low for all three altruist detection problems.

Is it possible that Stanford students simply do not know the meaning of the word "altruistic"? We thought this highly unlikely, but just to be sure we ran another 75 Stanford students (*n* = 25 per condition) on problems that were identical to the first three, except that the word "selflessly" was substituted for the word "altruistically." The word "selfless" effectively announces its own definition—less for the self. If there are inference procedures specialized for detecting altruists—or if social contract problems merely afford clear thinking—then surely subjects should be able to perform as well on

---

Cheater version

You are an anthropologist studying the Kaluame, a Polynesian people who live in small warring bands on Maku Island in the Pacific. You are interested in how Kaluame "big men"–chieftans–wield power.

"Big Kiku" is a Kaluame big man who is known for his ruthlessness. As a sign of loyalty, he makes his own subjects put a tattoo on their face. Members of other Kaluame bands never have facial tattoos. Big Kiku has made so many enemies in other Kaluame bands that being caught in another village with facial tattoo is, quite literally, the kiss of death.

Four men from different bands stumble into Big Kiku's village, starving and desperate. They have been kicked out of their respective villages for various misdeeds, and have come to Big Kiku because they need food badly. Big Kiku offers each of them the following deal:

"If you get a tattoo on your face, then I'll give you cassava root."

Cassava root is a very sustaining food which Big Kiku's people cultivate. The four men are very hungry, so they agree to Big Kiku's deal. Big Kiku says that the tattoos must be in place tonight, but that the cassava root will not be available until the following morning.

You learn that Big Kiku hates some of these men for betraying him to his enemies. You suspect he will cheat and betray some of them. Thus this is a perfect opportunity for you to see first hand how Big Kiku wields his power.

The cards below have information about the fates of the four men. Each card represents one man. One side of a card tells whether or not the man went through with the facial tattoo that evening and the other side of the card tells whether or not Big Kiku gave that man cassava root the next day.

Did Big Kiku get away with cheating any of these four men? Indicate only those cards(s) you definitely need to turn over to see if Big Kiku has broken his word to any of these four men.

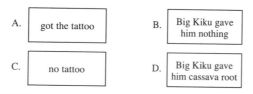

Figure 26.7. Both problems describe a social contract rule, but the problem on the left asks the subject to look for cheaters (individuals who took the benefit without paying the cost), whereas the problem on the right asks the subject to look for altruists (individuals who paid the cost but did not take the benefit to which this entitles them).

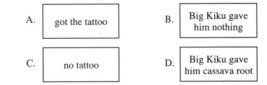

> **Altruist version:**
>
> You are an anthropologist studying the Kaluame, a Polynesian people who live in small warring bands on Maku Island in the Pacific. You are interested in how Kaluame "big men"—chieftans—wield power.
>
> "Big Kiku" is a Kaluame big man who is known for his ruthlesness. As a sign of loyalty, he makes his own subjects put a tattoo on their face. Members of other Kaluame bands never have facial tattoos. Big Kiku has made so many enemies in other Kaluame bands that being caught in another village with facial tattoo is, quite literally, the kiss of death.
>
> Four men from different bands stumble into Big Kiku's village, starving and desperate. They have been kicked out of their respective villages for various misdeeds, and have come to Big Kiku because they need food badly. Big Kiku offers each of them the following deal:
>
> "If you get a tattoo on your face, then I'll give you cassava root."
>
> Cassava root is a very sustaining food which Big Kiku's people cultivate. The four men are very hungry, so they agree to Big Kiku's deal. Big Kiku says that the tattoos must be in place tonight, but that the cassava root will not be available until the following morning.
>
> You learn that Big Kiku hates some of these men for betraying him to his enemies. You suspect he will cheat and betray some of them. However, you have also heard that Big Kiku sometimes, quite unexpectedly, shows great generosity towards others—that he is sometimes quite altruistic.Thus this is a perfect opportunity for you to see first hand how Big Kiku wields his power.
>
> The cards below have information about the fates of the four men. Each card represents one man. One side of a card tells whether or not the man went through with the facial tattoo that evening and the other side of the card tells whether or not Big Kiku gave that man cassava root the next day.
>
> Did Big Kiku get away with cheating any of these four men? Indicate only those cards(s) you definitely need to turn over to see if Big Kiku has broken his word to any of these four men.
>
> A. | got the tattoo | B. | Big Kiku gave him nothing |
>
> C. | no tattoo | D. | Big Kiku gave him cassava root |

Figure 26.7. (continued)

the "selfless" problems as they do on cheater detection problems.

Table 26.3 shows that this was not the case. Although performance was a bit higher on the problems that used "selfless" than on the problems that used "altruistic," performance was nowhere near the average of 74% that Cosmides (1989) found for comparable cheater detection problems.[17] In fact, performance on the selfless versions of the altruist detection problems was no better than performance on the familiar descriptive transportation problem (reported earlier). This indicates that people do not have inference procedures specialized for detecting altruists on social contracts, which is just what social contract theory predicted. More impor-

tant, it casts doubt on the hypothesis that cheater detection problems elicit high levels of performance merely because social contracts afford clear thinking.

ARE PEOPLE GOOD AT LOOKING FOR VIOLATIONS OF SOCIAL CONTRACTS WHEN THESE DO NOT INDICATE CHEATING? Gigerenzer and Hug

Table 26.3. Altruist Detection: Percent Correct (*not-P & Q*)

| | Personal Exchange | | |
	Ruthless	Generous	Law
Altruistic	28	8	8
Selfless	40	36	12

(in press) conducted a series of experiments designed to disentangle the concept of cheater detection from the concept of a social contract. The opportunity to illicitly benefit oneself is intrinsic to the notion of cheating. But one can construct situations in which the reason one is looking for violations of a social contract rule has nothing to do with looking for individuals who are illicitly benefiting themselves—i.e., one can construct situations in which looking for violations is not tantamount to looking for cheaters. Gigerenzer and Hug gave subjects Wason selection tasks in which all rules were framed as social contracts, but which varied in whether or not looking for violations constituted looking for cheaters.

Here is an example using the rule, "If one stays overnight in the cabin, then one must bring a load of firewood up from the valley." In the "cheating" version, it is explained that two Germans are hiking in the Swiss Alps and that the local Alpine Club has cabins at high altitudes that serve as overnight shelters for hikers. These cabins are heated by firewood, which must be brought up from the valley because trees do not grow at this altitude. So the Alpine Club has made the (social contract) rule, "If one stays overnight in the cabin, then one must bring along a bundle of firewood from the valley." There are rumors that the rule is not always followed. The subject is cued into the perspective of a guard whose job is to check for violations of the rule. In this version, looking for violations of the rule is the same as looking for cheaters.

In the "no cheating" version, the subject is cued into the perspective of a member of the German Alpine Association who is visiting a cabin in the Swiss Alps and wants to find out how the local Swiss Alpine Club runs the cabin. He sees people carrying loads of firewood into the cabin, and a friend suggests that the Swiss might have the same social contract rule as the Germans—"If one stays overnight in the cabin, then one must bring along a bundle of firewood from the valley." The story also mentions an alternative explanation: that members of the Swiss Alpine Club (who do not stay overnight in the cabin) bring wood, rather than the hikers. To settle the question, the subject is asked to assume that the proposed social contract rule is in effect, and then to look for violations of it. Note that the intent here is not to catch cheaters. In this situation, violations of the proposed social contract rule can occur simply because the Swiss Alpine Club never made such a rule in the first place.

In both versions, the rule in question is a social contract rule—in fact, exactly the same social contract rule. And in both versions, the subject is asked to look for violations of that rule. But in the cheating version, the subject is looking for violations because he or she is looking for individuals who are illicitly benefiting themselves, whereas in the no cheating version the subject is looking for violations because he or she is interested in whether the proposed social contract rule is in effect. If social contract problems merely afford clear thinking, then a violation is a violation is a violation: it shouldn't matter whether the violation constitutes cheating or not.[18] In contrast, if there are inference procedures specialized for cheater detection, then performance should be much better in the cheating version, where looking for violations is looking for illicitly taken benefits. Figure 26.8 shows the predictions and the results of four such experiments. On average, 83% of subjects correctly solved the cheating version, compared with only 44% on the no cheating version. Cosmides and Tooby (in prep. c) conducted a similarly designed experiment, with similar results. In both problems, it was stipulated that a social contract rule was in effect and that the people whose job it was to enforce the rule may have violated it. But in one version violations were portrayed as due to cheating, whereas in the other version violations were portrayed as due to innocent mistakes. We found 68% of subjects correctly solved the cheating version, compared with only 27% of subjects on the "mistake" (no cheating) version. Thus, using a different "no cheating" context in which it was stipulated that the social contract rule was in effect, we were able to replicate the difference that Gigerenzer and Hug found between their cheating and no cheating versions almost exactly (39 percentage points in Gigerenzer and Hug; 41 percentage points in Cosmides and Tooby).

These data indicate that social contract problems do not merely afford clear thinking. In addition, these results provide further evidence against the availability theories and the hypothesis that social contract content merely facilitates logical reasoning.

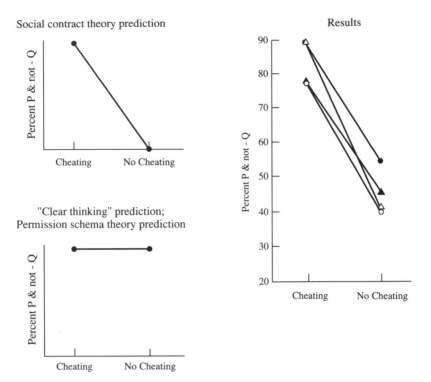

Figure 26.8. Is cheating necessary? Predictions and results. In these experiments, both conditions tested social contract rules, but in the "no cheating" condition looking for violations did not correspond to looking for cheaters. Social contract theory predicts a different pattern of results from both permission schema theory and the hypothesis that social contract content merely affords "clear thinking." Four separate experiments were conducted, testing the predictions the theories against one another. The results of the four experiments are indicated by filled and unfilled triangles, and filled and unfilled circles (from Gigerenzer and Hug, in press).

The results of these experiments are most parsimoniously explained by the assumption that people have inference procedures specialized for detecting cheaters: individuals who have illicitly taken benefits. Because these procedures operate on the cost-benefit representation of a problem, they can detect a violation only if that violation is represented as an illicitly taken benefit. They would not be able to detect other kinds of violations, nor would they detect altruists. These results provide further confirmation of a proposed design feature of the social contract algorithms: This bundle of cognitive processes appears to include inference procedures specialized for cheater detection.

Are cost-benefit representations necessary, or are subjects good at detecting violations of any rule involving permission? The social contract algorithms should contain decision rules that govern when one should engage in an exchange. A proposed contract should not be accepted unless the costs one incurs by providing a benefit to the other party are outweighed by the benefits one receives by engaging in the exchange. Consequently, the first stage of processing must be the assignment of cost-benefit weightings to the "benefit term"—the event, item, or state of affairs the contract entitles one to receive—and to the "cost term"—the event, item, or state of affairs that the other party requires of one. We have been calling these terms the "benefit" term and the "cost" term for ease of explication; we do not mean to prejudge the actual values that the parties to the exchange assign to these terms. For example, satisfying the requirement may actually benefit the person who satisfies it—the offerer's belief that the benefit she is requiring the other party to provide represents a cost to that party may be erroneous. But the offerer would not propose the contract in the first place unless she believed that the state of affairs she wants to bring about would not occur in the absence of the contract—it would be silly to offer you $20 for your watch if I believed you were going to give it to me anyway. Similarly, the offerer may be mistaken in her belief that she is offering a benefit to the other party, in which case her offer will not be accepted— you might value your watch more than you would value having an extra $20. In social contract theory, costs and benefits are defined with respect to the value systems of the participants, and relative to a zero-level utility baseline that represents how each party would behave in the absence of the contract. (The cost-benefit conditions that should adhere for an offerer to offer and the acceptor to accept a social contract are spelled out in Cosmides 1985, and Cosmides and Tooby 1989.)

Once the contract has been translated into cost-benefit terms, the decision rules for acceptance or rejection can operate on that representation. The cheater detection procedures should also act on that representation, causing one to investigate individuals who have not fulfilled the requirement specified in the cost term and individuals who have taken the benefit offered. By operating on this relatively abstract level of representation, the cheater detection procedures can detect cheaters no matter what the actual items of exchange are. Because humans are a technological species capable of exchanging a wide array of items, we hypothesized that human cheater detection procedures would operate on this abstract cost-benefit level of representation, rather than be tied to any particular item of exchange, as discussed earlier in this chapter. In other species, the constraint that cheaters must be detected might be implemented by algorithms that operate on other levels of representation (as discussed for the vampire bat).

Thus, a predicted design feature of human social contract algorithms is that they cause one to assign cost-benefit representations to a social contract, one for each party to the interaction. The presence of this design feature was confirmed by the perspective change experiments. Another predicted design feature is that cheater detection procedures operate on cost-benefit representations. Indeed, it is difficult to see how they could do otherwise, given that cheating is defined as accepting a benefit one is not entitled to. Technically, a violation that does not illicitly benefit one is not cheating.

If cheater detection algorithms operate on cost-benefit representations, then they should not be able to operate on rules that are similar to social contracts but that have not been assigned a cost-benefit representation. To test this prediction, we investigated Wason selection task performance on permission rules that did not afford the assignment of a cost-benefit representation.

Permission rules are prescriptive rules that specify the conditions under which one is allowed to take some action. Cheng and Holyoak (1985:398) define them as "regulations . . . typically imposed by an authority to achieve some social purpose". Their "permission schema theory" proposes that people have a schema for reasoning about permissions that consists of the following four production rules:

Rule 1: If the action is to be taken, then the precondition must be satisfied.

Rule 2: If the action is not to be taken, then the precondition need not be satisfied.

Rule 3: If the precondition is satisfied, then the action may be taken.

Rule 4: If the precondition is not satisfied, then the action must not be taken.

On a Wason selection task in the linguistic format of rule 1, the first production rule would cause one to choose the "action has been taken" card (P), and the fourth production rule would cause one to choose the "precondition has not been satisfied" card ($not\text{-}Q$). Rules 2 and 3 would not cause any card to be chosen. If a Wason selection task presented a rule in the linguistic format of rule 3 (a cognate to our switched social contracts), then the same two cards would be chosen for the same reason, but they would now correspond to the logical categories Q and $not\text{-}P$.

Cheng and Holyoak (1985) and Cheng, Holyoak, Nisbett and Oliver (1986) also propose the existence of "obligation schemas." These have the same implicational structure as permission schemas (and hence lead to the same predictions), but their representational format is "If condition C occurs, then action A must be taken." Because in any concrete case it is difficult to tell a permission from an obligation, we will refer to both kinds of rules under the rubric of permission schema theory.[19]

All social contracts are permission rules, but not all permission rules are social contracts. Social contract rules that have the form "If one takes the benefit, then one must pay the cost" are subsets of the set of all permission rules, because taking a benefit is just one kind of action that a person can take. Taking a benefit always entails taking an action, but there are many situations in which taking an action does not entail taking a benefit.

Permission schema theory has already been falsified by the experiment of Gigerenzer and Hug, described earlier. In permission schema theory, a permission rule has been violated whenever the action has been taken but the precondition has not been satisfied. It should not matter why subjects are interested in violations. Whether one is interested in violations because one is interested in finding cheaters or because one is interested in seeing whether the rule is in effect is irrelevant to permission schema theory. As long as the subject recognizes that the rule is a permission rule, the permission schema should cause the "action taken" and the "precondition not met" cards to be chosen. Consequently, permission schema theory would have to predict equally high levels of performance for the cheating and the no cheating versions of the social contract rules tested by Gigerenzer and Hug, as Figure 26.8 shows. Yet, even though both problems involved looking for violations of the same (social contract) permission rule, the cheating version elicited much higher performance than the no cheating version. Gigerenzer and Hug's perspective change experiments also falsify permission schema theory, and for a similar reason. Only one combination of values—"action taken" and "precondition not satisfied"—violates a permission rule in permission schema theory. What counts as a violation does not change depending on one's perspective; indeed, permission schema theory has no theoretical vocabulary for discussing differences of perspective. Yet the subjects' definition of violation depended on what role they were cued into, the employer's (P & not-Q) or the employee's (not-P & Q). Permission schema theory can account for the P & not-Q response, but not for the not-P & Q response.[20]

Permission schema theory and social contract theory differ in yet another way: The permission schema operates on the more abstract and inclusive action-precondition level of representation, whereas social contract algorithms construct and operate on the somewhat less general cost-benefit level of representation. Consequently, permission schema theory predicts that all permission rules will elicit high levels of performance, whether they have the cost-benefit structure of a social contract or not. In contrast, social contract theory does not predict high levels of performance for permission rules that do not afford the assignment of a cost-benefit representation. This is because cheating is *defined* as an illicitly taken benefit; where there are no benefits, there can be no cheating. By comparing performance on permission rules that do and do not afford the assignment of the appropriate cost-benefit representation, we can both test the prediction that cheater detection algorithms require a cost-benefit representation to operate and provide yet another test between social contract theory and permission schema theory.

In the first series of experiment (reported in Cosmides 1989), we used the same research strategy as before: Wason selection tasks using rules whose terms and relation would be unfamiliar to our subjects, surrounded by a story context that either did or did not afford the assignment of the cost-benefit structure of a social contract to the rule. But in these experiments, the non–social contract rule was a permission rule, not a descriptive rule. Let us illustrate the difference with an example: the school rule.

The school rule tested in both conditions was "If a student is to be assigned to Grover High School, then that student must live in Grover City." In the social contract version, the story explained that Grover High School is a much better high school than Hanover High, with a good record for getting students into college. Citizens of Grove City pay higher taxes for education than citizens of the town of Hanover, which is why Grover High is the better school. The story surrounding the rule thus portrays going to Grover High as a rationed benefit that must be paid for through higher taxes. Volunteers, some of whom are mothers with high-school-age children, are processing the school assignment documents, and it is rumored that some might have cheated on the rule in assigning their own children to a school. The subject is cued into the role of someone who is supervising these volunteers and must therefore look for cheaters.

In the non–social contract version, the same permission rule is used, but the surrounding story did not afford a cost-benefit interpretation of the terms of the rule. Grover High is not portrayed as any better than Hanover High, nor does the story mention any greater cost that is incurred by living in Grover City rather than Hanover. It is, however, explained that it is important that this rule for assigning students from various towns to the appropriate school district be followed, because the population statistics they provide allow the board of education to decide how many teachers need to be assigned to each school. If the rule is not followed, some schools could end up with too many teachers and others with too few. Thus the story context gives the rule a "social purpose." The subject is cued into the role of a person who is replacing the absent-minded secretary who was supposed to follow this rule in sorting the students' documents. Because the former secretary frequently made mistakes, the subject must check the documents to see if the rule was ever violated.

Although this rule is a permission rule—stating the conditions under which one is allowed to assign a student to Grover High School— nothing in the story affords the assignment of the cost-benefit structure of a social contract to this rule. There is no benefit to assigning someone to Grover rather than to Hanover High, and no cost associated with living in one city rather than the other. Moreover, there is no apparent way that the absent-minded secretary could have illicitly benefited from breaking the rule. Thus her mistakes would not constitute cheating. By hypothesis, cheater detection algorithms should not be able to operate on this problem, because they would have no cost-benefit representations to attach themselves to. Social contract theory, therefore, predicts a lower percent of correct responses for this version than for the social contract version. In contrast, permission schema theory predicts high levels of the correct responses for both rules, because both are permission rules: Both have the action-precondition representational format that permission schema theory requires. (For both theories, the "correct" response is P & not-Q for standard rules and not-P & Q for switched rules.)

The predictions and results of four experiment—two with standard rules, two with switched rules—are displayed in Figure 26.9. Across the four experiments, 75% of subjects chose the correct answer for the social contract permission rules, compared with only 21% for the non–social contract permission rules.

Using unfamiliar rules with a long story context has the advantage of giving the experimenter some control over the subject's mental model of the situation. The disadvantage of this method, however, is that it is difficult to create matching stories in which only one element varies. In the matched school rules, for example, two elements that distinguish permission schema theory and social contract theory varied: (a) whether the rule was given a cost-benefit structure, and (b) whether the potential violator was portrayed as a cheater or as a person who might have broken the rule by mistake. So we tackled the question of whether the rule must have a cost-benefit structure in another way as well: We tested minimalist problems that varied only in whether the subjects' past experience would cause them to interpret the antecedent of the rule as a benefit (Cosmides and Tooby, in prep., c). These problems had virtually no context: They simply explained that among the Kaluame (another fictitious culture) the elders make the laws, and one of the laws they made is, "If one is going out at night, then one must tie a small piece of red volcanic rock around one's ankle." The subject was then asked to see if any of four individuals had violated this law. The rule was based on one developed by Cheng and Holyoak (1989), but the context gave the rule no rationale or "social purpose."

We tested three versions of the rule that differed in only one respect: how much of a benefit the antecedent would seem to be. Among undergraduates, going out at night is a benefit: It represents fun, dating, adventure, and so on. Staying home at night is not as much fun, and taking out the garbage is even less so. Consequently, we compared performance on the "going out at night" rule to performance on two other rules: "If one is staying home at night, then one must tie a small piece of red volcanic rock around one's ankle" and "If one is taking out the garbage, then one must tie a small piece

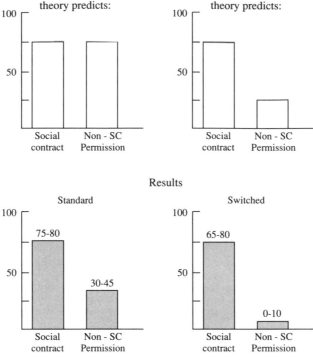

Figure 26.9. Are cost-benefit representations necessary? Social contract theory versus permission schema theory: Predictions and results (from Cosmides 1989, Experiments 5, 6, 8, and 9).

of red volcanic rock around one's ankle." If permission schema theory were correct, then all three of these permission rules would elicit equally high levels of *P & not-Q* responses.[21] But if social contract theory is correct, and the rule must have the cost-benefit structure of a social contract to elicit the effect, then performance should decline as the value of the antecedent declines. The more difficult it is to interpret the antecedent as a benefit, the more difficult it should be to see how one could illicitly benefit by breaking the rule.

The predictions and results are depicted in Figure 26.10. Performance decreases as the size of the benefit in the antecedent decreases, just as social contract theory predicts. Figure 26.10 also depicts the results of another, similar experiment with the so-called "Sears problem." As we removed the cost-benefit structure of the Sears problem, performance decreased. This experiment is also described in Cosmides and Tooby (in prep., c).

Manktelow and Over (1990, scenarios B and C) tested two obligation rules that lacked the cost-benefit structure of a social contract, with similar results. Cheng and Holyoak's theory predicts that both of these rules will elicit a high percentage of *P & not-Q* responses, yet they elicited this response from only 12% and 25% of subjects, respectively.

These experiments eliminate yet another by-product hypothesis: They show that reasoning on social contract problems is not a by-product of inference procedures for reasoning about a more general class of problems, permission problems. Permission rules elicit the effect only if the cost-benefit representation of a social contract can be assigned to them and if violating the rule would illicitly benefit the violator. These results confirm another predicted design feature: They show that cheater detection algorithms do not operate properly unless the appropriate cost-benefit representation can be assigned to the rule.

WILL ANY RULE THAT INVOLVES THE POSSI-
BILITY OF POSITIVE OR NEGATIVE PAYOFFS
ELICIT GOOD PERFORMANCE ON THE WASON SE-
LECTION TASK? Manktelow and Over (1990)
were interested in this question when they designed the experiments just described. Their
obligation rules lacked the cost-benefit structure of a social contract and, therefore, the property that one could illicitly benefit by cheating.
But in both scenarios a person would receive
high payoffs for following the rule. Violating
the rule would cause a person to incur a cost: a
small one in the case of one of the scenarios, a
large one in the case of the other. They found
that the possibility of payoffs, either positive or
negative, was not sufficient to elicit high levels
of *P & not-Q* responses. We found similar results in experiments testing rules concerning the
possibility that a food was poisonous (Cosmides and Tooby, in prep., a), rules such as "If
a person eats the red berries, then that person
will vomit."

These experiments eliminate another by-
product hypothesis: They show that the possibility of a payoff is not sufficient to elicit good

performance on the Wason selection task and,
therefore, not sufficient to explain the social
contract effect. To be good at detecting violations of a social contract rule, the violation has
to represent an illicitly taken benefit.

The possibility of payoffs is not sufficient to
explain the social contract effect. But heuristi-
cally, it is an important dimension to consider
when one is trying to discover specialized preference procedures. An evolutionary approach
would lead one to investigate domains in which
our foraging ancestors would have experienced
positive (fitness) payoffs for "correct" reasoning and negative (fitness) payoffs for "incorrect" reasoning. We place "correct" and "incorrect" in scare quotes because these notions
are defined with respect to the adaptive problem to be solved; "correct" does not necessarily mean the logically correct *P & not-Q*, just
as it did not in many of the social contract experiments reported here. In addition to social
contracts, there is now experimental evidence
suggesting the existence of specialized inference procedures for two other domains, both of
which involve large fitness payoffs: precautions

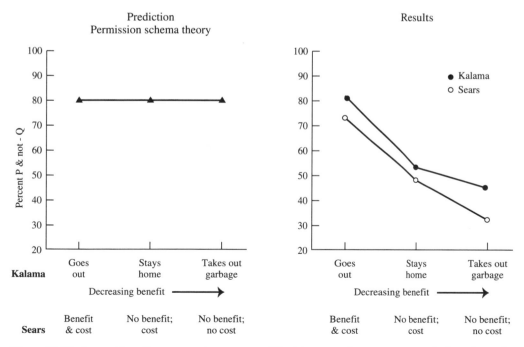

Figure 26.10. Are cost-benefit representations necessary? Social contract theory versus permission schema theory: Predictions and results (from Cosmides and Tooby, in prep., b).

(prudential obligations) and threats. Manktelow and Over (1990; scenario A) were the first to uncover the possibility of precaution schemas for rules of the general form "If one enters a hazardous situation, then one should take the appropriate precaution," and Cheng and Holyoak (1989) and we (Cosmides and Tooby, in prep., c) have provided evidence in support of the existence of precaution schemas. But the experiments to be reported in Cosmides and Tooby (in prep., c) also show that precaution rules are processed differently from social contract rules, in accordance with a different adaptive logic appropriate to that problem. This is also true of threats. Our tests of threat rules show that people are very good at detecting bluffs and double crosses in situations of threat, but again, the reasoning involved does not map on to cheater detection in social contract situations (Cosmides and Tooby, in prep., b).

Summary of Experimental Findings

Virtually all the experiments reviewed above asked subjects to detect violations of a conditional rule. Sometimes these violations corresponded to detecting cheaters on social contracts, other times they did not. The results showed that we do not have a general-purpose ability to detect violations of conditional rules. But human reasoning is well designed for detecting violations of conditional rules when these can be interpreted as cheating on a social contract. Based on our computational theory of social exchange, we predicted that reasoning about social contracts would exhibit a number of specific design features. The results of the experiments reviewed above confirm the existence of many of these design features and do not falsify any of them. They show the following:

1. The algorithms governing reasoning about social contracts include inference procedures specialized for cheater detection.
2. Their cheater detection procedures cannot detect violations that do not correspond to cheating (such as mistakes).
3. The algorithms governing reasoning about social contracts operate even in unfamiliar situations.
4. The definition of cheating that they embody depends on one's perspective.

5. They are just as good at computing the cost-benefit representation of a social contract from the perspective of one party as from the perspective of another.
6. They cannot operate so as to detect cheaters unless the rule has been assigned the cost-benefit representation of a social contract.
7. They embody implicational procedures specified by the computation theory (e.g., "If you take the benefit then you are obligated to pay the cost" implies "If you paid the cost, then you are entitled to take the benefit").
8. They do not include altruist detection procedures.

Furthermore, the highly patterned reasoning performance elicited by social contracts cannot be explained as a by-product of any of the more general-purpose reasoning procedures that have been proposed so far. The following by-product hypotheses were eliminated:

1. That familiarity can explain the social contract effect.
2. That social contract content merely activates the rules of inference of the propositional calculus.
3. That social contract content merely promotes, for whatever reason, clear thinking.
4. That permission schema theory can explain the social contract effect.
5. That any problem involving payoffs will elicit the detection of violations.
6. That a content-independent formal logic, such as the propositional calculus, quantificational logic, or deontic logic can explain the social contract effect.

These findings strongly support the hypothesis that the human mind includes cognitive procedures that are adaptations for reasoning about social exchange.

IMPLICATIONS FOR CULTURE

Cultural Forms Are Structured by Our Universal Evolved Psychology

Wherever human beings live, their cultural forms and social life are infused with social exchange relations (e.g., Malinowski 1922; Mauss 1925). Such relations appear in an enormous range of different guises, both simple and highly elaborated, implicit and explicit, deferred and simultaneous, practical and symbolic. The magnitude, variety, and complexity of our social exchange relations are among the most distinctive features of human social life, and differentiate us strongly from all other animal species (Tooby and DeVore 1987).

Antiquity, universality, and cross-cultural elaboration are exactly what one expects of behaviors that are the expression of universal, evolved information-processing mechanisms. From the child who gets dessert if her plate is cleaned, to the devout Christian who views the Old and New Testaments as covenants arrived at between humans and the supernatural, to the ubiquitous exchange of women between descent groups among tribal peoples, to trading partners in the Kula Ring of the Pacific—all of these phenomena require, from the participants, the recognition and comprehension of a complex set of implicit assumptions that apply to social contract situations. Our social exchange psychology supplies a set of inference procedures that fill in all these necessary steps, mapping the elements in each exchange situation to their representational equivalents within the social contract algorithms, specifying who in the situation counts as an agent in the exchange, which items are costs and benefits and to whom, who is entitled to what, under what conditions the contract is fulfilled or broken, and so on (Cosmides and Tooby 1989).

Without social exchange and the underlying constellation of cognitive adaptations that support it, social and mental life in every culture would be so different as to be unrecognizable as *human* life. If one removed from our evolutionary history and hence from our minds the possibility of cooperation and reciprocity—of mutually contingent benefit-benefit interactions arrived at through mutual consent—then coercion and force would loom even larger as instruments of social influence, and positive relationships would be limited primarily to self-sacrificial interactions among kin. Such conditions do, in fact, typify the social life of most other animal species. What psychological mechanisms allow humans to behave so differently?

According to the Standard Social Science Model, "culture" builds all concepts as sophisticated and as content-specific as social exchange from scratch, using only content-free general-purpose mental processes (see Tooby and Cosmides 1992). Yet the experiments reviewed herein have shown that no general-purpose process so far proposed can produce the sophisticated pattern of reasoning needed to engage in social exchange. Moreover, these experiments cast serious doubt on the claim that content-free general-purpose mechanisms were responsible for *building* the content-specific social contract algorithms. Although we have reasoning procedures elaborately tailored for solving this ancient adaptive problem, these experiments have demonstrated that we do not have reasoning procedures that are similarly specialized for solving many familiar problems that are routinely encountered in the modern social world—such as detecting whether someone has made a mistake, detecting whether someone has broken a prescriptive rule that is not a social contract, and detecting whether a situation exists that violates a descriptive rule. Yet, if we did have a content-free psychology that could build the necessary reasoning mechanisms "as needed," then one would expect to find elaborate reasoning procedures specialized for solving such problems. Procedures specialized for solving ancient adaptive problems, such as social exchange, would be no more likely to develop than procedures specialized for solving the many evolutionarily novel problems posed by life in a modern, postindustrial culture. Evaluating a scientific hypothesis about the effects of dietary cholesterol, detecting whether someone has misfiled a document, and following the string of "if-then" directions on one's tax returns would be as effortless—and require as little explicit instruction—as detecting cheaters in a situation of social exchange among members of an unfamiliar tribal culture who value cassava root and facial tattoos.

The claim that our only evolved psychological mechanisms are general-purpose and content-free, and that "culture" must therefore supply all the specific content of our minds, is exactly the issue on which evolutionary psychological approaches diverge most sharply from more traditional ones. In our view, instead of culture manufacturing the psychology of social exchange de novo, content-specific, evolved psychologies constitute the building blocks out of which cultures themselves are manufactured (Tooby and Cosmides 1992). These psychologies evolved to process information about ancient and important adaptive problems, such as social exchange, sexual jealousy, kin recognition, language acquisition, emotion recognition, and parenting. On this view, the social environment need not provide all of the (hypothetical) properties needed to construct a social exchange psychology from a set of content-free mental procedures (assuming this is possible at all), because the evolved architecture of the human mind already contains content-specific mechanisms that will cause a social exchange psychology to reliably develop in every normal human being. Because every human being will develop the same basic set of social contract algorithms, cultural forms that require their presence can emerge: traditions, rituals, institutions, linguistic conventions, symbols, and so forth can develop that rely on the stable features of this psychology, and that simply supply the specifics that activate and deploy it in each new situation.

Thus, there is an immediate difference between evolutionary psychological approaches and approaches that maintain that everything involving social interaction is "socially constructed." An evolutionary psychological perspective suggests that the universal evolved architecture of the human mind contains some content-specific algorithms that are shared across individuals and across cultures, and that, therefore, many things related to social exchange should be the same from place to place—as indeed they are. In contrast, a Standard Social Science Model approach would, if thoroughgoing, maintain that social exchange is culture-specific and historically contingent, existing in some places and not in others. Moreover, the Standard Model would have to predict that wherever social exchange is found to exist, it would have to be taught or communicated from the ground up. Because nothing about social exchange is initially present in the psychology of the learner, every structural feature of social exchange must be specified by the social environment as against the infinity of logically alternative branchings that could exist. It is telling that it is just this explicitness that is usually lacking in social life. Few individuals are able to articulate the assumptions that structure their own cultural forms—to do so usually requires considerable effort and is accompanied by the awareness that one is doing something unusual and artificial (Sperber 1975). We suggest that social exchange is learned without explicit enumeration of the un-

derlying assumptions. The surface forms are provided by specific cultures, but they are interpreted by content-specific information-processing devices containing implicit assumptions and procedures that evolved for exactly this purpose.

The issue of explicitness is particularly instructive. As Sperber and Wilson (1986) point out, if two individuals have no shared assumptions about the world, communication between them is impossible. The explicit part of the communicative process concerns those features of a situation that are known to the sender but not yet known to the receiver, but such transmissions are only interpretable because of what is already mutually understood. This point is particularly relevant to understanding human culture, because the learning of a culture itself in effect consists of successful communication between members of the culture and the individual who is learning about it. Consequently, for someone ignorant of a culture to learn it in the first place, it is necessary that she already share many assumptions with those from whom she is learning the culture. If human minds truly were initially tabula rasas, with no prior contentful structure, then no anthropologist or immigrant to a culture could ever learn about it (Quine 1969). More to the point, all children are immigrants, born into the world with no culturally specific knowledge at all. If the evolved architecture of the child's mind contained no meaningful content at all—that is, if it were truly content-free—then children could never learn the culture they are born into: They would have no reliable means of interpreting anything they saw and hence of placing the same construction on it that members of their culture do.

We suggest that domain-specific reasoning procedures such as social contract algorithms (Cosmides 1989; Cosmides and Tooby 1989) supply what is missing from traditional accounts of the acquisition of culture: that is, the necessary preexisting conceptual organization, which provides the shared assumptions humans need to interpret unfamiliar behavior and utterances and, in so doing, to acquire their culture. Such domain-specific algorithms embody both intrinsic definitions for the representations that they operate on (e.g., benefit, requirement, cheater) and cues for recognizing which elements in ontogenetically unfamiliar but evolutionarily recurrent situations correspond to those representations. This is why humans can barter or even form friendships where no common language is spoken. It is for this reason that we tested our subjects's ability to apply social contract algorithms to unfamiliar situations: Indeed, they did so as easily as they apply them to familiar contents. For all of the above reasons, we argue that such content-sensitive cognitive adaptations are a critical element in the process of cultural transmission. Culture would not be possible without them.

In any case, the way in which such a universal psychology would lead to cultural universals is straightforward, and the enumeration of cases of social exchange found cross-culturally would add little to furthering the discussion. For that reason, we would like to focus on two more interesting issues: (a) Assuming there is a universal, evolved psychology of social exchange, how might one explain and organize our understanding of cultural differences? That is, how can an underlying universal psychology express itself differently in different cultures? And (b) How can the ethnographic record inform us about additional aspects of our social exchange psychology, beyond those few algorithms and representations that have already been explored experimentally?

Intergroup Differences: Evoked Culture and Transmitted Culture

Human thought and behavior differs in an organized fashion from place to place, and these differences are typically termed "cultural" variation. In fact, it is considered a tautology by many to attribute this variation to the operation of culture—that is, to social transmission. Nevertheless, there are two complementary explanations for the existence of these within-location similarities and between-location differences in thought and behavior (Tooby and Cosmides 1989, 1992). The traditional explanation is that these systematic differences are caused by what is usually called *transmitted culture*, that is, the process whereby the thought and behavior of some individuals (usually from the preceding generation) is passed on to other individuals, thereby causing the present pattern. Indeed, we have already touched on how domain-specific cognitive adaptations make cultural transmission possible.

There is, however, a second way in which such local similarities can be brought about. Our universal, evolved information-processing mechanisms should be sensitively context-dependent: Different informational inputs should evoke different representational and behavioral outputs. Humans share the same evolved information-processing mechanisms, but they do not all live under the same circumstances. People living in the same location are likely to experience somewhat similar circumstances, which should evoke the same kind of response from each individual; people living in different locations are likely to experience somewhat different circumstances, which should evoke different responses from each individual. To take an obvious example, people in tropical forest environments all around the world tend to be at most only lightly clothed, something that has less to do with parental example than with heat load.

The more complex the set of species-typical psychological mechanisms, the more sensitively dependent behavior may be on local circumstances. This means that cultural forms may exist that are not primarily generated by cultural transmission at all. We call similarities triggered by local circumstances *evoked culture* (Tooby and Cosmides, this volume). Of course, these two explanations are by no means mutually exclusive and usually operate together to shape the distribution of human similarities and differences. The evolutionary psychology of social exchange shapes both evoked culture and transmitted culture, and the exploration of a few of these issues serves to illustrate how an evolutionary psychological approach to culture can diverge from traditional anthropological approaches.

Open Questions in the Psychology of Social Exchange

Before proceeding to discuss how an evolved, universal psychology can generate cultural variation, it is necessary to emphasize the limited nature of what we have done so far. We have tested only a small number of hypotheses about one mode of social exchange out of many. We have not discussed, much less experimentally explored, the rest of the intricate and complex psychology of social exchange. Anyone examining his or her own human experience will immediately identify large areas of the psychology of social exchange, such as the psychology of friendship, that are not captured well by the models introduced so far. More important, the other components of our evolved faculty of social cognition—for example, the psychological mechanisms that govern sexual relations, coalitional partnerships, status, revenge, threat, and parenting—will have to be mapped out and integrated with the psychological mechanisms governing social exchange before social exchange can be fully unraveled. Each component of the faculty of social cognition can be only incompletely understood when taken in isolation.

The computational theory that we have developed specifies certain contractual relationships and implicit inferences that people can be expected to make in social contract situations (Cosmides and Tooby 1989). It is, however, very far from a complete computational theory of social exchange and should not be mistaken for one: Instead, it is only an initial exploration of some of its major features. Many crucial questions were left unaddressed—questions that must be answered if we are to understand social exchange in all its various forms across cultures, or even within a single culture. For example, how many instances of cheating should the decision rule tolerate before it activates mechanisms causing one to sever one's relationship with an individual? Under what conditions should one cooperate with a person on a short-term basis, as opposed to a long-term basis? Should one's willingness to tolerate cheating differ in short-term versus long-term relationships? Will variance in the acquisition of the resources being exchanged affect the ways in which they are shared? What are the other bases for sharing, assistance, and friendship? What role do groups and coalitions play in shaping patterns of assistance? What is the role of aggression, retaliation, and status?

We expect that further evolutionary analyses will support the claim that different decision rules will be favored for long-term versus short-term relationships for high- versus low-variance resources, and for other variations in conditions that we have not considered here. If this turns out to be true, then although some decision rules governing social exchange should be common across situations, others will differ in ways that are sensitively dependent on context. In other

words, the social contract algorithms might contain different situation-specific modes of activation. For example, we expect the rules governing social exchange among close friends to differ somewhat from the rules governing social exchange among strangers.

Given an evolved architecture with a design of this kind, one can develop a coherent conceptual framework for understanding the ecological distribution of mental representations and expressed behaviors having to do with social exchange, both with and between groups (Sperber 1985). Although the analysis of individual and cultural variation with the context of a universal human nature is too complex to review fully here, extended discussions can be found in Cosmides and Tooby (1987), Tooby and Cosmides (1989, 1990a), and Brown (1991). Briefly:

1. By virtue of being members of the human species, all humans are expected to have the same adaptive mechanisms, either at the level of developmental programs, which govern alternative developmental pathways, or (more likely in the case of social exchange) universally developing cognitive specializations.

2. In consequence, certain fundamental ways of thinking about social exchange will be the same everywhere, without needing to be socially transmitted.

3. As is standardly believed, social transmission may indeed shape social exchange. But it does so not by manufacturing the concept of social exchange de novo. Instead, there are probably certain specific avenues through which social transmission can act: for example, by influencing the valuation placed on items or actions, by providing information that helps one identify appropriate partners, or by providing information that allows one to identify appropriate contexts.

4. Our social exchange psychology should be highly context-dependent. Consequently, many dimensions along which social exchange varies, both within and between cultures, may be instances of evoked culture. The presence or magnitude of certain cues, conditions, or situations should cause mechanisms within our social exchange psychology to be calibrated; to be activated or in-

hibited; or to be switched into alternative modes of activation. When local circumstances trigger a particular mode of activation of the social contract algorithms, for example, this may cause a highly structured, multi-individual behavioral outcome. Therefore, when one sees similar patterns of social exchange in widely different parts of the world, one cannot assume that the similarity is determined primarily by social transmission; the similarity may instead be an instance of evoked culture.

One simple illustration of evoked culture involves the decision rules governing reciprocity in food sharing. As we describe below, a contextual variable—the presence or absence of "luck" in food acquisition—appears to activate different decision rules governing food sharing.

Luck and Sharing

One finding from the literature of evolutionary ecology on optimal foraging is that different kinds of sharing rules benefit the individual in different situations (see Kaplan and Hill 1985a). For example, when the variance in foraging success of the individual is greater than the variance for the band as a whole, band-wide food sharing buffers the variance. This can happen when one individual's success on a given day is unconnected to that of another.

Luck, skill, and effort all affect whether an individual finds food on a given day, but for certain food sources, luck is much more important than skill and effort. When success in finding food randomly varies a great deal from day to day, consider what would happen to a person who ate only that which he or she individually acquired. Some days that person would be starving; other days that person would have more to eat than he or she could possibly consume. It would be a feast, or famine kind of life. Moreover, the temporary famines hit harder than the feasts can make up for. This is because (a) there is a zero point with food—death by starvation—and (b) the law of decreasing marginal utilities applies because we can only metabolize so much at one time—consequently, the fifth pound of meat eaten is far less valuable than the first pound. Under these circumstances, one is better off individually if one can redistribute food from periods of feast to peri-

ods of famine. There are two ways of doing this: through food storage or through pooling resources with others. Food storage is not an option for many hunter-gatherers, but pooling resources is: If two people average their returns, the variance decreases—one buys fewer periods of privation at the price of fewer periods of superabundance. By adding more individuals to the risk-pooling group, the variance may continue to decrease, making band-wide sharing an attractive system for hunter-gatherers facing certain conditions.

Thus, situations involving a random and frequent reversal of fortune can create substantial payoffs for cooperation. In effect, an individual can store food in the form of social obligations—by accepting food, others obligate themselves to reciprocate in the future. I may sacrifice by giving you some of my food today, but tomorrow I may be the one who is empty-handed and in need. For situations involving frequent, chance-driven reversals of fortune, the favored strategy involves sharing, from individuals who have food to those who do not. Luck plays an important role in hunting; consequently, hunter-gatherers frequently distribute game relatively equally to everyone in the band, no matter who found it or made a particular kill. Because it is a relatively high-variance activity, hunting may have been a particularly important driving force in the evolution of cognitive adaptations for social exchange (see Tooby and DeVore 1987, for discussion).

By the same token, when variance in foraging success for an individual is low, the average long-term payoffs to sharing are less. If everyone reliably has access to the same goals, there is no particular benefit to sharing—one gains nothing by swapping the same goods at the same time. In this circumstance, an individual may be better off sharing just within his or her family, in accordance with kin selection, mating, and parenting principles.

Under low-variance conditions, not only might there be no benefit to sharing, there may be definite costs. When luck is eliminated as a factor, skill and effort remain. The smaller the role played by chance, the more differences between individuals in amount of food foraged will reflect differences in skill and effort. Under such circumstances, band-wide food sharing would simply redistribute food from those who expend more effort or are more skilled, to those who expend less effort or are less skilled. Sharing under these circumstances offers few—if any—intrinsic payoffs for those who have acquired more food. Without chance creating reversals of fortune, there is little reason to expect that the future will be different from the present and, therefore, little reason to expect that those with less food now will be in a better position to reciprocate in the future. Under these circumstances, then, one expects that (a) potential recipients will welcome sharing, but (b) potential donors will be more reluctant to share.

Consequently, the degree and source variance in resource acquisition were selection pressures that should have shaped the evolved architecture of our social exchange algorithms. Information about variance in foraging success should activate different modes of operation of these algorithms, with high variance due to chance triggering a psychology of sharing. To modern social scientists, factors such as variance in food acquisition may seem arcane and implausible because of their lack of connection to modern (middle-class) experience. But for our ancestors, food acquisition was a daily problem, as consequential as breathing. Daily decisions with respect to sharing had an unremitting impact on their lives and reproductive success, over hundreds of thousands of generations. In consequence, it is hard to see how our social psychology would not have been shaped by factors of this kind.

Obviously, this analysis of selection pressures is restricted to factors internal to foraging success. There are, of course, many other selection pressures that have shaped human social psychology over evolutionary time and hence many other factors that may lead to food sharing other than simple social exchange—kinship, love, parenting, sex, coercion, and status, for example. Moreover, even within the context of social exchange, the return on sharing food may be something other than food. Selection may have produced psychological mechanisms that cause highly productive foragers to share food without expecting any return of food, if, for example, by so doing others valued them highly and were therefore more disposed to render them aid when they were threatened, protect their children, grant them sexual access, and so on (Kaplan and Hill 1985a). Complicated though it may be, a more comprehensive understanding of social ex-

change eventually can be built up, element by element, by examining each selection pressure in turn and seeing whether our psychological mechanisms have the design features these selection pressures would lead one to expect.

In other words, the selection pressures analyzed in optimal foraging theory are one component of a task analysis, or, in David Marr's terms, a "computational theory," of the adaptive problem of foraging. It defines the nature of the problem to be solved and thereby specifies constraints that any mechanism that evolved to solve this problem can be expected to satisfy. In this case, optimal foraging theory suggests (a) that we should have content-specific information-processing mechanisms governing foraging and sharing, and (b) these mechanisms should be sensitive to information regarding variance in foraging success, causing us to prefer one set of sharing rules for high-variance items and another set for low-variance items.

The Ache: Within-Group Evidence for Evoked Culture

Kaplan and Hill's (1985a) study of the Ache, a hunter-gatherer group living in eastern Paraguay, provides a particularly elegant test of the hypothesis just described, because it controls for "culture." Meat is a very high-variance food item among the Ache: On any given day, there is a 40% chance that a hunter will come back empty-handed (Kaplan, Hill, and Hurtado 1990). Collected plant foods, in contrast, are very low-variance items. Kaplan and Hill found that the Ache engage in band-wide sharing of meat, whereas they share plant foods primarily within the nuclear family. Thus the same individuals, in the same culture, engage in different patterns of sharing for different foods, depending on the variance they experience in obtaining them.

The fact that meat is such a high-variance item also creates problems in cheater detection. If a man brings back no meat for seven days in a row, has he just had a run of bad luck, or has he been shirking? An Ache man's life and the life of his family depend on the long-term reciprocity relationships he has with the other hunters in his band. To accuse someone of cheating and ostracize him from the reciprocity network is a very serious matter. If the charge is false, then not only will the ostracized man's survival be jeopardized, but each member of the band will have lost a valuable reciprocation partner. If one is not sure, or if the suspected cheater is providing a net benefit even though it is less than he could provide if he tried harder, it might be better to continue the relationship.

The anthropologists who study the Ache know who the best hunters are, because they have recorded and weighed what each man brings back over long periods of time. Presumably, the Ache know also. But H. Kaplan (personal communication 1991) reports that when he and his colleagues ask Ache men who the best hunters are, the question makes them very uncomfortable and they refuse to answer.[22] This is not due to a general cultural prohibition against accusing others of cheating. When the Ache are staying at a mission camp, acrimonious arguments erupt over whether various individuals are doing their fair share of work in the garden. Gardening, however, provides a low-variance source of food, making the punishment of cheaters less risky, and it occurs in a well-defined, observable location, making it easy to monitor who is, and who is not, cheating.

!Kung San Versus //Gana San: Between-Group Evidence for Evoked Culture

Resource variance can also explain differences between groups, evoking different cultures in response to different, variance-related local circumstances. For example, Cashdan (1980) found variance-related differences in sharing between groups of Kalahari San that mirror those found within Ache culture.

The Kalahari San are well known in anthropological circles for their economic and political egalitarianism. For example, the !Kung San, who experience extreme variability in the availability of food and water, have very strong social sanctions that reinforce sharing, discourage hoarding (calling someone "stingy" is a strong insult), and discourage displays of arrogance and authority. For example:

The proper behavior of a !Kung hunter who has made a big kill is to speak of it in passing and in a deprecating manner . . . ; if an individual does not minimize or speak lightly of his own accomplishments,

his friends and relatives will not hesitate to do it for him. (Cashdan 1980:116)

But it turns out that some San bands are more egalitarian than others, and their degree of egalitarianism is related to variance in their food supply. The //Gana San of the northeastern Kalahari are able to buffer themselves from variability in the food and water supply in ways that other San cannot, through a small amount of food cultivation (including a kind of melon that stores water in the desert environment) and some goat husbandry. In contrast to the !Kung, the //Gana manifest considerable economic inequality, they hoard more, they are more polygynous, and, although they have no clear-cut authority structure, wealthy, high-status //Gana men are quick to claim that they speak for others and that they are the "headman"—behavior that would be considered unconscionable among the !Kung. Again, even though the !Kung and the //Gana are culturally similar in many ways—they share the same encompassing "meme-pool," so to speak—their social rules regarding sharing and economic equality differ, and these differences track the variance in their food and water supplies.

Local Conditions and Evoked Culture

It is difficult to explain these phenomena simply as the result of cultural transmission, at least in any traditional sense. Among the Ache of Paraguay, the same individuals share food types with different variances differently. Halfway around the world, in Africa, two different groups of Kalahari San manifest what appear to be the same differential sharing patterns in response to the same variable—variance. A parsimonious explanation is that these social norms and the highly patterned behaviors they give rise to are evoked by the same variable.

Because foraging and sharing are complex adaptive problems with a long evolutionary history, it is difficult to see how humans could have escaped evolving highly structured domain-specific psychological mechanisms that are well designed for solving them. These mechanisms should be sensitive to local informational input, such as information regarding variance in food supply. This input can act as a switch, turning on and off different modes of activation of the appropriate domain-specific mechanisms. The experience of high variance in foraging success should activate rules of inference, memory retrieval cues, attentional mechanisms, and motivational mechanisms. These should not only allow band-wide sharing to occur, but should make it seem fair and appealing. The experience of low variance in foraging success should activate rules of inference, memory retrieval cues, attentional mechanisms, and motivational mechanisms that make within-family sharing possible and appealing, but that make band-wide sharing seem unattractive and unjust. These alternative modes of activation of the domain-specific mechanisms provide the core knowledge that must be mutually manifest (see Sperber and Wilson 1986) to the various actors for band-wide or within-family sharing to occur. This core knowledge can then organize and provide points of attachment for symbolic activities that arise in these domains.

If this notion of evoked culture is correct, then one should not expect cultural variation to vary continuously along all imaginable dimensions. The free play of human creativity may assign relatively arbitrary construals to elements in some areas of life, such as the number of gods or the appropriate decoration on men's clothing. But in other areas of life one might expect there to be a limited number of recurring patterns, both within and across cultures. For certain domains of human activity, people from very different places and times may "reinvent" the same kinds of concepts, valuations, social rules, and customs (see Tooby and Cosmides 1992). In short, such alternative modes of activation in psychological mechanisms can create alternative sets of complexly patterned social rules and activities. These will emerge independently, that is, in the absence of direct cultural transmission, in culture after culture, when the individual members are exposed to the informational cues that activate these alternative modes.

Cross-cultural studies of social exchange by Fiske provide support for this notion (Fiske 1990, 1991b). Based on his field studies of the Moose ("Mossi") of Burkina Faso and his review of the anthropological literature, Fiske argues that the human mind contains four alternative implicit models of how sharing should be conducted, which are used to generate and evaluate social relations. These models are implicit in the sense that they are acted on unreflectively and without conscious awareness; indeed, they may never have been explicitly stated by any member of the culture. Nevertheless "these shared but unanalyzed, tacit models for Moose social relations allow them to generate coordinated, consistent, and culturally comprehensible interactions of four contrasting types" (Fiske 1990:180–181). For example, one of Fiske's four models is communal sharing of the kind used by the Ache in distributing hunted meat; another is "market pricing"—the kind of explicit contingent exchange that occurs when two people explicitly agree to trade, say, honey for meat or money for milk.

Varieties of Hunter-Gatherer Exchange

Whether or not Fiske's specific taxonomy of four categories is exactly the correct way to capture and characterize the limited set of modes whereby humans engage in social exchange, we very much agree with this general framework for conceptualizing cultural variation in social exchange. If human thought falls into recurrent patterns from place to place and from time to time, this is because it is the expression of, and anchored in, universal psychological mechanisms. If there is a limited set of such patterns, it is because different modes of activation of the algorithms regulating social exchange solved different adaptive problems that hunter-gatherers routinely faced. Consequently, clues as to how many modes of activation the social contract algorithms have, what the structure of each mode might be, and what kinds of circumstances can be expected to activate each mode can be found by investigating the various forms of social exchange that hunter-gatherers engage in, as well as the conditions under which each form of exchange arises.

Despite the common characterization of hunter-gatherer life as an orgy of indiscriminate, egalitarian cooperation and sharing—a kind of retro-utopia—the archaeological and ethnographic record shows that hunter-gatherers engaged in a number of different forms of social exchange (for an excellent review of hunter-gatherer economics, see Cashdan 1989). Communal sharing does not exhaust the full range of exchange in such societies. Hunter-gatherers also engage in explicit contingent exchange—Fiske's "market pricing"—in which tools and other durable goods are traded between bands, often in networks that extend over vast areas. A common form of trade is formal gift exchanges with carefully chosen partners from other bands. For instance, aboriginal Australians traded tools such as sting ray spears and stone axes through gift exchanges with partners from neighboring bands. These partnerships were linked in a chain that extended 620 km, from the coast, where sting ray spears were produced, to the interior, where there were quarries where the stone axes could be produced. Here, environmental variation in the source of raw materials for tool making allowed gains from trade based on economic specialization, and the laws of supply and demand seemed to operate: At the coast, where sting ray spears were common, it took more of them to buy an ax than in the interior, where spears were dear and axes cheap (Sharp 1952). Similarly, the !Kung of the Kalahari desert engage in a system of delayed reciprocal gift giving called "hxaro" (Weissner 1982; Cashdan 1989), through which they trade durable goods such as blankets and necklaces.

Unpredictable variation in rainfall and game makes access to land and water resources another important "item of trade" between hunter-gatherer bands and creates situations in which a kind of implicit one-for-one reciprocity prevails (Fiske's "equality matching"). For instance, a !Kung band that is caught in a drought will "visit relatives" in a band that is camped in an area that is experiencing more rainfall (Cashdan 1989). Indeed, hxaro partners are chosen carefully, not only for their ability to confer durable goods, but also to provide alternative residences in distant places during times of local scarcity (Weissner 1982). And before using another band's water hole or land, the !Kung are expected to ask permission; reciprocity in access to water holes is extremely important to the !Kung, who live in a desert with few permanent sources of water. Although formal permission is almost always granted, as the implicit rules of one-for-one reciprocity require, if the hosts really don't want to accommodate their guests, they make them feel unwelcome, thereby subtly encouraging them to leave (Cashdan 1989).

Although authoritarian social relations are unusual among the few remaining modern hunter-gatherer groups, this is probably a by-product of their having been pushed into marginal environments by the peoples of agricultural and industrial cultures. Variance in the food supply is high in harsh environments like the Kalahari desert, and band-wide communal sharing is advantageous for high-variance resources. But as variance is buffered, as in the //Gana San example discussed earlier, more inequality and more authority-ranking relationships develop. This process was, for example, quite pronounced in the hunter-gatherer societies of the Pacific Northwest. The Pacific Northwest was so rich in fish and game that the hunter-gatherers living there could afford to be relatively sedentary. These people developed stable, complex societies that were so hierarchical that some of them even included a slave class formed from prisoners of war (Drucker 1983; Donald 1983). Of course, the distribution of goods and services that occurs between individuals of different rank is often determined by an uneasy mixture of coercion, threat, and exchange.

This is not the place to attempt a full computational theory of the various modes of activation of the social contract algorithms. But even these brief examples drawn from hunter-gatherer life provide some hints as to what might be relevant variables in such an analysis: variance in the food supply; degree of kinship; status or rank; whether a relationship is long- or short-term; whether one is in daily contact (communal sharing; implicit deferred reciprocity) or only rare contact (explicit contingent exchange); whether storage is possible; whether the group is sedentary enough for inequalities in wealth to accumulate; whether gaining a resource requires close, interdependent cooperation; whether people are trading different resources or dividing the same resource; whether an external, consensual definition of "equal portion" is feasible; whether an individual can control access to a resource, and thereby "own" it; and so on (see also McGrew and Feistner 1992).

To understand social exchange in all its various forms, the adaptive problems that selected for different decision rules must be precisely defined in the form of computational theories. The computational theories can then be used to generate hypotheses about the design features that characterize the different modes of activation of the social contract algorithms. Psychological experiments of the kind described earlier in this chapter would allow one to test among these hypotheses and thereby develop a detailed map of the situation-specific cognitive processes that create these different modes of activation. Once we know what situational cues activate each set of decision rules, we should be able to predict a great deal of cultural variation.

Interpreting Other Cultures and Understanding Cultural Change

Significant aspects of cultural variation in social exchange can be readily reconciled with a universal human nature through applying the concept of evoked culture. The various sets of decision rules governing social exchange will be universal, but which sets are activated will differ from situation to situation within a culture, as well as between cultures. For example, in American middle-class culture different exchange rules apply to different aspects of a dinner party (Fiske 1991a). Invitations are sometimes governed by one-for-one reciprocity—an implicit rule such as "If you had me to your home for dinner, then at some point I must invite you to dinner." But food sharing at the party is governed by the same kind of communal sharing rules that characterize Ache meat sharing. Obtaining the food that is served is governed by explicit contingent exchange at a grocery store, and seating at the dinner table is sometimes determined by rank or status (as for example, at diplomatic dinners, birthday parties, or in certain traditional families).

The point is that communal sharing, explicit contingent exchange, equality matching, and so on, are not unique to American culture: The same sets of decision rules appear in other cultures as well, but local circumstances cause them to be applied to different situations (Fiske 1990, 1991b). Whereas all food at an American dinner party is shared communally, this is not true on Ache foraging trips: Meat is shared communally at the level of the entire band, but plant foods are not. In many cultures, men engage in explicit contingent exchange to procure wives: One man will buy another man's daughter (see Wilson and Daly 1992). In other cultures, men do not buy wives, but instead can engage in explicit contingent exchange with a woman to gain temporary sexual access to her. In still other cultures, the use of explicit contingent exchange is illegal in both circumstances (but may still be understood and occasionally practiced).

Fiske argues that in relatively stable, traditional societies there is a tacit consensus about which decision rules to apply in which situation. To apply the wrong decision rules to a situation can be uncomfortable, insulting, or even shocking: At the end of an American dinner party, one does not pull out a wallet and offer to pay the hosts for their services. Similarly, when Americans are sitting with friends or coworkers, they might spontaneously offer to split a sandwich, but they almost never spontaneously pull out their wallets and offer money. Indeed, figuring out which decision rules a culture applies to which situations is part of what it means to understand another culture (Fiske 1990). On this view, "interpreting another culture" is not usually a matter of absorbing wholly new systems of culturally alien semantic relations. Instead, interpreting another culture is a matter of learning how the evolved set of meanings that we have come to assign to one set of objects or elements in a situation are, in another culture, assigned to a different set.

New events of all kinds, from migrations to natural disasters to new technologies, create culturally unprecedented circumstances in which there is no within-culture consensus about which exchange rules are appropriate. In the United States, for example, there is a vigorous debate over which form of exchange should apply when a woman wants to be a surrogate mother for an infertile couple. Many women prefer explicit contingent exchange in which they are paid money for their labor (so to speak). But other Americans argue that surrogacy should occur—if at all—only among close friends and relatives who participate in informal communal sharing relationships and that women should be legally prohibited from granting access to their wombs on the basis of explicit contingent exchange.

Where do the impulses—or, more accurately—the decision rules come from that lead individuals or entire cultures to reject an existing practice or to invent or adopt something new? Transmission models can account for stable transmission of existing attitudes and cultural forms but intrinsically have no way to account for cultural change, or indeed any nonimitated individual act. The existence of a species-typical evolved psychology fills in this missing gap. It provides a basis from which one can interpret individual action, minority dissent, and the emergence of a new consensus. Dramatic new circumstances may evoke new attitudes overnight, as when the Battle of Britain changed the attitudes and sharing practices of Londoners, or when depictions of earthquakes and other natural disasters prompt people to donate food and other assistance. Even where one is dealing with the spread of new cultural forms through transmission, however, the dynamics are powerfully structured by our content-sensitive evolved psychology (for a lucid discussion of the "epidemiology" of beliefs and other representations, see Sperber 1985, 1990).

Consider the political and moral debate concerning the homeless in the United States. Those with opposing postures concerning how much to help the homeless frame their positions in ways that exploit the structure of this evolved psychology. One persistent theme among those who wish to motivate more sharing is the idea "there but for fortune, go you or I." That is, they emphasize the random, variance-driven dimensions of the situation. The potential recipient of aid is viewed as worthy because he or she is the unlucky victim of circumstances, such as unemployment, discrimination, or mental illness. On the other hand, those who oppose an increase in sharing with the homeless emphasize the putatively chosen or self-caused dimensions of the situation. Potential recipients are viewed as unworthy of aid because they "brought it on themselves": They are portrayed as able-bodied but lazy, or as having debilitated themselves through choosing to use alcohol and other drugs. The counterresponse from those who want to motivate more sharing is to portray drug use not as a choice but as a sickness, and so on.

If cultural meanings were truly arbitrary, then, cross-culturally, donors would be just as likely to view people as "worthy of assistance" when they have "brought it on themselves" as when they have been "the victims of bad luck." Indeed, if all were arbitrary, somewhere one should find a culture in which potential donors are most eager to help those who are more fortunate than themselves, merely because the potential recipients are *more* fortunate (and not, say, *because* they hope for something in return).

Finally, although our cognitive mechanisms evolved to promote adaptive decisions in the Pleistocene, they do not necessarily produce adaptive decisions under evolutionarily novel modern circumstances (see Symons 1992). For example, if individual variance in obtaining alcohol is greater than group variance for homeless alcoholics who camp out in the same alley, this circumstance might activate decision rules that promote communal sharing of alcohol, even though these people's mutual generosity would be slowly killing them.

CONCLUSIONS

Human reason has long been believed to be the paradigm case of the impartial, content-blind, general-purpose process. Further, it has been viewed as the faculty that distinguished humans from all other animals, and the very antithesis of "instinct." But if even reasoning turns out to be the product of a collection of functionally specialized, evolved mechanisms, most of which are content-dependent and content-imparting, then this has implications far beyond the study of reasoning. The presumption that psychological mechanisms are characteristically general-purpose and content-free would no longer be tenable: Such hypotheses should no longer be accorded the privileged status and the near-immunity from questions that they have customarily received. Instead, domain-general and domain-specific hypotheses should be given equal footing and evaluated solely on their ability to be turned into genuine, well-specified models that actually account for observed phenomena. Guided by such tenets, we may discover that the human mind is structurally far richer than we have suspected and contains a large population of different mechanisms.

We have used as a test case the intersection of reasoning and social exchange. The results of the experiments discussed herein directly contradict the traditional view, they indicate that the algorithms and representations whereby people reason about social exchange are specialized and domain-specific. Indeed, there has been an accumulation of "evidence of special design" (Williams 1966a), indicating the presence of an adaptation. The results are most parsimoniously explained by positing the existence of "specialized problem-solving machinery" (Williams 1966a)—such as cost-benefit representations and cheater detection procedures—that are well designed for solving adaptive problems particular to social exchange. Moreover, they cannot be explained as the by-product of mechanisms designed for reasoning about classes of problems that are more general than social contracts, such as "all propositions," or even the relatively restricted class of "all permissions." In addition, the pattern of results indicates that this specialized problem-solving machinery was not built by an evolved architecture that is general-purpose and content-free (see Implications for Culture, this chapter, and Cosmides 1989). In other words, the empirical record is most parsimoniously explained by the hypothesis that the evolved architecture of the human mind contains functionally specialized, content-dependent cognitive adaptations for social exchange. Such mechanisms, if they exist, would impose a distinct social contract conceptual organization on certain social situations and impart certain meanings to human psychological, social, and cultural life. We suggest these evolved algorithms constitute one functional subunit, out of many others, that are linked together to form a larger faculty of social cognition (e.g., Jackendoff 1991).

The results of the experiments discussed herein undermine two central tenets of the Standard Social Science Model (Tooby and Cosmides 1992). First, they undermine the proposition that the evolved architecture of the human mind contains a single "reasoning faculty" that is function-general and content-free. Instead, they support the contrary contention that human reasoning is governed by a diverse collection of evolved mechanisms, many of which are functionally specialized, domain-specific, content-imbued, and content-imparting (see Tooby and Cosmides 1992). According to this contrary view, situations involving threat, social exchange, hazard, rigid-object mechanics, contagion, and so on each activate different sets of functionally specialized procedures that exploit the recurrent properties of the corresponding domain in a way that would have produced an efficacious solution under Pleistocene conditions. On this view, the human mind would more closely resemble an intricate network of functionally dedicated computers than a single general-purpose computer. The second tenet that these results undermine is the proposition that all contentful features of the human mind are socially constructed or environmentally derived. In its place, this research supports the view that the human mind imposes contentful structure on the social world, derived from specialized functional design inherent in its evolved cognitive architecture.

The conceptual integration of evolutionary biology with cognitive psychology offers something far more valuable than general arguments. The analysis of the computational requirements of specific adaptive problems provides a principled way of identifying likely new modules, mental organs, or cognitive adaptations, and thereby opens the way for extensive empirical progress. By understanding these requirements, one can make educated guesses about the design features of the information-processing mechanisms that evolved to solve them. Turning knowledge of the adaptive problems our ancestors faced over evolutionary time into well-specified computational theories can therefore be a powerful engine of discovery, allowing one to construct experiments that can capture, document, and catalog the functionally specialized information-processing mechanisms that collectively constitute much (or all) of our central processes. In effect, knowledge of the adaptive problems humans faced, described in explicitly computational terms, can function as a kind of Rosetta Stone: It allows the bewildering array of content effects that cognitive psychologists routinely encounter—and usually disregard—to be translated into meaningful statements about the structure of the mind. The resulting maps of domain-specific information-processing mechanisms can supply the currently missing accounts of how the human mind generates and engages the rich content of human culture, behavior, and social life.

Acknowledgments. We thank Jerry Barkow, David Buss, Martin Daly, Lorraine Daston, Gerd Gigerenzer, Steve Pinker, Paul Romer, Roger Shepard, Don Symons, Phil Tetlock, Dan Sperber, Valerie Stone, and Margo Wilson for productive discussions of the issues addressed in this chapter or for their useful comments on previous drafts. This chapter was prepared, in part, while the authors were Fellows at the Center for Advanced Study in the Behavioral Sciences. We are grateful for the Center's support, as well as that provided by the Gordon P. Getty Trust, the Harry Frank Guggenheim Foundation, NSF Grant BNS87-00864 to the Center, NSF Grant BNS85-11685 to Roger Shepard, and NSF Grant BNS91-57449 to John Tooby.

NOTES

1. For example, if C_i and B_i refer to decreases and increases in i's reproduction, then a decision rule that causes i to perform act Z if, and only if, C_i of doing $Z < 0$ would promote its own Darwinian fitness, but not its inclusive fitness. In contrast, a decision rule that causes i to perform act Z if, and only if, $(C_i$ of doing $Z) < (B_i$ of i's doing $Z) \times r_{ij}$ would promote its inclusive fitness, sometimes at the expense of its Darwinian fitness. The first decision rule would be at a selective disadvantage compared with the second one, because it can make copies of itself only through its bearer and not through its bearer's relatives. For this reason, designs that promote their own inclusive fitness tend to replace alternative designs that promote Darwinian fitness at the expense of inclusive fitness.

Although this example involves helping behavior, kin selection theory applies to the evolution of nonbehavioral design features as well, for example, to the evolution of aposematic coloration of butterfly wings. In principle, one can compute the extent to which a new wing color affects the reproduction of its bearer and its bearer's kin, just as one can compute the extent to which an action affects the reproduction of these individuals.

2. Other models of social exchange are possible, but they will not change the basic conclusion of this section: that reciprocation is necessary for the evolution of social exchange. For example, the Prisoner's Dilemma assumes that enforceable threats and enforceable contracts are impossibilities (Axelrod 1984), assumptions that are frequently violated in nature. The introduction of these factors would not obviate reciprocation—in fact, they would enforce it.

3. Following Marr 1982, we would like to distinguish between the cognitive program itself and an abstract characterization of the decision rule it embodies. Algorithms that differ somewhat in the way they process information may nevertheless embody the same decision rule. For example, the algorithms for adding Arabic numerals differ from those for adding Roman numerals, yet they both embody the same rules for addition (e.g., that $A + B = B + A$) and therefore yield the same answer (Marr 1982).

4. These selection pressures exist *even in the absence of competition for scarce resources.* They are a consequence of the game-theoretic structure of the social interaction.

5. The game "unravels" if they do. If we both know we are playing three games, then we both know we will mutually defect on the last game. In practice, then, our second game is our last game. But we know that we will, therefore, mutually defect on that game, so, in practice, we are playing only one game. The argument is general to any known, fixed number of games (Luce and Raiffa 1957).

6. The cost-benefit values that these algorithms assign to items of exchange should be correlated with costs and benefits to fitness in the environment in which the algorithms evolved; otherwise, the algorithms could not have been selected for. But these assigned values will not necessarily correlate with fitness in the modern world. For example, our taste mechanisms assess fat content in food and our cognitive system uses this cue to assign food value: We tend to like food "rich" (!) in fat, such as ice cream, cheese, and marbled meat. The use of this cue is correlated with fitness in a hunter-gatherer ecology, where dietary fat is hard to come by (wild game is low in fat). But in modern industrial societies, fat is cheap and plentiful, and our love of it has become a liability. The environment changed in a way that lowered the cue validity of fat for fitness. But our cognitive system, which evolved in a foraging ecology, still uses it as a cue for assigning food value.

Given the long human generation time, and the fact that agriculture represents less than 1% of the evolutionary history of the genus *Homo*, it is unlikely that we have evolved any complex adaptations to an agricultural (or industrial) way of life (Tooby and Cosmides 1990a). Our ancestors spent most of the last 2 million years as hunter-gatherers, and our primate ancestors before the appearance of *Homo* were foragers as well, of course. The very first appearance of agriculture was only 10,000 years ago, and it wasn't until about 5,000 years ago that a significant fraction of the human population was engaged in agriculture.

7. Interpreting the statement as a biconditional, rather than as a material conditional, will also lead to error. Consider a situation in which you gave me your watch, but you did not take my $20. This would have to be considered a violation of the rule on a biconditional interpretation, but it is not necessarily cheating. If I had not offered you the $20, then I would have cheated. But if I had offered it and you had refused to take it, then no cheating would have occurred on either of our parts. In this situation, your behavior could be characterized as altruistic or foolish, but not as cheating. Distinctions based on notions such as "offering" or intentionality are no part of the definition of a violation in the propositional calculus.

8. Indeed, one expects learning under certain circumstances: The genome can "store" information in the environment if that information is stably present (Tooby and Cosmides 1990a).

9. Of course, if two developmental trajectories have different reproductive consequences, one will be favored over the other.

10. The drinking-age problem is also a social contract from the point of view of those who enacted the law. Satisfying the age requirement before drinking beer provides those who enacted the law with a benefit: People feel that the roads are safer when immature people are not allowed to drink. Although satisfying the requirement in a social contract will often cause one to incur a cost, it need not do so (see Cosmides and Tooby 1989). The requirement is imposed not because it inflicts a cost on the person who must satisfy it, but because it creates a situation that benefits the recipient, which the recipient believes would not occur if the requirement were not imposed.

Consider the following social contract: "If you are a relative of Nisa's, then you may drink from my water hole." A hunter-gatherer may make this rule because she wants to be able to call on Nisa for a favor in the future. A given person either is, or is not, Nisa's relative: it would therefore be odd to say that being Nisa's relative inflicts a cost on one. Nevertheless, it is the requirement that must be satisfied to gain access to a benefit, and it was imposed because it creates a situation that can benefit the person who imposed it. This is why Cheng and Holyoak's (1989) distinction between "true" social exchange, where the parties incur costs, and "pseudo" social exchange, where at least one party must meet a requirement that may not be costly, constitutes a misunderstanding of social contract theory and the basic evolutionary biology that underlies it. Social exchange is the reciprocal provisioning of benefits, and the fact that the delivery of a benefit may prove costly is purely a by-product.

11. So far, the evidence suggests that we also have specialized procedures for reasoning about threats and precautions, for example.

12. No criticism of the experimenters is implied; these experiments were not designed for the purpose of testing social contract theory.

13. What if people read in a "may" that refers to obligation, rather than to possibility? That is, after all, a prediction of social contract theory. Logicians have tried to create "deontic logics": rules of inference that apply to situations of obligation and entitlement. Social contract theory is, in fact, a circumscribed form of deontic logic. But could subjects be using a generalized form of deontic logic? Manktelow and Over (1987) say that the answer is not clear because deontic logicians do not yet agree: According to some, no cards should be chosen on the switched social contracts; according to others, *not-P & Q* should be chosen. Because the rules of inference in social contract theory include the concepts of entitlement and obligation, it can be thought of as a specialized, domain-specific deontic logic. But we doubt that people have a generalized deontic logic. If they did, then non–social contract problems that involve obligation should elicit equally high levels of performance. But this is not the case, as will be discussed later in the chapter.

14. Even if this hypothesis were true, one would still have to explain why social contract problems are easier to understand, or more interesting, than other situations. After all, there is nothing particularly complicated about the situation described in a rule such as "If a person eats red meat, then that person drinks red wine." Social contract problems could be easier to understand, or more interesting, precisely because we do have social contract algorithms that organize our experience in such situations. Consequently, showing that social contract problems afford clear thinking about a wide variety of problems would not eliminate the possibility that there are social contract algorithms; it would simply cast doubt on the more specific claim that this set of algorithms includes a procedure specialized for cheater detection.

15. We would like to point out that the relationship between psychology and evolutionary biology can be a two-way street. For example, one could imagine models for the emergence of stable cooperation that require the evolution of a mechanism for altruism detection. If the selection pressures required by these models were present during hominid evolution, they should have left their mark on the design of our social contract algorithms. Finding that people are not good at detecting altruists casts doubt on this possibility, suggesting altruists are too rare to be worth evolving specialized mechanisms to detect, and hence gives insight into the kind of selection pressures that shaped the hominid line.

16. For example, instead of asking subjects to "indicate only those card(s) you definitely need to turn over to see if any of these boys have broken the law," the altruist version asked them to "indicate only those card(s) you definitely need to turn over to see if any of these boys have behaved altruistically with respect to this law."

17. Indeed, on the altruist detection problems in which the rule was a social law, more subjects detected *cheaters* than detected altruists! (This result was 64% in the altruist version; 44% in the selfless version.) It is almost as if, when it comes to a social law, subjects equate altruistic behavior with honorable behavior—i.e., with the absence of cheating. (This may be because for many social laws, such as the drinking age law, "society"—i.e., the individuals who enacted the law—benefits from the total configuration of events that ensues when the law is obeyed.) This was not true of the personal exchange laws, where it is easy to see how the other party benefits by your paying the cost to them but not accepting the benefit they have offered in return. (For the private exchange problems, only 16% of subjects chose the "look for cheaters" answer in the two altruist versions; 8% and 4%, in the selfless versions.)

18. Manktelow and Over (1987) point out that people do understand what conditions constitute a violation of a conditional rule, even when it is an abstract one. Hence the failure to perform well on the no cheating version cannot be attributed to subjects' not knowing what counts as a violation. (This fact may seem puzzling at first. But one can know what counts as a violation without being able to use that knowledge to generate falsifying inferences, as the failure to choose *P & not-Q* on abstract Wason selection tasks shows. Two separate kinds of cognitive processes appear to be involved. An analogy might be the ease with which one can recognize a name that one has been having trouble recalling.)

19. It is difficult to tell a permission from an obligation because both involve obligation and because there are no criteria for distinguishing the two representational formats ("If action is taken, then precondition must be satisfied" versus "If condition occurs, then action must be taken"). "Conditions" and "preconditions" can, after all, be "actions." The primary difference seems to be a time relation: If the obligation must be fulfilled before the action is taken, it is a permission. If the obligation can be fulfilled after a condition (which can be an "action taken") occurs, then it is an obligation. A social contract of the form, "If you take the benefit, then you must pay the cost" would be considered a permission if you were required to pay the cost before taking the benefit, but an obligation if you had first taken the benefit, thereby incurring the obligation to pay the cost.

20. To choose *not-P & Q*, one would have to interpret "If an employee gets a pension, then that employee must have worked for the firm for at least 10 years" as also implying "If an employee has worked for the firm for at least 10 years, then that employee must be given a pension." Social contract theory predicts that the one statement will be interpreted as implying the other, but permission schema theory does not. In fact, its translation rules (the four production rules) bar this interpretation. The rule presented to subjects—"If an employee gets a pension, then that employee must have worked for the firm for at least 10 years"—has the linguistic format of rule 1 of the permission schema—"If the action is to be taken, then the precondition must be satisfied." Rule 1 can be taken to imply rules 2, 3, and 4, but not other rules. By rule 3, the rule stated in the problem would translate to "If an employee has worked for the firm for at least 10 years, then that employee may be given a pension"—not that the employee *must* be given a pension.

21. Or equally low performance. Cheng and Holyoak have provided very little theory concerning what elements in a situation can be expected to activate the permission schema. Although they have suggested that the provision of a rationale or social purpose helps, they have never defined what counts as such and there are (social contract) permission rules that lack rationales that nevertheless produce the effect (Cosmides 1989). The problems that we tested here clearly stated that the rule is a law made by authorities which ought to clarify that they are permission rules and prevent subjects from interpreting them as descriptive rules. If this is sufficient to activate a permission schema, then performance on all three problems should be equally high. But none of the problems contains or suggests a rationale. So if one were to claim that rationales are necessary, then performance on all three problems should be equally low. Either way, performance should not vary across the three problems.

22. This is the kind of situation that Nesse and Lloyd (1992) suggest might call for benevolent self-deception. Although one memory module may be keeping an account of the other person's failure to contribute his fair share, this information might not be fed into the mechanisms that would cause an angry reaction to cheating. By preventing an angry reaction, this temporary encapsulation of the information would permit one to continue to cooperate with the suspected cheater. This situation would continue as long as one is still receiving a net benefit from the other person, or until it becomes sufficiently clear that the other person is cheating rather than experiencing a run of bad luck. At that point, the accounts kept by the one module would be fed into other modules, provoking an angry, recrimination-filled reaction.

27
Think Again

JOHN TOOBY
LEDA COSMIDES

As part of an effort to introduce an evolutionarily rigorous research framework into psychology and the other behavioral sciences (and to strengthen it within biology itself, where it is surprisingly rarely understood), we and a few others have introduced and used the term *evolutionary psychology*. Despite a widespread traditional conviction in many fields that behavior, social relations, culture, or mental phenomena are somehow outside of the scope of Darwinian analysis (see, for discussion, Tooby and Cosmides 1992), the principles of core Darwinism constitute an organism design theory whose engineering principles apply with as much force to the computational and neural machinery that produces behavior as to any other set of organs or tissues in the body (Cosmides and Tooby 1987). Indeed, increasingly accurate characterizations of the designs of these computational devices must eventually form the centerpiece of any meaningful theory of behavior, for any species, in any discipline (e.g., economics; see Cosmides and Tooby 1994).

In this sense, theories of behavior and theories of the structure of psychological mechanisms are simply two sides of the same coin. Observing patterns in behavior is one source of information that helps to reverse engineer the computational designs of the mechanisms that generate those patterns. Reciprocally, accurate knowledge of these designs yields precise theories of the behaviors that these designs generate. Evolution is logically linked to behavior only through its engineering impact on the psychological mechanisms that regulate behavior, and so evolutionary theories of behavior are, in-

evitably, psychological theories, whether their proponents explicitly recognize it or not. This is why behavioral measures and field studies are a regular part of evolutionary psychological research, along with a broad array of other methods, such as the study of focal brain damage, electromyography, hormone assays, psychophysics, cross-cultural comparison, experimental economic studies, neuroimaging, cognitive experimentation, psychopharmacological dissociations, the analysis of incidence rates from archive-derived data, and so on. Indeed, this is why evolutionary psychology and behavioral ecology are, in reality, essentially the same discipline. The only difference is that the term *evolutionary psychology* was adopted to identify a research program within modern evolutionary biology and behavioral ecology that adheres strictly to the logical structure of Darwinism and that is committed to characterizing the phenotypic designs of mechanisms, which are (usually complex) adaptations. Many researchers who identify themselves as behavioral ecologists share this program, but many do not.

By adaptations we mean inherited arrangements of elements in organisms that have been brought into their specific mutual relationship because that configuration, over evolutionary time, promoted the frequency of that inherited arrangement. In other words, adaptations are systems of functional machinery that assumed their improbably well-ordered functional relationships because, in the ancestral lineage's environment of evolutionary adaptedness, these relationships successfully accomplished tasks that increased the frequency of the alleles coding for those traits. Most phenotypic design consists of adaptations that are complex, that is, consisting of many components that depend for their existence on alleles at multiple loci. Because of sexual recombination and the combinatorics of alleles, most complex adaptations in humans and similar species will necessarily be species-typical and will depend on alleles at many loci being at or near fixation (for analysis, and appropriate qualifications, see Tooby and Cosmides 1990a).

With the foregoing as background, one can define the *environment of evolutionary adaptedness* for an adaptation as that set of selection pressures (i.e., properties of the ancestral world) that endured long enough to push each allele underlying the adaptation from its initial appearance to near fixation, and to maintain them there while other necessary alleles at related loci were similarly brought approximately to fixation. Because moving mutations from low initial frequencies to fixation takes substantial time, and sequential fixations must usually have been necessary to construct complex adaptations, almost all complex functional design in organisms owes its detailed organization to the complex and enduring structure of each species' past. Each design feature present in a modern organism is there because of a large and structured population of events in the past, and these event populations must be characterized if the design features are to be understood. It is a surprising lapse in many excellent evolutionary researchers' thought (see, e.g., Reeve and Sherman 1993) that they are not adaptationists in this strict Darwinian sense but focus instead on the present fitness consequences of a trait, which cannot logically play any role in explaining its existence (Tooby and Cosmides 1990b; Symons 1992).

Because selection is an antientropic process that operates across generations to build functional order into an organism's design, pushing upstream against entropy, the standards required to establish that a set of traits are an adaptation are probabilistic in nature (as they are in any good science). More specifically, one can use a knowledge of selection pressures, ancestral conditions, and computational principles to formulate hypotheses about the likely existence of various cognitive adaptations. To evaluate whether there is evidence for a particular adaptation, the question to be asked is: How im-

probably well ordered are the elements of the proposed adaptation, of one assumes its function was to reliably solve an adaptive problem or achieve an adaptive outcome in the organism's EEA? The metric is not optimality but rather, how much better than random is the adaptation at achieving biologically functional outcomes? In Williams's language, what is the evidence of special design (Williams 1966a)? That is, what is the evidence that the problem is solved with efficiency, reliability, economy, precision, and so on?

As one part of our research, we have been investigating the hypothesis that the human mind contains specialized information-processing adaptations designed to guide individuals successfully through social exchange. To provide a prototype of what an adaptationist psychological research paper might look like, we wrote "Cognitive Adaptations for Social Exchange," discussing selection pressures, ancestral conditions, predicted design features, and experimental evidence of special design, as well as the by-product counterhypotheses that had been eliminated experimentally. Since this paper, we and others have now produced a much larger body of evidence supporting the hypothesis that humans have specialized cognitive devices for this purpose (e.g., Gigerenzer and Hug 1995; Hoffman, McCabe, and Smith 1996a; Cosmides and Tooby, in prep.c; Fiddick, Cosmides, and Tooby, in prep.). One task is to show that any proposed complex psychological adaptation is effectively human universal, and not limited to some cultures but not others. Toward that end, these results have been replicated not only in a number of literate populations around the world but also using nonliterate subjects drawn from the Achuar, a hunter-horticulturalist population in the Amazonian region of Ecuador (Sugiyama, Tooby, and Cosmides, in prep.).

A second approach is to demonstrate that this specialized reasoning ability is a discrete, independent computational ability distinct from other abilities to reason, with its own unique properties and principles of activation. Toward this end, we have also accumulated a significant body of evidence supporting the existence of, and allowing us to separately characterize, three other reasoning adaptations (out of what we expect to be hundreds) with sharply differentiated functions and properties. These three include one for detecting lapses in taking precautions to avoid danger; one for detecting bluffs when one is threatened; and one for detecting double crosses when one is threatened. The most common counterhypothesis is that human reasoning is general-purpose and does not contain multiple reasoning specializations that operate according to domain-specific principles. If this were true, and there was only one psychological mechanism involved, then neither neurological impairments nor experimental manipulations should lead to dissociations in performance on tasks that differ only in whether they concern social contracts or precautions. To the human mind, these would all be instances of the same task, solved by the same mechanism, embodied in the same neural circuitry. However, subjects do experience experimentally induced dissociations that break down along the predicted lines—indicating that social exchange mechanisms and precaution mechanisms are cognitively real and separate mechanisms in humans (Fiddick, Cosmides, and Tooby, in prep.). We are presently collaborating on a study to identify the neural basis of these mechanisms, by identifying individuals who suffer selective impairments to one or another of these mechanisms, as the result of neurological damage. Indeed, Maljkovic (1987) has found that the ability to detect cheaters is maintained in schizophrenics, while other, more general deliberative reasoning abilities are impaired. This dissociation between social contract algorithms and general problem-solving ability constitutes another line of evidence suggesting that the social exchange mechanisms are a distinct and specialized competence. We are also collaborating on another study into the precaution and social exchange competences of individuals with autism. Autism is now believed to be a disorder caused by damage to part of an evolved faculty of social cognition—specifically, to the "theory of mind" module, a mechanism that causes people to infer that the actions of others are caused by unobservable mental attributes, such as beliefs and desires. Social exchange circuits are a part of social cognition, while precaution circuits need involve no social dimension. One intriguing possibility is that individuals with autism will be able to reason correctly about precautions, since they are nonsocial, but not about social exchanges. Another facet of this research program involves expanding the theoretical analysis from dyadic cooperation or social exchange to n-person cooperation, and mapping the set of computational devices that allow humans to form, participate in, manipulate, and abandon coalitions. The existence of a set of specialized cognitive devices that make sophisticated coalitional action possible is one central way in which human sociality differs from that of virtually all other species. Preliminary evidence suggests that at least some of the predicted coalitional mechanisms do exist.

In summary, a number of researchers have gone a long way toward establishing the existence of complex adaptive computational designs in the mind, designed to reason about social exchange. The weight of evidence now indicates that such mechanisms are species-typical. We anticipate that in the foreseeable future, we will be able to identify the neural basis of these mechanisms and their relationship to other related subsystems in human social cognition. What remains distant is the elucidation of the genetic bases and developmental biology of these adaptations.

III
COMPARATIVE AND HISTORICAL STUDIES

28

Tips, Branches, and Nodes: Seeking Adaptation through Comparative Studies

RUTH MACE
MARK PAGEL

The papers presented in this section share a "comparative approach" to testing ideas about the functional significance of cultural practices. Comparative studies test ideas about biological or cultural evolution by seeking relationships across a range of species or cultures or by making comparisons among groups within a culture. Comparative approaches have a long tradition in the human sciences, and the papers in this section span methodologies from narrative essays to quantitative empirical tests. Our task is to provide a critique of these papers in terms of how they have stood the test of time both in their conclusions and in the methods they employ.

Anthropologists are sometimes doubtful about the relevance of comparative study as a research method for understanding variation in cultural practices. The usual reason is that cultural practices and their precise causes are considered unique and their study in each single culture becomes an end in itself. There is a similar strand among that group of comparative biologists known as *cladists*. The cladistic view, named after the practice of defining clades of species, is that each evolutionary adaptation is unique and should be so studied (see Pagel 1994a). However, although one must acknowledge that at some level each cultural practice and each biological adaptation is unique, at another level—that of the functions they serve—there may be great convergence. Thus it may just be true that the reasons for the practice of having more than one wife, of passing wealth

along the male line, or of practicing infanticide are similar among cultures with similar practices. It is the promise that convergence of function across cultures holds for developing general statements about the evolution of human cultural practices that drives the field of comparative anthropology.

NARRATIVE ESSAYS

We have categorized the six papers in this section on comparative studies into two groups. In this first group of three papers, the authors—Mildred Dickemann, Laura Betzig, and Sarah Blaffer Hrdy—use a narrative-essay format to suggest and seek support for their ideas. By this we mean that these three authors do not rely upon explicit quantitative hypothesis tests. What distinguishes these papers from mere reviews, however, is that they seek to advance a particular idea and weigh the evidence for it in a narrative style. Accordingly, we shall critique these papers as scientific works and ask both specifically of them and more generally of the narrative-essay approach how well it succeeds.

Scientists should be immediately suspicious of the narrative-essay format as a way to test among competing ideas. Narratives rarely advance any explicit criteria for data collection; they frequently depend more upon the brute force of repeated assertions than on sophisticated use of control groups, whether naturally occurring or experimentally created; they seldom have any formal mechanism for weighing up the evidence; they may not directly test their hypothesis—indeed, there may not even be a formal hypothesis in some instances; and one cannot help but wonder if the strength of the authors' prior beliefs about the truth of their hypotheses influenced either their interpretation or sampling of events. We refer here to the large and influential literature on the effects of experimenter bias in research (e.g., Rosenthal 1976). Given these potential shortcomings, could an author's hypothesis ever be falsified by the narrative review? And, if not, to the extent that one finds these narratives believable, is it because the assertions they test are uncontroversial?

Narrative studies seldom confront the issue of what constitutes a contradiction to the hypothesis. In a quantitative test, ideally all of the evidence is summarized by some statistic and the hypothesis is judged. The number of data points "for" and "against" the hypothesis is, in principle, clear. But the piece-by-piece presentation of most narratives means that this "last judgment" may never happen. A relatively new set of techniques, known collectively as meta-analysis (Rosenthal 1991; Cooper and Hedges 1993), can be used to test a set of results for some overall level of significance, hence analyzing and summarizing a set of independent studies (see Arnqvist and Wooster 1995 for a recent review). Meta-analysis techniques would allow authors of narrative essays to sample from the domain of all tests or anecdotes and ask quantitatively whether that set provides support for their hypothesis. The use of meta-analysis techniques in narrative reviews would lend a salutary degree of discipline to these studies. Irons (1995) has used these techniques to summarize a range of independent studies seeking correlations between wealth and reproductive success in traditional societies.

Lacking sampling criteria, we may not be party to opposing pieces of evidence in the narrative review. One must, therefore, be mindful that contradictory evidence may exist. Reference to studies that contradict the hypothesis may be mentioned. But, even if authors assiduously sample the universe of anecdotes when constructing their narratives, the universe available to them may be biased. Journals frequently have a bias against "negative" results. Even the most comprehensive review of the published literature might lead us to believe that the ef-

fects described are stronger or more general than is in fact the case (this may be less of a problem when most of the relevant studies are conducted by those with a different disciplinary perspective, such as historians, although they may have another ax to grind). This is sometimes referred to as "the file drawer problem"; results that support fashionable hypotheses are more likely to get published, while those that do not languish in file drawers. Even meta-analysis cannot overcome this problem, but it can give an estimate of the number of unpublished studies that would have to exist for a significant finding to be overturned.

These are serious charges against the narrative essay as a form of science, and so perhaps we should dispense with the obvious defense of the essay: that it is not intended to be science. Indeed, in large branches of anthropology the idea that facts themselves should be considered as social constructs came into the ascendancy, and much of anthropology redefined itself as an interpretative humanity rather than as a science, concerning itself with cultural specifics. But anthropology does seem to have turned a corner, however, as the last decade especially has witnessed a great expansion in the study of many aspects of humanity as a scientific endeavor. We shall critique the papers in this section as contributions to this new human science.

Our view is that narrative essays can rarely be taken as tests of scientific hypotheses. In the face of the charges we have made against the narrative essay as a form of science, what role can they play? These narratives can be taken as works of advocacy—works that can, at their best, suggest ideas to be investigated further. In this role narrative essays can be very successful, and we include the three papers reviewed here in that category. This should not be surprising: Betzig, Dickemann, and Hrdy have all made outstanding contributions to the field, and their work deserves careful attention. If some of the arguments put forward now seem uncontroversial to those of us with evolutionary training, we should not forget that someone needed to start the ball rolling.

Dickemann was among the first to advance the case that specific cultural practices (dowry and purdah, to name but two) cannot be understood without biology in general and reproductive competition in particular. In her review of infanticide and delegated mothering, Hrdy argues that maternal effort is a limited resource that has to be spent selectively and saved either through infanticide or through the delegation of child care onto others should the opportunity to do so arise. There is a pervading view (no doubt fueled more by hope than experience) that disadvantaged children will receive more, not less, care from their parents. Articles such as Hrdy's force us to see the true meaning of selection. Finally, we would not like to have the job of defending the Romans against the accusation of spending their wealth on polygyny after reading Betzig's forty pages of relentless exposure to the sexual habits of Roman aristocracy.

Before moving on to reviewing the articles, we should make clear that we are not "data chauvinists." All of the concerns we express, about sampling, testing, and the like, are also true to varying degrees of quantitative surveys and field experiments. Nevertheless, our admonitions rest upon the fact that these other forms of study carry at least a veneer of expectation for scientific justification—something lacking from the essay. But more to the point: two wrongs do not make a right.

The Case of Sexual Perversity in Rome

Laura Betzig's eye-opening article on the sexual habits of wealthy Romans may be a paradigm case of the narrative-essay format: the argument is built and supported by means of the overwhelming accumulation of anecdotal evidence. Betzig wants to convince us that wealthy and powerful Romans enjoy higher reproductive success and do so on the backs of the poor and weak. She argues that wealthy Romans used their female slaves among other things, as large "breeding colonies." The treatment of different groups of slaves (female versus male, young versus old, slaves born on their master's estate versus slaves born elsewhere) is compared to support this assertion. The broad message is that wealth can procure increased reproductive success. The specific message is that Roman emperors used their wealth to have sex.

Exploitation of the poor not only for their work but also to produce children for the wealthy is the sort of charge that appeals to the liberal-minded. The real danger, however, is that by also being believable in the light of evolutionary theory, or even fashionable in the light of cynicism about the intentions of those in

power, the hypothesis may be too readily accepted. Has Betzig really made her case that Roman polygyny is a strategy of fitness maximization?

Are there systematic biases in the reporting of events by historians of the time or by later historians? History usually emphasizes—as does Betzig's paper—the wealthy and the powerful. How representative of wealthy Romans were a particularly notorious family of emperors? Perhaps very little is known about the poor, especially about their sexual habits. Slaveholders may have believed the children of their female slaves to be theirs, but what about the sexual habits of male slaves? Betzig cites, among other evidence, the fact that slaves are often freed when young to support the hypothesis that the children of slaves are frequently fathered by their owner. She mentions, briefly, that another historian believes the opposite to be true—that slaves are freed when old. Do other contradictory studies exist, and are they being given a fair hearing?

Sexual debauchery may not translate into large numbers of offspring. This is a critical assumption if the intention is to advance the idea that wealth used to procure women is being spent as a reproductive strategy. Powerful Romans had a habit of forcing other men's wives into sexual relationships, but how were any bastard children of unwilling mates treated, if allowed to survive at all? Were fertility and longevity so lowered in the sexually hyperactive by the sexually transmitted diseases that would inevitably arise that such behavior actually decreased fitness?

We raise these issues not because we disbelieve the arguments Betzig advances but to illustrate the difficulties of testing hypotheses with anecdotal evidence. Quantitative measures of reproductive success, if we had them, might be the only method by which we could answer these questions for certain. Betzig is of course aware of this, being a strong advocate of counting babies (Betzig 1995b). What she does here is invite us to see history in a new way, in the light of evolutionary theory. In this she succeeds. Indeed, the strategy of buying slaves for breeding, which Betzig highlights here, is not something we heard about in our history lessons, and it could be one of the more direct methods ever described of using wealth for reproductive purposes.

Claustration and Foot Binding: Mate Guarding or Honest Advertisement of Wealth?

Mildred Dickemann's pioneering essay reinterprets the claustration of women (including purdah) and the Chinese practice of foot binding as examples not simply of male control of females but of what is a more general phenomenon of the control of women for the purposes of mate guarding. As with the other essays, we should attempt to distinguish the immediate effects of these practices from what the author implies is their longer-term or evolutionary implication. We find Dickemann's implicit thesis that foot binding and claustration reduce the frequency of what behavioral ecologists would call "extra-pair copulations" eminently plausible, although anecdotes provide no direct information about this. It may even be possible for some wealthy women in harems or secluded accommodations to use their wealth to procure clandestine mates. A field behavioral ecologist would aim to keep track of the number of extra-pair copulations (i.e., the amount of sex outside of "marriage") among women with bound feet or claustrated compared with those who were not so treated.

Dickemann mentions in passing that some social scientists have considered claustration of women an example of "conspicuous consumption." This was Thorsten Veblen's (1899) term for the tendency of the wealthy to display their riches in highly conspicuous, ostentatious, and ultimately wasteful ways; F. Scott Fitzgerald's Gatsby is the archetype of the conspicuous consumer. At the time Dickemann wrote her article, evolutionary biology's contemporary incarnation of Veblen's conspicuous consumption—Zahavi's (1975) theory of costly signaling and honest advertisement—was not widely known. This may be why Dickemann does not discuss this aspect of claustration further in an evolutionary context. But now so-called "honest advertisement" is a central plank of signaling theory and of sexual signaling theory in particular. Low (1988b) has applied this evolutionary framework to body adornment in human populations.

We suggest that the claustration of women and their disablement by the mutilation of their feet could equally well be considered as honest signals of wealth and status rather than mate

guarding per se. Claustration and foot binding were largely confined to the upper classes. In poor families women worked in the fields, and poor families probably could not survive without women's labor. Bound feet could thus be an honest, costly signal that a girl was raised in a wealthy household—a signal that, unlike jewelry and other finery, could not be adorned by the nouveau riche or sold by those falling on hard times.

Signaling is in fact at the center of Dickemann's hypothesis for dowry—that a father signals his daughter's purity through dowry to enhance her chances in the competition for high-status husbands. But there is no reason given as to why wealth in general or dowry in particular should be an honest signal of chastity, which an evolutionary interpretation would require.

Delegating Mothering as a Means To Increase Fertility

Sarah Hrdy makes skillful use of the weight of anecdotal evidence to convince us that wet-nursing, adoption, and infanticide can be understood as reproductive strategies. With respect to wet-nursing, she cites the hyperfertility of some eighteenth-century Europeans, comparing it with more "natural" human birth rates (such as the presumed "Pleistocene" four-year birth interval), to convince us that wet nurses are used as a strategy to increase fertility. Hrdy provides an example of an individual woman of that period who gave birth to over twenty children.

That breast-feeding inhibits fertility is not controversial. In societies where fertility is high, women who breast-feed longer have been shown to have longer interbirth intervals (e.g., in Hutterites [Margulis et al. 1993]). Thus Hrdy's argument, that wet-nursing in humans may have been a strategy to reduce the interbirth interval, is believable. But Hrdy also tells us that fertility declined in the French aristocracy between the seventeenth and eighteenth centuries to levels well below that at which length of breast-feeding could be a relevant proximate cause; yet wet nurses were still used. Other explanations for wet-nursing may deserve further investigation. Could wet-nursing have been a manifestation of a desire to avoid tiring activities—ones we buy our way out of if we can afford to (like the modern practices of hiring a cleaner or a nanny or even bottle-feeding a baby)? Could decreased interbirth intervals have been an unwelcome side effect of wet-nursing that was eventually countered by changes in sexual practices?

Hrdy points out that mechanisms for retrenching maternal effort will vary according to the opportunities that the culture and ecology afford to women. She observes that wet-nursing was not always intended as a method to raise the child—it was sometimes a form of infanticide. Under these circumstances it seems unlikely that the parents would wish to conceive another child, and if they did it would likely meet the same end. That this has an evolutionary interpretation is quite plausible, but it does pose problems of falsifiability. If a hypothesis is not specific, and a number of different outcomes can all be explained in evolutionary terms, then how can statements be falsified? We doubt by narrative review. So how are Hrdy's assertions supported or contradicted by more detailed empirical studies?

Hrdy argues that adoption may be another case of delegating mothering for reproductive reasons. In a study of a population of Herero pastoralists in southern Africa, Pennington and Harpending (1993) investigated patterns of the fostering of children—a very common form of delegated mothering around the world, especially common in Africa. In one of the more detailed studies of its kind, they could find no evidence that the fostering out of a child decreased birth intervals in the natural mother, nor even that the practice occurred more often at ages that would make use of the mother's maximum potential fertility. They could not explain fostering as an adaptive strategy by the parents. They considered it most likely that fostered children were being "taken" by kin (presumably for their value as helpers) rather than being "given" by mothers attempting to retrench maternal investment.

Does this matter for the hypothesis that Hrdy is supporting in her paper that mothering is delegated to enhance future reproduction? It does not, in the sense that she need not find that every single case of delegated mothering can necessarily be understood as a reproductive strategy. It does not undermine the argument any more than the finding of a monogamous Roman emperor would undermine Betzig's central tenet.

But when the advancement of a hypothesis is based on literature review, we are again reminded that a review can never be complete (not least because some studies will not yet have been done), and this alerts us to the possibility that contradictory evidence may exist.

In each case discussed here, we would be able to answer some of the questions if we were to measure reproductive success. As it is not always possible to do this—not least if the people and practices are history—the authors make use of the anecdotal evidence available to them. It could be argued that truth will gradually emerge because opposing anecdotes will be brought to light by those with opposing hypotheses. But how, then, do we make a judgment between the opposing texts? How do we try to ensure that our hypotheses are more than just _informed storytelling_?

QUANTITATIVE COMPARATIVE TESTS

The three papers in this section on quantitative investigations are studies by Steve Gaulin and James Boster, John Hartung, and Bobbi Low. These authors all use quantitative information obtained from cross-cultural samples to test hypotheses about the function of various cultural practices. The cross-cultural samples are typically drawn from databases of information, such as the Human Relations Area Files. The information in such databases is generally compiled without any particular hypothesis in mind. Hypotheses are then tested by seeking an association between two or more variables across a range of cultures, in an attempt to determine whether the two variables co-occur across cultures more frequently than would be expected by chance.

Hartung investigates whether strongly male-biased wealth inheritance is more likely in polygynous societies (where wealth is presumed to be a stronger determinant of male than female reproductive success). Gaulin and Boster's paper is the other side of the same coin. They investigate whether the practice of paying a dowry is associated with monogamy and stratification in society, to put the case that dowry is a means by which the bride's family helps her to compete with other women for the most desirable husbands. In the third paper in this section, Low examines whether the training that boys and girls receive from their parents differs depending upon the marriage system and the degree of stratification in society.

Quantitative comparative investigations of the sort these authors use are expected to have most of the trappings of scientific studies—sampling criteria, appropriate controls or comparisons, statistical weighing of evidence, testable hypotheses—and this may give them an aesthetic advantage over narratives. The trappings of science can, however, be just as misleading as their absence, and therefore we shall also want to scrutinize very carefully the studies in this section.

Our task is focused by the fact that the three investigations share a common methodology—quantitative cross-cultural comparison. Cross-cultural comparative studies have long been bedeviled by the observation that cultures, owing to the fact that they evolve at least in part by a process of hierarchical descent, cannot be considered independent of each other for statistical purposes. This can render statistical tests misleading or even useless. Accordingly, a large part of our review in this section will be devoted to discussing how properly to conduct quantitative statistical tests across cultures. Along the way we shall comment on the three investigations and reanalyze data from Hartung's and from Gaulin and Boster's studies.

Phylogenetic Approaches to Cross-cultural Comparative Studies

Identifying independent instances of cultural change. The purpose of a cross-cultural comparative study is to seek evidence for the correlated evolution of two or more elements of culture. Evidence for correlated evolutionary change comes from repeated and independent instances of the *evolution* of these elements in different cultural groups. The outstanding problem of cross-cultural comparison has been to determine what constitutes a suitable sample of independent data points. We have discussed this problem at length elsewhere (Mace and Pagel 1994). In short, if cultures are related hierarchically (that is, cultures are descended from other cultures, thought to go back to a single origin in the past), then they cannot necessarily be considered as independent data points.

A correlation between two elements of culture could arise because both elements were inherited by daughter cultures from an ancestral

culture, rather than because those elements arose independently in each. However, a correlation arising from shared ancestry does not necessarily say anything about whether these traits are functionally linked. The elements may each have arisen once in the past for good functional reasons and then been retained in a large number of descendant cultures, even though the two elements are not related to each other.

Statistical tests of correlated evolution have to be based on independent instances of cultural change, which can only be identified by the construction of phylogenies of culture (Mace and Pagel 1994). An independent instance of cultural change could be de novo invention of a practice or custom, or the acquisition of that custom from another culture other than a mother culture (i.e., by horizontal transmission or diffusion). Figure 28.1a illustrates an instance in which an apparent correlation between two elements arises because of shared ancestry, even though only one instance of evolutionary change has occurred. In contrast, Figure 28.1b illustrates the same correlation based upon four instances of change on the phylogeny. Only the latter relationship is evidence for repeated and correlated evolutionary change.

Hartung appreciates the possibility of a cross-cultural correlation arising because of shared ancestry. He attempts to control for it by dividing his database into language groups and allowing each language group to contribute equally to the final statistical test of association, assuming, probably correctly, that the cultures within each of these groups will generally not be independent. Low attempts to exclude closely related cultures by drawing her sample of cultures from larger clusters that are thought to be independent. We have discussed elsewhere (Mace and Pagel 1994) why such approaches, while helping to reduce the possibility that correlations are artifacts of shared ancestry, do not identify independent instances of cultural change. They simply remove the problem of nonindependence to nodes farther down the tree (i.e., earlier in time). Such techniques can also waste a great deal of potentially relevant data. Low, for example, samples only every second culture available to her.

In the following we shall illustrate techniques that provide a principled solution to the problem of how to test cross-cultural comparative hypotheses by reanalyzing data from Gaulin

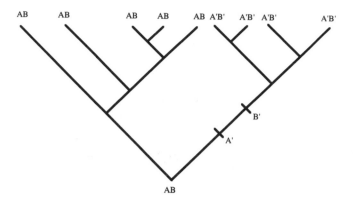

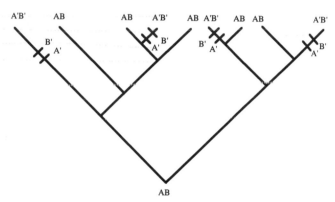

Figure 28.1. (a) A phylogeny where A changes to A′ and B changes to B′ only once. (b) A phylogeny where A changes to A′ and B changes to B′ in the presence of A′ on four separate occasions.

and Boster's work on the coevolution of dowry and monogamy, and from Hartung's study of wealth inheritance.

Parsimony methods. To identify independent instances of cultural change, we need first to construct a phylogeny of the cultures concerned. This could be done on the basis of genes (as with species phylogenies) or on the basis of language. Language behaves, to some extent, like a neutral genetic mutation—two separated languages diverge over time by the random accumulation of changes. Classifications of language based on the assumption that language evolves in a "phylogenetic" way correspond with phylogenies based on genetic similarity (Cavalli-Sforza et al. 1988, 1994; Torroni et al. 1992). This helps to convince us that such phy-

logenies do tell us something about the historical relationships between cultures.

Whether to use linguistic or genetic phylogenies will depend in part on which is most likely to best represent the history of the variables being studied. Language is likely to provide more clues to the history of a cultural custom such as dowry (and the genetic picture of Europe is particularly complex, not lending itself to the construction of phylogenetic trees (Cavalli-Sforza et al. 1994). We have used Ruhlen's (1991) classification of languages to construct the phylogenies given here.

Gaulin and Boster show, using simple cross-tabulations of dowry/no dowry versus monogamous/polygynous marriage system across cultures, that dowry and monogamy occur together very frequently (Table 1 in Gaulin and Boster and Figure 28.2a). The majority of the coincidence of dowry and monogamy occurs in Europe and East Asia. The majority of these cases occur within the Indo-Hittite (Indo-European) language group. Therefore, we selected this study in particular for reanalysis because it appears to be the most at risk of having generated a correlation as a result of shared ancestry or phylogenetic effects rather than from the repeated coevolution between the customs of interest (although we are not sure of the extent to which Low's results may suffer from this problem because she does not discuss how the traits of interest are "clumped" phylogenetically).

The linguistic phylogenetic tree for the Indo-Hittites is shown in Figures 28.3a and 28.3b. After reconstructing this tree, we assigned the character state of each of the two cultural elements to each of the cultures at the tips of the phylogeny. We then reconstructed the probable ancestral states of marriage system and dowry/no dowry using parsimony methods. These methods find the minimum number of

Marriage System

Dowry	Monogamy	Polygyny
Yes	11	0
No	6	13

Marriage System

Inheritance	Monogamy	Polygyny
High male bias	4	32
Low or no male bias	10	4

Figure 28.2. (a) The number of cultures showing dowry in the presence of monogamy and polygyny in the Indo-Hittites. (b) The number of cultures showing strongly male-biased inheritance in the presence of monogamy and polygyny in the Amerinds.

cultural changes that are required to produce the distribution of characters that currently exist. Computer programs are available to help calculate these (Maddison and Maddison 1992). Figure 28.3a shows the most parsimonious reconstruction of the possible evolution of monogamy. Monogamy arose perhaps only once, at the root of the tree, was lost in the Indo-Iranians, and gained once in the ancestral culture of the Vedda and Sinhalese.

28.3 Figure 28b shows the most parsimonious reconstruction of the evolution of dowry. Dowry may have arisen independently (i.e., other than by descent) only once in the Europeans and once in the Sinhalese, and was then lost in some European cultures.

Putting together Figures 28.3a and 28.3b, there is very little evidence in the Indo-Hittites for the repeated coevolution of dowry and monogamy because the number of occasions on which each arose is so small. The significant correlation between the two characters obtained from counting the states across the tips (i.e., the extant cultures) of the phylogeny (Figure 28.2a and 28.2b) says little about the likelihood that these two variables are evolutionarily linked. Both characters may be functional in their own right but could be maintained in these cultures for unrelated reasons.

Contrast these results with those obtained from a phylogenetic reanalysis of Hartung's data on the association between male-biased wealth inheritance and polygyny. Figures 28.4a and 28.4b show a phylogeny of Amerind peoples of North America, representing part of Hartung's data set. Monogamy (Figure 28.4a) and inheritance system (Figure 28.4b) have each arisen on a number of independent occasions among the Amerind. Although there are many ambiguities when reconstructing ancestral character states, there are enough unambiguous associations between changes in marriage system and inheritance to suggest that the correlation found by Hartung is real, that is, it is unlikely to be merely an artifact of shared ancestry.

However, there are a number of problems with considering these as the only, or even the most likely, reconstructions of history. There are many places on both trees, particularly at their roots, where a number of cultures emerge from a single node. This indicates that we do not know the precise hierarchy in which they

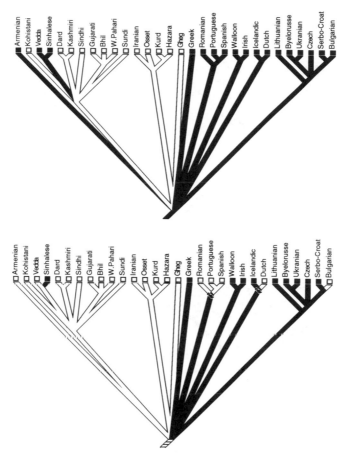

Figure 28.3. (a) The most parsimonious reconstruction of the evolution of monogamy (dark branches) in the Indo-Hittites. The phylogeny is based on the linguistic classification of Ruhlen 1991. (b) The most parsimonious reconstruction of the evolution of dowry (dark branches) on the same phylogeny. The symbol seen on two nodes indicates that a known ancestral culture had dowry.

arose. The assumptions we make here could change the number of occasions on which it is likely that either dowry or monogamy or male-biased inheritance may have arisen independently. This immediately highlights the problems of trying to find a unique set of ancestral character states on a phylogeny.

Pairwise comparison and other methods. A weakness in relying upon parsimony to estimate ancestral character states for cultural elements is that cultures evolve rapidly compared with most biological traits. Add to this the possibility of horizontal transmission of cultural elements and the assumption of parsimony becomes even shakier. An alternative approach is simply to make comparisons between pairs of cultures at the tips of the phylogeny, in which each pair shares an immediate common ancestor. This would be especially relevant if, as may be the case with many, rapidly evolving elements of culture, dowry is a relatively recent custom. If dowry is very recent (within one thousand years, for example), then it is not likely that all the European cultures acquired it by descent.

Pairwise comparisons in this context would proceed by comparing pairs of "sister cultures" in which one of the pair was monogamous and one was polygynous. If, within these pairs, dowry is more likely to have been adopted in

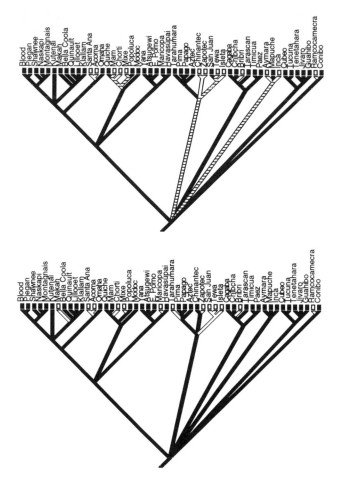

Figure 28.4. (a) The most parsimonious reconstruction of the evolution of monogamy (white branches) in the Amerinds. The phylogeny is based on the linguistic classification of Ruhlen 1991. (Hashed branches indicate that monogamy or polygyny are equally parsimonious assumptions.) Only those Amerind cultures that meet Hartung's (1982) definition of strong male-bias or low/no male-bias in inheritance are included. (b) The most parsimonious reconstruction of the evolution of strongly male-biased inheritance (dark branches) on the same phylogeny.

the monogamous culture, then this would be an independent data point in support of the hypothesis that dowry was evolving in the presence of monogamy. From the Indo-Hittite phylogeny in Figure 28.3a, however, it is clear that there are no such pairs at the tips in which marriage system differs. At the point where the Europeans separated from the other Indo-Hittites, it does appear that monogamy was maintained (or arose) in the Europeans and the other cultures became (or remained) largely polygynous, and that dowry only emerges in

the presence of monogamy. Thus there is at least one pairwise comparison in the direction of the hypothesis, albeit not at the tips of the tree.

There are some other pieces of evidence that may lead us to favor the hypothesis. The single appearance of dowry outside the European cluster is associated with one of the few non-European cultures practicing monogamy. Taking into account all possible ways the two events of the evolution of dowry could have evolved on the tree (see Maddison 1990), the probability that they would occur by chance in only monogamous branches is $p = .19$.

Comparative methods using maximum likelihood. Statistical tests such as those we have described here depend upon inferring, usually by parsimony, a single set of values at the internal nodes of the phylogenetic tree (Pagel 1994b). Any inferences about the relationship between two characters will depend upon the validity of the unique set of reconstructed values. Where characters evolve rapidly and repeatedly, such as in the Amerind phylogeny, parsimony methods may often give unreliable answers. Moreover, it is unusual in statistics that values inferred but not directly observed are nonetheless treated as actual observed data points in later tests.

Pagel (1994b) describes a method for the analysis of binary discrete characters that avoids the problem of inferring the pattern of changes at the internal nodes. The method finds evidence for correlated evolutionary change in two discrete characters by considering all possible transitions among states at each internal node. This avoids the logical problem of treating inferred values as actual observed data points and is especially valuable for evolutionarily labile traits, such as many behavioral or cultural characters, for which no single most parsimonious reconstruction of the states at the internal nodes of the tree will exist. The method can also make use of information on branch lengths and can test hypotheses about the direction of evolutionary change.   M^cPEEK ?

The test begins by fitting two alternative statistical models to a data set. The model of "independence" allows the two binary variables to evolve independently of one another, along each of the branches of the tree. The model of "dependent change" makes the probability of change in one variable dependent upon the state of the other variable. For example, one might be interested in whether the dependent variable Y is more likely to change from state 0 to state 1 when the independent variable is in state 0 rather than in state 1. The independent and dependent models of change are fitted to the data by a technique known as *maximum likelihood*, which chooses that set of values for the parameters of both models that make the observed data most likely, given the phylogenetic relationships among the cultures. This can deter-

mine whether the model of dependent change fits the data better than the model of independent change sufficiently well that we can disregard the latter as a useful description of the data. The test statistic compares the "log-likelihood" (a measure of goodness of fit) for the model of independence with that for the model of dependence.

To illustrate the method we have reanalyzed the data from Figures 28.3 and 28.4. The model of independence for Figure 28.3 yields a log-likelihood of -22.84; the model of dependent change has a log-likelihood of -18.74. Because these values are logarithms of probabilities, more strongly negative numbers represent probabilities closer to zero (the logarithm of zero is negative infinity), whereas the less strongly negative number is the logarithm of a number closer to one (the logarithm of one is zero). Therefore, we have some initial evidence that the model of dependent change is more probable.

To assess whether this difference is significant, one uses the likelihood ratio statistic, defined as $LR = -2\log[I/D] = -2[\log(I) - \log(D)]$ where I and D stand, respectively, for the models of independence and dependence. For the relationship between dowry and monogamy, $LR = 6.82$, which in this instance (see Pagel 1994b for testing procedures) is suggestive but not significant $(.05 < p < .1)$. Thus while Gaulin and Boster's cross-cultural correlations appear to have predictive power with respect to the circumstances in which dowry might occur, we cannot demonstrate that monogamy (or stratification) is in fact a force that causes dowry to evolve. We have not explored the worldwide occurrence, and a larger sample might give a different result, but we note that instances of the evolution of dowry are rare.

Applying the maximum likelihood method to the Amerind inheritance data of Figure 28.4, however, yields $LR = 18.47$, a highly significant value indicating that strongly male-biased inheritance and polygyny do coevolve. The method allows us to go further and to test explicit directional hypotheses. Figure 28.5 shows a diagram of the four states possible with two binary characters and the transitions among them. Arrows with associated p values that are less than .05 are labeled and indicate that the transitions between character states indicated by the transitions are significant. Thus, polyg-

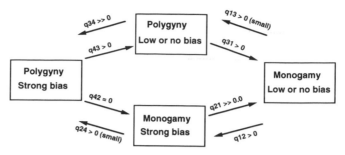

Figure 28.5. Likelihoods associated with transitions occurring between different states in the Amerind cultures.

ynous cultures with strongly male-biased inheritance never give rise to monogamous cultures with strongly male-biased inheritance, but all other transitions may occur at least occasionally. Both polygynous systems with low bias and monogamous systems with high bias appear to be unstable states, as the probability of moving to another state (polygyny with strong bias in the former case, and monogamy with low bias in the latter case) is very high. The transition from polygyny/high bias to monogamy/low bias is far more likely to occur via a state of polygyny with low bias than via monogamy with high bias. Transitions in the opposite direction, that is, from monogamy and no bias and polygyny and high bias, are more likely to occur via the intermediate state of monogamy with high bias. Both these findings suggest the intriguing possibility that inheritance systems may change prior to changes in marriage system. Hence, while most comparative studies can only show correlation, this method suggests the direction of change and may suggest further hypotheses for investigation.

Critiques of the Foundations Underlying Hypotheses

The comparative data from Indo-Hittites do not provide statistically significant evidence that the two practices of dowry and monogamy co-evolve. This does not necessarily mean that the theory is wrong, however. We emphasize, as with any empirical study, or even a narrative essay, that there may be other reasons for believing or not believing a research hypothesis. Both the theoretical and the empirical foundations need to be taken into account.

Dowry as female competition. That dowry is female competition is a point on which Gaulin and Boster and Dickemann agree, although Gaulin and Boster's case that dowry aids competition by increasing the wealth value of a bride seems to us to rest on firmer foundations than the idea that dowry is a signal of purity. If competition for wealth is to be given an evolutionary interpretation, then it should be true that wealth enhances reproductive success and thus plays a role in mate choice. Both assertions are well supported theoretically and empirically (e.g., Turke and Betzig 1985; Borgerhoff Mulder 1987a; Mace 1996; Irons 1995; Rogers 1996).

If there are too few independent instances of the evolution of dowry to make a case from cross-cultural comparison alone that dowry is female competition from investigating variation within societies (as Dickemann does) greatly strengthens that case. In hypergynous dowry societies, the fact that women can marry up but not down is what puts women in the upper strata in intense competition for mates; so the fact that dowry occurs only in the upper strata increases our confidence that dowry is used in female competition.

We did not examine stratification in our reanalysis because all Indo-European societies (with or without dowry) are stratified. Thus, sometimes monogamy and stratification do not occur with dowry. Wealth differences between men are not counted as "stratification," and there is no obvious reason why women should not be in competition over wealthy men in unstratified societies yet dowry is largely absent outside the Indo-Europeans. A complete theory of dowry would ideally explain why there are so many examples of monogamy with no dowry around the world, why dowry appears to have been lost in some stratified European cultures, and, most puzzling of all, why upper-class women are ever prevented from marrying down should they fail to secure an upper-class husband. This latter observation currently defies evolutionary interpretation, as theoretical investigations suggest that this would be of much greater fitness than remaining unmarried (Harpending and Rogers 1990).

As always, alternative explanations have to be entertained. Dowry is parental investment in a daughter, but that does not necessarily mean that its primary function is influencing male mate choice. Dowry may be a form of parental investment that is governed more by the returns achievable from investment in sons (with whom daughters are in direct competition for parental resources) than by competition with other women. As such, dowry may occur only where opportunities for male polygynous mating are severely constrained, perhaps by a particular religious system.

The training of children for future reproductive roles. The distinction that Low makes between the training of boys in stratified and unstratified polygynous societies rests on the assertion that men are not socially mobile in stratified societies. But is this generally true? Betzig gives examples of male ex-slaves reaching powerful positions in ancient Rome—either this is extraordinary or this aspect of male mobility should be examined further. In hypergynous societies, it is reported that men do not generally move up strata but that they can go down (Dickemann 1979b). Surely, competition to stay in the upper strata (as in the case of women in dowry societies) could be as important as competition to move up from a lower class? Thus, can we really be sure that males in stratified societies are subject to the reduced levels of competition, as Low's evolutionary interpretation of her results requires? Voland (1990) describes a stratified society where women are prepared to marry down but men are not. It may be that neither Low nor Gaulin and Boster can safely make cross-cultural generalizations about the movement of people of either sex through the levels of stratified societies.

Male-biased inheritance and marriage systems. The notion that male-biased inheritance and general polygyny co-evolve is supported empirically both by Hartung (1982) and by our re-analysis of his work. The evolutionary theory on which the hypothesis rests is also well founded (Fisher 1958; Orians 1969; Trivers 1972). Some findings do require additional explanations, such as the fact that male-biased inheritance occurs so frequently in monogamous cultures. It can be argued that monogamous marriage does not necessarily mean monogamous mating (e.g., Betzig 1993), which raises the issue of to what extent differences in marriage system are truly indicative of different mating systems, which an evolutionary interpretation of Hartung's findings does require. DNA typing opens up the theoretical, if not the practical, possibility of investigating this further. Indeed, every one of the hypotheses put forward here, whether by narrative or through quantitative test, could benefit from more information on how DNA moves around populations. That is, in the end, what we are talking about.

INTERPRETATION

If we are happy that we have chosen a meaningful test of a sound evolutionary hypothesis, a suitable sample, and have found a relevant association using statistics or other measures that truly demonstrate an association between some cultural practice and the circumstances in which it occurs, how do we interpret this result in the light of evolutionary theory?

What do we mean by a cultural adaptation? An evolutionary adaptation is generally taken to mean a trait that has arisen due to selection favoring the reproductive success of those individuals with that trait. If we believe this is so for a particular aspect of human behavior, then we can rightly describe that behavior as an adaptive strategy for that purpose. This is a separate question from whether or not the trait is genetic—culturally determined traits are inherited and have a fitness value too. All the papers we critique here argue that a cultural practice is an evolutionary adaptation, directly or indirectly enhancing the reproductive success of those who carry it. Casting aside any doubts we may have about methodology, if we take it that all the hypotheses discussed here are supported by data, then can we truly describe these behaviors as adaptations?

Imagine a behavior that enhances child survival has arisen over a short period of time, such as taking children for vaccination when a clinic is built in an area that previously had no medical facilities. Because the behavior is learned, this practice could become universal in the area within months, and thus could enhance child survival. But we could not describe it as an evolved adaptation, as not even one generation would have passed for any selection to act on. This behavior is adaptive, but it is the manifestation of the adaptation of a human psychology evolved to do the best for our children.

Roman orgies may be a manifestation of a psychological mechanism to seek pleasure, expressed in the small number of wealthy Romans who were able to indulge in such behavior. Wet-nursing may be a manifestation of the desire to avoid tiring activities. That both mechanisms are no doubt evolved does not necessarily make these behaviors adaptive strategies to increase fertility. Should such behaviors persist over many generations, always emerging in similar circumstances and always enhancing the reproductive success of those who practice them, then the case for calling them adaptations would increase.

This opens up the question of mechanisms. Our complex brains and the different transmission mechanisms of cultural traits and genetic traits make this an even more complex task than it would be if we were dealing with simple behaviors in species with limited cognitive ability. Behavioral ecologists have a long tradition of failing to address the mechanisms by which a correspondence between the observed pattern of occurrence of some behavior, and that predicted by evolutionary theory, might arise. Despite this neglect—in fact, probably because of it—the field has proven immensely successful at predicting and explaining animal behavior and life history. Frameworks drawn from the social sciences, which are frequently preoccupied with mechanisms, have not been so successful at predicting human behavior. Evolutionary theory provides such a strong paradigm that we would urge students of human behavior to pursue it without getting too concerned about definitions or the difficulty of elucidating mechanisms (as interesting as they are); a scientific framework will be judged in the end by what it can predict about the way we are.

We know so much more about variation in humans than in most other species that we find ourselves with much more to explain; and we will get away with less hand waving than do students of the behavior of some infrequently investigated animal. For example, history will throw up many problems. What we know of patterns of fertility suggests that post-Holocene fertility rates are rarely stable even for a century—if we have historical information about our population, not only do we have to explain the present behavior but our theory would only be really convincing if it also explained why the present is not the same as the past.

This necessitates high standards in the testing of hypotheses. As humans are not generally amenable to manipulation through experiments, then comparative studies are bound to feature prominently as a means of studying the function of human practices. Over the relatively short period of time that approaches from evolutionary ecology have been applied to humans, there have been many successes. If our guidelines to proceed with this approach can be summarized in a sentence, we would say: define your hypothesis specifically and base it on sound evolutionary theory, test it empirically in the best way that the data will allow, and do not use the fact that the study of the evolution of human behavior is difficult as an excuse not to do it.

Acknowledgments. Ruth Mace is funded by the Royal Society, and Mark Pagel is funded by the BBSRC and the NERC. We thank Laura Betzig for comments.

[handwritten annotations at top of page:]

♂ stratification → paternal invest. → confid. paternity
↳ operational sex ratio ↑
ave. R.S. of ♂ = ♀, so if some males "win" it is   guard.
29   over other males.

Paternal Confidence and Dowry Competition: A Biocultural Analysis of Purdah

MILDRED DICKEMANN   *[handwritten: stratification by sex & within ♂ taken as "given".]*

[handwritten: → asym. bargaining position results from lined of sex ratio]

> Why is there such interest in the sexuality of women rather than men?
>
> (Yalman, 1963).
>
> In the end, the question must be asked. Why? Why the emphasis on the bodily
> modesty of women, their seclusion, their chastity, their sexuality, their punishment,
> their protection, and their control? In short, why the modesty code?
>
> (Antoun, 1968)

The question is asked by anthropologists Nur Yalman, in an article "On the Purity of Women in the Castes of Ceylon and Malabar," and Richard Antoun, in an article "On the Modesty of Women in Arab Muslim Villages." Answers offered, both before and since by social scientists, historians, religious authorities, journalists, travelers, and feminists form an enormous and diverse corpus of materials. I add to it here to present an analysis from the perspective of social biology, which I believe sheds light on some central aspects of the seclusion of women. After a brief description of the forms of female claustration and veiling, I review previous explanations and then propose an explanation in terms of the theory of mating systems. Finally, I will comment on the adequacy of this sociobiological approach to the problem. (A review of some of the historical data is attached as an appendix.)

If women are secluded, veiled, protected, defended, controlled, we must look in explanation either to some value, some valued attribute, possessed by all women, or else to some attribute acquired by claustrated women alone. Claustration either protects a preexisting feminine quality, or it at once creates and maintains such a quality. The latter assumption is the obvious, if unstated, premise from which most explanations proceed: since not all women are so enclosed, both across societies and within societies, therefore the value of individual women varies. Second, admittedly or not, previous investigators are influenced by the testimony of practitioners, from authors of sacred dogma to village informants, and native testimony is overwhelmingly to the effect that what is being protected and controlled is female premarital chastity and marital fidelity. The "attribute" is one that any individual woman may or may not possess, but *only* women may possess. Once we articulate this generally unstated distinction, we note that the socially defined attribute of premarital *virginity* and marital *fidelity* is, in reproductive and physiological fact, not a unitary attribute at all. If veiling covers both these preparous and parous states, we must assume that female purity is a symbolic and social code standing for some unitary phenomenon lying behind these states or dependent upon them as well as for the means by which that phenomenon is produced.

These initial remarks may seem belabored to those who have anticipated my conclusion. I make them to demonstrate the value of close attention to unstated aspects of meaning for anthropologists concerned with unraveling function and to show that such attention may often reveal biological content. Read as metaphor for the facts and strategies of human reproduction, traditional and reli-

Reprinted with permission from R. D. Alexander and D. W. Tinkle (eds.), *Natural selection and social behavior*, pp. 417–38. New York: Chiron Press (1981).

gious justifications for human behavior make surprising good sense. In hindsight it is odd that, perhaps with some psychoanalytic exceptions, these metaphoric communications have gone so long unread. There is clearly an opportunity here for sustained analysis both of customary speech and of other symbolic communications, offering another evidence of the validity of biological perspectives on human behavior.

A GENERAL DEFINITION OF CLAUSTRATION AND VEILLNG

The claustration of women consists of their concealment, beginning at or before puberty in areas easily controlled by their natal or affinal kin, to prevent contact with males who are potential sexual partners, whether strangers or relatives. The *se*clusion of women is in fact the *ex*clusion of men. It must be emphasized, however, that the kin who enforce and maintain claustration are both *female* and male, and that women themselves voluntarily seek seclusion. The human socialization process makes claustration far more a matter of values than of force, values shared by the overwhelming majority of both sexes in the contexts in which it occurs.

Intersexual dining and socializing between adults are tabued, with exceptions in some cases for certain categories of kin, and public religion, especially in its most formal, prestigious aspects, is restricted to men. This segregation encourages the construction of architectural devices from the simplest of curtains or screens to the most elaborate of walled courtyards and recessed women's apartments; it may involve special modes of transportation in enclosed vehicles or palankeens, and the guarding of the women's quarters by nightwatchmen, eunuchs, elderly male, or female servants. Slaves, servants, or male members of the kingroup may take over public chores such as marketing or watercarrying, elsewhere assumed by women.

Seclusion is generally accompanied by forms of veiling, which covers, in increasing intensity, the nape of the neck, the hair and top of the head, the forehead, the chin, the face, and finally the whole body from top to toe, the greatest degree of covering being assumed in public and in the presence of certain categories of males. Veils or other stigma of claustration may be prohibited to women of outcaste status, such as slaves, prostitutes, or professional entertainers. Thus the *Koran* (Surah 34:59, M. M. Pick-

thall trans., my italics): "O prophet! Tell thy wives and thy daughters and the women of the believers to draw their cloaks close round them (when they go abroad). That will be better, *that so they may be recognized and not annoyed*" (cf. deVaux 1967). One function of the veil, then, is to state publicly that a male or males assume responsibility for the woman's reputation, a statement made in less claustrating cultures by other symbols such as the wedding ring.

Extreme forms of claustration result in an ideal of womanhood as unseen and unheard, reflected in strikingly parallel linguistic devices. In Japanese, another's wife is *okusan, okusama*, literally, interior or secluded (honorific), while *oku* is the interior apartments where she ideally dwells (Bacon 1902:254; Nelson 1974). In Arabic, the triliteral *hrm*, gives *hurma*, respectable woman or wife, *haram*, wife, sacred or sanctuary; *harīm* the women's quarters or its occupants; and *harām, s*acred, sin, sacrally prohibited (Antoun 1968). The Nambudiri Brahmins of South India refer to another's wife as *antarjanam*, interior being (Mencher and Goldberg 1967; Yalman 1963): presumably independent evolution of a metonomy has occurred, avoiding direct reference to the woman and emphasizing her ideal condition. Again, these examples (vide Cooper [1915]:122; Kahn 1972:34–37; Sorabji 1908:97; Urquhart 1927:30) suggest the value to sociobiologists of comparative linguistic analyses.

As well as being inculcated through socialization, claustration is supported by customary and formal legal sanctions: penalties for the loss of virginity may be inability to find a husband, rejection by the suitor, or even murder of the girl or her violator by her kinsmen; adulterous wives may suffer similar penalties. Murder of the violated woman or her violator is generally treated with less severity in law than are other homicides, and often with approval in fact. This is the "crime of honor," a concept recognized throughout the Mediterranean basin (Antoun

1968; Peristiany, ed. 1966; Pitt-Rivers, ed. 1963). In claustrating societies, the notions of "honor" and "shame" have as their core social meanings the defense of, and the loss of sexual morality of, the family's women. Each becomes, in Antoun's phrase, a "governing attribute" of one sex:

Although it would be an exaggeration to say that modesty is an exclusive attribute of the female and honor is an exclusive attribute of the male, the idioms translating these concepts into the uses of every day life cluster around the female on the one hand and the male on the other. . . . the woman, particularly the wife and mother, represents the family in its aspects as a moral corporation through her reputation for modesty. The man preserves his honor, in great part, by protecting the modesty of the woman. (Antoun 1968)

And, as Arabic 'ard means both "honor" and "woman,"

the height of immodesty, and thereby the greatest loss of honor, comes with the exposure of that which, above all, must remain protected and hidden, the pudenda. The symbolic unity of honor and modesty in the female genitalia is expressed by the fact that one of the worst insults one man can hurl at another is the phrase "your mother's genitals (kus immak)." (Antoun 1968)

Out of this opposition of male and female sexual roles emerges an extreme duality in the conception of male and female character and in the positive and negative aspects of feminine character as well. Men are assertive, strong, rational, capable of self-control, especially sexual control; women are vulnerable, weak, emotional, uncontrolled, and unreliable, especially sexually. Hence women threaten men as seducers, destroyers of masculine honor, so are typified and deified as temptresses, witches, evil goddesses. Yet as mothers preserving family modesty and honor, they are adored as well: the two Marys are products of a long tradition of at least moderate claustration and concern for feminine sexual purity, with equivalents in other claustrating societies.

It is significant that claustration, where it occurs at all, is always assumed at least by puberty, and that the moment of greatest ritual veiling is the wedding, while young girls and post-menopausal women may enjoy less severe concealment. (Widows, though, where remarriage is discouraged, may symbolize their chastity by rather intense veiling.) Wherever they occur, claustration and veiling are also prestige matters: the higher the socioeconomic status of the family, the greater the intensity of the practice, both as regards degrees of seclusion and of veiling and as regards their duration extending from the centerpoint of puberty toward the termini of birth and death. Women's modesty and the investment of energy into its maintenance become marks of family pride, major indices of public reputation. One example will suffice:

There is a saying [in Northern India] that you can tell the degree of a family's aristocracy by the height of the windows in the home. The higher the rank, the smaller and higher are the windows and the more secluded the women. An ordinary lady may walk in the garden and hear the birds sing and see the flowers. The higher grade lady may only look at them from her windows, and if she is a very great lady indeed, this even is forbidden her, as the windows are high up near the ceiling, merely slits in the wall for the lighting and ventilation of the room. (Cooper [1915]:121)

In those same societies in which we find intense claustration at the top of the social hierarchy, we are likely to find other expressions of concern for female chastity and fidelity at middle levels, namely, clitoridectomy and infibulation, and virginity tests such as the inspection and display of nuptial sheets. The overlap is not total, as these energetically less expensive forms have a wider distribution beyond the bounds of claustrating societies. Similarly correlated with claustration are the practice of early, often prepubertal betrothal and marriage, most common in the upper classes in most cases, and the transfer of wealth (dowry) from the bride's to the groom's family as the major marriage exchange, again an upper class form which is replaced by bride exchange, bride service, and bride price in lower strata. In examining claustration and veiling as here defined, we are focusing upon one end of a continuum of human concern for female sexual morality, milder in many societies but perhaps non-existent in none.

SOME PREVIOUS VIEWS OF THE MATTER

The preceding discussion will serve as a very generalized sketch of the central features of claustration. What explanations have been offered for it? Religious codes mandating the practice often contain both historical and functional explanations. Understandably, adherents of a religion assume the date of promulgation of their sacred laws as the origin of the practice, as most Muslims assume that purdah was created by the Prophet. Religious traditions may be justified not only by the divinity of their commands but by origin tales as well, as the *Koran* is accompanied by folk traditions (Hadith), expressing in personalistic terms the motivations of the "inventor." Masculine sexual jealousy is a common component of such origin tales. An equally common theme is the fear of stranger males, especially conquerors. In North India, where the most intense Indian forms of claustration occurred, the folk explanation commonly repeated by travelers, journalists, and even some anthropologists is that claustration either appeared or became widespread at the time of the Muslim conquest to protect wives and daughters of high status from rape and kidnap. Two embarrassing North Indian customs may be simultaneously justified: since "Islam forbids abduction of married women as slaves or concubines," so child marriage became common, but because Muslims then broke the law and began to abduct married women, therefore claustration was resorted to (Hauswirth 1932:64–65; cf. Cormack 1953:67). The recurrent themes of folk explanation are obviously not irrelevant to a biological analysis. They appear in even clearer form in some functional explanations provided by sacred dogma itself:

Men are in charge of women, because Allah hath made the one of them to excel the other, and *because they spend of their property (for the support of women)*. So good women are the obedient, guarding in secret that which Allah hath guarded. (*Koran*, Surah 4:34; M. M. Pickthall, trans., my italics)

Here is an overt recognition of the relation between masculine control over female sexuality and male investment of effort in offspring: an aspect of the phenomenon that has previously gone unnoticed by social scientists, so far as I can discover.

Other modern, secular explanations have been proposed besides those derived from folklore. Unilinear cultural evolutionist theory, deriving ultimately from Morgan and his contemporaries, is by no means out of fashion.

Engels, rejecting religious explanations, saw the development of the modern family as part of the "world historical defeat of the female sex" (1942:51). The transition from group marriage and matriarchy to polygynous and monogamous forms retained sexual freedom for men but denied it to women. This theory of early matriarchy and feminine devolution is popular in current feminist writing: it is the product of overgeneralization from scanty signs of early feminine authority, such as the occasional queen, confusion of the queen's role as regent of her infant son with independent power, and the overextension of royal statuses to other classes. (For examples and discussion see Lacey 1968:194–216; Pomeroy 1975:35ff. on Greece, especially Sparta and Crete; Grimal 1965 on Pharaonic Egypt; Pharr 1977 but Sansom 1936:28–29 on Japan.) Yet, to dismiss this evolutionary view entirely is also an oversimplification. If early matriarchy is mythical, still there is historical evidence for an increase in the intensity of claustration over time, corollary to significant declines in female control over property and legal and inheritance rights and to an increase in patrilineality, patrilocality, and unigeniture in the pre-industrial agrarian states of the Islamic Near East, South Asia, and the Far East. Unjustified is the projection backward from early patriliny to a non-existent matriarchal stage, as is the assumption that this historical change in the social relations of the sexes represents an inevitable unidirectional evolutionary process. In any case, unilineal evolutionary "theories" are not theories at all, but merely descriptive generalizations providing no causal explanation for the presumed progression through time.

Economic explanations focus on the status-grading of claustration as an example of "conspicuous" (or inconspicuous?) "consumption," yet fail to specify why these behaviors should be chosen for status display. Diffusionists, likewise, avoid functional explanation, appealing to some inevitable process of borrowing. Their works have, however, the virtue of revealing the antiquity and extensive distribution of the practice. One classic psychosocial analysis is Murphy's (1964) discussion of the masculine face-veiling of the Saharan Tuareg. I will not explore that case here, but note in passing that Tuareg males, though veiled, are never claustrated, and that Tuareg women engage in moderate status-graded veiling. Murphy's Tuareg do call our attention to the universal ethological substrate of veiling, the tendency of both sexes to cover the mouth and face in contexts of modesty, humility, and shame, even of intense emotion. There seems a parallel tendency to cover the head as a symbol of subordinacy. Although Leach (1958) has called attention to the magic of hair, I know of no general ethological analysis of these universal and probably genetic bases out of which the specific forms of veiling everywhere arise. Why, after all, should female sexuality be associated with the head and face? – *beauty*

The approaches to the problem summarized above are non-comparable, referring as they do to different aspects of the practice, its origin, and its local forms. It should be noted that none of them provides a causal hypothesis for the repeated appearance of this phenomenon in human history, in what must be to some degree independent historical contexts. It is, however, in the specifically functional analyses of social anthropologists that we see the social scientist grappling most directly with the sexual content of the custom emphasized above. I comment briefly on two classic analyses, those of Yalman (1963) and Antoun (1968), from which I have already quoted.

Yalman sought to explain not claustration and veiling but some South Indian female puberty ceremonies and the associated obsession with feminine sexual purity. He sees the concern for female sexuality as a means of maintaining caste purity in a content of hypergynous marriage systems. A few quotations will represent his views:

Thus the sexuality of men receives a generous *carte blanche*. But it always matters what the women do: (a) They may have sexual relations with superior and "pure" men. No harm comes to them in terms of purity. (b) They may have children from "pure" men; or from men of their own caste.

But, if they engage in sexual relations with men lower than themselves, then they get "internally" polluted. Moreover, they bear "polluted" children.

. . . It is clear that these rules of hypergamy are directly associated with systems in which membership in the group is acquired through both parents, but where the purity of the group is protected through women. . . . Hence, even though caste membership derives through both parents, there is a built-in asymmetry in all these systems.

. . . We are now in a position to understand the overwhelming interest in the sexuality of women rather than men. It is through women (and not men) that the "purity" of the caste-community is ensured and preserved. It is mainly through the women of the group (for the men may be of higher castes) that blood and purity is perpetuated. (Yalman 1963:42–43).

Yet this analysis fails to explain *why* purity is linked to hypergyny, let alone why hypergyny, with its peculiar inconsistency in approved male and female marriage patterns, exists. Further, Yalman's limitation of his analysis to caste societies denies its general applicability. As he concludes, "I certainly do not claim that customs concerning female purity must always be traced to caste. . . . There may be many reasons why certain societies single out the purity of women for attention." Yet, given this admission of inadequacy, there are some important perceptions in his analysis. These are the recognition that, in some way, paternity is involved, that female purity concerns are linked to hypergyny, and that there is a covert system of "inheritance of purity" operating through females even in societies whose formal descent systems are patrilineal. All of these are important components of a sociobiological analysis of claustration and its concomitant, female modesty.

In attempting to analyze Middle Eastern female sexual modesty, Antoun (1968) is no more definitive. He appeals to the interaction between Redfieldian "great" and "little" traditions (an essentially diffusionist position) and to the force of sacred dogma, confessing uncertainty regarding the historical origins of Near Eastern claustration. Reviewing a variety of local village cases in which the ideals of feminine purity are in conflict with other social norms, he identifies the differing commitments to the ideal on the part of differing social statuses and of the two sexes. Ultimately, he rejects the concern for blood paternity as an explanatory factor, because he feels the Islamic legal code, with its recognition of fictional paternity, offers contrary evidence. He retreats finally to the "logic of the beliefs themselves," that is, a historical justification of normative behaviors on the basis of pre-existing ideology regarding the attributes of men and women.

Like Yalman, Antoun points to the correlation of claustration and the ideology of feminine purity with other cultural traits: patriliny, child betrothal, and so forth. Neither list of correlates warrants repetition here, as each is based on a single cultural region, hence is in large part demonstrably false. Antoun's conclusion is as pessimistic as Yalman's. He confesses to having examined "various historical, psychological, and structural explanations for the persistence of the modesty code.... No single explanation was regarded as satisfactory." (For another critique of Antoun and Yalman, and a review of other theories, see Jacobson 1973:200–226.)

I have dwelt this long on previous views not merely to emphasize the weaknesses of social scientific approaches but to highlight two central qualities of their failure. Both of these authors are at pains to resolve apparent conflicts between behavior, ideology, and law. Thus, in the Near East, religion speaks clearly of paternity concerns, yet the law allows loopholes for adoption; observed social events appear to be products of a complex mixture of economic, political, and ideological motives, compromising stated principles. The analysts are likewise unable to choose between theories of origin and theories of maintenance, between ultimate and proximal causes. What is at issue here is the assignment of priorities to events in generating explanatory theories, the weighting of the significance of specific events on some basis other than mere frequency. In short, what is absent is a general theoretical framework that discriminates ultimate (phylogenetic) from proximate (ontogenetic) aspects, which is expressed in probabilistic terms, and which recognizes multiple causation.

Secondly, it is clear that these authors, like others venturing into the same area, find themselves continually confronted with the matter of sexuality. Yet each author ultimately rejects the facts of reproduction as analytically central and retreats in defeat. Again, what is lacking is a theoretical framework that makes sense of the obsession with female sexuality. It is precisely these capacities Darwinian theory offers.

The elemental puzzle for all commentators is indeed even more paradoxical than either Yalman or Antoun expresses. It is not just that there is "such interest in the sexuality of women rather than men" that confuses. It is that *female* sexuality and sexual purity, *not male*, is a concern of *men*, and indeed it is so in systems characterized by an overriding emphasis on masculine superiority, masculine authority and control, masculine alliance inheritance, and descent. This is the core paradox that only a theory of mating systems can unravel, illuminating at once the confusion of the anthropologist and the certainties of the *Koran*.

PROBABILITY OF PATERNITY AND DOWRY COMPETITION: A HYPOTHESIS

I have noted that folk and religious traditions about claustration often appear to refer to paternity concerns and that anthropologists likewise have repeatedly found themselves considering paternity as a possible source of the practice. I turn now to the biological literature on "confidence of paternity" or more accurately, probability of paternity, to make sense of the human phenomenon.

Concern for paternity is a consequence of the greater uncertainty of parenthood that males experience especially when fertilization occurs within the female body, while females do not experience such doubt. In these situations, specific mechanisms may evolve as a result of intrasexual competition to increase the inseminating male's probability of paternity, guaranteeing that the energy invested in searching and courtship was not wasted. A variety of such mechanisms occurs in vertebrates and invertebrates, including pre- and post-copulatory guarding of the female, attempts to determine her "virginity" prior to copulation, methods, either behavioral or pheromonic, of inducing receptivity or estrus in the female to increase the likelihood of fertilization, postcopulatory blocks or plugs to prevent inseminations by subsequent males, and finally, behavioral or pheromonic means of aborting or destroying a preexisting zygote or infant of the female that was sired by another male. These devices occur in organisms as diverse as flies and grasshoppers, ducks and doves, mice and langur monkeys (for a review of the literature see Dickemann [1978a]). Before suggesting how this body of data may relate to the human species, I call attention to some general attributes of human mating systems, that will suggest what kinds of probability of paternity mechanisms we might expect in our species and in what contexts (for theory of mating systems, see Campbell, ed. 1972; Emlen and Oring 1977; Orians 1969; Wilson 1975:314–335).

As in other mammals, human males compete for access to females, experiencing greater variance in reproductive success than the latter. Their lesser physiological investment in sperm production should mean that they are facultatively polygynous. Reliance on internal fertilization results in masculine uncertainty of parenthood. In addition, low efficiency of sperm utilization, low sperm viability, and random mixing of ejaculates in the inseminated female all result in low probability of conception both for each insemination and for each male (Bailey [1977]; Nag 1972). Hence multiple matings are advantageous to the male whether or not he has sole access to the female.

These considerations are aggravated by the design of the human ovulatory cycle: an absence of seasonality, general asynchrony of females, and the recurrence of ovulation at relatively short intervals make guarding of the female between cycles immensely more rewarding to the male who has the capacity to do so than mere sperm competition through repeated copulations. In addition, long pre- and postnatal female parental effort, especially where lactation may extend up to three years or more and the investment of all this effort in only a single offspring at a time must intensify competition between males not only for access to but for control over females, especially those in pre-conception status. Both the value of each offspring and the level of female investment are high: therefore, the ratio of benefit to cost is high. Almost four years of maternal effort (not including subsequent socialization) may be gained by a single male for his own offspring if he can pay whatever costs are involved in controlling (herding) the female for a month. We should anticipate, then, both pre- and post-copulatory guarding of females to increase probability of paternity through the exclusion of other males and probability of fertilization through repeated copulations.

The degree of investment of energy in confidence of paternity devices should be correlated with the degree to which mating is promiscuous or "bonded." Bonding means fundamentally the intention or existence of male parental care, and human matings are often characterized by significant amounts of male parental care. This effort is more variable than that of the female, being dependent upon the ecological opportunities and consequent social

structure of the specific breeding unit. Nevertheless, some paternal contribution, some specifically economic investment is universal in human societies, although it is not universal as regards individual reproducing males. We should expect, then, that Trivers' 1972 prediction would hold for humans: *ceteris paribus*, males who invest more heavily in their offspring should show greater concern for paternal confidence. Trivers restricted his prediction to monogamous males. But this is an artifact of the association between monogamy and paternal care in those species from which he induced his generalization. The human species teaches us that monogamy and paternal care are by no means necessarily associated.

If the above is true, then all human males should show some desire to control the fidelity of their mates even during casual liaisons, and this concern should increase in intensity and duration as the male's investment in his offspring (direct and indirect) increases. I do not review the data for the first assertion here, but I believe it can be shown to be reasonable: sexual jealousy is probably universal in human males, and attempts to control female sexual fidelity are by no means absent from even those societies and subcultures that involve a good deal of female promiscuity and short-term sexual liaisons (see Dickemann [1978]). They are, however, milder than the forms we are considering here.

The importance of male parental care depends upon another and more distinctive human attribute that plays a role in defining the character of confidence of paternity mechanisms, and that is the nature of the human breeding unit, a subject of much sociological disputation and confusion. Whether we call it a "domestic group," a "family," or whatever, the human unit is characterized by extreme variability in size and structure, that is, a capacity to expand into extended corporations usually associated with territory and based on ties of inclusive fitness or to contract to the minimal mother-infant pair. Where they are feasible, nepotistic extensions of the parenting unit enormously increase the capacity for energy investment in care of the young. It is their existence that makes possible the unusual simultaneous occurrence of intense male parental care and high levels of polygyny in some human groups.

But we may go much further than this. The precise cultural definition of group membership

OP. SEX RATIO

and expected degrees of kin investment of which our species is capable (i.e., kinship systems) make possible cooperation in much more than merely the care and socialization of the young. Human kin groups may take over the competitive searching and courtship roles of the mating pair: they *breed* their members as they breed their cows and camels. It should not surprise us to find that this ready-made organization would also assume responsibility for the control of paternal probability for members in whom they have nepotistic interest. These transfers of function are, I would guess, unique attributes of the human species and seem to me to be striking testimonials to the significance of inclusive fitness in our species.

The basic motivation for the formation of such groups seems to be the necessity to control and defend the means of production in competition against other breeding units. If such a competitive context is sufficient for the evolution of kin altruism in the care of the young, another requirement must prevail in order for polygyny to evolve simultaneously with extended parental care, since polygyny, in a species with a sex ratio near 50–50, must depend on some significant distortion of reproductive access. Biological theory tells us (Orians 1969; Verner and Willson 1966; Wilson 1975:327 ff.) that polygyny will occur where differences in resource access of males (or their families) are sufficient that a female gains more from association with an already-mated male than from association with an unmated male in a less reproductively advantageous environment. Extreme variance in masculine access to those environmental resources necessary for reproductive success is, of course, the hallmark of preindustrial stratified human societies. As competition produces increasing differences between families in access to and control over the primary means of production, variance in male *RS* increases by extension at both ends of the spectrum: while the rich get richer and more politically powerful, poorer males are excluded partially or totally from breeding, not only through the negative survival effects of poverty per se but through higher rates of mortality from warfare and homicide and through incarceration, exile, and castration. Thus the increasing intensity of social stratification increases the benefit to a female of matings with high-status males, that is, hypergyny. The excess of the *to-*

tality of females over the number of *high-status* males, in a pyramidally stratified society, makes harem polygyny possible (cf. Trivers and Willard 1973; Alexander 1974). And since kin groups, as we have seen, have already developed kin-inclusive forms of childcare, it is natural that their inclusive fitness interests, in a situation of intense competition for high-status mates, should produce hypergynous competition between families that control the courtship and mating of their sisters and daughters.

This may seem a long digression from claustration. Yet it is precisely those societies with the greatest extremes between the rich and poor, in which court and palace enjoy unimagined luxury while the masses live on a level always close to starvation, in which large numbers of beggars, outcasts, floater males, and celibates exist at the bottom while intense polygyny in the form of secondary wives, concubines, and harems occurs at the top that the most extreme forms of claustration, veiling, and incapacitation of women occur. And, as was noted, it is at the top that these forms of control are most intense.

It may at first appear senseless, to those familiar with the female supply networks that existed in these societies, that families should compete for matings of their women with high-status males. In all these claustrating societies, elaborate and often institutionalized systems evolved for the capture of women in warfare, the kidnapping and sale of wives and infants of the very poor, and their transmission through trade networks into the harems of the wealthy and the brothels that served them. This apparent contradiction is resolved by attention to the forms of mating involved. High-status men enjoyed not only promiscuous mating (many kings or lords, for example, having legal access to all subordinate women in their domains) but harem concubinage, while simultaneously holding several secondary wives and a single primary wife. These statuses are clearly distinguished in the linguistic and legal taxonomies of the cultures: the essential difference is the degree of paternal effort promised or given. Thus it is not at all irrational that families, insofar as they were able, should compete to place their daughters in association with upper-level males, regardless of the flood of other females filling their harems. What these families strove for was not merely sexual access to the preferred male's genes but the commitment of significant paternal care to the female and her offspring, including ultimately bequeathal of goods and political preferment to her descendants, which the preferred statuses of concubine and wife denote. For the very poor, placement of a daughter in the king's harem would surely increase her chances for survival and reproductive success over her peers who remained at the lowest levels of society; even she, like her sister in the brothel, might if fortunate find herself chosen as favorite and elevated to the status of preferred concubine or of wife, and her son, in consequence, polygynously powerful. But for the wealthy family, the goal was acceptance of their daughter as a stable primary or secondary consort whose probability of reproductive success was far greater.

Before demonstrating how this competition operated in cultural terms, I would like to underline some of the biologically peculiar, but nevertheless predictable, consequences of this intense mating competition in a stratified context. In a society with high male mortality and reproductive variance, parents should regard their bearing and rearing of boys as a high-risk, high-benefit strategy, and the rearing of girls as of lower risk but lower gain (cf. Trivers 1972; Hartung 1976). Female offspring give more reliability of genetic survival but less competitive advantage. However, this proposition presumes that offspring of both sexes operate within the same ecological context, i.e., under the same environmental determinants of mortality and reproduction. But where socioeconomic conditions of the offspring differ, then the relative value of each sex differs: thus in the hypergynous context under discussion, the proposition is reversed. With a hypergynous mating, a female offspring may convert her own physiologically lower RS into the higher RS of sons (grandsons of her strategy-designing parents). Further, the hypergynous female's advantage includes the probability that her own female offspring may make further hypergynous matings into a yet higher RS stratum. Thus, the rearing of females becomes a long-term rather than a short-term strategy (dependent upon the human cognitive capacity for long-range planning). But it is a high-risk, as well as high-benefit strategy, since the social pyramid has fewer and fewer grooms at the top, and the hypergynous society many suppliant brides. In-

deed it is in these situations that the risk may outweigh any possible benefit, and large numbers of females remain celibate or are removed by infanticide in the topmost strata (Alexander 1974; Dickemann 1979b).

The obverse of this biologically peculiar but predictable situation is that the competition for high-status grooms, associated with scarce reproductive resources, defines those grooms as the scarce, valuable sex, hence courted rather than courting, more selective than their mates (cf. Trivers 1972:153; Dawkins 1976:177–78). Desirable high-status grooms, or more exactly their kin groups, can now exact specific requirements from the suppliant family in exchange for the proffered bride. And they do exact a high price, in addition to her physical attractiveness, good health, and intelligence.

This brings us to the specific cultural form of this contest for grooms, and to the final ingredient in this analysis of claustration. The most visible and most widely discussed of these exactions is the dowry, defined here as any net economic benefit to the groom and his family transmitted in exchange from the bride's family. Dowry competition is the human, social structural, expression of the Verner-Willson-Orians effect in a context of regular kin altruism. At a minimum, in the lowest (land-associated) levels engaged in hypergynous competition or in less intensely stratified societies, dowry consists of a trousseau, a tangible piece of capital investment in the future household, materials, and machinery of lifelong worth for the mated pair and their young. The more wealthy may greatly enlarge the trousseau to include extensive furniture, clothing, heirlooms and jewelry, slave girls, and servants. It is the trousseau that is displayed in procession to the groom's residence, informing the community at large of the economic status of the bride's kingroup. At higher levels, dowry will include a monetary payment, often very large, and sometimes livestock and land as well. Whole provinces with their attached dependents, as we know, were the dowries of queens. In addition, in situations of intense competition, the dowry is accompanied by lifelong obligations of support and repetitive gift-giving from the bride's to the groom's family.

This is not the place for an extended analysis of dowry systems. Let me assert however that underneath the often deceptive folk terminologies and the frequent lack of accord between legal systems and customary behavior, I am convinced that it can be demonstrated that in all these societies there was a gradual transition from the net payment of bridewealth in the lowest classes, where the poor paid to acquire reproductively more valuable females, through transitional forms of exchange of equal value, to the payment of dowry or groomwealth at the top, where, as we have seen, association with higher-status grooms was bought. What this suggests is that, if the data could be obtained, a quantitative expression of the relation between the economics of marriage exchange and the probably relative RS of each sex at each level of society could be made.

If the desirable groom exacts a monetary price, he exacts as well something less tangible if no less public. In exchange for the promise of paternal investment of the resources of his higher-status household in the bride and her future offspring, his breeding unit demands a guarantee of high probability of paternity, insofar as it can be assured by the bride's kin. This, I believe, is a component of dowry competition heretofore neglected by most anthropologists. We can now understand why the most intense symbolic statement of female chastity-fidelity, one that persists even in societies and families that have little claim to the genuine article, is the bridal veil: a symbolic *bona fides*, true or deceitful, made at the moment of transfer of the woman from her own family to the groom's. We can understand as well the masculine obsession with feminine virginity, apparently characteristic of all stratified societies, seemingly so irrationally focussed on such an infinitesimal number of copulations. And most importantly, we can now see why claustration and veiling are universally status-graded. The higher the groom's status, the greater the degree of paternal investment of effort into his offspring, the greater the groom's demand for probability of paternity, the greater the competition between bridal families to demonstrate and assure confidence of paternity to future grooms.

Of what does this assurance consist? Of a good deal more than virginity at marriage, as will be seen. But first, let me propose that tests of virginity are not 100 per cent reliable, either because of variations in the morphology of the hymen, or its possible non-sexual rupture, or

the kin-altruistic machinations of experienced ladies in the bride's kingroup. Consequently these tests are relied upon only by those, in the middle strata of society, for whom cost-benefit ratios do not warrant any very great energetic investment in confidence of paternity. Where the investment is warranted, much more reliable methods, namely claustration, veiling, and incapacitation, are preferred.

These forms at once control the woman's freedom to engage in sexual activity of her own choosing and at the same time hide her from the gaze and even knowledge of any males who might be tempted to seek or to force copulations with her. I have not attempted here to unravel the difficult puzzle of the relative contributions of these two sources of danger in the evolution of claustration. On the one hand, ideological emphasis on female sexuality would lead one to suspect that women are largely at fault. So would the incapacitation of footbinding. But this may be partly masculine projection. I think it is important to recall that the societies we are examining were characterized not only by arbitrary sexual rights of lords and rulers but by large numbers of masculine floaters and promiscuous semi-floaters, beggars, bandits, outlaws, kidnappers, militia, and resentful slaves and serfs. "Out of sight, out of mind" was probably a sensible proposition for a high-status family in such a society.

I noted finally that the concept of feminine purity conflates premarital chastity and lifelong marital fidelity. To insure the latter, a woman must be more than guarded, she must be socialized to value feminine modesty, to submit to the goals and demands of her future husband and his kin, to maintain the honor of his family, and finally to socialize her own daughters into the ideology of female purity. This is what the public reputation of the bride's family and the formal symbolic displays are intended to attest. Hence a covert, but critical element in dowry competition is a competition to produce and make credible the ability to produce women of modesty. Thus it is that in the highest status groups, girls enter claustration long before menarche, and women continue in it long after menopause. Thus the dual definition of family honor that we have noted in these societies; for men, honor is the capacity and willingness to defend and enforce the purity of their female kin, which allows them to achieve reproductively successful matings for their daughters and sisters; for women, it is the possession of that which is defended, chastity and fidelity, sexual morality itself. The core of a family's honor is its ability to produce such women.

Again, let me point to some peculiarities of this situation. The emphasis on competition in the mating of females means that in these largely patrilineal groups, kin-inclusive fitness based on genetic relationships to daughters and sisters may be equally or more important to males than their own direct fitness. This is understandable in societies with high masculine mortalities, but it warns us that the overt forms of kinship and inheritance may be misleading as guides to reproductive strategies. (This is, of course, what Yalman was suggesting.) Concomitantly, we are analyzing societies in which masculine upward mobility, achieved through economic or political means, is rare and impermanent. Through dowry competition, the major means of upward mobility, and hence the major upward gene flow, is achieved by women, a point which I believe has gone unnoticed till now. Is there another such peculiar species, in which groups of genetic relatives engage, through manipulation of their females, in confidence-of-paternity competition?

SUMMARY AND CONCLUSIONS

I want to be clear that this very general theory of claustration has not explained many of the specifics of the practice as it appears in various times and places. I have not dealt with the local and regional variations nor the varying degrees to which the practice obtrudes downward into the lower classes. Nor have I dealt with the variation in forms that may be correlated with differing systems of exogamy and endogamy (for India, see Jacobson 1973:187–99, 482–98; 508–31). Nor such unusual phenomena as the masculine veiling of Tuareg nor the husband-wife avoidance that seems inevitably to evolve in conditions of intense claustration. Nor have I attempted here to elaborate in ecological terms exactly why some societies have evolved intense claustration and others only milder forms nor the fate of these practices in industrial societies though I believe that biologists familiar with the literature on mating systems and especially polygyny can read some of that between the lines.

Nevertheless, this analysis does explain the universal features of the phenomenon, both behavioral and ideological: the conjunction of virginity and fidelity, the double standard and dual code of honor, and the status-grading of the intensity of claustration, while illuminating some previously unidentified aspects of dowry competition. This hypothesis may have even more functional significance for our attempt to develop a theory of human biology if, as I believe, we have here a case of direct economic acquisition of reproductive success. In general, the ethnographic sources that I have used give very little indication that the dowry-producing family gains any reciprocal benefit from its time and energy investment, in the form of economic or political favors. Indeed, in the most extreme cases, as in Northern India, the subordinacy of the bride-giving family and the one-way, upward flow of economic value, are strongly emphasized. If this is so, then the transaction we have been analyzing cannot be reduced to purely economic or political terms. I have proposed that the bride's family, in exchange for dowry gifts and other economic obligations and for its guarantee of paternal confidence to the groom, *is purchasing increased probable RS*, for itself (inclusively), for its daughter and most directly for her as-yet unborn sons. We have here a clear case of the necessity, in Marvin Harris' (1975) words, to conjoin, in our analyses of human behavior, the "mode of reproduction" with the "mode of production," in short, to attend to Darwinian theory.

Darwinian theory does, I think I have shown, allow us to answer the initial question: "Why is there such interest in the sexuality of women rather than men?" "Why the emphasis on the bodily modesty of women, their seclusion, their chastity, their sexuality . . . their protection, and their control?" As the *Koran* had already told us, "Men are in charge of women . . . because they spend of their property for the support of women. So good women are obedient, guarding in secret that which Allah hath guarded."

APPENDIX A: A NOTE ON FOOTBINDING

Footbinding, which was invented sometime from the late Tang to early Sung Dynasty, spread during the subsequent Sung and Yüan and had become general by the Ming Dynasty

(1368–1644 A.D.). While some more psychologically oriented authors, van Gulik (1974) among them, deny its function as a claustrating device, focusing only on the erotic and esthetic connotations that it acquired, most social scientists and many Chinese authors are explicit that it was a means of restricting movement. Thus Lang (1946:45–46) asserts: "Whatever the origin, the purpose was clear. Bound feet kept women at home, made them safer, less movable property. . . . *Nu Erh Ching*, one of the numerous book about virtuous women, is . . . explicit: 'Feet are bound, not to make them beautiful as a curved bow, but to restrain women when they go outdoors.' " The intensity of footbinding varied both by region and by status, in precisely the same manner as do other forms of claustration. The very wealthy woman strove for a foot so small that "the longest walk she would take was from one room to the next, and she was obliged to sit down after walking a few steps on her marble floors. I have seen those whose feet were but two inches long upon the sole... Only the very rich can afford to be so helpless as such feet render their possessor, and there are not many who are very rich" (Fielde 1887:30). When moving short distances, these women leaned on a cane or a servant or were carried on the backs of natural-footed female slaves. Middle-class women were able to walk four or five miles a day (Fielde 1887:30). Among the poor, there was greater variation, both in the presence and absence of binding and its degree. The urban poor were more likely to be bound-footed than rural women, as is true of other forms of claustration as well. Perhaps most village women were large-footed, many of them merely wrapping their feet tightly to resemble the true deformation when going to town or festival or during their wedding ceremonies. Others began footbinding later than the higher-status woman, thus producing a larger, though nevertheless deformed foot. In the north of China, however, rural women had bound feet sufficiently crippled that it was necessary for them to do agricultural labor on their knees (Davin 1975; Nevius 1869:201–3).

The practice was variable in regard to prostitutes and courtesans, though it seems that a bound-footed courtesan was more desirable (Fielde 1887:31; Lang 1946:45–46; Nevius 1869:201–3). Slaves generally were natural-footed, as were Hakka women, and the outcaste "beggar" women of Kiangsu and Anhui were expressly forbidden to engage in the practice (Ch'ü 1965:130). By Ch'ing Dynasty, footbinding had reached its greatest extent and intensity: one Chinese historian referred to the period as "the age of small feet fools" (Ropp 1976:5–6). In spite of the fact that footbinding focuses upon the opposite ends of the human body than that involved in veiling, these parallels with other forms of control, both in evolution and in distribution, lead to the conclusion that it is a claustrating device. It appears less unique if placed in the context of other attempts to incapacitate through the modification of feminine shoes, such as the high geta of the Japanese courtesan or the high heel of the incapacitated modern Western woman.

APPENDIX B: BRIEF OVERVIEW OF OLD WORLD CLAUSTRATION, INCAPACITATION, AND VEILING

While there is no space here for a thorough presentation of the distribution and evolution of these customs, a brief review of some of the historical data may give some sense of the descriptive data involved. Some degree of control and claustration of women appears almost with the appearance of civilization, though it is difficult to determine its precise nature. Although many authorities agree that women's legal and political status was higher during the Old Babylonian period than subsequently (Batto 1974; Harris 1966; Oppenheim 1964:77), nevertheless, harems and concubinage existed, at least for kings, in addition to the queen and secondary wives (Batto 1974). Batto believes he may have discovered, in analysis of documents from Mari, the earliest reference to veiling (Batto 1974:39). This society shows other familiar aspects of the pattern: legal documents reveal demand for virginity and virginity tests, at marriage: the Code of Hammurapi imposed the death penalty for a girl who was unchaste while still in her father's house. Dowry competition also existed among the wealthy: excess daughters of kings, nobles and the upper merchant class were sent with dowry and other financial support into religious establishments as lifelong celibates (Batto 1974; Harris 1964). By middle Assyrian times, there is clear record of veiling in legal documents that required that wives and daughters of free men cover their heads when outside, but prohibited prostitutes, temple slaves, and servants from doing so. The first certain record of eunuchs employed to guard harems appears here (Oppenheim 1964:104). But nothing is known of the life of women of lower status, other than their appearance as slaves in private households, as harem servants, and as serfs and weavers attached to temple and palace. Some were war captives, but others were sold into slavery as wives and children of debtors or famine victims (Batto 1974:28; Crawford 1973; Oppenheim 1964:75–76, 96–97, 107). Other scattered evidence of veiling can be found in later periods: a study of surviving art would uncover more. Thus, the Kouyunjik reliefs of Sennacherib (705–681 B.C.) depicting the flight of Luli from Phoenician Tyre, show women with heads completely covered except for the face (Harden 1963:124, 132, Plate 50). Biblical veiling is something of a conundrum too. Women traveled with their faces uncovered, but Rebecca veiled herself on first meeting her betrothed (Genesis 24:65) and both the veil and latticed windows appear in Canticles (2:9, 5:7). But emphasis on female virginity is clear: the nuptial cloth was used as legal evidence and the unchaste bride was stoned to death (Deuteronomy 22:13–21). Whatever the situation at this time, veiling became common in postbiblical Judaism as the Mishnah (ca. 200 A.D.) describes Persian and Arabic women veiling during the Sabbath.

I have mentioned the latticed window: architectural history can yield important clues to claustration. By biblical times, both styles of claustrating architecture are present: the second storey with narrow or latticed windows, the common Phoenician (Harden 1963:132, pl. 61) and biblical (Judges 5:28; 2 Kings 9:30) form, and the walled or interior courtyard, probably represented by an early house model from Babylonian Mari (Mallowan 1965:85).

I do not review Egyptian materials here, but Vercoutter's (1965) careful analysis suggests that its reputation for matriliny and feminine freedom may be undeserved. Greek history also seems to involve claustration from Mycenean to Classical times, though there are great difficulties in the interpretation of Homeric and non-Athenian materials. Pomeroy (1975:35–42) maintains that the legal codes of Sparta, Cretan

Gortyn, and Athens reveal a chronological decline in the legal status of women. Homeric epics depict women as modest, chaste, traveling in public with escorts, apparently unveiled. Many secondary wives and concubines appear and female slaves captured in war (Lacey 1968:39–47; Pomeroy 1975:18–31). Classical Athenian forms, after the seventh century B.C., are clearer though there is still much dispute about details. The respectable Athenian woman was moderately veiled. A head veil, *xalyptra*, was rarely worn, instead a fold of the outer garment (*himation*) was brought over the head, and if occasion demanded, across the face, thus producing a favorite gesture of classical sculptors, the raised hand with drapery of the modest girl. But high-status women rarely left their homes: when they did they might be escorted by a servant carrying a parasol, but they relied on slaves to run errands, carry water and do other external chores and were excluded from most public events except religious festivals, almost certainly from the theater and games. The upper-status ideal was that the free woman be seen only by closely related men; the women's quarters (*gynecea*) consisted of rooms either at the rear of the house or in the upper storey. Wealthy country landowners might have walled gardens. Older women had some slight increase in freedom, but only the poor were seen regularly outside the house, in retail trade, small manufactures, going to wet-nurse, and in the country doing agricultural labor (deVaux 1967; Lacey 1968:138, 168–171, 175; Pomeroy 1975:78 ff., 238; Seltman 1957:94, 97). Polygyny occurred, but large harems do not seem to have been common nor were eunuchs used. Prostitution was of all grades from street prostitution to the well-known *hetaira* (Licht 1969:296ff.). These women were foreigners, slaves, girls too poor to marry, or the illegitimate offspring of slave girls and their owners. The rest of the pattern is familiar: dowry competition was intense in the upper classes, virginity highly valued and adultery severely punished, and the ideological definition of woman as merely vessel for her husband's seed, dependent upon father, brother and sons was predictably present (Flaceliere 1962:101–61; Lacey 1968 passim; Levy 1963; Pomeroy 1975 passim). Aristotle himself recognized a correlation between claustration and political structure: "A magistracy which controls the boys or the women . . . is suited to an aristocracy rather than to a democracy; for how can the magistrates prevent the wives of the poor from going out of doors? Neither is it an oligarchical office: for the wives of the oligarchs are too fine to be controlled" (*Politics*, Book 4 Chap. 15:1229–30).

Improvement in female freedom is said to have occurred during the Hellenistic period, but I have not reviewed the literature on this or on Roman and Byzantine periods. By Christian times, the face veil had been adopted by Jews, Christians, and Arabs at least in some communities in Greece, Yemen, and elsewhere. Arabs employed a veil covering all but the eyes, and their women traveled in covered camel-borne litters (deVaux 1967).

The evolution of Islamic claustration and veiling is again a matter of dispute among scholars, conservative religious scholars tending to regard them as unchanged since the time of the Prophet, and modernizing scholars in favor of relaxation proposing that extreme forms are not truly Islamic but developed or diffused as a later date. However, the evidence reviewed above and the *Koran* itself make clear that veiling was a common practice of respectable women (cf. von Grunebaum 1954:174). The less severe claustration of early Islam may merely reflect the middle rather than the upper-class origins of the sect; however, women were originally educated, prayed in the mosque with men and had some public authority. Nor is there any clear early evidence for the totally concealing modern *burka*. Harem claustration appeared with the first Ummayyad Caliphs (Walid II, 473–4 A.D.) as did eunuch guards, apparently copied from Byzantium (Hitti 1953:228–29; Khan 1972:31). Some authorities maintain complete claustration of respectable women had developed by the time of Harun al-Rashid (786–809 A.D.) (Levy 1957:125–31). Learning, like singing and dancing, became appropriate only to concubines and courtesans (Hitti 1953:342). Hitti (1953:333) dates full claustration a little later, in the tenth century. The influence of Byzantium and Persia, the latter especially at the Abbasid court, is noted by most authorities. By the mid–thirteenth century, in any case, claustration was entrenched and intense: Islamic scholars debated whether female hands and feet could be seen in public, while veiling, at least in Persia, was forbidden to

slaves and other women of low status (deVaux 1967; Khan 1972:26–34; von Grunebaum 1954:155–56, 174–75; Yarshater 1967). (Khan supports his reconstruction with architectural evidence, but more can be done here.)

Other aspects of the pattern are more or less clear. Patrilineal emphasis in inheritance had developed by the middle Abbasids (Khan 1972:50, footnote); by the eighteenth and nineteenth centuries women of middle and upper status regularly sacrificed their inheritance rights, guaranteed them by the *Koran*, to their brothers (Levy 1957:244–46; Rosenfeld 1958, 1960; Yarshater 1967). I believe it can be shown that dowry competition evolved in the upper strata, again in contradiction to Koranic marriage rules (Cooper [1915]:34; Fernea 1976:130–31; Jacobson 1973:217–18; Patai 1956:274–75; Smock and Youssef 1977); at least some upper-class elites practiced child betrothal and marriage (Churchill 1967).

There was, however, much variation over this vast region: Egypt is reported to have been less restrictive until the fifteenth century (Smock and Youssef 1977); Persia until the sixteenth–seventeenth centuries (Yarshater 1967); and Lebanon was reported to be less limiting until modern times (Patai, 1956:222–23). Jennings (1973, 1975), in a study of Anatolian Ottoman legal records, emphasizes the difficulty of generalizing from women's degree of claustration to their legal status. The reverse is also true: we do not know what the association of these various measures is. Some of these reports may be special pleading or the product of difficulties in making comparative judgments. Some may be the product of uneven attention to social class variation in each locale and especially inadequate attention to the upper classes. Nevertheless, there does seem to be a general consensus that claustration increased in severity from the Abbasids down to the eighteenth or nineteenth century.

One other continuity may be mentioned, that is, the growth of slavery on a scale far exceeding that of the Greeks: prevalent since Babylonian times, it had evolved into a large trading operation by the Ummayyad Dynasty. A prince might regularly hold about a thousand slaves in his retinue; a private in the army might have from one to ten as servants. Slave routes supplying slave girls and eunuchs led from southern Europe, India and Africa; poor Muslims sold their children into slavery although this was forbidden by Islam. This superabundance increased under the late Ummayyads and early Abbasids, and several Caliphs were themselves sons of slave concubines. The Abbasid Harun al-Rashid (786–809 A.D.) had 7,000 eunuchs in his service: Al-Muktadir (908–932 A.D.) had 11,000 mostly Greeks and Sudanese. Of concubines, Al-Mutawwakil (847–851 A.D.) is reputed to have had 4,000; other figures for harems range from 200 to 6,000 women (Hitti 1953:303, 341–43; Khan 1972:38–39; Lane 1973:183–86, 194; Levy 1957:76, 81ff.). It seems clear that levels of concubinage and slavery far exceeded those of Athenian Greece.

Received doctrine has it that "It was the Mohammedans who brought the 'purdah' system, or the seclusion of women, into India. Before the invasion of these warlike people the women of India went about freely" (Cooper [1915]:102). The greater intensity and universality of claustration in the North of India than in the South conveniently accords with the greater impact of Islam. Yet even in recent centuries it is not evident that Muslims secluded their women more than others. Indeed, North Indian Muslims blamed the Rajput nobility for carrying the practice to greater extremes than did any Muslims (Rothfeld [n.d.]:26, 86–87). These quarrels have little relation to historical reality.

The *Rig Veda* may depict men and unmarried women in free association, but the *Arthashastra* of the Mauryan Period (322–183 B.C.) records closely guarded harems, illegal entry into which was punished by burning alive, while rules and fines controlled women who left their houses without their husbands's permissions. Even if reduced to poverty, formerly upper-class women moved outside at dawn and dusk to avoid being seen. Polygyny, dowry, brideprice, and wife capture are all mentioned in the *Rig Veda*, before 900 B.C., as are dancing girls and slave girls (Basham 1967:119, 169, 174); during the same period, the first accounts of *satidaha* or widow immolation appear. Referred to in both the *Ramayana* and the *Mahabharata*, it became more common after the Period of Invasions (ca. 1–200 A.D.) (Basham 1967:188–90; Hauswirth 1932:50–61; Narain 1967).

By about 1 A.D., women along with "Sudras and servants" had been forbidden to hear or study the Vedas and were restricted to lesser literature, kitchen gods, husband worship, and the Tantric sects (paralleling the local saint worship of Islamic women). Failure to marry one's daughter before her puberty became a grave sin for the father, divorce became impossible for upper-class women, and woman's subservience to male kinsmen was clearly defined (Basham 1967:174; Hauswirth 1932:23–34). Polygyny had become the rule for those who could afford it; slave girls and prostitution are frequently referred to, a slave trade having been established with the Roman Empire (Basham 1967:154, 174–75).

There is controversy regarding the covering of women during these early periods because of ambiguities of art and the omissions of literature. Sculpture at Bharhut and Sanchi (second first centuries B.C.) shows "wealthy ladies, naked to the waist, lean[ing] from their balconies to watch processions . . ." "In some literary sources there are references to married women wearing veils, but there is no evidence that these were normally more than head coverings. . ."; "early Arab travelers remarked that queens were often to be seen in Hindu courts without veils," and in some sources respectable women attended temples and festivals without escorts. Nevertheless, "the ancient Indian attitude to women was . . . ambivalent. She was at once a goddess and a slave, a saint and a strumpet" (Basham 1967:180–83, 214). Again, architectural developments are suggestive: after the Gupta Period, flat roofs on which the family slept appear. Windows and balconies appear very early but are not covered with lattice until the Medieval Period (Basham 1967:204).

By Medieval times (after 540 A.D.), hypergynous dowry marriage had become the rule in upper and middle classes; Derrett (1964) believes upper-class female infanticide probably began during this period as a result of dowry competition. Widow remarriage, even for virgins, was prohibited; legal and inheritance rights of women steadily declined (Basham 1967:147–49; 187–88).

Prostitution is referred to from ancient times, and by the Middle Ages, an elaborate courtesan role, comparable to that of the Greek hetaira, had evolved, requiring training in literature, arts, and sports. In addition to his own harem of wives and concubines, the king retained salaried prostitutes for his own and his courtiers' use. State brothels were established and devadasis or temple prostitutes were legally recognized, some temples having hundreds on their staffs (Basham 1967:180, 184–87, 387; Derrett 1964). Slavery, temporary and permanent, was a part of Indian life from Vedic times, and by the date of the *Arthashastra* included war captives who were not ransomed and those sold into slavery for debt or crime. The Laws of Manu permitted the sale of one's children during dire emergency. Slave trade with the Roman Empire began at least by the early centuries A.D.: foreigners are reported selling their children to Hindus during the Medieval Period, and the slave trade continued into recent times in both directions, with Indian pilgrims to Mecca transporting children for sale (Basham 1967:137, 164; Derrett 1964; Levy 1957:81ff.).

As elsewhere, Indian claustration seems to be correlated with polygyny, dowry competition, and class stratification. It is instructive that none of the polyandrous societies of India claustrate their women to the degree that their polygynous neighbors do. If these Indian events can be dismissed as the product of a long series of contacts with Greeks, Persians, Scythians, Kushans, Huns, and other even more mysterious invaders from the Middle Eastern regions, the famous South Indian case of Nambudiri Brahmins is less easy to attribute to diffusion and appears to authorities to be independently evolved. A landed aristocracy of Kerala, in a political system comparable to feudal Europe, the Nambudiris claustrated both married and celibate women in separate apartments; even wedding festivals were observed from behind screens. Although they went with breasts uncovered at home, women left the house covered "with a long piece of cloth, leaving only the head and feet exposed. One end of the cloth is so held up in the hand which also holds the . . . umbrella" (Yalman 1963, quoting Iyer 1912) as to hide her face. She was preceded by a Nayar maidservant who called out to disperse people from her path. Women left their homes, in any case, only to visit temples or for occasional social visits: they rarely visited natal villages after marriage. The unchaste woman was stripped of her umbrella and covering cloth and outcasted (Yalman 1963). The context of this claustration and veiling was predictable: strong emphasis on patrilineal inheritance and patrilocality, intense dowry competition, and the only regular primogeniture reported from South In-

dia. Only the first son could marry; subsequent sons formed liaisons with women of lower-ranking castes or remained celibate. Excess Nambudiri women remained celibate most of their lives (Mencher 1966a, 1966b; Mencher and Goldberg 1967; Jacobson 1973:528–31).

Data relevant to the history of Chinese claustration have been synthesized by van Gulik (1974). Both he and Ropp (1976) present a picture of increasing intensity. As far back as their Former Chou Dynasty (1500–771 B.C.), women of royalty and nobility were segregated in their own apartments, served meals separately, and observed festivals from behind screens. Young girls were also secluded; virginity was a prerequisite for principal wife. Polygyny already involved formal distinctions between primary and secondary wives and concubines. The latter were supervised by court ladies; an upper-class or noble bride brought concubines with her as part of her dowry, a custom continuing down to modern times. Apparently commoners did not yet participate in these customs, however (van Gulik 1974:11–21).

By Later Chou Dynasty (770–222 B.C.) a literature of female obedience had begun to appear: female chastity and the complete separation of the sexes were enjoined; the "three obediences" of a woman to father, husband, son, were idealized. Respectable married women traveled in covered chariot, going out only to visit tombs and temples. Ideally they saw their husbands only at mealtimes and in bed although they might be present behind screens while their husbands entertained guests. Music, dancing, and literacy were abandoned by respectable women, and the professional female musician developed. Such women were sent by the wealthy as gifts and bribes to princes, judges, and other officials to add to their harems. Eunuchs supervised the king's harem. Common prostitution also developed: public brothels and tea houses were a response to the appearance of a mercantile class, which often bought its concubines from them (Kiang 1935:224–27; van Gulik 1974:29–106).

During Chin or Former Han Dynasty (221 B.C.–24 A.D.) women wore a shoulder shawl and covered their heads when outside the home (van Gulik 1974:64). Sometime between Tang and Sung Dynasties (908–1279 A.D.) footbinding was invented, becoming general by the Ming Dynasty. The role of footbinding as a form of claustration is reviewed in Appendix A. From Sung Dynasty onward, modesty required a high collar concealing the neck and a gown that disguised the shape of the female body (Cooper [1915]:223).

By Tang Dynasty (618–907 A.D.) a "full hetaira complex" of educated courtesans, playing important roles in literature and politics, had evolved. Palace agents recruited concubines and servants, while military brothels served lower-ranking officials and officers. One source mentions 3,000 women in the palace harem. An increase in brothels and wine shops was accompanied by traffic in kidnapping and sale of girls; numerous poor women became prostitutes when outcasted or condemned as criminals or the relatives of criminals or when taken captive in war (van Gulik 1974:108, 206).

By Yüan Dynasty (1279–1367 A.D.) the ideology of seclusion and separation of women was intense: heavy religious penalties were believed to result from touching a women, entering her quarters, debauching a married woman, a virgin, or nun. Divorce was disgraceful as was the remarriage of widows. During the Ming Dynasty (1369–1644 A.D.), the first Westerners entering China reported the absence of middle- or upper-class women on the streets, except for the very elderly; nor were they seen by visitors to their homes. Traveling was in enclosed chairs. Homes of the wealthy had the familiar courtyard pattern, with separate rooms for each wife and her offspring. In the upper classes, early betrothal was the rule (Cooper [1915]:212ff.; van Gulik 1974:246–49, 265). With government approval monuments might be erected to virtuous widows who remained chaste; the greatest virtue was to commit suicide. Female infanticide was intense, as was the slave trade, especially in females (Dickemann 1979a; Ropp 1976). Although dowry competition is not reflected in my historical sources, it may be inferred, as it was intense in recent times. Polygyny continued to be popular; many officials and merchants in the nineteenth century and early twentieth centuries had from two to ten wives (Cooper [1915]:230, 242–44; Dickemann 1978).

An evolutionary process is less clear in my Japanese sources. Patriliny, polygyny, and slavery are reported from the first two centuries A.D.: by the 600s, after the introduction of Buddhism, daughters of the nobility entered nunneries, hypergyny occurred in the upper classes, while slavery, banditry, and piracy were widespread (Sansom 1936:1–98). By Heian period (782–1068 A.D.) polygyny was common in the upper class; the empress, secondary wives, and concubines of the Emperor were housed in a "forbidden interior" of the palace, with the residences of ladies-in-waiting nearby (Sansom 1936:191). The Confucian ideology of yin-yang, of the three obediences and husband worship had been adopted: the upper-class woman was lodged inside a "twilight world" that Morris compares to Islamic purdah, hidden by screens and interior apartments from all men except her father and husband, traveling only in covered carriages. "Ghosts and women had best remain invisible," remarks a contemporary lady. However, women were still at this period able to inherit and own property, and virginity was expected only for principal wives. Yet dowry competition and child betrothal were already characteristic of the upper classes. Professional courtesans appeared during this period, but their social role was as yet unimportant (Morris 1969:211ff.). Private, public, and temple slaves originated in war captives, criminals, and the sale of women and children of the poor (Fréderic 1972:115–17; Sansom 1936:214–15). Degrees of claustration and veiling in later periods are not entirely clear. Sansom (1936:294) illustrates a picture of Kyoto ladies out-of-doors, after a Kamakura scroll, in which the hair but not the face is covered; one covers the side of the face in the Grecian gesture of modesty, with her garment in her raised hand. Fréderic (1972:82) describes the wide hat with gauze veil worn outside the house by feminine nobility in the twelfth century. All sources agree, however, that women's status declined during the thirteenth and fourteenth centuries: as unigeniture became common, their property rights declined, divorce became the husband's prerogative, and widow chastity was idealized. The Emperor's daughters, who could not find marriage partners of sufficient status, entered nunneries; many samurai women spent their lives as celibate servants to the nobility. The term "okusan" for wife dates from the Muromachi Period (1382–1573). By Tokugawa times, men had legal right to kill adulterous wives (Akroyd 1959; Asakawa 1955; Bacon 1902; Brown 1966; Fréderic 1972:47–48; Sansom 1936: 354–56). Nevertheless, among middle-class and rural women claustration seems never to have assumed the intensity that it did in China, India, or the Middle East (Akroyd 1959; Bacon 1902; Koyama et al. 1967; Pharr 1977). If Medieval Japan was more claustrating than Medieval Europe, it seems to fall closer to that feudal nation than to other societies reviewed.

Finally, a word on Europe itself. If Medieval European women, especially in the North, moved about more publicly and with less veiling, even in the middle and upper classes, the idea of feminine modesty was still present. Covering of the head except for the face with the wimple or a corner of the cloak or shawl, and even some chin covering were common; according to Higounet (1966) usual in France in the twelfth century, and even the face veil was not unusual though it was often gauzy (see illustrations throughout Grimal, ed. 1965–66, v. 2). In Southern Europe, in Greece, Italy, and especially Portugal and Spain, extreme claustration was usual among elites, persisting down to modern times and being carried to the New World. These are precisely those areas of Europe in which concubinage, slavery, and the Mediterranean slave trade network were most elaborate and enduring, in which patrilineal emphasis in residence and inheritance, the double standard and the crime of honor most accord with our previous definition. In Spain, face veiling in some public contexts persisted down to the eighteenth century (Pescatello 1976:20–47, 144–50, 168–73). Throughout Europe, we know that dowry competition and early betrothal characterized the upper classes, and the ideology of women as weak and sexually unreliable is familiar. Still, the greater economic independence of North European women and their greater ability to control and inherit property are consonant with their lesser claustration than in the South (vide Dickemann 1979a).

This cursory survey, while extremely uneven, does suggest possibilities for comparative analysis. If we view societies as points on a scale of intensity in claustration, we note a number of other coordinated variables. Besides the closely linked and expectable hypergyny and dowry competition, patrilocal-patrilineal emphasis in residence and inheritance, intensity of polygyny, extent of prostitution, concubinage and female slavery, extent of masculine involvement in banditry, vagrancy and criminality all seem to be involved. Even such apparently unrelated phenomena as evolution of the hetaira role, elite male homosexuality and male prostitution, the public restaurant, and the theater are in some ways part of this complex. Some of the ecological precursors are explored elsewhere (Dickemann 1979b); it is likely, however, that a single continuum will ultimately prove to be too simple a model to explain all of the historical variation reflected here.

Acknowledgments. This paper was made possible by a grant from the Harry Frank Guggenheim Foundation, for which I am very grateful. Thanks especially to John Hartung for advice, encouragement, and assistance with sources, to S. Parker and L. Tiger for encouragement, to P. Brucker, D. Jacobson, and R. Trivers for assistance with sources and to M. Rebhan for editorial advice and support. Responsibility for my errors is my own.

30
Cleo Unveiled

MILDRED DICKEMANN

Anthropology's antipathy to history, which it-self is none other than diachronic anthropology, grew out of an obsessive focus on ethnographic fieldwork, now dissipating. It was fortunately offset, in my case, by both Whitian and Boas-Kroeberian indoctrinations (both historical in their contrary ways), augmented by a realization that fieldwork was not a sympathetic pursuit. That history, in concert with a penchant for global theorizing, led me to employ data from both disciplines, as well as a variety of nonscholarly sources, in developing a provisional general model of stratified societies (Dickemann 1979a, 1979b), extended in this article. Resulting from a long interest in human ecology, and specific work on infanticide (Dickemann 1975), this effort put me in contact with others beginning to employ Darwinian theory.

While the mating system model has received several critiques (Kitcher 1985; Miller 1981; Stuard 1984; Wittenberger 1981a), all, I believe, based on misreadings (cf. Dickemann 1984b), the discussion of claustration has not been noticed outside the small circle of Darwinian anthropologists. Infanticide was at the time just coming to attention simultaneously among historians and social analysts, and therefore was of broader interest. Claustration, in contrast, concerned primarily feminists, who shied away from anything labeled "sociobiology" or "Darwin." That, and the article's appearance in a specialist anthology rather than a mainstream anthropology journal, guaranteed the loss of a primary audience.

Initial extensions of this work with reference to European religious celibacy were by Boone (1983, 1986, 1988a) and Hager (1992), while Boswell (1988) independently addressed the related subject of oblation. But an adequate analysis of religious claustration, in agrarian Europe and elsewhere, must specify the gains both to family and to institution, requiring an investigation of the role of the church as a financial institution. The explosion of feminist anthropology in the 1970s and 1980s has resulted in an enormous corpus of data on women's marital seclusion, especially in the Near East and India, too numerous to cite (though Morgen 1989 may provide entry), even resulting in coffee-table productions (Croutier 1989; Alloula 1986), while work on the ethos of honor and shame continues, though still largely with reference to the Mediterranean. Feminists have also devoted some attention to secular spinsterhood (e.g., Chambers-Schiller 1984; Vicinus 1988) but limited to Anglo-American societies. Some work has been done on female genital mutilation (El Saadawi 1982; Koso-Thomas 1987; Lightfoot-Klein 1989; Passmore Sanderson 1986, etc.), but I have seen nothing recent on footbinding, nor do we understand the reasons for the specific regional distributions of these forms. It is notable how topics seem stuck within the traditions of specific local histories and sociologies, rather than receiving world-wide attention, an annoyance for cross-cultural theorists.

There are other aspects still neglected. My own treatment underestimated the role of the threat of rape in inducing claustration of wives and daughters; I believe only one of my sources (Jacobson 1973) mentioned it. We are now aware that it is an inevitable concomitant of war and mass population upheavals (cf. Clark 1989). There has been no general cross-cultural synthesis, however, so the relative roles of ideology and economics in driving the system are unclear. We have before us today many examples of the reimposition of veiling, purportedly ideological in motivation, yet on examination underlying economic and political fears appear primary. Societies at the edge of industrial and demographic transition may be expected to revive past reproductive management practices as they fall back into the kind of patrilineal despotisms symptomatic of unstable, intensely competitive economic environments (Dickemann 1979b). Researchers now have the unpleasant opportunity to study the diachronic abandonment and reimposition of forms of gender oppression in a single locale, providing far better understanding of their genesis.

In conclusion, I must comment on one aspect of my work often remarked by critics, namely its nonquantitative, discursive nature. Whatever the science, initial reports and preliminary hypotheses are often so framed—in human sciences especially so, since the complexity of the domain means that variables may be defined in many alternate ways. Indeed, new hypotheses often force the redefinition of variables in ways contrary to past practice, something that has occurred repeatedly in Darwinian anthropology. I must plead guilty to a failure to offer alternate hypotheses: I could not think of any worth the paper. But after another decade and more observing spilled ink and wasted funds (in fields as diverse human genetics, demography, and cross-cultural comparison) due to the failure to begin with grassroots natural history of the subject at hand, leading to the isolation of meaningful variables, I must reaffirm my dedication to this method of doing science. Rigorous quantitative tests should follow, but they are not the first step.

Indeed, the world does not consist only of the statistically verifiable and nothing else. In our present state of knowledge, there are degrees of likelihood. Especially in dealing with the past, reasonableness, logical fit, and circumstantial evidence, supported by relevant theories drawn from analogous domains, will always be necessary. If this work from a couple of decades ago provokes further investigation, including more and better data and more refined testing, it will have done its job.

31

Polygyny and Inheritance of Wealth

JOHN HARTUNG

Polygamy is contrary to the Law of Nature and Justice, and to the Propagation of the Human Race; for where Males and Females are in equal number, if one man takes Twenty Wives, Nineteen Men must live in Celibacy, which is repugnant to the design of Nature; nor is it probable that Twenty Women will be so well impregnated by one Man as by Twenty.

—Dr. John Arbuthnott, 1710

The hypothesis to be tested here, that humans tend to transmit wealth to male descendants where polygyny is possible (Dr. Arbuthnott's assertions notwithstanding), follows from considering the difference in within-sex variance in reproductive success between males and females (Darwin 1859, 1871) and the fact that in polygynous societies multiple wives are acquired by men who can afford them.[1] That is, since "a male's reproductive success can be greatly enhanced by mating with many females, whereas a female can only be impregnated approximately once per year, regardless of the number of her mates," and since "wealth is a decisive parameter for securing multiple mates in polygynous cultures," "variance in male reproductive success is not simply a reflection of genetic variance within the sex, but is due in part to extraneous variables such as nongenetically determined resource status. It follows that ancestors (both male *and female*) would maximize the reproductive-success value of their transferable wealth by leaving it to offspring of the sex upon which it has the highest probability of having the largest positive effect"—usually males (Hartung 1976:607, 608; 1977:336).

In plainer English, if a set of parents left wealth to a son who could thereby afford an additional wife, that inheritance would, on average, increase their number of grandchildren more than if it were left to a daughter who was thereby able to gain an additional husband (see Fig. 31.1). This does not assume that parents calculate the potential effect of their wealth on various possible heirs and act accordingly or

that they are consciously motivated to enhance their long-range reproductive success. It does assume that if a pattern of behavior causes people to produce more descendants who also follow that pattern, the behavior will eventually come to predominate or be naturally selected. This should hold regardless of the mechanism of transmission of the behavior from parents to children.

AN ANALOGUE

An explanatory nonhuman analogue of this *polygyny → male bias* hypothesis can be drawn from blackbirds. Male blackbirds hold territories of varying quality, and females are attracted to an individual male by the quality of his territory (Orians 1969). Males with territories of high enough quality to put them over the "polygyny threshold" (Verner and Willson 1966) mate with two females per season, while males holding poor-quality territory go without (Pleszczynska 1978). Emlen and Oring (1977) have called this general phenomenon "resource polygyny" (see also Borgia 1979). Extending the analogy hypothetically, if parent blackbirds could enhance the quality of a male or female offspring's territory, they would be selected to enhance their male offspring's territory when the enhancement caused him to have an additional mate and them to have more grandoffspring. Thus, male bias in inheritance would be selected as a facultative response when polygyny is an option and the amount of heritable wealth is significant.

331

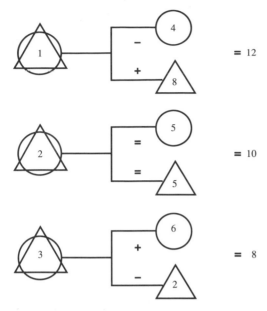

Figure 31.1. A simplified model of the relationship between female/male reproductive variance, inheritance, and fitness. Given a society in which the standard deviation in number of offspring for males is 3, the standard deviation in number of offspring for females is 1, the mean number of offspring for males/females is 5, and the sole differentiating variable for number of offspring is the proportion of wealth inherited, and three couples, each with offspring as shown, where Couple 1 leaves all wealth to the son, Couple 2 divides the wealth evenly, and Couple 3 leaves all wealth to the daughter, and assuming that inheritance permits the attainment of one standard deviation in number of offspring over others of the same sex and noninheritance results in a corresponding one standard deviation decrease, the total number of grandchildren for each couple will be as shown at right.

The hypothesis here is that such an effect can occur in humans and therefore a polygynous society's norm for inheritance will show a bias in favor of males. As with blackbirds, the hypothesis for humans assumes that variance in individual behavior is a facultative phenotypic response to variance in individual economic/mating conditions and that genetic variance across individuals or across cultures is irrelevant. That is, these behaviors (mate choice, heir choice, polygyny, etc.) are so important to reproductive success that they are unlikely to

have significant heritability and very likely to have a range of appropriate phenotypic responses which each individual has the potential to display according to his/her circumstances (Hartung 1980).

HUMAN RESOURCE-DEFENSE POLYGYNY

Two general categories of polygyny are _resource-defense polygyny_ and _mate-defense polygyny_. Mate-defense polygyny in humans would look something like the scenario one sees (or used to see) in cartoons in which a caveman drags women off by their hair while brandishing a large club to ward off anyone who might intervene (thereby "defending" his mates from access to/by other males). Substituting antlers or large canines for the club, this is a reasonable caricature for many mammals. The presumption necessary to my hypothesis, however, is that human polygyny, like polygyny in many birds, is resource-defense polygyny. That is, the hypothesis assumes that obtaining multiple wives requires substantial economic expenditure, or, as found by Clignet (1970:34), that "additional co-wives are a privilege reserved to individuals who initially hold higher than average positions." *why not mate-defense of resources*

Some indication as to whether this is the case can be gained by examining Murdock's (1967) variable "Mode of marriage—the prevailing mode of obtaining a wife." Two dichotomous modes of marriage are (1) "Bride-price or bride-wealth, i.e., transfer of a substantial consideration in the form of livestock, goods, or money from the groom or his relatives to the kinsmen of the bride" and (2) "Absence of any significant consideration or bridal gifts only." Of the 1,170 societies in the punch-card version of Murdock's *Ethnographic Atlas*, 850 have one of these modes of marriage and are also coded for prevalence of polygyny.[2] Figure 31.2 indicates a strong positive relationship between polygyny and bride-price, supporting the assumption that human polygyny is resource-defense polygyny.

The problem with Figure 31.2 is that since many of the cases cannot be assumed to be independent, a necessary assumption in any nonparametric analysis is violated. One solution is to use the Standard Cross-Cultural Sample (Murdock and White 1969)—a subset of 186

Mode of marriage

Polygyny	no cost	bride price
none	70 — 62.5%	42 — 37.5%
limited (<20%)	137 — 47.2%	153 — 52.8%
general (>20%)	41 — 9.2%	407 — 90.8%

Atlas

Figure 31.2. Mode of marriage by polygyny for the whole *Atlas*. $N = 850$, chi-square $= 192.9$, $p << .001$, Cramer's $V = .48$, Gamma $- .75$.

Mode of marriage

Polygyny	no cost	bride price
none	15.73 — 81.5%	3.56 — 18.5%
limited (<20%)	25.83 — 60.0%	17.20 — 40.0%
general (>20%)	9.16 — 35.7%	16.51 — 64.3%

Corrected atlas

Figure 31.4. Mode of marriage by polygyny for the *Atlas* corrected by language family. $N = 88$, chi-square $= 9.68$, $p < .008$, Cramer's $V = .332$, Gamma $= .544$.

societies each of which represents one of the world's major culture areas. Of these societies, 111 are coded on both variables, and Figure 31.3 indicates that the relationship evident in Figure 31.2 also holds here.

Mode of marriage

Polygyny	no cost	bride price
none	15 — 62.5%	9 — 37.5%
limited (<20%)	15 — 36.6%	26 — 63.4%
general (>20%)	10 — 21.7%	36 — 78.3%

Standard sample

Figure 31.3. Mode of marriage by polygyny for the Standard Sample. $N = 111$, chi-square $= 11.4$, $p < .01$, Cramer's $V = .32$, Gamma $= .50$.

Another solution to Galton's problem[3] is to correct for diffusion by counting language families instead of societies. The assumption here is that societies speaking languages from different language families are independent (see Whiting 1981). Accordingly, the number of cases in each whole *Atlas* cross-tabulation is reduced to the number of language families represented by those societies, and each cell is weighted by the proportion of each language family represented in it. For example, there are 331 Niger-Congo-speaking societies in the punch-card version of the *Atlas*. The distribution of the Niger-Congo-speaking societies of Figure 31.2 is as follows:

$$\begin{array}{cc} 0 & 2 \\ 2 & 4 \\ 0 & 245 \end{array}$$

This entire group is reduced to one case, and, for the corrected analysis, the numbers entered into the table for this language family are the percentages of 1 that fall in each cell:

$$\begin{array}{cc} 0 & .0079 \\ .0079 & .0158 \\ 0 & .9684 \end{array}$$

This procedure is repeated for each language family represented, and the proportions in each cell are added to give the numbers upon which statistics are calculated.[4] Figure 31.4 supports the contention that the relationship indicated in Figures 31.2 and 31.3 is not an artifact of cultural diffusion.

In addition to these nominally coded variables, data on the degree of polygyny (the percentage of females who share a husband) collected by J. Whiting and others in 1964 are available (see appendix). Although these data represent independent cultures from around the world, the criteria for independence are less rigorous than those for the Standard Cross-Cultural Sample. Since, however, the analysis of these data is not nonparametric, noise from diffusion would be more likely to obscure a real relationship than to indicate a false one.[5] Accordingly, while Figures 31.2, 31.3, and 31.4 show strong evidence of an association between bride-price and polygyny, Figure 31.5 presents the strongest indication of the degree of association.

Goody (1976) has argued that bride-price itself is often a form of inheritance or invest-

ment in sons. That is, in many societies the bride-price for a man's first wife is paid by his parents, who are effectively buying their son a spouse while providing themselves with an enhanced probability of vicarious reproductive success. In this sense, the correlation between bride-price and polygyny simultaneously supports the contentions that (1) human polygyny is resource-defense polygyny and (2) humans bias inheritance toward males under resource-defense polygynous conditions.

POLYGYNY → MALE BIAS

Murdock coded inheritance patterns separately for real property (land, house) and movable property (e.g., livestock, money) as follows:[6]

0 No information
1 No land rights/no inherited movable property/no rule governing the transmission of same
2 Matrilineal inheritance to a sister's son or sons
3 Inheritance by matrilineal heirs who take precedence over sister's son (e.g., younger brother)[7]
4 Inheritance by children, but with daughters receiving less than sons
5 Inheritance by children of either sex or both
6 Inheritance by patrilineal heirs who take precedence over sons (e.g., younger brother)
7 Patrilineal inheritance to son or sons

Two of these codes (2 and 7) indicate inheritance by males only, while two (4 and 5) prescribe at least some inheritance by females.[8] In order to maximize sample size and variable dichotomy, the following two categories were decided upon: *high-bias/males-only*, including societies coded 2 or 7 for both types of wealth, or one of these for each type, or one of these in combination with 1 (the most prevalent example of the latter being pastoral societies that transfer livestock to son with no land at issue); and *low-bias/no-bias*, including societies coded 5 for both types of wealth, or 5 for one and 4 for the other, or 5 for one and 1 for the other.[9] Figures 31.6–31.8 present cross-tabulations of low-bias/no-bias vs. high-bias/males-only by polygyny for the whole *Atlas*, the Standard Cross-Cultural Sample, and the *Atlas* corrected

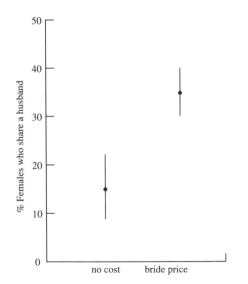

Figure 31.5. Mode of marriage by ratio data on polygyny. No cost: $N = 34$, mean $= 15.5$, 95% confidence interval $= 8.1$ to 22.8; bride-price: $N = 84$, mean $= 35.3$, 95% confidence interval $= 29.8$ to 40.8.

Polygyny	♂ Bias in inheritance: low/no	♂ Bias in inheritance: high/males only
none	32 42.1%	b 44 57.9%
limited (<20%)	27 20.3%	106 79.7%
general (>20%)	6 3%	196 97%

Atlas

Figure 31.6. Inheritance bias by polygyny for the whole *Atlas*. $N = 411$, chi-square $= 66.5$, $p < < .001$, Cramer's $V = .40$, Gamma $= .75$.

Polygyny	♂ Bias in inheritance: low/no	♂ Bias in inheritance: high/males only
none	7.84 48.7%	b 8.25 51.3%
limited (<20%)	4.83 17.4%	22.93 82.6%
general (>20%)	1.51 10.7%	12.63 89.3%

Corrected atlas

Figure 31.8. Inheritance bias by polygyny for the *Atlas* corrected by language family. $N = 58$, chi-square $= 7.35$, $p < .026$, Cramer's $V = .355$, Gamma $= .593$.

by language family. Figure 31.9 presents the ratio data. All of these analyses indicate a positive relationship between male bias in inheritance and polygyny.

Polygyny	♂ Bias in inheritance: low/no	♂ Bias in inheritance: high/males only
none	9 39.1%	b 14 60.9%
limited (<20%)	8 24.2%	25 75.8%
general (>20%)	2 7.1%	26 92.9%

Standard sample

Figure 31.7. Inheritance bias by polygyny for the Standard Sample. $N = 84$, chi-square $= 7.5, p < .03$, Cramer's $V = .30$, Gamma $= .56$.

Though the relationship indicated by Figures 31.6–31.8 is strong, it would be stronger if fewer cases fell in Cell *b*. That is, according to the hypothesis, one might expect even fewer monogamous societies to have a male bias in inheritance. However, "monogamy/polygyny" in these analyses refers to the marriage system, not the actual mating system. While it is reasonable to suppose that across-sex difference in within-sex variance for reproductive success (the index of sexual selection) is higher in societies with polygynous marriages, it is not safe to assume that the difference is negligible in societies without such marriages. Such societies can achieve considerable variance in male reproductive success through concubines or mistresses and other forms of institutionalized and/or noninstitutionalized, nonmarriage mating. Also, sequential monogamy (frequent divorce and remarriage) can increase male variance over female variance "if the remarriage-ability of a middle-aged male is higher than that of a middle-aged female and/or if the reproductive value of a middle-aged male is higher than that of a middle-aged female (which it is)" (Hartung 1977: 336). (Reproductive value is a measure of expected future fertility [Fisher

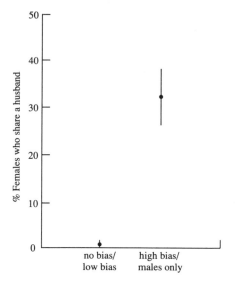

Figure 31.9. Inheritance bias by ratio data on polygyny. No-bias/low-bias: $N = 8$, mean = 0.5, 95% confidence interval = −0.39 to 1.39 high-bias/males-only: $N = 69$, mean = 32.8, 95% confidence interval = 26.9 to 38.7.

However, for most societies (as in mammals generally) females are probably the limiting sex and norms for inheritance of wealth are probably set primarily by those who have wealth—just as in our society norms for dress at the opera are set by those who go to the opera. If the amount of wealth some individuals transfer is so small as to be inconspicuous, that wealth can follow any pattern without establishing what an ethnographer would recognize as a norm—so individuals near the bottom of the economic order will usually be Code 1 (No property/no rule) for both types of wealth. (For an excellent case study of the interactions between wealth, polygyny [and/or serial monogamy], inheritance pattern, and reproductive success, see Irons [1976, 1979b, 1980].)

OEDIPUS: A DERIVATIVE HYPOTHESIS

The critical variable for the polygyny → male bias hypothesis is the index of sexual selection—the amount by which variance in male reproductive success is higher than variance in female reproductive success. However, large as this across-sex difference in within-sex variance may be, the prevailing rule that mammalian females have comparatively low variance applies only to the offspring generation (Hartung 1981a:393): "with any constant male variance across generations, the female variance must increase successively with reference to successive generations. That is, every male at the high end of the fitness distribution contributes to his female parent's F_2 [grandparent-generation] reproductive success. Accordingly, while that female may have been near the mean for number of offspring, she will be at the high end of the higher variance fitness curve for number of grandoffspring. This will necessarily follow whether the additive heritability of fitness is large or non-existent." Put more plainly, every highly successful male has a mother, and every mother with highly successful sons has an extraordinary number of grandchildren.

1958].) Such factors may account for some of the societies that fall in Cell b of Figures 31.6–31.8.

A logical extension of the hypothesis suggests that individuals in the lower economic strata of a society should transfer wealth to daughters, or without bias, regardless of the prevalence of polygyny. That is, if inherited wealth is not sufficient to put a male within reach of the "polygyny threshold" (in the marriage *or* mating sense), no increase in reproductive success will result. Dickemann (1979a) has investigated within-society splits in inheritance/investment norms in caste-stratified societies where high-status males are the limiting sex in the upper strata while females are the limiting sex only in the lower strata. Here lower-upper-stratum families (whose males cannot marry women from lower castes) pool their resources to accumulate a large enough dowry to permit one of their daughters/nieces to marry a male from the highest subcaste (hypergyny). In the upper upper strata, a high frequency of female infanticide and/or female celibacy lessens the probability of a daughter's marrying "down" (hypogyny) and taking family resources with her.

The point here is that females also have a means of attaining extraordinary reproductive success (or, more precisely, extraordinary vicarious reproductive success, or inclusive fitness [Hamilton 1964]). The critical difference between males and females, in this regard, is that males can have this success directly (by having many mates/offspring), but females must do so indirectly (by having sons that have many mates/offspring). Therefore, given a family with considerable resources (of the sort that could be spent on bride-price and/or other means of obtaining mates), one should expect mother and son to side against father over the issue of resource expenditure. That is, if resources can be either (1) conserved and passed on to the son so that he can gain multiple mates or (2) spent by the father to gain additional mates for himself, mother and son (and mother's mother)[10] should strongly prefer the first strategy.

Freud hypothesized that sons are sexually attracted to their mothers and that antagonism between fathers and sons stems from potential sexual competition for mother. While there is much evidence (e.g., from a 1977 Gallup poll) indicating that mother-son bonds are stronger and more positive than father-son relationships, data on incest indicate that father-daughter incest and even brother-sister incest are orders of magnitude more frequent than mother-son incest (which is practically nonexistent, despite the several-year period during which adolescent sons are physically dominant over their mothers and despite the reasonably frequent situation of adolescent sons in fatherless households [see Herman 1977]). Even father-son incest is more frequent than mother-son incest. Perhaps the classic family conflict perceived by Freud and interpreted by him as the "Oedipus complex" does stem from sexual competition between father and son, but not over mother— rather, over which family male will be a resource-defense polygynist.

CAVEAT AND CONCLUDING REMARKS

Culture is adaptive or "functional," subserving the basic needs of its carriers and altering through time by a sort of mass trial-and-error in a process which is truly evolutionary. (Murdock 1949:xii)

It has been assumed throughout this paper that humans behave as if influenced by the legacy of behaviors that served the reproductive success of their ancestors. Murdock was following the lead of Sumner and Keller (1927) when he wrote that culturally transmitted behavior is adaptive and that change in such behavior is the consequence of a process analogous to the process proposed by Darwin for genetic change.

That most cultural differences are differences in learned behavior, and that they result from differences in socialization, do not detract from their potential to be adaptive in a Darwinian sense. Like genes, culture is a mechanism that transmits instructions down family lines. It follows that if one culturally transmitted behavior causes its bearers/transmitters to have higher reproductive success than another, it will increase in frequency. Unlike genes, culture can also spread laterally across individuals within a given generation or, because of lateral spread, fail to decrease when it has a relatively negative effect on individual reproductive success. So culturally transmitted behaviors can spread comparatively quickly, decrease comparatively slowly, or even be perpetuated by "socio-cultural, economic, and political factors ... that decrease the individual and inclusive fitness of the individuals who practice them" (Beall and Goldstein 1981:11). In short, culture is comparatively ductile, and this ductility means that its carriers are subject to faster rates of evolution and/or extinction (the last Shaker died last year).

If humans tend to (1) invent new behaviors that are adaptive and (2) copy or avoid new behavior according to its adaptive merits (as opposed to simply reproducing or failing to reproduce), then adaptive culturally transmitted behavior should arise more frequently and spread more rapidly than adaptive genetically transmitted behavior. My own presumption is that both of these conditions hold and that the Lamarckian attributes of cultural evolution account for the conspicuous rapidity of human evolution. How people might judge, a priori, the potential adaptiveness of a novel behavior is a subject for investigation in itself (largely within the purview of psychology, I presume), as is how such behaviors spread across individuals and interact with general evolution (see Pulliam and Dunford 1980; Boyd and Richerson 1980; Cavalli-Sforza and Feldman 1981; Lumsden and Wilson 1981). However, the subject here is not the mechanics of culture per se, but the adaptive compatibility of particular combinations of cultural behaviors.

The data presented support the hypotheses they are analyzed to test, and in a general way they lend support to the Sumner-Keller-Murdock view of the relationship between culture and natural selection. It is important to keep in mind what is meant (and not meant) by the phrase "truly evolutionary." That is, it is important to recognize the nature of adaptation by natural selection—that it operates primarily at the level of the individual, that most individual lines become extinct, that most social groups become extinct, and that most species become extinct.

Natural selection does not insure the future success of its products—it only insures that its products *have had* relative reproductive success. It does not operate by design, but, through an effect like that of Adam Smith's "invisible hand" in economics, it can give rise to populations of individuals whose interactions are sufficiently coordinated to give the finished structure an appearance of design—or even the appearance of having evolved independently of its most elemental components. Natural selection does not have foresight, but it can cause the evolution of organisms that do have foresight. Whether it can generate an organism that has enough foresight to evolve by design remains to be seen.

Arbuthnott was wrong to equate *Justice* with the *Law of Nature*. Hepburn came closer to the truth when she put it to Bogart in *The African Queen*: "Nature, Mr. Allnutt, is what we are put into this world to rise above." I hope that investigating the influence of natural selection on our cultural legacy will facilitate changing it when major discrepancies exist between human nature as we would like it to be and human nature as we find it.

NOTES

1. I thank R. L. Trivers and E. O. Wilson for teaching me about evolution, and P. H. Harvey for the realization that in science you're wrong until you prove you might not be. I thank R. D. Alexander, P. van den Berghe, N. Chagnon, I. DeVore, M. Dickemann, P. Ellison, W. Irons, G. P. Murdock, J. Shepher, B. Smuts, and P. Whitten for valuable thoughts and encouragement.

2. Polygyny can be derived from Murdock's code on family organization from the variables Famorg and Marcomp in the SPSS punched version of the *Atlas*. See Murdock (1957) for the distinction between "limited" and "general" polygyny.

3. "Galton's problem" is the issue of independence of cases—whether some societies in an analysis are being counted more than once because they have been arbitrarily or artificially subdivided, each subdivision being counted as a case. PSEUDO REP.

4. The statistical problem with this correction is that a standard chi-square value calculated on the numbers in the finished table is an underestimate of the actual value. This is because large language families are very likely to be represented in more than one cell of the table. The effect of "splitting" many cases (each language family is treated as a single case) means that if the cases were randomly distributed (the theoretical expected distribution), skew in distribution of cases in the cells would be even less likely than if cases could not "split." This increases kurtosis and decreases variance in the expected distribution. Accordingly, if the observed chi-square value is below an acceptable significance level (as is the case here) the problem is not critical (one simply has a stronger result than actually indicated). However, if the chi-square value indicated a probability that was not quite significant, one could falsely fail to reject the null hypothesis. In other words, the procedure is safe (robust) but lacks power. A modified chi-square calculation is being developed to deal with this problem (see Tomberlin, Greene, and Hartung, 1981).

5. My presumption here is that while marriage system may be subject to diffusion, given polygyny, its actual degree (e.g., 9% vs. 14%) is not likely to result from cultural borrowing. Economic practices that lead to a particular range of degree of polygyny may diffuse, but the degree itself is the result of functional relationships. Accordingly, if the nominal/ordinal variable involved were distributed by diffusion (independently of a functional relationship with degree of polygyny), then variance around a mean for the ratio data would be increased rather than decreased—extending rather than shortening the confidence interval.

6. In response to an inquiry, Murdock has said that he has no reservations about the accuracy of the 1967 data but feels that the codes are "too crude" (personal communication, June 1980). Further research would profit from refinement of these codes, especially 1, 3, and 6.

7. See the inheritance codes listed by Textor (1966:112) and the HRAF *Atlas* codebook.

8. Code 2 can be left out of the analysis without significant effect, slightly strengthening the *Atlas* result (32 cases) and slightly weakening the Standard Sample result (3 cases). For a separate analysis of matrilineal inheritance, see Hartung (1981b) and references therein.

9. Several other reasonable groupings were run, and all produced essentially the same results (some a bit stronger, some somewhat weaker, all in the predicted direction). Codes 6 and 3 usually mean inheritance by brother (see n. 7) and can be classified as high-bias/males only, but since Murdock did not specify brother and since examining each of the nearly 200 societies coded 3 or 6 would be a major project, these data were not utilized (see also n. 8). Code 4 *for both types of property* was not used because "daughters less" is not sufficiently specific to indicate to which category such cases belong.

10. This is perhaps a contributing factor in mother-in-law avoidance.

Appendix: Table 31.1. Societies Coded for Degree of Polygyny by Whiting et al., and for Inheritance Bias and/or Mode of Marriage by *Ethnographic Atlas*

Name	EA No.	% Females Who Share A Husband	Inheritance Bias[a]	Mode of Marriage[b]
Alorese	IC02	22	0	1
Amba	AE01	49	2	0
Andamanese	EH01	0	0	2
Aranda	ID01	59	2	0
Arapaho	NE09	9	0	2
Arapesh	IE03	46	2	2
Armenians	CI10	0	0	1
Ashanti	AF03	72	0	1
Atayal	IA01	0	2	1
Aymara	SF02	0	2	2
Azande	AI03	57	0	1
Baiga	EG09	66	0	1
Bali	AE49	12	2	1
Bari	AJ08	30	2	1
Baya	AI07	40	2	1
Bete	AF07	81	0	1
Bhil	EF05	13	2	1
Bijogo	AG18	5	0	2
Bulgarians	CH05	0	0	2
Cayapa	SF03	0	0	2
Chiricahua	NH01	18	0	2
Chukchee	EC03	49	2	2
Dobu	IG05	0	2	0
Dzem	AE40	61	2	1
Egyptians	CD02	7	0	1
Falasha	CA31	0	0	2
Fang	AE03	42	2	1
Fipa	AD19	46	0	1
Ganda	AD07	44	2	1
Gheg	CE01	41	2	1
Gilyak	EC01	3	2	1
Gujarati	EF09	2	2	1
Gusii	AD12	63	2	1
Hausa	CB26	59	0	1
Havasupai	ND03	19	2	0
Hehe	AD08	59	0	1
Iban	IB01	0	1	2
Ifaluk	IF04	0	0	2
Iranians	EA09	1	0	1
Irish	CG03	0	2	0
Iroqouis	NG10	0	0	2
Jivaro	SE03	90	2	0
Jordanians	CJ06	22	0	1
Jukun	AH02	5	2	1
Kachin	EI05	2	2	1

Appendix: Table 31.1. (continued)

Name	*EA* No.	% Females Who Share A Husband	Inheritance Bias[a]	Mode of Marriage[b]
Kadara	AJ19	64	2	0
Kagoro	AH20	55	2	1
Kapauku	IE01	39	0	1
Katab	AH01	68	2	0
Kazak	EB01	67	2	1
Khasi	EI08	0	0	2
Khmer	EJ05	5	0	1
Kikuyu	AD04	32	2	1
Kissi	AF02	17	2	1
Konso	CA01	76	0	2
Koryak	EC05	24	2	0
Kurd	CI11	7	0	1
Kurtachi	IG03	50	0	1
Kutenai	ND07	19	2	2
Kwoma	IE12	55	2	1
Lapps	CG04	0	0	2
Lepcha	EE03	35	2	1
Lesu	IG04	21	0	1
Lolo	ED02	5	2	1
Lovedu	AB14	49	0	1
Lozi	AB03	66	2	0
Luba	AE06	49	0	1
Luo	AJ06	62	2	1
Macassarese	IC01	8	0	1
Malays	EJ08	5	0	1
Mamvu	AI05	47	0	1
Mapuche	SG02	64	2	1
Maria Gond	EG03	4	0	1
Marquesans	IJ03	0	1	0
Marshallese	IF03	0	0	2
Mbundu	AB05	45	2	1
Mende	AF05	79	0	1
Minchia	ED08	14	2	1
Mossi	AG47	42	2	1
Nambicuara	SI04	55	0	2
Nandi	AJ07	18	2	1
Naskapi	NA05	29	2	2
Ndob	AE55	61	2	1
New England	CF01	0	1	2
Ngonde	AD16	70	0	1
Ngoni	AC09	29	0	2
Nuer	AJ03	75	2	1
Nupe	AF08	82	0	1
Nyakyusa	AD06	68	0	1
Nyoro	AD02	66	2	1
Ojibwa	NF01	13	2	2
Okinawans	ED07	0	2	0
Otoro	AI10	77	2	1
Paiute	ND22	18	0	2
Palaung	EI18	29	0	1
Papago	NI02	49	2	2
Pawnee	NF06	54	0	2
Pondo	AB10	21	2	1
Quinault	NB25	13	2	0
Riffians	CD03	46	2	1
Rundi	AE08	33	2	0
Sandawe	AA06	20	0	1
Semang	EJ03	3	1	2
Seri	NI04	0	0	1
Shawiya	CD08	0	2	1

Appendix: Table 31.1. (continued)

Name	*EA* No.	% Females Who Share A Husband	Inheritance Bias[a]	Mode of Marriage[b]
Shilluk	AI06	37	2	1
Shluh	CD05	0	0	1
Siamese	EJ09	1	1	0
Siriono	SE01	38	0	2
Siwans	CC03	5	0	1
Songhai	CB03	5	0	1
Sonjo	AD39	18	2	1
Sotho	AB08	18	2	1
Suku	AC17	41	0	1
Swazi	AB02	37	2	1
Tallensi	AG04	62	0	1
Tapirape	SD02	0	0	2
Telugu	EG10	9	2	0
Temne	AF57	49	0	1
Teso	AJ01	45	2	1
Tewa	NH11	0	1	2
Tibetans	EE04	0	2	0
Timbira	SJ04	0	1	0
Tiv	AH03	52	2	0
Tiwi	ID03	85	0	1
Toda	EG04	0	2	0
Tonga	II12	35	0	2
Trobrianders	IG02	39	2	1
Trukese	IF02	0	2	2
Tswana	AB13	21	2	1
Tuareg	CC09	0	0	1
Tubatlabal	NC02	0	0	1
Vedda	EH04	0	2	0
Vugusu	AD41	30	2	1
Wogeo	IE04	53	2	0
Wolof	CB02	61	0	1
Yanzi	AC26	54	0	1
Yao	AC07	30	0	2
Yoruba	AF06	29	0	1
Zapotec	NJ10	0	1	2
Zuni	NH04	0	0	2

[a]0 = code not used; 1 = low-bias/no bias; 2 = high-bias/males-only.
[b]0 = code not used; 1 = bride-price; 2 = not cost.

Appendix: Table 31.2. Societies Coded for
Degree of Polygyny by Whiting et al. and lacking
Codes for Inheritance Bias and Mode of Marriage

Name	EA No.	% Females Who Share A Husband
Apinaye	SJ07	0
Balinese	IB03	35
Bemba	AC03	52
Camayura	SI05	18
Carib	SC03	37
Cuna	SA01	2
Dogon	AG03	24
Kaonde	AC32	33
Kaska	NA04	0
Klamath	NC08	35
Koma	AI46	5
Konkomba	AG10	57
Kung	AA01	9
Lamba	AC05	9
Luvale	AC11	26
Mambila	AH04	18
Manus	IG09	11
Maori	IJ02	2
Mataco	SH01	5
Mbuti	AA05	10
Murngin	ID02	57
Navaho	NH03	13
Ndembu	AC06	26
Nootka	NB11	23
Serbs	CH01	0
Tanala	EH03	49
Tehuelche	SG04	2
Tikopia	II02	7
Trumai	SI02	22
Yagua	SE04	0
Yaruro	SC02	17

Appendix: Table 31.3. Societies for Which the Two Data Sources Are in Conflict or Potential Conflict

Name	EA No.	% Females Who Share A Husband	Inheritance Bias[a]	Mode of Marriage[b]
Ainu	EC07	0	0	2
Ambo	AB19	0	0	1
Ambonese	IC11	3	2	1
Bajun	AD01	5	1	1
Bontok	IA08	5	1	0
Burmese	EI03	5	1	0
Chenchu	EG01	4	2	1
Chin	EI19	0	2	1
Comanche	NE03	0	0	2
Copper Eskimo	NA03	10	1	0
Daka	AH29	5	0	0
Dorobo	AA02	5	0	1
Eastern Pomo	NC18	0	2	2
Hottentots	AA03	0	2	0
Inca	SF01	27	2	2
Ingasasana	AI04	5	0	0
Javanese	IB02	0	1	0
Kalmyk	CI01	5	2	0
Karen	EI07	5	1	2
Koreans	ED01	2	2	2
Lau	IH04	0	0	0
Lebanese	CJ07	1	2	2
Mbugwe	AD05	5	2	1
Merina	EH02	0	1	0
Miao	ED04	0	2	1
Miskito	SA09	0	0	0
Nicobarese	EH05	0	1	2
Northern Pomo	NC17	0	0	2
Omaha	NF03	0	2	0
Samoans	II01	0	0	0
Sanpoil	ND04	0	0	0
Tarasco	NJ08	0	2	2
Terena	SH02	0	0	2
Tupinamba	SJ08	0	0	0
Tzeltal	SA02	0	0	0
Yahgan	SG01	0	0	0
Yapese	IF06	5	0	2
Yokuts	NC03	0	0	2
Yukaghir	EC06	0	2	0
Yurak	EC04	0	0	1
Yurok	NB04	0	0	1

Note: Of these 41 cases, 14 are rated monogamous by the *Atlas* but considered to show 1–5% of females sharing a husband; 25 are rated polygynous by the *Atlas* but judged to have no females sharing a husband. (Since the Whiting group's codings were sometimes based on samples smaller than 100 marriages, the latter are likely to be cases in which polygyny is permitted but the degree of polygyny was too low to be protected.) The remaining cases, Copper Eskimo and Inca, are rated monogamous by the *Atlas* but considered by Whiting et al. to have 10% and 27% of females sharing a husband. None of these were used in analysis.
[a]0 = code not used; 1 = low-bias/no bias; 2 = high-bias/males-only.
[b]0 = code not used; 1 = bride-price; 2 = not cost.

32

If I Had It to Do Over

JOHN HARTUNG

First, I would have made the "no cost *versus* bride-price" comparison trichotomous—to "dowry *vs* no cost *vs* bride-price"—in order to clarify the relevance and prevalence of resource competition in human marriage systems. Given the potential difference in within-sex variance in reproductive success between men and women, the hypothesis that general polygyny will prevail in cultures where there is resource competition for spouses between husbands' families (bride-price) is logically complemented by the hypothesis that monogamy will prevail in cultures where there is resource competition for spouses between wives' families. As put by van den Berghe (1979), in stratified societies, "Through the bait of a dowry, upper-status women (and their fathers) can ensnare upper-status men against stiff competition by lower-status women who are quite happy to be had for free" (p. 101). But why "snare an upper-status man" if he is going to put your money into an account that enables him to support so many legitimate sons by so many legal wives that your son's/grandson's share of his bequeathed wealth will be a small piece of the cake? So it is that dowry associates even more strongly with monogamous marriage than bride-price associates with polygynous marriage (Table 32.1 $p < 6.6 \times 10^{-58}$, *Ethnographic Atlas* sample not corrected for Galton's problem, from Hartung 1983; cf. Hartung 1982, Fig. 2):

As is the case in bride-price societies, the initial competitors in dowry societies are parents of both genders, and the descendants who bring return on investment are male—in bride-price societies sons, in dowry societies grandsons. The dowry payoff is appreciated when male descendants are born into high-status, long-lived lineages in which monogamously married men are able to augment their reproductive success through serial monogamy and extramarital mating with those "lower-status women who [would be] quite happy to be had for free" as marriage partners, who require only somewhat more material compensation as extramarital partners, who give birth to daughters whose biological father does not supply dowry, and give birth to sons to whom their biological father does not bequeath wealth. Winners of dowry competition have grandsons who can have their cake and eat it too.

So the "female-competition" perspective on dowry (Gaulin and Boster 1990), and van den Berge's gender-challenged parenthetical remark, both supply an important piece of the picture. In dowry societies the initial payoff is shifted forward by one generation—that is, parents compete to have their daughters' sons born into wealthy families (Dickemann 1976, 1981) instead of competing to have their sons marry polygynously (see Josephson 1993 for an analogous frame shift among Mormons).

Table 32.1.

	Dowry	No Cost	Bride-Price
MONOGAMY	20 (80%)	70 (28%)	42 (7%)
OCCASIONAL POLYGYNY	3 (12%)	137 (55%)	153 (25%)
GENERAL POLYGYNY	2 (8%)	41 (17%)	407 (68%)

Second, because at least a dozen colleagues have asked in a tone of voice that would be the envy of most IRS auditors, if I had it to do over I would explain why the hypothesis put forth in "On Natural Selection and Inheritance of Wealth" (1976) and tested in "Polygyny and Inheritance of Wealth" (1982) was not presented as a test of Trivers and Willard's "Natural Selection of Parental Ability to Vary the Sex Ratio of Offspring" (1973). Paraphrasing and abbreviating what is taken by the auditors to be the relevant prediction, <u>Trivers and Willard hypothesized that within breeding populations of polygynous mammals, parents in relatively good condition will bias parental investment toward male offspring while parents in relatively poor condition will bias investment toward female offspring</u> (cf. Betzig, introduction).

The variable in Trivers and Willard's argument is parental investment whose disbursement is not influenced by cultural norms, whose magnitudes include amounts that are large enough to enhance a daughter's reproductive success but are too small to put a son over the polygyny threshold, and whose form of investment cannot be readily purloined by an offspring's mate—all types of investment that humans make but seldom, if ever, as inherited wealth.

A small percentage of societies in the *Ethnographic Atlas* are lumped into the code "no land rights/no inherited movable property, or no rule governing the transmission of same" for both movable and real property—that is, perhaps no inherited wealth, and no cultural norm in either case. If any of these societies have substantial amounts of inherited wealth but do not have rules governing it transmission (this is not delineated in the codes) such that individuals would not be influenced by cultural norms, and they are not highly stratified but are substantively polygynous, and women can protect inherited wealth for their own use, I would expect the female bias component of Trivers and Willard's hypothesis to have some effect.

With regard to the stratification stipulation, in societies where the Trivers and Willard hypothesis would otherwise apply, a subset of daughter-biasing decedents should only be found among parents whose bequeathed wealth is sufficient to enhance the reproductive success of a daughter but not sufficient or not of a type that would equally enhance the reproductive success of a son. However, if a society is highly stratified, with a small group of rich families and a large group of poor families, I would expect the prevailing norm to be a bias toward sons—because even a small inheritance can enhance a man's access to a large pool of poor women. Viewed from the other end of the wealth distribution, poor people in highly stratified societies may bias parental investment toward daughters, but that will seldom be in the form of inherited wealth because they seldom have any. The confounding relationship here is that polygyny, stratification, and wealth are usually covariates in traditional societies.

Even where there is a middle class, I would not expect daughter bias in inheritance of real or movable property (e.g., land and money) if such wealth and/or the income that it generates is subject to being used by a daughter's husband to pursue his reproductive interests in a manner that is to her and her parents' disadvantage—that is, by enabling him to afford additional wives or extramarital mates (this problem does not occur for types of nonpartible parental investment considered by Trivers and Willard—like skewing sex ratio toward females, nursing females longer, or investing in their subsequent health and nurture).

Under any condition, testing the Trivers and Willard hypothesis with inherited wealth would require information about the practices of individual decedents within societies—as distinct from inheritance norms across societies (a limiting attribute of the data I analyzed is that they refer to inheritance norms for whole societies, as distinct from individuals within societies). Smith, Kish, and Crawford (1987) analyzed individual inheritance practices in a nontraditional society by examining one thousand wills probated by the Supreme Court of British Columbia. They found statistically significant evidence for a bias toward daughters among the less wealthy and toward sons among the more wealthy. According to the authors, this is what Trivers and Willard's hypothesis would predict. My view is that the Trivers and Willard effect would not be precluded in such societies because they are not highly stratified, the range of economic status includes people who are wealthy enough to bequeath wealth but not wealthy enough to put sons over the serial monogamy or extramarital polygyny threshold, and being modern, relatively egalitarian, legalistic societies like Canada, a woman is reasonably capable of preventing her husband from using wealth derived from her parents to become polygynous. Nevertheless, what would be the advantage of biasing wealth toward daughters in a society where men are as likely as women to be married or otherwise reproductively engaged during their reproductive years—that is, where there is not a substantive pool of men whose parents have wealth to bequeath but who remain below an economic mating threshold? Put differently, why would a small or modest inheritance not help even a monogamous son as much as a daughter? My guess is that the daughter bias found by Smith, Kish, and Crawford results from uncertainty of grandpaternity and grandmaternity (Hartung 1985)—a risk that is outweighed when the amount of wealth bequeathed would make a son more likely to be a cuckolder than a cuckold, more likely to have an unmarried lover, and more likely to seek divorce than to be divorced.

Another complication in humans is that the correlation between economic status and genetic status is weak compared with the correlation between physical condition and genetic status in other mammals. In addition, wealth dissipates with degree of polygynous marriage in human males, whereas genetic superiority does not dissipate in consequence of polygynous mating in other male mammals. That is, a man with five wives has less wealth to pass on to his mother-in-laws' daughters' children than would the same man with one wife, but a nonhuman male mammal with superior genes passes those genes to his descendants almost without regard to the number of his mates. Each of these factors diminishes the prospect that biasing wealth toward daughters would enable them to obtain a mate that would cause a larger return, in terms of number or quality of grandchildren, than would non-gender-biased inheritance.

Inherited wealth has always appeared to me to be a variable for which hypotheses that apply to mammals generally often do not apply directly to humans (cf. Judge and Hrdy 1992). Trivers and Willard (1973:91) stated that "application of the model to humans is complicated by the tendency for males to invest parental effort in their young (which reduces variance in

male RS), and by the importance of kin interactions among adults." Indeed, and this appears to be particularly the case when the parental investment under consideration is inherited wealth, which might explain why none of over 1,200 societies in the *Ethnographic Atlas* are coded as favoring daughters—and even in polyandrous households, property is bequeathed to sons.

I presume that the preceding realizations explain why Trivers, with whom I began correspondence about this issue in January 1974 (see following), and whose student I have remained for more than twenty years, has not been among the auditors. That or my obtuseness in this regard explains why I am in anesthesiology!

Third, of course, if I had it to do over I would adapt the Mace/Pagel/Cowlishaw correction for Galton's problem (Mace and Pagel 1994; Cowlishaw and Mace 1996). Their procedure is an important refinement in general, and in particular, it reveals that the problem of not having "fewer cases in Cell b" is even larger than I perceived. Indeed, there is no difference between monogamy and limited polygyny when corrected by the "phylogenetic approach," but the reasons remain, I think, those which I elaborated—that is, the difference between marriage systems and mating systems, with polygynous mating swamping the difference between monogamous marriage and low-frequency polygynous marriage; for detailed investigations of polygynous mating in nominally monogamous societies, see Betzig 1992c; Pérusse 1993).

That said, I do not think that uncorrected analyses of *Ethnographic Atlas* societies are useless, though inferences should be limited to appropriate taxa. If we took a single large culture and arbitrarily divided it into one hundred subdivisions by placing it on a grid, assigning a separate identity to the people in each square, and found that individuals in subdivisions with higher frequencies of polygyny tend to favor sons in inheritance of wealth, we would be likely to have learned something true about that culture. And if cultural differences are driven by differences in economic, ecological, and social circumstances, rather than the other way around, then our finding would be generalizable to those circumstances in that culture. And if the subdivisions were not arbitrary but were instead based upon distinctions made by people within the subdivisions and so by anthropologists—even though those distinctions were not of sufficient magnitude to qualify any subdivision, or protoculture, as phylogenetically independent—then inferences about relations between economic, ecological, and social circumstances would extend to phylogenetically related subcultures.

In distinction, if we failed to find a relationship, we would be likely to make a false-negative inference from uncorrected analyses if we inferred a lack of relationship. That is, Galton's problem, or the lack of independence of societies considered as representing separate cultures, is like noise in a signal. It is more likely to obscure true relationships than to generate false ones. If we hear a weather report through much static but are able to detect a forecast of rain, we should pack the umbrella and leave the sun hat. However, if the reception is so bad that we cannot detect a forecast, we should pack both, pack neither, or stay home—but we should not decide, on that basis, to pack the sun hat and leave the umbrella. As the phylogenetic approach gains statistical power consequent to increased taxonomic delineation, it may prove more useful for detecting relationships that were previously obscure than for obscuring relationships that were previously evident.

That said, I think the great leap forward in cross-cultural analysis will be realized when Cowlishaw and Mace's phylogenies are sufficiently resolved to fulfill the promise of Maddison's (1990) and Pagel's (1994a) methods for ferreting out the causal direction of cultural change. Then we will be able to estimate the power of culture as a driving and/or inertial force (I think it is primarily the latter), factor it out, and make direct inferences about human nature from cross-cultural data—inferences about the nature of the beast independent of culture, inferences about culture independent of human nature, and inferences about interactions between the two.

Fourth, if I had it to do over, given Haig's reintroduction of the importance of differential reproduction of genes independent of differential reproduction of individuals, and specifically the potential importance of reproduction of imprinted genes (1992, 1993, 1995) on cross-cultural differences in human behavior (1994), I would have reiterated "The Chromosomal Corollary to Patrilineage" (Hartung 1976) in "Polygyny and the Inheritance of Wealth" (Hartung 1982).

For selection purposes, the entire Y chromosome can be considered to be imprinted, and on that basis alone or in combination with the potential paths of genes on a man's X chromosome, a male's fitness will be enhanced if his heritable wealth is passed to his son, his son's son, etc. And for genes on a woman's X chromosomes:

While this is not the ideal line of descent for a female (hers will be son's daughter's son's daughter's son, etc), some degree of male bias will provide a more effective fitness-maximizing effect than will transmission down a line of daughters. (Even though the descendent with the outstanding coefficient of relationship is not male, access to that descendent will depend on transmission through first-generation sons with some degree of male favoritism thereafter). (Hartung 1976:608, cf. Hartung 1985)

Perhaps these phenomena account for some son bias that is not due to the reproductive success of individuals (cf. Borgerhoff Mulder 1989b).

Last but not least, if I had it to do over, I would have made it clearer that inherited wealth, unlike money generally, is a source of much evil. Alfred Russel Wallace considered inherited wealth to be one of the four "root causes of evil": "it may be defined as *social injustice*, inasmuch as the *few* in each generation are allowed to inherit the stored-up wealth of all preceding generations, while the *many* inherit nothing. The remedy is to adopt the principle of equality of opportunity for all, or of universal *inheritance by the State in trust for the whole Community*" (1913, italics in original).

Today, in the United States, 40 percent of the nation's wealth is concentrated in only 1 percent of American households, and the principle of equality of opportunity is being eroded because less than 5 percent of the population possesses, by virtue of inheritance, more than six times the amount of wealth distributed across the bottom 50 percent of the population. Accordingly, our average modern-day aristocrat possesses, independent of contribution to the economy, more than sixty-three times the amount of wealth possessed by the average person who is not on the top half of the economic ladder, and this disparity is increasing (see Har-

tung 1988, references therein; Bradsher 1995).
I fancy that Wallace would have agreed with
the conclusion that "cross-generational congestion at the top of the economic scale necessarily causes chronic congestion at the bottom. It
is the people who start the ten-lap race on lap
four, or five . . . or nine who ultimately cause
our penal and mental institutions to be over-
crowded. . . . [and although] the connection between mental disorder and lack of economic opportunity is indirect . . . ultimately it is only
more subtle than the connection between mental disarray and a gunshot wound to the head"
(Hartung 1988).

Darwin, being a big-time heir himself, waf-
fled on the issue. Although he believed that "the
children of the rich have an advantage over the
poor in the race for success, independently of
bodily or mental superiority," he held that "the
inheritance of property by itself is very far from
an evil; for without the accumulation of capital
the arts could not progress; and it is chiefly
through their power that the civilized races have
extended, and are now everywhere extending
their range, so as to take the place of the lower
races" . . . and . . . "The presence of a body of
well-instructed men, who have not to labour for
their daily bread, is important to a degree which
cannot be over-estimated; as all high intellectual work is carried on by them, and on such
work, material progress of all kinds mainly depends, not to mention other and higher advantages."

Darwin even proffered a eugenic effect of inherited wealth: "Men who are rich through primogeniture are able to select generation after
generation the more beautiful and charming
women; and these must generally be healthy in
body and active in mind" (1871). Begging the
question of Isaac Newton and Thomas Paine,
Darwin's penchant for straightforward common
sense left him altogether when contemplating
his ability to hold tightly to his own: "My sole
and poor excuse is much ill-health and my mental constitution, which makes it extremely difficult for me to turn from one subject or occu-

pation to another. I can imagine with high satisfaction giving up my whole time to philan-
thropy, but not a portion of it; though this would
have been a far better line of conduct" (1887).

Charles Darwin—not able to walk and chew
gum at the same time? Wallace had it right.

Begging the reader's indulgence, I will end this
commentary with a bit of (a bit more?) self-in-
dulgence. In the spring of 1973, when I penned
the male-bias hypothesis for my senior thesis
as an undergraduate in anthropology at the University of Pennsylvania, the professor who received it was perplexed and forwarded a copy
to a newly arrived Professor Frank Johnston.
Johnston called me into his office, introduced
himself, and said, almost apologetically, that
my paper was important and that he thought I
was right—and that fewer than half a dozen anthropologists in the world would understand
what I was on about. As I left, Johnston suggested that I try some people at Harvard. He
mentioned Trivers, whom I presciently mistook
to be an anthropologist.

In January 1974 I sent the manuscript to
Trivers, who replied quickly with a construc-
tive, insightful, encouraging letter. Having no
sense of propriety in my youth, I also sent the
paper to Claude Lévi-Strauss. His return letter
was less encouraging (parentheses not added):
"To avail myself of Laplace's famous reply to
Napoleon about the place of God in his system,
my personal feeling is that we (i.e. anthropologists) do not need those hypotheses."

Work done in human sociobiology over the
ensuing years, only a speck of which can be presented in this volume, shows that Lévi-Strauss
was wrong and Trivers was right. Anthropologists are in desperate need of any testable hypotheses, and they are especially in need of
testable hypotheses that are grounded in evolutionary theory. Moreover, I am of the conviction
that Laplace, one of the greatest theorists and em-
piricists to have ever graced the endeavor of science, would have sided with sociobiologists in
this and all other important regards.

33

Cross-Cultural Patterns in the Training of Children: An Evolutionary Perspective

BOBBI S. LOW

Considerable data concerning patterns of child rearing in different cultures exist (e.g., Barry, Bacon, and Child 1957; Barry, Josephson, Lauer, and Marshall 1976). As Konner (1981) noted, cross-cultural research on children's behavior in natural circumstances has suggested that sex or gender differences we observe in American and English children are not limited to Anglo-Saxon cultures (e.g., Blurton-Jones and Konner 1973; Whiting and Edwards 1973; Whiting and Whiting 1975) and that there are both differences and similarities cross-culturally in how boys versus girls are treated.

However, previous analyses of sex differences in child rearing (Ember 1981; Rosenblatt and Cunningham 1976) have not found any clear logical patterns in the existing variation. In part, this may have arisen from a failure to use the extraordinary advances in evolutionary theory of the past decade, something Konner (1981) has urged. A false dichotomy may have persisted between biological and social causes, both defined narrowly; often only proximate mechanisms are considered in hypotheses. For example, biological hypotheses typically concerned whether sex differences could be clearly related to hormonal or brain lateralization differences. Biological determinism has often been inferred from such situations as a behavior that occurs in all cultures, a behavior that occurs at a typical age, and so forth. Konner and Ember correctly criticized such arguments, which simply make assumptions on the basis of analogy. It is at the least misleading to assume a dichotomy between some sort of biological-genetic determinism, assumed to be fixed and immutable, and social causes of behavior, assumed to have no correlation with genotype. All behavior is the result of interactions between alleles and environment, and experience and ontogeny are important for all species, not just humans.

The purpose of this article is to test hypotheses derived from evolutionary theory about the functional significance of sex differences in child-rearing practices across cultures. The evolutionary paradigm, both simple and broad, has helped elucidate complex patterns of social behavior in nonhuman species (e.g., Daly and Wilson 1983; Krebs and Davies 1984). Although human societies are clearly more complex and more variable than those of any other species, this paradigm can be used to generate testable hypotheses.

The theoretical background is simple: The array of traits exhibited by organisms is postulated to be, directly or indirectly, the result of differential reproduction of individual organisms of different genetic composition. The simple statement might read "every trait of every organism" but, as Dobzhansky (1961) noted, although inheritance is particulate, development is unitary. Organisms are complex arrays and combinations of traits, and their relative success can seldom be dissected into any particular trait, independent of others. Thus, (a) heritable variation exists; and (b) in any environment not all variants survive and reproduce equally well.

Reprinted with permission from *Journal of Comparative Psychology* 103:311–19 (1989).

These assumptions are made in order to produce hypotheses on why and how a particular trait, such as a child-rearing pattern, might advance individual genetic success and why different strategies might be predicted under different circumstances. Natural selection is only one part of the evolutionary process, but the effects of genetic drift (accidentally biased losses of genetic material) and new mutations (which are, of course, acted on by selection) are minor compared to the impact of selection and apparently produce no pattern in the direction of change (Alexander 1979; Williams 1966a).

Some early attempts to examine evolutionary patterns in human behavior have been criticized as deterministic, given human flexibility. It is important to note, however, that behavior in other species is far more complex and flexible than widely recognized and involves alternate strategies and learning. My approach here, like many other recent attempts, is a behavioral ecological one, focusing on the ecological correlates of training rather than on the mechanisms or the relative contribution of genetic versus cultural factors.

This does not mean that the only behaviors appropriate for analysis are those for which we can establish a clear one allele/one behavior correlation. Some genetic basis is assumed for purposes of hypothesis making. It does not mean that any behavior is *programmed* in the sense of developing without environmental influence. It does mean that certain correlations ought to exist between environmental conditions (including social conditions) and behaviors (including learned behavior) and that if we can describe the selective environment appropriately, we may be able to predict the characteristics of behaviors that will have evolved because they raise fitness. The patterns may be mediated either genetically or culturally; in fact, the tendency for transmission to be more or less genetic or cultural is subject to natural selection and can be predicted, given appropriate information about the environment (Boyd and Richerson 1985).

HYPOTHESES ABOUT CHILD-REARING PRACTICES FROM EVOLUTIONARY THEORY

In other species, patterns of parental care, offspring development, and play are related to the mating system, trophic level, and degree of sociality and group-living of the species (Daly and Wilson 1983; Fagen 1981; Krebs and Davies 1981, 1984; Trivers 1985; Wittenberger 1981a). Sex differences are more pronounced in polygynous than in monogamous species, and the exaggeration of male traits is related to competition for resources, mates, or both.

The evolutionary background of humans appears to be polygynous (cf. Alexander 1979), and 1,078 out of 1,158 (93%) societies for which data exist are polygynous (Murdock 1967, 1981). Polygynous marriage systems constitute a social institution with great biological impact. Biologists (e.g., Krebs and Davies 1984) often define polygyny as a situation in which a male mates with several females, whereas females mate with only one male. Anthropologists (e.g., Kottak 1978) typically define it as a marital relationship that involves multiple wives. Polygyny in humans, however,

can be more varied and complex than in other species (e.g., White 1988). Co-wives may be sisters or unrelated, may live together or apart. In some societies, bravery in war or success in accumulating resources may be sufficient for a man to acquire more than one wife. In other societies, the number of wives may be restricted according to class or rank. A few societies have reproductive despotism in which the leader may have hundreds of wives or concubines (Betzig 1986).

Both anthropologists and biologists have recently become interested in sexual selection and the ecological and cultural correlates of marriage systems. In biological terms, the degree (percentage) and intensity (maximum harem size) of polygyny, other things being equal, reflect opportunity for and intensity of sexual selection. Determining whether other things are equal may, however, be a serious problem (Low 1988a; White 1988), as noted above.

The result of polygyny is that, other things being equal, fewer males than females contribute to each generation (Alexander et al. 1979), and thus the variance in male reproductive success typically is greater than the variance in female reproductive success (Bateman

1948). More men than women in any generation fail to have any children, and more men than women have very large numbers of children. Thus males may be constrained to expend considerable effort to get mates. This is likely to be true not only for formally polygynous systems but also for socially imposed monogamous and promiscuous polygynous systems.

This asymmetry in variance between the sexes reflects the relative intensity of sexual selection: The greater the variance, the more intense the selection (Wade and Arnold 1980; cf. Falconer 1981; Low 1988a). Because the intensity of sexual selection differs between the sexes, it seems likely that men and women, like males and females of other polygynous species, have maximized their reproductive success through different sets of behaviors throughout their evolutionary history. If this is true, and if the behavioral differences follow the same patterns as those of other polygynous species:

1. Sons and daughters ought to be trained differently in all societies; and

2. Sons ought to be inculcated more strongly than daughters in competitive behaviors that are likely to result in the acquisition and control of resources useful in getting mates.

These are not powerful predictions; even a cursory examination of Barry et al.'s (1976) data suggests that they are likely to be upheld. Furthermore, they predict nothing more than universal sex differences in training. The following are an attempt to generate less obvious and more specific predictions:

3. The more polygynous the society, the more boys ought to be taught to strive. The variance in reproductive success increases for men as the degree of polygyny increases (Low 1988a), and a very few men may be extremely successful, whereas many men may fail entirely (e.g., Betzig 1986; White 1988). In such situations, the rewards for training boys to strive may be great.

4. In stratified societies, whether the stratification is by wealth or heredity, the impact of striving on reproductive success for men may be muted. That is, whereas women may marry up to a higher class, men are seldom able to do so. Furthermore, stratified societies frequently have rules that limit not only the males' status but the number of wives allowed to men of different statuses. Thus, the more stratified the so-

ciety (the more reduced the correlation between striving and possible reproductive payoffs to males), the less boys are taught to strive openly (though sneaky competition may exist). Because there is some association between stratification and polygyny (stratified societies tend to be polygynous), but the impacts of polygyny and stratification are opposed, it is important to separate the impacts of the two conditions.

5. Stratified polygynous societies with hypergyny ought to show stronger inculcation of daughters in sexual restraint and obedience than in other societies, because these increase a woman's apparent value to prospective high-status husbands.

6. Because male-male coalitions are well developed and important in patrilocal societies (see Flinn and Low 1986), sons in patrilocal societies ought to be strongly inculcated in traits useful in potential new coalition members (e.g., obedience, but also traits like fortitude).

7. Regardless of the inheritance system, and even in patrilineal societies, women may sometimes have considerable control over real resources in day-to-day life (Low 1990b; Whyte 1978). The more actual control women have over resources (the less dependent they must be on men for those resources), the less daughters ought to be taught to be submissive and obedient.

8. The larger the group, the greater the potential for numerous and varied individual conflicts of interest; Alexander (1979) and others have argued that this has led to the imposition of monogamy on individual persons by the group (or by powerful leaders or coalitions within the group). Getting large groups of men to cooperate in hunts or raids, for example, when their (reproductive) interests diverge and may be in serious conflict, can be difficult. Chagnon (1979a, 1982) has found that the polygynous and aggressive Yanomamö live in villages of no more than 200. When the group becomes larger than approximately 200, interfamilial conflicts of interests become severe, and the group splits, or fissions, into two smaller villages. The fissions occur along family lines and follow genetic-reproductive confluences of interest.

Powerful leaders in large groups clearly have an interest in minimizing intragroup conflict.

Both hunters and warriors cooperate more effectively and safely when internecine feuds are absent or minimized—and nothing gives rise to such feuds more powerfully than conflicts over women. Manson and Wrangham (1991) found that in 75 societies in which warfare was conducted, women (including abductions, failure to deliver a promised bride, etc.) were cited as the cause or reward of conflict in 34 (45%); women were the most frequently cited cause. In a further 29 (39%) societies, resources (useful for bride-price or correlated with increased reproductive success) were cited as the cause or reward of conflict. Thus, conflicts of interest over women, among the men in a large group, may seriously impair the effectiveness of the group when interacting with other groups or societies. Group unity and effectiveness are likely to be promoted by powerful leaders or subgroups that urge or impose monogamy, even though monogamy may carry a reproductive cost compared with polygyny for richer, more powerful, or more able men.

The same logic leads to the prediction that the larger the group size, the more children, particularly boys, ought to be taught to be industrious, obedient, and restrained in order to minimize friction within the group.

METHOD

The sample comprised the odd-numbered societies of the standard cross-cultural sample, which are stratified for geographical location and language group, and for which available ethnographies are by qualified ethnographers resident with the society for a considerable period of time.

Data for inculcation of children were taken from Barry et al. (1976). Data from Barry et al. (1957), which reported greater differences between the sexes (cf. Ember 1981), were deliberately not used, because the hypotheses tested here predicted sex differences. Barry et al.'s (1976) categories were highly specific: (a) *fortitude*, the suppression of visible reaction to pain, exertion, and so forth; (b) *aggression*, overt and covert training of aggressive behavior toward persons or animals; (c) *competitiveness*, achievement of superiority over others, especially peers, for example, in competitive games or crafts; (d) *self-reliance*, initiative and encouragement of unsupervised activity; (e)

achievement, demand for acquisition of skills and excellence in skills (but self-referential rather than in open competition against peers); (f) *industriousness*, diligence on the basis of the requirement that the child keep busy on responsible jobs; (g) *responsibility*, regular performance of duties or economic activities without continual supervision; (h) *obedience*, the degree to which children are expected to obey specific requests by parents and other authority figures; (i) *self-restraint*, the degree to which children openly express emotions, including crying, anger, or effusiveness; and (j) *sexual restraint*, restrictions on erotic play, masturbation, and heterosexual play. Barry et al. (1976) constructed the following summary categories as simple averages of types of inculcation that covaried: (a) *toughness*, fortitude, aggression, and competition; (b) *maturity*, self-reliance and achievement; (c) *dutifulness*, industry and responsibility; (d) *submission*, obedience and sexual restraint. These summary categories are useful in analyzing broad trends. All codes in the original paper ranged from 1 to 5, with plus and minus modifiers for some levels. In all, 11 levels were represented; for this analysis, these were converted to a simple ordinal scale: $1 = 1$, $2- = 2$, $2 = 3$, $2+ = 4$, $3- = 5$, $3 = 6$, $3+ = 7$, $4- = 8$, $4 = 9$, $4+ = 10$, $5 = 11$. Early childhood begins when the child is walking and talking proficiently or when "the society considers the child past infancy," and late childhood begins at approximately 7, 9, or 11 years, depending on the society, and is marked by "important changes in treatment or status" (Barry et al. 1976, p. 85).

Eighty-nine percent (83 of 93) of the societies in this sample were polygynous. Codes for degree of polygyny were taken from Low (1988a); the code combines the percentage of men polygynously married and the percentage of women polygynously married, in order to reflect the potential variance in reproductive success for men versus for women. Codes for the maximum number of wives or concubines were taken from Betzig (1986); this represents the maximum reproductive payoff available for men in any society, but the measure is complicated by the fact that very large maximum harem sizes occur in societies with stratification, which can severely limit the reproductive opportunities for most men. Codes for stratification were taken from Murdock (1967, 1981).

Codes for women's ability to control resources, who has authority over children, and systematic male absence were taken from Whyte (1978).

Because data were categorical and ordinal, nonparametric statistics were used. When relationships were predicted to be linear, Spearman's rho was calculated (Conover 1980). When differences between or among categories were predicted, Wilcoxin matched-pair rank-sum and Kruskal-Wallis statistics were calculated (Conover 1980). Calculations were performed with the MIDAS statistical package of the Michigan Terminal System.

RESULTS

In this sample, as in Barry et al.'s (1976) original study, there are society-wide correlates in the training of boys and girls. For all of the traits examined, the intensity of training of boys and girls across societies covaried; rho ranged from .60 (industriousness) to .91 (competition) and the pattern was strong ($p < .0001$ in all cases). Thus, societies in which boys are trained to show considerable fortitude, for example, are also the societies in which girls are trained to show fortitude. These trends show only that some societies train their children more intensely than others. These broad, non-sex-specific differences in intensity of training are reflected in the different parenting styles reported by Whiting and Edwards (1988), who found three broad different inculcation styles: *training* mothering styles (e.g., in sub-Saharan Africa), by mothers who used prosocial commands and recruited their children to help them work at an early age; *controlling* mothers (e.g., in the Philippines and Mexico), who used reprimands and threats in child training rather than task assignments; and *sociable* mothers (e.g., in the U.S.) who had more opportunity for play and information transfer.

There are, in addition, significant differences in the training of boys and girls within societies, independent of broad differences in training intensity. Across all societies, boys are taught, in early and late childhood, to show more fortitude and be more self-reliant than girls (Table 33.1 and Figure 33.1). Girls are taught, in early and late childhood, to be more industrious, responsible, obedient, and sexually restrained than boys (Table 33.1 and Figure 33.1). The

Table 33.1. Comparison (Wilcoxin Rank-Sum Test) of the Inculcation of Boys and Girls

Trait and period	Sex more inculcated	n	p
Fortitude			
Early	Boys	63	<.001
Late	Boys	73	<.001
Aggression			
Early	—	52	.065
Late	Boys	59	.002
Competition			
Early	—	53	.500
Late	—	69	.065
Self-Reliance			
Early	Boys	77	.004
Late	Boys	75	<.001
Achievement			
Early	—	70	.455
Late	—	78	.585
Industriousness			
Early	Girls	84	<.001
Late	Girls	87	<.001
Responsibility			
Early	Girls	77	.004
Late	Girls	78	.002
Obedience			
Early	Girls	78	.002
Late	Girls	78	.002
Self-Restraint			
Early	Girls	65	.012
Late	—	66	.804
Sexual Restraint			
Early	Girls	71	<.001
Late	Girls	78	<.001

Note: Data are from Barry et al. (1976); sample is the odd-numbered societies of the standard cross-cultural sample. A dash indicates no significant difference between boys and girls.

strength of inculcation is more striking in later childhood (when children begin to assume responsibility; Barry et al. 1976) than in early childhood for most traits, as expected, and the probable impact of training is greater in later childhood than in infancy. Further analysis was restricted to later childhood.

Polygyny and Stratification

The greater the degree of polygyny, measured as the percentage of men and the percentage of women polygynously married (cf. Low 1988a), the more boys are taught to show fortitude, aggression, and industriousness (Table 33.2). Marginally significant trends exist for self-reliance and obedience. As the maximum harem size allowed increases (cf. Betzig 1986), so does intensity of training for boys to show for-

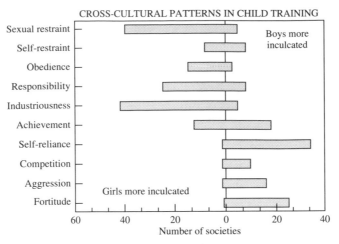

Figure 33.1 Comparison of the number of societies in which boys or girls are more strongly inculcated for each of the traits. (The overall length of the bar indicates the similarity or difference in training. The shorter the bar, the more boys and girls are similarly trained in the societies in this sample. The direction of difference is indicated by the left-right placement of the bar. Bars that extend to the left of the vertical line reflect traits inculcated more strongly in girls in more societies and bars that extend to the right reflect traits that are taught more strongly in boys in more societies.)

Table 33.2. Patterns of Training of Sons: Intensity of Each Trait for Boys Versus Maximum Harem Size and the Percentage of Polygyny

Trait	n	ρ	p
Fortitude			
Maximum harem size	44	.287	.065
Degree of polygyny	81	.234	.037
Aggression			
Maximum harem size	39	.141	.394
Degree of polygyny	74	.233	.046
Competition			
Maximum harem size	39	.208	.224
Degree of polygyny	74	.071	.529
Self-Reliance			
Maximum harem size	41	−.148	.344
Degree of polygyny	79	.208	.068
Achievement			
Maximum harem size	45	.186	.212
Degree of polygyny	80	.033	.699
Industriousness			
Maximum harem size	47	.348	.022
Degree of polygyny	88	.300	.004
Responsibility			
Maximum harem size	43	.327	.035
Degree of polygyny	82	.106	.352
Obedience			
Maximum harem size	44	.258	.084
Degree of polygyny	80	.203	.081
Self-Restraint			
Maximum harem size	38	−.024	.923
Degree of polygyny	68	.045	.707
Sexual Restraint			
Maximum harem size	45	.100	.513
Degree of polygyny	79	−.074	.528

titude, industriousness, responsibility, and obedience (Table 33.2).

Many societies with very large maximum harem size are also stratified societies, in which the reproductive opportunities are severely constrained for many men (those in lower classes), and the impacts of stratification should oppose those of polygyny. Stratification is not simply redundant with polygyny, however; 43 of 80 polygynous societies in this sample were stratified (3 had no data on stratification), as were 4 of 7 of the monogamous societies and 1 of 3 of the polyandrous societies. I therefore separated stratified from nonstratified societies (Figure 33.2).

The correlations between the degree of polygyny (Low 1988a) and male training in fortitude, aggression, obedience, toughness, and dutifulness arise solely from the pattern displayed by the nonstratified societies (Figure 33.2). The correlations between maximum harem size and male inculcation for fortitude ($n = 44$, $\rho = .29$, $p = .06$), industriousness ($n = 97$, $\rho = .35$, $p = .02$), obedience ($n = 44$, $\rho = .26$, $p = .08$), toughness, and dutifulness also are a consequence of the pattern solely in nonstratified societies. Furthermore, the correlations between training for submissiveness and degree and intensity of polygyny are not sig-

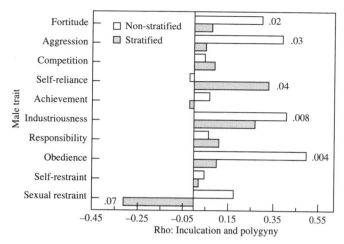

Figure 33.2. The rho values for relationships between degree of polygyny and inculcation traits are reported separately for stratified versus nonstratified societies. (Significance values from Table 33.2 do not arise equally from stratified and nonstratified societies and are reported above appropriate bars. Values in Table 33.2 for fortitude, aggression, obedience, and industriousness arise solely from the pattern displayed by nonstratified societies. The relationship between degree of polygyny and self-reliance is related solely to the pattern displayed by stratified societies. See text for further explanation.)

nificant overall but are significant for nonstratified societies. Training for competitiveness and maximum harem size similarly are not significantly correlated, except for nonstratified societies ($n = 19$, $\rho = .76$, $p = .0009$). These patterns suggest that the limitations on variance in reproductive success imposed by stratification have important impacts on the training for sons to strive. If a man's reproductive success is largely set by his social or class position and unlikely to be changed much by (potentially expensive and dangerous) striving, parents are unlikely to inculcate value of striving.

Conversely, other correlations with degree of polygyny arise solely from the pattern displayed by stratified societies. The more rigidly stratified the society, the less older boys are trained to be self-reliant ($n = 77$, $\rho = -.37$, $p = .001$), and the more they are trained to be industrious ($n = 85$, $\rho = .27$, $p = .02$), and to a lesser extent obedient ($n = 77$, $\rho = .19$, $p = .10$). The patterns of inculcation for male industriousness and male sexual restraint also do not covary in stratified versus nonstratified societies. In stratified societies, as the maximum harem size increases, so does intensity of inculcation for industriousness ($n = 22$, $\rho = .51$, $p = .02$; Table 33.2). No pattern is evident for nonstratified societies. Inculcation for male

sexual restraint increases somewhat with maximum harem size ($n = 18$, $\rho = .42$, $p = .06$) for nonstratified societies. For stratified societies, an opposite pattern is evident with the degree of polygyny; as the degree of polygyny increases, inculcation for male sexual restraint decreases somewhat ($n = 22$, $\rho = -.28$, $p = .08$).

Because broad patterns in the intensity of training of boys and girls generally covary, it is possible that the patterns in boys' training simply reflect general patterns in child training and are not the result of sexual selection, as proposed in the hypotheses; to eliminate this possibility, we must eliminate the possibility that the traits of interest simply covary for boys and girls.

There are 12 traits that show some pattern in the training of boys or girls, with the degree or intensity of polygyny, in stratified or nonstratified societies. Seven of these are exclusive to one sex; 6 are exclusive to boys, one to girls (cf. Barry et al. 1976, who noted that the intensity of training is greater for boys). As intensity (maximum harem size) of polygyny increases, boys, but not girls, are trained to show fortitude, competitiveness, sexual restraint, and obedience (nonstratified societies), or industriousness (stratified societies). As the degree of polygyny (the percentages of men and of women polygynously married) increases, boys, but not girls, are taught to show fortitude and to be aggressive and industrious (nonstratified societies). In stratified societies, as the degree of polygyny increases, boys are taught to show less sexual restraint and more self-reliance. Girls, but not boys, are trained to be responsible in nonstratified polygynous societies. For girls, training in responsibility and industriousness increases with both intensity and degree of polygyny in both stratified and nonstratified societies. No such general pattern is evident for boys. Thus, the observed patterns do not appear to be due simply to covariance in the training of boys and girls.

In stratified societies, hypergyny is common. A woman who marries up may not have more children than a woman who marries within her class, but her children are likely to be better-invested and survive better. The traits expressed as desirable in wives in stratified societies are chastity and obedience (cf. Dickemann 1979b). The more stratified the society, the more older girls (Hypothesis 5) are taught to be sexually restrained ($n = 77$, $\rho = .33$, $p = .004$) and obedient ($n = 75$, $\rho = .22$, $p = .05$), and the less they are urged to be self-reliant ($n = 73$, $\rho = -.32$, $p = .006$).

Table 33.3. Relationship of Group Size to Training

Trait	n	ρ	p
Male Training			
Fortitude	79	.0486	.5787
Aggression	73	.1465	.2222
Competition	73	.1521	.1738
Self-Reliance	77	−.2344	.0442
Achievement	78	.0527	.6064
Industriousness	86	.1662	.1130
Responsibility	80	.0303	.7902
Obedience	78	.3252	.0040
Self-Restraint	66	.2197	.0636
Sexual Restraint	77	.3719	.0013
Toughness	87	.1200	.2157
Maturity	84	−.0740	.5224
Dutifulness	86	.1392	.1924
Submissiveness	85	.3822	.0005
Female Training			
Fortitude	72	−.1845	.1246
Aggression	58	.0131	.9166
Competition	69	.1231	.2807
Self-Reliance	73	−.2672	.0214
Achievement	77	.0514	.6178
Industriousness	86	.1415	.1762
Responsibility	77	−.0680	.5465
Obedience	77	.2953	.0100
Self-Restraint	64	.1111	.3673
Sexual Restraint	78	.4255	.0001
Toughness	82	−.0446	.7505
Maturity	83	−.1043	.3982
Dutifulness	86	.1071	.3110
Submissiveness	84	.4137	.0001

Other Hypotheses

In patrilocal societies, in which male-male coalitions are important and older men in established coalitions have considerable say over younger men's rise in such coalitions, sons are taught to be obedient to a greater degree than in any other marital residence pattern ($n = 71$, KW $= 4.93$, df $= 1$, $p = .03$).

The more women actually control important resources or exercise power, the less daughters are taught to be submissive (Hypothesis 7). For example, the more women are able to inherit property, the less daughters are taught to be obedient ($n = 63$, $\rho = .55$, $p = .00001$). The more formal power women have within the kin group, the more daughters are taught to be aggressive ($n = 43$, $\rho = .31$, $p = .05$), and the less they are trained to be industrious ($n = 61$, $\rho = .27$, $p = .04$). In societies in which women can hold political office, daughters are more strongly inculcated in achievement ($n = 62$, $H = 2.9$, $p = .09$) and striving ($n = 70$, $H = 3.1$, $n = .08$) than in societies in which women

cannot hold office, although the difference is only marginally significant. The more authority women have over children older than four (Whyte 1978), the less daughters are taught to be obedient ($n = 59$, $\rho = -.42$, $p = .001$).

The larger the size of the social group, the less both sons and daughters are taught to be self-reliant, and the more they are taught to be obedient, sexually restrained, and submissive (Table 33.3). In this test the inculcation of boys and girls covaried; there is thus no evidence of sex differences in training to maximize success in getting a mate. Rather, as group size increases, inculcation of both sexes becomes stronger for traits that reduce friction within the group. These results support the argument of Alexander (1979) and others that as group size increases, so do societal constraints on individual persons, and are consistent with Barry et al.'s (1976) discussion of political complexity and inculcation in self-reliance, obedience, and sexual restraint.

DISCUSSION

My results suggest that sons and daughters are trained differently in ways that relate to the evolutionary history of reproductive success of the two sexes. Such results would hardly be surprising when reported for any other polygynous mammal (e.g., Clutton-Brock, Guinness, and Albon's 1982 meticulous study of red deer was subtitled "The Ecology of Two Sexes"), but the suggestion of differential paths to reproductive success for the two sexes in humans throughout evolutionary time may seem almost offensive to some. It is important, however, to understand past selective pressures if we wish to understand male-female differences or to be successful in modifying male-female patterns of behavior toward equality in our own society.

Several cautions are important here. The original categories include conclusions by ethnographers from observation and from discussions. Clearly, what people say they do may not, in fact, be what occurs. Even if only observational data were included, data from all societies are not from comparable periods, and different ethnographers may have vastly different interests in child-training practices—thus the depth of data for different societies may vary. The discussions are also largely with adult respondents; however, in some societies, peers have a large role in child care, and peer inculcation can differ significantly from adult inculcation (cf. Draper and Harpending 1986).

More important, and much more fruitful from the point of view of future research directions, is the fact that the categories used here (Barry et al. 1976) report one level of intensity for each society, probably what the ethnographer considered the mode; yet it is obvious that the optimum strategies for all parents in any society are not identical. In stratified societies, for example, sons of high- and low-status parents are predicted to gain from quite different training (cf. Dickemann 1979b). We have no information on whether systematic differences exist, although there is evidence that the nature and dynamics of parent-offspring relationships are correlated with individual characteristics (Hinde and Stevenson-Hinde 1986).

Despite the strong inference provided by these data that childhood inculcation is a parental response to ecological and social pressures that affect reproductive success, I know of no direct data on the relative reproductive success of parents training their sons and daughters differently within any society. Data that male reproductive success is related to resource control and status (Betzig 1986; Betzig, Borgerhoff Mulder, and Turke 1988; Hill 1984; Low 1989b) do exist for a number of societies, however, and thus show that boys who learn to be successful in obtaining resources, status, or both grow up to be reproductively successful men.

Betzig's (1986) work showed clearly that in many societies there are clear formal reproductive rewards for achievement: High-status men have more wives. In the Turkmen, Irons (1979a, 1979b) found that richer men had more wives and children than poorer men. A similar pattern exists in Trinidad, and men of different status pursue quite different strategies to get mates (Flinn 1983). On Ifaluk, men who hold power have more wives and better surviving children (Turke and Betzig 1985). Even in apparently egalitarian societies in which few or no physical resources are owned or controlled, differences may be dramatic. Chagnon (1979a) found that variance in male reproductive success, as measured by the number of children and grandchildren, was extreme and correlated with status in the Yanomamö. Chagnon (1979a, 1982, 1988) noted that male kin available for coalitions are, in fact, a major resource for the Yanomamö and that men manipulate kinship terminology in ways that maximize the availability of women as mates and of powerful men as coalition partners. In the Yanomamö, political status (becoming a chief) is reproductively advantageous; so is becoming an established revenge killer, *unokai* (Chagnon 1988). All chiefs are *unokai* and have large male kin groups. Hill (1984), reviewing less detailed data, found a positive relationship between resource control or prestige and reproductive success for men in several other cultures: the !Kung, Murngin, Nuer, Tallensi, Rajput, and Chinese. In two other societies, the Tlingit and the Nupe, he found that men could control excess resources and that these were frequently used in ways apparently unrelated to reproduction.

Even during and after the demographic transition, wealth may have reproductive impacts. In 19th-century Sweden, men who owned more than the average amount of farmland had more children than men with less than the average amount (Low 1991a). In the United States, Essock-Vitale (1984) and Daly and Wilson (1983) found that reproductive success had a positive relationship to wealth. Vining (1986) argued that no such differences exist, but he had incomplete data and used proxies such as IQ and education for resource control.

The positive relationship seems to hold generally for technological and nontechnological and for egalitarian and stratified societies, with a variety of subsistence bases. It is therefore not surprising that across all societies boys are trained to strive.

Data on the correlates of women's reproductive success are more elusive, despite the fact that maternity is easier to assign than paternity. In the majority of societies for which there are data, polygynously married women tend to have fewer children than monogamously married women (reviewed by Daly and Wilson 1983); most of that difference arises because second and subsequent wives have fewer children than first wives of polygynous men. In the United States (perhaps surprisingly, because of the demographic transition), wives of affluent men have more children earlier in life than the wives of poorer men (Daly and Wilson 1983). I know of no data on other correlates predicted in this paper.

Barry et al. (1976) noted that intercorrelations among traits were stronger for boys than girls; boys are trained more intensely and consistently. The observation that male reproductive success varies more than female reproductive success in polygynous systems may support an argument that the reproductive payoffs for parents are higher for successful training of sons than of daughters. In this context, it is interesting that in our society children themselves quickly show sex differences in perceptions of dominance and aggression. By age 3, boys play in larger groups and play more aggressive games than girls (Freedman 1974; Omark and Edelman 1975). By age 4, boys tend to advertise themselves as toughest (Omark and Edelman 1975); by age 6, they form dominance hierarchies, perceive them accurately, and attempt to manipulate their position (Freedman 1980)—whereas girls find the entire question irrelevant! Consistent with these studies, Piaget (1932) found girls more tolerant in their attitudes toward rules and more willing to make exceptions.

Not only do boys play more often than girls in large age-heterogeneous groups and play more competitively, boys' games last longer than girls' (Lever 1976). This is apparently not because boys' games are more complex or less boring, but because continual disputes over rules arise and boys engage in conflict resolution. In Lever's study, boys were "seen quarreling all the time, but not once was a game terminated because of a quarrel, and no game was interrupted for more than seven minutes" (p. 482). It almost appeared that the negotiation of rules was as important as the game itself; certainly it was more constant—whatever the game, boys argued about the rules. Among girls, the occurrence of a dispute tended to end the game; in a sense the girls sacrificed the continuation of the game for the continuation of the relationship (as if no options for negotiation within the coalition or for changing coalitions existed). These differences are understandable if in evolutionary history women have enhanced their reproductive success by cooperating in the household sphere with sisters and co-wives—that is, in situations in which they could not gain through open conflict or by attempting to change coalitions. Men have enhanced their reproductive success by cooperating with both related and nonrelated men to get resources and power—situations in which open assertion of dominance may frequently gain (Low 1990b). The data from this study and the cross-cultural patterns in inculcation of children suggest that this may indeed have been the case.

The interplay between the effects of polygyny and stratification on possible reproductive success for men and boys's training are particularly interesting. The greater the possible reproductive rewards, the more boys are taught to be industrious, obedient, and aggressive and to show fortitude, but the variation is great only in nonstratified societies. An examination of ethnographies highlights the significance of this pattern. In nonstratified polygynous societies, inheritance tends to be male-biased (Hartung 1982, 1983), and coalitions of related men are likely to be powerful, particularly in patrilocal societies (Boone 1986; Flinn and Low 1986). To be successful, a boy must not only show traits useful in getting and managing resources, but also traits recommending him to his elders in the coalition whose help he will need to bargain for wives. In stratified societies, male coalitions may also be important, but in these large societies, they are likely to be among non-related men, and a man's ability to move up the hierarchy may be severely constrained (see Betzig 1986).

There is thus some evidence that patterns of child training across cultures vary in ways predictable from evolutionary theory, differing in specifiable ways between the sexes, and varying with group size, marriage system, and stratification. The link to variance in reproductive success is not firmly established and represents a fruitful focus for research.

Acknowledgments. A number of persons provided helpful criticism. In addition to three anonymous reviewers, I am particularly indebted to John Alcock, Steve Frank, Robert Hinde, Margo Wilson, Elisabeth Cashdan, Nancy Thornhill, Monique Borgerhoff Mulder, R. D. Alexander, and members of the Evolution and Human Behavior Program of the University of Michigan.

34

Comparing Snakes and Snails and Puppy-Dog Tails to Sugar and Spice: Reflections on Cross-Cultural Testing of Hypotheses

BOBBI S. LOW

The central hypothesis of this paper was, first, that if parents profit reproductively by training their sons and daughters differently, reliable differences will exist in how sons versus daughters are trained cross-culturally, and second, that the extent of such differences will vary in predictable ways with the strength of selection (whether genetic or cultural) for such differences. Grafen's (1991) phenotypic gambit was assumed—that conditions were stable and reflected a history of selection. No genetic mechanisms were assumed, and both cultural and natural selection were assumed to operate.

The data used were previously published data on the Standard Cross-Cultural Sample of 186 societies, stratified for geographic distribution and (within geographic region) language group. I used the odd-numbered half sample (which probably is less than optimal, since a doubled sample size is always preferable), and thus had data on 93 societies (not all published data were available for all societies). Although the sample attempts to get rid of some obvious sources of data bias, in anthropology, widespread bias exists in some anthropological circles against use of cross-cultural data (e.g., see review by Barry 1981). Some of this bias is based on failure to understand how comparative method works; for example, it is not true that "comparative method lacks controls" (e.g., see Harvey et al. 1987; Harvey and Pagel 1991). But, as I explore in the following, these data have serious limitations, and anyone working with them should understand those limitations clearly.

A major assumption in any such study is that what people report reflects what they actually do—and of course this is frequently not the case in systems in which we have enough information to tell. Thus the codes from Barry et al. may be a better assessment of people's normative beliefs about child training than a clear reflection of what they do. Further, just as in many historical studies, what some people report doing may indeed reflect what they—but not others—do. The codes are "typological," as if all individuals in each society behaved similarly, and the codes will thus miss intrapopulation variation. In smaller, less stratified societies, the risk of significant unrecognized intrapopulation variation may be somewhat lower than in highly stratified societies, but the risk exists in all cases, and the codes will not reflect within-society variation. Thus, to have great confidence that these results reflect a real and selective outcome, I would want data from within a sample of societies about the marriage system, the preferred traits of successful adult males and females, the training of sons and daughters by parents in different circumstances, and the actual outcomes for the children trained by different parents in various ways. (Were I working on another species, clearly I would prefer to move from comparative method to experimental manipulation, but as others have noted, humans are notoriously hard to culture in the lab.)

It is currently popular to assume, since most texts from which data like these come were written by white males, that significant bias exists and that all such data are simply unreliable. It is very difficult to tell how much validity such claims have. My own approach has been twofold. First, for any codes relying on interpretation, I look for published codes, since these have at least been exposed to the peer-review process; second, I prefer using data, like those of Martin King Whyte (1978, 1979), for which intercoder agreement scores are published. Darwin himself noted that a bad theory isn't fatal, since others will work toward disproving it, but bad data can be, since detecting what's wrong will be difficult.

The results are simply correlational: they are consistent with the hypotheses tested but do not prove any causality. Further, the data may be consistent with other hypotheses. Barry et al.'s original paper argued that child-training practices may be tied to the economics of traditional societies; that agriculturalists and herders stress compliance, because they cannot afford departures from established routines, while hunter-gatherers stress individual assertiveness, since initiative will not interfere with daily food intake (which may be rather uncertain anyway). While every effort was made to identify alternate hypotheses for comparison and falsification, I can't be sure I have identified them all, much less falsified them. The results I got suggest that in nonstratified polygynous societies, males who are assertive and show initiative are likely, other things being equal, to marry earlier and more often than others, and to have more children. What we need to test now is within-society data: do males who are identified as "movers and shakers" in their society marry earlier and have more children? Some data exist (e.g., Chagnon 1988 for the Yanomamö, Borgerhoff Mulder 1987a for the Kipsigis; see review by Low 1993); these support the hypotheses I tested. And within-society analyses of other traits, like that of Hawkes (1991) on why hunters hunt, also suggest that the hypotheses are probably widely true. But no systematic studies exist, and the data remain correlational.

These are culturally transmitted patterns, and the rules or frequency at equilibrium differ between culturally and genetically transmitted traits (e.g., Boyd and Richerson 1985). Presumably some genetic transmission is involved, if only with regard to traits that make possible the complex behaviors, but whatever portion that represents is unknown, and probably small and not specific to any of these behaviors. Cultural transmission of the patterns could be not only vertical from parent to child (in a manner analogous to genetic transmission) but oblique (e.g., from nonrelated adults to children), horizontal (within peer groups), and in these last two modes, across cultures (e.g., Cavalli-Sforza and Feldman 1981). Cultural transmission across cultures certainly complicates interpretation of patterns: suppose that boys in African societies are really trained strongly to strive and that African societies are relatively polygynous. Geographically close societies are known to share cultural patterns ("cultural diffusion"), from food preferences to marriage preferences. Clearly, there is some possibility that child-training patterns could be shared from societies in which they were profitable to societies with different characteristics, in which they could be deleterious. In comparing human societies, as in comparisons of other species, we are utilizing the "phenotypic gambit" (Grafen 1991); we are assuming that whatever the relationship between the mode of transmission (genes, culture) and the trait, enough time has passed that the relationship is in equilibrium, and what we see reflects what selection favors. In the case of traits whose transmission and selection are largely cultural (and thus can shift very rapidly), our risk of seeing a trait that is not in equilibrium (e.g., is widespread even though it is deleterious) is greater than if we were examining a nonsocial trait (see Williams 1992).

In sum, I found it an interesting exercise to generate and begin to test a set of hypotheses derived from evolutionary theory using these data—but I certainly wouldn't want to interpret them without considering all the above caveats. I think the evolutionary/behavioral ecological paradigm is particularly useful in generating new hypotheses that would not arise from existing anthropological, psychological, or sociological paradigms, and that analyses like this one are of use to help us explore these hypotheses. Making a final determination of the relative strength of competing hypotheses will typically require more detailed data, as well as within-society analysis and cross-cultural comparisons.

35
Dowry as Female Competition

STEVEN J. C. GAULIN
JAMES S. BOSTER

Bridewealth is common and dowry is rare. Based on recently corrected codes (Schlegel and Eloul 1987; Schlegel 1988), brideprice and brideservice (collectively called bridewealth by Goody [1973] and others) are found in 97 of the 186 (52%) societies in the Standard Cross-Cultural Sample (Murdock and White 1969) and 839 of the 1,267 (66%) societies in the *Ethnographic Atlas* (Murdock 1986). In contrast, dowry is normative in only 12 of the 186 (6%) societies in the corrected Standard Cross-Cultural Sample and 35 of the 1,267 (3%) societies in the *Ethnographic Atlas*.[1]

Furthermore, dowry is essentially restricted to circum-Mediterranean and East Asian societies, a fact that Jackson and Romney (1973) interpret as due to its recent origin. However, even there it is far from universal. Thus, there remains the question as to what factors explain its distribution within this region.

In this article, we attempt to explain not only the rarity of dowry but also why it occurs in the societies it does. Our model builds on theory derived from behavioral ecology and views dowry as a form of competition among women for husbands. Before developing our model we review an alternative explanation of dowry that views this practice as an outcome of the sexual division of agricultural labor (Boserup 1970).

Boserup (1970) emphasizes women's agricultural labor as a determinant of whether brideprice or dowry will be paid. She describes two major types of societies. Brideprice societies are characterized by high female contribution to agricultural work (typically swidden systems), high female reproductive and economic autonomy, and a high incidence of polygynous marriage. Dowry societies feature low female contribution to agriculture (typically plow-cultivation systems), high levels of dependence of women and children on husband's economic support, and low incidence of polygyny (1970:48–50). In essence, her model views dowry as a payment made by women that guarantees future support for them and their children under circumstances where their own contributions to subsistence are relatively small. We refer to Boserup's model as the *labor-value* model, and we test it below in parallel with our own.[2]

THE MODEL: DOWRY AS FEMALE COMPETITION

The female competition model assumes that, in *Homo sapiens* as in other animals, the behaviors associated with pair formation can be interpreted as (possibly unconscious) reproductive tactics. We interpret the bias in marriage transactions as reflecting a bias in competition for marriage partners. On this view, the wide distribution of bridewealth and the rarity of dowry suggest that men frequently compete for wives, whereas competition among women for husbands is seldom of equal intensity. Men's

Reprinted with permission from *American Anthropologist* 92:994–1005 (1990).

frequent willingness to pay high stakes for wives suggests that it usually matters to them whom, when, and how often they marry. In contrast, the societies where women have driven up the stakes for husbands are few. In this article, we explore the causes of this bias.

This view of competition for mates does not assume that the suitors are the only relevant participants in marriage arrangements. Regardless of whether dowry or bridewealth is paid, parents and other kin frequently aid in amassing the transferred wealth and often negotiate the marriage contract. These facts are consistent with the generalization that humans invest in their offspring (and other kin) over many years. From a neo-Darwinian perspective, individuals should allocate resources so as to maximize their own genetic representation in future generations. Such investment of resources should extend to marriage transactions whenever contributions to dowry or bridewealth aid in this maximization, for example, by securing fitter mates or earlier marriages for kin (typically offspring). The question is, should such resources flow to dowry or bridewealth, to improve the reproductive prospects of female or male kin? In our model, the answer hinges on where the resources will produce a greater reproductive benefit.[3]

In our own species, as in most mammals, the average female and the average male enjoy equal reproductive success. However, in some cases the distribution of reproductive success differs by sex, with one sex (usually, but not always, males) exhibiting higher variance (Trivers 1972; Wade 1979). This has important evolutionary consequences because if, for example, males have higher variance in reproductive success, the most successful males will produce more offspring than the most successful females, and the least successful males will produce fewer offspring than the least successful females. Wherever such patterns prevail, parents should correspondingly adjust the flow of their resources to offspring. The issue is, will a given investment by parents produce more grandchildren when expended on a son or when expended on a daughter? We expect bridewealth to become common in the former case and dowry to become common in the latter.

Further development of the female-competition model requires an explication of the "polygyny threshold" (Orians 1969), an idea first used to explain the distribution of mating systems across avian species. Orians realized that males should almost always prefer polygyny because more female partners would result in more offspring. Why then, he asked, is polygyny not universal? His answer was that mating systems result from the dynamic tension between female and male interests, and that polygyny may emerge because females also prefer it.

Orians's polygyny threshold model (also called the "resource-defense polygyny" model), while not the only evolutionary path to polygyny (Alcock 1989:443–456), can be used to analyze any case where males provide or control access to resources that are useful to females in producing offspring. In such cases females should prefer the males who provide the best supply of resources, because females who do so would have the highest reproductive success. This insight leads to clear predictions about the distribution of monogamy and polygyny across species. If all males offer essentially similar resources, no male will be differentially attractive to females. Thus, with even resource distributions, the optimal female strategy is to pair only with an unmated male, thereby gaining exclusive access to his resources; any female who chose to share a male and his resources with another female would receive less resources and therefore have lower reproductive success than a female who chose monogamy.

By a very similar logic, uneven resource distributions promote polygyny. When males offer resources that differ substantially in quantity or quality, the wealthier males are more attractive potential mates because their superior resources can be translated into more offspring.[4] Under these conditions, a female should pair with the wealthiest male. The next female to pair should choose the second wealthiest, and so on. But at some point the polygyny threshold is reached: a female considers the nth wealthiest unmated male and sees a superior option, because half of what the wealthiest (already mated) male has exceeds all of what this n^{th} wealthiest male has to offer. At this point the female should choose polygyny because so choosing maximizes the resources she will have available for reproduction. For simplicity, this process is described as if it were sequential, although this is not an essential feature of the polygyny threshold model. What is important is merely that each female chooses, at the time

of pairing, the male with the best available resources, taking into account each male's resource commitments to current partners. The
outcome of this process, if females make the
best (that is, evolutionarily rational) choice, is
what we call *ideal free polygyny* (cf. Fretwell
and Lucas 1969). Under ideal free polygyny
there is a perfect positive correlation between a
male's wealth and the number of his female
partners.

An ironic result of ideal free polygyny is that
it precisely cancels the differential attractiveness of males. If, as the model assumes, a male
who is five times wealthier than the average has
five times as many mates as the average, and a
male who is four times wealthier has four times
as many mates, and so on, then all females receive equal shares of resources, no matter how
many or how few "cowives" they have. The
benefits of choosing a wealthy male are diluted
by the choices of other females in direct proportion to the male's wealth. Thus, within any
local population, a male's reproductive success
should increase with the number of his mates,
while females are expected to have roughly
equal reproductive success regardless of
whether they are monogamously or polygynously mated. Research on nonhuman populations supports these expectations (Carey and
Nolan 1975; Pleszczynska 1978), as do recent
carefully controlled studies of human populations (Borgerhoff Mulder 1987a).[5]

To summarize, when males control essentially similar resources, females will distribute
themselves one to a male. When males control
unequal resources, females will cluster with the
wealthy males (in the absence of other constraints). In neither case are there significant
differences among females in terms of the share
of resources that each receives. Hence, there are
no resource-related differences in female reproductive success and no resource-related reasons for females to compete for particular
males.

Under the type of monogamy described
above, the variance in male and female reproductive success should be roughly equal because, barring significant reproduction outside
the pair, each male will be limited to the offspring his sole partner can produce. However,
under polygyny, the variance in male reproductive success increases because some males
are able to produce offspring with more than a

single female. This means that human parents
could increase their numbers of grandchildren
by investing in bridewealth for their sons. Neither condition would seem to render dowry payments advantageous, and indeed we should not
expect them under either of the mating systems
described so far. But these patterns do not exhaust the range of human marriage systems.

Some societies are characterized by high levels of stratification and strong wealth differentials among males but are nevertheless monogamous. Betzig (1986) and Alexander (1975)
have previously noted these exceptions to the
polygyny threshold model (Alexander's cases
of "socially imposed monogamy") and have offered similar, plausible explanations. Our focus
is not on explaining the factors that precipitate
such cases of monogamy in stratified societies,
but rather to consider the conditions they create. They are important to our analysis because
they define the environment in which we expect dowry to emerge.

In stratified, monogamous societies, large
differences in wealth exist among men that are
not diluted by their acquisition of additional
wives, as in polygynous societies. Any female
who marries such a wealthy male monogamously can expect to have the bulk of his resources for her offspring and thereby enjoy
greater reproductive success than females who
are not so well mated. Thus, we interpret dowry
as a means of female competition for desirable
(that is wealthy) husbands in monogamous societies. Parents (and other kin) should be expected to collaborate in such competition whenever a well-married daughter will gain more or
less exclusive access to (although not necessarily control over) her husband's resources.
The simplest operationalization of this hypothesis is that dowry should be present in nonpolygynous, stratified societies, but absent
elsewhere. We test our model by examining the
accuracy of this prediction.

The key parameters of this behavioral ecological model take combinations of values
among humans that they apparently never take
among other animals (i.e., the conjunction of
monogamy with large differentials in male resources). Thus, it would be inappropriate to im-
port, uncritically, models of reproductive relations derived from birds or apes, for example.
Instead, we have extended the reasoning of evolutionary biology to interpret the dynamics and

adaptive consequences of a situation that is unique to humans. Employing this reasoning to understand dowry in no way implies that dowry itself has a direct genetic basis. Rather, we assume that humans seek efficient tactics for reproduction and that the efficiency of particular tactics depends on local conditions. In our model of dowry, the novel combinations of parameter values present novel problems, requiring novel solutions, all of which are cultural in nature.

METHODS

Each hypothesis to be tested predicts that dowry will occur only under a special conjunction of circumstances. Comparative or "cross-cultural" methods are ideal for testing such hypotheses. The analysis presented below examines the extent to which each model accurately predicts the distribution of dowry among the 1,267 societies of the *Ethnographic Atlas* (Murdock 1986) and within various subsamples of this large data set.

Operationalization of the Variables

Dowry is our dependent variable, but there may be some dispute over what range of practices ought to count as dowry. Goody (1973, 1976) and more recently Schlegel and Eloul (1987) have emphasized that many societies coded in the *Ethnographic Atlas* as having brideprice actually practice what these authors call "indirect dowry." In recognizing this category, they are marking an important distinction. In cases of true brideprice, a groom (often with the material aid of his kinsmen) passes items of value to the male relatives of the bride. These recipients may use the acquired wealth as they see fit; quite often they use it to purchase wives themselves. Cases of indirect dowry are superficially similar, but instead of retaining the brideprice for their own purposes, the male kin of the bride convey some nontrivial portion (in extreme cases, all of it) to the bride herself.

For our purposes, this complication is easily resolved using the principle articulated by Schlegel and Eloul:

If one is interested in who gives payment, then indirect dowry can be considered along with bride-price, since the source in both cases is the groom or his kin. If the purpose is to determine the recipient, however, then indirect dowry belongs with dowry given by the bride's family, since in both cases the goods go to the household of the new conjugal couple. (Schlegel and Eloul 1987:119–120)

Thus, Goody (1973, 1976), because he focuses primarily on the flow and dispersion of wealth within societies, has grouped dowry with indirect dowry in his analyses. Conversely, because we focus on competition for mates, we must attend to the source of payments and thus we separate indirect dowry from dowry proper.

This dependent variable and all the independent variables discussed below were drawn from the electronic version of the *Ethnographic Atlas* (Murdock 1986); all column numbers refer to the formatting of this 1986 version. We created a dichotomous code based on the mode of marriage (col. 6), coding dowry as present for those societies in which dowry is the normal practice, and coding dowry as absent in all other cases.

The independent variables in the female-competition model are social stratification and marital form. We grouped the existing categories to create dichotomous variables. We regarded a society as stratified if it was coded (col. 65) as having "elite," "dual," or "complex" stratification, and as nonstratified otherwise. With respect to marital form, the important issue is whether a woman is at risk of having to share her husband's resources with cowives. In polygyny a woman may have to compete with cowives for her husband's resources, whereas in monogamy or polyandry she will not. Thus we regarded these resources as shared (i.e., vulnerable to being shared and thus not worth competing for) if polygyny was at least "occasional," and as unshared otherwise (col. 9). Finally, we added an interaction term for each society, which was computed as the product of the dichotomous stratification and marital form variables.

The independent variables in the labor-value model are mode of subsistence and relative labor inputs of women and men to subsistence. Here again, we grouped categories to create dichotomous variables. The labor-value model predicts dowry in cases where there is a significant reliance on agriculture but women perform little of the agricultural labor. Societies were regarded as importantly agricultural only if they derived more than 45% of their subsistence from this source (col. 5), and regarded as relatively nonagricultural otherwise. Women were regarded as contributing substantial amounts of agricultural labor unless such work was carried out by males "alone or almost alone" or "appreciably more" than females (col. 64). As we did for the female-competition model, we defined an interaction term as the product of the two independent variables, agricultural dependence and female labor.

Boserup (1970) offers a second operationalization of her model. She suggests that, because of the physical effort involved, plow-based agricultural systems will depend mainly on male labor. Hence, she sees the plow as a prime cause of dowry. But this way of thinking is not entirely consistent. Boserup (1970) argues that dowry emerges when women provide little of their own support and must therefore "buy" a subsistence guarantee. If this argument is correct, the type of agricultural technology should not matter: the only relevant factor should be the level of female contribution to agricultural labor. Because its key independent variable (female agricultural labor) is directly coded in the *Ethnographic Atlas*, we feel that the most logically consistent test of the labor-value model is the one already outlined. Nevertheless, we performed a separate test of the "plow version" of the labor-value model. Agricultural dependence is coded as above, but type of agriculture (col. 39) substitutes for female labor as the second independent variable. Societies were regarded as having plow-based agriculture if the plow was coded as "aboriginal" or "well established." Again, an interaction term was computed as the product of the two independent variables.

Analytical Techniques

Jackknife discriminant analysis, as implemented by BMDP (Jennrich and Sampson 1985), was our primary statistical tool for measuring the predictive accuracy of the two models. Drawing on a set of independent variables, discriminant analysis builds an equation to predict the presence or absence of a single dependent variable, dowry in this study. The program then evaluates the usefulness of the predictive model by comparing its predictions with the actual presence or absence of dowry on a case-by-case basis. If the independent variables chosen for use in the discriminant equation are the ones that actually influence the presence or absence of dowry, then most of the model's case-by-case predictions will be correct. If variables irrelevant to the occurrence of dowry are used to build the equation, many of the predictions will be incorrect. The discriminant analyses evaluating each model or operationalization were done twice: once for all world societies and again for those societies of the circum-Mediterranean and East Asia.

As has often been noted, there are coding errors in the cross-cultural data base. It has also been recognized that this situation does not generally threaten the validity of positive findings because random errors are expected to weaken rather than intensify any irregularities in the data (Kobben 1967). Nevertheless, we evaluated the extent to which a model's predictive failures were due to errors in coding rather than to errors in modeling.[6] Our analysis capitalizes on the fact that Schlegel and Eloul (1987) recently reviewed original ethnographic sources to correct the marriage transaction codes for the Standard Cross-Cultural Sample (SCCS; Murdock and White 1969), a 186-society subsample of the 1,267-society *Ethnographic Atlas*. Schlegel and Eloul recoded 8 of the 186 SCCS societies with respect to the presence or absence of (direct) dowry.

For each model, we performed a discriminant analysis on the entire 1,267-society data set, including the *uncorrected* version of the 186-society SCCS subsample.[7] Our first estimate of a model's accuracy was the percentage of its predictions that were correct. We next narrowed our focus to the predictions for the 186 societies of the SCCS. We identified those societies where the model's predictions were apparently in error (either predicting dowry where it is reported to be absent or predicting its absence where it reportedly occurs) and asked if these were the societies that Schlegel and Eloul (1987) had found to be incorrectly coded.[8] In essence, we treat a prediction error by a model as a guess that a society was miscoded. A perfect model would have made only 8 prediction errors among the 186 SCCS societies, corresponding to the 8 dowry-related coding errors found by Schlegel and Eloul (1987). To estimate a model's accuracy, we used probability theory (Polimeni and Straight 1985) to assess whether the model found more of these coding errors than would have been expected by chance, given the number of prediction errors it made (see the Appendix).

Table 35.1. The distribution of dowry by stratification and marital form among the societies of the *Ethnographic Atlas*.

	Nonstratified		Stratified	
	Monogamous and		Monogamous and	
Dowry	**Polygynous**	**Polyandrous**	**Polygynous**	**polyandrous**
Absent				
Europe and East Asia	73	19	81	30
Rest of world	551	80	182	15
Total	624 7 2 3	99	263 3 0 ⊂	45
Present				
Europe and East Asia	0	2	4	27
Rest of world	1	0	1	0
Total	1 3	2	5 3 ㄴ	27

Note: Entries are raw counts; *n* = 1,066 due to missing data for dowry, stratification, or marital form.

RESULTS

Previous work has established that dowry is essentially restricted to circum-Mediterranean and East Asian societies (Jackson and Romney 1973). Beyond this geographic restriction, the female-competition model predicts that dowry will be restricted to societies with significant stratification and a nonpolygynous marriage system. Table 35.1 shows that the actual distribution of dowry is skewed in the expected way. In total, there are 994 societies that should lack dowry: all polygynous societies whether stratified or not, and those monogamous and polyandrous societies that are unstratified. Of these 994 societies, fewer than 1% are reported to have dowry. In contrast, dowry is normative in 37.5% of stratified nonpolygynous societies.

The distribution of dowry is shown for the two versions of the labor-value model in Tables 35.2 and 35.3. The labor-value model predicts dowry in societies that are agricultural but have low female subsistence labor. This column does show an elevated proportion of dowry cases: 9.6% for female labor and 21.8% for plow-based agriculture. Neither of these values approaches the 37.5% figure for the female-competition model, but all three tables represent significant deviations from randomness. Thus we turn to discriminant analysis to evaluate which model provides a better fit to the data.

Evaluation of the Models

Both the labor-value model and the female-competition model provide a better-than-chance basis for predicting the actual occur-

Table 35.2. The distribution of dowry by agricultural dependence and female subsistence among the societies of the *Ethnographic Atlas*.

	Substantial Female Labor Agriculture		Low Female Labor Agriculture	
Dowry	**Unimportant**	**Important**	**Unimportant**	**Important**
Absent				
Europe and East Asia	28	65	15	63
Rest of world	302	299	25	106
Total	330	364	40	169
Present				
Europe and East Asia	0	10	2	17
Rest of world	1	0	0	1
Total	1	10	2	18

Note: Entries are raw counts; *n* = 934 due to missing data for dowry, agricultural dependence, or female subsistence labor.

Table 35.3. The distribution of dowry by agricultural dependence and agricultural technology among the societies of the *Ethnographic Atlas*.

| | Plow Absent Agriculture | | Plow Present Agriculture | |
Dowry	Unimportant	Important	Unimportant	Important
Absent				
Europe and East Asia	61	76	19	82
Rest of world	355	517	0	22
Total	416	593	19	104
Present				
Europe and East Asia	1	1	2	29
Rest of world	1	1	0	0
Total	2	2	2	29

Note: Entries are raw counts; $n = 1,167$ due to missing data for dowry, agricultural dependence, or agricultural technology.

rence of dowry. Nevertheless, in comparison to the labor-value model, the female-competition model is clearly superior in predictive accuracy.

Table 35.4 compares the performance of the labor-value model and the female-competition model with respect to our first measure of predictive accuracy. For the *Ethnographic Atlas* as a whole, discriminant functions based on the two models met with varying degrees of success. Consider first the performance of the basic models, each with two independent variables and an interaction term. For the world as a whole, the female-competition model predicts the presence or absence of dowry with only a 5.3% overall error rate (100 − 94.7). Depending on how it is operationalized, the labor-value model has error rates between 11.6% and 23.8%, two to four times higher. For the circum-Mediterranean and East Asia, the error rates are higher for all models, but the female-competition model is still demonstrably superior with a 16.9% overall error rate. For this region, the two operationalizations of the labor-value model have error rates between 33.9% and 37.5%, roughly twice as high.

Turning to the second measure of predictive accuracy, we see that both models can identify errors in dowry codes among the SCCS societies (Table 35.5); however, the female-competition model identifies them much more efficiently. For this subsample of 186 societies, the female-competition model makes only 13 prediction errors, 6 of which turn out to be data errors. This is remarkably successful given that there are only 8 errors to be found and that the a priori chance of "hitting" a data error with any

given prediction error is therefore only 8/186 (see the Appendix). Under these conditions, only about once in 1,180,000 times could we expect to hit 6 data errors with 13 guesses. In these probabilistic terms the labor-value model, while successful, is orders of magnitude less so. In its more straightforward operationalization, its hit rate is 5 in 47, a result that could be expected by chance

Table 35.4. Discriminant analysis results for two models of dowry among the societies of the *Ethnographic Atlas*, and for the societies of the circum-Mediterranean and East Asia.

| | Dowry[a] | | |
Model	Absent	Present	Total
Apparently correct predictions (%) for the world			
1. Labor value			
a. Female labor	76.6	63.0	76.2
$n =$	(907)	(27)	(934)
b. Plow	88.7	77.4	88.4
$n =$	(1,136)	(31)	(1,167)
2. Female competition	95.3	74.2	94.7
$n =$	(1,035)	(31)	(1,066)
Apparently correct prediction (%) for the circum-Mediterranean and East Asia			
1. Labor value			
a. Female labor	62.9	60.0	62.5
$n =$	(175)	(25)	(200)
b. Plow	64.0	82.8	66.1
$n =$	(242)	(29)	(271)
2. Female competition	83.6	79.3	83.1
$n =$	(207)	(29)	(236)

Note: Entries are percentages; *n* varies from model to model due to the unique pattern of missing values for each variable.
[a]Percentage of apparently correct prediction regarding the occurrence of dowry, given separately for societies where dowry is coded as absent and societies where it is coded as present.

Table 35.5. Ability of two models to find errors in the Standard Cross-Cultural Sample.

Model	Apparently incorrect predictions		
	Total[a]	Data-error "hits"[b]	P-value
1. Labor value			
a. Male-biased labor	47	5	0.026
b. Plow	30	7	0.00011
2. Female competition	13	6	0.00000085

Note: Entries are raw counts; $n = 186$

[a]Number of apparently incorrect predictions regarding the presence or absence of dowry, out of a possible 186.

[b]Number of apparently incorrect predictions that were actually correct due to data errors previously uncovered by Schlegel and Eloul (1987).

once in 39 times. The version of the labor-value model that incorporates plow agriculture shows an intermediate level of success.

DISCUSSION AND CONCLUSIONS

All models tested in this study perform well. Even at its worst, the labor-value model makes accurate predictions about the occurrence of dowry in five-eighths of circum-Mediterranean and East Asian societies and identifies coding errors in the SCCS at a better-than-chance rate. This is a reasonable fit, given the complexity of social science data. However, because the female-competition model accurately predicts the occurrence of dowry in nearly 95% of all world societies (83% of circum-Mediterranean and East Asian societies) and because it identifies coding errors in the SCCS with extreme efficiency, we conclude that it is somewhat closer to the way the world works than is any form of the labor-value model.[9]

In sum, dowry is about 50 times more common in stratified, nonpolygynous societies than it is elsewhere. We predicted this pattern on the assumption that females (typically with the aid of their parents and other kin) compete through dowry for wealthy husbands whose resources will not be diluted by the acquisition of additional wives. Dowry societies also typically have plow agriculture, low female contribution to subsistence (Boserup 1970), inheritance rules that minimize male bias (Goody 1973, 1976), and are more or less restricted to the western, southern, and eastern margins of Eurasia (Jackson and Romney 1973).

In other words, dowry is part of a unique complex of institutions in a geographically de-

limited set of state- and near-state-level societies. The co-occurrence of monogamy with stratification is also largely restricted to this set of societies (for an explanation of this association see Betzig 1986). Thus, the high intercorrelations among these societal features help account for the fact that at least one alternative explanation of dowry (labor-value) also finds some support in the cross-cultural record. This problem of multicollinearity suggests that an examination of within-society variation in dowry practices might provide further clarification of the specific factors that cause this institution. In particular, if the female-competition model is correct, we would expect the largest dowry payments to flow from the middle class to the elite, as women in the middle tier compete for husbands in the highest.

We are left with the puzzle of why many stratified, nonpolygynous societies lack dowry.[10] One line of inquiry would explore other possible forms of female competition for mates, such as elaborate fashion[11] and direct generation of income. These alternatives may be preferred by women over dowry systems because they indicate either greater individual autonomy in the choice of a marriage partner or a higher degree of economic security and independence. Perhaps dowry is restricted to those stratified nonpolygynous societies where alternative forms of female competition for mates are unavailable: societies where women are either barred from the workplace (thus preventing income competition) or where marriages are arranged by families and are not an individual decision (thus thwarting competition through personal display).

We have outlined two directions for future research on dowry. First, it would be important to conduct detailed within-society studies to discover who is paying how much to whom. Second, further cross-cultural studies may illuminate whether dowry is less common in stratified, nonpolygynous societies where alternative forms of female competition are available.

Acknowledgments. We thank L. Agostino for provoking the model developed in this article by asking why dowry exists. H. Barry III, C. Ember, and A. Oyuela-Caycedo called our attention to especially useful references. G. Benjamin, C. Ember, H. Nutini, J. Roberts, A. Roth, R. Scaglion, and R. Watson provided stimulating discussion of the ideas developed here. A. K. Romney was especially helpful in his thoughtful criticism and careful reanalysis of our model. M. Salmon and G. Whitehead assisted with probability theory, M. Freilino assisted with data management, and M. Wartell unveiled Pascal's triangle. Special thanks are due to D. White for all his work on the electronic journal, *World Cultures*.

APPENDIX

Let g = the number of guesses (i.e., prediction errors) made by a particular model, and let h = the number of those guesses that "hit" societies that Schlegel and Eloul (1987) have identified as miscoded. There are 186 cases in the Standard Cross-Cultural Sample, of which 8 were known to be miscoded with respect to dowry. The probability of getting a hit on a single guess is thus 8/186 and the probability of h hits given g guesses is:

$$\frac{\dfrac{8!}{h! \times (8 - h)!} \times \dfrac{178!}{(g - h! \times (178 - (g - h))!}}{\dfrac{186!}{g! \times (186 - g)!}}$$

But what we require is the probability of getting h *or more* hits in g guesses; thus, we sum the above probability with the similarly computed probability for the more extreme results, $h + 1, h + 2 \ldots 8$, which is the maximum number of possible hits. This technique yields the value reported in the text and in Table 35.5.

NOTES

1. With this contrast, we are not suggesting that dowry and bridewealth are mirror images in all respects. For example, with certain exceptions (see Schlegel and Eloul 1987), bridewealth payments go to the male kin of the bride, whereas dowry goes to the bride herself. Nevertheless, in regard to the source of the payments—the groom's family for bridewealth and the bride's family for dowry—the two practices are symmetrical opposites. Because our model focuses on who bears the cost of marriage transactions, we find it useful to contrast these two practices.

2. Goody (1973, 1976) views dowry, indirect dowry (any case where the recipients of bridewealth payments return at least a portion of these payments to the bride), and the inheritance of real or movable property by women as components of a wealth transfer system that he calls *diverging devolution*. His principal aim is to explain the societal consequences of such wealth transfer systems, although he also uses a clustering technique (Goody 1976:27–28) to search for factors underlying diverging devolution in the societies of the *Ethnographic Atlas*. Because Goody treats direct dowry as one of several indicators of a more general system (diverging devolution), because he mainly uses diverging devolution as an independent variable, and because he uses post hoc techniques to search for its causes, we find it difficult to tease from his account a testable causal model of dowry itself.

3. It could be argued that competition for mates is more concerned with status (or wealth) seeking than with fitness maximization. Several authors have demonstrated a high correlation among wealth, status, and reproductive success (Irons 1979a; Chagnon 1980b; Turke and Betzig 1985; Mealey 1985; Flinn 1986; Boone 1986; and especially Borgerhoff Mulder 1987a), so discriminating among these models would be difficult. Darwin's theory can also explain status seeking. We know of no causal model of status seeking that can similarly subsume reproductive motivations. Nor has a theory of status competition led to a predictive model of dowry. Single-culture studies could help evaluate the extent to which individuals choose status or fitness when the two are in conflict. Such studies could also help determine what factors govern the distribution of parental resources among same-sex progeny.

4. We use "wealthy" to refer to an individual who controls more or better-quality resources than other males. In this sense it can be used to describe both human and nonhuman mating systems.

5. Data from human populations are more difficult to interpret in this respect due to frequent fertility differentials between head wives and their cowives (Isaac 1980).

6. One approach, often called "deviant case analysis," would be to reread the ethnographic sources for any societies where the model's predictions do not agree with the reported real-world situation. Any coding errors discovered among these cases could be corrected and the model's "accuracy score" thereby improved. This approach would be biased, however, unless one also checked all those societies where the model's prediction appeared accurate; any coding errors discovered among these cases would reduce the model's accuracy score. In other words, the only fair approach would seem to involve rereading the primary sources for all 1,267 societies.

7. We had initially hoped that log-linear analysis would elegantly uncover the pattern in the cross-cultural distribution of dowry. Unfortunately, it proved unstable, producing radically different solutions on the corrected and uncorrected data sets. Thus, discriminant analysis was chosen as a more robust and interpretable alternative.

8. We did not discuss our model with Schlegel and Eloul and they offer no causal model of dowry, focusing mainly on the distinction between direct and indirect dowry (Schlegel and Eloul 1987). Thus, we can assume that their corrections are independent of the model developed here.

9. One reviewer notes that a model that denies the existence of dowry performs favorably in comparison to the models evaluated here. Granted, any rare phenomenon could be "modeled" quite successfully by mere denial, but such an approach offers no genuine causal explanation of the phenomenon.

10. We thought Boserup's labor-value model might explain some of this residual variance. To test this possibility, we performed a discriminant analysis limited to the 67 stratified, nonpolygynous societies for which data on agricultural labor patterns were available. Unfortunately, female contribution to agriculture did not help discriminate between those stratified nonpolygynous societies with and without dowry.

11. Kroeber and Richardson's (1940) demonstration of the cyclic nature of fashion may have its explanation here: apparently arbitrary shifts in fashion serve to indicate who can keep up with the current style. Given the expense of high fashion, stylishness is an effective clue to a woman's health.

36

When Are Husbands Worth Fighting For?

STEVEN J. C. GAULIN
JAMES S. BOSTER

As indicated by our title, our motivation in developing and testing an explanatory model of dowry was to explore the factors that could precipitate significant female-female competition. Bridewealth had been consistently interpreted by evolutionarily inclined social scientists (e.g., Daly and Wilson 1983; Borgerhoff Mulder 1988c) as an aspect of male-male competition for valuable reproductive opportunities. It seemed logical to start with the premise that in the opposite case—when the bride's family must forfeit stuff of value to contract the marriage—a significant element of female-female competition must be present. Thus we asked ourselves, why would females ever compete for males? Of course polyandry would trigger female-female competition, but polyandry is vanishingly rare across human societies (Murdock 1986); we had to look elsewhere for an explanation. Building on Orians's (1969) polygyny threshold model and Alexander's notion of socially imposed monogamy (Alexander et al. 1979), we developed an argument about the novel mating dynamics that would develop in stratified, nonpolygynous societies.

The "self-critique" that follows is liberally seasoned with the criticisms and suggested refinements of colleagues. Although Dickemann (e.g., 1979a, 1979b) was an early advocate of the evolutionary approach to social science, her (1991) criticisms of our model seem misplaced. She argued that dowry did not represent female-female competition because the dowry is contributed by the bride's parents, and that our analysis thus misrepresents the extent of female autonomy. She is correct that in dowry societies women are not free to enter the marriage market and compete for whatever man they like; but the same could often be said of men in bridewealth societies (e.g., Borgerhoff Mulder 1988c). In introducing our model we noted that it:

does not assume that the suitors are the only relevant participants in marriage arrangements. Regardless of whether dowry or bridewealth is paid, parents and other kin frequently aid in amassing the transferred wealth and often negotiate the marriage contract. These facts are consistent with the generalization that humans invest in their offspring (and other kin) over many years. (chapter 36:363)

Moreover, we specifically argued that female-female competition was likely to be expressed in the form of dowry where female autonomy was low.

Dickemann's second criticism emphasizes the unreliable character of the ethnographic database on which all cross-cultural research rests. She argued that there are numerous errors as well as systematic class biases in the database. First, if data errors represent random noise, they will make any real-world pattern more difficult to discover and any model more difficult to verify. After all, it would not be surprising for a watch to shatter into pieces if hurled at a wall, but it would be startling to hurl watch parts at the wall and get a working watch. Second, while this same critique applies to all cross-cultural studies, we found it surprising to have it targeted at ours because we examined the impact of errors on our analysis. Schlegel and Eloul (1987) recently corrected the relevant parts of the Standard Cross-Cultural Sample. All the dowry models we tested gave a better fit to the corrected than to the uncorrected data set, suggesting that the apparent pattern is not a consequence of data errors but is instead somewhat obscured by the errors. Thus, while both of Dickemann's (1991) observations are true, they do not constitute especially relevant criticisms of our model, our argumentation, or our method (Gaulin and Boster 1991).

A somewhat more serious analytical issue concerns independence, or, as it is sometimes called, Galton's problem. Societies, typically treated as separate cases in cross-cultural research, have histories of interaction. If interaction causes the joint diffusion of sets of traits, then the resultant statistical association between traits within such sets might be mistaken for a functional relationship. Our efforts to deal with this problem consisted of testing our model not only on the *Ethnographic Atlas* (Murdock 1986) but also on the Standard Cross-Cultural Sample (Murdock and White 1969). The latter sample was specifically selected to include just one culture from each world "sampling province" in order to maximize the statistical independence of the cases. A model that performs less well on the Standard Cross-Cultural Sample than on the *Ethnographic Atlas* can be suspected of deriving some false support from joint diffusion. Fortunately, the female-competition model performs equally well on these two data sets. Regardless of this encouraging result, there are recent developments in the analysis of dependent data (e.g., Mace and Pagel 1994) that could be applied in testing the female-female competition model; this should be done.

Schlegel (1993; Schlegel and Eloul 1988) has focused on the causes and consequences of dowry and indirect dowry—a marriage transaction in which wealth originating with the groom's kin is transferred all or in part to the newlyweds (Goody 1973). She argues that such systems arise where there is substantial private property and that they serve to concentrate this property within lineages. She claims that dowry and indirect dowry create competition, "but it is competition among men for affinal alliances and the social, political and sometimes economic benefits to be gained through them" (Schlegel 1993:156). The differences in our viewpoints are easy to summarize. First, Schlegel assumes that dowry *generates* competition, whereas we argue that it is a manifestation of competition and would never emerge except where there is already a resource worth

competing for. Second, we cannot comfortably regard dowry and indirect dowry as equivalent since in the former the bride's family must pay and in the latter the groom's must do so. At a market the one who stands to gain the most bids the most, and when active bidders fall silent everyone knows that something has changed. If the bride's family is silent in some societies and the groom's silent in others, can a single social dynamic be the cause? Differences in viewpoint aside, empiricism reigns; systematic cross-cultural tests of Schlegel's model show that it is as accurate in predicting the distribution of dowry as earlier formulations by Boserup (1970) but that both are markedly less accurate than ours (Gaulin and Boster 1993).

Lang (1993) used Boolean analysis to evaluate our model. He found that, while our model accurately predicts where dowry will *not* occur, the model performs less well at predicting where it will occur (62 percent of stratified, nonpolygynous societies lack dowry). This was apparent to us, and we noted it in our original publication, but not because we viewed it as a weakness of the model. Our principal objective was to explain why females would ever compete for mates. We interpreted dowry as one manifestation of such female-female competition but explicitly pointed out that it was not the only such manifestation. Thus, we argued that there would be no need for any form of female-female competition, and hence no dowry, unless significant stratification coincided with a prohibition on polygyny (and the tests strongly support this prediction). Lang, however, seems to believe that we claimed the opposite, that every stratified, nonpolygynous society would have dowry. We made no such claim; rather, we argued that they would be characterized by female-female competition, nothing that various forms of female-female competition are possible.

For those who, like Lang, are interested in developing a model of dowry per se (rather than a model of female-female competition), it will be important to specify alternative modes of female-female competition and to determine what factors channel this competition toward or away from dowry. We suggested two alternative modes of female-female competition: elaborate fashion and direct generation of income. In traditional societies, elaborate dress was probably stylistically conservative but costly to acquire due to its reliance on scarce materials and intricate ornamentation. In more modern settings fashion is costly because it cycles rapidly and thereby requires sustained expenditures. Either would have signaled considerable wealth and thus an attractive potential mate. Similarly, where females have considerable wealth-generating potential, the education, standing, or position to realize this potential could be a potent vehicle of female-female competition. These modes of female competition might be viewed as emerging along a continuum of female autonomy. Thus when females are free to enter the marketplace and use their talents to generate an ongoing income stream, their own economic potential—a college education rather than a dowry—would be a means of attracting the best husbands. Further analysis along these lines might be undertaken if these alternative modes of female-female competition are assessable from the cross-cultural record.

To test this or any model of dowry one might also turn to within-culture comparisons. For example, if dowry does represent competition among females for the wealthiest husbands, then the value of the dowry should be more strongly correlated with the husband's wealth than with the bride's wealth. Similarly, a historical approach might be used. Some societies have recently ceased the practice of dowry (see, e.g., Nazzari 1991). Our analysis suggests one of three causes: a marked reduction in stratification, the adoption of polygyny (neither especially likely), or a significant increase in female autonomy and concomitant development of alternate forms of female-female competition such as income generation.

Might there be circumstances other than those we have outlined that would lead to significant female-female competition? In a very original paper, Low (1990a) drew on Hamilton's (1980) "pathogen theory" of sexual reproduction to argue that, where pathogens constitute a significant selective force, good-genes sexual selection would cause female preference to converge on a small number of disease-resistant males as optimal mates. Such a situation, she reasoned, would foster polygyny, and her cross-cultural tests were supportive, indicating a significant association between the incidence of polygyny and parasite load. Although Low made no such claim, an issue to consider is whether high pathogen load would generate significant female-female competition for disease-resistant mates. We suggest that it typically would not. From a wife's point of view, sharing her husband's genes with other females is typically much less costly than sharing his economic resources—and a male will more readily contribute his genes than his wealth to an extramarital encounter. The point is that, to be of value, a man's economic resources must be available as a sustained flow. Any disruption of that flow threatens his partner's fitness. A reallocation of some of his sperm is much less damaging. Hence women are more likely to compete over men's resources than over their genes. For a parallel argument in the psychological domain see Buss et al. (1992).

Laura Betzig (personal communication) has suggested a reasonable, and we think friendly, amendment to our model. Remember that we argue that the conjunction of stratification and nonpolygynous marriage fosters female competition for exclusive rights to the resources of wealthy males. Betzig's point is that what matters is not protection from cowives per se but protection from the inheritance claims of cowives' children. Hence, it would not matter how many wives or concubines a wealthy or powerful man might have; if the children of the head wife (queen, etc.) reap special benefits (e.g., succession), then such benefits would be worth competing for *despite polygyny*. We agree; resources are the issue, and thus what matters is monogamous resource flow, not monogamous marriage. We encourage a careful reanalysis of the data in this regard.

The single most important idea contained in our paper is that, if wealth and power differentials are protected from the dilution that occurs with polygyny, a novel mating dynamic emerges in which females can gain reproductively by forming long-term unions with males who control disproportionate shares of these resources. Such situations should engender relatively high levels of female-female competition. One next step is to develop a more precise formulation of the factors that foster particular avenues of female-female competition (e.g., low female autonomy leading to dowry, high autonomy to fashion and income competition). Another is to apply this model to explain within-culture variance in dowry as Borgerhoff Mulder (1988c) has done for brideprice.

37

Roman Polygyny

LAURA BETZIG

Sir Ronald Syme, in a paper on "Bastards in the Roman Aristocracy," asked: Where are they? Plenty of illegitimates were talked about, he pointed out, in early modern Italy, England, France, and Spain; but ancient Romans kept quiet about them. As Syme complained, "there is a singular dearth of evidence about aristocratic bastards. . . . it is not easy to produce an authentic bastard anywhere, let alone the bastard of a *nobilis*" (1960:324).

Weren't there any? Most historians seem as skeptical as Syme. From Juvenal's second-century satires through Augustine's fourth-century sermons, there was praise and disgust for blue bloods' lust (e.g., Juvenal, *Satires* viii.181–2; Augustine, *Sermons* 153.5.6). Most historians take that much for granted; some go so far as to refer to Roman "harems" (e.g., Carcopino 1940:101–2; Veyne 1987:76, 204). Roman marriage was unquestionably monogamous: no man took more than one wife at once. But Roman mating might have been polygynous: a majority of women might have mated with a minority of men (see Kleiman 1977; Wittenberger and Tilson 1980; Daly and Wilson 1983:152 for definitions of monogamy and polygyny).

There are two good reasons to suspect they did. The first is Darwin's theory of sexual selection. Darwin argued that for the vast majority of species males should have evolved to compete for mates; men were no exception. The reason has become clear in the last hundred years. Most males can raise their reproduction by mating with many females; few females can do the same by mating with many males. If Darwin was right—if we've evolved *to* reproduce—then men can be expected to compete for women (Darwin 1871:571, 581; Bateman 1948; Clutton-Brock and Vincent 1991). The Roman empire, like every other empire, was filled with competition; and the men who won came off with spoils enough to attract and support many more women and children than the many who lost.

The second reason to suspect polygyny in the Roman aristocracy is the comparative record. If powerful Roman men weren't polygynous, they may be the only powerful men in any preindustrial society who were *not*. The evidence across cultures is consistent. In the simplest societies, like the !Kung in Botswana or the Yanomamö in Venezuela, the strongest men typically kept up to ten women; in medium-sized societies that organized above the local level, like the Samoans and other Polynesians, men at the top kept up to a hundred women; and in the biggest societies, including the "pristine" empires in Mesopotamia and Egypt, India and China, Aztec Mexico and Inca Peru, and in many empires that came later, powerful men kept hundreds, or thousands, or even tens of thousands of women—along with one, or two, or three at most, legitimate *wives*; lesser men kept progressively fewer women (Betzig 1982, 1986, 1988a, 1991, 1993; see too Dickemann 1979a, 1979b and van den Berghe 1979).

Was Roman mating, like Roman marriage, monogamous? Or was monogamous *marriage* in Rome, like monogamous marriage in other empires, a way that polygynously *mated* men passed

Reprinted with permission from *Ethology and Sociobiology* 13:309–49 (1992).

harems on to their sons? It may not be a trivial question. Polygyny, or reproductive inequality, requires economic and political inequality: a man with ten times as many women and children must either work ten times as hard to support them, or take what he needs from other men (Chagnon 1979a). Across space and time, polygyny has overlapped with despotism, monogamy with egalitarianism (Betzig 1982, 1986, 1991). The Roman empire was not marked by egalitarianism (e.g. Garnsey 1970; Duncan-Jones 1982; Garnsey and Saller 1987). How much was the economic and political inequality in the Roman empire matched by reproductive inequality, or polygyny?

This paper uses two kinds of evidence to answer that question. First are some original sources. Most of the Latin historians, including Tacitus, Suetonius, Cassius Dio, the Greek writer Herodian, and the compilers of the *Scriptores Historiae Augustae*, had a lot to say about emperors' lives, including their personal lives. Second are studies. To get at how most other men and women, rich or poor, lived and reproduced, modern historians have looked at other kinds of evidence, including literary, legal, and especially inscriptional—at epitaphs. Both the Latin and modern historians are asked: How polygynous *were* Roman aristocrats?

SOURCES

More than half a century ago, Otto Kiefer was the first to try a systematic survey of the Caesars' sex lives. The funny thing is, he wasn't interested. He had little respect for Tacitus's or Suetonius's "malevolent gossip" and went on, "besides, are we better off for knowing that the great man gave his love to this or that woman outside the confines of his marriage?" He found it "much more interesting and important to learn that Caesar was an epileptic" (1934:298). The problem wasn't that the Latin historians weren't credible otherwise. Tacitus was a senator under the emperor Vespasian, consul under Nerva, and governor of Western Anatolia under Trajan late in the first and early in the second century; Suetonius was chief secretary to the emperor Hadrian early in the second century; and Dio was a senator late in the second century under the emperor Commodus. The problem was that little could be known of personal affairs—even emperors' personal affairs—*except* through gossip (Momigliano 1971:56–57).

On that basis, most modern historians before and after Kiefer have discounted these sources altogether. Syme, for instance, suggests that the tradition of slanderous rhetoric in Rome was strong. He says, "the best of arguments was personal abuse. In the allegation of disgusting immorality, degrading pursuits or ignoble origin the Roman politician knew no compunction" (1939:149). More recently, Richard Saller looked at a sample of 52 anecdotes from Suetonius and found, compared to other versions of the same stories in other sources, the time,

place, supporting cast, and subjects all changed more often than they stayed the same (1980). For three reasons, though, I'm unwilling to disregard Tacitus, Suetonius, and Dio entirely. First, there *is* consistency across authors: the punch lines in the stories stay the same. Second, there is consistency across emperors: though there are variations, they turn around a few themes. Third, and most important, there is consistency across authors on *other* empires: from the *Rig Veda* and other Indian texts, to Chinese sex handbooks from the Sui and other dynasties, to reassembled Egyptian temple reliefs, to a half-bred Inca's accounts of his ancestors, to Franciscans' accounts of conquered Aztecs, and beyond, the gossip about emperors is stunningly often the same (see Table 37.1).

There is no doubt, of course, that one or two or more Romans' slander is worth what hundreds of modern historians—who have had access to the full range of surviving sources, literary, legal, and archaeological—have written. For that reason, I've kept these "sources" apart from their "studies." But, because the Latin sources have so much in common with sources on other empires, and because they're consistent with much in the modern studies, I can't leave them out. Just how "malevolent" are they? Are some Roman emperors—or even most Roman emperors—supposed to have held harems? Or did they "radiate marital propriety?" How often are they said to have lived up to model speeches in which writers were advised, as in Menander's *Epideictica*, to add: "Because of the emperor, marriages are chaste. . . . As for the rest of womankind, he does not so much as

Table 37.1. Polygyny in the First Six Civilizations, and in Rome (after Betzig 1993, 1986, and text)

Empire	Place	Focus in Time	A Focal Emperor	Number of Women	How Recruited	Who Recruited	How Kept Chaste	Rights to Others' Women	Number of Wives
Babylonian	Mesopotamia	1700 BC	Hammurabi	1000s of slaves??			In fortified palace; eunuchs present??	Temple prostitution??	One wife; "secondary" slave wives
Egyptian	Egypt	1300 BC	Akhenaten	317 plus "droves"	Procured as tribute	"Very beautiful women"	Behind a "battlemented enclosure"; watched by "overseers"	"All the wives of his subjects were his"	One "Great Wife," many concubines and consorts
Aztec	Mesoamerica	1500 AD	Montezuma	4000 "concubines"	Procured as tribute	Young and pretty women	On Tenochtitlan, a "natural fort"	Social structure "rested on sexual licence" by noble Aztecs	One *ciuatlanti* "asked for woman"; many concubines and consorts
Inca	Peru	1500 AD	Atahuallpa	1500 in each "house of virgins"	Inca asks	Of good lineage, beautiful, under age 8 at admission	In last recess down narrow passage; guarded by "mama cunas"	Inca asks	One queen, concubine cousins, commoners who mothered "bastards"
Indian	India	From 500 BC	Udayama	Up to 16,000		Young women; "free from disease or menstruation"	In inner apartments, ringed by fire; guarded by eunuchs	A Brahamin's right, by "ancient custom"	One Maharani, several ranis, many consorts
Chinese	China	From 700 BC	Fei-ti	10,000	Palace agents would "scour the empire"	"Young women whose breasts have not yet developed"; fifth day after menstruation	In innermost part of palace; guarded by eunuchs	Married women "debauched"	One queen, three consorts, nine wives of second rank etc.
Roman	Mediterranean	From 27 BC	Augustus	Women of rank; 1000s of slaves?	Livia procured some	Virgins	Eunuchs present??	Married women, divorced, debauched, and/or prostituted	One

know that they exist" (ii.i. 396; in Brown 1988:16)? How often are they not?

Tacitus, Suetonius, and Dio all wrote about the first twelve Caesars, that is, about Julius Caesar and the first eleven Roman emperors. What follows sums up what they had to say about their personal lives. These Caesars: had sex with many women; preferred rich and pretty women; and had a privileged right to other men's wives. Many emperors seem to have been studies in sexual selection: they drove chariots, fought wild beasts, cultivated the arts, and covered themselves with make-up and fancy clothes; and they showed off a lot of the food and protection that might be spent on some of their women and children.

Collecting Women

Again, Roman emperors, like other emperors, liked sex with many women, liked rich and pretty women, and liked to have women procured for them.

Here's what Suetonius says of Julius Caesar: "His affairs with women are commonly described as extravagant." He elaborates. His women included many queens—Cleopatra, who might have got her son Caesarion by him, the most famous of them (but see Syme 1980). They also included many provincials. Caesar's soldiers got up this verse on his behalf:

> Home we bring our bald
>   whoremonger;
> Romans, lock your wives away!
> All the bags of gold you lent him
> Went his Gallic tarts to pay.

But Caesar's greatest honor, or indictment, was Helvius Cinna's. Cinna, in Caesar's absence, had a bill drawn up for the commons to pass legitimizing his union "with any woman, or women, he pleased—'for the procreation of children' " (Suetonius, *Julius Caesar*, 50–52; see too Dio, *History*, xliv.7.3).

So much for Julius Caesar. What of his great-nephew, the first emperor? Augustus is often remembered for his simplicity and humility: he often walked rather than rode through the streets of Rome; and he was horrified and insulted to be called "my Lord" (Suetonius, *Augustus*, 53). He is remembered, too, for his devotion to Livia, his third wife. But devotion didn't necessarily involve exclusion. Augus-

tus's second wife, Scribonia, had been divorced for her "moral perversity," specifically, for her failure to tolerate *his* adultery; Livia was much more accommodating (Suetonius, *Augustus*, 62; Balsdon 1962:68). Suetonius says, "the charge of being a womanizer stuck, and as an elderly man he is said to have still harboured a passion for deflowering girls—who were collected for him from every quarter, *even by his wife*" (*Augustus*, 71, italics mine). Augustus was a great adulterer; like Caesar his predecessor, and like several of his successors, he had women requisitioned from far and wide. "His friends used to behave like Toranius, the slave-dealer, in arranging his pleasures for him—they would strip mothers of families, or grown girls, of their clothes and inspect them as though they were for sale" (Augustus, 69).

The third Caesar, Rome's second emperor, Augustus's step-son Tiberius, was much more notoriously lascivious. Dio writes, "his sensual orgies which he carried on shamelessly with persons of the highest rank, both male and female, brought him ill repute" (*History*, lviii.22.2). Tiberius followed Caesar and Augustus's precedent in having sex partners procured for him; in this case, the service was done by his slaves. To Tacitus, Tiberius's "criminal lusts" were "worthy of an oriental tyrant." He liked freeborn children best. "He was fascinated by beauty, youthful innocence, and aristocratic birth." The slaves who searched them out "rewarded compliance, overbore reluctance with menaces and—if resisted by parents or relations—kidnapped their victims, and violated them on their own account. It was like the sack of a captured city" (*Annals*, v. 10). According to Dio, when one father high in imperial favor, Sextus Marius, sent his "strikingly beautiful" daughter away "in order to prevent her from being outraged by Tiberius," both he and his daughter were killed (*History*, lviii.22.2–4). Tiberius closed his career on the isolated island of Capreae; as Tacitus points out, its climate was mild, its views were exceptionally lovely, and all of its landings could be controlled by sentries. "On this island then, in twelve spacious, separately named villas, Tiberius took up residence. His former absorption in State affairs ended. Instead he spent the time in secret orgies" (Tacitus, *Annals*, iv.66–67). Tiberius preferred a private "sporting-house" for his "sexual extravagances"; the whole scene is extremely "oriental." Suetonius says: "A number of small rooms were furnished with the most indecent pictures and statuary obtainable, also certain erotic manuals from Elephantis in Egypt; the inmates would know from these exactly what was expected of them." Outside was also nice. There were "little nooks of lechery" in the woods; "bevies" of girls and boys would dress up as nymphs and Pans in Capreae's caverns and grottoes (Suetonius, *Tiberius*, 43). Tacitus says Tiberius's lusts didn't abate till death (*Annals*, vi.47).

If Tiberius was notorious, Caligula, the great-nephew who succeeded him, was infamous. Caligula began his short but spectacular career under his uncle's tutelage. Tiberius had him brought to Capreae at eighteen; "yet even in those days he could not control his natural brutality and viciousness" (Suetonius, *Gaius*, 11). He loved executions by day, gluttony and adultery by night. Was Tiberius pleased? "'I am nursing a viper for the Roman people'" he is supposed to have said (*Gaius*, 11). According to Dio, Caligula "not only emulated but surpassed his predecessor's licentiousness and bloodthirstiness" (Dio, *History*, lix.4.1). Unlike Augustus, Caligula was glad to be called a god; he liked to say he'd copulated with the moon, and to pose as Neptune, Bacchus, Apollo, and Jupiter; "he made this a pretext for seducing numerous women, particularly his sisters" (lix.26.5). According to Suetonius, he made it a "habit" to commit incest with all three of his sisters; he "ravished" one, Drusilla, before he came of age; later he took her from her husband, "openly treating her as his lawfully married wife" (*Gaius*, 24). The rights of other husbands were no better respected; Caligula "had not the slightest regard for chastity, either his own or others'. . . . He made advances to almost every women of rank in Rome." They would be invited to dinner with their husbands, and "he would slowly and carefully examine each in turn while they passed his couch, as a purchaser might assess the value of a slave." Then he'd send for whatever woman he liked best, take her out, and come back "commenting on her sexual performance." Now and then he'd register divorces in their husbands' names (Suetonius, *Gaius*, 36).

After Caligula's excesses provoked his assassination, the fifth Caesar, his uncle Claudius, succeeded him. Claudius, like Augustus, is re-

membered as relatively benign. His ambition might have been muted in childhood by diseases that left him, in Suetonius's words, "stumbling," "stammering," and "slobbering." In spite of that, he became emperor at fifty, "by an extraordinary accident"; and then he was a humble one, for instance, turning the title "Imperator" down (Suetonius, *Claudius*, 2, 10, 12, 30). But he was bold enough to follow a few precedents with respect to sex. Suetonius says, "his feelings for women were extremely passionate"; Dio writes of his "insatiable" inclination to sexual intercourse and of his "many amours with women" (Suetonius, *Claudius*, 34; Dio, *History*, lx.2.5–6). Again, these women were sometimes procured for him; and, after Augustus's example, the procuring was sometimes left to his wife. Dio says Messalina "took care" of her husband "by giving him sundry housemaids to lie with" (lx.18.3). And when Claudius finally became aware of Messalina's own infidelities, it was through Calpurnia and Cleopatra, two "favourites" among many mistresses (Tacitus, *Annals*, xi.29).

But the best, or worst, of the Julio-Claudian dynasty came last. The sixth Caesar was Claudius's great-nephew, his step-son, and his son-in-law, Nero. Tacitus says this about the young emperor about town: "Disguised as a slave, he ranged the streets, brothels, and taverns with his friends, who pilfered goods from shops and assaulted wayfarers. . . . Rome by night came to resemble a conquered city" (*Annals*, xiii.24; cf. Suetonius, *Nero*, 26). At home, Nero liked to tie naked girls and boys to stakes, put on the hide of a wild beast, and "satisfy his brutal lust under the appearance of devouring parts of their bodies" (Dio, *History*, lxiii.13.2). In making ready for war, his main concern was with "arranging for the concubines who would accompany him to have male haircuts and be issued with Amazonian shields and axes" (Suetonius, *Nero*, 44). Even en route his needs would be met. "Whenever he floated down the Tiber to Ostia, or cruised past the Gulf of Baiae, he had a row of temporary brothels erected along the shore, where married women, pretending to be inn-keepers, solicited him" (*Nero*, 27).

When Nero finally fled, and was assisted in the suicide that ended his thirteen-year reign, he was succeeded by three emperors who ruled altogether for a year and a half. Galba, the first, is described as "old and feeble;" though he's discredited with brutality and greed, little is said about his lust (Tacitus, *Histories*, i.4). We know more about the second. Otho's ambition was "a court and life of pleasure like Nero's, liaisons, marriages and all the gratifications of tyranny" (*Histories*, i.22, 30); Dio accuses him of wickedness, impiousness, and "disgraceful" living (Dio, *History*, lxiii.15.1). Vitellius, the third, is supposed to have been a little like Otho; Tacitus calls them "the two most despicable men in the whole world by reason of their unclean, idle, and pleasure-loving lives, apparently appointed by fate for the task of destroying the empire" (Tacitus, *Histories*, i.50). Dio adds that Vitellius was "addicted" to "luxury and licentiousness," and "no longer cared for anything else either human or divine" (Dio, *History*, lxiv.2.1).

The Flavian dynasty followed: Vespasian, the father, the tenth Caesar, then Titus and Domitian, his sons. As in the Julio-Claudian case, abuses seemed to increase over time. Vespasian is another emperor fondly remembered. Having begun of an admittedly obscure family, he was "bewildered" to have become emperor, and was "from first to last modest and lenient" (Suetonius, *Vespasian*, 1, 7, 12). In ten years of ruling Rome he may have grown notorious for avarice, but not for lust. Still, according to Suetonius, he did find time in his daily routine for an afternoon nap "with one of the several mistresses whom he had engaged" after Caenis, his freedwoman mistress, had died (*Vespasian*, 21).

Vespasian's first son, Titus, is also kindly remembered, though his failings included cruelty and "immorality" as well as greed. Suetonius called him immoral on account of his "troop of inverts and eunuchs" and his cohabitation in Rome with a Hebrew queen (*Titus*, 7). Titus lasted just over two years.

He was succeeded by Domitian, his younger brother, who ruled for fifteen years. Suetonius, Dio, and Tacitus all say Domitian was promiscuous. Tacitus recalls his "crowd" of dancing courtiers (*Agricola*, 40); Dio remembers him as "profligate and lewd towards women and boys alike" (*History*, lxvii.6.4); to Suetonius "Domitian was extremely lustful, and called his constant sexual activities 'bed-wrestling,' as though it were a sport" (*Domitian*, 22).

So much for the first twelve Caesars. Both Tacitus's and Suetonius's accounts end with

them; Dio and two other sources, Herodian and the *Scriptores Historiae Augustae*, go on. But Herodian is much more superficial, especially about sex. In fact, Echols, his translator, writes that his "decision to ignore the sexual experiments of many of the emperors is odd in the extreme" (1961:7). And the *SHA* are notoriously unreliable; Syme calls them "mythistoria" (1983:13), and Magie, their translator, concedes they may be little better than "literary monstrosities" (1922:xxiv). Though the writers of the *Scriptores* are sometimes interested in sex, they often eschew the subject, and refer the reader in disgust to Marius Maximus or Aelius Junius Cordus, neither of whom survives in print. Still, there are a few sex lives in these biographies that are too striking to leave out. Commodus's and Elagabalus's stand out.

Marcus Aurelius, the imperial philosopher, was Commodus's father. He was, according to the *Scriptores*, "pre-eminent among emperors in purity of life" (*Marcus Antoninus*, i.1). His son, on the other hand, was "base and dishonourable, and cruel and lewd, defiled of mouth, moreover, and debauched" (*Commodus Antoninus*, i.7). Herodian is, as usual, terse. "Night and day, without interruption, licentious pleasures of the flesh made him a slave, body, and soul" (*Marcus Aurelius and Commodus*, xiii.7, xvii.9); his orgies were "endless and excessive" (*Pertinax, Didius Julianus*, i.3). Dio doesn't add much: "Commodus was wholly devoted to pleasure" (*History*, lxxiii.10.2). The *Scriptores* flesh the story out. Commodus "herded together women of unusual beauty, keeping them like purchased prostitutes in a sort of brothel for the violation of their chastity" (*Commodus Antoninus*, v.8). How many women? Somebody counted in this case. He "rioted" in the palace, at banquets and in baths, "along with 300 concubines, gathered together for their beauty and chosen from both matrons and harlots, and with minions, also 300 in number, whom he had collected by force and by purchase indiscriminately from the common people and the nobles solely on the basis of bodily beauty" (*Commodus Antoninus*, v.4). This is remarkably "oriental" again and, as it turns out, remarkably universal. Nor is it likely that harems like this were unique to Commodus in Rome. For instance his immediate successor, the much more moderate Pertinax, ordered an auction of Commodus's concubines, except those who had been procured by force. "However, many were soon brought back to his service and ministered to the pleasures of the old man" (*Pertinax*, vii.8–9). And Severus, in a speech to the senate, defended Commodus in view of the fact that most senators "led worse lives"—out nights with women in leopard skins, and so on (Dio, *History*, lxxvia.8.1).

In Elagabalus's case nobody counted, but words make the point. Elagabalus "never had intercourse with the same woman twice except with his wife"; and, like so many other emperors, he used the palace as a brothel "for his friends, his clients, and his slaves" (SHA, Antoninus *Elagabalus*, xxiv.2–3). They had fun. Elagabalus would have them to twenty-two course banquets, "and between each course he and his guests would bathe and dally with women," all swearing by oath that they were having a good time (*Antoninus Elagabalus*, xxx.3). Sometimes he wasn't as generous: sometimes he'd shut his friends up on the road "with old hags from Ethiopia," and not let them out until morning. He traveled in style himself, hitching his chariots to "women of the greatest beauty . . . in fours, in twos, or in threes or even more," driving them about in the buff, "usually naked himself" (*Antoninus Elagabalus*, xxxii.5, xxix.2). On the other hand, men like Severus Alexander, Elagabalus's immediate successor, were said to have been "temperate" in love. "His chief amusement consisted of having young dogs play with little pigs" (SHA, *Severus Alexander*, xli.5).

Collecting Other Men's Women

Roman emperors, like other emperors, could be great adulterers. From Lucretia's rape at least, heads of state took liberties with their subjects' wives (Livy, *History of Rome*, i.57–60). Sometimes they took other men's wives and married them; sometimes they took other men's wives and had sex with them; sometimes they took other men's wives and prostituted them to third parties. None of these acts of "adultery" seem to have been committed infrequently.

Augustus took his third and last wife, Livia, from her husband, Tiberius Claudius Nero, when she was nineteen years old, mother of a four-year-old son, and six months pregnant with her second child. That Claudius "gave her away" when she married Augustus (Balsdon

1962:68–71; cf. Suetonius, *Augustus*, 4; Tacitus, *Annals*, i.10). If Suetonius is right, she might already have been given up for a night—like other wives Augustus had had provisioned—at least. Suetonius writes, "when, three months after her marriage to Augustus, Livia gave birth to Decimus (later Nero) Drusus—the father of the emperor Claudius—people naturally suspected that he was the product of adultery with his stepfather" (Suetonius, *Claudius*, 1). Another epigram was got up:

> How fortunate those parents are for whom
> Their child is only three months in the womb!

Suetonius makes this sound at least a little plausible. Augustus seems to have left the empire to his first step-son, Tiberius, with regret; he is reported, for instance, to have pitied "poor Rome, doomed to be masticated by those slow-moving jaws" (*Tiberius*, 21). But for Livia's second son, Drusus, Augustus is supposed to have felt "so deep a love" that he considered him no less an heir than Gaius and Lucius, his only legitimate grandsons. "Nor did he think it enough to have an adulatory inscription carved on Drusus's tomb in verses of his own composition: he also wrote his biography in prose" (Suetonius, *Claudius*, 1). Augustus picked Drusus, not his elder brother Tiberius, to wed Antonia, daughter of his sister Octavia; and when Drusus died he forced Tiberius to adopt Germanicus, Drusus and Antonia's eldest son (see Hallett 1984:324). Drusus was not just father to Germanicus and Claudius; he was grandfather to Caligula and great-grandfather to Nero.

Other emperors followed Augustus's precedent. Caligula took Ennia, wife of his Commander of the Guards, swearing in writing to marry her if he became emperor; he took Livia Orestilla from her husband, Piso, on their wedding day, telling the groom "hands off my wife!," and divorcing her a few days later; and he took Lollia Paulina, wife of a provincial governor, "because somebody had remarked that her grandmother was once a famous beauty," but soon divorced her as well (Suetonius, *Gaius*, 12, 25; Tacitus, *Annals*, vi.45). Domitian took Domitia from her husband, Aelius Lamia, made her "one of his mistresses," and then his wife; later Titus took Domitia from his brother (Dio, *History*, lxv.3.4; lxvi.26.4). After Domitian had taken Domitia from her husband, Titus encouraged Lamia to marry again. "What? You are not wanting a wife, too, are you?" was his reply; it cost him not a wife, but his life (Suetonius, *Domitian*, 10).

Most emperors followed Caesar in having sex with other men's wives; some might have got children by them. Caesar notoriously enjoyed, according to Suetonius, the wives of Servius Sulpicius, Aulus Gabinius, Marcus Crassus, and Pompey; "but Marcus Brutus's mother Sevilia was the woman whom Caesar loved best" (*Julius Caesar*, 50). In that case, Caesar's murder may have been a parricide (Syme 1980). Otho's father, who was brought up in Livia's house, "was generally supposed to be a bastard of Tiberius, to whom the boy was very dear, and bore a close resemblance" (Suetonius, *Otho*, 1). Hadrian, who was "addicted" to adulteries with married women (SHA, *Hadrian*, xi.7), but left no legitimate issue, adopted Aelius and appointed him his successor; he also adopted Antoninus Pius on condition that he in turn adopt Lucius Verus, Aelius's son. To Balsdon, Hadrian's devotion to Aelius's family was "inexplicable," "unless," as he added in a footnote, Aelius was his bastard son (1962:140–141). According to Carcopino, he was (1958:143–222; but see Syme 1980). Finally, Herodian and the *SHA* agree that Elagabalus's mother's affair with Caracalla was so well known that he was commonly assumed to be the emperor's bastard (SHA, *Antoninus Elagabalus*, ii.1; Herodian, *Macrinus, Elagabalus*, iii.10).

But the most amazing thing Roman emperors did with other men's women was to pimp them. Caligula turned quite a profit. Dio says he set apart rooms in the palace, and shut up "the wives of the foremost men as well as the children of the most aristocratic families . . . using them as a means of milking everybody alike." Some women were willing, others were not; most "rejoiced" at the emperor's "licentiousness, and in the fact that he used to throw himself each time on the gold and silver collected from these sources and roll in it" (Dio, *History*, lix.28.9–10). Nero seems to have done the same. Tacitus describes a spectacular feast on an artificial lake, the quays covered with brothels "stocked with high-ranking ladies"; they included "the most beautiful and distin-

guished in the city" of the oldest families, both "virgins and married women" (Tacitus, *Annals*, xv.37; Dio, *History*, lxii.15.4). Nero, other nobles, gladiators, and an "indiscriminate rabble" of men "had the privilege of enjoying whichever one he wished, as the women were not allowed to refuse anyone" (Dio, *History*, lxii.15.5). The *SHA* are terse about Elagabalus, but they make the same point: "He opened brothels in his house for his friends, his clients, and his slaves" (*Antoninus Elagabalus*, xxiv.2). Messalina seems to have made money and friends the same way (Dio, *History*, lx.l8.1–2, lxi.31.1).

Showing Themselves Off

Roman emperors were studies in sexual selection (see Darwin 1871). That is inevitably so in one sense: they had what it took to win at *intra*sexual selection. Emperors had, by definition, won the imperial power struggle; they'd out*competed* everybody else for the title that got them the right to more riches—and so, perhaps, to more women—than any other man in Rome. But sometimes they also excelled at *inter*sexual selection. They made ostentatious efforts to *attract* members of the opposite sex, showing off their intellects, their athleticism, and their good looks.

Most Roman emperors, like emperors all over the world, were devotees of the arts. Some practiced rather than watched. Hadrian was a poet and flautist; Elagabalus sang, danced, and played the organ (SHA, *Hadrian*, xiv.8; *Antoninus Elagabalus*, xxxii.8). On the day Caligula died, he'd meant to make his stage debut. He'd already rehearsed in private. Suetonius says he asked three men of consular rank to a stage in the palace one night, burst onto it "amid a tremendous racket of flutes and clogs," did a little song and dance, and disappeared (*Gaius*, 54). But the most artistic emperor must have been Nero. He was exceedingly interested in music, and from an early age loved to sing. He "conscientiously undertook all the usual exercises for strengthening and developing his voice." He'd lie on his back under a slab of lead, use enemas and emetics to keep his weight down, and abstain from apples and other edibles that might hurt his vocal chords (Suetonius, *Nero*, 20). Unlike Caligula, Nero actually made a stage debut—in an earthquake; after that he performed in public contests whenever he got a chance. He was a jealous competitor, ordering busts of earlier winners be taken down, dragged away with hooks, and hurled into public lavatories (*Nero,* 22, 24). Most infamously of all, when Rome burned in a six-day fire, he watched the conflagration from the Tower of Maecenas, enraptured by what he called "the beauty of the flames"; then put on his tragedian's costume and sang *The Sack of Illium* from beginning to end (*Nero*, 38).

Other emperors were athletes. Some of the more modest were avid hunters, Marcus Aurelius among them (SHA, *Marcus Antoninus*, iv.8). Others, Caligula for one, were charioteers (Dio, *History*, lix.l7.3–5). But the most daring, like Commodus and at least seven others, were gladiators. Commodus, according to Dio, devoted his life "to combats of wild beasts and of men." Once, with his bare hands, he was supposed to have done two elephants and five hippopotami in (*History*, lxxiii.10.2–3), according to the *Scriptores*, he fought 735 bouts in all (*Commodus Antoninus*, ixi.12). Roman women loved a gladiator. At Pompeii they were commemorated as "heart-throbs" and "netters of young girls by night;" an excavated terra-cotta helmet is shaped like a phallus; even the word *gladius*, literally "sword," meant "penis" on the street (Hopkins 1983:6–7, 20–23; cf. Geertz 1973).

Many emperors were fancy dressers. For instance Caligula, in his chariot, wore the breastplate of Alexander "(or so he claimed)," a purple silk mantle covered with precious stones, a tunic embroidered in gold, and an oak leaf garland (Dio, *History*, lix.17.3–5; cf. Suetonius, *Gaius,* 51). Commodus, in combat, wore a lion's skin and gold and purple robes and called himself Hercules, son of Zeus (Herodian, *Marcus Aurelius and Commodus*, xiv.8). Elagabalus, at home, wore jewels on his shoes, tunics made of purple or gold or studded with stones, and a gemmed crown; "at such times he would say that he felt oppressed by the weight of his pleasures" (SHA, *Antoninus Elagabalus*, xxiii.4–5, xxxii.1; cf. Herodian, *Macrinus, Elagabalus* v.3 vi.10).

Showing Money Off

Roman emperors didn't just show off their personal attractions, they showed off their provisions. Men are, of course, among the males of many species who offer more to their mates than sperm; collecting a harem often involves defending, and displaying, resources as well as bodies (e.g., Emlen and Oring 1977). Consumption can get to be conspicuous (e.g., Codere 1950). Roman emperors could be cases in point.

They ate wonderfully. Consider generous Augustus whose banquet, "The Feast of the Divine Twelve," in the midst of a famine caused a public scandal (Suetonius, *Augustus*, 70). Hadrian, another generous emperor, loved to eat "tetrapharmacum" made of pastry, pheasant, sow's udders, and ham (SHA, *Hadrian*, xxi.4). Elagabalus fed his dogs on goose livers; Caligula offered golden barley to his horse (SHA, *Antoninus Elagabalus*, xxi.l; Dio, *History*, lix.l4.7).

They lived in nice houses. The nicest of all was, no doubt, Nero's Golden House. It stretched from the Palatine to the Esquiline, across landscaped gardens, vineyards, pastures, and woods stocked with menageries, around a pool "like a sea." Parts of the house were overlaid with gold, pearl, ivory, and precious stones; panels slid back to let in showers of flowers; baths were filled with sulphur water. How did he pay for it? Nero told his magistrates: " 'You know my needs! Let us see to it that nobody is left with anything' " (Suetonius, *Nero*, 31–32).

They didn't work hard for the money. Roman aristocrats, like most aristocrats, led a leisurely life. Domitian is the most stupefying example. He "hated to exert himself" but hit, early in his reign, on a way to pass the time. "Domitian would spend hours alone every day doing nothing but catch flies and stabbing them with a needle-sharp pen" (Suetonius, *Domitian*, 19, 3).

Collecting Men

Again, in all these respects—in collecting lots of women, in having sexual access to other men's women, in showing themselves off, and in showing their money off—Roman emperors were very much like emperors everywhere else; and in all these respects they seem to have been striving, consciously or not, to reproduce (cf. Betzig 1982, 1986, 1993). But in another respect Roman emperors stand out. They apparently liked, very much, to have sex with men.

It is not clear how few or many precedents that follows. Bisexuality seems to have penetrated aristocracies in Polynesia and Greece at least; in ancient India and China, on the other hand, semen conservation was a religious concern, and nobles took trouble to limit their emissions to women likely to conceive (Sagan 1985: 204–210; Dass 1970:22; van Gulik 1974:46, 339–345). Neither is it at all clear that bisexuality in the Roman aristocracy follows from Darwinian theory. Given a choice, and Roman emperors apparently had one, sex with men seems less likely than sex with women to result in reproduction.

In a couple of cases, sex among men in Rome seems to have had something to do with political advancement. Early in his career, for instance, Caesar wasted so much time at King Nicomedes's court that people suspected an affair (Suetonius, *Julius Caesar*, 2). Vitellius is supposed to have been among Tiberius's "male prostitutes" at Capreae (Suetonius, *Vitellius*, 3). And Otho is thought to have become Nero's favorite by what Suetonius calls their "decidedly unnatural" involvement (Suetonius, *Otho*, 2).

In many other cases, it just seems to have been the thing to do (see Veyne 1985). Suetonius calls Galba a "homosexual invert" (Suetonius, *Galba*, 21); Dio says Trajan was "devoted to boys" (Dio, *History*, lxviii.7.4); and the *Scriptores* refer to Hadrian's "passion for males" (SHA, *Hadrian*, xi.7). Suetonius takes the trouble, on Claudius's behalf, to point out that "boys and men left him cold" (*Claudius*, 33). Most emperors seem to have collected boys as well as girls.

Some were flamboyant about it. Nero was a groom, and then a bride, to a pair of young men. He tried—or managed—to turn Sporus, the first, into a girl by castration. Then he gave him a dowry, put him in a veil, invited a crowd to the ceremony, and "treated him as his wife." Afterwards, he dressed Sporus up like an empress and took him to fairs, "kissing him amorously now and then" (Suetonius, *Nero*, 28; Dio, *History*, lxii.28.2–3; lxiii.13.1–2). Nero later became a bride himself to his freedman Doryphorus, making the "screams and moans of a girl being deflowered" on his wedding night (Suetonius, *Nero*, 29). Elagabalus's interest in his own sex was even more amazing. The *Scriptores* say "even at Rome he did nothing but send out agents to search for those who had

particularly large organs and bring them to the palace in order that he might enjoy their vigour." He had the city, the baths, and the wharves scoured for "*onobeli*," men who resembled asses. Elagabalus preferred to play Venus to Anchises, particularly to Zoticus, the athlete from Smyrna whose bride he became (SHA, *Antoninus Elagabalus*, v.3–4, viii.6–7, x.5; cf. Dio, *History*, lxxx.16). According to Dio, he went to the extent of asking his surgeons to make him a vagina by incision; according to the *Scriptores*, he went so far as to "infibulate" himself (Dio, *History*, lxxx. 16.7; SHA, *Antoninus Elagabalus*, vii.2). "Indeed, for him life was nothing except a search after pleasures" (SHA, *Antoninus Elagabalus*, xix.6).

STUDIES

There is enough in these sources to make a case for polygyny at the top of the Roman aristocracy. But what about everybody else? There is an enormous amount of evidence on the Roman family—in literary sources, from letters to love poems; in legal sources, like Justinian's *Digest*; and in the thousands of epitaphs left on the tombs that line the roads from Rome. And there has been an enormous number of studies.

How right was Livy? How much did wealth bring "sensual excess" to Rome (*History of Rome*, i.1)? In other empires, social status was matched by sexual access to women—and so, arguably, by the production of children (e.g., Betzig 1982, 1986, 1993). How much did power parallel polygyny in the Roman aristocracy? There is plenty of evidence, of course, that wealth in Rome bought access to at least one kind of women—to slaves. Slaves were a part of the Roman family: neither word commonly used for family in Rome, *domus* or *familia*, excluded slaves; in fact, the word *familia* itself is derived from *famel*, or slave; the word *puer*, "child," took in all the children of a household, slave or free; and many Romans, like Cicero, commonly referred to their families by the simple adjective, "my (people)," *mei* (see Saller 1984; Corbier 1991:129; Wiedemann 1989:33; Bradley 1991b:97). There is a consensus that slaves were more concentrated in Italy than in the rest of the empire, in Rome than in the rest of Italy, and in the most powerful households in Rome. How much did Roman polygyny involve slavery?

The literature on Roman slavery is huge (e.g., Wiedemann 1987). There's enough there, I think, to suggest: that rich Romans kept as many slaves as they could afford, often hundreds and sometimes thousands; that many of those slaves were women; and that slave women could be picked and praised for their ability to bear children. So much is only a little controversial; it has often been said that slave women were bought to breed slaves (e.g., Biezunska-Malowist 1969; Kolendo 1976; Bradley 1984). But to most who have made that case, slaves were bred for economic reasons. I think another case can be made that slave women were kept to breed their masters' bastards. Why? Because there is so much evidence that rich Romans: had sexual access to their slave women; punished other men who sought sexual access; invested heavily in slave children, freed so many slaves and freed them so young, and provided them with great wealth, high position, and paternal affection.

How Many Slaves?

How many slaves might a rich man have? Most estimates are large. P. A. Brunt guessed there were about 2,000,000 slaves in a total population of around 5,000,000 in Italy in 225 B.C.; William Harris guessed there might have been about 10,000,000 slaves in a population of around 50,000,000 in the whole Roman empire in the first century A.D. (Brunt 1971:121, 124; Harris 1982:118). How evenly distributed were they?

Tacitus tells how Lucius Pedanius Secundus, one of the richest men in Rome, was killed by a slave at home while another 400 failed to act in his defense (*Annals*, xiv.42–3). Many more slaves, as Brunt points out, may have lived on Secundus's farms, earning the income he needed to live so well in town (1971:125). Augustus's *lex Fufia Caninia* of 2 B.C. limited the number who could be freed by will to 20% for holders of more than 100 slaves. That law also limited the absolute number of slaves freed by will to 100 (e.g., Westermann 1955:89), suggesting that holdings of 500 and more might not have been rare. Pliny the Younger, whose fortune was thought to be "modest," probably had around 500 (Brunt 1971:125). Susan Treggiari counted 204, 634, and 642 slaves and freed slaves from surviving inscriptions in tombs of

three noble families of the first century A.D. (1975a:395). Again many other slaves—like those on country farms—may not have earned an inscription; the last of these three tombs, Augustus's wife Livia's, held 3,000 burial urns, most for her freedmen and slaves (Hopkins 1983:216). The biggest holding on record comes from early in the fifth century A.D.; the Christian noblewoman Melania is said to have freed 8,000 of her 24,000 slaves (e.g., Finley 1980:123). But the biggest *familia* of all was probably the imperial *Familia*. "It is beyond doubt that thousands of slaves, scattered throughout the empire, were owned by the emperor, who was himself the greatest slave-owner of all" (Bradley 1984:16). Over 4,000 imperial slaves and freedmen are listed in the inscriptions; their numbers grew over time (Weaver 1972:3, 32). After the third century A.D., the emperor's house is supposed to have held 1,000 cooks, 1,000 barbers, more than 1,000 cupbearers, "hives" of table servants, and many other slaves (Friedlander 1908 v.1:66). There's undoubtedly hyperbole here; but the numbers were undoubtedly large. In Rome, as in other empires, households varied enormously in size (e.g., Wallace-Hadrill 1991). Bigger houses housed more slaves.

Descriptions put meat on figures like these. Rich Romans squandered their slaves' labor just to show off their numbers. Slaves served as torch-bearers, lantern-bearers, and chief sedan-chair bearers. The emperor kept a slave for every piece in his closet: a *veste privata* for what he wore at home, a *veste forensi* for what he wore in the city, a *veste triumphali* for what he wore on parade, a *veste gladiatorial* for what he wore to the show. There was an imperial slave assigned to every type of utensil: some for silver, some for rock crystal, some for gold. Some slaves kept track of time; some kept track of names; others were kept to remind people to eat or sleep. There were thousands of slaves in a senator's palace. Some cost 100,000 or 200,000 sesterces or more—1,000,000 qualified a man to enter the senate (Friedlander 1908 v.1:114, v.2:219–221; Carcopino 1940:70–1).

How Many Slave Women?

But harems are filled with women; and many of these slaves were men. In the inscriptions, in fact, males outnumber females by about two to one. Treggiari counted 129 males and 75 females in inscriptions for the Volusii family, 421 males and 213 females for the Statilii, and 440 males and 212 females in the *Monumentum Liviae* (1975a:395). Interestingly, Beryl Rawson found the same sex ratio, 276:139, in inscriptions for *alumni* in the city of Rome. *Alumni* were, loosely translated, foster children. She found a similar sex ratio, 381:183, among *vernae*, slaves born and bred in their masters' homes (1986a:173, 179). In the emperor's family, P. R. C. Weaver found 440 male and 290 female children born to imperial slaves and freed slaves, counting just those children who lacked any formal status indication. But in the *Familia Caesaris* proper, that is, among children with formal imperial status, he found a much smaller proportion of girls—in Italy just 6% (1972:172–173, 177). Sex ratio biases like these have made Treggiari wonder, more than once, where all the women went (1975a: 400–401; 1979:201; see also Pomeroy 1975; Oldenziel 1987). They might have been killed more often; they might have been bought less often; they might just have been less apt to leave their names inscribed in stone (see Hopkins 1966 on selective commemoration; see Trivers and Willard 1973; Alexander 1974; and discussion in Betzig 1992b on how male bias might raise reproduction).

The evidence suggests women were at least as likely to be bought and sold as men. As Harris among others points out, *the* major source of slaves in the republic was by capture in war (1982:121–122; cf. Westermann 1955:84–85; Hopkins 1978:102). Across cultures, war captives tend to be women rather than men (e.g., Chagnon 1983, 1988a; Manson and Wrangham 1991). The Latins agree. Livy, for instance, in his *History of Rome* of the first century B.C., notes a consistent female bias in captives; Sallust and Tacitus say that at Capsa and Volandum men were killed and women captured and sold; and Augustine says that in a raid on an Algerian village slave-dealers killed the men and took the women and children. This habit persisted; according to Gregory of Tours, in his sixth-century *History of the Franks*, soldiers were advised to kill "everyone who could piss against the wall," and capture the others (in Bradley 1987:51; Whittaker 1987:98).

After the empire was established, slaves were less likely to be recruited by capture. At that point, other than slave breeding, the most important source may have been foundlings (Harris 1982). According to John Boswell, as many as 20–40% of children born in Rome might have been abandoned during the first three centuries A.D., and most were probably girls (1988:135). The axiom "everyone raises a son, including a poor man, but even a rich man will abandon a daughter" was 800 years old when it was quoted by Stobaeus in the fifth century A.D. (pp. 101–102). In other words, more female slaves should still have been bought and sold.

What Were Slave Women For?

Slaves are often economic assets. That fact is so obvious that it's seldom been asked if they might be good for anything else. If slaves are valued mainly for manual labor, it makes sense that men should be valued more than women. But then why keep slave women at all? Several historians have answered that question: in order to breed more hard-working men (e.g., Biezunska-Malowist 1969; Kolendo 1976; Bradley 1978). From the republic into the empire, the slave population grew by leaps and bounds. An arguable proportion—perhaps most of them—were slave women's children (e.g., Westermann 1955:86; Brunt 1971:131; Bradley 1987:42). How many might have been? Home-breeding was arguably the most important source of new slaves under the empire; it was a significant source of slaves under the republic as well (e.g., Harris 1982; Bradley 1987). Bradley's guess is that for late republican Italy roughly 100,000 new slaves were recruited annually; for the whole Roman empire around the first two centuries A.D. more than 500,000 new slaves may have been needed every year (1987:42). Even if a minority in each case were homeborn, the numbers must have been very large. In Roman Egypt the word *oikogenesis* is listed with "great frequency" on papyri; the term *vernae* is listed on inscriptions outside of Rome; both mean homeborn (e.g., Westermann 1955:86; Rawson 1986a).

Other evidence suggests slave breeding, too. In the inscriptions, slave women are seldom ascribed other jobs. In literary, legal, and medical sources, and in Egyptian papyri, slave women are sometimes bought with their breeding potential in mind and rewarded for having borne children. And in legal and especially literary sources, slave women are sent to the country to gestate and give birth on their masters' estates.

Susan Treggiari has looked at the jobs ascribed to female slaves in Rome. There weren't many. On Livia's staff, "one striking factor in the job structure is the low proportion of women"; only 18 of the 79 slaves who were specifically attested as having worked for Livia were female, and only 3 of the 75 freed slaves who worked for her were women (1975b:58). In aristocratic households, there are no job titles for women who worked outdoors, and women rarely seem to have worked in the public parts of houses. Administrators, reception room staff, and dining room staff were all male. Slave women, when jobs are attested at all, usually seem to have waited on other women. They were dressers, hair dressers, clothes menders, clothes folders, massagers, midwives, and wet-nurses; sometimes, they were spinners and weavers. But "there are many women in the *columbaria* whose jobs are not known" (Treggiari 1976:94). What did they do? Maybe they bore and brought up children.

Suetonius says Julius Caesar would pay top dollar for a pretty slave (*Julius Caesar*, 47); he wasn't the only one. Martial refers more than once to the high price friends paid for nice-looking slaves (*Epigrams*, ii.63, ix.21); and evidence from Egyptian papyri suggests that "physical attractiveness" was taken into account in determining a slave's price (in Westermann 1955:100). To Ulpian, the *Digest* jurist, "slave-girls are not generally acquired as breeders"; on the other hand, evidence from other jurists suggests that sterility might have been considered a defect in female slaves at the time of their sale (*Digest*, 5.3.27pr., see Gardner 1986:206; Wiedemann 1981:120).

Keith Bradley did a systematic study of the ages at which slaves were sold in Roman Egypt. He looked at twenty-nine records from papyri, and found an age range from 4 to 35 years, with a mean for the twenty-two "adult" women, 14 or older, of just over 22 years. Bradley concludes that such evidence "seems to indicate a correlation between the ages of adult female slaves at time of sale and the period of expected female reproductivity." He adds, "this can hardly be an accident," and, even more strongly, that the data suggest "that female slaves were bought and sold with their potential for breeding acting as a prime consideration for buyers and sellers" (Bradley 1978:245–246; see too Dalby 1979). But it is important to note that Bradley's own data on ages of *male* slaves at time of sale, from another twenty-one Egyptian records, follow a similar pattern. In this case the range is from 2 to 40 years, with a mean, for eleven "adults," 14 or older, of less than 27 years (Bradley 1984:57). It makes sense to invest in young breeders; but it makes sense, too, to invest in young workers.

Other evidence, from medical texts, suggests that Romans placed a premium on fertile women—in *spite* of the notorious fact that they made strenuous efforts to limit *legitimate* family size (e.g., Dio, *History*, lvi.5). This was anticipated by Greek tradition: According to Aline Rouselle, every book in the *Hippocratic Collection* on female illness has to do with the uterus. Rouselle writes, "conception and pregnancy were thought of as the remedy for all female ailments, for a pregnant woman was a healthy woman" (1988:24, 28). Keith Hopkins, in a study of Roman contraception, looked at 22 ancient medical writers and found that though only 11 suggested contraceptive methods, 18 mentioned methods of aiding conception (1965:132–133). Soranus, the best-known medicine man in Rome before Galen, called a section of his *Gynaecology* "What is the best time for fruitful intercourse?" He answered: when menstruation is ending, appetite for coitus is present, and "a pleasant state exists in every respect" (i.x.36). There was a preoccupation with gynecological disorders in discussions of disabilities affecting female slaves (Treggiari 1979:187). The *Digest* refers to love potions and fertility drugs (*Digest*, 48.8.3.2, 48.19.38.5; see Gardner 1986:159).

Both Columella and Varro, writing on Roman agriculture, advised that female slaves be encouraged to breed; incentives included exemption from work for mothers of three children, and manumission for mothers of four or more. Evidence from the *Digest* also suggests that some slave women were given freedom on condition of having borne a specified number of children; Arethusa, freed after the birth of her third child (who was, as it turned out, one of twins or triplets) offered the "textbook" case (*Digest* 1.5.15; 16, 34.5.10(11).1; see Gardner 1986:208–209).

The best evidence that Romans valued female slaves' fertility may be literary. Horace, in a bucolic passage, attributes the "joy" of seeing sheep, oxen, and "home-bred slaves (the swarm of a thriving house)" to Alfius, a money-lender turning farmer (*Epodes*, ii.62–67). Martial criticizes Linus's cheap country life, where home-bred slaves wait on his table; but he advises Publius to keep pages "fresh from the farm," the "sons of your herd reeking from the stable"; and he loves his friend Faustinus's Baian villa for its corners packed with grain, stalls stocked with bulls, and "young slaves born on the farm, with skins as white as milk, set in a circle round the bright fireside" (*Epigrams*, iv.66, x.98, iii.58). Tacitus, in his *Annals,* refers to slaves "born on the same estates, in the same homes, as their masters, who had treated them kindly since birth" (xiv.44). And in Petronius's *Satyricon*, the best-known example, Trimalchio's accountant interrupts the party to let him know that on July 26th: 10,000,000 sesterces had been deposited in his strongroom; a fire had started at his Pompeian estate; and, on his estate at Cumae, there had been 30 male and 40 female births (xv.53).

Sketches like these are matched by legal and inscriptional evidence. Two passages in the *Digest*, by Paulus and Marcianus, refer to slave accouchements taking place on country estates as a matter of course (*Digest*, 32.99.3, 50.16.210; see Treggiari 1979:189). And Rawson, in her study of 564 inscriptions of *vernae*, found over three-quarters of those of specified age to be between 1 and 14; very few were over 20; and only 2% were infants of under one year (1986a:191). Where were the babies? Maybe at Baiae, at Cumae, or on some other estate in the Roman countryside. Treggiari suggests, and Rawson and others concur, that slave women—who had few jobs to do in town—may have spent much of their lives gestating, birthing, and nursing children in the country. Treggiari writes,

The Romans realised the importance of fresh air, exercise and a healthy diet for pregnant women and small children. It would be better for their *vernae* to be born and brought up in the country. Besides, it would be cheaper and easier to feed them on a farm, and it would save overcrowding the limited accommodation of a town house. So we might guess that some of the pregnant women in the urban *familia* would be packed off to bear their children at a villa,

and that then, for some time at least, the children might be reared in the country. (1979:189)

But *Whose* Children Were They?

That is, I think, the critical question. If slave women are bred for economic reasons, then it shouldn't much matter to masters who are the fathers. If, on the other hand, slave women are bought and bred for the sake of their master's own reproduction, then paternity becomes a huge concern (e.g., Trivers 1972; Alexander and Borgia 1979). Most historians seem satisfied that slave men fathered slave women's children (e.g., Rawson 1966; Flory 1978; Treggiari 1981b). But at least three facts mitigate against that. First is masters' concern with chastity in slave men; second is masters' concern with chastity in slave women; third, but not least, is masters' own use of slaves for sex.

There is plenty of legal and inscriptional evidence of "slave families" in Rome. Though Alan Watson suggests that "it is not easy to find legal texts that show slaves as holders of family relationships," there are *Digest* references to slave women bringing slave men "dowries," to slave families given together as legacies, and to incest avoidance and parricide among slave fathers and children (e.g., *Digest*, 23.3.39.pr, 33.7.12.33, 33.7.20.4, 23.2.14.2; see Watson 1987:78–80, 96). Though slaves couldn't legally marry, hundreds are listed as *contubernales* in the inscriptions, and others listed as *collibertus* and *colliberta* were legally married after they were freed (e.g., Flory 1978:92 n. 18, 23). Inscriptions refer to slave children with slave mothers *and* slave fathers; for instance, *CIL 6* 6698 says simply, "set up to Narcissus, who lived 2 years, 4 months and 13 days, by Tychus his mother and Narcissus his father," all of them slaves (thanks to Jane Gardner, personal communication).

But what sorts of slaves were most likely to have become fathers? Beryl Rawson put some of the first work on slave families into a paper on life among the Roman "lower class." In a sample of 1572 freed or freeborn children commemorated in the inscriptions, she found 73 had two slave parents, 591 had two free parents, and 751 had one free and one slave parent (1966:73). In another paper, on slave "marriages," Treggiari found 260 inscriptions (of a sample of 39,340 in *CIL 6*) listing a man and a woman in *contubernium*, an informal union. In 68 of these cases, both partners were probably slaves; in another 37, the man was a slave and the woman free (1981b). But the slave "husbands" and fathers in these two studies are unlikely to have been "lower class" in the sense of lacking influence or wealth or both. Since both samples were drawn from inscriptions, they left out the mass of people too powerless or poor to be remembered in an epitaph, many of whose remains were thrown into *puticuli* pits outside Rome (e.g., Hopkins 1983:208). Many of the fathers in these inscriptions were, or are likely to have resembled, slaves in the emperor's house, that is, the *Familia Caesaris*. When Rawson found 184 inscriptions of freeborn Romans who inserted the term *spurii filius* in their names—children of male slaves and free women— she concluded that "most of the slaves in these relationships are imperial slaves" (1989:30). Similarly, Treggiari concluded of her *contubernales* that most men in the mixed unions "were imperial civil servants or belonged to women of the imperial family or dependents of the emperor" (1981b:15). P. R. C. Weaver, in his detailed study of the emperors' families, found 462 wives of imperial slaves, most of them free or freed (1972:114). Of all slaves in the inscriptions, men in the *Familia Caesaris* were most likely to marry; and their wives were most likely to be freeborn (Weaver 1972:114; 1986:115).

But what of the others? Certainly, some humbler slaves had "wives" and were fathers (e.g., Flory 1978). But the majority might not have been offered sexual access to women or encouraged to have children. Most male slaves, especially the "barbarians" not lucky enough to have been home-grown, did not live comfortably with their masters in town. They lived and worked on the farms, and in the mines (e.g., Treggiari 1969:9). Women were rare in both spots. In the mines, the work was dangerous, the mortality rate was high, and women were next to none. "None of these conditions favoured the formation of family units" (Bradley 1984:77). On the farms, Columella's "humanitarian" recommendations included attention to the sick, availability of a large kitchen, and sturdy clothes. On the other hand, the housing was not conducive to family living: "The individual cells in which chained slaves are housed should be built so as to admit some

sunlight, while the *ergastulum*, although subterranean, should be well lit and as healthy as possible," so long as the windows were kept out of reach (*De Re Rustica*, i). Hopkins says that "agricultural slaves were usually male and celibate" (1978:106); exceptions, according to Varro and Columella, were foremen, each of whom was to be rewarded with a woman (see Westermann 1955:119). Even in town, where slave men were surrounded by women, they might have been made to mind their manners. As far as Juvenal was concerned, "if a slave takes a lick at a tart, we give *him* a licking" (*Satires*, ix.5–6). Slaves seem very seldom to have been accompanied by fathers when they were sold: in Delphic manumission records, mothers are freed with children 29 times, father with child only once; and in records from Roman Egypt, the overwhelming majority of sales concern individual slaves, mothers are rarely sold with young children, and no man on record is sold with a wife or child (Gardner 1986:213; Bradley 1978:246). Cato, according to Plutarch, let some of his slave men into his "female slave quarters," but charged them a fee for admission (Plutarch, *Cato*, xxi.2). Again, slaves had no "*conubium*"; they were legally barred from marriage (e.g., Watson 1987:77).

Slaves weren't the only men kept away from slave women. Martial, in a well-known epigram, said a slave girl "whose reputation one could smell from here to her street corner in the slums" was auctioned off for a paltry sum (vi.66). In the *Digest*, a buyer had an action against the seller should a slave woman sold as a virgin turn out not to be one; and pregnancy could be considered a defect at the time of sale (*Digest*, 19.1.1.5; see Gardner 1986:206–207). None of this makes sense if slaves were bred for economic reasons; in that case, contributions of semen should be welcomed, especially in large households (Betzig 1989a:661–662). When women were deflowered, the penalties could be severe. Commodus found out his powerful freedman, Cleander, had "begotten sons" by some of his 300 women; those sons, their mothers, and Cleander were all put to death (SHA, *Commodus Antoninus*, vii.2–3). In the *Digest*, seducing another man's slave might involve the seducer in a suit (*Digest*, 47.10.9.4, 47.10.25, 48.5.6.pr.; see Treggiari 1979:193). And in particular, under the *Lex Aquilia*, a Roman damage legislation, an action might be brought if a virgin slave were debauched (e.g., Gardner 1986:119, 207, 220). Seneca thought particularly profligate masters most likely to insist on fidelity in their slaves (*Ira*, 2, 28, 7; in Treggiari 1979:193). Later on, in the early Middle Ages, the rape of slave women was punished in Frankish and Burgundian law; to the Franks a man who slept with another man's slave was an "adulterer," and the adulterer himself was enslaved (Rouche 1987:466, 472).

Sarah Pomeroy has made a point of contrasting the Greek *gynaeceum*, in which women were carefully hidden, with the relative freedom of Roman women (1975). Cornelius Nepos did the same; Roman matrons, in particular, moved physically and socially "in the middle of male life" (in Wallace-Hadrill 1988:51; but see p. 52, note 32). That may be so; but certainly Roman women, especially slave women, were not altogether free. Women gave birth attended by midwives—always women; and they were probably cared for in segregated wards (e.g., Treggiari 1976:87; Rawson 1991:11). Slaves often slept apart; many probably lived on second stories. In the Casa del Menandro at Pompeii, service areas are accessible only down long corridors; in Nero's Domus Aurea, a small suite of rooms off the north peristyle, with a small garden, and with paintings from feminine mythology, has been called a *gynaeceum*; and in at least one picture from Pompeii, possibly based on a Greek version, women lay about and talk in a "*gynaeceum* scene" (Westermann 1955:107; Wallace-Hadrill 1988:79, 81, 52, note 32; Stambaugh 1988:164, 170; Veyne 1987:38). And slaves often worked apart: slave women are absent from apprenticeship documents in Roman Egypt; and in Rome they were kept from any public or outdoor employment: "the more elegant the household, the less women servants appeared before visitors" (Bradley 1991a:108; Treggiari 1981b:11). It is worth mentioning, too, that whether they slept or worked, women in Rome might be surrounded by eunuchs. Ovid feels sorry for Bagoas, his mistress' "attendant": "Poor guardian, you're neither man nor woman; / The joys of mutual love you cannot know" (*Amores*, ii.3.1–2); Juvenal weighs the relative merits of eunuchs on whom surgeons work before and after their "testicles ripen and drop" (Juvenal, *Satires*, vi.365–379); Martial finds eunuchs even on the Baian farm (*Epigrams*, iii.58). Eu-

nuchs seem to have been fairly common from early in the empire; by the third century, there were "hives" of them in the imperial household; eventually, the "Superintendent of the Sacred Bedchamber" was in Rome, as in other empires, a powerful castrated man (e.g., Friedlander 1908 v.1:66; Treggiari 1975b:49; Hopkins 1978: chapter 4). Eunuchs may have been deprived of several motivations; fertilization was one of them (e.g., Dickemann 1981; contrast Coser 1964). Eunuchs have guarded harems all over the world (e.g., Dickemann 1981; Betzig 1986, 1993).

Masters themselves, on the other hand, were free to have sex with their slaves. "The whole area remains a terribly understudied subject" (Shaw 1987:30). Still, there are some well-known examples. Carcopino thought that, although the "better Romans" saved face by resisting temptation, others, "preoccupied solely with their own ease and pleasure, as indifferent to the duties of their position as to the dignity of the honours they enjoyed, . . . held it preferable to rule as pashas over the slave harems which their riches permitted them to maintain" (1940:102). He cites the case of Larcius Macedo, another master apparently assassinated by his slaves; afterwards "his concubines ran up, screaming frantically," and he revived (Pliny the Younger, *Letters*, iii.14). Treggiari, in her paper on concubinage, notes that use of the word "*concubina*" is often vague. But, she adds, "it is most commonly used . . . of whole harems of women kept by emperors and members of the upper classes," and "this usage is a commonplace of invective and hardly helps us to establish facts" (1981a:60–61; see too 1991b:52). She cites the case of Fabius Valens, who advanced "with a long and luxurious train of harlots and eunuchs," and was caught "dishonouring the homes of his hosts by intrigues with their wives and daughters" when he fought for Vitellius (Tacitus, *Histories*, iii.40–41).

Lots of evidence that masters used slaves for sex is literary. Moses Finley, for instance, says slaves' unrestricted sexual availability "is treated as a commonplace in Graeco-Roman literature from Homer on; only modern writers have managed largely to ignore it" (1980:95; see too Kiefer 1934:56, 179; Biezunska-Malowist 1977:113–116; Kolendo 1976). Handbooks advised Greek wives to abide husbands' infidelities with *hetaerae*: Plutarch advised Roman women to put up with husbands' "pecca-dilloes," that is, with their "debauchery, licen-tiousness, and wantonness" with their slaves (see Treggiari 1991b:201; Plutarch, *Moralia*, 140B). Most moralists from Plato to Cato and later were concerned that men stay away from other men's *wives* (Treggiari 1991b); most writers took sex with other women for granted. Horace, for instance, asks:

> When your organ is stiff, and a
>   servant girl
> Or young boy from the household is
>   near at hand and you know
> You can make an immediate assault,
>   would you sooner burst with
>   tension?
> Not me. I like sex to be there and
>   easy to get

(*Satires*, i.ii.16–19). Martial writes to Sosib-ianus: "Your mother was a slave; but though you guess it / Why call your father 'Master' and confess it?" He writes about Quirinalis:

> Children he wants, but fears the
>   marriage bond;
> Yet his dislikes and fancies
>   correspond;
> For kindly handmaids set the matter
>   right;
> The fields and mansions of the
>   worthy knight
> Are well supplied with slavelings—
>   knightlings rather;
> To each of whom he is a proper
>   father.

And he writes against Sila, who said she'd be his wife at any price, that he'd need: a dowry of a million sesterces, a bedroom separate from hers, and mistresses and slaves to fill his own bed—even while she was looking on (*Epi-grams*, i.81, i.84, xi.23; see too xi.98, xii.49). As Juvenal jokes:

> Hey there, *you*,
> Who do you think you're fooling?
>   Keep this masquerade
> For those who believe it. I'll wager
>   that you're one hundred
> Per cent a man. It's a bet. So will
>   you confess,
> Or must the torturer rack the truth
>   from your maids?

Or, more philosophically, "led helpless / By ir-rational impulse and powerful blind desires / We ask for marriage and children" (*Satires*, vi, x.350–352). They didn't necessarily intersect.

Other evidence that masters sired slaves is le-gal. There are many references to slaves as *filii naturales* in the *Digest* and other documents (see Crook 1967; Gardner 1986; Watson 1987). A blood tie between master and slave is as-sumed in legal discussions of manumission, damage assessments, and inheritance (e.g., Rawson 1989:23–29 and below). And a legal inconsistency, on usufruct, makes sense if a "natural" relationship between master and slave is assumed. Buyers of livestock automatically acquired a life interest in a mother's offspring, but when a slave woman was sold her children stayed with her original owner. Hardly human-itarian, if slave children were best looked after by their mothers. But it might have made sense if owners, or their sons, were the fathers. "Hence ownership of the child is being given, reasonably, to those among whom is the puta-tive father" (Watson 1987:104).

Still more evidence of aristocratic polygyny is architectural. Carcopino says Tiberius "al-most created a scandal" by decorating his bed-room with a Bride of Parrhasius and other erot-ica; in Nero's Golden House, the "love chambers" were covered with pearls (Car-copino 1940:152; Friedlander 1908 v.2:192; Suetonius, *Nero*, 31). John Stambaugh, de-scribing Roman mansions, says that even in the republic the master's bedroom sat in an elevated place on the main axis of the house, and "dom-inated everything that happened" (1988:164–165). Later, under the empire, houses lost much of their outward public function, tended to turn inward on private life, and centered on court-yard gardens. The best was, again, in Nero's house, filled with acres of meadows, trees, and flowers, "imitating the 'paradise' or pleasure gardens of the old Persian kings" (pp. 168-169). The names of imperial palaces of the third and fourth centuries imply that imitation went on; the "House of Amor and Psyche" and "House of Nymphaeum" at Ostia are two (p. 193). Un-fortunately, little remains architecturally of the most luxurious houses; most of the Campanian coast, covered with the villas of the Roman up-per classes, including its emperors, is now un-der water or under volcanic ash (e.g., D'Arms 1970; Gazda 1991). But in Roman Africa, remaining mosaics often invoke Dionysus and "transform products of nature into symbols of fertility"; others are filled with dancers and courtesans; bedrooms, in particular, are covered with sensual scenes. "It was there that the prevailing morality was most shockingly transgressed—a place of adultery, incest, and unnatural intercourse" (Thébert 1987:370, 378–379). Marianne Maaskant-Kleibrink, in a paper on "nymphomania," describes the *nymphaeum*, a Roman garden filled with waterfalls, artificial springs, and architectural backdrops with sculptures and mosaics of nude or semi-nude girls (1987:280). More straightforwardly, imperial Romans might protect themselves against the "evil eye" by painting phalli in their doorways (Veyne 1987:177). Phalli are common, of course, in public architecture too. The Column of Trajan, nearly thirty vertical meters of marble, is a conspicuous example. Elagabalus, according to the *Scriptores Historiae Augustae*, planned to outdo it, but "could not find enough stone" (SHA, *Antoninus Elagabalus*, xxiv .7).

Caring for *Vernae*

The best evidence of all that aristocratic Romans mated with slave women is that they spent so much time, love, and *money* on those women's children. Xenophon said raising slaves wasn't a profitable practice (in Biezunska-Malowist 1969:91). In some cases, at least, he must have been right. Some slave children, especially home-grown ones, were: pampered from birth; freed young; and lavished with status, sesterces, and love. Interestingly, though slave fathers of slave, freed, and free children are sometimes attested in the inscriptions—especially well-off slave fathers, like those from the *Familia Caesaris*—natural parents are seldom attested for *vernae* (Rawson 1986a). Rawson draws this fairly sweeping conclusion. "There may be owners' illegitimate children among the many *vernae* ('home-born slaves') recorded: this term often has parental-filial overtones, and *vernae* seem to have had a privileged position and not infrequently to have become their masters' heirs" (1989:18; see too Treggiari 1979:188; Bradley 1987:57; and below).

Iza Biezunska-Malowist seems to have convinced many historians that slave breeding was profitable after all. She found bills of sale for 24 infants from Roman Egypt, and argues that "buying infant slaves proves, beyond a doubt, that it was profitable to raise infants from their birth" (Biezunska-Malowist 1969:93). But, as Bradley points out, slaves were sold much more often as adults than as children; if it were more profitable to rear slaves than to buy them full grown, the opposite should hold (1978:247).

The ideal was always that slaves be born at home (e.g., Treggiari 1979:188; Wiedemann 1981:7, 120; Rawson 1986a:186). These weren't always cheap to bring up. Some *vernae*, at least, shared wet nurses, tutors, and quarters with legitimate children. Bradley looked at wet nursing contracts from Roman Egypt; they listed 19 slave nurslings, and just 2 free (1980:325). He looked then at Roman inscriptions, and found the word *nutrix* in 69 of them; in this case, nearly half of the nurslings were of equestrian or senatorial rank, but at least a fifth were slaves. In several cases, such slaves were nursed by someone other than their mother in spite of the fact that their mother was alive (1986:203–209; see too Bradley 1991a:14–22). There is some legal evidence of slave nursing, too: in the *Digest*, a husband was expected to provide a wet nurse for children born to slave women who came as part of a wife's dowry (*Digest*, 24.1.28.1; see Gardner 1986:242). Lactational amenorrhea—the fact that nursing suppresses cycling—was appreciated by Soranus (*Gynaecology*, i.15); Plutarch appreciated the fact that a mother who gave her child to a nurse would get pregnant again sooner as a result; it had already been appreciated by Aristotle (in Bradley 1986:212; Garnsey 1991:61). This is consistent with modern evidence that interbirth intervals are lengthened, and fertility is lowered, by lactation (e.g., Wood 1989). Rich men all over the world, at least from Sumerian times on, have provided wet nurses for their children—and so probably raised their own reproduction (e.g., Fildes 1986, 1988; Betzig 1993; Hrdy 1992). Galen recommended that nursing last three years (in Bradley 1991a:26–27); Soranus specified a number of conditions that the ideal nurse should meet (*Gynaecology*, ii.19–20). According to Westermann, in some nursing contracts, whether the child was free or slave the same demands were made of the nurse (1955:102).

Other contracts, for teachers, are the same whether the child was slave or free (Westermann 1955:102). In Livia's household, Treggiari found evidence that *paedagogi* were provided for some of the slaves (1975b:56). Bradley found inscriptional evidence of a number of *nutritores*, *educatores*, and *paedagogi* with slave charges. In fact, he suggests that "it was not at all uncommon" for slave children to be provided with tutors and other caretakers. Some of these slaves were from the *Familia Caesaris* (1991a:42–43, 62). In the *paedagogium Caesaris*, boy slaves were trained for court service later in life; as Bradley points out, the same sort of institution probably existed in lesser houses; the younger Pliny, for instance, may have maintained one (1991a:63). *Alumni* and *vernae* might share their nutritores with the master's legitimate daughters and sons (Dixon 1988:151, 159).

Bradley cites literary and legal evidence that slaves might sleep with their owners, that legitimate children might sleep with grown slaves, and that slave children and legitimate children might be brought up together as "familiar companions" (1991a:9, 150). *Vernae* are sometimes referred to as *collacteus*, that is, nursed together, or at least reared together, with a legitimate son or daughter (Rawson 1986a:187). Cato is supposed to have intended that some of his slave children, nursed by the same women, grow particularly attached to his legitimate son (in Dixon 1988:33). Legitimate and "natural" children shared quarters in Rome, as they did later in Europe and in other places and times (Wallace-Hadrill 1991:222–223; cf. Duby 1983; Betzig 1993, 1995). And some slave children, like legitimate children, were given an "allowance." *Peculium*, the money a father allotted a son, was also allotted to slaves. In both cases, the money technically belonged to the paterfamilias, but the son, daughter, or slave was free to administer it (e.g., Rawson 1986b:17). In the *Digest*, *peculium* given to slaves is not discussed separately from that given to daughters and sons (see Crook 1967:110). In regard not just to peculium, but in many other regards, "the legal position of a slave was very similar to that of a son" (Watson 1987:46, 98–100).

In Rome, *vernae* weren't just given good nurses, good tutors, and good accommodations; some of them seem to have been loved. A little evidence is in the histories. Dio describes Livia, at home in the imperial palace, surrounded by naked slave girls and boys (*History*, xlviii.44.3). Herodian describes boys kept about Commodus's palace, "who went about bare of clothes but adorned with gold and costly gems" (*Marcus Aurelius and Commodus*, xvii.3). One in particular, a very little boy called "Philocommodus," often slept with the emperor—as did other slave boys with other powerful masters.

More evidence is in the poets. Martial and friends were fond of a few young slaves. One epigram describes the grave of a freed slave, Glaucias, loved by his mentor, Melior—he was "pure," "fair," and dead at twelve years; two other epigrams describe Martial's own slave, Erotion, who died at five (Martial, *Epigrams*, 6.28; 5.34; 10.61). Both of the last are full of tenderness; at least one is worth reprinting:

> To you, my parents, I send on
> This little girl Erotion,
> The slave I loved, that by your side
> Her ghost need not be terrified
> Of the pitch darkness underground
> Or the great jaws of Hades' hound.
> This winter she would have
>   completed
> Her sixth year had she not been
>   cheated
> By just six days. Lisping my name,
> May she continue the sweet game
> Of childhood happily down there
> In two such good, old spirits' care.
> Lie lightly on her, turf and dew:
> She put so little weight on you.

Rich Romans were often surrounded by slave children, girls and especially boys; they called them *delicia*. "Great men playing with children for relaxation is a motif known in literature from Euripides on" (Slater 1974:134; see too Wiedemann 1989:31). Some of these *deliciae* were bought in the market; others must have been *filii naturales* of their masters (e.g., Treggiari 1969:212; Rawson 1986a:196). They seem to have surrounded women as often as men; husbands, fathers, brothers, or sons might have fathered some of them. According to Treggiari, "their relationship with their owners was like that between parents and children"; legitimate children were called *delicia*, too (1975b: 53–54; see too Rawson 1986a:186).

Other evidence is inscriptional. According to Wiedemann, names masters picked for slaves were often associated with luxury or divinity (Wiedemann 1987:23). Both suggest affection. So do commemorations of slave children by their *tatae* and *mamae*—literally, or metaphorically, daddies and mommies. In 49 *tatae* and 61 *mamae* inscriptions, Bradley finds children most often of slave status, and *tatae* and *mamae* most often of free status. Sometimes, natural parents other than these *tatae* and *mamae* are mentioned in, or inferred from, the inscriptions; more often, they are not (1991a:76–87).

Manumission

Keith Hopkins asks the question: "Why did the Romans free so many slaves?" (1978:115). He and others offer an answer: slaves were freed for economic reasons. Liberty might have been a reward for hard work. At the same time, Hopkins and others offer another answer: slaves were freed for reproductive reasons. Masters freed young slaves because they were their illegitimate children; and they freed female slaves so that their children would be freeborn.

Manumission was common. It was more likely for some than others. Young slaves, female slaves, homegrown slaves, and slaves in Rome, especially members of the *Familia Caesaris*, were most often freed.

Roman manumissions were especially common. According to Lily Ross Taylor, in two-thirds of the inscriptions of Roman citizens, it is not clear whether status is freed or freeborn. But of the remaining one-third, probably three-fourths of the epitaphs belong to freed slaves. As Taylor adds, freedmen, rather than freeborn, were more likely to have left status off their epitaphs—so, overall, the proportion of inscriptions belonging to freedmen might have been quite a bit higher than three in four. She concludes: "It seems likely that most of the Roman populace eventually had the blood of slaves in their veins" (1961:117–120, 132). On the other hand, it is generally agreed that agricultural slaves, and slaves in the mines, were seldom freed (e.g., Treggiari 1969:9, 11, 106–110; Brunt 1971:122; Harris 1982:118; Bradley 1984:103–104; Wiedemann 1987:23). Manumission was less common, too, in the provinces: Taylor says that only about 37% of the commemorated citizens of Italian towns other than

Rome were freed rather than freeborn; that's about half the ratio she found at the capital. Manumission was most common in the emperor's family (e.g., Wiedemann 1985:163). As Dio put it: "The freedmen of Caesar were many and wealthy" (*History*, liv.21.2).

Slaves were often freed young. James Harper averaged ages at death in inscriptions of slaves, freedmen, and freeborn; he found the mean age for freedmen to be around 25 years, and argued that slaves who survived to maturity in Rome had a "considerable" chance of being freed (1972:342). In the *Familia Caesaris*, Weaver concluded that manumission was not uncommon before age 30, but was most common from 30 to 40—that makes early manumission less common for imperial slaves (1972:103–104; cf. Wiedemann 1985:163).

Female slaves were freed more often. This is true, at least, for a couple of groups. In a sample of 998 records of Delphic manumissions, 63% of freed slaves were women; and in a sample of 173 freed slaves from the *Familia Caesaris* whose ages at death were recorded, 27, or almost 16%, were women—twice the proportion of women found in the *Familia Caesaris* overall (Hopkins 1978:139; Weaver 1972:101–102; see too Rawson 1986a:188–190).

Last but not least, *vernae* were especially likely to be freed. The best evidence comes from records of Delphic manumissions. From 200 B.C. to A.D. 100, 357 freed slaves were homeborn, 259 were known aliens, and another 621 were of unknown origin. In other words, 58% of known origins were homeborn (Hopkins 1978:140; see too Westermann 1955:98). It is consistent that in Rawson's study of Roman inscriptions, 78% of 322 *vernae* of specified age were under 15. It seems reasonable to guess that older *vernae* were *liberti*—freed (Rawson 1986a:188–191; compare Shaw 1991:81). Interestingly, a similar pattern holds for *alumni*, the "foster" children for whom patrons also felt a "paternal affection" and who sometimes, Rawson says, might have been their natural children. Of 194 *alumni* of specified age, 77% were under 15—again, older *alumni* often might have been freed (pp. 173–180).

Why were so many slaves freed? Many have answered: to turn a profit (e.g., Treggiari 1969:19–20; Hopkins 1978:131–132; Bradley 1984:83–84). As Hopkins points out, "Roman society was not marked by altruism"

(1978:117). Freedom might have been the most effective incentive to good work and a good worker might have paid a high price to be freed. Hopkins found over 70 references, mainly in the *Digest*, to slaves who bought manumission; slaves at Delphi and elsewhere sometimes paid considerable sums for their freedom. Hopkins suggests that they saved up their *peculium* for that purpose, and that masters profited further by services performed, e.g., as *operae*, after these slaves were freed (pp. 125–30, 158–63). It makes sense that some reward should be held out to slaves who worked hard. But there are a few holes in this argument. First, it is not clear how often slaves paid to get freed. Some passages in the *Digest* suggest slaves freed *inter vivos* were automatically given their *peculium*, and that sometimes *peculium* was given to slaves freed by will (e.g., *Digest*, 15.1.53, 33.8.8.7; see Watson 1987:96–97). Second, couldn't masters have extracted services, more or less equivalent to *operae*, more easily from slaves who hadn't been freed? To give a slave his freedom was, by definition, to lose control of him at least to some extent. Finally why, if liberty was an incentive to work, should young, female, homegrown slaves in and around Rome most often have got their freedom? Why free a young slave with his productive life ahead of him? Why favor females who, as Treggiari's work suggests, had less work to do? Why favor *vernae* over slaves who could be hand-picked at auction for their physical or mental ability to do a job? And why not hold out the carrot of manumission to provincial slaves, and even to agricultural slaves, more often?

Why else free slaves? Others have answered: to legitimize children. That might be done in two ways. One, since children inherited their mothers' status, was to free a future mother. The other was to free her children. The biases to free female slaves, and to free them young, make sense if women were manumitted to be married. Other facts fit too. In the *Institutes of Gaius*, "just causes" for early manumission— before age 30—include: blood relationship (*filii naturales*); foster relationship (*alumni*); future services (if the slave was over 18); and intent to marry (e.g., Weaver 1972:97). Weaver finds the last condition explicit in inscriptions of imperial freedwomen (1972:99–100); several references to marriage with freedwomen exist in the *Digest* (see Treggiari 1979:200). But who

married them? Masters, or others? According to Hopkins, money paid to free young Delphic women may have been put up by suitors from other houses; masters might have retained a lien on the women's services, and some of their children, besides (1978:169). Alternatively, Romans might have freed slave women in order to marry them themselves. As Treggiari and others agree, "freeing a slave mistress might be a sensible move to ensure the free birth of the children" (1969:213; see too Brunt 1971:144; Hopkins 1978:127; Harris 1982:120). In this case, masters gained reproductive assets— daughters and sons, though they lost economic assets—slaves.

Last but not least, Romans might have freed their bastard children. Again, several facts fit. Among slaves, the homegrown variety were more likely to be *filii naturales*—this explains why *vernae* were more likely to be freed. In the *Institutes*, blood relationship was one cause for early manumission—this explains why slaves were freed young. And if polygyny paralleled power in the Roman empire, as it did in other empires, then both the number of a man's slave women and of his bastard children should have increased with proximity to the emperor—this explains why slaves were freed least often on the latifundia and in the mines, less often in the provinces, more often in Rome, and most often in the *Familia Caesaris*. That there are "very many" freedmen in the inscriptions under 30 suggests masters and slaves shared a blood relationship (e.g., Rawson 1986b:12–13); so do expressions like *patronus et frater* and *filius et libertus* in the epitaphs (Weaver 1972:184). It seems that, in some cases, rich Romans may have used a few of their slave women as rich men in other empires used their concubines— as bearers of contingency heirs. Given monogamous marriage, and a barren wife, a concubine's children have advanced to the status of heirs (see Goody 1976, 1983, 1990; Betzig 1993, 1995). Among concubines mentioned in the *Digest*, the most common are a man's freedwomen (e.g., *Digest*, 24.1.3.1, 25.7.1. pr., 25.7.2; see Treggiari 1979:193). In other cases, Romans may have used their slave women as men in other empires used most of their harem women—as bearers of children without rights to inheritance or succession. The bulk of a man's estate went to children by his legitimate wife. Still, other children by his slave women *anecdotes ≠ 'science'!*

may have been left gleanings enough to make them rich and powerful—and even polygynous?—freedmen.

Wealth, Position, Wives, and Children

If some historians are surprised that Romans freed so many slaves, others are amazed that freedmen could have so much money. Ludwig Friedlander goes on at length. "To be as rich as a freedman was proverbial" (1908 v.1:43). Narcissus, at 400,000,000 sesterces, was the richest Roman of his time; Pallas was worth 300,000,000 sesterces; others of Claudius's freedmen had almost as much. Men like these "outbid the Roman aristocracy in luxury"; "their parks and gardens were the largest and most beautiful in the city"; "their palaces were the most pretentious in all Rome" (p. 45). How did they get so rich? Their patrons helped. Freedmen, like Petronius's Trimalchio, were notoriously good at commerce; but then as now it took money to make it. Patrons provided *peculium*; they offered lucrative jobs, like procuratorships, by which slaves might build on that capital; and they often returned the enhanced *peculium* on freedom (e.g., Friedlander 1908; Hopkins 1978; Watson 1987). Freedmen, like knights, got rich in commerce and trade—as younger sons, disinherited by primogeniture, have across empires (e.g., Betzig 1992b). But most important of all, where they lacked legitimate sons, patrons occasionally left a *bona fide* inheritance to their freedmen and slaves. That slaves could be heirs is confirmed in Horace and other literary sources, which say men without sons made freedmen their heirs; it's confirmed in the inscriptions, in which rich men and women often leave property to their freedmen and women; it's confirmed in the *Institutes*, the *Digest*, and the *Codex*, in which slaves and freedmen were made heirs with or without adoption (Horace, *Satires*, ii.3.122; Balsdon 1962:194; Watson 1987:26–29, 81–82). That slaves could be heirs is suggested, too, by the fact that slaves and freedmen were trusted with family financial matters; slaves, like sons, might enter into contracts on behalf of their *paters*; freedmen, like brothers, might be obliged to serve as tutors or guardians of their dead masters' estates; and freedmen were "curiously" left their master's instructions to keep properties within his family (Watson 1987:90; Saller

1991a:43, 45; Johnston 1988:88–97). Last but not least, that slaves could be heirs is consistent with the facts that freedmen so often earned a place in their masters' tombs ("burial and commemoration were so closely associated with heirship"—Saller and Shaw 1984:126), and that freed slaves were given their masters' *nomen* ("one's own freedmen, who took the same gentile name, were seen as substitute descendants"—Treggiari 1991b:368). Edward Champlin, who looked at what fragments of evidence exist on Roman testation, from literary sources, legal sources, papyri, and inscriptions, concluded that testators were much more likely to leave estates to friends and freedmen than to cousins or other more distant kin; as Champlin says himself, "the slave named as heir might have been an illegitimate child of the testator," left the inheritance in the absence of legitimate sons (1991:126, 137). Even when legitimates got the lion's share of an estate, freedmen and women might be left with scavengers' surfeits; there are literary examples of this, and a whole title in the *Digest* is devoted to the subject (*Digest*, 34.1; see Gardner 1986:181). Slaves might even be left money by third parties as a favor to their masters: Herod left 500 talents to Augustus's wife, children, friends and freedmen; Marcus Aurelius gave "many privileges and much honour and money" to the freedman of his co-regent, Lucius Verus (Friedlander 1908 v.1:38; SHA, *Marcus Antoninus*, xx.5). According to Treggiari, "a freedman might make a respectable fortune in trade . . . , but most of the outstandingly rich freedmen won their money either by exploiting the position won for them by their patron's status . . . , or by inheriting from a childless patron" (1969:239). Her ellipses are filled with examples.

There is as much consensus that freedmen could have high status. It was apparent to Tacitus that "ex-slaves are everywhere." Most voters, public servants, and officials' attendants were freedmen; most knights, and many senators, had a freed ancestor (*Annals*, xiii.27). So did a few emperors. Otho, according to Suetonius, was grandson of a knight and a humble girl who "may not even have been freeborn"; according to the *Scriptores*, Pertinax was the son of a freedman, and "Macrinus under the reign of Commodus was a freedman and a public prostitute" (Suetonius, *Otho*, 1: SHA, *Pertinax*, i.1; *Opellius Macrinus*, iv.3). One honorary consul, under Caligula, was the son of "an attractive ex-slave," and called the emperor his father (Tacitus, *Annals*, xv.73). A "cautious estimate," overall, is that about one in five of the Italian aristocracy was descended from slaves (Weaver 1991:173). And freedmen who fathered the Roman aristocracy often did well themselves. Hopkins, in his study of succession to the Roman senate, found seats were seldom passed from father to son. Instead, a "patrimonial administration" emerged, "centered on the imperial palace": this was the administration of imperial slaves and freedmen (1983:124–125). In Hopkins's words, "during the republic, Roman senators had been masters of the world. Now they had to subserve an emperor; and in order to acquire favours from him, they often had to fawn on his slaves and ex-slaves" (p. 77). As Weaver says, men in the imperial civil service were "almost entirely the emperor's freedmen and slaves"; they were, among other things, in charge of petitions, chief secretary, and head of the finance administration (1972:1–2; Dio, *History*, lxi.30.6). Outside of Rome, imperial freedmen were generals, admirals, provincial governors, and tax collectors (Hopkins 1978:116; SHA, *Antoninus Elagabalus*, xi.1). When, early in the second century, Pliny inaugurated Trajan with his panegyric, he accused earlier emperors of having been "both lords over citizens and slaves of freedmen" (*Panegyricus*, 88.1–2). But even Trajan wasn't immune from their influence; Hadrian might have got Trajan to adopt him partly by "wooing and bribing" his freedmen. Even if the influence of freedmen abated a little under a few "good" emperors, in the long run it seems to have grown (e.g., Westermann 1955; Hopkins 1978, 1983; Wiedemann 1987). The "elusive" explanation might have something to do with filiation: the senatorial aristocracy of the Roman republic might have been, over the empire, replaced by an imperial dynasty made up—at least in part—of the emperor's illegitimate sons (cf. Hopkins 1983:176ff).

Finally freedmen, like free men, seem to have used money and status themselves to find women and father children. Imperial freedmen, in particular, could be promiscuous. For instance Verus, Marcus Aurelius' co-regent, "built an exceedingly notorious villa on the Clodian Way" where he "revelled" for days at a time in "boundless extravagance" with his friends and freedmen (SHA, *Verus*, viii.8); un-

der Commodus, imperial freedmen "refrained from no form of mischief" indulging, among other things, in "wantonness and debauchery" (Dio, *History*, lxxiii.10.2). Again, imperial freedmen, and imperial slaves, very much unlike the unfortunate masses of provincial, agricultural, and mining slaves, got "married" and sired *spurii filii* and other commemorated children (Treggiari 1975a, 1981a, 1981b; Rawson 1966, 1974, 1989). It seems plausible, then, that well-to-do freedmen followed in the footsteps of their well-to-do patrons (see Betzig 1992b). When they could, they got legitimate children by free, well-connected, and well-to-do wives (e.g., Dixon 1985; Treggiari 1984, 1991a; Corbier 1991); and they got illegitimate children by promiscuity, and by slavery. Rich freedmen, like rich patrons, might father two or three legitimate children; and rich freedmen, like rich patrons, often owned hundreds, or even thousands, of slaves—one of the Metelli family, early in the first century A.D., bequeathed 4,116 (e.g., Treggiari 1975a:400; Pliny the Elder, *Natural History*, xxxiii.134). And when they died "scores" of these freedmen, along with their children and their children's children, were saved a place in their patrons' tombs (e.g., Carcopino 1940:102).

DISCUSSION

Let's be skeptical. How much did the Roman family resemble families in our own society; how much did it resemble families in other empires?

What's in the sources? How much evidence is in the Latin histories that Roman emperors, like other emperors, had sexual access to women other than their wives? These sources are thin: they are thickest on Julius Caesar and the first eleven emperors; both Tacitus's and Suetonius's accounts, probably the best we have, end with the Flavian Dynasty. And these sources are purely descriptive: except in Commodus's case, nobody bothered to count an emperor's consorts; and the 300 concubines ascribed to Commodus are nothing, of course, but a guess. On the other hand, these sources are consistent: with the single exception of "old and feeble" Vespasian, every one of the first twelve Caesars is explicitly said to have enjoyed sexual access to several women; a majority of them is explicitly said to have taken married women from their husbands; and at least three—Augustus, Tiberius, and Claudius—are explicitly said to have had women procured for the sake of sex, sometimes by force. This picture is not just consistent on the first twelve Caesars. It fits with fragments of evidence on later emperors. And it fits with evidence on emperors in other empires. It seems safe to say that Roman emperors did not "radiate marital propriety," if "propriety" means "fidelity"; most of them were promiscuous, some of them extremely.

What's in the studies? Enough to suggest that there were millions of slaves in the Roman empire; that women were bought and sold at least as often as men; and that they often functioned as breeders. Sexual access to slave women was taken for granted by their masters but taken at risk by other men; and masters cared materially and emotionally for some of their slave women's children, often manumitted them, and gave some of them great wealth, high position, and a place in their family tombs. Access to slaves varied with wealth and power; lesser aristocrats early in the empire, like Pliny the Younger, might have had several hundred; greater aristocrats later in the empire, like Melania the Christian, had tens of thousands. Emperors were the greatest slave owners of all.

All of which suggests that Syme was right about aristocratic bastards. Most of them were sons and daughters of slaves. "The bastard followed the civil status of his mother" (1960:325). Paternity, never assured, wasn't even ascribed.

Why bother to look for bastards in the Roman aristocracy? For lots of reasons. For one, family history is intrinsically interesting to most people. For another, it's part and parcel of history in a larger context. As, for instance, Richard Saller and David Kertzer point out in the introduction to their new book on the Roman family, families effect and are caused by demographics, economics, politics, and religion (1991:8). But family history is most important because, if Darwin was right, reproduction is the reason we do everything else. As Darwin (1859:52) said himself:

Nothing is easier than to admit in words the truth of the universal struggle for life, or more difficult—at least I have found it so—than constantly to bear this struggle in mind. Yet unless it be thoroughly engrained in the mind, the whole economy of nature, with every fact on distribution, rarity, abundance, ex-

tinctions and variation, will be dimly seen or quite misunderstood.

In this light, everything we do or have ever done—from demographics to economics to politics to religion—might be understood, more or less, as reproductive competition.

There is, again, plenty of evidence for competition in the Roman empire; and there is plenty of evidence that winners in Rome, as in other empires, came off much better than losers. Consider modest Augustus's fortune: he left 1,500,000 gold pieces to his heirs (Suetonius, *Augustus*, 101). Consider mild-mannered Claudius's despotism: he killed men "on unsupported charges," including 35 senators and 300 knights, with "little apparent concern" (Suetonius, *Claudius*, 29). Were wealth and power like this ends in themselves? Or were they means to the spread of genes? I think the evidence here, though not conclusive, is suggestive. Power in the Roman empire, as in other empires, seems to have made polygyny possible. Politics seems, at least in part, to have been a means to reproductive ends.

That leaves me with my favorite question. When, and why, did polygyny and despotism end, and monogamy and democracy begin? Some people have said the Roman empire was monogamous (e.g., Murdock and Wilson 1972; MacDonald 1990). This evidence isn't persuasive. Others have said monogamy began in the Middle Ages under the Catholic Church (e.g., Duby 1983; Herlihy 1985). But political, economic, and even reproductive inequality seem to have characterized medieval Europe too (Betzig 1995). It seems to me that one event changed all that: the switch to an industrial economy in Europe in the past few centuries (Betzig 1982, 1986, 1991). Reproductive inequality, and the economic and political inequality that are prerequisite to it, seem to have declined in that one space and time. *Why* is another matter.

Acknowledgments. It gives me real pleasure to thank the historians who saved me, line by line, from mistakes of etiquette, interpretation, and fact. Susan Treggiari, Richard Saller, Jane Gardner, and Beryl Rawson sent reprints, lists of references, and even class handouts; they gave good general criticism; and they corrected errors as particular as typos. I've never had more fun, and they're partly to blame.

38

Why a Despot?

LAURA BETZIG

"Roman Polygyny" is bad science, in two respects. First, *the data are crude.* There are no DNA fingerprints; there are no complete reproductive histories; there aren't even a few sets of spotty parish records to help us tell how good or bad rich Romans were at spreading genes. There are only Tacitus's, Suetonius's, and Dio's histories; Ovid's love poems, Horace's satires, and Martial's epigrams; the *Digest* and other legal documents; records of slave sales on Egyptian papyri; manumission records from Delphi; the phallus of Priapus (and other phalli on wall paintings, floor mosaics, ceiling hangings, pots, rooftops, and doorways) from Pompeii; and the tens of thousands of inscriptions on Roman tombstones—which, with the help of computers, have revolutionized the study of Roman demography over the last couple of decades. These patches of evidence all tell the same story: rich Romans were promiscuous; they had sexual access to tens, or hundreds, or thousands of slave women; and by those women they begat tens, or hundreds, or thousands of slave children.

There is a real-life parable about probabilities in history. Two living giants in the study of modern England are Peter Laslett and Lawrence Stone. Laslett, having gotten over an early infatuation with "belletristic" evidence, discovered numbers in the form of parish records in the middle of his career. Eventually, over the '60s and '70s, his Cambridge Group for the History of Population and Social Structure "crystallized physically around 20 Silver Street" in pleasant "coffee and tea breaks" where "history ceased to be the concern of the researcher contemplating his or her own navel." More profoundly, it took form in the gathering, punching, and computer analyzing of hundreds of parish records. The result was a statistical picture of the births, marriages, and deaths of thousands of otherwise inaccessible middling early modern English from the "world we have lost."

Lawrence Stone took the other road. He continued to read chronicles, diaries, letters, literature, law books, and so on; and he tabulated smaller sets of numbers—on knighthoods, numbers of country houses, and clandestine marriages, for instance. Stone's focus has been the British aristocracy, the Cambridge Group's the average man; Stone has, largely as a result, accessed a large variety of documents on a small sample of people, the Cambridge Group a small variety of documents on a large sample of people. By the standard of data *quantity*—the number of numbers, and the precision of statistical manipulations—the Cambridge Group wins hands down. But by the standard of data *quality*—the richness of information on every individual in the sample—Lawrence Stone has no peer.

At worst, the Cambridge Group has plugged garbage in and gotten garbage out; at worst, Stone has told a story about a vanishingly small and impotent group. The best critics, in either case, are hostile critics. Critics hostile to the Cambridge Group's sort tell them when their large samples are biased misrepresentations of whole populations, when their data points are inaccurate or incomplete, and when their statistical analyses are inept. Critics hostile to Stone's sort let them know when they've picked their anecdotes to make their points, why there's reason to believe their sources were penned by biased hands, and how much or little can be inferred about history from small samples. *The best "science" does what it can with the best data at hand.*[1]

The other thing wrong with "Roman Polygyny" is that *the model is cruder*. That is, in part, an effect of problem number one—there's little point testing a complex model with a crude data set. My defense is that crude models can be good models. Life is messy; many variables determine what happens. But most of the variance may be explained by a few. Despotism explains differential reproduction. Power predicts polygyny, in Rome, and apparently everywhere else.[2]

In Mesopotamia, where civilization began, Hammurabi's Code started out: "That the strong may not oppress the weak [and] so to give justice to the orphan [and] the widow, I have inscribed my precious words." But his words are full of "skew": rich men were better than poor men, who were better than slaves. Law 8 (a typical law) recommends that the thief of an ox, sheep, ass, swine, or boat pay a noble owner back thirtyfold, pay a peasant owner back tenfold, and lose his life if he is unable to pay. In Egypt, temple reliefs were covered with armed guards; and Akhenaten (the famous monotheist) worshiped the sun god Re—in an oppressive equatorial climate on an often shadeless landscape. In the New World, Incan emperors (like other emperors) took lives for lèse-majesté; adulterers, in particular, paid heavily—their wives, children, servants, kin, friends, and flocks were all put to death, their villages were pulled down, and the sites were strewn with stones. Aztec kings (like other kings) killed singers who sang out of tune. In India, he who harmed a Brahmin's cow lost his head—the Artharvaveda said, "Snatch thou the hair from off his head, and from his body strip the skin; tear out his sinews, cause his flesh to fall in pieces from his frame." And China, through the twentieth century, was ruled by tyrants deliberately or indifferently responsible for the deaths of their subjects. The Romans weren't dramatic exceptions. The *Digest*, like Hammurabi's and other codes, is harder on poor men than on rich men. And early in the empire, under Tiberius, "every crime became a capital one, even the utterance of a few careless words"; the bodies of the guilty "were flung on the Stairs of Mourning, and dragged to the Tiber with hooks—as many as twenty a day, including women and children."

The point of all that power was sex.

Mesopotamians, Egyptians, Incas, Aztecs, Indians, Chinese, and Romans had harems of tens (for upper-middle-class types), or hundreds (for nobles), or thousands (for kings), or tens of thousands (figures quoted exclusively for most exalted emperors) of women. And the point of sex was the proliferation of genes.[3]

But all that only raises what is, to me, a much more interesting question. What accounts for power? If power is, after all, a means to reproductive ends, then what makes for reproductive inequality, and what makes for reproductive equality? What makes despotism, and what makes democracy?

Ornithologists have had some luck with these questions. And their answers have, in the past few years, been of some use to entomologists and mammologists—to name a few.[4] To sum up: Societies are "skewed" when subordinates get trapped. Poor fighters stick around with good fighters when they've nowhere better to go. Two factors determine the relative merits of leaving or staying. One is ecological: poor fighters may gain if the quality of food, shelter, or climate is better where they are than it is anywhere nearby. The other is social: good fighters may offset the costs they inflict, in part, by being good food finders, predator detectors, kin, or mates. If good fighters take, say, two-thirds of what can be had in one spot, and if no other spot is, say, one-third as good, then it makes sense for poor fighters to put up with the "skew."

It was as late as 1840 when de Tocqueville wrote, "I go back from age to age up to the remotest antiquity, but I find no parallel to what is occurring before my eyes"—meaning the fall of kings and rise of the common man.[5] What made it happen at last? Part of the answer lies in the division of labor. Skills proliferated; poor fighters suddenly had more "social benefits" (e.g., textile weaving or shotgun inventing) to offer. The other part of the answer has to do with mobility. Poor fighters may or may not have gained much geographic mobility in the last few centuries, but the "ecological benefits" of staying in any one spot were lost to the extent that cash—their new subsistence source—came to them. Over the farmers of history, from Mesopotamian planters to Roman peasants and chained gangs to medieval small farmers and serfs, strong arms extended themselves by force. Traders have something that farmers have lacked. When strong arms reach out in their direction, they are at liberty to "walk."

" ..... credible threat to leave. "

NOTES

1. On the Cambridge Group see Laslett's (1984) *The World We Have Lost*, and Bonfield, Smith, and Wrightson's (1986) *The World We Have Gained*; much of the latter is a critique of Stone. Contributions by Stone alluded to here include *The Crisis of the Aristocracy* (1965), *An Open Elite* (Stone and Stone 1984), and *The Road to Divorce* (1990); he's compared his own approach to that of the Cambridge Group in *The Past and Present Revisited* (1987, 37–38). Although I venerate the Cambridge Group, I'm more of Stone's ilk, and can't resist quoting this part of his critique: "There are many dangers inherent in such projects, the most serious of which is that to some extent the conclusions drawn from these highly costly and labour-intensive quantitative studies still depend on the utility and reliability of the variables selected for study.... Some may turn out to be rather like the project to put a man on the moon, more remarkable for the evidence they provide of man's vaulting ambition, vast financial resources, and technical virtuosity in the 1960s than for their scientific results in the advancement of knowledge" (pp 37–38).

2. On power and polygyny, see Betzig (1982, 1986, 1991, 1992c, 1993, 1994, 1995, 1996a, and review in the first chapter of this book).

3. On sex and despotism in "the first six civilizations," see Betzig (1993). On Mao's China, see Zhisui (1994). On bias in Roman law, see Garnsey (1970); on Tiberius see Suetonius (*Tiberius*, 61), also Tacitus (*Annals*, ii.29–49) and Dio (*History*, lix).

4. Pioneering ornithologists addressing the subject of "cooperative breeding" include Brown (1987), Emlen (1991), and Vehrencamp (1983a). Entomologists interested in democracy and despotism include West-Eberhard (1978, 1981) and Reeve (Reeve and Nonacs 1992; Reeve and Ratneiks 1993); mammologists interested in the same problem include Creel (Creel and Creel 1991) and Sherman, Jarvis, and Alexander (1991; also Reeve 1992). Human applications include Betzig (1994).

5. De Tocqueville (1840, 319).

39

Fitness Tradeoffs in the History and Evolution ?ⁱⱼ ₙₛ ? of Delegated Mothering with Special Reference to Wet-Nursing, Abandonment, and Infanticide

SARAH BLAFFER HRDY

> *Early European accounts of infanticidal savages bristled with ethnocentric*
> *moralizing ... And yet as we read the tragic accounts ... from one society to*
> *another, it is not the inhumanity of the unfortunate perpetrators that confronts us,*
> *but rather their humanity.*

—Martin Daly and Margo Wilson (1988b:59)

I. INTRODUCTION: MOTHERHOOD AS COMPROMISE

The dilemma confronting working mothers in the Western world today has universal dimensions.[1] To imagine that there is anything new in the conflicts faced by modern women is to adopt a mythologized concept of self-sacrificing motherhood. For motherhood has always meant compromise, compromise between subsistence needs of the mother and the time, energy, and resources needed to mate and reproduce (reproductive effort). In addition to conflicts between the mother's own needs and a general commitment to reproduction, iteroparous mothers (breeding over a lifetime) must also partition their reproductive effort among different offspring. Parental investment of time, energy, or resources in the production or nurturing of one offspring can diminish a mother's ability to invest in older offspring or in her ability to produce additional offspring in the future (Trivers 1972).

As Robert Trivers pointed out (1974), individual infants may attempt to extract greater investment from their parents than the parents have been selected to give. Herein lies the source of the chronic tension between parental commitment to the survival and well-being of offspring and parental frustration at the frequency and insistence of infant demands. Although a primate infant should rarely seek to extract more reproductive effort from a mother than is compatible with her survival, it might well seek to extract additional parental investment when it would come at the expense of future siblings rather than the mother's survival. In this paper I will be dealing with maternal dilemmas and decision making at two levels: (1) at the level of reproductive effort—her own survival versus that of her progeny; and (2) at the level of parental investment—investment in one particular infant versus investment in infants of another sex, born with different qualities and/or under different circumstances.

In most mammals, and all primates, newborns are dependent on their mother for warmth, protection, locomotion, and nutrition. Substitute providers of these functions occasionally crop up in evolutionary history (e.g., van Lawick 1973 for wild dogs; Hrdy 1976; Thierry and Anderson 1986 for primates) and have even been common during some periods in human history. More often than not, how-

Reprinted with permission from *Ethology and Sociobiology* 13:409–42 (1992).

ever, survival of the infant depends on the mother's survival. From an evolutionary perspective, then, it is the mother who is the critical unit of selection and the mother's survival would always have priority except in the case of older or incapacitated mothers with low probabilities of reproducing again, that is, mothers with very low reproductive value. Even here maternal survival should take priority if survival of the infant depends on her nurturing.

Where parental rank is correlated with the survival and breeding prospects of selected offspring, even the maintenance of parental status may take precedence over the survival of less favored infants. Some of the best-documented examples derive from human parents who cloister in convents or actually destroy daughters whose dowry costs jeopardize family socioeconomic status, or destroy daughters who threaten to injure family standing or honor (Dickemann 1979b; Manzoni 1961:134ff; Boone 1986).

In other mammals who produce either sequential young or litters parents respond to local conditions in evaluating the worth of a particular offspring in terms of probabilistic assessments of future conditions and "as a function of the proportion that this child represents of his total future reproductive prospects" (Dawkins and Carlisle 1976:132). That is, parents respond with what Daly and Wilson (1980, 1983) refer to as "discriminative parental solicitude"—an amalgam derived from assessments of probable degree of relatedness (clearly more important in the case of males and egg layers than for most female mammals), worth of the offspring in terms of its ability to translate parental investment into subsequent reproduction, and finally consideration of alternate uses to which the parent could devote the resources, such as diverting resources to a stronger child, a child of a preferred sex, or sustaining the parent until more favorable opportunities to breed should present themselves. In humans these levels of solicitude are tempered (albeit rarely overridden completely) by cultural ideals, especially ideals about continuation of the household or the lineage, ideals which are in turn shaped through historical time by the changing productive and reproductive value of children (Hrdy 1990).[2]

Here I focus on fitness tradeoffs made by mothers through human history. In humans, however, as in so many species, maternal sub-

sistence and especially the survival of her offspring are so heavily influenced by other group members that it is impossible to consider the mother in isolation from the web of fitness tradeoffs by other individuals in the social network she is part of (see Hill and Kaplan 1988 for an exemplary case study exploring how reproductive decisions "mutually constrain one another" and involve complex tradeoffs between alternative behavioral options among Ache hunter-foragers of Paraguay). Relevant individuals may include former and future mates of the mother, biological relatives, affines and unrelated individuals linked to her in either cooperative or competitive arrangements, subordinate individuals she exploits as well as dominant individuals exploiting her. For the purposes of this paper, I will sometimes substitute the term "parental" for maternal when my knowledge of the situation is too limited to separate maternal from paternal interests, or when in fact there is good reason to assume they coincide.

II. FITNESS TRADEOFFS IN DETERMINING THE LEVEL AND TYPE OF SOLICITUDE

For the purposes of this article, I assume that infanticide (were information available) could be documented for virtually all human populations, although frequencies differ markedly, ranging from near zero to over 40% of live births (section IV-B). The main functional classes of infanticide that have been described for nonhuman animals (Hrdy 1979) can all be documented among humans, if only anecdotally. Nevertheless, the patterning of infanticide in humans is considerably different. For example, in other primates unrelated males are the most likely perpetrators of infanticide (Hrdy 1977, 1979; Leland, Struhsaker, and Butynski 1984). While the close proximity to the mother of males unrelated to her infant (either captors or stepfathers) can represent a threat to human infants (e.g., see Biocca 1971; Hill and Kaplan 1988 for Amazonian hunter-foragers; Exodus 1:16 and Matthew 2:16 for ancient Near Eastern pastoralists; Daly and Wilson 1988b for contemporary North American populations), biological parents are responsible for the largest portion of infanticides, and marriage and inheritance systems, religious beliefs, and social norms concerning individual and family honor play central roles in parental decisions to terminate investment in these human infants. Furthermore these parental decisions are informed by a unique awareness of history, the future and longterm goals for family survival. Hence although thresholds for parents to invest may be set by evolved motivational processes (Daly and Wilson 1980, 1988b) adjustments in parental investment are consciously calculated to achieve culturally as well as biologically defined goals, and are played out in specific demographic and cultural contexts (e.g., see Korbin 1981; Skinner 1988, 1993).

By far the most common goal for parents committing infanticide involves the manipulation of family size, composition, or the adjustment of the timing of parental investment by the mother and/or father. In fact, however, infanticide in the sense of Langer's (1974) classic definition ("the willful destruction of newborn babies through exposure, starvation, strangulation, smothering, poisoning, or through the use of some lethal weapon") represents only the extreme end of a continuum of behaviors which function to reduce the costs (in terms of time, energy risk, and resources) that offspring impose upon parents. In contrast to rodents and other mammals who may cannibalize supernumerary infants (Day and Galef 1977; Gandelman and Simon 1978), thereby recouping nutrients, there are virtually never any benefits to killing one's own offspring apart from perceived benefits in rare cases of child sacrifice (e.g., points to be won with a god for sacrificing a valued son, Genesis 22; see Stager and Wolff 1984 for ancient Carthage). And quite often, there are costs.

Hence, we would expect infanticide involving direct destruction of the young to occur only as a last resort when other options for reducing postpartum investment are constrained by legal sanctions which make abandonment riskier than murder, by the lack of supportive kin networks or other potential caregivers, or else by particular sorts of environmental hazards which make abandonment impractical. A different set of constraints may also pertain in the upper reaches of stratified societies where the continued existence of a child may represent a threat to social status, family "honor," or orderly succession. Although it is very common to read in the literature on infanticide that parents were

responding to scarcity by eliminating their infants, limited resources by themselves (except in special circumstances, see section IV-A) are no reason to destroy an infant. Scarcity is merely a reason for parents to *reduce* investment in a current infant, perhaps abandon it. There exist a wide array of alternatives to infanticide whose availability varies according to specific historical and ecological contexts.

These means of reducing parental investment in offspring have received relatively less emphasis in the literature than has infanticide per se. Nevertheless, such retrenchments from the "primate ideal" of a Pleistocene mother emotionally bonded and physically in contact with her continuously suckling offspring (Konner 1976) are for most societies far more common, and sociologically and demographically more important than actual infanticide (exceptions are discussed in section IV-B). I list below seven different ways of dealing with infants, each of which functions to mitigate or terminate parental investment without outright destruction of the infant. This list is by no means exhaustive:

1. *Exploitation of the infant as a resource, usually selling the infant*, which entails some immediate (usually small) gain to the parents (e.g., see Boswell 1988:170–171; Fildes 1986:6). Although prostitution or slavery would be likely fates for offspring sold (Boswell 1988) some children could conceivably end up with improved prospects of survival or even reproduction.

2. *Abandonment of the infant* where the parents leaves the infant, typically out of harm's way so that there is some prospect that the infant will be taken up and cared for by someone else (Trexler 1973b; Boswell 1988; see Exodus 2 for the story of Moses). In the most benign form of abandonment, children are relinquished for adoption (Bachrach et al. 1992). Admittedly there can be a fuzzy distinction between abandonment and infanticide when real or imagined parental optimism comes up against the realities of infant starvation or hypothermia. Nevertheless, the practice common in Medieval Europe of abandoning infants with identifying tokens indicates—at least for those cases—the existence of a parental mind set where retrieval of the infant one day remained a possibility. Some parents found solace by fantasizing fab-

ulous destinies of upward social mobility for abandoned progeny (e.g., Romulus, who founds a dynasty; see Boswell 1988 for other European examples).

3. *Fostering out* the infant either through arrangements with relatives who can rear children more cheaply (a grandmother in a rural area) or provide them special opportunities (education in an urban area) or through the more common practice of an "invented" kin tie whereby infants, or more often children past weaning, are sent to a distant household to live and one or both parents pay (in cash, goods, or current or future favors) someone (often an older woman) to care for an infant (Goody 1969; Isiugo-Abanihe 1985 for West Africa; Pennington 1989 for South Africa; Shahar 1990 for Medieval Europe). Although typically infants going to foster mothers are weaned, the distinction between "fostering out" and "wet-nursing" can become blurred when the foster mother does provide milk (Bledsoe and Isiugo-Abanihe 1989: note 1). Because children fostered out tend to be older, there is also a much higher likelihood that a foster parent (as opposed to a wet-nurse) can set them useful tasks, and the use of foster children as helpers and child minders may explain the fact that among Botswana pastoralists daughters are more often sent (Pennington 1989).

4. *Wet-nursing* when the mother or both parents contract with another woman to suckle their infant (for overview see Fildes 1988), an arrangement which encumbers the wet-nurse but frees the mother both for status or labor-related pursuits and simultaneously also renders the mother fertile for subsequent pregnancies—an artifact of wet-nursing that may or may not be intended; see next section.

5. *Oblation* when one or both parents leaves the children in the custody of a religious institution, usually, but not always, irrevocably (Boswell 1988: Chapter 8; Fuchs 1984).

6. *Reducing overall reproductive effort* so that parents continue to rear their own children but at a lower level of resource and energy expenditure, or a lower level of direct involvement, delegating care to others such as locally available kin, particularly older siblings as is characteristic today in much of Bantu East and South Africa (e.g., Weisner 1987; Draper 1989).

7. *Reducing parental investment in particular children,* often weak ones, or else supernumerary daughters destined to be economic or social liabilities, or in later born sons in societies with primogeniture, etc. (Cain 1977; Miller 1981; DeVries 1984; Boone 1986; Das Gupta 1987; Voland 1988). Such reduced investment may be motivated either by insufficient resources, by probable absence or loss of paternal investment (e.g., Schepher-Hughes 1985 for mothers in Brazilian shantytowns), or by the advantages which may accrue to families channeling resources toward selected progeny in high-density, stratified societies (see Dickemann 1979b; Levine 1987:293).

In the last five or so thousand years such "mitigating strategies" accounted for the fates (both survivals and deaths) of far more infants than did infanticide, even though infanticide as a phenomenon has attracted more attention from anthropologists and biologists. Indeed, patterns of continued investment with retrenchments (7 and 8 above) are so common in human societies as to be—at least in their milder forms—completely unremarkable both to the ethnographer in tribal societies or to the sociologist surveying contemporary Western populations. These patterns represent the investing end of a continuum that ranges from termination of investment at the one extreme to total self-sacrifice of the parent on behalf of offspring at the other—what might be termed the "Stella Dallas" strategy. Although I would expect such maternal self-sacrifice to be more common in fiction than in life, real-life examples can be documented.[3]

Globally, I suspect that retrenchment of parental investment would have pertained to more infant survivals and deaths than all the other strategies, including infanticide, combined. Nevertheless, depending on the time and place, one or another of these patterns can become demographically more important. Wet-nursing, which affected large segments of the population in seventeenth- and eighteenth-century France, is a case in point and is discussed below.

From the perspective of reproductive strategies, abandonment of an infant should be the default divestment strategy for parents terminating investment; infanticide would only be a last resort when this option is curtailed. Hence when parents destroy their children, it is certainly important to ask what factors diminished parental solicitude toward their offspring (Daly and Wilson 1984), but it is also useful to identify the ecological, social and cultural constraints which prevented parents from abandoning the baby or from attempting to mitigate the cost of rearing an infant through some other means (Granzberg 1973). In this review I focus on the decision-making process of parents, and inquire: what social, economic and environmental factors shape parental cost-benefit analyses? If indeed the various mitigating strategies outlined above are all functionally similar, why do parents opt for one strategy rather than another? What is the role of historical precedents, history, and local ecology in these decisions? What factors predispose or forestall pursuit of alternative strategies to mitigate parental effort?[4]

III. WET-NURSING AS A CASE STUDY IN TRADEOFFS

A. Diluting the Costs of Reproductive Effort

It is widely believed that the use of wet-nurses in premodern Europe was in fact a disguised, nonprosecutable form of infanticide. This interpretation is implicit in terms for wet-nurses such as the English "angelmaker" and the German "Engelmacherin." Wet-nurses were viewed as "surrogates upon whom parents could depend for a swift demise for unwanted children" (H. F. Smith 1984:64C). "It must have been common knowledge," writes Maria Piers in her book on *Infanticide*, that the wet nurse "was a professional feeder and a professional killer" (1978:52). Critics of wet-nursing, such as the reformer Dr. Alexander Mayer, giving testimony before the Roussel Committee in France at the end of the nineteenth century, just before the Roussel Law of 1874[5] was passed, claimed that the artisans of Paris sent their infants off to wet-nurses "with the desire of not seeing them again . . ." (cited from court records by Sussman 1982:123).

In fact, however, even during the European heyday of wet-nursing at the end of the eighteenth century when up to 90% of infants born

in urban centers such as Paris and Lyon were nursed by women *other* than their biological mother (20,000 of 21,000 infants born in the famous statistic given by Paris lieutenant general of police for Paris, LeNoir 1780:63), wet-nursing is best understood as a strategy to reduce the costs of reproductive effort for individual mothers. Wet-nursing represented an alternative to worse outcomes (death of infant and maternal destitution) rather than a covert means of destruction. There can be little doubt that wet-nursing varied according to circumstances of parents, and that under some circumstances this form of delegated mothering was associated with high levels of mortality. But these cases involved parents with poor access to resources and dismal alternatives.

The risks that parents took with the lives of their infants cannot be understood without reference to both local customs (e.g., a well established tradition of wet-nursing among elites that had long exposed rural poor in many parts of France to the practice) and prevailing ecological conditions. By the eighteenth century, France was in the throes of a tremendous increase in population (from 20 million in 1720 to 27 million by the end of the century, Hufton 1974:14). In the countryside, poor harvests and especially fractionalization of small landholdings among several sons swelled the numbers of the dispossessed. There was a proliferation of people who found it difficult to provide themselves with the bare necessities. A man by himself, without a working wife, could not expect to earn enough to support more than himself and perhaps one child. The arrival of additional children could reduce the family to destitution.

Moving to the city could not have been much improvement. Rapid urbanization combined with slow industrialization meant that opportunities were few—not only for parents but for children who survived to mature. Incomes were low, rents high. Around 60% of these French mothers sending their infants to wet-nurses belonged to the large class of artisans. In his detailed analysis of wet-nursing commerce, George Sussman writes that "a majority of the working people of eighteenth-century Paris was engaged in a perpetual struggle to avoid insolvency and indigence, a struggle that became more difficult as the cost of living and particularly bread rose faster than wages" (1982:58).

Even for this "bourgeoisie" then, maintenance of that status was precarious. In Sussman's calculation of a typical budget for a family of the artisan class, a husband would earn about twenty-five livre a month, the wife another fifteen. Of this, 40–50% would go for food, 15% for clothing, 6% for light and heat, and another 13% for rent. In addition, each wet-nursed child would cost about eight livre a month (or 20% of the total budget per child) as long as the parents chose to keep up the payments (see below).

B. Reconstructing the History of Wet-Nursing

Such was the ecological context for eighteenth-century France. Let us proceed then by trying to put the phenomenon of wet-nursing in broad evolutionary and comparative perspective, and then examine its antecedents in human history. From a comparative perspective we can certainly locate examples of communal suckling and "delegated mothering" in other animals. As we further attempt to reconstruct the use of wet-nurses in prehistoric times it seems probable that this curious phenomenon initially functioned either to (1) enhance foraging (or labor) opportunities for mothers who would otherwise be burdened by infants, or (2) to reduce the physiological costs of lactation. In either case, the ultimate outcome would be enhanced reproductive success for the mother, either due to her own or her infant's improved survival prospects and/or her own shorter inter-birth intervals.

In the animal literature, biological relatedness looms large in the evolution of communal suckling (e.g., McCracken 1984; Lee 1989). Although there exist primate cases where lactating females adopt unrelated (or distantly related) individuals under natural conditions adoption of close relatives (siblings, grandchildren) is the more common pattern (Thierry and Anderson 1986; Goodall 1986:101–103; 383–384). As in allomaternal caretaking generally, kinship tends to play an important role (Hrdy 1976; Sommer 1992). Although care of these adopted young may not include suckling, several spectacular cases involve older female monkeys who resume lactating when caring for grand-offspring (see Auerbach 1981; Auerbach and Avery 1981 for evidence of induced lacta-

tion in women other than the biological mother).

The presence of matrilineal kin might have been problematic, however, for early humans—just as it is for most contemporary humans. It would be ill-advised to extrapolate to humans from cercopithecine and colobine monkeys which are predominantly matrilineal and female philopatric.[6] By contrast, human societies are most often characterized as patrilineal and patrilocal (Murdock 1934), that is, humans are most often "male philopatric," a tendency that may be quite ancient (Ghiglieri 1987), characterizing as it does four of five hominoid species. Males remain in their natal range, while females migrate out to breed in gorillas, common chimps, bonobos, and the majority of human societies. If early hominid allomothers only chose to suckle infants born to close kin, they might then have had few opportunities to do so (i.e., allomaternal suckling would have been limited to cases where two sisters were married to the same man or to brothers; or else lactating relatives of the father). Biocca describes for the Amazonian Yanomamö a case where the mother had decided not to rear her son. The paternal grandmother intervenes and the infant is suckled by the father's sister in addition to suckling her own new infant (1971:299).

It is perhaps not surprising then that in contrast to most examples of communal suckling in animals, co-residence and the potential for reciprocity appear to be more important than kinship in sustaining shared nursing in traditional societies. Where kinswomen are available to nurse, all three factors (relatedness, co-residence, and reciprocity) may be at issue (see Tronick et al. 1987 for Ituri Forest pygmies in Central Zaire). Furthermore, it is probably not a coincidence that kin-based fostering out (as opposed to commercial daycare and boarding schools or paid wet-nursing) is most richly developed in West Africa and other parts of the world where matrilineal kinship systems are strongly developed and intact (e.g., see Bledsoe and Isiugo Abanihe 1989; Draper 1989).

Assuming that most women in early human societies were living in patrilocal (male philopatric) systems, wet-nursing in its earliest manifestations was probably a reciprocal favor among co-wives or neighbors. Among the Andaman Islanders, for example, any lactating woman supposedly would give her breast to any crying child (Radcliffe-Brown 1922:76; see also Tronick, Morelli, and Winn 1987 for Efe pygmies in Zaire). In addition to incorporating infants into a network of caretakers, mothers presumably gain from being able to forage more efficiently while another female holds her infant (Hrdy 1976; Whitten 1982). Hurtado has recorded significantly lower rates of food acquisition by Ache food gatherers who are lactating (1985); to compensate, women shared food with the inefficient gatherer. Among Solomon Islanders, where taboos prevented mothers from nursing their babies in the place where they garden, a mother might leave her infant with a lactating sister-in-law for an hour or so while she goes to work in the fields (Akin 1983 and personal communication). Indeed, among the Arunta, where women nurse one another's children, disputes may arise over which mother is to stay in camp and which is to go and forage (Murdock 1934:35).

These wet-nursing relationships are best characterized as casual opportunistic cooperation among women—affines, neighbors, and blood kin—who are in a position to reciprocate help. Some voluntary wet-nurses may look forward to future support from a grown charge who owes his life to her (e.g., Biocca 1971:214 for the case of a captured woman who nurses the orphaned daughter of a headman). In some societies, wet-nursing arrangements have become more formalized. In Arab culture, such relationships are institutionalized and Islamic law actually allows for three kinds of kinship: kinship by blood, by marriage, and by the happenstance of two individuals having suckled milk from the same woman (see for example Altorki 1980). The same incest rules pertain to children who suckled from the same woman as for true siblings.

Wet-nursing on a large scale probably did not emerge until there were stratified societies in which one class could command or purchase the services of lower-ranking mothers. But this situation was probably neither that rare nor that recent in human history. Enforced suckling involving females of different dominance statuses occurs in a wide range of animals (e.g., see van Lawick 1973 for wild dogs; Rood 1980 for dwarf mongooses; O'Brien 1988 for cebus monkeys; reviewed in Lee 1989), and it is likely that "enforced suckling" among humans predates its appearance in the historical record. In

the most famous animal example of enforced suckling, the dominant female in a pack of wild dogs kills all but one of the pups of a subordinate female, designated by van Lawick as "Angel." Angel's single pup is sufficient to sustain the subordinate female's lactation so that at a later date the dominant female's ten-week-old pups can preferentially nurse from her, at the expense of the lone, stunted, survivor who is not competitive for her milk with these older and larger pups (van Lawick 1973).

Although enforced wet-nursing among humans is no doubt even older, the earliest written records of one woman suckling another's infant in a context that was neither kin-based nor rooted in reciprocal cooperation date from 3000 B.C. (see Fildes 1988: Chapter 1 for a review of wet-nursing in antiquity). Consider a Sumerian lullaby from the late third millennium B.C. As the wife of Shulgi, ruler of Ur, sings her son to sleep she promises him first a wife and then a son—complete with wet-nurse. "The nursemaid, joyous of heart, will sing to him; The nursemaid, joyous of heart, will suckle him" (from Wallis Budge 1925, cited in Fildes 1986:6). Some of these nurses were themselves from privileged backgrounds, their status elevated still higher through contact with their charges. Fildes (1988:3–4) points out that for Ancient Egypt wet-nurses were recruited from the harems of senior officials, and subsequently appeared on the guest lists for royal funeral feasts; the child of one royal wet-nurse from Ancient Egypt was permitted to use the title "milk-sister to the king." Similar respect could be accorded wet-nurses in India, China, Japan, and the Near East (Fildes 1988:4). Less fortunate wet-nurses were actually, or effectively, slaves. Furthermore, not all wet-nurses were living under close supervision of the parents, since Near Eastern authorities clearly had some reason for fearing wet-nurses were substituting another infant for one that had died when they outlawed the practice (cited by Fildes 1988:24 from the Code of Hammurabi, ca. 1700 B.C.).

In South Asia, in the period just prior to the Buddha's lifetime (566?–480 B.C.), references in the *Caraka Samhita*, an encyclopedic collection of Ayurvedic beliefs, made it clear that the use of wet-nurses was widespread among the elites and that great care was taken to assure nurses of appropriate caste, color, and character, a common theme through the history of wet-nursing (Fildes 1988). In Hellenistic Egypt, from about 300 BC, the Greek ruling class used slaves as wet-nurses;[7] however, free women as well turned to wet-nursing for income (see Pomeroy 1984:139 for evidence from Greek papyri). In some cases, people who planned to rear a foundling as a future slave hired one of these wet-nurses to suckle it (personal communication from S. Pomeroy). Nursing contracts from the subsequent period of Roman rule in Egypt also survive (Bradley 1980).

By the second century A.D., wet-nursing in parts of Europe was an organized commercial activity. In Rome it was centered about particular columns in the vegetable market at the Forum Holitorium specifically referred to as "lactaria." From Medieval times onward, wet-nurses, paid, indentured, or enslaved, were used by royalty and elites in many European countries. Typically, propertied families would hire women to suckle their children under conditions of close supervision, so that only one infant was nursed at a time by a nonpregnant woman with a healthy supply of milk. Although more costly, wet-nursing in this form ensured high rates of infant survival (Sussman 1982 for

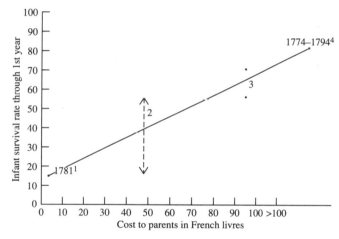

Figure 39.1. Linear relationship between amount expended by parents to pay wet-nurses and the probability of infant survival.

Notes on how survival rates and costs were calculated:

1. Mortality rates during the first year of life for infants deposited in Parisian foundling hospitals reached 68.5% in 1751, and rose to 85.7% by 1781. Ninety-two percent of these children would die by their eighth birthday (Sussman 1982:62–64).

2. Roughly 10% of parents who sent children to rural wet-nurses subsequently defaulted on their payments with the result that their infants were eventually deposited in foundling homes (Sussman 1982:62). Infants abandoned after six months of paid wet-nursing nevertheless tended to have higher prospects of survival than did those infants abandoned at birth (Delasselle 1975). The cost here is calculated at one-half the yearly rate for a rural wet-nurse.

3. A Parisian artisan might earn 20–25 livres per month, his wife one-half that. Seven to eight livres per month went to pay the rural wet-nurse (Sussman 1982:59). Sussman estimates mortality for these wet-nursed infants at 25–40% (1982:67). Mortality rates rose somewhat over time as good wet-nurses became increasingly hard to find. By the period 1871–74 mortality reached 42% according to records kept by the Bureau of Wet-Nursing.

4. Infants tended at home by live-in wet-nurses enjoyed roughly the same prospects of survival as infants nursed by their own mothers. Based on information recorded for 11,923 babies born in 19 parishes in suburbs south of Paris and nursed by their own mothers during the period 1774–84, Galliano (1966) estimates that mortality rates were around 18% (Sussman 1982:67). Data collected by Maurice Garden (1970:125) for Lyon during the period 1785–88 indicate a comparable rate of mortality for mother-nursed infants, only 16% died in their first year of life.

eighteenth-century France; Klapisch-Zuber 1986a for fifteenth-century Italy). Infant mortality in the French case of in-house wet-nursing hovered around 20 percent— about the same or only slightly higher than if a French mother of that period suckled her own offspring (see Fig. 39.1, note 4).

Not much is known about wet-nurses themselves, but there can be little doubt that in most cases their occupation curtailed the opportunities that their own infant had to nurse, and may have led to its death. In Renaissance Italy, nearly 30 percent of the infants sent to foundling homes—where probability of survival would be low—were in fact the offspring of slave women whose milk would subsequently be used or sold to the benefit of her owner (Trexler 1973a:270; Klapisch-Zuber, 1986a:141 and 141, n. 33). There are dozens of texts and manuals describing attributes of a good wet-nurse. Virtually all advise parents not to select a nurse who is either pregnant or still suckling her own infant—even when they also recommended choosing mothers with very new milk. The wet-nurse's own infant might be farmed out to an even less well paid wet-nurse, or else "dry-nursed." Klapisch-Zuber expresses the suspicion that fourteenth- and fifteenth-century Florentine slaveowners may have hastened the death of "certain socially condemned infants" through abandonment in order to obtain a wet-nurse (1986a:140). In the rich correspondence between Margherita Dattini and her Renaissance merchant husband for whose client she was seeking a suitable wet-nurse, Margherita conveys her disappointment that the infant of one prospective candidate had survived after all (Origo 1957:200–201; see also Trexler 1973a for more of the same). In other cases a lactating nurse might simply sustain milk production over years (Jane Austen, born 1775 in Hampshire, was the seventh of eight of her siblings to be suckled by the same nurse).

Given that any shift away from breastmilk would have introduced new opportunities for infection and lowered survivorship for infants thus deprived of milk their mothers provided to the children of others, wet-nurses were directly contributing to the death of their own offspring. Maternal decision-making in these instances must however be examined in social context. The wet-nurse's behavior benefited nonrelatives more powerful than she (although in some of these instances, fitness tradeoffs will be complicated by biological relatedness between the infant and a male householder who fathered it). The price paid by these mothers for remaining within the system at all (perceived by them with some accuracy as synonymous with survival?) was to redirect their own milk to nonrelatives—a forced decision not unlike that made by "Angel," the subordinate wild dog mother.

C. Reproductive Consequences of Wet-Nursing

Although it is difficult to precisely document what happened to the wet-nurse's own infants, demographic consequences for the women on whose behalf they were hired are better known, largely through family diaries and birth records. Non-nursing mothers gave birth at a higher rate (Dupaquier and Lachiver 1964:1399)—as often as annually in some extreme cases instead of every three or four years as one might expect if they nursed their own infants. Maurice Garden's remarkable study of the demography of eighteenth-century Lyon documents nearly annual births in the families of butchers and silk-makers, with mothers routinely producing twelve to sixteen children (Garden 1970:95–97). One of the women in his sample of butchers' wives produced twenty-one children in twenty-four years (see 1970: Tableau VII "Les enfants de Jacques Gantillon le cadet"). A similar hyperfertility is documented for upper class British women, but the situation is more complicated for French elites for whom the average number of births per marriage fell from 6.15 in the seventeenth century to 2.79 in the eighteenth century (Johansson 1987b) despite continued use of wet-nurses.[8] Of fifty women focused on in Judith Lewis's study of childbearing among the British aristocracy between 1760–1860, the Duchess of Leinster was the most fecund, giving birth to her first child at sixteen, only a year after her marriage, and continuing to reproduce until her twenty-first and last child was born thirty years later when the Duchess was forty-six (1986:123–124). For the entire group of fifty, the *median* span of childbearing from marriage to last birth was eighteen years, resulting in an average of eight children each. Twenty-three of these women gave birth to their second child within a year or less of their first.[9] (Contrast this with the four-year birth intervals, and average of five children per female thought to have characterized Pleistocene hunter-gatherers during most of human history, Short 1976b; Lancaster and Lancaster 1987). There can be little doubt that the anemia, poor health, prolapsed uteruses, and other obstetrical difficulties documented in such lurid detail by Shorter (1982) was in fact the toll taken on women's bodies by nearly annual births during the first decade of marriage, followed by a second decade of production at a slower—but still "unnaturally" high—rate. In the years before the availability to women of birth control, any behavior that circumvented lactational amenorrhea resulted in increased fertility so that wet-nursing was well-suited to achieve (primarily male?) pronatalist goals.

For those who combined these high levels of fertility with relatively low levels of mortality (i.e., 20% or less), wet-nurses meant large completed family sizes such as those recorded for aristocratic British women between 1760 and 1860 (Lewis 1986). There is little reason to doubt Stone's assessment that prior to the demographic transition the wealthy had larger completed family sizes than the poor (Stone 1977:64).[10] Even as late as the nineteenth century in parts of Sicily, the landed aristocracy using wet-nurses produced significantly more children (an average of seven per family) and children were born at shorter intervals (two years) than was the case for families lower in the social hierarchy and among those foregoing the services of wet-nurses (four children on average, with a birth interval of 4.3 years) (Schneider and Schneider 1984).

D. Different Fitness Tradeoffs in the Social Transformation of Commercial Wet-Nursing in Europe

Shorter birth intervals, greater fertility, and high infant survivorship were outcomes of wet-nursing for families at the higher end of the social scale whose power and resources permitted them to engage or enforce the highest quality wet-nurses and have them perform their services under close supervision in the parents'

place of residence. In time, wet-nurses themselves may have become a sort of status symbol which members of the sub-elites struggled to retain, even if it meant sending their infants out to wet-nurses further and further from the parental abode. Klapisch-Zuber (1986a) documents this transition from a primarily upper-class to a middle-class child rearing practice for Renaissance Italy. Using data gleaned from domestic diaries or "ricordanze" she shows that between 1302 and 1399 only two of fifteen fathers who put children out to nurse did not come from prominent families. After 1450, however, half the families were of modest rank. From the middle of the fifteenth century onward, nursing by a paid wet-nurse or slave was the norm for all but the poorest women. "It is probable," writes Klapish-Zuber, "that the demand for nurses among proper Florentines motivated the *popolo minuto*—particularly those who . . . had professional dealings with the merchants and the families of the highest society—to dispatch their children to the country as soon as they were born so that they could offer the wife's milk to the burghers who found it unthinkable that their own wives be allowed to breast-feed" (1986a:138). The practice spread not only by direct emulation, but also through "ricochet" effects as wealthier babies displaced poorer ones and so on down the line.

It seems possible then that this upper-class practice, increasingly adopted by sub-elites, served as a model for artisans and marginal members of the bourgeoisie, who for quite different reasons—in order to maintain the wife's labor within the family business—adopted what had begun as an elite pronatalist strategy. Working women began to purchase wet-nursing services from still poorer women (e.g., see Sussman 1982 for France). Garden's data for Lyon document the use of wet-nurses in order to retain a mother's labor. The more involved the wife was in helping her husband in the butcher shop or in silk-making or other trades—the more likely the family was to use wet-nurses (1970:137).

By this point, historical links with traditional patterns of reciprocal wet-nursing as in the Solomon Islands or pygmy cases have become very remote. Enforced wet-nursing through exploitation of slaves (as in the Classical and Oriental examples) provides a more apt precedent for commercial wet-nursing in premodern Europe.

One striking feature of commercial wet-nursing to emerge from the French and Italian case studies is the linear relationship between extent of parental outlay (cost of wet-nurse) and infant survivorship (Fig. 39.1). This finding is consistent with the idea that parents are using wet-nurses to lower the overall cost of producing infants, but it is important to note that the nature of the costs may be quite different from group to group. For the elites engaged in this game early on, wet-nurses meant shorter birth intervals, and greater reproductive success (since higher fertility was not offset by greater infant mortality). As even the elites confronted greater and greater competition for suitable wet-nurses, later-born children and non-heirs would have to settle for inferior care. The amount that parents were willing to spend for wet-nurses depended on the reproductive value of the nursling. That is, given the system of primogeniture, what was this son's prospect for translating parental investment into subsequent reproduction? Given a system in which dowries were larger for daughters lower in the birth order, what was this daughter's prospects? The firstborn of each sex was likely to be at an advantage over same-sex siblings, and sons favored over daughters.

E. The Role of Postpartum Sex Taboos

Among the elite, it seems likely that wet-nurses do indeed free mothers for status-enhancing social functions. The process by which ambitious women obtain favors for their families by service at court is well described in writings from the period (e.g., Lafayette 1678). The primary original function of wet-nurses for this group may have been to not only circumvent lactational amenorrhea, but also postpartum sex taboos.

Although historians tend to regard postpartum sex taboos as a uniquely European phenomenon, strictures against husbands sleeping with lactating wives are in fact very widespread in traditional societies. These taboos can be documented in cultures as geographically diverse as the Eipo of New Guinea, the !Kung and Herrero of South Africa, the Mende and other tribes of West Africa, the Yanamamö, Nambikwara, and other South American tribes as well as the North American Sioux (Schiefenhovel 1989; Howell 1979; Pennington 1989; Isiugo-Abanihe 1985:72, n. 8; Early and Peters 1990).

This custom, so common in traditional societies, can be documented in Europe at least by the second century AD. In his medical writings, Galen ordered all nursing women to abstain completely from sexual relations. The Alexandrian physician Soranus, writing around the same period, maintained that "coitus cools the affection toward nursing by the diversion of sexual pleasure and moreover spoils and diminishes the milk or suppresses it entirely . . . by bringing about conception" (cited in Bradley 1980:322). Similar versions of this postpartum sex taboo persisted through the eighteenth century in Britain, France, and other parts of Europe, although there is some question as to how strictly parents abided by these taboos (Fildes 1986:105). Nevertheless, one reason why the Catholic church so strongly supported the practice of sending babies to wet-nurses was that the use of wet-nurses (who were also not supposed to be sleeping with their husbands) permitted the women who hired them "to provide for the frailty of her husband by paying the conjugal due" (cited in Fildes 1986:105). (Note that the position of the Catholic church may help explain why wet-nursing was more common in France than in primarily Protestant England.)

A common belief associated with postpartum taboos is the notion that the milk of a mother who has intercourse will damage any infant (her own or others') that partakes of it. How these taboos came into existence is simply not well understood but once practiced would clearly constrain a couple's sex life. Given that frequent suckling over a 24-hour period would in any event contribute to long inter-birth intervals (Konner and Worthman 1980) the occasionally stated explanation that the taboo was used to prevent closely spaced births seems redundant and impractical. If postpartum sex taboos were really intended to *protect* babies it would have made more sense to keep babies with their mothers but permit them to suckle often enough both night and day to suppress ovulation (Konner and Worthman 1980). It seems an odd premise that babies were sent to wet-nurses—often with very detrimental consequences—in order to spare them ingesting the spoilt milk of a sexually active mother.

If protection of the baby was really the point, breaking the taboo seems so much more practical. For this reason, male pronatalist sentiment provides a more convincing explanation for husbands to ship babies out of the house as soon as possible. And indeed, whether for Britain, France, or Italy, there is little doubt that husbands played key roles in insisting on the use of wet-nurses and in lining up the desired service, sometimes seeing that the baby was removed from the house almost before the mother could see it (e.g., the eighteenth-century observations of Madame Rolande, cited in Sussman 1982:80; Klapisch-Zuber 1986a:143). Whatever its cause, this early separation of mother and infant would inhibit the bonding of mother with infant. Mothers of the new mother or mothers-in-law could play key roles in this process, criticizing new mothers who insisted on nursing their own baby (Lewis 1986:61).

Is it possible that the widespread postpartum sex taboo is a cultural outgrowth of male (and lineage) pronatalist interests? The prevalence of these taboos combined with the absence of any obvious rationale for believing that sex spoils milk (although a subsequent pregnancy might, Palloni and Tienda 1986:31) makes this a problem that clearly deserves further research. In any event, whether it was to preserve fertility for pronatalist purposes among the elite, or to preserve the woman's labor for family ends among the artisan class, the outcome of wet-nursing was the same: shorter birth intervals for the paying mother, far longer ones for the paid nurse. This higher fertility among elites would have come linked to high survivorship of their offspring, but be linked to high infant mortality among workers. The paid wet-nurse in this system would suffer both lower fertility and higher mortality for her offspring.

F. Differential Treatment of Wet-Nursed Charges

Among elites, artisans, and peasants, parents used wet-nurses to reduce the labor-intensive tasks of nurturing slow-maturing human young. But for each group, the costs and benefits were quite different. Furthermore, the strategies pursued were changing through time in response to social and economic competition, costs of superfluous children (e.g., the increasing cost of providing dowries for elite daughters, see

Klapisch-Zuber 1986b:215 for Renaissance Italy; Boone 1986 for Medieval Portugal) and fluctuations in the availability and cost of wet-nurses and other resources that mitigated the costs of parenting.

Elites for example were clearly fine-tuning investment in children in line with quite specific social and reproductive needs. One family out of three in Klapisch-Zuber's Florentine sample were more likely to keep sons than daughters at home, to nurse them longer, and to use a higher quality wet-nurse. Twenty-three percent of boys were entrusted for relatively long periods to a wet-nurse who lived in casa, compared to 12% of girls (1986a:138). Conversely, 69% of daughters born compared to 55% of sons were sent to wet-nurses in the country. Assuming that the nurse in casa cost eighteen to twenty fiorini annually, compared to eight to fifteen for a nurse in the country (Klapisch-Zuber 1986a:136), parents were clearly paying more for sons. Furthermore, parents were more likely to wean daughters abruptly while paying extra for sons to enjoy a supplementary transition period, which may in part account for the fact that boys spent on average one and one-half months longer at wet-nurses than daughters did (1986a: Table 7:7). Similar preferences can be documented for first versus later-born children.

Given such prejudices, it might appear at first glance surprising that infant boys sent out to wet-nurses did not survive any better than girls. In fact, the tendency was slightly in the opposite direction with 18.1% of 144 boys and 15.8% of 139 girls in Klapisch-Zuber's sample dying. However, if we take into account that the primary male heirs were kept at home and not sent out to begin with, these high mortality rates would be impinging upon sons who were already designated heirs to spare.[11]

Strategic allocation of resources to children varies according to circumstances (Hrdy and Judge 1993). Furthermore, within families such strategies might be altered over time in line with specific events. The life of Charles Maurice de Talleyrand-Perigord (1754–1838), the French diplomat and statesman, provides a poignant case in point. Talleyrand's ancient and powerful but not overly wealthy family, with one son in hand, sent their second son to a less expensive wet-nurse in the suburbs of Paris. Unfortunately, the firstborn son died, and when his parents sent for young Charles Maurice, they learned that sometime between his third or fourth year, the surplus son had fallen from a chest and injured his foot, rendering the newly needed heir crippled for life. Nevertheless, young Talleyrand was brought home to be groomed for his future role. But when his mother gave birth to yet another son, a family council was convened. In the interests of the family, it was decided that the crippled child should forfeit the right of primogeniture. Once again relegated to a secondary position, Talleyrand was educated for a career in the church—a vocation he soon abandoned. The rest, as they say, is history.

IV. CHOOSING BETWEEN ALTERNATIVE MEANS TO REDUCE PARENTAL EFFORT

If one accepts that wet-nursing, fostering-out, abandonment, and infanticide all function to reduce outlays of parental effort (albeit with potentially quite different outcomes for the infant), we are still left with the question of why parents opt for one solution rather than another. Why for example is fostering-out of weaned babies the choice of some 30–40% of West African mothers,[12] while among their eighteenth-century French counterparts, parents were electing en masse to hire paid wet-nurses? Why do some 20–40% of infant births end in infanticide among some Amazonian and Papuan tribes, while abandonment of infants accounted for comparable mortality in premodern Europe?

Sociobiologists have been able to identify several predictors for the retrenchment of parental solicitude. They focus on such variables as the high reproductive value of the mother combined with poor current prospects; low potential for paternal support in environments where such support is critical; or poor prospects of either productive or reproductive returns from investment in the infant (Alexander 1974; Daly and Wilson 1980; Hrdy 1987, 1990; Hill and Kaplan 1988).

These predictors probably apply to all types of retrenchment discussed here and the same "ultimate explanations" may be invoked. For example, Bugos and McCarthy have shown for South American Ayoreo, and Daly and Wilson have shown for contemporary North Americans that mothers with high reproductive values,

with many additional years of potential reproduction ahead of them, are significantly more likely to commit infanticide than are older mothers nearing the end of their reproductive careers. In a West African setting where infanticide is very rare, this same group of young, high reproductive value mothers, is significantly more likely to send infants to foster homes (Isiugo-Abanihe 1985: Table 4 and p. 67). Purely from the perspective of maternal workload, one might expect higher parity birth order mothers, those with a number of children already, to send children away. The fact that it is instead lower parity mothers who reduce their investment in children is consistent with the hypothesis that these young women are keeping options open for future reproductive opportunities. Similarly, whereas lack of male support is a "risk factor" for infanticide for children born in Amazonian and New Guinea societies (see Bugos and McCarthy 1984 for the Ayoreo; Hill and Kaplan 1988 and Hill and Hurtado 1996 for the Ache; Schiefenhovel 1989 for the Eipo), it is a "risk factor" for fostering in African societies where paternal support is needed. Pennington, for example, found for patrilineal Herrero pastoralists in Southern Africa that unmarried mothers were nearly twice as likely as those in a stable union to send children to foster mothers (1989).

These parallels illustrate a highly facultative maternal response system that varies in line with life-history stage and socioenvironmental conditions. Examining this response system from a sociobiological vantage may help us understand why a mother would abandon her infant to a foundling home rather than continue to invest heavily by nursing the infant herself.[13] But we must seek explanations at a different level for why a mother chooses to leave her infant in a foundling home versus a relative's rural hut, or why she abandons an infant versus fostering him out? Why bury alive versus abandon, and so forth. Such decisions are made within the framework of culturally imaginable and available options, as well as social (particularly family structure) and environmental constraints. Hence by identifying constraints which prevent people from selecting alternative tactics for reducing parental effort we go a long way toward understanding the proximate causes of infanticide. Here sociobiology meets the traditional concerns of cultural ecologists and historians. Or rather, traditional but with an important twist. Instead of the "group," the focus is upon the decisions made by individuals in accordance with their assessments of maternal survival or lineage prospects.

A. Abandonment Versus Infanticide: Opportunities and Constraints

In his 1988 book *The Kindness of Strangers*, John Boswell documents a widespread traffic in European babies from Antiquity to the Renaissance, as couples without children and perhaps especially slave-dealers gathered up those infants that their parents did not choose to rear. High population densities meant that even if no one in the mother's immediate vicinity was known to want her baby there might well be "strangers" willing to rear the foundling. Furthermore, compared to tropical forests with stinging insects and Amazonian jaguars and other predators, there was a reasonable chance that an exposed infant might survive long enough to be found. By the end of the Middle Ages, infant abandonment had become so widespread in the West, that throughout Europe public institutions were formed to cope with this epidemic of foundlings whose supply now clearly exceeded demand.

Between the thirteenth and sixteenth century charitable groups (whose motivations are outside the scope of this paper) set up hospitals and foundling homes. In one particularly well-documented case, the commune of Florence, together with the local silk guild, joined to build an asylum called Santa Maria degl'Innocenti. By 1445 the doors were opened to a small flood of "innocents." No doubt numbers of abandoned children rose and fell with economic conditions, but the numbers also increased in response to the opportunity to reduce parental effort without necessarily killing infants that was created by these institutions.

In what was a fairly general pattern for such institutions in continental Europe and Russia, the Innocenti in its early years was a fairly benign environment for infants. Death rates during the first year of life were around 26 percent for 1445, down to 23 percent during the Innocenti's second year (compared to ca. 21% for the population at large). However, by 1448, as the Innocenti became a magnet for abandoned babies from all over the dominion, these rates

doubled to 53.6% mortality. By 1451, six years after the institution opened, death rates soared to 57.6% (Trexler 1973a: Table V).

At the outset, in "a hospital of minimum crowding, and with a sufficient supply of *balie* (wet-nurses), spared famine and pestilence, the first innocents had as good a chance as any children" (Trexler 1973a:276). And many foundlings left at the Innocenti would definitely have been better off there. These were the illegitimate children of slaves and servants who according to Trexler would have died at triple the rates of legitimate children. The decision by a mother to deposit her baby in the *tour* (rotating barrel) at the foundling home could be construed as in the baby's best interests.

But what of the same decision once mortality rates in foundling homes reached the catastrophic levels which almost inevitably, they eventually did, as more and more parents made the same choice? (See Trexler 1973a for Italy; Dupoux 1958 for France.) Dupoux's statistics for Parisian foundling homes at the end of the eighteenth century indicate that 92% of these children died before their eighth birthday. Death rates of 70–85% were not unusual. Were parents depositing their infants in the *tours* aware of the prognosis for survival of the abandoned baby? Surviving documents from fifteenth-century Florence strongly suggest that parents depositing children at the Innocenti certainly were not only aware of the risks, but were capable of making shrewd assessments concerning the survival chances of a baby kept in Florence versus a baby farmed out by the foundling home to distant wet-nurses. "Some parents, in abandoning their child to the Innocenti pleaded that the hospital keep it and not send it to an outside nurse . . ." (Herlihy and Klapisch-Zuber 1985:147).

Parents would deposit their infants with various mementos and identifying signs—an indication that they were gambling on a good outcome and that they harbored some hope of one day retrieving their child. Nevertheless, at some point, parents must have become aware of the high death rates suffered by the babies they abandoned.

Volker Hunecke records case studies from 18th and 19th century Milan of a tailor "Filippo A . . ." who keeps his first son and then deposits the next six (in the space of five and a half years) at the nearest tour. When his first wife dies, Filippo remarries "Cecilia B . . ." who deposits there five infants in five years. After a year and a half, Cecilia tries to retrieve them, but only two had survived long enough for her to be able to. "Francesco G . . ." and his wife "Amalia S . . ." similarly produced twelve infants in thirteen years. The first of these died shortly after birth. All the others were left at foundling homes, and only one of them, a girl, survived.

The point here is that these outcomes were not a secret. Parents were in a position to have some sense of the high mortality, and being human would have communicated what they knew to their neighbors. Granted that it is difficult, even for trained social scientists, to obtain accurate estimates of infant mortality (and these were after all illiterate people with neither time nor facilities to study the situation), still I don't think we can assume that many parents remained ignorant of the prospects for their abandoned children. Yet even if parents were aware of high mortality, it does not mean that parents opting for the *tour* were merely seeking a legal way to kill an infant. More plausible is the hypothesis that parents were making their calculations based on immediate costs (mother's lost employment; cost of a wetnurse). This information was likely to carry more weight than rumored events behind distant walls. Indeed, Garden's information for silk-makers and butchers in eighteenth-century Lyon suggest that whether or not the mother helped in the family business was a better predictor of whether or not babies were sent to wetnurses than were mortality rates.

Given the long history of child abandonment in the West (or indeed, currently tolerated child mortality rates in industrialized countries like the U.S. today, Gibbs 1990:43) there is a certain irony about the readiness of people from "civilized" (e.g., Western-oriented) backgrounds to condemn infanticide among tribal societies. For as I will argue in the next section, infanticide has far more to do with family structure, ecology, and the absence of alternative means of mitigating parental investment than it does with morality.

B. High Versus Low Rates of Infanticide

Infanticide is everywhere an uncommon event and tends to be poorly documented. By and large, reviews of infanticide in human societies have used ethnographic accounts to conduct surveys to try to determine whether infanticide is present or absent for a particular culture. Where infanticide occurs, special attention is given to the stated circumstances (Dickemann 1975; Daly and Wilson 1984). In the most extensive such review, Daly and Wilson took a representative sample of sixty cultures described in the Human Relations Area Files; infanticide was reported for thirty-nine of these, and in thirty-five, the circumstances surrounding at least some cases were known. They were able to identify sets of circumstances that pertained to virtually all reported cases; these circumstances were compatible with their sociobiological analysis: the infant killed was probably sired by a man other than the woman's current mate; the infant was defective or considered to be of poor quality or else was one of a pair of twins; there was a problem in the timing of the birth (short interbirth intervals); or else for some other reason (mother dead, no male support, poor economic conditions) parental resources were inadequate to rear the child. At the time of these surveys, virtually no data existed on the frequency of infanticide.

Scarcity of information is exacerbated both by the discomfort or grief that perpetrators feel in discussing infanticide (Bugos and McCarthy 1984) and the prospect of disapproval by public or religious bodies, or the prospect of legal sanctions. In contemporary Brazil, a woman may abandon or neglect her infant, thereby indirectly killing it, but if she commits infanticide, she is imprisoned (Schepher-Hughes 1985). This situation is currently complicated by the accusation that anthropologists who attribute violent practices to tribal people (and infanticide is considered a violent practice) are in fact playing into the hands of forces who wish to manipulate or eliminate these tribes (see Booth 1989 for a South American case).[14] For this reason, several of those anthropologists who for the first time actually have quantitative data on infanticide are now reluctant to publish them; they have specifically requested that I delete their data from this paper.

In spite of these difficulties, a limited amount of data have emerged over the last decade, and permit us for the first time to move beyond largely anecdotal ethnographic accounts and examine actual rates. Hence, it is now possible

Table 39.1. Infanticide in Nine Traditional Societies in Africa, Amazonia, and New Guinea Where Available Information Permits the Calculation of Rates of Infanticide for a Sample of Liveborn Infants

Culture and Location	Subsistence Type	No. Reported Cases Infanticide/No. Live Births	Proportion Infant Mortality Due to Infanticide (%)	Source
1. **EFE** Ituri Forest, Zaire	Specialized hunter-gatherer	≈0/530 (≈0%)	≈0	Bailey 1989; and pers. com. from Bailey and Peacock
2. **LESE** Ituri Forest, Zaire	Horticulture	≈0/777 (≈0%)	≈0	Bailey 1989; and pers. com. from Bailey and Peacock
3. **DATOGA** N. Tanzania	Pastoralism	0/762 (0%)	0	Borgerhoff Mulder pers. comm.
4. **KIPSIGIS** S. W. Kenya	Agro-pastoralism	0/2,190 (0%)	0	Borgerhoff Mulder pers. comm.
5. **SAN** Kalahari Desert Botswana	Hunter-gatherer	6/500 (1%)	3	Howell 1979
6. **MUCAJI YANAMAMÖ** N. Brazil	Horticulture and hunting	17/283 (6%)	44	Early and Peters 1990
7. **ACHE** Paraguay	Hunter-gatherer	26/223 (12%)[b,c] 11 males (.09) 15 females (.16)	39[c]	Hill and Hurtado 1996 and pers. com.
8. **AYOREO** S. W. Bolivia and N. Paraguay	Horticulture and foraging	54/141 (38%)[d] 31 males (.41) 16 females (.27)	Unknown	Bugos and McCarthy 1984
9. **EIPO** Highland Central New Guinea	Horticulture	20/49 (41%)[e] 5 males (.21) 15 females (.60)	≈81[e]	Schiefenhovel 1989: Fig. 10.8

[a]It is not possible to state with certainty that infanticide never occurred. It was suspicious for example that in these 777 births, only two sets of twins were reported, and in both cases only one twin survived (one was stillborn, the other twin died shortly after birth). Nevertheless, for the purposes of this paper the Efe and Lese qualify as groups with very low rates of infanticide.

[b]These 26 Ache cases includes children who are killed up to five years of age, and some of these cases involve nonparents.

[c]These figures are only for the last decade prior to peaceful contact (1960–1970), and represent only a fraction of Hill's total data base. Hill believes that data from this period provide the most accurate estimate of infant mortality since his data suggest an increasing tendency not to report infants who die in cohorts born in the more distant past.

[d]This is an inflated rate because Bugos and McCarthy only included in the sample of women known to commit infanticide. Apparently most women committed infanticide, but from the article it is impossible to say how many women were left out. Note that sex of infant was unknown in seven cases.

[e]These data are for the period 1974–1978. Under mission influence, infanticide rates fell to 10% after 1978. The proportion of infant mortality due to infanticide is calculated from Schiefenhovel's estimation that "normal" infant mortality, excluding infanticide is around 50 per thousand (1989: p.174). Counting infanticide, total infant mortality would be 480 per thousand.

to compare populations known to have very low rates of infanticide, approaching zero (epitomized here by the various African cases), with populations exhibiting high rates of infanticide.[15] Table 39.1 summarizes information from nine traditional societies in which it has been possible for anthropologists to record the (acknowledged) proportion of livebirths that were killed, yielding minimum rates of infanticide. These rates range from zero or near zero in African hunter-gatherer, horticultural, and pastoralist groups and one percent among San hunter-gatherers in the Kalahari, to the extra-ordinarily high rate of 41% of livebirths among the Eipo.[16] Interviews by ethnographer Wulf Schiefenhovel among the (up to that point) largely uncontacted Eipo tribespeople in the West New Guinean mountains revealed that thirty-one of the forty-two infants killed in the period 1974–1978 were female. These data combined with interview data make it clear that the desire for sons is implicated in this very high rate.[17] Preference for sons is also apparent in the Ache data where 16% of daughters born and 9% of sons were killed. Other Amazonian groups exhibited much lower rates—5–6% of live births without such marked son preference. The Ayoreo rate is inflated upwards, not by son preference but by several other factors. In particular, Bugos and McCarthy (1984) only included women in their sample who had committed infanticide, and it is not clear how many non-infanticidal mothers were excluded.

These high rates of infanticide for New Guinea and Amazonia are consistent with the general ethnographic literature for these areas. That is, even though rates were not available, anthropologists were by and large aware that infanticide was going on (e.g., Neel and colleagues estimated that infanticide was occurring at a rate around 15–20% among the Yanamamö, Neel 1970). This situation contrasts markedly with the published literature on Africa, where infanticide is rare and largely confined to destruction of defective offspring or twins (Granzberg 1973), although other circumstances are sometimes also cited (see review in Daly and Wilson 1984). For large segments of subsaharan Africa, an area where there is an exceptionally high desire for parenthood and a real horror of subfertility (Page 1989), infanticide is unthinkable. Several African ethnographers I asked about infanticide either have no information on its occurrence ("the rate is zero") or point out how puzzled their informants would be by the notion (personal communications from R. Bailey for Lese, and M. Borgerhoff Mulder and Lee Cronk for Nilotic Kipsigis and Mukogodo Ma-speaking people). The main exceptions to this would be for Africa's nomadic gathering people, who regard infanticide as a mother's right even if it is not one commonly exercised. In the words of demographer Nancy Howell, who studied the Khoisan-speaking San hunter-gatherers: "infanticide is part of a mother's prerogatives and responsibilities, culturally prescribed for birth defects and for one of each pair of twins" (1979). Of six San cases Howell knew about (out of five hundred livebirths), two involved low probability of male support. Anecdotal reports of infanticide in early ethnographies for the Masai, Bemba, Lozi, and other African tribal groups (cited in Daly and Wilson 1984) appear to involve similar circumstances. A sense of the cultural difference between San and Bantu in respect to infanticide is conveyed by Nancy Howell's account of a San woman who gives birth to a defective infant. Although tra-

ditionally, the delivering mother would have been alone, on this occasion, Bantu women were present. The mother of the defective infant felt it her duty to dispose of the infant, but the Bantu women prevented her (Howell 1979:119–120).

For the present, I accept these findings at face value, and conclude that by and large infanticide is not a salient feature in the lives of many Bantu and other African peoples. The key I think to the general low incidence of infanticide over much of Africa is linked to the same set of factors that lead to the persistent high fertility in contemporary (and presumably also traditional) Africa (Caldwell and Caldwell 1990): (1) children are highly desired for symbolic reasons involving ancestor worship and perpetuation of the lineage; (2) they reportedly cost their parents, particularly their fathers, very little to rear (though this is changing now with more emphasis on the need for education and payment of school fees); and (3) such costs as there are, are borne by the mother and by an assortment of caretakers, the infant's older siblings, real and fictive "grannies," and other patrilineal and especially matrilineal kin. Indeed, the Caldwells's claim in their famous argument (1982, 1990) that "wealth flows" from children to parents, that children eventually become net assets to parents although to date there are few empirical studies to support this claim (for an exception see Cain 1977, who has tried to measure benefits to parents from the labor of their offspring). Matrilineal social organization combined with female-centered horticultural practices mean that by and large male investment is not critical for child survival and well-being at the same time that the mother's social network makes available to her a range of options for delegating some of the necessary caretaking to other people—either older siblings and other related caretakers (Weisner 1987; Draper 1989) or fostering adults (Page 1989; Isiugo-Abanihe 1985). A fifth reason would be that few of these groups exhibit any strong preference for sons since daughters are often valued for their labor and the bridewealth they bring,[18] obviating any pressure for sex-preferential infanticide.

The African cases contrast markedly with primarily patrilineal and virilocal horticultural/hunting/fishing societies in South America and New Guinea. Male protection and support are essential for the well-being of children, and orphans or children of inappropriate paternity are at high risk of dying before adulthood. Among the Ache horticultural hunters of Paraguay, Hill and Kaplan demonstrate that children whose reported biological fathers die before the children reach fifteen years of age are significantly more likely to die (43.3% of 67 such children) compared to children whose fathers remain with the mother (only 19.3% of 171 such children) (Hill and Kaplan 1988:298). Such children are at high risk from being killed by the mother's subsequent mate. Furthermore, because of their poor prospects, infants no longer under the protection of the acknowledged father are at risk of being eliminated by the mother herself (e.g., see Murphy and Murphy 1974:166 for Mundurucu; Bugos and McCarthy 1984 for Ayoreo; Hill in press for Ache). In contrast to Africa, men in the South American cases provide the bulk of protein and calories for the village, and children without a male protector are discriminated against (Hill and Hurtado 1996).

As described by Bugos and McCarthy (1984), Ayoreo mothers—caught in transition between war and missionized settlement—confronted especially difficult socioecological conditions contributing to unstable marriages and exacerbating the need for male support. One mother, "Asago," with poor prospects of male support from her first three husbands buries at birth the first six of the ten children she will eventually bear in her lifetime. As extreme as this case is, Asago loses no more children to live-burial than did "Amalia S." to nineteenth-century Milanese foundling homes. Hill reports similar (if less extreme) cases for the Ache. Many of these Ache children were either considered defective in some way or stood a high chance of eventually being murdered by a stepfather or other male had the mother not eliminated them at birth (Hill and Kaplan 1988; and Hill and Hurtado 1996). As in Medieval Europe, compassion for deformed, sick, or unwanted children was not a luxury that traditional societies in South America could readily afford, and events which would strike contemporary Europeans, Americans, or Africans as astoundingly callous are commonplace (e.g., Biocca 1971, and Chagnon, personal communication for the Yanamamö; Hill and Hurtado 1996 for Ache). Among the Ache, children under the age of fifteen who are reared by a

woman other than their biological mother suffer higher mortality rates (36.1% of 61 children) than do children reared in intact families (25% of 184 children died) (Hill and Kaplan 1988: 798). For children under two years of age, 100% of the four whose mothers died, also died (contrasted with 33% mortality for children under two whose mothers remained alive). The decision to terminate investment in a fatherless or motherless child, sooner rather than later, can be seen as rational. But why ever smother (e.g., Early and Peters 1990:77 for Yanamamö) or bury an infant alive (a very widespread practice throughout the Amazon, Gregor 1985:89 for the Mehinacu; Hill and Hurtado 1996 for Ache; Milton p.c. 1991 for the Arawete; Wagley 1977:137 for the Tapirape)? Why this shift in emphasis away from such default strategies as abandonment to either relatives or to "the kindness of strangers"?

The answer I think must be a culturally mediated, and also common sense, assessment of what use abandonment could possibly be. If in small, isolated villages, someone was going to take on responsibility for an unwanted child (see Biocca 1971 for cases involving a grandmother, a sister-in-law, and a captured woman) they would have made themselves known. Furthermore, fertility is high and people tend to have as many children as they want. In addition, stringent ecological conditions forestall abandonment. Whether lying on the forest floor or hanging from trees (the early European custom), no infant could survive long within the Amazonian context; any infant left unattended would soon die from the bites of stinging insects (see Hill and Kaplan 1988; Hurtado et al. 1985) or from predation. Jaguars in this area are a major source of mortality—even for adult males. An infant left in the forest would not only be doomed but would "condition" jaguars to a small human search image, increasing the predation hazard for wanted children as well. (A dissatisfied child may threaten parents with going off into the forest to be eaten by a jaguar, cited in Johnson 1981:60). If Amazonian infanticide rates seem incredibly high, one must take into account ecological conditions that forestall European-style child abandonment.

Once a tradition of infanticide is developed, customs encouraging psychological distancing between mother and neonate become institutionalized.[19] Hence even as conditions become altered (e.g., by settlement) infanticide is more likely to remain in the cultural repertoire than if mother-infant bonding were encouraged from the outset (as it currently is in delivery rooms in progressive modern hospitals). Beliefs which withhold full human identity to newborns until after some specific milestone or ritual (baby takes food; cries; receives a soul; receives a name—the traditional Greek "amphidromia" ceremony comes to mind) or customs which transfer the responsibility for survival to the infant (very different from our own culture where parents hold themselves responsible for infant survival) illustrate ways of looking at the world which facilitate infanticide. Hence even after ecological conditions have changed, infanticide may be more possible than in cultures where mother-infant bonding is promoted with little delay or where newborns are regarded as fully "human." Where psychological distancing from the newborn is culturally entrenched, parents are more likely to resort to infanticide as an option rather than inventing new alternatives for mitigating costs of parental effort. Where other alternatives (e.g., giving children away to relatives or unrelated childless adults) also exist, one or the other traditions may become more

emphasized. For example, increased contact between native South Americans and outsiders from urban areas has created many more opportunities for Indians to give children away. At the same time, infanticide has been becoming less common (Bugos and McCarthy 1984). An obvious conclusion from this analysis is that high rates of infanticide are inversely correlated with alternative opportunities to reduce parental effort.

Acknowledgments. I thank L. Betzig, M. Borgerhoff Mulder, J. Chisholm, M. Daly, B. Hanawalt, K. Hill, D. Judge, S. Pomeroy, and M. Wilson for valuable criticisms. R. C. Bailey, L. Cronk, K. Hill, M. Borgerhoff Mulder, and N. Peacock provided unpublished data. I thank Alexander Harcourt, Volker Sommer and Ekhart Voland for references. I am particularly grateful to Fred vom Saal, Bruce Svare and Stephano Parmigiani for soliciting this overview, originally prepared for the 1990 Erice Conference on The Protection and Abuse of Infants. I thank Doris and Gene Minor for bibliographic and other assistance. Finally I thank Lupe de la Concha for permitting me to delegate some of my own maternal responsibilities.

NOTES

1. This review was prepared for the conference on "The protection and abuse of infants" organized by S. Parmigiani, B. Svare, and F. vom Saal at the Ettore Majorana Centre for Scientific Culture, Erice, Sicily, June 13–20, 1990. A previous version appears in the proceedings of that conference entitled *Infanticide and Parental Care*, edited by S. Parmigiani and Fred vom Saal and published by Harwood Academic Publishers. This revised version is reprinted with the permission of Harwood Academic Publishers.

2. Whether individuals are primarily motivated by a desire to perpetuate a biological lineage (i.e., reproductive success) or whether parental investment strategies are geared to perpetuation of the social or economic status of a family or household (containing affines and adopted members) is not always clear. Perhaps this is because over past generations these two outcomes have been so closely interconnected. Other ideological factors influencing cultural attitudes toward children are clearly important, but beyond the scope of this paper.

3. Stephen Lock (1990:397) discusses the case of a mother who risks her life for her unborn child. A twenty-weeks pregnant woman informed by her doctor that she has cancer of the cervix must choose between immediate treatment and sacrifice of the pregnancy with an 80 percent chance of complete cure versus delayed treatment until the baby could survive with only a 10% chance of cure. The mother opted to save the baby.

4. It is important to note that I do not consider here the infant's "point of view." Nor do I address ethical implications of the behaviors I describe. These are separate issues.

5. The primary intent of the Roussel law was to protect infants from the worst abuses of commercial wet-nursing.

6. That is, females remain in their natal group while males migrate away to breed.

7. After the Augustan period, some of these enslaved wet-nurses would have been abandoned daughters who had been reared by "foster parents" and subsequently sold. "Foster parents" in this context are in fact slave dealers (Pomeroy 1984:138).

8. According to Johansson (1987b), fixed incomes among continental elites coincided with a new enlightenment ethic which called for parents to treat children equally. Anxious to maintain their high social status, these parents reduced fertility since only by producing few children could they both treat heirs equally and provide them large legacies.

9. Note that Lewis disagrees with both Stone (1977) and Trumbach (1978) over how late British women continued to use wet-nurses. Although Trumbach assumed that most aristocratic women were breastfeeding their own infants by 1780, the data from Lewis' sample causes her to assume that wet-nursing continued much later, and she can come up with no other feasible explanation for short birth intervals. "While there may well have been more women breastfeeding by the 1780s than in earlier generations, it had become by no means a uniform practice . . ." (Lewis 1986:209). Some women—apparently fully aware of the contraceptive effects of breastfeeding—adjusted their use of wet-nurses accordingly—using a wet-nurse with the first children and breastfeeding later ones for long periods so as to deliberately avoid additional impregnations (Lewis 1986:212).

10. But note for the reasons given in footnote 9, Stone would probably not concur with my assessment of the role of wet-nurses in maintaining this differential—at least not for Britain.

11. We can not of course rule out the alternative hypothesis that these sons were simply more vulnerable to harsh conditions.

12. One out of three Ghanian women and 40% of Liberian women between the ages of fifteen and thirty-four had a child living in another household. Forty-six percent of Sierra Leonian women aged thirty to thirty-four fostered children out. These figures derive from interview data reported in Isiugo-Abanihe 1985; see also Page 1989: Table 399.1 for similar data from Cameroon, Lesotho, and Ivory Coast; slightly lower levels of fostering out exist in Kenya, Nigeria, and Sudan.

13. Although it is commonly argued that the facultative withholding of maternal investment proves that maternal responses must be "socially constructed" rather than "biological" in origin (e.g., Badinter 1980; Schepher-Hughes 1985), this conclusion is based on a misunderstanding of what an evolutionary approach means (Hrdy 1990).

14. The notion of violence is apparently crucial to the moral condemnation of infanticide, as lethal levels of child neglect in urban and shantytown areas of the same part of the world (Schepher-Hughes 1985; Gruson 1990) are not so condemned.

15. There is an obvious reporting problem here. Anthropologists tend to go to greater lengths to determine that neonatal deaths are or are not due to infanticide in societies where infanticide is thought to be an important phenomenon or in areas where it is already the subject of debate—as it is for Amazonia (e.g., the famous debate begun by Divale and Harris 1976 and still ongoing; Chagnon 1983; Early and Peters 1990). Where infanticide rates are near zero, the matter is not pursued in demographic interviews with the results that investigators then hesitate to publish a rate of infanticide: they assume it is very low, but don't know it for sure.

16. The Eipo and Ache rates may seem unbelievably high to some. For example, in a now famous computer simulated analysis, Schrire and Steiger (1974) demonstrated that if even 8 percent of female births are terminated through infanticide the practice will lead to extinction of the population. And indeed, few would like to argue that such high infanticide rates represent a stable situation. Nevertheless, one flaw in such critiques is the assumption that children killed and those kept have equivalent survival rates. Children killed are often those whose survival prospects are in any event compromised.

17. If the data were comparably quantitative, rates of infanticide per live birth would probably be at least as high for those areas of early China and North India which practiced female-biased infanticide. In particular, in some nineteenth-century North Indian clans, no daughter was ever allowed to live (Cave-Brown 1857; Parry 1979; Miller 1981; Dickemann 1979b). Obviously, such stringent preference for sons would yield infanticide rates on the order of 50%. In spite of the greater public outcry today (Hull 1990; Rao 1986), the contemporary frequency of female foeticide and infanticide in India and China is almost certainly lower than historically they have been.

18. These generalizations, entrenched as they are in the literature on Africa, should nevertheless be regarded with caution (see especially critique by Turke 1989). Following the Caldwells, Draper, Page, and others I stress the high value placed on children and the prevalence in Africa of fostering. Yet there are signals in the literature that this story may be more complicated. Levine and Levine (1981) cite a Gusii saying that "another woman's child is like cold mucus," referring to something unattractive which clings. Furthermore, the Levines reported that five of eight children under the age of five who died were either illegitimate or were being reared by grandmothers. In short, although there is general agreement that African children are being reared by farflung assemblages of relatives and childless nonrelatives, and that this "complex web of dependency weakens the relations between the number of children the woman bears and the number she supports" (Caldwell and Caldwell 1990), we need more information on precisely which individuals comprise this web, and how much each actually provides to their charges. At the same time, unpublished information for Yanamamö and other South

American tribes (personal communication from Napoleon Chagnon) indicates that there is a great deal of adoption of unwanted children by relatives, which may in fact resemble fostering.

19. In addition to cultural customs, individual decisions, or institutional policies can have profound effects on the development of mother-infant bonds For example, practices which discourage prolonged close contact between mothers and infants in the days or months after birth weaken maternal attachment to the infant while customs (such as breastfeeding or rooming-in) enhance it. Rachel Fuchs provides a tantalizing illustration of this point from her study of child abandonment by nineteenth-century French mothers giving birth in a government-sponsored hospital for indigent women. Those mothers who spent eight days or more nursing their infants were significantly less likely to decide to give the baby up when they left the hospital than did mothers who spent less than eight days in association with the new baby (Fuchs 1987:65).

40

Mainstreaming Medea

SARAH BLAFFER HRDY

This review grew out of the ashes of a failed effort to use archival sources from eighteenth-century France to quantify the amount mothers and fathers from different socioeconomic backgrounds were willing to pay wet nurses to nurture sons versus daughters. Inspired by Mildred Dickemann's extraordinary essays interpreting son preference in stratified Asian societies, and, like Dickemann, extending a hypothesis originally proposed by Trivers and Willard (1973), I postulated that a general preference for sons over daughters found through much of the Western world would be exaggerated among elites and reversed among the poor.

Rooted in evolutionary theory, the Trivers-Willard hypothesis (and subsequent refinements of it) was based on the expectation that sons, through sequential monogamy, polygyny, and concubinage, would be better able to translate the advantages of privileged upbringing and high status into reproductive success than would daughters. For daughters, ovulation, gestation, and lactation would set a ceiling on reproductive success, even though under some circumstances social status and access to resources might correlate with reproductive success among women as well.

For this reason, I anticipated complications in the stratified societies of eighteenth-century Europe. Compared with more egalitarian traditional societies, celibacy, reproductive failure, and high infant mortality among the dispossessed would contrast sharply with the high fertility of the advantaged who used wet nurses and thereby reaped the reproductive benefits of short birth intervals and high infant survivorship. These patterns would have had to augment variance in female reproductive success. Yet even when the discrepancy between male and female variance in reproductive success is less pronounced than commonly supposed, preferences for sons can persist. This implies that other factors are at work. Recently, attention has turned to these other factors, especially the greater capacity of sons to enhance the value of local resources (Gowaty and Lennartz 1985; Sieff 1990) by maintaining their lineage's hold over family possessions (Hrdy and Judge 1993), as well as the relative capacities of sons versus daughters to pay back parents for the cost of rearing them (Sieff 1990).

Wishing to learn more about parental preferences, I consulted the Archives of L'Assistance Publique in Paris. There I found such treasures as Anne Françoise Gou Delaunay's register of infants placed among wet nurses between 1732 and 1735.[1] This remarkable *recommandaresse* (a woman who earns her living matchmaking nurslings with nurses) had noted the sex and name of each infant, the name of the parents, and her certification specifying the qualifications of the wet nurse with whom the baby was placed. But alas, from this point on, further payments and such correspondence as there was passed directly between parents and the wet nurse. Only in the case of infants whose expenses were no longer paid for by their parents, but taken over by the state, could I find (in the extraordinarily detailed *Direction des Nourrices*)[2] systematic long-term records of transactions from placement of baby with the wet nurse to either death or retrieval of the infant. Since I was interested in parental, not governmental, decisions, these large samples of abandoned infants and orphans were of little use for studying parental investment decisions.

In order to reconstruct histories of infants paid for by parents, what was needed were household diaries and correspondence, such as Christiane Klapisch-Zuber has used to such advantage for Renaissance Italy. But it was sobering to note that locating and studying household records, and correlating information they contain with local tax surveys, censuses, and birth and death records, is a life's work.

Not accidentally, therefore, it was at roughly this time that I embarked, in collaboration with Debra Judge, on an in-depth study of American testators. For although we were forced to focus on transfers of resources to offspring that take place during only one life phase, after the parents' deaths, at least among the musty probate files we could obtain quantitative information from centralized archives for large samples of individuals spanning quite different economic and social circumstances over several centuries (Judge and Hrdy 1992; Judge 1996; Judge and Hrdy 1996).

As originally defined by Trivers (1972), parental investment refers to any investment by the parent that increases the offspring's chance of survival and eventual reproductive success at the expense of the parent's ability to invest in other offspring. Researchers have pointed out how difficult it is to quantify the time, energy, and risk that men and women commit to reproduction, and to compare costs from one domain to another (Knapton 1984). More problematic still is measuring how investment in one offspring detracts from the parent's ability to invest in another (Clutton-Brock 1991), and inferring causality.

Such objections have persuaded many researchers to focus instead on measurable contributions from parent to offspring, often referred to as "parental care." Here, then, is the central trade-off researchers in this area face: Do we confine investigation to what is readily quantifiable (e.g., the amount of a legacy; how much was paid to a wet nurse)? Or do we range more broadly so as to include the complex, interactive, and often unmeasurable "parental investment strategies" that individuals devise and gradually parcel out in response to a lifetime of imperfectly predictable economic events and demographic contingencies?

For humans, at least, I concur with Dickemann that Trivers's initial insight into how parents weigh investment in one particular off-spring against parental well-being, family status, and the potential to invest in other offspring comes close to the mark. For this reason, at this early stage of our understanding I advocate combining attempts to measure costs of parental care with "thicker description" of the local ecological and cultural contexts within which parental logic plays itself out in observable "decisions."

Comprehending the conservative and bet-hedging strategies parents devise will require researchers to combine practically quantifiable measures of "parental care" with more subjective, ethnographically, ecologically, and historically based analyses. Such a tack assumes, as Trivers initially proposed, that parents do take into account implications for their own survival and future reproduction, as well as the prosperity of other offspring and long-term prospects for the lineage, when making decisions about investing in a particular infant. Testing these assumptions at a psychological level would be a key area for future research.

In the process of discovering limitations to the theory and the data available to me, I remained fascinated by the eighteenth-century traffic in European babies. Across France, Italy, Spain, and Russia, detailed archival records document streams of babies, many of them flowing from the city out to wet nurses in the country in one direction, and from poor peasant households in the countryside into urban foundling homes. (The fantastical illustrations of Maurice Sendak's ominous classic *Outside over There* come to mind—columns of babies floating mysteriously over bridges and down paths.) Rates of infant mortality in the hospitals and foundling homes where such babies ended up have to be among the highest in human history and prehistory, in extreme cases, climbing to 80% or higher.

Many historians actually suggested that wet nurses and foundling homes provided a legally sanctioned form of infanticide available to parents who hired these "angelmakers" or abandoned their babies in specially designed rotating crèches that guaranteed anonymity. (See, Sherwood 1988, chap. 8 for an excellent discussion of whether mortality in such depositories could be construed as legalized infanticide.) More recently, in the wake of John Boswell's monumental scholarship in *The Kindness of Strangers*, attention shifted from the murderous intentions of parents to the altruism of allomaternal "volunteers."

Yet such explanations relied on assumptions that strike Darwinians as odd. Hence, when Fred vom Saal asked me to present an overview of human infanticide at the 1990 Erice Conference on the Protection and Abuse of Infants (Parmigiani and vom Saal 1994), out came instead an essay on this bizarre traffic in babies. In it, I began to identify and describe the wide range of tactics parents used to mitigate the costs of rearing human infants. Across the entire span of human history, such "mitigating behaviors" must have been both more common and also demographically more significant than the more notorious parental practice of infanticide—which even if not necessarily better documented is certainly much more often discussed.

The resulting essay calls attention to the fact that families in a position to contract with wet nurses on advantageous terms were in a position to produce a large number of surviving young without compromising their legitimacy within monogamous marriage/inheritance systems. Such parents imported carefully screened and monitored wet nurses into their homes and tried to hire only newly delivered, healthy wet nurses—practices that ensured high rates of survivorship for infants wet-nursed under these conditions.

Freed from lactation, a single legal wife could ovulate again within a few months of giving birth. Infants were born fast and furious—annually during the mother's prime reproductive years. In the wake of a hyperfertility that tripled or quadrupled the typical clutch size that Pleistocene mothers would have been adapted for (perhaps four to five babies in a lifetime), these "privileged" women endured a range of problems ranging from chronic anemia to prolapsed uteruses. Their plight should alert us to the identities of the prime movers (if not the only beneficiaries) from relieving wives of the "drudgery" of nursing: these were most likely husbands, patrilines, and grandparents.

It was typically when hired wet nurses lived at greater distances from the household that survivorship of wet-nursed charges started to decline in line with the amount paid out. The farther away from urban areas, the cheaper were the wet nurses, but the trip was also longer and more arduous, and supervision impossible. Infant mortality rates rose inversely with the amount paid out and with the payments to the wet nurse, but this mortality was offset by enhanced fertility in mothers who, freed from lactation, soon ovulated again.

An obvious prediction of this model is that these wives of butchers and artisans enjoyed (suffered, might be a better word) higher reproductive success than did wives in the same borderline economic position where the wife's work was also essential but who nursed their offspring while working and presumably gave birth at slower intervals. The rub at present is the dearth of records for working mothers not using wet nurses; I could not locate any.

Out-and-out losers (apart from infants, who even if they survived, one assumes must have suffered psychologically from ruptured attachments) were the wet nurses, whose limited options in life put them in a biologically lose-lose predicament, combining very low survival rates for their own offspring with very low fertility caused by prolonged suckling of the offspring of others.

By visualizing wet nursing as one set of strategies along a continuum of strategies for mitigating the heavy costs of maternal effort among humans, and by placing such "mitigating strategies" in a Darwinian framework, specific predictions are generated. Hopefully, future historians will be sufficiently challenged by the notion of "mitigating strategies" to reconstruct measures of their costs and relate them to reproductive outcomes for individuals. Does there actually exist a positive linear correlation between parental outlays for wet nursing and infant survival outcomes, as suggested in this essay (Figure 39.1)? Are current economic conditions within the family, or future reproductive prospects of the mother, actually better predictors of parental decisions to abandon infants than the survival rates of infants at foundling homes? Such predictions are empirically testable if only the appropriate records can be located. Dealing with the mentally and emotionally consuming construct of "parental investment" will, however, be more problematic.

Acknowledgments. Thanks to Monique Borgerhoff Mulder, Debra Judge, Mary Towner, George Williams, and Dan Hrdy for criticisms, to Peter Riviere for correction of errors, and to Laura Betzig for encouragement.

NOTES

1. Archives de l'Assistance Publique. #283. Enfants trouvés. Registre pour Anne Françoise Gou Delaunay, l'une des quatre Recomanderesses de la Ville et fauxbourgs de Paris, Juillet 1732–Mai 1735. Avec, au premier feuillet, la declaration du Roy portant reglement pour les recommanderesses et les nourrices, donné a Versailles le 29 Janvier 1715.

2. Archives de l'Assistance Publique, Paris. #224. *Direction des Nourrices.* Service exterieur. Payement des mois de nourrice et dépenses accessoires Registre d'Epernay.

References

Abramson, P. R., and I. W. Handschumacher. 1978. The Mosher sex guilt scale and the college population: A methodological note. *Journal of Personality Assessment* 42:6. [20]

Abramson, P. R., and D. L. Mosher. 1979. An empirical investigation of experimentally induced masturbatory fantasies. *Archives of Sexual Behavior* 8:27–39. [20]

Adair, L. S., B. Popkin, and D. Guilkey. 1993. The duration of breast-feeding: How is it affected by biological, sociodemographic, health sector, and food industry factors? *Demography* 30:63–80. [8]

Akin, K. Gillogly. 1983. Changes in infant care and feeding practices in East Kwaio, Malatia. Paper presented at Symposium on Infant Care and Feeding in Oceania, Annual Meeting of the Association of Social Anthropology in Oceania, March 9–13. [39]

Akroyd, Joyce. 1959. Women in feudal Japan. Transactions, *Asiatic Society of Japan*, 3d series, no. 7:31–68. [29]

Alatalo, R. V., A. Lundberg, and C. Glynn. 1986. Female pied flycatchers choose territory quality and note male characteristics. *Nature* 323:152–53. [11]

Alatalo, R. V., A. Lundberg, and K. Stahlbrandt. 1982. Why do pied flycatchers mate with already-mated males? *Animal Behaviour* 30:585–93. [11]

———. 1984. Female mate choice in the pied flycatcher *Ficedula hypoleuca*. *Behavioural Ecology and Sociobiology* 14:253–261. [11]

Albert, Bruce. 1989. Yanomamö "violence": Inclusive fitness or ethnographer's representation? *Current Anthropology* 30:637–40. [10]

Alcock, John. 1984. *Animal behavior*. Sunderland, Mass.: Sinauer. [24]

———. 1989. *Animal behavior*, 4th ed. Sunderland, Mass.: Sinauer. [35]

Alcock, John, and Paul Sherman. 1994. The utility of the proximate-ultimate distinction in ethology. *Ethology* 96:58–62. [15]

Ales, Catherine. 1984. Violence et ordre social dans une societe amazonienne: Les Yanomamö du Venezuela. *Etudes Rurales* 95–96:89–114. [10]

Alexander, Richard D. 1974. The evolution of social behavior. *Annual Review of Ecology and Systematics* 5:325–83. [13, 29, 37, 39]

———. 1975. The search for a general theory of behavior. *Behavioral Science* 20:77–100. [24, 35]

———. 1979. *Darwinism and human affairs*. Seattle: University of Washington Press. [1, 9, 15, 24, 33]

———. 1985. Evolution and human moral systems. *Zygon* 1:27–42. [9]

———. 1986. Ostracism and indirect reciprocity: The reproductive significance of humor. *Ethology and Sociobiology* 7:105–22. [24]

———. *The biology of moral systems*. Hawthorne, N.Y.: Aldine–de Gruyter. [1, 9, 15, 24]

———. 1988. Evolutionary approaches to human behavior: What does the future hold? In L. Betzig et al. (eds.), *Human reproductive behaviour*, pp. 317–41, Cambridge: Cambridge University Press. [15]

———. 1989. The evolution of the human psyche. In P. Mellars and C. Stringer (eds.), *The human revolution*, pp. 455–513. Princeton, N.J.: Princeton University Press. [15, 24]

———. 1990. Epigenetic rules and Darwinian algorithms. *Ethology and Sociobiology* 11:241–303. [15]

Alexander, Richard D., and Gerald Borgia. 1978. Group selection, altruism, and the levels of organization of life. *Annual Reviews of Ecology and Systematics* 9:449–74. [9]

———. 1979. On the origin and basis of the male-female phenomenon. In M. Blum and N. Blum (eds.), *Sexual selection and reproductive competition in insects*, pp. 417–40. New York: Academic Press. [37]

Alexander, Richard D., John H. Hoogland, Richard D. Howard, Katharine M. Noonan, and Paul W. Sherman. 1979. Sexual dimorphisms and breeding systems in pinnipeds, ungulates, primates and humans. In N. A. Chagnon and W. Irons (eds.), *Evolutionary biology and human social behavior: An anthropological perspective*, pp. 402–35. North Scituate, Mass.: Duxbury Press. [1, 24, 33, 36]

Alexander, Richard D., and Katherine Noonan. 1979. Concealment of ovulation, parental care, and human social evolution. In N. A. Chagnon and W. Irons (eds.), *Evolutionary biology and human social behavior: An anthropological perspective,* pp. 436–53. North Scituate, Mass.: Duxbury Press. [1, 18, 24]

Alloula, Malek. 1986. *The colonial harem,* trans. M. and W. Godzich. Minneapolis: University of Minnesota Press. [30]

Altmann, Jeanne. 1980. *Baboon mothers and infants.* Cambridge, Mass.: Harvard University Press. [8]

The numbers in brackets denote the chapters where references appear.

Altmann, Stuart A., S. F. Wagner, and S. Lenington. 1977. Two models for the evolution of polygyny. *Behavioral Ecology and Sociobiology* 2:397–410. [11]

Altorki, S. 1980. Milk-kinship in Arab society: An unexplored problem in the ethnography of marriage. *Ethnology* 19:233–43. [39]

Alvard, Michael. 1993. Testing the "ecologically noble savage" hypothesis: Interspecific prey choice by Piro hunters, Amazonian Peru. *Human Ecology* 2:335–87. [1]

Anderson, C. M. 1986. Female age: Male preference and reproductive success in primates. *International Journal of Primatology* 7:305–26. [18]

Anderson, Judith L., and Charles B. Crawford. 1993. Trivers-Willard rules for sex allocation. *Human Nature* 4:137–74. [1]

Anderson, Judith L., Charles B. Crawford, Joanne Nadeau, and Tracy Lindberg. 1992. Was the Duchess of Windsor right? A cross-cultural review of the socioecology of ideals of female body shape. *Ethology and Sociobiology* 13:197–227. [1]

Anderson, Roy, and Robert May. 1991. *Infectious diseases of humans.* New York: Oxford University Press. [1]

Andersson, M., and J. R. Krebs. 1978. On the evolution of hoarding behaviour. *Animal Behaviour* 26:707–11. [2]

Antonovics, J. 1987. The evolutionary dis-synthesis: Which bottles for which wine? *American Naturalist* 129:321–31. [15]

Antoun, Richard T. 1968. On the modesty of women in Arab Muslim villages: A study in the accommodation of traditions. *American Anthropologist* 70:671–97. [29]

Arbuthnott, J. 1710. An argument for divine providence, taken from the constant regularity observed in the births of both sexes. *Philosophical Transactions* [of the Royal Society, London] 27 for 1710, 1711, and 1712:186–90. [31]

Aristotle. *Politics,* trans. by B. Jowett. In R. McKern (ed.), *The basic works of Aristotle,* pp. 1113–316. New York: Random House, 1941. [29]

Armitage, Kenneth B. 1986. Marmot polygyny revisited: Determinants of male and female reproductive strategies. In D. Rubenstein and R. Wrangham (eds.), *Ecological aspects of social evolution,* pp. 303–31. Princeton, N.J.: Princeton University Press. [11]

Armstrong, D. P. 1991. Levels of cause and effect as organizing principles for research in animal behavior. *Canadian Journal of Zoology* 69:823–29. [15]

Arndt, W. B., J. Foehl, and F. E. Good. 1985. Specific sexual fantasy themes: A multidimensional study. *Journal of Personality and Social Psychology* 48:472–80. [20]

Arnqvist, Göran, and Locke Rowe. 1996. Conflicts of interests between the sexes: A morphological adaptation for control of mating in a female insect. *Proceedings of the Royal Society of London, B* 261:123–127. [25]

Arnqvist, Göran, and D. Wooster. 1995. Meta-analysis: Synthesizing research findings in ecology and evolution. *Trends in Ecology and Evolution* 10:236–40. [28]

Asakawa, Kan-ichi, ed. 1955. *The documents of Iriki,* 2d ed. Tokyo: Japan Society for the Promotion of Science. [29]

Auerbach, K. G. 1981. Extraordinary breast feeding: Relactation/induced lactation. *Journal of Tropical Pediatrics* 27:52–55. [39]

Auerbach, K. G., and J. L. Avery. 1981. Induced lactation: A study of adoptive nursing by 240 women. *American Journal of Diseases of Children* 135:340–43. [39]

Augustine. 1966. *Selected sermons,* transl. by Quincy Howe. New York: Holt, Rinehart and Winston. [37]

Aunger, Robert. 1994. Are food avoidances maladaptive in the Ituri forest of Zaire? *Journal of Anthropological Research* 50:277–310. [1]

———. 1995. On ethnography: Storytelling or science? *Current Anthropology* 36:97–130. [1]

———. 1996. Acculturation and persistence of traditional food avoidances in the Ituri forest of Zaire. *Human Organization* 55. [1]

Austad, Steve. 1993. Ovarian aging: An evolutionary perspective. *Experimental Gerontology.* [14]

Axelrod, Robert. 1984. *The evolution of cooperation.* New York: Basic Books. [9, 26]

Axelrod, Robert, and William D. Hamilton. 1981. The evolution of cooperation. *Science* 211:1385–90. [1, 9, 15, 26]

Bachrach, C. A. 1983. Children in families: Characteristics of biological, step-, and adopted children. *Journal of Marriage and the Family* 45:171–79. [16]

Bachrach, C. A., K. S. Stolley, and K. A. London. 1992. Relinquishment of premarital births: Evidence from national survey data. *Family Planning Perspectives* 24:27–32. [39]

Bacon, Alice. 1902. *Japanese girls and women.* Boston: Houghton, Mifflin. [29]

Bacon-Smith, Camille. 1992. *Enterprising women: Television fandom and the creation of popular myth.* Philadelphia: University of Pennsylvania Press. [21]

Badcock, Christopher. 1991. *Evolution and human behavior: An introduction to human sociobiology.* Oxford: Basil Blackwell. [1]

Badinter, E. 1980. *L'Amour en plus.* Paris: Flammarion. [39]

Bailey, F. G. 1969. *Strategems and spoils.* New York: Schocken Books. [9]

Bailey, J. Michael, Steven Gaulin, Yvonne Agyei, and Brian Gladue. 1994. Effects of gender and sexual orientation on evolutionarily relevant aspects of human mating psychology. *Journal of Personality and Social Psychology* 66:1081–93. [1]

Bailey, Robert. 1977. Variations in the live-birth sex ratio. Manuscript. [29]

———. The demography of foragers and farmers in the Ituri forest. Paper presented at the 88th annual meeting of the American Anthropological Association, Washington D.C. [39]

———. 1991. *The behavioral ecology of Efe Pygmy men in the Ituri forest, Zaire.* Ann Arbor: University of Michigan Museum of Anthropology. [1]

Bailey, Robert, Mark Jenike, Peter Ellison, Gillian Bentley, Alisa Harrigan, and Nadine Peacock. 1992. The ecology of birth seasonality among agriculturalists in central Africa. *Journal of Biosocial Science* 24:393–412. [1]

Baker, Robin, and Mark A. Bellis. 1988. "Kamikaze" sperm in mammals? *Animal Behaviour* 36:937–80. [1]

———. 1989. Number of sperm in human ejaculates varies in accordance with sperm competition. *Animal Behaviour* 37:867–69. [1]

———. 1993a. Elaboration of the kamikaze sperm hypothesis: A reply to Harcourt. *Animal Behaviour* 46:865–67. [1]

———. 1993b. Human sperm competition: Ejaculate manipulation by females and a function for the female orgasm. *Animal Behaviour* 46:861–86. [1]

———. 1995. *Human sperm competition: Copulation, masturbation and infidelity.* London: Chapman and Hall. [1]

Balsdon, J. 1962. *Roman women.* London: The Bodley Head. [37]

Bancroft, J. 1984. Hormones and human sexual behavior. *Journal of Sex and Marital Therapy* 10:3–27. [20]

Barash, David. 1977. *Sociobiology and behavior.* New York: Elsevier. [9, 22]

Barclay, A. M. 1973. Sexual fantasies in men and women. *Medical Aspects of Human Sexuality* 7:205–16. [20]

Barkow, Jerome H. 1977. Conformity to ethos and reproductive success in two Hausa communities: An empirical evalution. *Ethos* 5:409–25. [4]

———. 1984. The distance between genes and culture. *Journal of Anthropological Research* 40:367–79. [16]

———. 1989. *Darwin, sex, and status.* Toronto: University of Toronto Press. [1]

Barron, F. 1963. *Creativity and psychological health.* Amsterdam: Van Nostrand. [18]

Barry, H. 1981. Uses and limitations of ethnographic descriptions. In R. Monroe et al. (eds.), *Handbook of Cross-cultural human development,* pp. 91–111. New York: Garland Press. [33]

Barry, H., M. K. Bacon, and I. L. Child. 1957. A cross-cultural study of some sex differences in socialization. *Journal of Abnormal and Social Psychology* 55:327–32. [33]

Barry, H., L. Josephson, E. Lauer, and C. Marshall. 1976. Traits inculcated in childhood: Cross-cultural codes 5. *Ethnology* 15:83–114. [33]

Barth, Frederick. 1966. Models of social organization. Royal Anthropological Institute, Occasional Paper no. 23. London: Royal Anthropological Institute. [9]

———. 1967. On the study of social change. *American Anthropologist* 69:661–69. [9]

Basham, A. L. 1967. *The wonder that was India: A survey of the history and culture of the Indian sub-continent before the coming of the Muslims,* 3d ed. London: Sidgwick and Jackson. [29]

Bateman, A. J. 1948. Intrasexual selection in *Drosophila. Heredity* 2:349–68. [18, 33, 37]

Bateson, Patrick, ed. 1983. *Mate choice.* Cambridge: Cambridge University Press. [18]

Batten, Mary. 1992. *Sexual strategies.* New York: Putnam. [1]

Batto, Bernard F. 1974. *Studies on the women at Mari.* Baltimore, Md.: Johns Hopkins University Press. [29]

Beall, C. M., and M. C. Goldstein. 1981. Tibetan fraternal polyandry: A test of sociobiological theory. *American Anthropologist* 83:5–12. [31]

Becker, Gary. 1976. Altruism, egoism, and genetic fitness: Economics and sociobiology. *Journal of Economic Literature* 14:817–26. [1]

———. 1981. *A treatise on the family.* Cambridge, Mass.: Harvard University Press. [1]

Becker, S., A. Chowdhury, and H. Leridon. 1986. Seasonal patterns of reproduction in Matlab, Bangladesh. *Population Studies* 40:457–72. [1]

Beckerman, Stephen. 1983. Carpe diem: An optimal foraging approach to Bari fishing and hunting. In R. Hames and W. Vickers (eds.), *Adaptive responses of native Amazoniana,* pp. 269–99. New York: Academic Press. [1, 5]

Bell, G., and V. Koufopanou. 1986. The cost of reproduction. In R. Dawkins (ed.), *Oxford surveys in evolutionary biology*, pp. 83–131. Oxford: Oxford University Press. [13]

Bellis, Mark A., and Robin Baker. 1990. Do females promote sperm competition: Data for humans. *Animal Behaviour* 40:997–99. [1]

Belsky, Jay, and L. Steinberg. 1978. The effects of daycare: A critical review. *Child Development* 49:929–49. [39]

Belsky, Jay, L. Steinberg, and Patricia Draper. 1991. Childhood experience, interpersonal development, and reproductive strategy: An evolutionary theory of socialization. *Child Development* 62:647–70. [1]

Benshoof, L., and Randy Thornhill. 1979. The evolution of monogamy and concealed ovulation in humans. *Journal of Social and Biological Structures* 2:95–106. [24]

Bentley, Gillian, Tony Goldberg, and Grazyna Jasienska. 1993. The fertility of agricultural and non-agricultural traditional societies. *Population Studies* 47:269–81. [1]

Bereczkei, Tamas and Andras Csanaky. 1996. Mate choice, marital success, and reproduction in a modern society. *Ethology and Sociobiology* 17:17–36. [1]

Bergstrom, Theodore. 1994. Primogeniture, monogamy, and reproductive value in a stratified society. University of Michigan, Department of Economics Working Paper No. 94–10. [1]

———. 1995. On the evolution of altruistic ethical rules for siblings. *American Economic Review* 85:58–81. [1]

Bergstrom, Theodore, and Oded Stark. 1993. How can altruism prevail in an evolutionary environment? *American Economics Association Papers and Proceedings* 83:149–55. [1]

Bernstain, L., and T. Wade. 1983. Intrasexual selection and male mating strategies in baboons and macaques. *International Journal of Primatology* 4:201–35. [18]

Berté, Nancy A. 1988. Kékch'i horticultural labor exchange: Productive and reproductive implications. In L. Betzig et al. (eds), *Human reproductive behaviour*, pp. 83–96, Cambridge: Cambridge University Press. [1, 6]

Betzig, Laura. 1982. Despotism and differential reproduction: A cross-cultural correlation of conflict asymmetry, hierarchy, and degree of polygyny. *Ethology and Sociobiology* 3:209–21. [1, 37, 38]

———. 1986. *Despotism and differential reproduction: A Darwinian view of history*. Hawthorne, N.Y.: Aldine–de Gruyter. [1, 4, 9, 11, 33, 35, 37, 38]

———. 1988a. Mating and parenting in Darwinian perspective. In L. Betzig et al. (eds), *Human reproductive behaviour*, pp. 1–20. Cambridge: Cambridge University Press. [1, 37]

———. 1988b. Redistribution: Equity or exploitation? In L. Betzig et al. (eds), *Human reproductive behaviour*, pp. 49–63. Cambridge: Cambridge University Press. [1]

———. 1989a. Causes of conjugal dissolution: A cross-cultural study. *Current Anthropology* 30:654–76. [1, 19, 37]

———. 1989b. Rethinking human ethology: A response to some recent critiques. *Ethology and Sociobiology* 10:315–24. [15]

———. 1991. History. In M. Maxwell (ed.), *The sociobiological imagination*, pp. 131–40. Albany: State University of New York Press. [37]

———. 1992a. Of human bonding: Cooperation or exploitation? *Social Science Information* 31:611–42. [38]

———. 1992b. Roman monogamy. *Ethology and Sociobiology* 13:351–83. [1, 37, 38]

———. 1992c. Roman polygyny. *Ethology and Sociobiology* 13:309–49. [1, 15, 19, 28, 32, 37, 38]

———. 1993. Sex, succession, and stratification in the first six civilizations: How powerful men reproduced, passed power on to their sons, and used their power to defend their wealth, women, and children. In L. Ellis (ed.), *Social stratification and socioeconomic inequality*, pp. 37–74. New York: Praeger. [1, 28, 37, 38]

———. 1994. The point of politics. *Analyse and Kritik* 15:20–37. [38]

———. 1995. Medieval monogamy. *Journal of Family History* 20:181–215. [1, 37, 38]

———. 1996a. British polygyny. Manuscript. [1, 38].

———. 1996b. Not whether to count babies but which. In C. Crawford and D. Krebs (eds.), *Evolution and human behavior: Issues, ideas, and applications*. Hillsdale, N.J.: Erlbaum. [28]

Betzig, Laura, Monique Borgerhoff Mulder, and Paul Turke, eds. 1988. *Human reproductive behaviour*. Cambridge: Cambridge University Press. [15, 18, 33]

Betzig, Laura, and Leslie Hodgkins Lombardo. 1992. Who's pro-choice and why. *Ethology and Sociobiology* 13:49–71. [1]

Betzig, Laura, Alisa Harrigan, and Paul Turke. 1989. Childcare on Ifaluk. *Zeitschrift für Ethologie* 114:161–77. [1]

Betzig, Laura, and Paul Turke. 1986a. Food sharing on Ifaluk. *Current Anthropology* 17:397–400. [1, 6]

———. 1986b. Parental investment by sex on Ifaluk. *Ethology and Sociobiology* 7:29–37. [1]

Betzig, Laura, and Samantha Weber. 1993. Polygyny in American politics. *Politics and the Life Sciences* 12:45–52. [1]
———. 1995. Presidents preferred sons. *Politics and the Life Sciences* 14:61–64. [1]
Biezunska-Malowist, I. 1969. Les enfants-esclaves á la lumiére des papyrus. In J. Bibauw (ed.), *Homages á Marcel Renard, II*, pp. 91–96. Brussels: Revue d'Études Latines. [37]
———. 1977. *L'Esclavage dans l'Egypte gréco-romaine.* Wrocław. [37]
Biggers, J. D., C. A. Finn, and A. McLaren. 1962. Long-term reproductive performance of female mice, I: Variation of litter size with parity. *Journal of Reproductive Fertility* 3:303–12. [13]
Binmore, Ken. 1994. *Playing fair.* Cambridge, Mass.: MIT Press. [1]
Biocca, E. 1970. *Yanoama: The narrative of a white girl kidnapped by Amazonian Indians.* New York: Dutton. [9, 39]
Bird, Doug and Rebecca Bliege Bird. 1996. Contemporary shellfish gathering strategies among the Meriam of the Torres Strait Islands, Australia: Testing predictions of a central place foraging model. *Journal of Archaeological Science,* in press. [1]
Birkhead, Tim, and Anders Møller. 1992. *Sperm competition in birds: Evolutionary causes and consequences.* London: Academic Press. [1]
Blass, T. 1984. Social psychology and personality: Toward a convergence. *Journal of Personality and Social Psychology* 47:1304–9. [22]
Bledsoe, C., and U. Isiugo-Abanihe. 1989. Strategies of child fosterage among Mende grannies in Sierra Leone. In R. Lesthaeghe (ed.), *Reproduction and social organization in sub-saharan Africa,* pp. 442–74. Berkeley: University of California Press. [39]
Block, E. 1952. Quantitative morphological investigations of the follicular system in women: Variations at different ages. *Acta Anatomica* 14:108–23. [13]
Bliege Bird, Rebecca and Doug Bird. 1996. Delayed reciprocity and tolerated theft: The behavioral ecology of food sharing strategies. *Current Anthropology* 37, in press. [1]
Blurton Jones, Nicholas. 1986. Bushman birth spacing: A test for optimal interbirth intervals. *Ethology and Sociobiology* 7:91–105. [1]
Blurton Jones, Nicholas. 1987a. Bushman birth spacing: Direct tests of some simple predictions. *Ethology and Sociobiology* 8:183–204. [1, 8]
———. 1987b. Tolerated theft, suggestions about the ecology and evolution of sharing, hoarding and scrounging. *Social Science Information* 26:31–54. [6]
———. 1994. A reply to Dr. Harpending. *American Journal of Physical Anthropology* 93:391–97. [8]
Blurton Jones, Nicholas, Kristen Hawkes, and Patricia Draper. 1994. Foraging returns of !Kung adults and children: Why didn't !Kung children forage? *Journal of Anthropological Research* 50:217–48. [8]
Blurton Jones, Nicholas, Kristen Hawkes, and James O'Connell. 1989. Modelling and measuring costs of children in two foraging societies. In V. Standen and R. Foley (eds.), *Comparative socioecology* pp. 367–90. Oxford: Blackwell Scientific. [8]
———. 1991. Demography of the Hadza. Manuscript. [13]
———. 1996. The global process and local ecology: How should we explain differences between the Hadza and the !Kung? In S. Kent (ed.), *Cultural diversity among twentieth-century foragers: An African perspective.* Cambridge: Cambridge University Press. [8]
Blurton Jones, Nicholas, and Melvin Konnor. 1973. Sex differences in the behavior of London and Bushman children. In J. Crook and R. Michael (eds.), *Comparative ecology and behavior of primates,* pp. 689–750. New York: Academic Press. [33]
Blurton Jones, Nicholas, and R. M. Sibly. 1978. Testing adaptiveness of culturally determined behaviour: Do bushman women maximise their reproductive success by spacing births widely and foraging seldom? In N. Blurton Jones and V. Reynolds (eds.), *Human behaviour and adaptation* pp. 135–58. London: Taylor and Francis. [2, 7, 8]
Blurton Jones, Nicholas, L. C. Smith, James O'Connell, Kristen Hawkes, and C. L. Kamuzora. 1992. Demography of the Hadza, an increasing and high density population of savanna foragers. *American Journal of Physical Anthropology* 89:159–81. [8]
BMDP. 1985a. Statistical software manual. Berkeley: University of California Press. [11]
BMDP. 1985b. Technical report no. 80, example 4. Berkeley: University of California Press. [11]
Boehm, Christopher. 1984. *Blood revenge: The anthropology of feuding in Montenegro and other tribal societies.* Lawrence: University Press of Kansas. [9]
Bonfield, Lloyd, Richard Smith, and Keith Wrightson, eds. 1986. *The world we have gained.* Oxford: Basil Blackwell. [38]
Boone, James. 1983. Noble family structure and expansionist warfare in the late Middle Ages. In R. Dyson-Hudson and M. Little (eds.), *Rethinking human adaptation* pp. 79–96. Denver: Westview Press. [30]

————. 1986. Parental investment and elite family structure in preindustrial states: A case study of late medieval–early modern Portuguese genealogies. *American Anthropologist* 88:859–78. [1, 4, 30, 33, 35, 39]

————. 1988a. Parental investment, social subordination and population processes among the 15th and 16th century Portuguese nobility. In L. Betzig et al. (eds.), *Human reproductive behaviour,* pp. 201–19, Cambridge: Cambridge University Press. [1, 4, 30]

————. 1988b. Second- and third-generation reproductive success among the Portuguese nobility. Paper presented at the 87th annual meetings of the American Anthropological Association, Phoenix, Arizona. [39]

Booth, W. 1989. Warfare over Yanomamö Indians. *Science* 243:1138–43. [39]

Borgerhoff Mulder, Monique. 1987a. On cultural and reproductive success, with an example from the Kipsigis. *American Anthropologist* 89:617–34. [1, 4, 9, 11, 34, 35, 28]

————. 1987b. Resources and reproductive success in women, with an example from the Kipsigis. *Journal of Zoology* 213:489–505. [1, 11]

————. 1988a. Early maturing Kipsigis women have higher reproductive success than later maturing women, and cost more to marry. *Behavioral Ecology and Sociobiology* 24:145–53. [1]

————. 1988b. Is the polygyny threshold model relevant to humans? Kipsigis evidence. In C. Mascie-Taylor and A. Boyce (eds.), *Mating patterns,* pp. 209–30. Cambridge: University Press. [11, 12]

————. 1988c. Kipsigis bridewealth payments. In L. Betzig et al. (eds.), *Human reproductive behaviour,* pp. 65–82. Cambridge: Cambridge University Press. [1, 11, 18, 21, 36]

————. 1988d. Reproductive consequences of sex-biased inheritance. In V. Standon and R. Foley (eds.), *Comparative socioecology of mammals and man,* pp. 405–27. London: Basil Blackwell. [1, 32]

————. 1988e. Reproductive success in three Kipsigis cohorts. In T. H. Clutton-Brock (ed.), *Reproductive success,* pp. 419–35. Chicago: University of Chicago Press. [1, 11, 12]

————. 1989a. Menarche, menopause and reproduction in the Kipsigis of Kenya. *Journal of Biosocial Science* 21:179–92. [13].

————. 1989b. Polygyny and the extent of women's contributions to subsistence: A reply to White. *American Anthropologist* 90:179–81. [1, 2]

————. 1989c. The polygyny-fertility hypothesis: New evidence from the Kipsigis of Kenya. *Population Studies* 43:285–304. [1, 11, 12]

————. 1990. Kipsigis women's preferences for wealthy men: Evidence for female choice in mammals? *Behavioral Ecology and Sociobiology* 27:255–64. [1]

————. 1991. Human behavioral ecology. In J. R. Krebs and N. B. Davies (eds.), *Behavioural ecology: An evolutionary approach,* 3d ed., pp. 69–98. Oxford: Blackwell Scientific. [1]

————. 1992a. Reproductive decisions. In E. A. Smith and B. Winterhalder (eds.), *Evolutionary ecology and human behavior,* pp. 339–74. Hawthorne, N.Y.: Aldine–de Gruyter. [8].

————. 1992b. Women's strategies in polygynous marriage: Kipsigis, Datoga, and other East African cases. *Human Nature* 3:45–70. [11]

————. 1995. Bridewealth and its correlates: Quantifying changes over time. *Current Anthropology* 36:573–603. [1, 12]

————. 1996. Responses to environmental novelty: Changes in men's marriage strategies in a rural Kenyan community. In J. Maynard Smith (ed.), *Evolution of social behavior patterns in primates and man.* London: British Academy Press. [1, 12]

Borgerhoff Mulder, Monique, Nancy Wilmsen Thornhill, Ekhart Voland, and Peter Richerson. 1996. The place of behavioural ecology in the evolutionary social sciences. In P. Weingart et al. (eds.), *Human by nautre.* Hillsdale, N.J.: Erlbaum. [12]

Borgia, Gerald. 1979. Sexual selection and the evolution of mating systems. In M. Blum and N. Blum (eds.), *Sexual selection and reproductive competition in insects.* New York: Academic Press. [31]

Boserup, Esther. 1970. *Woman's role in economic development.* New York: St. Martin's Press. [35, 36]

Bosler, B. 1990. Underpaid, overworked and from the Philippines. *New York Times,* August 26. [39]

Boswell, John 1988. *The kindness of strangers: The abandonment of children in western Europe from late antiquity to the Renaissance.* New York: Random House. [30, 37, 39]

Bowlby, John. 1982. *Attachment.* 2d ed. New York: Basic Books. [20]

Boyd, Robert. 1988. Is the repeated prisoner's dilemma a good model of reciprocal altruism? *Ethology and Sociobiology* 9:211–22. [26]

Boyd, Robert, and Peter J. Richerson. 1980. Sociobiology, culture, and economic theory. *Journal of Economic Behavior and Organization* 1:97–121. [31]

————. 1985. *Culture and the evolutionary process.* Chicago: University of Chicago Press. [1, 2, 33, 34]

Brabin, L. 1984. Polygyny an indicator of nutritional slack in African agricultural societies. *Africa* 54:31–45. [11]

Bradie, Michael. 1995. *The secret chain: Evolution and ethics*. Albany: State University of New York Press. [1]

Bradley, Keith. 1978. Age at time of sale of female slaves. *Arethusa* 11:243–52. [37]

———. 1980. Sexual regulations in wet-nursing contracts from Roman Egypt. *Klio* 62:321–25. [37, 39]

———. 1984. *Slaves and masters in the Roman Empire: A study in social control*. Brussels: Revue d'Études Latines. [37]

———. 1986. Wet-nursing at Rome: A study in social relations. In B. Rawson (ed.), *The family in ancient Rome: New perspectives*, pp. 201–29. Ithaca, N.Y.: Cornell University Press. [37, 39]

———. 1987. On the Roman slave supply and slavebreeding. In M. Finley (ed.), *Classical slavery*. London: Frank Cass. [37]

———. 1991a. *Discovering the Roman family: Studies in Roman social history*. New York: Oxford University Press. [37]

———. 1991b. Remarriage and the structure of the upper-class Roman family. In B. Rawson (ed.), *Marriage, divorce, and children in ancient Rome*. Oxford: Clarendon. [37]

Bradsher, Keith. 1995. America's opportunity gap. *New York Times*, June 4, p. 4E. [32]

Bribiescas, Richard. 1996. Testosterone levels among Ache hunter-gatherer men. *Human Nature* 7:163–88. [1]

Brickman, J. 1978. Erotica: Sex differences in stimulus preferences and fantasy content. Ph.D. diss., University of Manitoba. [20]

Brown, Charles, and Bruce Ronnala. Relatedness and conflict over optimal group size. *Trends in Ecology and Evolution* 9:117. [6]

Brown, Charles, Mary Bomberger Brown, and Martin Shaffer. 1991. Food-sharing signals among socially foraging cliff swallows. *Animal Behaviour*. 42:551–65. [6]

Brown, Donald. 1991. *Human universals*. New York: McGraw-Hill. [26]

Brown, Jerram. 1982. Optimal group size in territorial animals. *Journal of Theoretical Biology* 95:793–810. [5]

———. 1987. *Helping and communal breeding in birds*. Princeton, N.J.: Princeton University Press. [38]

Brown, Keith. 1966. Dozoku and the ideology of descent in rural Japan. *American Anthropologist* 68:1129–51. [29]

Brown, Peter. 1988. *The body and society: Men, women and sexual renunciation in early Christianity*. New York: Columbia University Press. [37]

Brunt, P. A. 1971. *Italian manpower: 225 BC–AD 14*. Oxford: Clarendon. [37]

Bugos, Paul, and Lorraine McCarthy. 1984. Ayoreo infanticide: A case study. In G. Hausfater and S. B. Hrdy (eds.), *Infanticide* pp. 503–20. Hawthorne, N.Y.: Aldine–de Gruyter. [1, 16, 39]

Buikstra, Jane E., and Lyle W. Konigsberg. 1985. Paleodemography: Critiques and controversies. *American Anthropologist* 87:316–33. [13]

Bulatao, Ronald, and R. D. Lee, eds. 1983. *Determinants of fertility in developing countries*. New York: Academic Press. [1]

Burnstein, Eugene, Christian Crandall, and Shinobu Kitayama. 1994. Some neo-Darwinian decision rules for altruism: Weighing cues for inclusive fitness as a function of the biological importance of the decision. *Journal of Personality and Social Psychology* 67:773–89. [1]

Buss, David M. 1985. Human mate selection. *American Scientist* 73:47–51. [18]

———. 1987. Sex differences in human mate selection criteria: An evolutionary perspective. In C. Crawford et al. (eds.), *Sociobiology and psychology: Issues, ideas, applications*. Hillsdale, N.J.: Erlbaum. [18]

———. 1988a. The evolution of human intrasexual competition: Tactics of mate attraction. *Journal of Personality and Social Psychology* 54:628–61. [1, 18]

———. 1988b. From vigilance to violence: Mate guarding tactics. *Ethology and Sociobiology* 9:291–317. [1, 18, 19]

———. 1989a. Conflict between the sexes: Strategic interference and the evocation of anger and upset. *Journal of Personality and Social Psychology* 56:735–47. [1]

———. 1989b. Sex differences in human mate preferences: Evolutionary hypotheses tested in 37 cultures. *Behavioral and Brain Sciences* 12:1–49. [1, 15, 20, 22, 23]

———. 1991. Conflict in married couples: Personality predictors of anger and upset. *Journal of Personality* 59:663–88. [1]

———. 1994. *The evolution of desire: Strategies of human mating*. New York: Basic Books. [1, 19, 21]

———. 1995a. Evolutionary psychology: A new paradigm for psychological science. *Psychological Inquiry* 6:1–30. [1, 15]

———. 1995b. The future of evolutionary psychology. *Psychological Inquiry* 6:81–87. [1]

Buss, David M., and M. Barnes. 1986. Preferences in human mate selection. *Journal of Personality and Social Psychology* 50:559–70. [1, 18, 22]

Buss, David M., and Lisa Dedden. 1990. Derogation of competitors. *Journal of Social and Personal Relationships* 7:395–422. [1, 18]

Buss, David M., R. J. Larsen, D. Westen, and Jennifer Semmelroth. 1992. Sex differences in jealousy: Evolution, physiology, and psychology. *Psychological Science* 3:251–55. [1, 36]

Buss, David M., and David Schmitt. 1993. Sexual strategies theory: An evolutionary perspective on human mating. *Psychological Reviews* 100:204–32. [1, 19, 23]

Buss, David M., and Neil Malamuth, eds. 1996. *Sex, power, and conflict: Evolutionary and feminist perspectives.* New York: Oxford University Press. [1]

Cain, Mead. 1977. The economic activities of children in a village in Bangladesh. *Population and Development Review* 3:301–7. [39]

Calder, C. 1967. Breeding behavior of the roadrunner *Geococcyx californianus. Aux* 84:597–98. [18]

Caldwell, John. 1982. *Theory of fertility decline.* New York: Academic Press. [39]

Caldwell, John, and P. Caldwell. 1990. High fertility in sub-Saharan Africa. *Scientific American* 263:118–25. [39]

Campbell, Anne. 1995. A few good men: Evolutionary psychology and female adolescent aggression. *Ethology and Sociobiology* 16:99–123. [1]

Campbell, Benjamin, and Paul Leslie. 1995. Reproductive ecology of human males. *Yearbook of Physical Anthropology* 38:1–26. [1]

Campbell, Bernard, ed. 1972. *Sexual selection and the descent of man 1871–1971.* Chicago: Aldine. [9, 29]

Caraco, T. 1982. Risk-sensitivity and foraging groups. *Ecology* 62:527–31. [5]

Caraco, T., and L. Wolf. 1975. Ecological determinants of group sizes of foraging lions. *American Naturalist* 109:343–52. [5]

Carcopino, Jerome. 1940. *Daily life in ancient Rome*, trans. E. O. Lorimer. London: Routledge and Sons. [37]

———. 1958. *Passion et politique chez les Césares.* Oxford: Clarendon. [37]

Carey, M., and V. Nolan. 1975. Polygyny in indigo buntings: A hypothesis tested. *Science* 190:1296–97. [35]

Carlson, E. R., and C. E. Coleman. 1977. Experimental and motivational determinants of the richness of an induced sexual fantasy. *Journal of Sex Research* 45:528–42. [20]

Carneiro, Robert L. 1970. A theory of the origin of the state. *Science* 169:733–38. [9]

Carneiro da Cunha, Maria Manuela. 1989. To the editor. *Anthropology Newsletter* January. [10]

Caro, Timothy et al. 1994. Termination of reproduction in nonhuman and human female primates. Working Paper, Department of Biology, University of California-Davis. [14]

Carroll, Joseph. 1995. *Evolution and literary theory.* Saint Louis: University of Missouri Press. [1]

Cashdan, Elizabeth. 1980. Egalitarianism among hunters and gatherers. *American Anthropologist* 82:116–20. [26]

———. 1989. Hunters and gatherers: Economic behavior in bands. In S. Plattner (ed.), *Economic Anthropology*, pp. 21–48. Stanford, Calif: Stanford University Press. [26]

———. 1993. Attracting mates: Effects of paternal investment on mate attraction strategies. *Ethology and Sociobiology* 14:1–24. [1]

———. 1994. A sensitive period for learning about food? *Human Nature* 5:279–91. [1]

———. 1995. Hormones, sex and status in women. *Hormones and Behavior* 29:354–366. [1]

Casimir, Michael and Aparna Rao. 1995. Prestige, possessions, and progeny: Cultural goals and reproductive success among the Bakkarwal. *Human Nature* 6:241–72. [1]

Catchpole, C., B. Leisler, and H. Winkler. 1985. Polygyny in the great reed warbler, *Acrocephalus arundinaceus:* A possible case of deception. *Behavioral Ecology and Sociobiology* 12:169–80. [11]

Cavalli-Sforza, Luigi Luca, and Marcus W. Feldman. 1981. *Cultural transmission and evolution: A quantitative approach.* Princeton, N.J.: Princeton University Press. [1, 2, 3, 34]

Cavalli-Sforza, Luigi, P. Menozzi, and A. Piazza. 1994. *History and geography of human genes.* Princeton, N.J.: Princeton University Press. [28]

Cavalli-Sforza, Luigi, A. Piazza, P. Menozzi, and J. Mountain. 1988. Reconstruction of human evolution: Bringing together genetic, archaeological and linguistic data. *Proceedings of the National Academy of Sciences* 85:6002–6. [28]

Cave-Brown, J. 1857. *Indian infanticide: Its origins, progress and suppression.* London: W. H. Allen. [39]

Chagnon, Napoleon A. 1966. Yanomamö warfare, social organization and marriage alliances. Ph.D. diss., Dept. of Anthropology, University of Michigan. Ann Arbor, Mich.: UMI. [9]

———. 1968a. The culture-ecology of shifting (pioneering) cultivation among the Yanomamö Indians. *Proceedings, Eighth International Congress of Anthropological and Ethnological Sciences* 3:249–55. [9, 39]

———. 1968b. Yanomamö social organization and warfare. In M. Fried et al. (eds.), *War: The anthropology of armed conflict and aggression*, pp. 109–59. Garden City, N.Y.: Natural History Press. [9]

————. 1972. Social causes for population fissioning. In G. Harrison and A. Boyce (eds.), *The structure of human populations*, pp. 252–82. Oxford: Oxford University Press. [9]

————. 1974. *Studying the Yanomamö*. New York: Holt, Rinehart and Winston. [9]

————. 1979a. Is reproductive success equal in egalitarian societies? In N. A. Chagnon and W. Irons (eds.), *Evolutionary biology and human social behavior: An anthropological perspective*, pp. 374–402. North Scituate, Mass.: Duxbury Press. [1, 33, 37]

————. 1979b. Mate competition, favoring close kin, and village fissioning among the Yanomamö Indians. In N. A. Chagnon and W. Irons (eds.), *Evolutionary biology and human social behavior: An anthropological perspective*, pp. 86–132. North Scituate, Mass.: Duxbury Press. [1, 9]

————. 1980a. Highland New Guinea models in the South American lowlands. In R. Hames (ed.), *Working papers on South American Indians*, vol. 2, pp. 131–37. Bennington, Vt.: Bennington College. [9]

————. 1980b. Kin selection theory, kinship, marriage and fitness among the Yanomamö Indians. In G. Barlow and I. Silverberg (eds.), *Sociobiology: Beyond nature/nurture?*, pp. 545–71. Boulder, Colo.: Westview Press. [1, 35]

————. 1981. Terminological kinship, genealogical relatedness, and village fissioning among the Yanomamö Indians. In R. Alexander and D. Tinkle (eds.), *Natural selection and social behavior*, pp. 490–508. New York: Chiron Press. [1, 9]

————. 1982. Man the rule breaker. In King's College Sociobiology Group (eds.), *Current problems in sociobiology*, pp. 291–318. Cambridge: Cambridge University Press. [1, 9, 33]

————. 1988a. Life histories, blood revenge, and warfare in a tribal population. *Science*, 238:985–92. [1, 4, 37]

————. 1988b. Male Yanomamö manipulations of kinship classifications of female kin for reproductive advantage. In L. Betzig et al. (eds), *Human reproductive behaviour*, pp. 23–48. Cambridge: Cambridge University Press. [1, 9]

————. 1990. Reproductive and somatic conflicts of interest in the genesis of violence and warfare among tribesmen. In J. Haas (ed.), *The anthropology of war*, pp. 77–104. Cambridge: Cambridge University Press. [9]

————. 1992. *Yanomamö* 4th ed. New York: Holt, Rinehart and Winston. [4, 9, 37, 39]

————. 1995. L'ethnologie du deshonneur: Brief response to Lizot. *American Ethnologist*, 22:187–89. [10]

————. 1996. Chronic problems in understanding tribal violence and warfare. CIBA Foundation Symposium no. 194. [10]

Chagnon, Napoleon A., and Paul Bugos. 1979. Kin selection and conflict: An analysis of a Yanomamö ax fight. In N. A. Chagnon and W. Irons (eds.), *Evolutionary biology and human social behavior: An anthropological perspective*, pp. 213–38. North Scituate, Mass.: Duxbury Press. [1, 9]

Chagnon, Napoleon A., Mark V. Flinn, and Thomas Melancon. 1979. Sex ratio variation among the Yanomamö Indians. In N. A. Chagnon and W. Irons (eds.), *Evolutionary biology and human social behavior: An anthropological perspective*, pp. 290–320. North Scituate, Mass.: Duxbury Press. [1, 4]

Chagnon, Napoleon A., and Raymond B. Hames. 1979. Protein deficiency and tribal warfare in Amazonia: New data. *Science* 203:10–15. [9]

Chagnon, Napoleon A., and William Irons, eds. 1979. *Evolutionary biology and human social behavior: An anthropological perspective*. North Scituate, Mass.: Duxbury Press. [9]

Chamberlain, Wilt. 1991. *A view from above*. New York: Random House. [1]

Chambers-Schiller, Lee V. 1984. *Liberty, a better husband: Single women in America, the generations of 1780–1840*. New Haven, Conn.: Yale University Press. [30]

Champlin, Edward. 1991. *Final judgements: Duty and emotion in Roman wills*. Berkeley: University of California Press. [37]

Charlesworth, Brian. 1980. *Evolution in age-structured populations*. Cambridge: Cambridge University Press. [13, 14]

Charnov, Eric. 1976. Optimal foraging: The marginal value theorem. *Theoretical Population Biology* 9:129–36. [1, 2]

————. 1982. *The theory of sex allocation*. Princeton, N.J.: Princeton University Press. [1]

————. 1991. Evolution of life history variation among female mammals. *Proceedings of the National Academy of Sciences* 88:1134–37. [13]

————. 1993. *Life history invariants*. New York: Oxford University Press. [1, 8]

Cheney, Dorothy, and Robert Seyfarth. 1990. *How monkeys see the world*. Chicago: University of Chicago Press. [13]

Cheng, P., and K. Holyoak. 1985. Pragmatic reasoning schemas. *Cognitive Psychology* 17:391–416. [26]

———— 1989. On the natural selection of reasoning theories. *Cognition* 33:285–313. [26]

Cheng, P., K. Holyoak, R. Nisbett, and L. Oliver. 1986. Pragmatic versus syntactic approaches to training deductive reasoning. *Cognitive Psychology,* 18:293–328. [26]

Cherlin, Andrew. 1978. Remarriage as an incomplete institution. *American Journal of Sociology* 84:634–50. [16]

Chick, D., and S. R. Gold. 1987–88. A review of influences on sexual fantasy: Attitudes, experience, guilt and gender. *Imagination, Cognition and Personality* 7:61–76. [20]

Chisholm, James, and Victoria Burbank. 1991. Monogamy and polygyny in southeast Arnhem Land: Male coercion and female choice. *Ethology and Sociobiology* 12:291–313. [1, 12]

Christie, J. H. 1983. Female choice in the resource-defense mating system of the sand fiddler crab, *Uca pugilator. Behavioral Ecology and Sociobiology* 12:169–80. [11]

Ch'ü, T'ung-tsu. 1965. *Law and society in traditional China.* Paris: Mouton. [29]

Clark, Alice. 1989. Limitations on female life chances in rural central Gujarat. In J. Krishnamurty (ed.), *Women in colonial India,* pp. 27–51. Delhi: Oxford University Press. [30]

Clark, Colin, and Marc Mangel. 1986. The evolutionary advantages of group foraging. *Theoretical Population Biology* 30:45–74. [6]

Clark, R. D., and E. Hatfield. 1989. Gender differences in receptivity to sexual offers. *Journal of Psychology and Human Sexuality* 2:39–55. [23]

Clarke, Alice L., and Bobbi S. Low. 1992. Ecological correlates of human dispersal in 19th-century Sweden. *Animal Behaviour* 44:677–93. [1]

Clignet, R. 1970. *Many wives, many powers: Authority and power in polygynous families.* Evanston, Ill.: Northwestern University Press. [31]

Clingempeel, W. G., E. Brand, and R. Ievoli. 1984. Stepparent-stepchild relationships in stepmother and stepfather families: A multimethod study. *Family Relations* 33:465–73. [16]

Clutton-Brock, Timothy H. 1991. *The evolution of parental care.* Princeton, N.J.: Princeton University Press. [1, 8, 13, 40]

———, ed. 1988. *Reproductive success.* Chicago: University of Chicago Press. [1]

Clutton-Brock, Timothy, Fiona Guinness, and Steve Albon. 1982. *Red deer: The ecology of two sexes.* Chicago: University of Chicago Press. [33]

Clutton-Brock, Timothy H., and Anne Vincent. 1991. Sexual selection and the potential reproductive rates of males and females. *Nature* 351:58–60. [1, 37]

Coale, A. J., and P. Demeny. 1966. *Regional model life tables and stable populations.* Princeton, N.J.: Princeton University Press. [3]

Codere, Helen. 1950. *Fighting with property.* New York: J. J. Augustin. [37]

Coles, C. D., and M. Shamp. 1984. Some sexual, personality and demographic characteristics of women readers of erotic romances. *Archives of Sexual Behavior* 13:187–209. [20]

Columella. 1941–55. *De re rustica.* Cambridge, Mass.: Classical Library. [37]

Comaroff, J. L., and J. Comaroff. 1981. The management of marriage in a Tswana chiefdom. In E. Krige and J. Comaroff (eds.), *Essays on African marriage in Southern Africa,* pp. 24–49. Capetown: Juta. [11]

Comfort, Alex. 1956. *The biology of senescence.* New York: Rinehart. [13]

Connor, Richard C. 1995. The benefits of mutualism: A conceptual framework. *Biological Reviews* 70:425–457. [1, 6]

Conover, W. J. 1980. *Practical nonparametric statistics,* 2d ed. New York: Wiley. [33]

Copper, Elizabeth. 1915. *The harem and the purdah: Studies of Oriental women.* New York: Century. [29]

Cooper, H. M., and L. V. Hedges, eds. 1993. *Handbook of research synthesis.* New York: Russel Sage Foundation. [28]

Corbier, Mirielle. 1991. Constructing kinship in Rome: Marriage and divorce, filiation and adoption. In D. Kertzer and R. Saller (eds.), *The family in Italy from antiquity to the present.* New Haven, Conn.: Yale University Press. [37]

Cormack, Margaret. 1953. *The Hindu woman.* New York: Columbia University Press. [29]

Coser, L. 1964. The political functions of eunuchism. *American Sociological Review* 29:880–85. [37]

Cosmides, Leda. 1985. Deduction or Darwinian algorithms? An explanation of the "elusive" content effect on the Wason selection task. Ph.D. diss. Dept. of Psychology, Harvard University. Ann Arbor, Mich.: University Microfilms International. [26]

———. 1989. The logic of social exchange: Has natural selection shaped how humans reason? *Cognition* 31:187–276. [1, 20, 26]

Cosmides, Leda, and John Tooby. 1981. Cytoplasmic inheritance and intragenomic conflict. *Journal of Theoretical Biology* 89:83–129. [1]

———. 1987. From evolution to behavior: Evolutionary psychology as the missing link. In J. Dupré (ed.), *The latest on the best: Essays on evolution and optimality,* pp. 277–306. Cambridge, Mass.: MIT Press. [1, 15, 20, 24, 26, 27]

———. 1989. Evolutionary psychology and the generation of culture. Part II. Case study: A computational theory of social exchange. *Ethology and Sociobiology* 10:51–98. [1, 15, 24, 26]

———. 1992. Cognitive adaptations to social exchange. In J. Barkow et al. (eds.), *The adapted mind,* pp. 163–228. New York: Oxford University Press. [1, 12, 15]

———. 1994. Evolutionary psychology and the invisible hand. *American Economic Review* 84:327–32. [27]

———. In prep. a. Is the Wason selection task an assay for production rules in mentalese? [26]

———. In prep. b. The logic of threat: Evidence for another adaptation? [26]

———. In prep. c. Social contracts, precaution rules, and threats: How to tell one schema from another. [2, 27]

Cowlishaw, Guy, and Ruth Mace. 1996. Cross-cultural patterns of marriage and inheritance: A phylogenetic approach. *Ethology and Sociobiology* 17, in press. [1, 32]

Cox, D. R. 1972. Regression model and life-tables (with discussion). *Journal of the Royal Statistical Society* 34:186–220. [11]

Crawford, Charles B. 1993. The future of sociobiology: Counting babies or proximate mechanisms? *Trends in Ecology and Evolution* 8:183–86. [15]

Crawford, Charles B., and Dennis Krebs, eds. 1996. *Evolution and human behavior: Issues, ideas, and applications.* Hillsdale, N.J.: Erlbaum. [1]

Crawford, Charles B., Dennis Krebs, and Martin Smith, eds. 1987. *Sociobiology and psychology: Issues, ideas, applications.* Hillsdale, N.J.: Erlbaum. [1]

Crawford, Charles B., Brenda Salter, and Kerry Lang. 1989. Human grief: Is its intensity related to the reproductive value of the deceased? *Ethology and Sociobiology,* 10:297–307. [1]

Crawford, Charles B., Martin Smith, and Dennis Krebs. 1991. Sociobiology: Is it still too hot to handle? *Contemporary Psychology* 35:408–11. [24]

Crawford, H. E. W. 1973. Mesopotamia's invisible exports in the third millennium B.C. *World Archaeology,* 5:232–41. [29]

Creel, Scott, and Nancy Creel. 1991. Energetics, reproductive suppression and obligate communal breeding in carnivores. *Behavioural Ecology and Sociobiology* 28:267–70. [38]

Creighton, S. J. 1985. An epidemiological study of abused children and their families in the United Kingdom between 1977 and 1982. *Child Abuse and Neglect* 9:441–48. [17]

Creighton, S. J., and P. Noyes. 1989. *Child abuse trends in England and Wales, 1983–1987.* London: National Society for the Prevention of Cruelty to Children. [17]

Cronin, Helena. 1991. *The ant and the peacock.* Cambridge: Cambridge University Press. [1]

Cronk, Lee. 1989a. From hunters to herders: Subsistence change as a reproductive strategy among the Mukogodo. *Current Anthropology* 30:224–34. [1]

———. 1989b. Low socioeconomic status and female-biased parental investment: The Mukogodo example. *American Anthropologist* 91:414–29. [1, 39]

———. 1991a. Human behavioral ecology. *Annual Reviews in Anthropology* 20:25–53. [1]

———. 1991b. Wealth, status, and reproductive success among the Mukogodo of Kenya. *American Anthropologist* 93:345–60. [1, 4, 28]

———. 1994. Evolutionary theories of morality and the manipulative use of signals. *Zygon* 29:81–101. [1]

———. 1995. Is there a role for culture in human behavioral ecology? *Ethology and Sociobiology* 16:181–205. [1]

Crook, John. 1967. *Law and life of Rome.* Ithaca, N.Y.: Cornell University Press. [37]

Crook, John H., and Stamati J. Crook. 1988. Tibetan polyandry: Problems of adaptation and fitness. In L. Betzig et al. (eds.), *Human reproductive behaviour,* pp. 97–114. Cambridge: Cambridge University Press. [1]

Croutier, Alev. 1989. *Harem: The world behind the veil.* New York: Abbeville Press. [30]

Croze, H. A. K. Hillman, and E. M. Lang. 1981. Elephants and their habitats: How do they tolerate each other? In C. W. Fowler and T. D. Smith (eds.), *Dynamics of large mammal populations,* New York: Wiley. [13]

Csillag, Pál. 1976. *The Augustan laws on family relations.* Budapest: Akadémiai Kiadó. [37]

Cunningham, Michael R. 1986. Measuring the physical in physical attractiveness: Quasi-experiments in the sociobiology of female facial beauty. *Journal of Personality and Social Psychology* 50:925–35. [1]

Cunningham, Michael R., A. Barbee, and C. Pike. 1990. What do women want? Facialmetric assessment of multiple motives in the perception of male facial physical attractiveness. *Journal of Personality and Social Psychology* 59:61–72. [1]

Cunningham, Michael R., Alan Roberts, Anita Barbee, Perri Druen, and Cheng-Huan Wu. 1995. "Their ideas of beauty are, on the whole, the same as ours:" Consistency and variability in the cross-cultural perception of female physical attractiveness. *Journal of Personality and Social Psychology* 68:261–279. [1]

Curley, R. T. 1973. *Elders, shades and women: Ceremonial change in Lango, Uganda.* Berkeley: University of California Press. [11]

Dahl, Edgar. 1994. *Die gene der liebe: Vom weigen kampf der geschlechter.* Hamburg: Carlsen. [1]

Dalby, Andrew. 1979. On female slaves in Roman Egypt. *Arethusa* 12:255–59. [37]

Daly, Martin, L. S. Singh, and Margo Wilson. 1993. Children fathered by previous fathers: A risk factor for violence against women. *Canadian Journal of Public Health* 84:209–10. [17]

Daly, Martin, and Margo Wilson. 1980. Discriminative parental solicitude: A biological perspective. *Journal of Marriage and the Family* 42:277–88. [16, 39]

———. 1981a. Abuse and neglect of children in evolutionary perspective. In R. Alexander and D. Tinkle (eds.), *Natural selection and social behavior,* pp. 405–16. New York: Chrion Press. [1, 16]

———. 1981b. Child maltreatment from a sociobiological perspective. *New Directions for Child Development* 11:93–112. [16]

———. 1982. Whom are newborn babies said to resemble? *Ethology and Sociobiology* 3:69–78. [1]

———. 1983. *Sex, evolution, and behavior,* 2d ed. Boston: Willard Grant. [1, 9, 11, 18, 20, 22, 23, 24, 33, 36, 37, 39]

———. 1984. A sociobiological analysis of human infanticide. In G. Hausfater and S. B. Hrdy (eds.), *Infanticide: Comparative and evolutionary perspectives,* pp. 487–502. Hawthorne, N.Y.: Aldine–de Gruyter. [16, 39]

———. 1985. Child abuse and other risks of not living with both parents. *Ethology and Sociobiology* 6:155–76. [1, 15]

———. 1987. Evolutionary psychology and family violence. In C. Crawford et al. (eds.), *Sociobiology and psychology: Issues, ideas, and applications.* Hillsdale, N.J.: Erlbaum. [16]

———. 1988a. Evolutionary social psychology and family homicide. *Science* 242:519–24. [17]

———. 1988b. *Homicide.* Hawthorne, N.Y.: Aldine–de Gruyter. [1, 9, 17, 20, 21, 23, 24, 39]

———. 1988c. The Darwinian psychology of discriminative parental solicitude. *Nebraska Symposium on Motivation* 35:91–144. [17]

———. 1994a. Discriminative parental solicitude and the relevance of evolutionary models to the analysis of motivational systems. In M. S. Gazzaniga (ed.), *The cognitive neurosciences* Cambridge, Mass.: MIT Press. [17]

———. 1994b. Some differential attributes of lethal assaults on small children by stepfathers versus genetic fathers. *Ethology and Sociobiology* 15:207–17. [17]

———. 1994c. Stepparenthood and the evolved psychology of discriminative parental solicitude. In S. Parmigiami and F. vom Saal (eds.), *Infanticide and parental care.* Chur, Switzerland: Harwood Academic. [17]

———. 1996. Evolutionary psychology and marital conflict: The relevance of stepchildren. In D. M. Buss and N. Malamuth (eds.), *Sex, power, and conflict.* New York: Oxford University Press. [17]

Daly, Martin, Margo Wilson, and Suzanne Weghorst. 1982. Male sexual jealousy. *Ethology and Sociobiology,* 3:11–27. [1, 9, 18]

D'Arms, John. 1970. *Romans on the Bay of Naples.* Cambridge, Mass.: Harvard University Press. [37]

Darwin, Charles. 1859. *On the origin of species.* New York: Modern Library reprint of edition published by John Murray, London. [1, 18, 22, 31, 37]

———. 1871. *The descent of man and selection in relation to sex.* New York: Modern Library reprint of edition published by John Murray, London. [1, 9, 18, 31, 32, 37]

———. 1887. *Autobiography,* ed. Gavin de Beer. New York: Oxford University Press, 1983. [1, 32]

Das Gupta, M. 1987. Selective discrimination against female children in rural Punjab, India. *Population and Development Review* 13:17–100. [39]

Dass, Diwan Jarmani. 1970. *Maharaja.* Delhi: Hind. [37]

Davie, M. 1929. *The evolution of war: A study of its role in early societies.* New Haven, Conn.: Yale University Press. [9]

Davies, Nick. 1989. Sexual conflict and the polygyny threshold. *Animal Behaviour* 38:226–34. [11, 12]

Davies, Nick, and and A. I. Houston. 1986. Reproductive success of dunnocks, *Prunella modularis,* in a variable mating system. II. Conflicts of interest among breeding adults. *Journal of Animal Ecology* 55:139–54. [11]

Davies, Paul, James Fetzer and Thomas Foster. 1995. Logical reasoning and domain specificity: A critique of the social exchange theory of reasoning. *Biology and Philosophy* 10:1–37. [1]

Davin, Delia. 1975. Women in the countryside of China. In M. Wolf and R. Witke (eds.), *Women in Chinese society,* pp. 243–73. Stanford, Calif.: Stanford University Press. [29]

Davison, G. C., and J. M. Neale. 1982. *Abnormal psychology,* 3d ed. New York: Wiley. [22]

Dawkins, Richard. 1982. *The extended phenotype: The gene as the unit of selection.* San Francisco: Freeman. [1, 24, 26]

———. 1986. *The blind watchmaker.* New York: Norton. [1, 24, 26]

———. 1989. *The selfish gene,* rev. ed. London: Oxford. [1, 2, 3, 9, 24, 29]

———. 1995. *River out of Eden.* New York: HarperCollins. [1]

Dawkins, Richard, and T. R. Carlisle. 1976. Parental investment, mate desertion and a fallacy. *Nature* 262:131–33. [39]

Dawkins, Richard, and John Krebs. 1978. Animal signals: Information or manipulation? In J. Krebs and N. Davies (eds.), *Behavioural Ecology: An Evolutionary Approach.* Sunderland, Mass.: Sinauer. [15]

Day, C. S. D., and Bennet Galef. 1977. Pup cannibalism: One aspect of maternal behavior in golden hamsters. *Journal of Comparative and Physiological Psychology* 91:1179–89. [39]

de Catanzaro, Dennis. 1980. Human suicide: A biological perspective. *Behavioral and Brain Sciences* 3:265–290. [1]

———. 1981. *Suicide and self-damaging behavior: A sociobiological perspective.* New York: Academic Press. [1]

———. 1991. Evolutionary limits to self-preservation. *Ethology and Sociobiology* 12:13–28. [1]

———. 1995. Reproductive status, family interactions, and suicidal ideation. *Ethology and Sociobiology* 16:385–394. [1]

Degler, Carl. 1991. *In search of human nature.* New York: Oxford University Press. [1]

Delasselle, C. 1975. Les enfants abandonnés a Paris au XVIIIe siecle. *Annales: Economies, Societés, Civilisations* 30:187–218. [39]

Dennett, Dan. 1995. *Darwin's dangerous idea.* New York: Simon and Schuster. [1]

Derrett, J. Duncan. 1964. Law and the social order in India before the Muhammadan conquests. *Journal of Economic and Social History of the Orient* 7:73–120. [29]

Deslypere, J. P., and A. Vermeulen. 1984. Leydig cell function in normal men: Effect of age, lifestyle, residence, diet and activity. *Journal of Clinical Endocrinology and Metabolism* 59:955–62. [13]

DeVaux, Roland. 1967. Sur le voile des femmes dans l'Orient ancien: A propos d'un bas-relief de Palmyre. *Bible et Orient,* pp. 407–23. Paris: Éditions du Cerf. [29]

DeVries, M. 1984. Temperament and infant mortality among the Masai of East Africa. *American Journal of Psychiatry* 141:1189–94. [39]

Dew, J. L., T. R. Spoon, and Mary Towner. 1994. Mating systems: Anthropologists and behavioral ecologists combine perspectives. *Evolutionary Anthropology* 3:111–12. [12]

Dewsbury, Donald. 1992. On the problems studied in ethology, comparative psychology, and animal behavior. *Ethology* 92:89–107. [15]

Diana, L. 1985. *The prostitute and her clients.* Springfield, Ill.: Charles Thomas. [20]

Dickemann, Mildred. 1975. Demographic consequences of infanticide in man. *Annual Review of Ecology and Systematics* 6:107–37. [30, 39]

———. 1978. Confidence of paternity mechanisms in the human species. Manuscript. [29]

———. 1979a. The ecology of mating systems in hypergynous dowry societies. *Social Science Information* 18:163–95. [1, 11, 29, 30, 31, 36, 37]

———. 1979b. Female infanticide, reproductive strategies, and social stratification: A preliminary model. In N. A. Chagnon and W. Irons (eds.), *Evolutionary biology and human social behavior: An anthropological perspective,* pp. 321–67. North Sciuate, Mass.: Duxbury Press. [1, 11, 28, 29, 30, 32, 33, 36, 37, 39]

———. 1981. Paternal confidence and dowry competition: A biocultural analysis of purdah. In R. Alexander and D. Tinkle (eds.), *Natural selection and social behavior.* New York: Chrion Press. [1, 18, 28, 32, 37]

———. 1982. Commentary on Hartung. *Current Anthropology* 23:1–12. [11]

———. 1984a. Concepts and classification in the study of human infanticide. In G. Hausfater and S. B. Hrdy (eds.), *Infanticide: Comparative and evolutionary perspectives,* pp. 427–37. Hawthorne, N.Y.: Aldine–de Gruyter. [39]

———. 1984b. Medieval muddles and modern modles: A reply to Stuard. *American Anthropologist* 86:683–86. [30]

———. 1991. Woman, class, and dowry. *American Anthropologist* 93:944–46. [36]

The Digest of Justinian, trans. Alan Watson. Philadelphia: University of Pennsylvania Press. [37]

Dio, Cassius. 1925. *History,* trans. Earnest Cary. New York: G. P. Putnam's Sons. [37, 38]

Divale, William T., and Marvin Harris. 1976. Population, warfare and the male supremacist complex. *American Anthropologist* 78:521–38. [39]

Dixon, Suzanne. 1985. The marriage alliance in the Roman elite. *Journal of Family History* 10:353–78. [37]

———. 1988. *The Roman mother.* London: Croon Helm. [37]

Dixon, W. J., ed 1981. *BMDP statistical software.* Berkeley: University of California Press. [7]

Dobzhansky, T. 1961. Discussion. In J. S. Kennedy (ed.), *Symposium of the Royal Entomological Society of London*, p. 11. London. [33]

Donald, L. 1983. Was Nuu-chah-nulth-aht (Nootka) society based on slave labor? Ecology and political organization in the Northwest Coast of America. In E. Tooker (ed.), *The development of political organization in native North America*, pp. 108–19. Washington, D.C.: American Ethnological Society. [26]

Donald, Robyn. 1992. Mean, moody, and magnificent: The hero in romance literature. In J. Krentz (ed.), *Dangerous men and adventurous women: Writers on the appeal of the romance*. Philadelphia: University of Pennsylvania Press. [21]

Draper, Patricia. 1989. African marriage systems: Perspectives from evolutionary ecology. *Ethology and Sociobiology* 10:145–69. [39]

Draper, Patricia, and Jay Belsky. 1990. Personality development in evolutionary perspective. *Journal of Personality* 58:141–62. [1]

Draper, Patricia, and Henry Harpending. 1982. Father absence and reproductive strategies: An evolutionary perspective. *Journal of Anthropological Research* 38:225–73. [1]

———. 1986. Parental investment and the child's environment. In J. Lancaster et al. (eds.), *Parenting across the lifespan*, pp. 207–35. Hawthorne, N.Y.: Aldine–de Gruyter. [33]

Drucker, P. 1983. Ecology and political organization in the Northwest coast of America. In E. Tooker (ed.), *The development of political organization in native North America*, pp. 86–96. Washington, D.C.: American Ethnological Society. [26]

Duberman, L. 1975. *The reconstituted family: A study of remarried couples and their children*. Chicago: Nelson-Hall. [16]

Duby, Georges. 1983. *The knight, the lady, and the priest: The making of modern marriage in medieval France.* trans. Barbara Bray. New York: Pantheon. [37]

Dugatkin, Lee. 1996. *Cooperation among animals: An evolutionary* perspective. New York: Oxford University Press. [1]

Dunbar, Robin. 1987. Demography and reproduction. In B. Smuts et al. (eds.), *Primate societies*, pp. 240–49. Chicago: University of Chicago Press. [13]

Dunbar, Robin, Amanda Clark, and Nicola Hurst. 1994. Conflict and cooperation among the Vikings: Contingent behavioral decisions. *Ethology and Sociobiology* 16:233–246. [1]

Duncan, P. 1975. Topi and their food supply. Ph. D. diss. University of Nairobi. [11]

Duncan-Jones, R. 1982. *The economy of the Roman Empire: Quantitative studies*, 2d ed. Cambridge: Cambridge University Press. [37]

Dupaquier, J., and M. Lachiver. 1964. Sur les débuts de la contraception en France ou les deux Malthosianismus. *Annales E. S. C.* 1391–406. [39]

Dupoux, A. 1958. Sur les pas de Monsieur Vincent: Trois cents ans d'histoire Parisienne de l'enfance abandonée. *Revue de l'Assistance Publique*. Paris. [39]

Durden-Smith, D., and J. DeSimone. 1983. *Sex and the brain*. New York: Warner Books. [20]

Durham, William. 1991. *Coevolution: Genes, culture, and human diversity*. Stanford, Calif.: Stanford University Press. [1]

Durnin, J., and R. Passmore. 1967. *Energy, work and leisure*. London: Heinemann. [5]

Eals, Marion, and Irwin Silverman. 1994. The hunter-gatherer theory of spatial sex differences: Proximate factors mediating the female advantage in recall of object arrays. *Ethology and Sociobiology* 15:95–105. [1]

Early, J. D., and J. F. Peters. 1990. *The population dynamics of the Mucajai Yanomamö*. New York: Academic Press. [13, 39]

Eaton, S. Boyd, Malcom Pike, Roger V. Short, Nancy Lee, James Trussell, Robert Hatcher, James Wood, Carol M. Worthman, Nicholas Blurton-Jones, Melvin Konner, Kim Hill, Robert Bailey and A. M. Hurtado. Women's reproductive cancers in evolutionary context. 1994. *Quarterly Review of Biology* 69:353–67. [1]

Eaton, Boyd, Marjorie Shostak, and Melvin Konnor. 1988. *The Paleolithic prescription*. New York: Harper and Row. [1]

Eberhard, William G. 1985. *Sexual selection and animal genitalia*. Cambridge, Mass.: Harvard University Press. [25]

Echols, E. 1961. Introduction to Herodian's *History of the Roman Empire*. Berkeley: University of California Press. [37]

Eckert, C. G., and P. J. Weatherhead. 1987. Male characteristics, parental quality and the study of mate choice in the red-winged blackbird *(agelaius phoenicus). Behavioral Ecology and Sociobiology* 20:35–42. [11]

Egeland, B. 1987. Issues related to the developmental consequences of child maltreatment. In R. Gelles and J. Lancaster (eds.), *Biosocial perspectives on child abuse and neglect*. Hawthorne, N.Y.: Aldine–de Gruyter. [16]

Einon, Dorothy. 1994. Are men more promiscuous than women? *Ethology and Sociobiology* 15:131–43. [1]

Einstein, E. 1982. *The stepfamily*. New York: Macmillan. [16]

El-Faedy, M. A., and L. L. Bean. 1987. Differential paternity in Libya. *Journal of Biosocial Science* 19:395–403. [13]

Ellis, Bruce J. 1992. The evolution of sexual attraction: Evaluative mechanisms in women. In J. Barkow et al. (eds.), *The adapted mind*. New York: Oxford University Press. [18, 20]

———. 1995. Investment in dating relationships. Ph.D. diss. Dept. of Psychology, University of Michigan. Ann Arbor Mich.: University Microfilms International. [1]

Ellis, Bruce J., and Donald Symons. 1990. Sex differences in sexual fantasy: An evolutionary psychological approach. *Journal of Sex Research* 27:527–55. [1, 15]

Ellis, Lee. 1995. Dominance and reproductive success: A review of the evidence. *Ethology and Sociobiology* 16:253–333. [1]

Ellison, Peter. 1994a. Advances in human reproductive ecology. *Annual Reviews of Anthropology* 23:255–75. [1]

———. 1994b. Extinction and descent. *Human Nature* 5:155–165. [1]

———. 1996. Understanding natural variation in human ovarian function. In R. Dundar (ed.), *Human reproductive decisions*, pp. 22–51. London: Macmillan. [1]

Ellison, Peter, Nadine Peacock, and Catherine Lager. 1989. Ecology and ovarian function among Lese women of the Ituri forest, Zaire. *American Journal of Physical Anthropology* 78:519–26. [1]

Ember, Carol R. 1981. A cross-cultural perspective on sex differences. In R. H. Munroe et al. (eds.), *Handbook of cross-cultural human development,* pp. 531–80. New York: Garland. [33]

Emlen, Stephen. 1982. The evolution of helping. II: The role of behavioral conflict. *American Naturalist* 119:40–53. [5]

———. 1991. Evolution of cooperative breeding in birds and mammals. In J. Krebs and N. Davies (eds.), *Behavioural ecology: An evolutionary approach,* 3d ed. pp. 301–37. Oxford: Blackwell Scientific. [38]

Emlen, Stephen, and L. W. Oring. 1977. Ecology, sexual selection, and the evolution of mating systems. *Science* 197:215–23. [11, 18, 29, 31, 37]

Engels, Frederick. 1942. *The origin of the family, private property, and the state*. New York: International Publishers. [29]

Essock-Vitale, Susan M. 1984. The reproductive success of wealthy Americans. *Ethology and Sociobiology,* 5:45–49. [1, 4, 33]

Essock-Vitale, Susan M., and Michael T. McGuire. 1980. Predictions derived from the theories of kin selection and reciprocation assessed by anthropological data. *Ethology and Sociobiology* 1:233–43. [1]

———. 1985a. Women's lives viewed from an evolutionary perspective: I. Sexual histories, reproductive success, and demographic characteristics of a random sample of American women. *Ethology and Sociobiology* 6:138–54. [1]

———. 1985b. Women's lives viewed from an evolutionary perspective: II. Patterns of helping. *Ethology and Sociobiology* 6:155–73. [1]

———. 1988. What 70 million years have wrought: Sexual histories and reproductive success of a random sample of American women. In L. Betzig et al. (eds.), *Human reproductive behavior,* pp. 123–48. Cambridge: Cambridge University Press. [4]

Euler, Harold and Barbara Weitzel. 1996. Discriminative grandparental solicitude as reproductive strategy. *Human Nature* 7:39–59. [1]

Evans, J. St. B. T. 1984. Heuristic and analytic processes in reasoning. *British Journal of Psychology* 75:457–68. [26]

Evans-Pritchard, Edward E. 1940. *The Nuer*. Oxford: Oxford University Press. [11]

Ewald, Paul. 1980. Evolutionary biology and the treatment of signs and symptoms of infectious disease. *Journal of Theoretical Biology* 86:169–76. [1]

———. 1994a. *The evolution of infectious disease*. New York: Oxford University Press. [1]

———. 1994b. Evolution of mutation rate and virulence among human retroviruses. *Proceedings of the Royal Society of London, B* 346:333–43. [1]

Fagen, R. 1981. *Animal play behavior*. Oxford: Oxford University Press. [33]

Fairbanks, Lynn. 1996. Maternal behavior of Old World monkeys. In P. Whitehead and C. Jolly (eds.), *Old World monkeys*. New York: Cambridge University Press. [8]

Fairbanks, Lynn, and Michael T. McGuire. 1986. Age, reproductive value, and dominance-related behavior in vervet monkey females: Cross-generational social influences on social relationships and reproduction. *Animal Behaviour* 34:1718–21. [13]

Falconer, D. S. 1981. *Introduction to quantitative genetics,* 2d ed. London: Longeman. [33]

Farrell, W. 1986. *Why men are the way they are*. New York: McGraw-Hill. [20]

Faust, B. 1980. *Women, sex, and pornography*. New York: Macmillan. [20]

Faux, S. F., and H. Miller. 1984. Evolutionary speculations on the oligarchic development of Mormon polygyny. *Ethology and Sociobiology* 5:15–31. [1, 4]

Feingold, Alan. 1990. Gender differences in effects of physical attractiveness on romantic attraction: A comparison across five research paradigms. *Journal of Personality and Social Psychology* 59:981–93. [1]

———. 1991. Sex differences in the effects of similarity and physical attractiveness on opposite-sex attraction. *Basic and Applied Psychology* 12:357–67. [1]

———. 1992. Gender differences in mate selection preferences: A test of the parental investment model. *Psychological Bulletin* 112:125–39. [1]

Ferguson, R. Brian. 1989. Do Yanomamö killers have more kids? *American Ethnologist* 16:564–65. [10]

Fergusson, D. M., J. Fleming, and D. O'Neill. 1972. *Child abuse in New Zealand.* Wellington: Government of New Zealand Printer. [16]

Fernea, Elizabeth W. 1976. *A street in Marrakech.* Garden City, N.Y.: Doubleday. [29]

Ferri, E. 1984. *Stepchildren: A national study.* Windsor, Engl.: NFER-Nelson. [17]

Festing, M. F. W., and D. K. Blackmore. 1971. Life span of specified pathogen-free (MRC category 4) mice and rats. *Laboratory Animal Bulletin* 5:179–92. [13]

Fiddick, Larry, Leda Cosmides, and John Tooby. in prep. Dissociations between reasoning modules: Evidence from priming studies. [27]

Fielde, Adele M. 1887. *Pagoda shadows: Studies from life in China.* London: T. Oglivie Smith. [29]

Figueredo, Aurelio José, and Laura Ann McCloskey. 1993. Sex, money, and paternity: The evolutionary psychology of domestic violence. *Ethology and Sociobiology* 14:353–79. [1, 17]

Fildes, Valerie. 1986. *Breasts, babies, and bottles.* Edinburgh: Edinburgh University Press. [37, 39]

———. 1988. *Wet nursing: A history from antiquity to the present.* New York: Oxford University Press. [37, 39]

Finkelhor, D. 1984. *Child sexual abuse: New theory and research.* New York: Free Press. [24]

Finley, Moses. 1980. *Ancient slavery and modern ideology.* New York: Viking, [37]

Fischer, E. A. 1988. Simultaneous hermaphroditism, tit-for-tat, and the evolutionary stability of social systems. *Ethology and Sociobiology* 9:116–36. [26]

Fisher, Helen E. 1989. Evolution of human serial pairbonding. *American Journal of Physical Anthropology* 78:331–54. [1]

———. 1992. *The anatomy of love.* New York: Norton. [1]

Fisher, Ronald A. 1958. *The genetical theory of natural selection,* 2d ed. New York: Dover. [1, 18, 28, 31]

Fisher, W. A., D. Byrne, D. White, and K. Kelley. 1988. Erotophobia-erotophilia as a dimension of personality. *Journal of Sex Research* 25:123–51. [20]

Fiske, A. P. 1990. Relativity within Moose ("Mossi") culture: Four incommensurable models for social relationships. Ethos 18:180–204. [26]

———. 1991a. Innate hypotheses and cultural parameters for social relations. Paper presented at the Society for Philosophy and Psychology, San Francisco. [26]

———. 1991b. *Structures of social life: The four elementary forms of human relations.* New York: Free Press. [26]

Flaceliere, Robert. 1962. *Love in ancient Greece,* trans. J. Cleugh. New York: Crown. [29]

Flinn, Mark V. 1981. Uterine vs. agnatic kinship variability and associated cousin marriage preferences: An evolutionary biological analysis. In R. D. Alexander and D. W. Tinkle (eds.), *Natural selection and social behavior,* pp. 439–75. New York: Chiron Press. [1]

———. 1983. Resources, mating, and kinship: The behavioral ecology of a Trinidadian village. Ph.D. diss., Dept. of Anthropology, Northwestern University. Ann Arbor, Mich.: University Microfilms International. [33]

———. 1986. Correlates of reproductive success in a Caribbean village. *Human Ecology* 14:225–43. [1, 4, 35]

———. 1987. Mate guarding in a Caribbean village. *Ethology and Sociobiology* 8:1–29. [1, 18]

———. 1988a. Household composition and female strategies in a Trinidadian village. In A. Rasa et al. (eds.), *The sociobiology of sexual and reproductive strategies,* pp. 206–33. London: Chapman and Hall. [1]

———. 1988b. Parent-offspring interactions in a Caribbean village: Daughter guarding. In L. Betzig et al. (eds.), *Human reproductive behaviour,* pp. 189–200. Cambridge: Cambridge University Press. [1]

———. 1988c. Step and genetic parent/offspring relationships in a Caribbean village. *Ethology and Sociobiology* 9:1–34. [1, 17]

———. 1996. Endocrine, immunologic, and health responses to household dynamics in Caribbean children. In C. Panter-Brick and C. Worthman (eds.), *Hormones, health, and behavior.* New York: Cambridge University Press. [1]

Flinn, Mark V., and Richard D. Alexander. 1982. Culture theory: The developing synthesis from biology. *Human Ecology* 10:383–400. [15]

Flinn, Mark V., and Barry England. 1995. Childhood stress and family environment. *Current Anthropology* 36:854–66. [1]

———. 1996. Social economics of childhood glutocorticoid stress response and health. *American Journal of Physical Anthropology,* in press [1]

Flinn, Mark V., and Bobbi S. Low. 1986. Resource distribution, social competition, and mating patterns in human societies. In R. Wrangham and D. Rubenstein (eds.), *Ecological aspects of social evolution,* pp. 217–43. Princeton, N.J.: Princeton University Press. [1, 11, 33]

Flinn, Mark V., R. Quinlan, M. Turner, S. Decker, and B. England. 1996 Male female differences in effects of parental absence on glucocorticoid stress response. *Human Nature* 7:125–62. [1]

Flory, M. B. 1978. Family in *familia:* Kinship and community in slavery. *American Journal of Ancient History* 3:78–95. [37]

Fodor, J. A. 1983. *The modularity of mind.* Cambridge, Mass.: MIT Press. [26]

Follingstad, D. R., and C. D. Kimbrell. 1986. Sex fantasies revisited: An expansion and further clarification of variables affecting sex fantasy production. *Archives of Sexual Behavior* 15:475–86. [20]

Ford, C. S., and F. A. Beach. 1951. *Patterns of sexual behavior.* New York: Harper and Row. [18]

Forsberg, Anna J. L., and Birgitta S. Tullberg. 1995. The relationship between cumulative number of cohabiting partners and number of children for men and women in modern Sweden. *Ethology and Sociobiology* 16:221–232. [1]

Fowler, C. W., and T. D. Smith, eds. 1981. *Dynamics of large mammal populations.* New York: Wiley. [13]

Frank, E. S. M. Turner, B. Stewart, M. Jacob, and D. West. 1981. Past psychiatric symptoms and the response to sexual assault. *Comprehensive Psychiatry* 22:479–87. [24]

Frank, Robert. 1988. *Passions within reason.* New York: Norton. [1]

Frank, Steven A. 1990. Sex alloction theory for birds and mammals. *Annual Review of Ecology and Systematics* 21:13–55. [1]

Fréderic, Louis. 1972. *Daily life in Japan at the time of the samurai, 1185–1603,* trans. E. M. Lowe. London: George Allan and Unwin. [29]

Fredlund, Eric. 1984. The use and abuse of kinship when classifying marriages: A Shitari Yanomamö case study. *Ethology and Sociobiology* 6:17–25. [1]

Freedman, Daniel G. 1974. *Human infancy: An evolutionary perspective.* Hillsdale, N.J.: Erlbaum. [33]

———. 1980. Sexual dimorphism and the status hierarchy. In D. Omark et al. (eds.), *Dominance relations,* pp. 261–71. New York: Garland. [33]

Fretwell, S. D. 1972. *Populations in a seasonal environment.* Princeton, N.J.: Princeton University Press. [11]

Fretwell, S. D., and H. L. Lucas. 1969. On territorial and other factors influencing distribution in birds, I: Theoretical development. *Acta Biotheoretica* 19:16–36. [35]

Fricke, H. W., and S. Fricke. 1977. Monogamy and sex change by aggressive dominance in coral reef fish. *Nature* 266:830–32. [1]

Friedlander, Ludwig. 1908. *Roman life and manners under the early empire,* trans. Leonard Magnus. New York: George Routledge. [37]

Frumhoff, P. C., and J. Baker. 1988. A genetic component to division of labour within honey bee colonies. *Nature* 333:358–61. [26]

Frumhoff, P. C., and S. Schneider. 1987. The social consequences of honey bee polyandry: The effects of kinship on worker interactions within colonies. *Animal Behaviour* 35:255–62. [26]

Fuchs, R. 1984. *Abandoned children: Foundlings and child welfare in nineteenth-century France.* Albany: State University of New York Press. [39]

———. 1987. Legislation, poverty and child-abandonment in nineteenth-century Paris. *Journal of Interdisciplinary History* 18:55–80. [39]

Gagnon, J. H., and W. Simon. 1973. *Sexual conduct.* Chicago: Aldine. [20]

Galliano, P. 1966. La mortalité infantile (indigenes et nourrissons) dans la banlieue sud de Paris a la fin du XVIIIe siecle (1774–1794). *Annales de Démographie Historique.* Paris: Editions Sirey. [39]

Gamboa, G. J., H. K. Reeve, and D. W. Pfennig. 1986. The evolution and ontogeny of nestmate recognition in social wasps. *Annual Reviews of Entomology* 31:432–54. [15]

Gandelman, R., and N. G. Simon. 1978. Spontaneous pup-killing by mice in response to large litters. *Developmental Psychobiology* 11:235–41. [39]

Gangestad, Steven W., and David M. Buss. 1993. Pathogen prevalence and human mate preferences. *Ethology and Sociobiology* 14:89–96. [1]

Gangestad, Steven W., and Jeffry A. Simpson. 1990. Toward an evolutionary history of female sociosexual variation. *Journal of Personality* 58:69–76. [1]

Gangestad, Steven W., Jeffry A. Simpson, Kenneth DiGeronimo, and Michael Biek. 1992. Differential accuracy in person perception across traits: Examination of a functional hypothesis. *Journal of Personality and Social Psychology* 62:668–98. [1]

Gangestad, Steven W., and Randy Thornhill. 1995. An evolutionary psychological analysis of human sexual selection: Developmental stability, male sexual behavior, and mediating features. *Psychological Science.* [1]

———. 1996a. The evolutionary psychology of extrapair sex: The role of fluctuating asymmetry. *Ethology and Sociobiology.* [1]

———. 1996b. Human sexual selection and developmental stability. In J. Simpson and D. Kenrick (eds.), *Evolutionary social psychology.* Hillsdale, N.J.: Erlbaum. [1]

Gangestad, Steven W., Randy Thornhill, and Ronald A. Yeo. 1993. Facial attractiveness, developmental stability, and fluctuating asymmetry. *Ethology and Sociobiology* 15:73–85. [1]

Garden, M. 1970. La démographie lyonnaise: L'analyse des comportements. *Lyon et les Lyonnais au XVIIe Siecle.* Bibliotheque de la Faculte des Lettres de Lyon, pp. 83–169. Paris. [39]

Gardner, Jane. 1986. *Women in Roman law and society.* London: Croon Helm. [37]

Garnsey, Peter. 1970. *Social status and legal privilege in the Roman Empire.* Oxford: Clarendon. [37, 38]

———. 1991. Child rearing in ancient Italy. In D. Kertzer and R. Saller (eds.), *The family in Italy from antiquity to the present.* New Haven, Conn.: Yale University Press. [37]

Garnsey, Peter, and Richard Saller. 1987. *The Roman Empire: Economy, society and culture.* Berkeley: University of California Press. [37]

Garson, P. J., W. Plezczynska, and C. Holm. 1981. The "polygyny threshold" model: A reassessment. *Canadian Journal of Zoology* 59:902–10. [11]

Gaulin, Steven J. C. 1980. Sexual dimorphism in the human post-reproductive lifespan: Possible causes. *Human Evolution* 9:227–32. [13]

Gaulin, Steven J. C., and James Boster. 1985. Cross-cultural differences in sexual dimorphism: Is there any variance to be explained? *Ethology and Sociobiology* 6:219–25. [1]

———. 1990. Dowry as female competition. *American Anthropologist* 92:994–1005. [1, 28, 32]

———. 1991. Dowry and female competition: A reply to Dickemann. *American Anthropologist* 93:946–48. [36]

———. 1993. Testing explanatory models of dowry: A reply to Schlegel. *American Anthropologist* 95:157–59. [36]

Gaulin, Steven, J.C., and Harol Hoffmann. 1988. Evolution and development of sex differences in spatial ability. In L. Betzig et al. (eds.), *Human reproductive behaviour,* pp. 129–52. Cambridge: Cambridge University Press. [1]

Gaulin, Steven J. C., and Carole Robbins. 1991. Trivers-Willard effect in contemporary North American society. *American Journal of Physical Anthropology* 85:61–69. [1]

Gaulin, Steven J. C., and Alice Schelgel. 1980. Paternal confidence and parental investment: A cross-cultural test of a sociobiological hypothesis. *Ethology and Sociobiology* 1:301–09. [1]

Gazda, Elaine. 1991. *Roman art in the private sphere.* Ann Arbor: University of Michigan Press. [37]

Gazzaniga, Michael. 1992. *Nature's mind.* New York: Basic Books. [1]

Geary, David C., Michael Rumsey, C. C. Bow-Thomas, and Mary K. Hoard. 1995. Sexual jealousy as a facultative trait: Evidence from the pattern of sex differences in adults from China and The United States. *Ethhology and Sociobiology* 16:355–383. [1]

Geertz, Clifford. 1973. Deep play: Notes on the Balinese cock fight. In *The interpretation of cultures,* chap. 15. New York: Basic Books. [37]

Gelles, Richard, and J. W. Harrop. 1991. The risk of abuse violence among children with nongenetic caretakers. *Family Relations* 40:78–83. [17]

George Washington University Medical Center. 1975. Population reports, series J, no. 8: Family planning programs. Washington, D.C.: Department of Medical and Public Affairs. [13]

Ghiglieri, M. 1987. Sociobiology of the great apes and of the hominid ancestors. *Journal of Human Evolution* 16:319. [39]

Gibbard, Alan. 1992. *Apt feelings and wise choices.* Cambridge, Mass.: Harvard University Press. [1]

Gibbs, N. 1990. Shameful bequest to the next generation. *Time Magazine,* October 8, pp. 42–46. [39]

Gigerenzer, Gerd. 1995. Rationality: Why social context matters. In P. Baltes and U. Staudinger (eds.), *Interactive minds: Life-span perspectives on the social foundation of cognition.* Cambridge: Cambridge University Press. [1]

Gigerenzer, Gerd, and H. Hug. 1995. Domain-specific reasoning: Social contracts, cheating and perspective change. *Cognition* 43:127–71. [27]

———. 1996. Reasoning about social contracts: Cheating and perspective change. Salzburg: Insitut für Psychologie. [26]

Giles-Sims, J. 1984. The stepparent role: Expectations, behavior and sanctions. *Journal of Family Issues* 5:116–30. [16]

Giles-Sims, J., and D. Finkelhor. 1984. Child abuse in stepfamilies. *Family Relations* 33:407–13. [16]

Giraldeau, Luc-Alain. 1988. The stable group and the determinants of foraging group size. In C. N. Slobodchikoff (ed.), *The ecology of social behavior*, pp. 33–53. San Diego: Academic Press. [6]

Giraldeau, Luc-Alain and Thomas Caraco. 1993. Genetic relatedness and group size in an aggregation economy. *Evolutionary Ecology* 7:429–438. [6]

Glasse, R. 1968. *Huli of Papua.* Paris: Mouton. [9]

Godin, G., and R. J. Shephard. 1973. Activity patterns of the Canadian Eskimo. In O. Edholm and E. Gunderson (eds.), *Polar human biology,* pp. 193–215. London: Heinemann. [5]

Goldberg, L. R. 1981. Language and individual differences: The search for universals in personality lexicons. In L. Wheeler (ed.), *Personality and social psychology review,* vol. 2, pp. 141–65. Beverly Hills, Calif.: Sage. [22]

Goldman, N., and M. Montgomery. 1989. Fecundability and husband's age. *Social Biology* 36:146–66. [13]

Goldschmidt, W. 1986. *The Sebei: A study in adaptation.* New York: Holt, Rinehart and Winston. [11]

Goodall, Jane. 1986. *The chimpanzees of Gombe: Patterns of behavior.* Cambridge, Mass.: Harvard University Press. [13, 39]

Goodenough, Oliver R. 1995. Mind viruses: Culture, evolution and the puzzle of altruism. *Social Science Information* 34:287–300. [1]

Goodenough, Oliver R., and Richard Dawkins. 1994. The St. Jude mind virus. *Nature* 371:23–24. [1]

Goody, Esther. 1969. Kinship fostering in Gonja: Deprivation or advantage? In P. Mayer (ed.), *Socialization,* pp. 137–65. London: International African Institute. [39]

———. 1975. Delegation of parental roles in West Africa and West Indies. In J. Goody (ed.), *Changing social structure in Ghana.* London: International African Institute. [39]

Goody, Jack. 1973. Bridewealth and dowry in Africa and Eurasia. In J. Goody and S. J. Tambiah (eds.), *Bridewealth and dowry.* Cambridge: Cambridge University Press. [35, 36]

———. 1976. *Production and reproduction: A comparative study of the domestic domain.* Cambridge: Cambridge University Press. [31, 35, 37]

———. 1983. *The development of the family and marriage in Europe.* Cambridge: Cambridge University Press. [37]

———. 1990. *The Oriental, the ancient, and the primitive.* Cambridge: Cambridge University Press. [37]

Gordon, M. 1989. The family environment of sexual abuse: A comparison of natal and stepfather abuse. *Child Abuse and Neglect* 13:121–30. [17]

Gordon, M., and S. J. Creighton. 1988. Natal and non-natal fathers as sexual abusers in the United Kingdom: A comparative analysis. *Journal of Marriage and the Family* 50:99–105. [17]

Gosden, R. G. 1987. Follicular status as menopause. *Human Reproduction* 2:617. [13]

Gottlieb, J. F. 1985. Sex and handedness differences in the use of autoerotic fantasy and imagery: A proposed explanation. *International Journal of Neuroscience* 26:259–68. [20]

Gough, H. G. 1973. Personality assessment in the study of population. In J Fawcett, (ed.), *Psychological perspectives on population,* New York: Basic Books. [18]

Gould, Stephen Jay. 1980. Sociobiology and the theory of natural selection. In G. Barlow and J. Silverberg (eds.). *Sociobiology: Beyond nature/nurture?,* pp. 257–72. Boulder, Colo.: Westview Press. [15]

———. 1989. *Wonderful life: The Burgess shale and the nature of history.* New York: Norton. [1]

Gowaty, Patty. 1995. Battles of the sexes and the origins of the monogamy. In J. Black (ed.), *Partnerships in birds.* Oxford: Oxford University Press. [12]

Gowaty, P., and M. Lennartz. 1985. Sex ratios of nestling and fledgling red-cockaded woodpeckers *(Picoides borealis)* favor males. *American Naturalist* 126:347–53. [40]

Grafen, Alan. 1984. Natural selection, kin selection and group selection. In J. Krebs and N. Davies (eds.), *Behavioural ecology: An evolutionary approach,* 2d edition, pp. 62–84. Oxford: Blackwell Scientific. [1, 6, 24]

———. 1991. Modelling in behavioural ecology. In J. Krebs and N. Davies (eds.) *Behavioural ecology: An evolutionary approach,* 3d edition, pp. 5–31. Oxford Blackwell Scientific. [34]

Grammer, Karl. 1993a. 5-•a-androst-16-en-3a-on: A male pheromone? A brief report. *Ethology and Sociobiology* 14:201–08. [1]

———. 1993b. *Signale der liebe die biologischen gesetze der partherschaft.* Hamburg: Hoffman and Campe. [1]

Grammer, Karl, John Dittami, and Bettina Fischmann. 1994. Changes in female sexual advertisement according to menstrual cycle. Poster presented at 23rd International Ethological Conference (IEC) in Torremolinos (Spain). [1]

Grammer, Karl, and Randy Thornhill. 1994. Human *(Homo sapiens)* facial attractiveness and sexual selection: The role of symmetry and averageness. *Journal of Comparative Psychology* 3:233–42. [1]

Grant, Peter. 1986. *Ecology and evolution of Darwin's finches.* Princeton, N.J.: Princeton University Press. [1]

Gray, Patrick. 1985. *Primate sociobiology.* Pittsburgh: HRAF Press. [1, 11]

Gray, Patrick, and Linda Wolfe. 1980. Height and sexual dimorphism of stature among human societies. *American Journal of Physical Anthropology* 53:441–56. [1]

Granzberg, G. 1973. Twin-infanticide-A cross-cultural test of materialist explanation. *Ethos* 1:405–12. [39]

Greenlees, I. A., and William C. McGrew. 1994. Sex and age differences in preferences and tactics of mate attraction: Analysis of published advertisements. *Ethology and Sociobiology* 15:59–72. [1]

Greer, Arlette, and David Buss. 1994. Tactics for promoting sexual encounters. *Journal of Sex Research* 31:185–201. [1, 19]

Gregor, Thomas. 1985. *Anxious pleasures: The sexual lives of an Amazonian people.* Chicago: University of Chicago Press. [39]

Greiling, Heidi, and David Buss. 1996. Women's sexual strategies: The hidden dimension of short-term mating. Manuscript. [19]

Griggs, R. A., and J. R. Cox. 1982. The elusive thematic-materials effect in Wason's selection task. *British Journal of Psychology* 73:407–20. [26]

Grimal, Pierre, ed. 1965–66. *Histoire mondiale de al femme.* Paris: Nouvelle Librairie de France. [29]

Grinnell, Jon, Craig Packer, and Anne Pusey. 1995. Cooperation in male lions: Kinship, reciprocity or mutualism? *Animal Behaviour* 49:95–105. [6]

Gross, Daniel. 1975. Protein capture and cultural development in the Amazon Basin. *American Anthropologist* 77:526–49. [9]

Groves, R. M. 1989. *Survey error and survey cost.* New York: Wiley. [1]

Groves, R. M., and R. L. Kahn. 1979. *Surveys by telephone: A national comparison with personal interviews.* New York: Academic Press. [16]

Gruson, L. 1990. Remembering a tortured child who lived in the streets of Guatemala City. *New York Times,* OCtober 14, p. 3. [39]

Guemple, L. 1976. The institutional flexibility of Inuit social life. In M. Freeman (ed.), *Inuit land use and occupancy project,* vol. 2, pp. 181–86. Ottawa: Department of Indian and Northern Affairs. [5]

———. 1979. *Inuit adoption.* Canadian Ethnology Service, Mercury Series, no. 47. Ottawa: National Museums of Canada. [5]

Gulliver, P. A. 1963. *Social control in an African society.* New York: New York University Press. [11]

Haas, A. 1979. *Teenage sexuality.* New York: Macmillan. [7]

Hager, Barbara J. 1992. Get thee to a nunnery: Female religious claustration in medieval Europe. *Ethology and Sociobiology* 13:385–407. [1, 30]

Haig, David. 1992. Genomic imprinting and the theory of parent-offspring conflict. *Seminal Developments in Biology* 3:153–60. [1, 32]

———. 1993. Genetic conflicts in human pregnancy. *Quarterly Review of Biology* 68:495–532. [1, 32]

———. 1994. Cohabitation and pregnancy-induced hypertension. *Lancet* 344:1633–34. [1, 32]

———. 1995. Placental hormones, genomic imprinting and maternal fetal communication. Manuscript. [32]

Hallett, Judith. 1984. *Fathers and daughters in Roman society.* Princeton, N.J.: Princeton University Press. [37]

Hames, Raymond B. 1979. Relatedness and interaction among the Ye'kwana: A preliminary analysis. In N. A. Chagnon and W. Irons (eds.), *Evolutionary biology and human social behavior: An anthropological perspective,* pp. 239–49. North Scituate, Mass.: Duxbury Press. [1]

———. 1987. Garden labor exchange among the Ye'kwana. *Ethology and Sociobiology* 8:259–84. [1, 5]

———. 1990. Adaptations to risk among the Yanomamo. In E. Cashdan (ed.), *Risk and uncertainty in tribal and peasant economies.* Boulder, Colo.: Westview Press. [6]

———. 1996. The costs and benefits of monogamy and polygyny for Yanomamö women. *Ethology and Sociobiology* 17:1–19. [1, 12]

Hames, Raymond B., and William Vickers. 1982. Optimal foraging theory as a model to explain variability in Amazon hunting. *American Ethnologist* 9:358–78. [1]

———, eds. 1983. *Adaptive responses of native Amazonians.* New York: Academic Press. [9]

Hamilton, William D. 1963. The evolution of altruistic behavior. *American Naturalist* 97:354–56. [1]

———. 1964. The genetical evolution of social behavior. *Journal of Theroetical Biology* 7:1–52. [1, 5, 6, 9, 13, 19, 24, 26, 31]

———. 1966. The moulding of senescence by natural selection. *Journal of Theoretical Biology* 12:12–45. [1, 13]

———. 1967. Extraordinary sex ratios. *Science* 156:477–88. [1]

————. 1971. Geometry for the selfish herd. *Journal of Theoretical Biology* 31:295–311. [1]

————. 1972. Altruism and related phenomena, mainly in the social insects. *Annual Reviews of Ecology and Systematics* 3:193–232. [1]

————. 1980. Sex versus non-sex versus parasite. *Oikos* 35:282–90. [1, 36]

————. 1996a. *Narrow roads of gene land.* Vol. 1. *Evolution of social behaviour.* Oxford: W. H. Freeman. [1]

————. 1996b. *Narrow roads of gene land.* Vol. 2. *Sex and sexual selection.* Oxford: W. H. Freeman. [1]

Hamilton, William D., Robert Axelrod, and Reiko Tanese. 1990. Sexual reproduction as an adaptation to resist parasites (a review). *Proceedings of the National Academy of Science USA* 87:3566–73. [1]

Hamilton, William D., and Marlene Zuk. 1982. Heritable true fitness and bright birds: A role for parasites? *Science* 218:384–87. [1, 19]

Hammerstein, Peter, and Geoff Parker. 1987. Sexual selection: Games between the sexes. In J. Bradbury and M. Anderson, *Sexual selection: Testing the alternatives,* pp. 119–42. New York: Wiley. [25]

Hanken, J., and Paul W. Sherman. 1981. Multiple paternity in Belding's ground squirrel litters. *Science* 212:351–53. [26]

Hanschu, Richard. 1996. Potential role of M.H.C. in human mate preference. Manuscript. [1]

Harcourt, Alexander, Paul Harvey, S. Larson, and R. Short. 1981. Testis weight, body weight, and breeding system in primates. *Nature* 293:55–57.

Harden, Donald. 1963. *The Phoenicians.* London: Thames and Hudson. [29]

Harner, Michael. 1962. Jívaro souls. *American Anthropologist* 64:258–272. [9]

Harpending, Henry. 1994. Infertility and forager demography. *American Journal of Physical Anthropology* 93:385–90. [8]

Harpending, Henry, and Alan Rogers. 1993. Fitness in stratified societies. *Ethology and Sociobiology* 11:497–509. [28]

Harpending, Henry, Alan Rogers, and Patricia Draper. 1987. Human sociobiology. *Yearbook of Physical Anthropology* 30:127–50. [1]

Harper, D. G. C. 1991. Communication. In J. Krebs and N. Davies (eds.), *Behavioural ecology: An evolutionary approach,* 3d ed., pp. 374–97. Oxford: Blackwell Scientific. [15]

Harper, J. 1972. Slaves and freedmen in imperial Rome. *American Journal of Philology* 93:341–42. [37]

Harris, Marvin. 1975. Mode of production and mode of reproduction. Paper presented in an American Association for the Advancement of Science symposium on Mode of Production, New York. [29]

————. 1979a. Protein and pilfering. In B. Ferguson (ed.), *Warfare, culture and environment,* pp. 111–140. Orlando, Fla.: Academic Press. [9]

————. 1979b. The Yanomamo and the causes of war in band and village societies. In M. Margolies and W. Carter (eds.), *Brazil: Anthropological perspectives,* pp. 121–32. New York: Columbia University Press. [9]

————. 1984. Animal capture and Yanamomö warfare. *Journal of Anthropological Research* 40:183–201. [9]

Harris, Rivkah. 1964. The naditu woman. In R. M. Adams (ed.), *Studies presented in A. Leo Oppenheim,* pp. 106–135. Chicago: Oriental Institute of the University of Chicago. [29]

————. 1966. Review of Histoire mondiale de la femme. *Journal of Economic and Social History of the Orient.* 9:308–9. [29]

Harris, William V. 1982. Towards a study of the Roman slave trade. *Memoirs of the American Academy in Rome* 36:117–40. [37]

Hart, C. W., and A. R. Pilling. 1960. *The Tiwi of north Australia.* New York: Holt, Rinehart and Winston. [18]

Hartung, John. 1976. On natural selection and the inheritance of wealth. *Current Anthropology* 17:607–13. [1, 3, 29, 31, 32]

————. 1977. More on natural selection and inheritence. *Current Anthropology* 18:336. [31]

————. 1980. On the geneticness of traits: Beyond $h^2 = V_g/V_p$. *Current Anthropology* 21:131–32. [31]

————. 1981a. Genome parliaments and sex with the red queen. In R. D. Alexander and D. W. Tinkle (eds.), *Natural selection and social behavior,* pp. 382–402. New York: Chiron Press. [31]

————. 1981b. Paternity and the inheritance of wealth. *Nature* 291:652–54. [31]

————. 1982. Polygyny and the inheritance of wealth. *Current Anthropology* 23:1–12. [1, 11, 28, 32, 33]

————. 1983. In defense of Murdock: A reply to Dickemann. *Current Anthropology* 24:125–26. [32, 33]

————. 1985. Matrilineal inheritance. New theory and analysis. *Behavioral and Brain Sciences* 8:661–88. [1, 32]

————. 1988. Deceiving down: Conjectures on the managements of subordinate status. In J. Lockhard and P. Paulhus (eds.), *Self-deception: An adaptive mechanism.* Englewood Cliffs, N.J.: Prentice-Hall. [32]

Harvey, Paul, R. D. Martin, and Tim Clutton-Brock. 1987. Primate life history in comparative perspective. In B. Smuts et al. (eds.), *Primate societies* pp. 181–96. Chicago University of Chicago Press. [34]

Harvey, Paul, and S. Nee. 1991. How to live like a mammal. *Nature* 350:23–24. [13]

Harvey, Paul, and Mark Pagel. 1991. *The comparative method in evolutionary biology.* Oxford: Oxford University Press. [1, 34]

Hasluck, M. 1954. *The unwritten law in Albania.* Cambridge: Cambridge University Press. [9]

Hass, A. 1979. *Teenage sexuality.* New York: Macmillan. [20]

Hauser, Marc. 1996. *Evolution of communication.* Cambridge, Mass: MIT Press. [1]

Hauswirth, Frieda. 1932. *Purdah: The status of Indian women.* London: Kegan Paul, Trench, Trubner. [29]

Hawkes, Kristen. 1983. Kin selection and culture. *American Ethnologist* 10:345–63. [1]

———. 1990. Why do men hunt? Some benefits for risky strategies. In E. Cashdan (ed.), *Risk and uncertainty,* pp. 145–66. Boulder, Colo.: Westview Press. [1, 6]

———. 1991. Showing off: Tests of another hypothesis about men's foraging goals. *Ethology and Sociobiology* 11:29–54. [1, 6, 34]

———. 1992. Sharing and collective action. In E. A. Smith and B. Winterhalder (eds.), *Evolutionary ecology and human behavior,* pp. 269–300. Hawthorne, N.Y.: Aldine–de Gruyter. [1, 6]

———. 1993. Why hunter-gatherers work: An ancient version of the problem of public goods. *Current Anthropology* 34:341–61. [1, 6]

Hawkes, Kristen, Kim Hill, and James F. O'Connell. 1982. Why hunters gather: Optimal foraging and the Ache of eastern Paraguay. *American Ethnologist* 9:379–98. [1]

Hawkes, Kristen, Kim Hill, James F. O'Connell, and Eric Charnov. 1985. How much is enough? Hunters and limited needs. *Ethology and Sociobiology* 6:3–15. [1]

Hawkes, Kristen, James F. O'Connell, and Nicholas Blurton Jones. 1989. Hardworking Hadza grandmothers. In V. Standen and R. Foley (eds.), *Comparative socioecology,* pp. 341–66. London: Basil Blackwell. [1, 13]

———. 1991. Hunting income patterns among the Hadza: Big game, common goods, foraging goals and the evolution of the human diet. *Philosophical Transactions of the Royal Society London, B* 334:243–51. [1]

Hazen, H. 1983. *Endless rapture: Rape, romance and the female imagination.* New York: Charles Scribner's Sons. [20]

Heffley, S. 1981. Northern Athapaskan settlement patterns and resource distributions: An application of Horn's model. In B. Winterhalder and E. A. Smith (eds.), *Hunter-gatherer foraging strategies,* pp. 125–47. Chicago: University of Chicago Press. [5]

Heider, K. 1970. *The Dugum Dani.* Chicago: Aldine. [9]

Herlihy, David. 1985. *Medieval households.* Cambridge, Mass.: Harvard University Press. [37]

Herlihy, David, and Christianne Klapisch-Zuber. 1985. *Tuscans and their families.* New Haven, Conn.: Yale University Press. [39]

Herman, J. 1977. Father-daugher incest. *Signs* 2:735–56. [31]

Herodian of Antioch. 1961. *History of the Roman Empire,* trans. Edward Echols. Berkeley: University of California Press. [37]

Hessellund, H. 1976. Masturbation and sexual fantasies in married couples. *Archives of Sexual Behavior* 5:133–47. [20]

Hewlett, Barry S. 1988. Sexual selection and paternal investment among Aka Pygmies. In L. Betzig et al. (eds.), *Human reproductive behaviour: A Darwinian perspective,* pp. 263–76. Cambridge University Press. [1]

———. 1991. Demography and childcare in preindustrial societies. *Journal of Anthropological Research* 2:78–88. [8]

Higashi, M., and N. Yamamura. 1993. What determines animal group size? Insider-outsider conflict and its resolution. *American Naturalist* 142:553–64. [6]

Higounet, Arlette. 1966. La femme du Moyen age en France dans la vie politique, economique et sociale. In P. Grimal (ed.), *Histoire mondiale de la femme,* vol. 2, pp. 135–84. Paris: Nouvelle Librairie de France. [29]

Hill, Elizabeth M., and Bobbi S. Low. 1992. Contemporary abortion patterns: A life-history approach. *Ethology and Sociobiology* 13:35–48. [1]

Hill, Elizabeth M., Elaine Nocks, and Lucinda Gardner. 1987. Physical attractiveness: Manipulation by physique and status displays. *Ethology and Sociobiology* 8:143–54. [1]

Hill, J. 1984. Prestige and reproductive success in man. *Ethology and Sociobiology* 5:77–95. [1, 4, 33]

Hill, Kim. 1988. Macronutrient modifications of optimal foraging theory: An approach using indifference curves applied to some modern foragers. *Human Ecology* 16:157–97. [1]

———. 1993. Life history theory and evolutionary anthropology. *Evolutionary Anthropology* 2:78–88. [8]

Hill, Kim, and Kristen Hawkes. 1983. Neotropical hunting among the Ache of eastern Paraguay. In R. Hames and W. Vickers (eds.), *Adaptive responses of native Amazoniana,* pp. 223–67. New York: Academic Press. [1, 5, 6]

Hill, Kim, and Ana Magdalena Hurtado. 1989. Hunter-gatherers of the New World. *American Scientist* 77:436–43. [13]

———. 1991. The evolution of premature reproductive senescence and menopause in human females: An evaluation of the "grandmother" hypothesis. *Human Nature* 2:313–50. [1, 13]

———. 1996. *Ache life history.* Hawthorne, N.Y.: Aldine–de Gruyter. [1, 6, 8, 13, 14, 15, 39]

Hill, Kim, and Hillard Kaplan. 1988. Tradeoffs in male and female reproductive strategies among the Ache. In L. Betzig et al. (eds.), *Human reproductive behaviour,* pp. 277–305. Cambridge: Cambridge University Press. [1, 17, 39]

Hill, Kim, Hillard Kaplan, Kristen Hawkes, and Ana Magdalena Hurtado. 1987. Foraging decisions among Ache hunter-gatherers: New data and implications for optimal foraging models. *Ethology and Sociobiology* 8:1–36. [1, 15]

Hill, R. 1945. Campus values in mate selection. *Journal of Home Economics* 37:554–58. [18]

Hinde, Robert A. 1984. Why do the sexes behave differently in close relationships? *Journal of Social and Personal Relationships* 1:471–501. [22, 33]

Hinde, Robert A. and Joan Stevenson-Hinde. 1986. Relating childhood relationships to individual characteristics. In W. Hartup and Zkubin (eds), *Relationships and Development,* pp 27–50. Hillsdale, NJ: Erlbaum. [33]

Hippel, Arndt von, 1994. *Human evolutionary biology.* Anchorage, Alaska: Stone Age Press. [1]

Hirshleifer, Jack. 1977. Economics from a biological viewpoint. *Journal of Law and Economics* 20:1–54. [1]

———. 1978. Natural economy vs. political economy. *Journal of Social and Biological Structures* 1:319–37. [1]

———. 1995. Anarchy and its breakdown. *Journal of Political Economy* 103:26–42. [1]

Hitti, Philip K. 1953. *History of the Arabs: From the earliest times to the present.* London: Macmillan. [29]

Hobcraft, J., J. McDonald, and S. Rutstein. 1983. Child-spacing effects on infant and early child mortality. *Population Index* 49:584–57. [7, 8]

Hoebel, E. A. 1968. The law of primitive man. In M. Fried et al. (eds.), *War: The anthropology of armed conflict and aggression,* pp. 208–10. Garden City, N.Y.: Natural History Press. [9]

Hoffman, Elizabeth, Keven McCabe, and Vernon Smith. 1996a. Behavioral foundations of reciprocity: Experimental economics and evolutionary psychology. Manuscript. [1, 27]

———. 1996b. On expectations and the monetary stakes in ultimatum games. *International Journal of Game Theory,* in press. [1]

———. 1996c. Social distance and other-regarding behavior in dictator games. Manuscript. [1]

Hoffman, Elizabeth, Kevin McCabe, Keith Shacht, and Vernon Smith. 1994. Preferences, property rights, and anonymity in bargaining game. *Games and Economic Behavior* 7:346–80. [1]

Hogan, R. 1982. A socioanalytic theory of personality. In M. Page (ed.), *Nebraska Symposium on Motivation,* pp. 55–89. Lincoln: University of Nebraska Press. [22]

Holcomb, Harmon. 1993. *Sociobiology, sex, and science.* Albany: State University of New York Press. [1]

Holecamp, K. E., and P. W. Sherman. 1989. Why male ground squirrels disperse. *American Scientist* 77:232–39. [15]

Holmes, Warren, and Paul W. Sherman. 1982. The ontogeny of kin recognition in two species of ground squirrels. *American Zoologist* 22:491–517. [16, 26]

Hopkins, Keith. 1965. Contraception in the Roman Empire. *Comparative Studies in Society and History* 8:124–51. [37]

———. 1966. On the probable age structure of the Roman population. *Population studies* 20:245–64. [37]

———. 1978. *Conquerors and slaves.* Cambridge: Cambridge University Press. [37]

———. 1983. *Death and renewal.* Cambridge: Cambridge University Press. [37]

Horace. 1980. *Odes and epodes,* trans. W. G. Shepherd. Harmondsworth: Penguin. [37]

———. 1979. *Satires and epistles,* trans. Niall Rudd. Harmondsworth: Penguin. [37]

Houston, A. I., C. W. Clark, J. M. McNamara, and M. Mangel. 1988. Dynamic models in behavioral and evolutionary ecology. *Nature* 332:29–34. [2]

Howard, Richard D. 1979. Estimating reproductive success in natural populations. *American Naturalist* 114:221–31. [15]

———. 1988. Reproductive success in two species of anurans. In T. Clutton-Brock (ed.), *Reproductive success,* pp. 99–113. Chicago: University of Chicago Press. [15]

Howell, Nancy. 1979. *Demography of the Dobe area !Kung.* New York: Academic Press. [7, 8, 13, 39]

————. 1982. Village composition implied by a paleodemographic life table: The Libben site. *American Journal of Physical Anthropology* 59:263–69. [13]

Howie, P. W., and A. McNeilly. 1982. Effects of breast feeding patterns on human birth intervals. *Journal of Reproductive Fertility* 65:545–57. [7]

Hrdy, Sarah Blaffer. 1976. The care and exploitation of nonhuman primate infants by conspecifics other than the mother. *Advances in the Study of Behavior* 6:101–58. [39]

————. 1977. The puzzle of langur infant-sharting. In *The Langurs of Abu: Female and male strategies of reproduction.* Cambridge, Mass.: Harvard University Press. [39]

————. 1979. Infanticide among mammals: A review, classification, and examination of the implications for the reproductive strategies of females. *Ethology and Sociobiology* 1:13–40. [39]

————. 1987. Sex-biased parental investment among primates and other mammals: A critical evaluation of the Trivers-Willard hypothesis. In J. Lancaster and R. Gelles (eds.), *Child abuse and neglect: Biosocial dimensions,* pp. 97–147. Hawthorne, N.Y.: Aldine–de Gruyter. [1, 39]

————. 1990. Sex bias in nature and in history. *Yearbook of Physical Anthropology* 33:1–13. [39]

————. 1992. Fitness trade-offs in the history and evolution of delegated mothering with special reference to wet-nursing, abandonment, and infanticide. *Ethology and Sociobiology* 13:409–42. [1, 8, 28]

Hrdy, Sarah Blaffer, and Debra Judge. 1993. Darwin and the puzzle of primogeniture. *Human Nature* 4:1–45. [1, 39, 40]

Hudson, J. W., and L. F. Henze. 1969. Campus values in mate selection: A replication. *Journal of Marriage and the Family* 31:772–75. [18]

Hufton, O. 1974. *The poor in eighteenth-century France 1750–1789.* Oxford: Oxford University Press. [39]

Hughes, Austin. 1983. Kin selection of complex behavioral strategies. *American Naturalist* 112:181–90. [4, 5]

————. 1986. Reproductive success and occupational class in eighteenth-century Lancashire, England. *Social Biology* 33:109–15. [1]

————. 1988. *Evolution and human kinship.* New York: Oxford University Press. [1]

Hull, T. H. 1990. Recent trends in sex ratios at birth in China. *Population and Development Review* 16:63–83. [39]

Humphrey, Nicholas K. 1976. The social function of the intellect. In P. Bateson and R. Hinde (eds.), *Growing points in ethology,* pp. 303–17. Cambridge: Cambridge University Press. [24]

————. 1980. Nature's psychologists. In B. Josephson and V. Ramachandran (eds.), *Consciousness and the physical world,* pp. 57–80. Oxford: Pergamon Press. [24]

————. 1981. Having feelings and showing feelings. In D. Wood-Gush et al. (eds.), *Self-awareness in domesticated animals,* pp. 37–39. Hertfordshire: The Universities Federation for Animal Welfare. [24]

————. 1983. *Consciousness regained.* Oxford: Oxford University Press. [1]

Hunecke, V. 1985. Les enfants trouvés: Contexte européen et cas Milanais (XVIIIe–XIXe siecles). *Revue d'Histoire Moderne et Contemporaine* 32:3–29. [39]

Hunt, M. 1974. *Sexual behavior in the 1970s.* New York: Dell. [20]

Hurd, James. 1983. Kin relatedness and church fissioning among the "Nebraska" Amish of Pennsylvania. *Social Biology* 30:59–66. [1]

————. 1985. Sex differences in mate choice among the "Nebraska" Amish of Central Pennsylvania. *Ethology and Sociobiology* 6:49–57. [1]

————, ed. 1995. *The biology of morality.* Hawthorne, N.Y.: Aldine–de Gruyter. [1]

Hurst, Lawrence D. 1990. Parasite diversity and the evolution of diploidy, multicellularity and anisogamy. *Journal of Theoretical Biology* 144:429–43. [1]

————. 1992. Intragenomic conflict as an evolutionary force. *Proceedings of the Royal Society, B* 248:135–48. [1]

Hurtado, Magdi. 1985. Women's subsistence strategies among Ache hunter-gatherers of eastern Paraguay. Ph.D. thesis, Dept. of Anthropology, University of Utah. Ann Arbor, Mich.: University Microfilms International. [39]

Hurtado, Magdi, Kristen Hawkes, Kim Hill, and Hilly Kaplan. 1985. Female subsistence strategies among Ache hunter-gatherers of eastern Paraguay. *Human Ecology* 13:1–28. [8, 39]

Hurtado, Magdi, and Kim Hill. 1990. Seasonality in a foraging society: Variation in diet, work effort, fertility, and the sexual division of labor among the Hiwi of Venezuela. *Journal of Anthropological Research* 46:293–346. [13]

Hurtado, Magdi, Kim Hill, Hilly Kaplan, and Inez Hurtado. 1992. Trade-offs between female food acquisition and child care among Hiwi and Ache foragers. *Human Nature* 3:185–216. [1]

Ireland, E. 1989. Why some Waura are killed and not buried, and why some are buried and not killed. Paper presented at 88th annual meeting of the American Anthropological Association, Washington, D.C. [39]

Ireland, E., and Thomas Gregor. 1986. Interring the "thing that created itself." Paper presented at 85th annual meeting of the American Anthropological Association, Philadelphia. [39]

Irons, William. 1975. *The Yomut Turkmen: A study of social organization among a central Asian Turkic-speaking population.* Anthropological Paper no. 58, Museum of Anthropology, University of Michigan. [3, 4]

———. 1976. Emic and reproductive success. Paper read at the 75th annual meeting of the American Anthropological Association, Washington, D.C. [4, 31]

———. 1977. Evolutionary biology and human fertility. Paper presented at annual meetings of the American Anthropological Association. [3]

———. 1979a. Cultural and biological success. In N. A. Chagnon and W. Irons (eds.), *Natural selection and social behavior,* pp. 257–72. North Scituate, Mass.: Duxbury Press. [1, 4, 9, 13, 33, 35]

———. 1979b. Natural selection, adaptation, and human social behavior. In N. A. Chagnon and W. Irons (eds.), *Natural selection and social behavior,* pp. 4–39, North Scituate, Mass: Duxbury Press. [3]

———. 1979c. Investment and primary social dyads. In N. A. Chagnon and W. Irons (eds.), *Natural selection and social behavior,* pp. 181–212. North Scituate, Mass.: Duxbury Press. [31, 33]

———. 1980. Is Yomut social behavior adaptive? In G. Barlow and J. Silverberg (eds.), *Sociobiology: Beyond nature/nurture?* Boulder, Colo.: Westview Press. [3, 4, 31]

———. 1981. Why lineage exogamy? In R. Alexander and D. Tinkle (eds.), *Natural selection and social behavior,* pp. 476–89. New York: Chiron Press. [9]

———. 1983. Human female reproductive strategies. In S. Waser (ed.), *Social behavior of female vertebrates,* pp. 169–213. New York: Academic Press. [11]

———. 1991. How did morality evolve? *Zygon* 26:49–89. [1]

———. 1995. Meta-analysis of studies on wealth and reproductive success. Working Paper, Department of Anthropology, Northwestern University. [28]

———. 1996. Morality, religion, and human evolution. In W. M. Richardson and W. Wildman (eds.), *Building bridges between theology and the natural sciences.* New York: Natural History Press. [1]

Isaac, B. 1980. Female fertility and marital form among the Mende of rural upper Bambara chiefdom, Sierra Leone. *Ethnology* 19:297–313. [35]

Isaac, Glynn. 1978. The food-sharing behavior of protohuman hominids. *Scientific American* 238:90–108. [26]

Isuigo-Abanihe Unche, C. 1985. Child fosterage in West Africa. *Population and Development Review* 11:53–73. [39]

Iwawaki, S., and G. Wilson. 1983. Sex fantasies in Japan. *Personality and Individual Differences* 4:543–45. [20]

Jackendoff, R. 1991. Is there a faculty of social cognition? Presidential address to the Society for Philosophy and Psychology, San Francisco. [26]

Jackson, G. B., and A. K. Romney. 1973. Historical inference from cross-cultural data: The case of dowry. *Ethos* 1:517–20. [35]

Jacobson, Dorothy. 1973. *Hidden faces: Hindu and Muslim purdah in a central Indian village.* Ph.D. diss., Columbia University. Ann Arbor Mich.: University Microfilms International [29, 30]

Jacoby, S. 1983. *Wild justice: The evolution of revenge.* New York: Harper and Row. [9]

Jank, Margaret. 1977. *Mission: Venezuela. Reaching new tribes.* Sanford, Fla.: Brown Gold Publications Bookroom. [10]

Jankowiak, William R., Elizabeth M. Hill, and J. M. Donovan. 1992. The effects of sex and sexual orientation on attractiveness judgements: An evolutionary interpretation. *Ethology and Sociobiology* 13:73–85. [1]

Jasienska, Grazyna, and Peter Ellison. 1993. Heavy workload impairs ovarian function in Polish peasant women. *American Journal of Physical Anthropology* 16:117–18. [1]

Jelliffe, D. B., and Patrice Jelliffe. 1978. The volume and composition of human milk in poorly nourished communities: A review. *American Journal of Clinical Nutrition* 31:492–515. [7]

Jencks, C. 1979. *Who gets ahead? Determinants of economic success in America.* New York: Basic Books. [18]

Jenkins, Henry. 1992. *Textual poachers: Television fans and participatory culture.* New York: Routledge. [21]

Jennings, Ronald C. 1973. Loans and credit in early 17th-century Ottoman judicial records: The Sharia court of Anatolian Kayseri. *Journal of Economic and Social History of the Orient* 16:168–216. [29]

———. 1975. Women in early 17th-century Ottoman judicial records—the Sharia court of Anatolian Kayseri. *Journal of the Economic and Social History of the Orient* 18:53–114. [29]

Jennrich, R., and P. Sampson. 1985. Stepwise discriminant analysis. In W. J. Dixon (ed.), *BMDP Statistical Software Manual*. Berkeley: University of California Press. [35]

Jensen-Campbell, Lauri A., William Graziano and Stephen West. 1995. Dominance, prosocial orientation, and female preferences. Do nice guys really finish last? *Journal of Personality and Social Psychology* 68:427–40. [1]

Johansson, Sheila R. 1987a. Centuries of childhood/centuries of parenting: Philippe Ariés and the modernization of privileged infancy. *Family History* 12:343–65. [39]

———. 1987b. Status anxiety and demographic contraction of privileged populations. *Population and Development Review* 13:439–70. [39]

Johnson, A., and T. Earle. 1987. *The evolution of human societies: From foraging group to agrarian state*. Stanford, Calif.: Stanford University Press. [9]

Johnson, Earvin "Magic." 1992. *My life*. New York: Random House. [1]

Johnson, H. C. 1980. Working with stepfamilies: Principles of practice. *Social Work* 25:304–8. [16]

Johnson, O. 1981. The socioeconomic context of child abuse and neglect in native South America. In J. Korbin (ed.), *Child abuse and neglect*, pp. 56–70. Berkeley: University of California Press. [39]

Johnson, Steven B., and Ronald C. Johnson. 1991. Support and conflict in kinsmen in Norse earldoms, Icelandic families and the English royalty. *Ethology and Sociobiology* 12:211–20. [1]

Johnson-Laird, P. N. 1982. Thinking as a skill. *Quarterly Journal of Experimental Psychology* 34A:1–29. [26]

———. 1983. *Mental models: Towards a cognitive science of language, inference and consciousness*. Cambridge, Mass.: Harvard University Press. [26]

Johnston, D. 1988. *The Roman law of trusts*. Oxford: Oxford University Press. [37]

Johnston, Victor, and Melissa Franklin. 1993. Is beauty in the eye of the beholder? *Ethology and Sociobiology* 14:183–99. [1]

Johnstone, Rufus. 1994. Female preference for symmetrical mates as the by-product of selection for mate recognition. *Nature* 372:172–75. [1]

Jones, Doug. 1995. Sexual selection, physical attractiveness, and facial neoteny: Cross-cultural evidence and implications. *Current Anthropology* 36:723–48. [1]

Jones, Doug, and Kim Hill. 1993. Criteria of facial attractiveness in five populations. *Human Nature* 4:271–96. [1]

Jones, E. C. 1975. The post-reproductive phase in mammals. In P. van Keep and C. Lauritzen (eds.), *Frontiers of hormone research*, pp. 1–20. Basel: Karger. [13]

Jones, J., and D. Barlow. 1987. *Self-reported frequency of sexual urges, fantasies, and masturbatory fantasies in heterosexual males and females*. Paper presented at the annual meeting of the Association for the Advancement of Behavior Therapy. [20]

Jones, R. E. 1988. A hazards model analysis of breastfeeding variables and maternal age on return to menses postpartum in rural Indonesian women. *Human Biology* 60:853–71. [1]

Josephson, Steve C. 1993. Status, reproductive success, and marrying polygynously. *Ethology and Sociobiology* 14:391–96. [1, 12, 32]

Judge, Debra. 1996. American legacies and the variable life histories of men and women. *Ethology and Sociobiology* 17 in press. [40]

Judge, Debra, and Sarah Blaffer Hrdy. 1992. Allocation of accumulated resources among close kin: Inheritance in Sacramento, California. *Ethology and Sociobiology* 13:495–522. [1, 32, 40]

———. 1996. Historical change in patterns of property allocations at death: Case studies from New England and California. Manuscript. [1, 40]

Juvenal. 1974. *The sixteen satires*, trans. Peter Green. Harmondsworth: Penguin. [37]

Kacelnik, A. 1984. Central place foraging in starlings (*Sturnus vulgaris*). I. Patch residence time. *Journal of Animal Ecology* 53:283–99. [2]

Kacelnik, A., and I. C. Cuthill. 1987. Starlings and optimal foraging theory: Modelling in a fractal world. In A. C. Kamil et al. (eds.), *Foraging theory*, pp. 303–33. New York: Plenum Press. [2]

Kadushin, A., and F. W. Seidl. 1971. Adoption failure: A social work postmortem. *Social Work* 16:32–38. [16]

Kaplan, Hillard. 1994. Evolutionary and wealth flows theories of fertility: Empirical tests and new models. *Population and Development Review* 20:753–91. [1, 8]

———. 1996. The competitive labor market theory of the demographic transition: An evolutionary-economic theory of human fertility and paternal investment. *Behavioral and Brain Sciences*, in press. [1]

Kaplan, Hillard, and Kim Hill. 1985a. Food sharing among Ache foragers: Tests of explanatory hypotheses. *Current Anthropology* 26:233–45. [1, 5, 6, 26]

———. 1985b. Hunting ability and reproductive success among male Ache foragers. *Current Anthropology* 26:131–33. [1, 4]

———. 1992. The evolutionary ecology of food acquisition. In E. A. Smith and B. Winterhalder (eds.), *Evolutionary ecology,* pp. 167–201. Hawthorne, N.Y.: Aldine–de Gruyter. [1]

Kaplan, Hillard, Kim Hill, Kristen Hawkes, and Ana Magdalena Hurtado. 1984. Food sharing among the Ache hunter-gatherers of eastern Paraguay. *Current Anthropology* 25:113–15. [1, 5, 6]

Kaplan, Hillard, Kim Hill, and Ana Magdalena Hurtado. 1990. Risk, foraging, and food sharing among the Aché. In E. Cashdan (ed.), *Risk and uncertainty in tribal and peasant economies,* pp. 107–44. Boulder, Colo.: Westview Press. [1, 6, 26]

Kaplan, Hillard, Jane B. Lancaster, John A. Bock, and Sara E. Johnson. 1995a. Fertility and fitness among Albuquerque men: A competitive labour market theory. In R. Dunbar (ed.), *Human reproductive decisions: Biological and social perspectives,* pp. 96–136. London: Macmillan. [1]

———. 1995b. Does observed fertility maximize fitness among New Mexican men? *Human Nature* 6:325–60.

Keegan, William F. 1986. The optimal foraging analysis of horticultural production. *American Anthropologist* 88:92–107. [1]

Keesing, Roger. 1970. Kwaio fosterage. *American Anthropologist* 72:991–1020. [39]

Kelley, K. 1984–85. Sexual fantasy and attitudes as functions of sex of subject and content of erotica. *Imagination, Cognition, and Personality* 4:339–47. [20]

Kelsen, H. 1946. *Society and nature: A sociological inquiry.* London: Kegan Paul, Trench and Trubner. [9]

Kenrick, Douglas T. 1986. How strong is the case against contemporary social and personality psychology? A response to Carlson. *Journal of Personality and Social Psychology* 50:839–44. [22]

———. 1987. Gender, genes, and the social environment. In P. Shaver and C. Hendrick (eds.), *Review of personality and social psychology: Sex and gender,* pp. 14–43, Newbury Park, Calif.: Sage. [22]

Kenrick, Douglas T., Gary E. Groth, Melanie R. Trost, and Edward K. Sadalla. 1993. Integrating evolutionary and social exchange perspectives on relationships: Effects of gender, self-appraisal, and involvement on level of mate selection. *Journal of Personality and Social Psychology* 58.97–116. [1, 23]

Kenrick, Douglas T., and Richard C. Keefe. 1989. Time to integrate sociobiology and social psychology. *Behavioral and Brain Sciences* 12:24–25. [22]

———. 1992. Age preferences in mates reflect sex differences in human reproductive strategies. *Behavioral and Brain Sciences* 15:75–133. [1, 23]

Kenrick, Douglas T., D. Montelo, and S. MacFarlane. 1985. Personality: Social learning, social cognition, or sociobiology? In R. Hogan and W. Jones (eds.), *Perspectives in personality,* vol. 1, pp. 201–34. Greenwich, Conn.: JAI Press. [22]

Kenrick, Douglas T., Edward Sadalla, Gary Groth, and Melanie Trost. 1990. Evolution, traits, and the stages of human courtship: Qualifying the parental investment model. *Journal of Personality* 58:97–116. [1, 15]

Kenrick, Douglas T., and Virgil Sheets. 1993. Homicidal fantasies. *Ethology and Sociobiology* 14:231–46. [1]

Kenrick, Douglas T., D. O. Stringfield, W. Wagenhals, R. Dahl, and H. J. Ransdell. 1980. Sex differences, androgyny, and approach responses to erotica: A new variation on the old volunteer problem. *Journal of Personality and Social Psychology* 38:517–24. [22, 23]

Kenrick, Douglas T., and Melanie R. Trost. 1987. A biosocial theory of heterosexual relationships. In K. Kelly (ed.), *Females, males, and sexuality,* pp. 59–100. Albany: State University of New York Press. [22]

———. 1989. Reproductive exchange model of heterosexual relationships: Putting proximate economics in ultimate perspective. In C. Hendrick (ed.), *Review of personality and social psychology,* vol. 10, pp. 92–118. Newbury Park, Calif.: Sage. [22]

Khan, Mazhar ul Haq. 1972. *Purdah and polygamy: A study in the social pathology of the Muslim society.* Peshawar: Nashiran-e-Ilm-o-Taraqiyet. [29]

Kiang, Kang-hu. 1935. *Chinese civilization: An introduction to sinology.* Shangahi: Chung Hwa Book. [29]

Kiefer, Otto. 1934. *Sexual life in ancient Rome.* London: Routledge and Kegan Paul. [37]

Kim, K., and B. Ko. 1990. An incidence survey of battered children in two elementary schools of Seoul. *Child Abuse and Neglect* 14:273–76. [17]

Kings' College Sociobiology Study Group, ed. 1982. *Current problems in sociobiology.* Cambridge: Cambridge University Press. [9]

Kinsey, Alfred, W. B. Pomeroy, and C. E. Martin. 1948. *Sexual behavior in the human male.* Philadelphia: Saunders. [20, 22]

Kinsey, Alfred, W. B. Pomeroy, C. E. Martin, and P. H. Gebhard. 1953. *Sexual behavior in the human female.* Philadelphia: Saunders. [20, 22]

Kitchen, D. W. 1974. Social behavior and ecology of the pronghorn. *Wildlife Monographs* 38:1–96. [11]

Kitcher, Philip. 1985. *Vaulting ambition: Sociobiology and the quest for human nature.* Cambridge, Mass.: MIT Press. [1, 15, 30]

Klapisch-Zuber, Christianne. 1986a. Blood parents and milk parents: Wet nursing in Florence, 1300–1530. In *Women, family, and ritual in Renaissance Florence*, pp. 132–64. Chicago: University of Chicago Press. [39]

———. 1986b. The Griselda complex. Dowry and marriage gifts in the quattrocento. In *Women, family and ritual in Renaissance Florence*, pp. 213–46. Chicago: University of Chicago Press. [39]

Kleiman, Devra. 1977. Monogamy in mammals. *Quarterly Review of Biology* 52:39–60. [37]

Kleinman, M. D., L. Jacobson, E. Hormann, and W. A. Walker. 1980. Protein values of milk samples from mothers without biologic pregnancies. *Journal of Pediatrics* 97:612–15. [39]

Klindworth, Heike and Eckart Voland. 1995. How did the Krummhörn elite males achieve above-average reproductive success? *Human Nature* 6:221–40. [1]

Kline, J., Z. Stein, and M. Susser, 1989. *Conception to birth: Epidemiology of prenatal development*. New York: Oxford University Press. [13]

Kluger, Matt. 1979. *Fever: Its biology, evolution, and function*. Princeton, N.J.: Princeton University Press. [1]

Knafo, D., and Y. Jaffee. 1984. Sexual fantasizing in males and females. *Journal of Research in Personality*, 18:451–62. [20]

Knapton, R. W. 1984. Parental investment: The problem of currency. *Canadian Journal of Zoology*, 62:2673–74. [40]

Knauft, Bruce. 1987a. Divergence between cultural success and reproductive fitness in preindustrial cities. *Cultural Anthropology* 2:94–114. [4]

———. 1987b. Reconsidering violence in simple human societies. *Current Anthropology* 28:457–82. [9]

Knight, Chris. 1991. *Blood relations: Menstruation and the origins of culture*. New Haven, Conn.: Yale University Press. [1]

Knoth, R., K. Boyd, and B. Singer. 1988. Empirical tests of sexual selection theory: Predictions of sex differences in onset, intensity, and time course of sexual arousal. *Journal of Sex Research* 24:73–89. [20]

Kobben, J. F. 1967. Why exceptions? The logic of cross-cultural analysis. *Current Anthropology* 8:3–34. [35]

Koch, K-F. 1974. *War and peace in Jalémo: The management of conflict in highland New Guinea*. Cambridge, Mass.: Harvard University Press. [9]

Kolendo, J. 1976. Les Femmes esclaves de e'Empereur. *Actes du Colloque 1970/71/72/73 sur l'esclavage*, pp. 399–416. [37]

Kompara, D. R. 1980. Difficulties in the socialization process of step-parenting. *Family Relations* 29:69–73. [16]

Konner, Melvin. 1976. Maternal care, infant behavior, and development among the !Kung. In R. Lee and I. DeVore (eds.), *Kalahari hunter-gatherers: Studies of the !Kung San and their neighbors*. Cambridge, Mass.: Harvard University Press. [39]

———. 1981. Evolution of human behavior development. In R. H. Munroe et al. (eds.), *Handbook of cross-cultural development*, pp. 3–51. New York: Garland. [33]

———. 1982. *The tangled wing: Biological constraints on the human spirit*. New York: Holt, Rinehart and Winston. [1]

Konner, Melvin, and Carol Worthman. 1980. Nursing frequency, gonadal function and birth spacing among !Kung hunter-gatherers. *Science* 207:788–91. [7, 39]

Korbin, J. E., ed. 1981. *Child abuse and neglect: Cross-cultural perspectives*. Berkeley: University of California Press. [39]

Koso-Thomas, Olayinka. 1987. *The circumcision of women: A strategy for eradication*. London: Zed Books. [30]

Kottak, Conrad. 1978. *Anthropology: The exploration of human diversity*, 2d ed. New York: Random House. [33]

Koyama, Takashi, H. Nakamura, and M. Hiramatsu. 1967. Japan. In R. Patai (ed.), *Women in the modern world*, pp. 290–314. New York: Free Press. [29]

Krebs, John. 1978. Optimal foraging: Decision rules for predators. In J. Krebs and N. Davies (eds.), *Behavioural ecology: An evolutionary approach*, pp. 23–63. Oxford: Blackwell Scientific. [5]

Krebs, John and Nick Davies. 1984. *Behavioural ecology: An evolutionary approach*, 2d ed. Sunderland, Mass.: Sinauer. [24, 33]

———. 1987. *An introduction to behavioral ecology*, 2d ed. Oxford: Blackwell Scientific. [11, 33]

Krebs, John, A. Kacelnik, and P. Taylor. 1978. Tests of optimal sampling by foraging great tits. *Nature* 275:27–31. [2]

Krebs, John, D. Sherry, S. D. Healy, V. H. Perry, and A. L. Vaccarino. 1989. Hippocampal specialization of food-storing birds. *Proceedings of the National Academy of Sciences*, USA 86:1388–92. [2]

Kretz, Jayne Ann, ed. 1992. *Dangerous men and adventurous women: Romance writers on the appeal of the romance*. Philadelphia: University of Pennsylvania Press. [21]

Kroeber, Alfred, and J. Richardson. 1940. Three centuries of women's dress fashions: A quantitative analysis. Cambridge, Mass.: Papers of the Peabody Museum of American Archaeology and Ethnology, vol. 47. [35]

Kuchikura, Y. 1988. Efficiency and focus of blowpipe hunting among Semaq Beri hunter-gatherers of peninsular Malaysia. *Human Ecology* 16:271–305. [1]

Kundera, Milan. 1984. *The unbearable lightness of being,* trans. Michael Henry Heim. New York: Harper-Collins. [1]

Kurian, G., ed. 1979. *Cross-cultural perspectives of mate-selection and marriage.* Westview, Conn.: Greenwood Press. [18]

Kurland, Jeffrey. 1979. Paternity, mother's brother, and human sociality. In N. A. Chagnon and W. Irons (eds.), *Natural selection and social behavior.* North Scituate, Mass.: Duxbury Press. [31]

Kurland, Jeffrey, and Steven J. C. Gaulin. 1979. Testing kin selection: Problems with r. *Behavioral Ecology and Sociobiology* 6:81–83. [5]

Lacey, W. K. 1968. *The family in classical Greece.* London: Thames and Hudson. [29]

Lack, David. 1940. Pair formation in birds. *Condor* 42:269–86. [18]

Lafayette, M-M. 1678. *Princesse de Cleves.* Paris. [39]

Laland, Kevin. 1993. The mathematical modeling of human culture and its implications for psychology and the human sciences. *British Journal of Psychology* 84:144–69. [1]

Laland, Kevin, Jochen Kumm, and Marcus Feldman. 1995. Gene-culture coevolutionary theory: A test case. *Current Anthropology* 36:131–156. [1]

Lamb, Patricia, and Diana L. Veith. 1986. Romantic myth, transcendence, and *Star Trek* zines. In D. Palumbo (ed.), *Erotic universe: Sexuality and fantastic literature,* New York: Greenwood. [21]

Lancaster, Jane B., and B. J. King. 1985. An evolutionary perspective on menopause. In J. K. Brown and V. Kerns (eds.), *In her prime,* pp. 13–20. Boston Massachusetts: Bergin and Garvey. [13]

Lancaster, Jane B., and Chet S. Lancaster. 1987. The watershed: Change in parental investment and family formation strategies in the course of human evolution. In J. Lancaster et al. (eds.), *Parenting across the lifespan.* Hawthorne, N.Y.: Aldine–de Gruyter. [39]

Landolt, Monica, Martin Lalumiére, and Vernon Quinsey. 1995. Sex differences in intra-sex variations in human mating tactics: An evolutionary approach. *Ethology and Sociobiology* 16:3–23. [1]

Lane, Edward W. 1973. *An account of the manners and customs of modern Egyptians,* 5th ed. New York: Dover. [29]

Lang, H. 1993. Dowry and female competition: A Boolean reanalysis. *Current Anthropology* 34:775–78. [36]

Lang, Olga. 1946. *Chinese family and society.* New Haven, Conn.: Yale University Press. [29]

Langer, W. 1974. Infanticide: A historical survey. *History of Childhood Quarterly* 1:353–65. [39]

Laslett, Peter. 1984. *The world we have lost,* 3d ed. London: Macmillan. [1, 38]

Lasselle, C. de. 1975. Les Enfants abandonnés a Paris au XVIIIe siecle. *Annales E. S. C.,* 30:187–218. [39]

Lawick, Hugo van. 1973. *Solo: The story of an African wild dog puppy and his pack.* London: Collins. [39]

Leach, Edmund R. 1958. Magical hair. *Journal of the Royal Anthropological Institute* 88:147–64. [29]

Lee, Phillis C. 1989. Family structure, communal care and female reproductive effort. In V. Standen and R. Foley (eds.), *Comparative socioecology,* pp. 323–40. London: Blackwell Scientific. [39]

Lee, Richard B. 1972. Population growth and the beginnings of sedentary life among the !Kung bushmen. In B. Spooner (ed.), *Population growth: Anthropological implications.* Cambridge, Mass.: MIT Press. [7]

———. 1979. *The !Kung San: Men, women, and work in a foraging society.* Cambridge: Cambridge University Press. [7, 9]

Lee, Richard B., and I. DeVore, eds. 1968. *Man the hunter.* Chicago: Aldine. [26]

Lehrman, D. S. 1970. Semantic and conceptual issues in the nature-nurture problem. In L. Aronson et al. (eds.), *Development and evolution of behavior,* pp. 17–52. San Francisco: Freeman. [15]

Leland, L., T. Struhsaker, and T. Butynski. 1984. Infanticide by adult males in three primate species of the Kibale forest, Uganda: A test of hypotheses. In G. Hausfater and S. B. Hrdy (eds.), *Infanticide: Comparative and evolutionary perspectives,* pp. 151–72. Hawthorne, N.Y.: Aldine–de Gruyter. [39]

Lenington, S. 1980. Female choice and polygyny in red-winged blackbirds. *Animal Behaviour* 28:347–61. [11]

———. 1981. Child abuse: The limits of sociobiology. *Ethology and Sociobiology* 2:17–29. [1, 16]

LeNoir, J-C-P. 1780. Détail sur quelques établissements de la ville de Paris, demandé par sa majesté impériale, la reine de Hongrie. *Paris: Document in Bibliotheque Nationale.* Paris. [39]

Leslie, P. W., and P. H. Fry. 1989. Extreme seasonality of births among nomadic Turkana pastoralists. *American Journal of Physical Anthropology* 79:103–15. [1]

Lessing, Doris. 1952. *A proper marriage.* New York: Simon and Schuster. [1]

Lever, J. 1976. Sex differences in the games children play. *Social Problems* 23:478–87. [33]

Levine, N. 1987. Differential child care in three Tibetan communities: Beyond son preference. *Population and Development Review* 13:281–304. [39]

Levine, S., and R. Levine. 1981. Child abuse and neglect in sub-Saharan Africa. In J. Korbin (ed.), *Child abuse and neglect: Cross-cultural perspectives,* pp. 35–55. Berkeley: University of California Press. [39]

Lévi-Strauss, Claude. 1944. The social and psychological aspects of chieftainship in a primitive tribe: The Nambikuara of northwestern Matto Grosso. *Transactions of the New York Academy of Sciences* 7:16–32. [9]

Levy, Harry L. 1963. Inheritance and dowry in classical Athens. In J. Pitt-Rivers (ed.), *Mediterranean countrymen: Essays in the social anthropology of the Mediterranean,* pp. 137–43. Paris: Mouton. [29]

Levy, Reuben. 1957. *The social structure of Islam.* Cambridge: Cambridge University Press. [29]

Lewis, J. S. 1986. *In the family way: Childbearing in the British aristocracy 1760–1860.* New Brunswick, N.J.: Rutgers University Press. [39]

Licht, Hans. 1969. *Sexual life in ancient Greece,* trans. J. H. Freese. London: Panther Books. [29]

Lightcap, Joy, Jeffrey Kurland, and R. Burgess. 1982. Child abuse: A test of some predictions from evolutionary theory. *Ethology and Sociobiology* 3:61–67. [1, 16]

Lightfoot-Klein, Hanny. 1989. *Prisoners of ritual: Odyssey into female genital circumcision in Africa.* New York: Harrington Park Press. [30]

Littlefield, C., and Philip Rushton. 1986. When a child dies. *Journal of Personality and Social Psychology* 51:797–802. [1, 9]

Livy. 1971. *The early history of Rome,* trans. Aubrey de Sélincourt. Harmondsworth: Penguin. [37]

Lizot, Jacques. 1977. The Yanomamö *Man* 12:496. [9]

———. 1984. *Les Yanomami centraux.* Paris L'Ecole des Hantes Etudes. [9]

———. 1985. *Tales of the Yanomami.* Cambridge: Cambridge University Press. [9]

———. 1989. Sobre la guerra: Una respuesta a N. A. Chagnon. *La Iglesia en Amazonas* 44:23–34. [10]

———. 1994. On warfare: An answer to N. A. Chagnon. *American Ethnologist* 21:841–58. [10]

Llewellyn-Jones, D. 1974. *Human reproduction and society.* New York: Pitman. [13]

Lock, S. 1990. Right and wrong: Book reviews. *Nature* 345:397. [39]

Low, Bobbi S. 1979. Sexual selection and human ornamentation. In N. A. Chagnon and W. Irons (eds.), *Evolutionary biology and human social behavior: An anthropological perspective,* pp. 197–213. North Scituate, Mass.: Duxbury Press. [1]

———. 1988a. Measures of polygyny in humans. *Current Anthropology* 29:189–94. [33]

———. 1988b. Pathogen stress and polygyny in humans. In L. Betzig et al. (eds.), *Human reproductive behaviour,* pp. 115–27. Cambridge: Cambridge University Press. [28]

———. 1989a. Cross-cultural patterns in the training of children. *Journal of Comparative Psychology* 103:311–19. [1, 28]

———. 1989b. Occupational status and reproductive behavior in 19th-century Sweden: Locknevi Parish. *Social Biology* 36:82–101. [33]

———. 1990a. Marriage systems and pathogen stress in human societies. *American Zoologist* 30:325–39. [1, 36]

———. 1990b. Sex, power, and resources: Male and female strategies. *International Journal of Contemporary Sociology* 27:45–71. [33]

———. 1991a. Occupational status, land ownership, and reproductive behavior in 19th-century Sweden: Tuna Parish. *American Anthropologist* 92:115–26. [4, 33]

———. 1991b. Reproductive life in 19th-century Sweden: An evolutionary perspective on demographic phenomena. *Ethology and Sociobiology* 12:411–48. [1]

Low, Bobbi S., and Alice L. Clarke. 1992. Resources and the life course: Patterns through the demographic transition. *Ethology and Sociobiology* 13:463–94. [1, 4, 15]

Luce, R. D., and H. Raiffa. 1957. *Games and decisions: Introduction and critical survey.* New York: Wiley. [26]

Lumsden, Charles, and Edward O. Wilson. 1981. *Genes, mind, and culture: The coevolutionary process.* Cambridge, Mass.: Harvard University Press. [1, 31]

———. 1982. *Promethean fire: Reflections on the origin of mind.* Cambridge, Mass.: Harvard University Press. [1, 9]

Luttbeg, B., Monique Borgerhoff Mulder, and Marc Mangel. 1996. Persistent polygyny: Dynamic modelling of a male allocation problem. Working Paper, Department of Anthropology, University of California–Davis. [12]

Maaskant-Kleibrink, M. 1987. Nymphomania. In J. Blok and P. Mason (eds.), *Sexual asymmetry.* Amsterdam: J. C. Geiben. [37]

Maccoby, Elinor and C. N. Jacklin. 1974. *The psychology of sex differences.* Palo Alto, Calif: Stanford University Press. [18]

MacDonald, Kevin. 1990. Mechanisms of sexual egalitarianism in Western Europe. *Ethology and Sociobiology* 11:1–27. [37]

———, ed. 1988. *Social and personality development: An evolutionary synthesis.* New York: Plenum. [1]

Mace, Ruth. 1993a. Nomadic pastoralists adopt subsistence strategies that maximize long-term household survival. *Behavioral Ecology and Sociobiology* 33:363–82. [1]

———. 1993b. Transitions between cultivation and pastoralism in sub-Saharan Africa. *Current Anthropology* 34:363–82. [1]

———. 1996a. When to have another baby: A dynamic model of reproductive decision-making and evidence from the Gabbra pastoralists. *Ethology and Sociobiology* 17, in press. [1]

———1996b. Biased parental investment and reproductive success in babbra pastoralists. *Behavioral Ecology and Sociobiology* 38:75–81. [1, 28]

Mace, Ruth, and Mark Pagel. 1994. The comparative method in anthropology. *Current Anthropology* 35:549–64. [28, 32, 36]

Maddala, G. S. 1983. *Limited dependent and qualitative variables in econometrics.* Cambridge: Cambridge University Press. [11]

Maddison, William. 1990. A method testing the correlated evolution of two binary characters: Are gains or losses concentrated on certain branches of a phylogenetic tree? *Evolution* 44:539–57. [28, 32]

Maddison, W. P., and D. R. Maddison. 1992. MacClade: Analysis of phylogeny and character evolution. Version 3.0 Sunderland, Mass.: Sinauer. [28]

Magie, David. 1922. The scope and literary character of the *Historia Augusta.* Introduction to the *Scriptores Historiae Augustae,* David Magie (ed.). New York: G. P. Putnam's Sons. [37]

Majerus, M. 1986. The genetics and evolution of female choice. *Trends in Ecology and Evolution* 1:1–7. [18]

Malek, Doreen Owens. 1992. Mad, bad, and dangerous to know: The hero as challenge. In J. A. Krentz (ed.), *Dangerous men and adventurous women: Romance writers on the appeal of the romance,* Philadelphia: University of Pennsylvania Press. [21]

Malinowski, Bronislaw. 1992. *Argonauts of the western Pacific.* New York: Dutton. [26]

Maljkovic, V. 1987. Reasoning in evolutionarily important domains and schizophrenia: Dissociation between content-dependent and content-independent reasoning. Unpublished graduate honors thesis, Dept. of Psychology, Harvard University. [26, 27]

Malkin, C. M., and Michael E. Lamb. 1994. Child maltreatment: A test of sociobiological theory. *Journal of Comparative Family Studies* 25:121–33. [1, 17]

Mallowan, M. E. L. 1965. *Early Mesopotamia and Iran.* Cambridge: Cambridge University Press. [29]

Mangel, M., and C. W. Clark. 1988. *Dynamic modeling in behavioral ecology.* Princeton, N.J.: Princeton University Press. [2]

Manktelow, K. I. and J. St. B. T. Evans. 1979. Facilitation of reasoning by realism: Effect or non-effect? *British Journal of Psychology* 70:477–88. [26]

Manktelow, K. E. and D.E. Over. 1987. Reasoning and rationality. *Mind and Language* 2:199–219. [26]

———. 1990. Deontic thought and the selection task. In K. J. Gilhooly et al. (eds.), *Lines of Thinking.* London: Wiley. [26]

Mann, Janet. 1992. Nurturance or negligence: Maternal psychology and behavior preference among preterm twins. In J. Barkow et al. (eds.), *The adapted mind,* pp. 367–90. New York: Oxford University Press. [1]

Mannarino, A. P., and J. Cohen. 1987. Psychological symptoms of sexually abused children. Paper presented at the third National Family Violence Conference, Durham, N.H. [24]

Manners, R. A. 1967. The Kipsigis of Kenya: Culture change in a "model" East African tribe. In J. Steward (ed.), *Contemporary change in traditional societies,* vol. 1, pp. 207–359. Urbana: University of Illinois Press. [11]

Manning, J. T. 1995. Fluctuating asymmetry and body weight in men and women: Implications for sexual selection. *Ethology and Sociobiology* 16:145–53. [1]

Manson, Joseph, and Richard W. Wrangham. 1991. Intergroup aggression in chimpanzees and humans. *Current Anthropology* 32:369–90. [1, 33, 37]

Manzoni, A. 1961. *The betrothed,* translated from the 1840–1842 original. New York: Dutton. [39]

Marcus, S. 1966. *The other Victorians: A study of sexuality and pornography in mid-nineteenth century England.* New York: Basic Books. [20]

Margulis, S. W., Jeanne Altmann, and Carole Ober. 1993. Sex-biased lactation in a human population and its reproductive costs. *Behavioural Ecology and Sociobiology* 32:41–45. [28]

Marr, David. 1982. *Vision: A computational investigation into the human representation and processing of visual information.* San Francisco: Freeman. [26]

Marr, David, and H. K. Nishihara. 1978. Visual information processing: Artificial intelligence and the sensorium of sight. *Technology Review* 17:28–49. [26]

Marschak, J., and R. Radner. 1971. *The economic theory of teams.* New Haven, Conn.: Yale University Press. [5]

Marsh, H., and T. Kasuya. 1986. Evidence for reproductive senescence in female cetaceans. *Report of the International Whaling Commission,* special issue, 8:57–74. [13]

Martial. *Epigrams,* J. A. Pott and F. A. Wright provide a complete translation. London: George Routledge and Sons, n.d. All direct quotes are drawn from James Michie's translation. Harmondsworth: Penguin. [37]

Masters, Roger. 1989. *The nature of politics.* New Haven: Yale University Press. [1]

Mauss, Marcel. 1925. *The gift: Forms and functions of exchange in Archaic societies,* trans. I. Cunnision. New York: Norton. [26]

Maxwell, Mary, ed. 1991. *The sociobiological imagination.* Albany: State University of New York Press. [1]

Maynard Smith, John. 1964. Group selection and kin selection. *Nature* 201:1145–47. [9, 26]

———. 1982. *Evolution and the theory of games.* Cambridge: Cambridge University Press. [1, 26]

Maynard Smith, John, and G. R. Price. 1973. The logic of animal conflict. *Nature* 246:15–18. [1]

Mayr, Ernst. 1983. How to carry out the adaptationist program. *American Naturalist* 121:324–34. [1, 24]

Mazur, Allan, Carolyn Halpern, and Richard Udry. 1994. Dominant looking male teenagers copulate earlier. *Ethology and Sociobiology* 15:87–94, [1]

McCahill, Thomas, Linda Meyer, and Arthur Fischman. 1979. *The aftermath of rape.* Lexington, Mass.: Heath. [24, 25]

McCracken, G. 1984. Communal nursing in Mexican free-tailed bat maternity colonies. *Science* 223:1090–91. [39]

McDougall, W. 1908. *Social psychology: An introduction.* London: Methuen. [22]

McGinnis, R. 1958. Campus values in mate selection. *Social Forces* 35:368–73. [18]

McGrew, William C. and Anna T. Feistner. 1992. Two nonhuman primate models for the evolution of human food sharing: Chimpanzees and callitrichids. In J. Barkow et al. (eds.), *The Adapted Mind* pp. 229–43. New York: Oxford University Press. [26]

McGuire, Michael T., Issac Marks, Randolph Nesse, and Alfonso Troisi. 1992. Evolutionary psychobiology: A basic science for psychiatry. *Acta Psychiatrica Scandinavica* 86:89–96. [1]

McGuire, Michael T., and Alfonso Triosi. 1996. *Evolutionary psychiatry.* Cambridge, Mass.: Harvard University Press. [1]

Mealey, Linda. 1985. The relationship between social status and biological success: A case study of the Mormon religious hierarchy. *Ethology and Sociobiology* 6:249–57. [1, 4, 35]

———. 1995. Sociopathy. *Behavioral and Brain Sciences* 18:401–47. [1]

Mealey, Linda, Christopher Daood and Michael Krage. 1996. Enhanced memory for faces of cheaters. *Ethology and Sociobiology* 17:119–28. [1]

Mealey, Linda, and Wade Mackey. 1990. Variation in offspring sex ratio in women of differing social status. *Ethology and Sociobiology* 11:83–95. [1]

Mednick, R. A. 1977. Gender specific variances in sexual fantasy. *Journal of Personality Assessment* 41:248–54. [20]

Meggitt, M. 1977. *Blood is their argument: Warfare among the Mae Enga tribesmen of the New Guinea highlands.* Palo Alto, Calif.: Mayfield. [9]

Melancon, Thomas. 1982. Marriage and reproduction among the Yanomamo Indians of Venezuela. Ph.D. Diss. Dept. of Anthropology, Pennsylvania State University. Ann Arbor, Mich.: University Microfilms International. [9, 13]

Mencher, Joan P. 1966a. Kerala and Madras: A comparative study of ecology and social structure. *Ethnology* 5:135–71. [29]

———. 1966b. Namboodiri Brahmins: An analysis of a traditional elite in Kerala. *Journal of Asian African Studies* 1:183–96. [29]

Mencher, Joan, P., and H. Goldberg. 1967. Kinship and marriage regulations among the Namboodiri Brahmins of Kreala. *Man,* n.s., 2:87–106. [29]

Mesterson-Gibbons, Michael, and Lee Alan Dugatkin. 1992. Cooperation among unrelated individuals: Evolutionary factors. *Quarterly Review of Biology* 67:267–81. [6]

Michod, Richard. 1982. The theory of kin selection. *Annual Reviews of Ecology and Systematics* 13:23–55. [5]

Mildvan, A. S., and B. L. Strehler. 1960. A critique of theories of mortality. In B. L. Strehler (ed.), *The biology of aging.* Washington DC: American Institute of Biological Sciences. [13]

Millar, J. S., and R. M. Zammuto. 1983. Life histories of mammals: An analysis of life tables. *Ecology* 64:631–35. [13]

Miller, Barbara D. 1981. *The endangered sex: Neglect of female children in rural North India.* Ithaca, N.Y.: Cornell University Press. [30, 39]

Miller, Geoffrey F. 1996a. *Evolution of the human brain through runaway sexual selection*. Cambridge Mass.: MIT Press. [1]

————. 1996b. The history of passion: A review of sexual selection and human evolution. In C. Crawford and D. Krebs (eds.), *Evolution and human behavior: Issues, ideas, and applications*. Hillsdale, N.J.: Erlbaum. [1]

————. 1996c. Protean primates: The evolution of adaptive unpredictability in competition and courtship. In A. Whiten and R. Byrne (eds.), *Machiavellian intelligence II*. Oxford: Oxford University Press. [1]

Miller, W. R., A. Williams, and M. Bernstein. 1982. The effects of rape on marital and sexual adjustment. *American Journal of Family Therapy* 10:51–58. [24]

Mills, D. M. 1984. A model for stepfamily development. *Family Relations* 33:365–72. [16]

Mizrooh, S. A. 1981. Analysis of some biological parameters in the antarctic fin whale. *Report of the International Whaling Commission* 31:425–34. [13]

Møller, Anders. 1994. *Sexual selection in swallows*. Oxford: Oxford University Press. [1]

Møller, Anders, and Andrew Pomiankowski. 1993. Fluctuating asymmetry and sexual selection. *Genetica* 89:267–79. [1]

Møller, Anders Pape, Manuel Soler, and Randy Thornhill. 1995. Breast asymmetry, sexual selection, and human reproductive success. *Ethology and Sociobiology,* 16:207–19. [1]

Momigliano, A. 1971. *The development of Greek Biography*. Cambridge, Mass.: Harvard University Press. [37]

Monberg, T. 1970. Determinants of choice in adoption and fosterage on Bellona Island. *Ethnology* 9:99–136. [39]

Money, J., and A. Ehrhardt. 1972. *Man & woman, boy & girl*. Baltimore, Md.: Johns Hopkins University Press. [20]

Moore, James. 1984. The evolution of reciprocal sharing. *Ethology and Sociobiology* 5:4–14. [6]

Moore, John. 1990. The reproductive success of Cheyenne war chiefs: A contrary case to Chagnon's Yanomamö. *Current Anthropology* 31:322–30. [10]

Morgan, C. J. 1979. Eskimo hunting groups, social kinship, and the possibility of kin selection in humans. *Ethology and Sociobiology* 1:83–86. [5]

Morgen, Sandra, ed. 1989. *Gender and anthropology: Critical reviews for research and teaching*. Washington, D.C.: American Anthropological Association. [30]

Morokoff, P. J. 1985. Effects of sex guilt, repression, sexual "arousability," and sexual experience on female sexual arousal during erotica and fantasy. *Journal of Personality and Social Psychology* 49:177–87. [20]

Morris, Ivan. 1969. *The world of the shining prince: Court life in ancient Japan*. Baltimore, Md.: Penguin. [29]

Mosher, D. L., and P. Abramson. 1977. Subjective sexual arousal to films of masturbation. *Journal of Consulting and Clinical Psychology* 45:796–807. [20]

Mosher, D. L., and H. J. Cress. 1971. Sex guilt and premarital experiences of college students. *Journal of Consulting and Clinical Psychology* 36:27–32. [20]

Mulhern, C. I. 1989. Japanese Harlequin romances as transcultural woman's fiction. *Journal of Asian Studies* 48:50–70. [20]

Müller, Ulrich. 1991. The reproductive success of the elites in Germany, Great Britain, Japan and the USA during the 19th and 20th centuries. ZUMA working paper 91/22. [1]

Murdock, George Peter. 1934. *Our primitive contemporaries*. New York: Macmillan. [39]

————. 1949. *Social structure*. New York: Macmillan. [31]

————. 1957. World ethnographic sample. *Americal Anthropologist* 59:664–87. [31]

————. 1967. *Ethnographic atlas*. Pittsburgh: University of Pittsburgh Press. [18, 31, 33]

————. 1981. *Atlas of world cultures*. Pittsburgh: University of Pittsburgh Press. [33]

————. 1986. Ethnographic Atlas. *World Cultures* 2:4. [18, 35, 36]

Murdock, George Peter, and Douglas White. 1969. Standard cross-cultural sample. *Ethnology* 8:329–69. [31, 35, 36]

Murdock, George Peter, and Suzanne Wilson. 1972. Settlement patterns and community organization: Cross-cultural codes 3. *Ethnology* 11:254–97. [37]

Murphy, Robert F. 1964. Social distance and the veil. *American Anthropologist* 66:1257–74. [29]

Murphy, Y., and R. Murphy. 1974. *Women of the forest*. New York: Columbia University Press. [39]

Murstein, B. 1986. *Paths to marriage*. New York: Sage. [18]

Mussel, K. 1984. *Fantasy and reconciliation: Contemporary formulas of women's romance fiction*. Westport, Conn.: Greenwood Press. [20]

Nag, Moni. 1972. Sex, culture and human fertility: India and the United States. *Current Anthropology* 13:231–37. [29]

Narain, Vatsala. 1967. India. In R. Patai (ed.), *Women in the modern world,* pp. 21–41. New York: Free Press. [29]

Nazzari, M. 1991. *Disappearance of the dowry: Women, families, and social change in Sao Paulo, Brazil (1600–1900).* Stanford, Calif.: Stanford University Press. [36]

Neel, James V. 1970. Lessons from a "primitive" people. *Science* 170:815–22. [39]

———. 1980. On being "headman." *Perspectives in Biology and Medicine* 23:277–94. [4]

Neel, James V., and Kenneth Weiss. 1975. The genetic structure of a tribal population, the Yanomamö Indians. XII. Biodemographic studies. *American Journal of Physical Anthropology* 42:25–51. [9]

Nelson, Andrew N. 1974. *The modern reader's Japanese-English character dictionary,* 2d ed. Rutland, Vt.: Charles Tuttle. [29]

Nesse, Margaret, ed. 1995. Bio-aesthetics: Bridging the bap between evolution and the arts. *Human Nature* 6:95–196. [1]

Neese, Randolph and Alan Lloyd. 1992. The evolution of psychodynamic mechanisms. In Barkow et al. (eds.), *The Adapted Mind,* pp. 601–24. New York: Oxford University Press. [26]

Neese, Randolph, and George C. Williams. 1994. *Why we get sick.* New York: Times Books. [1, 25]

Nevius, John L. 1869. *China and the Chinese: A general description of the country and its inhabitants.* New York: Harper. [29]

NHRC. 1979. *Research to establish present levels of native harvesting: Harvest by the Inuit of northern Quebec. Phase II (year 1976).* Montreal: James By and Northern Quebec Harvesting Research Committee. [5]

Nicholas, R. 1965. Tribal politics. In M. Banton (ed.), *Political systems and the distribution of power,* pp. 21–61. London: Tavistock. [9]

Nielsen, François. 1994. Sociobiology and sociology. *Annual Reviews of Sociology* 20:267–303. [1]

Nietschmann, B. 1980. The limits to protein. In R. B. Hames (ed.), *Working papers on South American Indians,* vol. 2, pp. 131–37. Bennington, Vt.: Bennington College. [9]

Nisbet, I. 1973. Courtship feeding, egg-size and breeding success in common terns. *Nature* 241:141–42. [18]

Nishida, T., H. Takasaki, and Y. Takahata. 1990. Demography and reproductive profiles. In T. Nishida (ed.), *The chimpanzees of Mahale Mountains.* Tokyo: University of Tokyo Press. [13]

Nitecki, Matthew, and Doris Nitecki. 1994. *Evolution and ethics.* Albany: State University of New York Press. [1]

Nonacs, Peter, and H. Kern Reeve. 1995. The ecology of cooperation in social wasps: Causes and consequences of alternative nesting strategies. *Ecology* 76:753–967. [15]

Nudds, T. D. 1977. Convergence of group size strategies by mammalian social carnivores. *American Naturalist* 111:957–60. [5]

Nunally, J. 1978. *Psychometric theory.* New York: McGraw-Hill. [18]

O'Brien, R. G., and M. K. Kaiser. 1985. MANOVA method for analyzing repeated measures designs: An extensive primer. *Psychological Bulletin* 97:316–33. [22]

O'Brien, T. 1988. Parasitic nursing in the wedge-capped capuchin monkey *(Cebus olivaceus). American Journal of Primatology* 16:341–44. [39]

O'Connell, James, and Kristen Hawkes. 1981. Alyawara plant use and optimal foraging theory. In E. A. Smith and B. Winterhalder (eds.), *Hunter-gatherer foraging strategies,* pp. 99–125. Chicago: University of Chicago Press. [1]

———. 1984. Food choice and foraging sites among the Alyawara. *Journal of Anthropological Research* 40:504–35. [1]

O'Kelly, C., and L. Carney. 1986. *Women and men in society: Cross-cultural perspectives on gender stratification.* New York: Wadsworth. [18]

Oldenziel, Ruth. 1987. The historiography of infanticide in antiquity: A literature stillborn. In J. Blok and P. Mason (eds.), *Sexual asymmetry.* Amsterdam: J. C. Geiben. [37]

Omark, D. R., and M. S. Edelman. 1975. A comparison status hierarchy in young children: An ethological approach. *Social Science Information* 14:87–107. [33]

Oppenheim, A. Leo. 1964. *Ancient Mesopotamia: Portrait of a dead civilization.* Chicago: University of Chicago Press. [29]

Orchardson, I. Q. 1961. *The Kipsigis.* Nairobi: Kenya Literature Bureau. [11]

Orians, Gordon H. 1969. On the evolution of mating systems in birds and mammals. American Naturalist 103:589–603. [11, 29, 28, 31, 35, 36]

———. 1980. Habitat selection: General theory and applications to human behavior. In J. S. Lockard (ed.), *The evolution of human social behavior.* Chicago: Elsevier. [21]

Orians, Gordon H. and Judith Heerwagen. 1992. Evolved responses to landscapes. In J. Barkow et al. (eds.), *The adapted mind*, pp. 555–79. New York: Oxford University Press. [1]

Origo, R. 1957. *The merchant of Prato*. Boston: Godine. [39]

Otterbein, Keith. 1970. *The evolution of war: A cross-cultural study*. New Haven, Conn.: HRAF Press. [9]

Ovid. 1990. *The love poems*. Include *Amores, The art of love*, and *The cures for love*, trans. A. D. Melville. New York: Oxford University Press. [37]

Owen-Smith, N. 1977. On territoriality in ungulates and an evolutionary model. *Quartely Review of Biology* 52:1–52. [11]

Packer, Craig. 1977. Reciprocal altruism in *Papio anubis. Nature* 201:441–43. [26]

Packer, Craig, and Anne Pusey. 1982. Cooperation and competition within coalitions of male lions: Kin selection or game theory? *Nature* 296:740–42. [6]

Packer, Craig, and Lore Ruttan. 1988. The evolution of cooperative hunting. *American Naturalist* 132:159–98. [6]

Page, H. J. 1989. Childrearing versus childbearing: Coresidence of mother and child in sub-Saharan Africa. In R. Lesthaeghe (ed.), *Reproduction and social organization in sub-Saharan Africa*, pp. 401–41. Berkeley: University of California Press. [39]

Pagel, Mark. 1994a. The adaptationist wager. In P. Eggleton and R. Vane-Wright (eds.), *Phylognetics and ecology*, pp. 29–51. London: Academic Press. [28, 32]

———. 1994b. Detecting correlated evolution on phylogenies: A general method for the analysis of discrete data. *Proceedings of the Royal Society of London, B* 255:37–45. [28]

Palloni, A., and M. Tienda. 1986. The effects of breastfeeding and pace of childbearing on mortality at early ages. *Demography* 23:31–52. [39]

Palmer, Craig. 1992. The use and abuse of Darwinian psychology: Its impact on attempts to determine the evolutionary basis of human rape. *Ethology and Sociobiology* 13:289–99. [15]

Pamilo, P., and R. H. Crozier. 1982. Measuring genetic relatedness in natural populations: Methodology. *Theoretical Population Biology* 21:171–73. [5]

Panter-Brick, Catherine. 1991. Lactation, birth spacing and maternal work-loads among two castes in rural Nepal. *Journal of Biosocial Science* 23:137–54. [1]

Panter-Brick, Catherine, Deborah Lotstein, and Peter Ellison. 1993. Seasonality of reproductive function and weight loss in rural Nepali women. *Human Reproduction* 8:684–90. [1]

Parker, Geoff. 1970. Sperm competition and its evolutionary consequences in insects. *Biological Reviews* 45:525–67. [1]

———. 1979. Sexual selection and sexual conflict. In M. Blum and N. Blum (eds.), *Sexual selection and reproductive competition in insects*, pp. 123–66. New York: Academic Press. [12, 25]

Parker, Geoff, Robin Baker, and V. G. F. Smith. 1972. The origin and evolution of gamete dimorphism and the male-female phenomenon. *Journal of Theoretical Biology* 36:529–33. [1]

Parker, Geoff, and R. A. Stuart. 1976. Animal behavior as a strategy optimizer. *American Naturalist* 110:1055–76. [1]

Parker, Patricia G., Thomas Waiste, Bernd Heinrich, and John Marzluff. 1994. Do common ravens share ephemeral food resources with kin? DNA fingerprinting evidence. *Animal Behaviour* 48:1085–94. [6]

Parmigiani, Stefano, and Frederick S. vom Saal, eds. 1994. *Infanticide and parental care*. Switzerland: Hardwood Academic. [40]

Parry, J. 1979. *Caste and kinship in Kangra*. London: Routledge and Kegan Paul. [39]

Partridge, Linda, and T. Halliday. 1984. Mating patterns and mate choice. In J. Krebs and N. Davies (eds.), *Behavioural ecology: An evolutionary approach*, 2d ed. pp. 222–50. Oxford: Blackwell Scientific. [11]

Patai, Raphael, ed. 1956. *The republic of Lebanon*, vol. 1. New Haven, Conn.: HRAF Press. [29]

Patterson, C. 1985. "Not worth the rearing": The causes of infant exposure in ancient Greece. *Transactions of the American Philological Association* 115:103–23. [39]

Pavelka, M., and Linda Fedigan. 1991. Menopause: A comparative life history perspective. *Yearbook of Physical Anthropology* 34:13–38. [14]

Peccei, J. S. 1994a. A hypothesis for the origin and evolution of menopause. Manuscript. [14]

———. 1994b. The origin and evolution of menopause: The altriciality-lifespan hypothesis. Manuscript. [14]

Peccei, J. S., and R. D. Peccei. 1994. A model for testing the altriciality-lifespan hypothesis for the origin and evolution of menopause. Manuscript. [14]

Pelton, L. H. 1978. Child abuse and neglect: The myth of classlessness. *American Journal of Orthopsychiatry* 48:608–17. [16]

Penley, Constance. 1992. Feminism, psychoanalysis, and the study of popular culture. In L. Grossberg et al. (eds.), *Cultural studies: Now and in the future*. New York: Routledge. [21]

Pennington, Renée. 1989. Child fostering as a reproductive strategy among Southern African pastoralists. Paper presented at meetings of the American Anthropological Association, Washington, D.C. [39]

Pennington, Renée, and Henry Harpending. 1988. Fitness and fertility among Kalahari !Kung. *American Journal of Physical Anthropology* 77:303–19. [8]

—. 1993. *The structure of an African pastoralist community: Demography, history and ecology of the Ngamiland Herero.* New York: Oxford University Press. [1, 8, 28]

Peristiany, J. G. 1939. *The social institutions of the Kipsigis.* London: Routledge and Kegan Paul. [11]

—, ed. 1966. *Honour and shame: The values of Mediterranean society.* Chicago: University of Chicago Press. [29]

Perkins, T. F., and J. P. Kahan. 1979. An empirical comparison of natural-father and stepfather family systems. *Family Process* 18:175–83. [16]

Perlez, J. 1990. In AIDS-stricken Uganda area, the orphans struggle to survive. *New York Times,* June 10. [39]

Pérusse, Daniel. 1993. Cultural and biological success in industrial societies. *Behavioral and Brain Sciences* 9:267–322. [1, 4, 15, 32]

—. 1994. Mate choice in modern societies: Testing evolutionary hypotheses with behavioral data. *Human Nature* 5:256–78. [1]

Pescatello, Ann M. 1976. *Power and pawn: The female in Iberian families, societies, and cultures.* Westport Conn.: Greenwood Press. [29]

Petronius. 1969. *The Satyricon,* trans. J. P. Sullivan. Harmondsworth: Penguin. [37]

Pfennig, D. W., and Paul Sherman. 1995. Kin recognition. *Scientific American* 272:98–103. [15]

Pharr, Susan J. 1977. Japan: Historical and contemporary prespectives. In J. Giele and A. Smock (eds.), *Women: Roles and status in eight countries,* pp. 217–55. New York: Wiley. [29]

Piaget, Jean. 1932. *The moral judgement of the child.* New York: Free Press. [33]

Pickthall, Mohammed M., ed. 1953. *The meaning of the glorious Koran, an exemplary translation.* New York: New American Library. [29]

Piers, M. 1978. *Infanticide: Past and present.* New York: Norton. [39]

Pinker, Steven. 1994. *The language instinct.* New York: William Morrow. [1]

—. 1996. *How the mind works.* New York: Norton. [1]

Pinker, Steven and Paul Bloom. 1992. Natural language and natural selection. In J. Barkow et al. (eds.), *The Adapted Mind,* pp. 451–93. New York: Oxford University Press. [26]

Pitt-Rivers, Julian, ed. 1963. *Mediterranean countrymen: Essays in the social anthropology of the Mediterranean.* Paris: Mouton. [29]

Pleszczynska, W. K. 1978. Microgeographic prediction of polygyny in the lark bunting. *Science* 201:935–37. [12]

Pliny the Elder. 1962. *Natural History,* transl. H. Rackham. Cambridge, Mass.: Harvard University Press. [37]

Pliny the Younger. 1969. *Letters,* trans. Betty Radice. Harmondsworth: Penguin. [37]

—. 1969. *Panegyricus.* transl. Betty Radice. Cambridge Mass.: Harvard University Press. [37]

Plutarch. 1927–76. *Moralia,* trans. F. C. Babbit. London: Loeb Classical Library. [37]

—. *Lives of the noble Grecians and Romans,* trans. John Dryden and A. H. Clough. New York: Modern Library. 1932. [37]

Plutchik, R., and H. Kellerman, eds. 1980. *Emotion: Theory, research, and experience.* New York: Academic Press. [24]

Polimeni, A. D., and H. J. Straight. 1985. *Foundations of discrete mathematics.* Monterey, Calif.: Brooks/Cole. [35]

Pollard, P. 1982. Human reasoning: Some possible effects of availability. *Cognition* 10:65–96. [26]

Pomeroy, Sarah B. 1975. *Goddesses, whores, wives and slaves: Women in classical antiquity.* New York: Schocken Books. [29, 37]

—. 1984. *Women in Hellenistic Egypt.* New York: Schocken Books. [39]

Pomiankowski, Andrew, Y. Iwasa, and S. Nee. 1991. The evolution of costly mate preferences, I: Fisher and biased mutation. *Evolution* 45:1422–30. [1]

Pospisil, Leopold. 1954. Laws of inheritance and kinship terminology. Manuscript. [31]

Prentice, A. M., et al. 1983. Dietary supplementation of lactating Gambian women. I: Effect on breast-milk volume and quality. *Human Clinical Nutrition* 37:53–64. [1]

Profet, Margie. 1991. The function of allergy: Immunological defense against toxins. *Quarterly Review of Biology* 66:23–62. [1]

—. 1992. Pregnancy sickness as adaptation: A deterrent to maternal ingestion of teratogens. In J. Barkow et al. (eds.), *The Adapted Mind,* pp. 327–65. New York: Oxford University Press. [1]

—. 1993. Menstruation as a defense against pathogens transported by sperm. *Quarterly Review of Biology* 68:335–86. [1]

—. 1995. *Protecting your baby to be: Preventing birth defects in the first trimester.* New York: Addison-Wesley. [1]

Promislow, Dan, and Paul Harvey. 1990. Living fast and dying young: A comparative analysis of life-history variation among mammals. *Journal of Zoology* 220:417–37. [13]

Pryor, E. T. 1983. Census of population (part 1): Demographic highlights. *Canadian Statistical Review,* p. viii. [16]

Pryzbyla, D. P. J., D. Byrne, and K. Kelley. 1983. The role of imagery in sexual behavior. In A. Sheikh (ed.), *Imagery: Current theory, research, and application.* New York: Wiley. [20]

Pugesek, B. H. 1981. Increased reproductive effort with age in the California gull *(Larus californicus). Science* 212:822–23. [16]

Pulliam, H. Ronald, and Thomas Caraco. 1984. Living in groups: Is there an optimal group size? In J. Krebs and N. Davies (eds.), *Behavioural ecology: An evolutionary approach,* 2d ed., pp. 122–47. Oxford: Blackwell Scientific. [5, 6]

Pulliam, H. Ronald, and C. Dunford. 1980. *Programmed to learn: An essay on the evolution of culture.* New York: Columbia University Press. [1, 31]

Pyke, G. H., H. R. Pulliam, and E. Charnov. 1977. Optimal foraging: A selective review of theory and tests. *Quarterly Review of Biology* 52:137–54. [5]

Quine, W. V. O. 1969. *Ontological relativity and other essays.* New York: Columbia University Press. [26]

Radcliffe-Brown, A. R. 1922. *The Andaman Islanders: A study in social anthropology.* Cambridge: Cambridge University Press. [39]

Radway, J. 1984. *Reading the romance: Women, patriarchy, and popular literature.* Chapel Hill: University of North Carolina Press. [20]

Ramanamma, A., and U. Bambawale. 1980. The mania for sons: An analysis of social values in South Asia. *Social Science Medicine* 14B:107–10. [39]

Rankin, J. H. 1983. The family context of delinquency. *Social Problems* 30:466–79. [16]

Rannala, Bruce, and Charles Brown. 1994. Relatedness and conflict over optimal group size. *Trends in Ecology and Evolution* 9:117–19. [6]

Rao, R. 1986. Move to stop sex-test abortion. *Nature* 324:202. [39]

Rappaport, Roy. 1968. *Pigs for the ancestors.* New Haven, Conn.: Yale University Press. [4]

Ravenholt, R. T., and J. Chao. 1974. World fertility trends. Population reports, series J, no. 2. Washington, D.C.: Department of Medical and Public Affairs, George Washington University Medical Center. [13]

Rawson, Beryl. 1966. Family life among the lower classes at Rome in the first two centuries of the Empire. *Classical Philology* 61:71–83. [37]

———. 1974. Roman concubinage and other *de facto* marriages. *Transactions of the American Philological Association* 104:279–305. [37]

———. 1986a. Children in the Roman *Familia.* In B. Rawson (ed.), *The family in ancient Rome: New perspectives.* Ithaca, N.Y.: Cornell University Press. [37]

———. 1986b. The Roman family. In B. Rawson (ed.), *The family in ancient Rome: New perspectives.* Ithaca, N.Y.: Cornell University Press. [37]

———. 1989. *Spurii* and the Roman view of illegitimacy. *Antichthon* 23:10–41. [37]

———. 1991. Adult-child relationships in Roman society. In B. Rawson (ed.), *Marriage, divorce, and children in ancient Rome.* Oxford: Clarendon. [37]

Reeve, H. Kern. 1989. The evolution of conspecific acceptance thresholds. *American Naturalist* 133:407–35. [15]

———. 1992. Queen activation of lazy workers in colonies of the eusocial naked mole-rat. *Nature* 358:147–49. [38]

Reeve, H. Kern, and Peter Nonacs. 1992. Social contracts in wasp societies. *Nature* 359:823–25. [38]

Reeve, H. Kern, and Floyd Ratneiks. 1993. Queen-queen conflicts in polygynous societies: Mutual tolerance and reproductive skew. In L. Keller (ed.), *Queen number and sociality in insects.* New York: Oxford University Press. [38]

Reeve, H. Kern, and Paul W. Sherman. 1993. Adaptation and the goals of evolutionary research. *Quarterly Review of Biology* 68:1–32. [1, 15, 27]

Regalski, Jeanne, and Steven J. C. Gaulin. 1993. Whom are Mexican infants said to resemble? Monitoring and fostering paternal confidence in the Yucatan. *Ethology and Sociobiology* 14:97–113. [1]

Republic of China. 1987. *1986 Taiwan-Fukien demographic fact-book.* Taiwan: Ministry of the Interior. [18]

Richards, Robert. 1987. *Darwin and the emergence of evolutionary theories of mind and behavior.* Chicago: University of Chicago Press. [1]

Richardson, S. J., V. Senikas, and J. F. Nelson. 1987. Follicular depletion during the menopausal transition: Evidence for accelerated loss and ultimate exhaustion. *Journal of Clinical Endocrinology and Metabolism* 65:1231–37. [13]

Ridley, Mark. 1983. *The explanation of organic diversity: The comparative method and adaptations for mating.* Oxford: Oxford University Press. [1]

Ridley, Matt. 1994. *The red queen: Sex and the evolution of human nature.* New York: Macmillan. [1]

———1996. *The origins of virtue.* Harmondsworth: Penguin. [1]

Robinson, J. 1982. Intrasexual competition and mate choice in primates. *American Journal of Primatology* supplement, 1:131–44. [18]

Rodman, Peter S. 1981. Inclusive fitness and group size with a reconsideration of group sizes in lions and wolves. *American Naturalist* 118:275–83. [5]

Roff, D. A. 1992. *The evolution of life histories: Theory and analysis.* New York: Chapman and Hall. [8]

Rogers, Alan. 1990. Evolutionary economies of human reproduction. *Ethology and Sociobiology* 11:479–95. [1]

———. 1993. Why menopause? *Evolutionary Ecology* 7:406–20. [14]

———. 1994. Evolution of time preference by natural selection. *American Economic Review* 84:460–82. [1]

———. 1996. For love or money: The evolution of reproductive and material motivations. In R. Dunbar (ed.), *Human reproductive decisions: Biological and social perspectives.* London: Macmillan. [1, 28]

Rood, J. 1980. Mating relationships and breeding suppression in the dwarf mongoose. *Animal Behaviour* 28:143–50. [39]

Ropp, Paul S. 1976. The seeds of change, reflections on the condition of women in the early and mid-Ch'ing. *Signs* 2:5–34. [29]

Rose, Michael R. *Evolutionary biology of aging.* New York: Oxford University Press. [1, 14]

Rosenblatt, P., and M. R. Cunningham. 1976. Sex differences in cross-cultural perspective. In B. B. Lloyd and J. Archer (eds.), *Explorations in sex differences,* pp. 71–94. New York: Academic Press. [33]

Rosenfeld, Henry. 1958. Processes of structural change within the Arab village extended family. *American Anthropologist* 60:1127–39. [29]

———. 1960. On determinants of the status of Arab village women. *Man* 60:66–70. [29]

Rosenthal, Robert. 1976. *Experimenter effects in behavioural research.* New York: Irvington. [28]

———. 1990. An evaluation of procedures and results. In K. W. Wachter and M. L. Straf (eds.), *The future of meta-analysis,* pp. 123–34. New York: Sage. [4]

———. 1991. *Meta-analytical procedures for social research.* New York: Sage. [28]

———. 1996. Parametric measures of effect size. In *Handbook of Research Synthesis* in press. [4]

Røskaft, Eivin, A. Wara, and Å. Viken. 1992. Human reproductive success in relation to resource-access and parental age in a small Norwegian farming parish during the period 1700–1900. *Ethology and Sociobiology* 13:443–61. [1, 4]

Ross, Eric. 1978. Food taboos, diet, and hunting strategy: The adaptation to animals in Amazon cultural ecology. *Current Anthropology* 19:1–36. [9]

Roston, Homes, ed. 1995. *Biology, ethics, and the origins of life.* London: Jones and Bartlett. [1]

Rothfeld, Otto. N.d. *Women of India.* London: Simpkin, Marshall Hamilton, Kent. [29]

Rouche, M. 1987. The early Middle Ages in the West. In P. Veyne (ed.), *From pagan Rome to Byzantium,* trans. Arthur Goldhammer. Cambridge, Mass.: Harvard University Press. [37]

Rouselle, A. 1988. *Porneia: On desires and the body in antiquity,* trans. Felicia Pheasant. New York: Basil Blackwell. [37]

Rubenstein, Dan. 1978. On predation, competition, and the advantages of group living. In P. Bateson and P. Klopfer (eds.), *Perspectives in ethology,* vol. 3, pp. 205–31. New York: Plenum. [5]

Rubenstein, Dan, and Richard Wrangham, eds. 1986. *Ecological aspects of social evolution.* Princeton, N.J.: Princeton University Press. [24]

Ruhlen, M. 1991. *A guide to the world's languages: Classification.* Stanford, Calif.: Stanford University Press. [28]

Ruse, Michael. 1982. *Darwinism defended.* Reading, Mass.: Addison-Wesley. [1]

———. 1995. *Evolutionary naturalism: Selected essays.* New York: Routledge. [1]

Rushton, J. P., R. Russell, and P. A. Wells. 1984. Genetic similarity theory: Beyond kin selection. *Behavior Genetics* 14:179–93. [18]

Russ, Joanna. 1985. *Magic mommas, trembling sisters, Puritans and perverts.* Trumansburg, N.Y.: Crossing Press. [21]

Russell, D. 1984. *Sexual exploitation: Rape, child sexual abuse and sexual harassment.* Beverly Hills, Calif.: Sage. [24]

———. 1986. *The secret trauma: Incest in the lives of girls and women.* New York: Basic Books. [17]

Saadawi, Nawal el. 1982. *The hidden face of Eve: Women in the Arab world.* Boston: Beacon Press. [30]

Sacher, G. A. 1975. Maturation and longevity in relation to cranial capacity in hominid evolution. In R. H. Tuttle (ed.), *Primate functional morphology and evolution,* pp. 417–41. The Hague: Mouton. [13]

Sadalla, Edward K., and M. Fausal. 1980. Dominance and heterosexual attraction: A field study. Manuscript. [22]

Sadalla, Edward K., Douglas T. Kenrick, and Beth Vershure. 1987. Dominance and heterosexual attraction. *Journal of Personality and Social Psychology* 52:730–38. [1, 22]

Sade, Donald, K. Cushing, P. Cushing, Janet Dunaif, A. Figueroa, J. R. Kaplan. C. Laver, D. Rhodes, and J. Schneider. 1976. Population dynamics in relation to social structure on Cayo Santiago. *Yearbook of Physical Anthropology* 20:253–62. [13]

Sagan, Eli. 1985. *At the dawn of tyranny.* New York: Routledge. [37]

Sahlins, Marshall. 1972. *Stone age economics.* Chicago: Aldine. [3]

Saller, Richard. 1980. Anecdotes as historical evidence for the principate. *Greece and Rome* 27:69–83. [37]

———. 1984. *Familia, domus,* and the Roman concept of the family. *Phoenix* 38:336–55. [37]

———. 1987. Slavery and the Roman family. In M. Finley (ed.), *Classical slavery.* London: Frank Cass. [37]

———. 1991a. Corporal punishment, authority, and obedience in the Roman household. In B. Rawson (ed.), *Marriage, divorce, and children in ancient Rome.* Oxford: Clarendon. [37]

———. 1991b. Roman heirship strategies in principle and in practice. In D. Kertzer and R. Saller (eds.), *The Family in Italy from antiquity to the present.* New Haven, Conn.: Yale University Press. [37]

Saller, Richard, and Brent Shaw. 1984. Tombstones and Roman family relations in the principate: Civilians, soldiers, and slaves. *Journal of Roman Studies* 74:124–56. [37]

Saller, Richard and David Kertzer. 1991. Historical and anthropological perspectives on Italian family life. In D. Kertzer and R. Saller (eds.). *The family in Italy from antiquity to the present.* New Haven: Yale University Press. [37]

Saltman, M. 1977. *The Kipsigis: A case study in changing law.* Cambridge, Mass.: Schenkman. [11]

Sanderson, Lilan Passmore. 1986. *Female genital mutilation: Excision and infibulation: A bibliography:* London: The Anti-Slavery Society for the Protection of Human Rights. [30]

Sansom, George B. 1936. *Japan, a short cultural history.* New York: D. Appleton Century. [29]

Sapolsky, Robert. 1994. *Why zebras don't get ulcers.* New York: Freeman. [1]

SAS Institute, Inc. 1986. *SUGI supplemental library users guide,* version 5 edition. Cary, N.C.: SAS Institute Inc. [13]

Scarr, S. 1989. Sociobiology: The psychology of sex, violence and oppression? *Contemporary Psychology,* 34:440–43. [24]

Schaffer, W. 1978. A note on the theory of reciprocal altruism. *American Naturalist* 112:250–53. [5]

Scheib, Joanna E. 1994. Sperm donor selection and the psychology of female mate choice. *Ethology and Sociobiology* 15:113–29. [1]

Schepher-Hughes, Nancy. 1985. Culture, scarcity and maternal thinking. *Ethos* 13:291–317. [39]

Schiefenhovel, W. 1989. Reproduction and sex-ratio manipulation through preferential female infanticide among the Eipo, in the highlands of western New Guinea. In A. Rasa et al., (eds.), *The sociobiology of sexual and reproductive strategies,* pp. 170–93. London: Chapman and Hall. [39]

Schlegel, Alice. 1988. Errata. *Behavioral Science Research* 22:111. [35]

———. 1993. Dowry: Who competes for what? *American Anthropologist* 95:155–57. [36]

Schlegel, Alice, and R. Eloul. 1987. A new coding of marriage transactions. *Behavioral Science Research* 21:118–40. [35, 36]

———. 1988. Marriage transactions: Labor, property, status. *American Anthropologist* 90:291–309. [36]

Schneider, J., and P. Schneider. 1984. Demographic transitions in a Sicilian rural town. *Journal of Family History* 12:245–72. [39]

Schoener, T. W. 1971. Theory of feeding strategies. *Annual Review of Ecology and Systematics* 2:369–404. [5]

Schrire, C., and W. Steiger. 1974. A matter of life and death: An investigation into the practice of female infanticide in the Arctic. *Man* 9:161–84. [39]

Scriptores Historiae Augustae, trans. David Maggie. 1922. London: William Heinemann. [37]

Searcy, W. A. 1979. Female choice of mates: A general model for birds and its application to red winged blackbirds. *American Naturalist* 114:77–100. [11]

Searcy, W. A., and K. Yakusawa. 1989. Alternative models of territorial polygyny in birds. *American Naturalist* 134:4323–43. [11, 12]

Seltman, Charles. 1957. *Women in antiquity,* 2d ed. London: Pan. [29]

Shahar, S. 1990. *Childhood in the Middle Ages.* London: Routledge. [39]

Sharp, L. 1952. Steel axes for stone age Australians. *Human Organization* 11:17–22. [26]

Shaw, Brent. 1987. The family in late antiquity: The experience in Augustine. *Past and Present* 115:3–51. [37]

———. 1991. The cultural meaning of death: Age and gender in the Roman family. In D. Kertzer and R. Saller (eds.), *The family in Italy from antiquity to the present.* New Haven, Conn.: Yale University Press. [37]

Shepher, J., and J. Reisman. 1985. Pornography: A sociobiological attempt at understanding. *Ethology and Sociobiology* 6:103–14. [22]

Sherman, Paul W. 1977. Nepotism and the evolution of alarm calls. *Science* 197:1246–53. [15, 26]

———. 1981. Reproductive competition and infanticide in Belding's ground squirrels and other animals. In R. Alexander and D. Tinkle (eds.), *Natural selection and social behavior,* pp. 311–31. New York: Chiron Press. [15]

———. 1988. The levels of analysis. *Animal Behaviour* 36:616 19. [15]

———. 1989a. The clitoris debate and the levels of analysis. *Animal Behaviour* 37:697–98. [15]

———. 1989b. Mate guarding as paternity insurance in Idaho ground squirrels. *Nature* 338:418–20 [15].

Sherman, Paul W., and Warren Holmes. 1985. Kin recognition: Issues and evidence. In B. Holldobler and M. Lindauer (eds.), *Experimental behavioral ecology and sociobiology,* pp. 437–60. Stuttgart: Fischer Verlag. [15]

Sherman, Paul W., J. U. M. Jarvis, and R. D. Alexander, eds. 1991. *The biology of the naked mole-rat.* Princeton, N.J.: Princeton University Press. [38]

Sherwin, B. B., M. Gelfand, and W. Brender. 1985. Androgen enhances sexual motivation in females: A perspective, crossover study of sex steroid administration in the surgical menopause. *Psychosomatic Medicine* 47:339–51. [20]

Sherwood, Joan. 1988. *Poverty in eighteenth-century Spain: The women and children of the Inclusa.* Toronto: University of Toronto Press. [40]

Short, Roger. 1976a. The evolution of human reproduction. *Proceedings of the Royal Society, B* 195:3–24. [1, 18]

——— 1976b. Lactation—the central control of reproduction. In *Breastfeeding and the mother,* Ciba Foundation Symposium 45, pp. 73–86. New York: Elsevier. [39]

Shorter, Edward. 1982. *A history of women's bodies.* New York: Basic Books. [39]

Sibly, R. M. 1983. Optimal group size is unstable. *Animal Behaviour* 31:947–48. [5, 6]

Sieff, Daniela. 1990. Explaining biased sex ratios in human populations: A critique of recent studies. *Current Anthropology* 31:25–48. [1, 39, 40]

Siegel, S. 1956. *Nonparametric statistics of the behavioral sciences.* New York: McGraw-Hill. [11]

Silk, Joan B. 1980. Adoption and kinship in Oceania. *American Anthropologist* 82:799–820. [1]

———. 1987a. Adoption among the Inuit. *Ethos* 15:320–30. [1]

———. 1987b. Social behavior in evolutionary perspective. In B. Smuts et al. (eds.), *Primate societies,* pp. 318–29. Chicago: University of Chicago Press. [6]

———. 1990. Human adoption in evolutionary perspective. *Human Nature* 1:25–52. [1]

Silverman, Irwin, and Marion Eals. 1992. Sex differences in spatial abilities: Evolutionary theory and data. In J. Barkow et al. (eds.), *The adapted mind,* pp. 533–49. New York: Oxford University Press. [1]

Silverman, Irwin, and Krista Phillips. 1993. Effects of estrogen changes during the menstrual cycle on spatial performance. *Ethology and Sociobiology* 14:257–70. [1]

Simpson, Jeffry A., and Steven W. Gangestad. 1991. Individual differences in sociosexuality: Evidence for convergent and discriminant validity. *Journal of Personality and Social Psychology* 50:870–83. [1]

———. 1992. Sociosexuality and romantic partner choice. *Journal of Personality* 60:31–51. [1]

Simpson, Jeffry A., Steven W. Gangestad, and Michael Biek. 1993. Personality and nonverbal social behavior: An ethological perspective of relationship initiation. *Journal of Experimental Social Psychology* 29:434–61. [1]

Simpson, Jeffry A., Steven W. Gangestad, and Margaret Lerma. 1990. Perception of physical attractiveness: Mechanisms involved in the maintenance of romantic relationships. *Journal of Personality and Social Psychology* 59:1192–201. [1]

Singer, B. 1985a. A comparison of evolutionary and environmental theories of erotic response. Part I: Structural features. *Journal of Sex Research* 21:229–57. [20]

———. 1985b. A comparison of evolutionary and environmental theories of erotic response. Part II: Empirical arenas. *Journal of Sex Research* 21:345–74. [20]

Singh, Devendra. 1993a. Adaptive significance of waist-to-hip ratio and female physical attractiveness. *Journal of Personality and Social Psychology* 65:298–307. [1, 21]

———. 1993b. Body shape and women's attractiveness. The critical role of waist-to-hip ratio. *Human Nature* 4:297–321. [1]

———. 1994. Is thin really beautiful and good? Relationship between waist-to-hip ratio (WHR) and female attractiveness. *Personality and Individual Differences* 16:123–32. [1, 21]

———. 1995a. Female health, attractiveness, and desirability for relationships: Role of breast asymmetry and waist-to-hip ratio. *Ethology and Sociobiology* 16:465–481. [1]

———. 1995b. Female judgement of male attractiveness and desirability for relationships: Role of waist-to-hip ratio and financial status. *Journal of Personality and Social Psychology* 69:1089–1101. [1]

————. 1996. Effect of maternal body morphology morning sickness and pregnancy complications on fluctuating asymmetry and body fat distribution in young women. Manuscript. [1]

Singh, Devendra, and Suwardi Luis. 1995. Ethnic and gender consensus for the effect of waist-to-hip ratio on judgement on women's attractiveness. *Human Nature* 6:51–65. [1]

Singh, Devendra, and Robert K. Young. 1995. Body weight, waist-to-hip ratio, breasts, and hips: Role in judgments of female attractiveness and desirability for relationships. *Ethology and Sociobiology* 16:483–507. [1]

Skinner, G. W. 1988. Reproductive strategies, the domestic cycle, and fertility among Japanese villagers, 1717–1869. Paper presented to Rockefeller Foundation workshop on women's status in relation to fertility and mortality, Bellagio, Italy. [39]

————. 1993. Conjugal power in Tokugawa Japanese families: A matter of life and death. In B. Miller (ed.), *Sex and gender hierarchies*. Cambridge: Cambridge University Press. [39]

Slagsvold, T., J. T. Lijfield, G. Stenmark, and T. Breiehagen. 1988. On the costs of searching for a male in female pied flycatchers, *Ficedula hypoleuca*. *Animal Behaviour* 36:433–42. [11]

Slater, W. J. 1974. *Pueri, turba minuta*. *Bulletin of the Institute of Classical Studies* 21:133–40. [37]

Slatkin, M., and J. Maynard Smith. 1979. Models of coevolution. *Quarterly Review of Biology* 54:233–63. [5]

Small, Meredith. 1995. *What's love get to do with it?* New York: Doubleday. [1]

Smith, B. Holly. 1991. Dental development and the evolution of life history in *Hominidae*. *American Journal of Physical Anthropology* 86:157–74. [13]

Smith, D. D. 1976. The social content of pornography. *Journal of Communication* 26:16–25. [20]

Smith, Eric Alden. 1979. Data and theory in sociobiological explanation: Critique of van den Berghe and Barash. *American Anthropologist* 81:360–63. [5]

————. 1980. Evolutionary ecology and the analysis of human foraging behavior: An Inuit example from the east coast of Hudson Bay. Ph.D. diss., Dept. of Anthropology, Cornell University. Ann Arbor, Mich.: University Microfilms International. [5]

————. 1981. The application of optimal foraging theory to the analysis of hunter-gatherer group size. In B. Winterhalder and E. A. Smith (eds.), *Hunter-gatherer foraging strategies,* pp. 36–65. Chicago: University of Chicago Press. [5, 6, 7]

————. 1983. Anthropological applications of optimal foraging theory: A critical review. *Current Anthropology* 24:625–51. [5, 6]

————. 1985. Inuit foraging groups. *Ethology and Sociobiology* 6:27–47. [1]

————. 1988. Risk and uncertainty in the "original affluent" society: Evolutionary ecology of resource sharing and land tenure. In T. Ingold et al. (eds.), *Hunters and gatherers,* pp. 222–52, Oxford: Berg. [6]

————. 1991. *Inujjuamiut foraging strategies: Evolutionary ecology of an Arctic hunting economy.* Hawthorne, N.Y.: Aldine–de Gruyter. [1, 6]

————. 1992a. Human behavioral ecology: I. *Evolutionary Anthropology* 1:20–25. [1]

————. 1992b. Human behavioral ecology: II. *Evolutionary Anthropology* 1:50–55. [1]

————. 1995. Inuit sex ratio: A correction and an addendum. *Current Anthropology* 36:658–59. [1]

Smith, Eric Alden, and Robert Boyd. 1990. Risk and reciprocity: Hunter-gatherer socioecology and the problem of collective action. In E. Cashdan (ed.), *Risk and uncertainty in tribal and peasant economies,* pp. 167–91. Boulder, Colo.: Westview Press. [6]

Smith, Eric Alden, and S. Abigail Smith. 1994. Inuit sex-ratio variation. *Current Anthropology* 35:595–624. [1, 6]

Smith, Eric Alden, and Bruce Winterhalder, eds. 1992. *Evolutionary ecology.* Hawthorne, N.Y.: Aldine–de Gruyter. [1]

Smith, H. F. 1984. Notes on the history of childhood. *Discovery Supplement, Harvard Magazine,* July–August, pp. 64G–64H. [39]

Smith, Martin, Bradley Kish, and Charles Crawford. 1987. Inheritance of wealth as human kin investment. *Ethology and Sociobiology* 8:171–82. [1, 32]

Smith, Robert L. 1984. Human sperm competition. In R. Smith (ed.), *Sperm competition and the evolution of mating systems,* pp. 601–59. New York: Academic Press. [1, 20]

Smith, T., and T. Polacheck. 1981. Reexamination of the life table for northern fur seals with implications about population regulatory mechanisms. In C. W. Fowler and T. D. Smith (eds.), *Dynamics of large mammal populations.* New York: Wiley. [13]

Smith, Vernon. 1994. Economics in the laboratory. *Journal of Economic Perspectives* 8:113–31. [1]

Smock, Audrey C., and N. H. Youssef. 1977. Egypt: From seclusion to limited participation. In J. Giele and A. Smock (eds.), *Women: Roles and status in eight countries,* pp. 33–79. New York: Wiley. [29]

Smuts, Barbara B. 1986. *Sex and friendship in baboons*. Hawthorne, N.Y.: Aldine–de Gruyter. [26]
———. 1987. Sexual competition and mate choice. In B. Smuts et al. (eds.), *Primate societies*. Chicago: University of Chicago Press. [18]
———. 1992. Male aggression against women. *Human Nature* 3:1–44. [12]
Smuts, Barbara B., and Robert W. Smuts. 1993. Male aggression and sexual coercion of females in nonhuman primates and other mammals: Evidence and theoretical implications. *Advances in the Study of Behavior* 22:1–63. [25]
Smuts, G. L. 1977. Reproduction and population characteristics of elephants in the Kruger National Park. *Journal of the African Wildlife Management Association* 5:1–10. [13]
Smuts, Robert W. 1991. The present also explains the past. *Ethology and Sociobiology* 12:77–82. [15]
Snowdon, D. A., et al. 1989. Is early menopause a biological marker of health and aging? *American Journal of Public Health* 79:709–14. [13]
Sommer, V. 1992. Infant mistreatment in langur monkeys—sociobiology tackled from the wrong end. In A. Rasa et al. (eds.), *The sociobiology of sexual and reproductive strategies*, pp. 110–27. London: Chapman and Hall. [39]
Sorabi, Cornelia. 1908. *Between the twilights: Being studies of Indian women by one of themselves*. London: Harper and Brothers. [29]
Soranus. *Gynaecology*, trans. Owsei Temkin. Baltimore, Md.: Johns Hopkins University Press, 1956. [37].
Sperber, Dan. 1975. *Rethinking symbolism*, transl. by A. Morton Cambridge: Cambridge University Press. [26]
———. 1985. Anthropology and psychology: Towards an epidemiology of representations. *Man (N.S.)* 20:73–89. [26]
———. 1990. The epidemiology of beliefs. In C. Fraser and G. Geskell (eds.), *Social psychological studies of widespread beliefs*. Oxford: Clarendon. [26]
———. 1994. The modularity of thought and the epidemiology of representations. In L. Hirschfeld and R. Gelman (eds.), *Mapping the mind*. Cambridge University Press: Cambridge. [2]
Sperber, Dan, and D. Wilson. 1986. *Relevance: Communication and cognition*. Oxford: Blackwell. [26]
Spielman, Richard. 1971. Ph.D. diss., Dept. of Anthropology, University of Michigan. Ann Arbor, Mich.: University Microfilms International. [9]
———. 1973. Do the natives all look alike? *American Naturalist* 107:694. [9]
Spielman, Richard, et al. 1972. Amazonian blood groups. *American Journal of Physical Anthropology* 37:345. [9]
Spinage, C. A. 1969. Territoriality and social organization of the Uganda defassa waterbuck *Kobus defassa ugandae* Neumann. In V. Geist and F. Walther (eds.), *The behaviour of ungulates and its relation to management*, pp. 635–43. Morges: IUCN New Series no. 24. [11]
Sponsel, L. 1983. Yanomamö warfare, protein capture, and cultural ecology. *Interciencia* 8:204–10. [9]
SPSSx. 1983. *User's guide*. Chicago: McGraw-Hill. [11]
Stager, L. E., and S. R. Wolff. 1984. Child sacrifice at Carthage: Religious rite or population control? *Biblical Archaeology Review*. [39]
Stambaugh, J. E. 1988. *The ancient Roman city*. Baltimore, Md.: Johns Hopkins University Press. [37]
Statistics Canada. 1982. *Census tracts*. Population, occupied private dwellings, private households, census families in private households, Hamilton. Ottawa: Minister of Supplies and Services Canada. [16]
Steadman, L. 1971. Tribal conflict. Ph.D. dissertation. Dept. of Anthropology, Australian National University, Canberra. Ann Arbor, Mich.: University Microfilms International. [9]
Stearns, Stephen. 1992. *The evolution of life histories*. New York: Oxford University Press. [1, 8]
Stenning, D. J. 1959. *Savannah nomads*. Oxford: Oxford University Press. [11]
Stephens, David, K. Nishimura, and K. Toyer. 1995. Error and discounting in the iterated prisoner's dilemma. *Journal of the Theoretical Biology* 176:457–69. [1]
Stephens, David, and Eric Charnov. 1982. Optimal foraging: Some simple stochastic models. *Behavioral Ecology and Sociobiology* 10:251–63. [5]
Stephens, David, and John Krebs. 1986. *Foraging theory*. Princeton, N.J.: Princeton University Press. [1, 2]
Stone, Lawrence. 1965. *The crisis of the aristocracy*. Oxford: Clarendon. [38]
———. 1977. *The family, sex and marriage in England 1500–1800*. New York: Harper and Row. [39]
———. 1987. *The past and present revisited*. New York: Routledge and Kegan Paul. [38]
———. 1990. *The road to divorce*. Oxford: Oxford University Press. [38]
Stone, Lawrence, and Jeanne C. F. Stone. 1984. *An open elite? England 1540–1880*. Oxford: Clarendon. [38]
Stone, Valerie, and Leda Cosmides. In prep. Do people have causal reasoning schemas? [26]
Strassmann, Beverly. 1981. Sexual selection, parental care, and concealed ovulation in humans. *Ethology and Sociobiology* 2:31–40. [1]

———. 1992. The function of menstrual taboos among the Dogon: Defense against cuckoldry? *Human Nature* 3:89–131. [1]

———. 1996a. The evolution of endrometrial cycles and menstrual bleeding. *Quarterly Review of Biology* 71:179–220. [1]

———. 1996b. Menstrual hut visits by Dogon women: A hormonal test distinguishes deceit from honest signalling. *Behavioral Ecology.* [1]

———. 1996c. Polygyny is a risk factor for child mortality among the Dogon of Mali. Manuscript. [1]

Studd, Michael, and Urs Gattiker. 1991. The evolutionary psychology of sexual harassment in organizations. *Ethology and Sociobiology* 12:249–90. [1]

Sue, D. 1979. Erotic fantasies of college students during coitus. *Journal of Sex Research* 15:299–305. [20]

Suetonius. 1982. *The twelve Caesars,* trans. Robert Graves, revised by Michael Grant. Harmondsworth: Penguin. [37, 38]

Sugiyama, J., John Tooby, and Leda Cosmides. in prep. Cheater-detection in a Yanomamö population. [27]

Sulloway, Frank. 1996. *Born to rebel: Radical thinking in science and social thought.* New York: Pantheon. [1]

Sumner, W. G., and A. Keller. 1927. *The science of society.* New Haven, Conn.: Yale University Press. [31]

Sussman, G. D. 1982. *Selling mothers' milk: The wet-nursing business in France 1715–1914.* Urbana: University of Illinois Press. [39]

Swarz, M., Victor Turner, and Arthur Tuden, eds. 1966. *Political anthropology.* Chicago: Aldine. [9]

Syme, Ronald 1939. *The Roman revolution.* Oxford: Oxford University Press. [37]

———. 1960. Bastards in the Roman aristocracy. *Proceedings of the American Philological Society,* 104:323–37. [37]

———. 1980. No son for Caesar? *Historia* 29:422–37. [37]

———. 1983. *Historia Augusta papers.* Oxford: Clarendon. [37]

Symons, Donald 1979. *The evolution of human sexuality.* New York: Oxford University Press. [1, 9, 18, 20, 21, 22, 23]

———. 1987a. Can Darwin's view of life shed light on human sexuality? In J. Geer and W. O'Donohue (eds.), *Theories of human sexuality.* New York: Plenum. [18, 20]

———. 1987b. If we're all Darwinians, what's the fuss about? In C. Crawford et al. (eds.), *Sociobiology and psychology: Issues, ideas, and applications,* pp. 121–46. Hillsdale, N.J.: Erlbaum. [15, 16, 18, 20, 24]

———. 1989. A critique of Darwinian anthropology. *Ethology and Sociobiology* 10:131–44. [15, 24]

———. 1990. Adaptiveness and adaptation. *Ethology and Sociobiology* 11:427–44. [15]

———. 1992. On the use and misuse of Darwinism in the study of human behavior. In J. Barkow et al. (eds.), *The adapted mind: Evolutionary psychology and the generation of culture,* pp. 137–59. New York: Oxford Universtiy Press. [15, 26, 27]

Symons, Donald, and Bruce Ellis. 1989. Human male-female differences in sexual desire. In A. Rasa et al. (eds.), *The sociobiology of sexual and reproductive strategies,* pp. 131–46. London: Chapman and Hall. [1, 20]

Tacitus. 1988. *The Agricola,* trans. H. Mattingly, revised by S. A. Handford. Harmondsworth: Penguin. [37]

———. 1989. *The annals of imperial Rome,* trans. Michael Grant. Harmondsworth: Penguin. [37, 38]

———. 1990. *The histories,* trans. Kenneth Wellesley. Harmondsworth: Penguin. [37]

Tatar, M., and J. R. Carey. 1994. Nutrition mediates reproductive costs in the beetle *Calosobruchus maculatus.* Manuscript. [14]

Taylor, Lily Ross. 1961. Freedmen and freeborn in the epitaphs of imperial Rome. *American Journal of Philology* 82:113–32. [37]

Tennov, D. 1979. *Love and limerence: The experience of being in love.* New York: Stein and Day. [20]

Textor, Robert B. 1966. *A cross-cultural summary.* New Haven, Conn.: HRAF Press. [31]

Thébert, Y. 1987. Private life and domestic architecture in Roman Africa. In P. Veyne (ed.), *From pagan Rome to Byzantium.* Cambridge, Mass.: Harvard University Press. [37]

Thierry, B., and J. R. Anderson. 1986. Adoption in anthropoid primates. *International Journal of Primatology* 7:191–216. [39]

Thiessen, D., and B. Gregg. 1980. Human assortative mating and genetic equilibrium. *Ethology and Sociobiology* 4:63–99. [18]

Thiessen, D., R. K. Young, and R. Burroughs. 1993. Lonely hearts advertisements reflect sexually dimorphic mating strategies. *Ethology and Sociobiology* 14:209–29. [1]

Thompson, S. 1955. *Motif-index of folk literature.* Bloomington: Indiana Unviersity Press. [17]

Thornhill, Nancy Wilmsen. 1989. The evolutionary significance of incest rules. *Ethology and Sociobiology* 10:113–29. [1]

———. 1990. The comparative method of evolutionary biology in the study of the societies of history. *International Journal of Contemporary Sociology* 27:7–27. [1]

————. 1991. An evolutionary analysis of rules regulating human inbreeding and marriage. *Behavioural and Brain Sciences* 14:247–93. [1]

Thornhill, Nancy Wilmsen, and Randy Thornhill. 1990a. Evolutionary analysis of psychological pain of rape victims: I. The effects of victim's age and marital status. *Ethology and Sociobiology* 11:155–76. [1, 15]

————. 1990b. An evolutionary analysis of psychological pain following human rape: II. The effects of stranger, friend and family-member rape. *Ethology and Sociobiology* 11:177–90. [24, 25]

————. 1990c. An evolutionary analysis of psychological pain following human rape: III. The effects of force and violence. *Aggressive Behavior* 16:297–320. [24, 25]

————. 1991. An evolutionary analysis of psychological pain following human rape: IV. The effect of the nature of the sexual assault. *Journal of Comparative Psychology* 105:243–52. [24, 25]

Thornhill, Randy. 1990. The study of adaptation. In M. Bekoff and D. Jamieson (eds.), *Interpretation and Explanation in the Study of Behavior*. Boulder, Colo.: Westview Press. [24, 26]

Thornhill, Randy, and John Alcock. 1983. *The evolution of insect mating systems*. Cambridge, Mass.: Harvard University Press. [24]

Thornhill, Randy, and Steven W. Gangestad. 1994. Human fluctuating asymmetry and sexual behavior. *Psychological Science* 5:297–302. [1]

————. 1995. The evolution of human sexuality. *Trends in Ecology and Evolution* 11:98–102. [1]

Thornhill, Randy, Steven W. Gangestad, and Randall Comer. 1996. Human female orgasm and mate fluctuating asymmetry. *Animal Behaviour*, in press. [1]

Thornhill, Randy, and Nancy Wilmsen Thornhill. 1983. Human rape: An evolutionary analysis. *Ethology and Sociobiology* 4:63–99. [18, 24]

————. 1987. Human rape: The strengths of the evolutionary perspective. In C. Crawford et al. (eds.) *Sociobiology and psychology*, pp. 269–91. Hillsdale, N.J.: Erlbaum. [24]

————. 1989. The evolution of psychological pain. In R. Bell and N. Bell (eds.), *Sociobiology and the social sciences*, pp. 73–107. Lubbock: Texas Tech University Press. [24, 25]

Thornhill, Randy, Nancy Wilmsen Thornhill, and G. Dizinno. 1986. The biology of rape. In R. Bell (ed.), *Sociobiology and the social sciences*, pp. 73–103. Lubbock: Texas Tech University Press. [24]

Tiger, Lionel. 1987. *The manufacture of evil: Ethics, evolution, and the industrial system*. New York: Harper and Row. [1]

Tiger, Lionel, and Robin Fox. 1966. The zoological perspective in social science. *Man* 1:75–81. [9]

————. 1971. *The imperial animal*. New York: Holt, Rinehart and Winston. [1]

Tinbergen, J. M. 1981. Foraging decisions in starlings (*Sturnus vulgaris* L.). *Ardea* 69:1–67. [2]

Tinbergen, Niko. 1963. On aims and methods of ethology. *Zeitschrift für Tierpsychologie* 20:410–33. [1]

Tocqueville, Alexis de. 1840. *Democracy in America*, vol. 2. New York: Random House. [38]

Tomberlin, T. J., P. J. Greene, and J. Hartung. 1981. A correction for diffusion. Paper presented at the annual meeting of the American Statistical Association, Detroit. [31]

Tooby, John. 1982. Pathogens, polymorphism and the evolution of sex. *Journal of Theoretical Biology* 97:557–76. [1]

————. 1985. The emergence of evolutionary psychology. In D. Pines (ed.), *Emerging syntheses in science*. Santa Fe, N.M.: The Santa Fe Institute. [26]

Tooby, John, and Leda Cosmides. 1989. Evolutionary psychology and the generation of culture. Part I: Theoretical considerations. *Ethology and Sociobiology* 10:29–49. [1, 15, 24, 26]

————. 1990a. On the universality of human nature and the uniqueness of the individual: The role of genetics and adaptation. *Journal of Personality* 58:17–67. [26, 27]

————. 1990b. The past explains the present: Emotional adaptations and the structure of ancestral environments. *Ethology and Sociobiology* 11:375–424. [15, 26, 27]

————. 1992. The psychological foundations of culture. In J. Barkow et al. (eds.), *The adapted mind*, pp. 19–136. New York: Oxford University Press. [1, 2, 4, 15, 26, 27]

Tooby, John, and Irv DeVore. 1987. The reconstruction of hominid behavioral evolution through strategic modeling. In W. Kinzey (ed.), *Primate models of hominid behavior*. Albany: State University of New York Press. [26]

Tooke, William, and Lori Camire. 1991. Patterns of deception in intersexual and intrasexual mating strategies. *Ethology and Sociobiology* 12:345–64. [1, 19]

Torroni, A., T. Schur, C. Yang, et al. 1992. Native-American Mt-DNA analysis indicates that the Amerind and the NaDene populations were founded by two independent migrations. *Genetics* 130:153–62. [28]

Townsend, John M. 1987. Sex differences in sexuality among medical students: Effects of increasing socioeconomic status. *Archives of Sexual Behavior* 16:425–44. [1]

————. 1989. Mate selection criteria: A pilot study. *Ethology and Sociobiology* 10:241–53. [1]

———. 1993. Sexuality and partner selection: Sex differences among college students. *Ethology and Sociobiology* 14:305–30. [1]

———. 1995. Sex without emotional involvement: An evolutionary interpretation of sex differences. *Archives of Sexual Behavior* 24:171–204. [1]

Townsend, John M., Jeffrey Kline, and Timothy Wasserman. 1995. Low-investment copulation: Sex differences in motivations and emotional reactions. *Ethology and Sociobiology* 16:25–51. [1]

Townsend, John M., and Gary D. Levy. 1990a. Effects of potential partners' costume and physical attractiveness on sexuality and partner selection. *Journal of Psychology* 124:371–89. [1]

———. 1990b. Effects of potential partners' physical attractiveness and socioeconomic status on sexuality and partner selection. *Archives of Sexual Behaviour* 371:149–64. [1]

Townsend, John M., and Laurence W. Roberts. 1993. Gender differences in mate preference among law students: Divergence and convergence of criteria. *Journal of Psychology* 127:507–28. [1]

Townsend, John M., and Timothy H. Wasserman. 1996a. Sex differences in sexual emotions and perception of sexual attractiveness. *Behavioral and Brain Sciences,* in press. [1]

———. 1996b. The perception of sexual attractiveness: Sex differences in variability. *Archives of Sexual Behaviour,* in press. [1]

Tracer, David P. 1991. Fertility-related changes in maternal body composition among the Av of Papua New Guinea. *American Journal of Physical Anthropology* 85:393–406. [13]

Treggiari, Susan. 1969. *Roman freedmen during the late republic.* Oxford: Clarendon. [37]

———. 1975a. Family life among the staff of the Volusii. *Transactions of the American Philological Association* 105:393–401. [37]

———. 1975b. Jobs in the household of Livia. *Papers of the British School at Rome* 43:48–77. [37]

———. 1976. Jobs for women. *American Journal of Ancient History* 1:76–104. [37]

———. 1979. Questions on women domestics in the Roman West. *Schiavit'u, Manomissione e Clawssi Dipendenti nel Mondo Antico,* pp. 184–201. [37]

———. 1981a. *Concubinae. Papers of the British School at Rome* 49:59–81. [37]

———. 1981b. *Contubernales* in *CIL* 6. *Phoenix* 35:42–69. [37]

———. 1984. *Digna condicio:* Betrothals in the Roman upper class. *Classical Views* 3:419–51. [37]

———. 1987. Women as property in the early Roman Empire. In D. K. Weisberg (ed.), *Women and the law.* Cambridge, Mass.: Schenkman. [37]

——— 1991a. Ideals and practicalities in matchmaking in ancient Rome. In D. Kertzer and R. Saller (eds.), *The family in Italy from antiquity to the present.* New Haven, Conn.: Yale University Press. [37]

———. 1991b. *Roman marriage: Iusti coniuges from the time of Cicero to the time of Ulpian.* Oxford: Clarendon. [37]

Trexler, R. 1973a. The foundlings of Florence, 1395–1455. *History of Childhood Quarterly* 259–84. [39]

———. 1973b. Infanticide in Florence: New sources and results. *History of Childhood Quarterly* 1:98–116. [39]

Trivers, Robert L. 1971. The evolution of reciprocal altruism. *Quarterly Review of Biology* 46:35–57. [1, 9, 26]

———. 1972. Parental investment and sexual selection. In B. Campbell (ed.), *Sexual selection and the descent of man,* pp. 136–79. Hawthorne, N.Y.: Aldine–de Gruyter. [1, 13, 15, 18, 19, 20, 22, 28, 29, 35, 37, 39, 40]

———. 1974. Parent-offspring conflict. *American Zoologist* 14:249–64. [1, 19, 39]

———. 1985. *Social evolution.* Menlo Park, Calif.: Benjamin/Cummings. [1, 18, 22, 24, 33]

———. 1991. Deceit and self-deception. In M. Robinson and L. Tiger (eds.), *Man and beast revisited,* pp. 175–91. Washington, D.C.: Smithsonian Institution Press. [15]

Trivers, Robert L., and Hope Hare. 1976. Haplodiploidy and the evolution of social insects. *Science* 191:249–63. [26]

Trivers, Robert L., and Dan E. Willard. 1973. Natural selection of parental ability to vary the sex ratio of offspring. *Science* 191:249–63. [1, 29, 32, 37, 40]

Tronick, E. Z., G. Morelli, and S. Winn. 1987. Multiple caretaking of Efe (Pygmy) infants. *American Anthropologist* 89:96–106. [39]

Trumbach, Randolph. 1978. *The rise of the egalitarian family: Aristocratic kinship and domestic relations.* New York: Academic Press. [39]

Turke, Paul W. 1984. Effects of ovulatory concealment and synchrony on protohominid mating systems and parental roles. *Ethology and Sociobiology* 5:33–44. [1]

———. 1988. Helpers at the nest: Childcare networks on Ifaluk. In L. Betzig et al. (eds.), *Human Reproductive Behaviour,* pp. 173–88, Cambridge: Cambridge University Press. [1, 8, 13]

———. 1989. Evolution and the demand for children. *Population and Development Review,* 15:61–90. [1, 4, 39]

————. 1990a. Just do it. *Ethology and Sociobiology,* 11:445–63. [15]

————. 1990b. Which humans behave adaptively, and why does it matter? *Ethology and Sociobiology,* 11:305–39. [1, 4, 15]

————. 1995a. The evolution of the hundred year lifespan. Manuscript. [1]

————. 1995b. Microbial parasites versus developing T cells: An evolutionary "arms race" with implications for the timing of thymic involution and HIV pathogenesis. *Thymus* 24:29–40. [1]

Turke, Paul W., and Laura Betzig. 1985. Those who can do: Wealth, status, and reproductive success on Ifaluk. *Ethology and Sociobiology* 6:79–87. [1, 4, 15, 28, 33, 35]

Turnbull, S. K., and J. M. Turnbull. 1983. To dream the impossible dream: An agenda for discussion with stepparents. *Family Relations* 32:227–30. [16]

Turney-High, H. 1971. *Primitive war: Its practice and concepts.* Columbia: University of South Carolina Press. [9]

Tutin, Caroline. 1980. Reproductive behaviour of wild chimpanzees in the Gombe National Park, Tanzania. *Journal of Reproductive Fertility* (supplement) 28:43–57. [7]

Udry, R., J. Billy, N. Morris, T. Groff, and M. Raj. 1985. Serum androgenic hormones motivate sexual behavior in adolescent boys. *Fertility and Sterility* 43:90–94. [20]

Udry, R., and B. K. Eckland. 1984. Benefits of being attractive: Differential payoffs for men and women. *Psychological Reports* 54:47–56. [19]

Udry, R., L. Talbert, and N. Morris. 1986. Biosocial foundations for adolescent female sexuality. *Demography,* 23:217–27. [20]

United Nations. 1988. *Demographic yearbook.* New York: United Nations. [18]

Urquhart, Margaret M. 1927. *Women of Bengal: A study of the Hindu pardanasins of Calcutta,* 3d ed. Calcutta: Association Press. [29]

Utian, W. H. 1980. *Menopause in modern perspective.* London: Prentice Hall. [13]

Valero, H. 1984. *Yo soy napëyoma.* Caracas: Fundación La Salle de Ciencias Naturales. [9]

Van de Castle, R. 1971. *The psychology of dreaming.* Washington, DC: General Learning Corporation. [20]

Van den Berghe, Pierre L. 1979. *Human family systems.* New York: Elsevier. [1, 9, 32, 37]

Van den Berghe, Pierre L., and Gene Mesher. 1980. Royal incest and inclusive fitness. *American Ethnologist* 7:300–17. [1]

Van Gulik, R. H. 1974. *Sexual life in ancient China.* London: E. J. Brill. [29, 37]

Van Wagenen, G. 1972. Vital statistics from a breeding colony. *Journal of Medical Primatology* 1:3–28. [13]

Veblen, T. 1899. *The theory of the leisure class.* London. [28]

Vehrencamp, Sandra. 1983a. A model for the evolution of despotic versus egalitarian societies. *Animal Behaviour* 31:667–82. [5, 38]

————. 1983b. Optimal degree of skew in cooperative societies. *American Zoologist* 23:327–55. [6]

Vercoutter, Jean. 1965. La femme en Egypte ancienne. In P. Grimal (ed.), *Histoire mondiale de la femme,* vol. 1, pp. 61–152. Paris: Nouvelle Librairie de France. [29]

Verner, Jared. 1964. Evolution of polygamy in the long-billed marsh wren. *Evolution* 18:252–61. [11]

Verner, Jared, and M. F. Willson. 1966. The influence of habitats on mating systems in North American passerine birds. *Ecology* 47:143–47. [11, 29, 31]

Veyne, Paul. 1985. Homosexuality in ancient Rome. In P. Ariés and A. Béjin (eds.), *Western sexuality.* Oxford: Basil Blackwell. [37]

————. 1987. The Roman Empire. In P. Veyne (ed.), *From pagan Rome to Byzantium.* Cambridge, Mass.: Harvard University Press. [37]

Vicinus, Martha. 1988. *Independent women.* Chicago: University of Chicago Press. [30]

Vining, Daniel R. 1986. Social versus reproductive success: The central theoretical problem of human sociobiology. *Behavioral and Brain Sciences* 9:167–216. [1, 4, 33]

Voland, Eckart. 1984. Human sex-ratio manipulation: Historical data from a German parish. *Journal of Human Evolution* 13:99–107. [1]

————. 1988. Differential infant and child mortality in evolutionary perspective: Data from late 17th to 19th century Ostfriesland (Germany). In L. Betzig et al. (eds.), *Human reproductive behaviour,* pp. 253–76. Cambridge: Cambridge University Press. [1, 17, 39]

————. 1990. Differential reproductive success within the Krummhörn population (Germany, 18th and 19th centuries). *Behavioural Ecology and Sociobiology* 26:65–72. [1, 28]

————. 1993. *Grundris der soziobiologie.* Stuttgart. [1]

Voland, Eckart, and Robin Dunbar. 1995. Resource competition and reproduction: The relationship between economic and parental strategies in the Krummhörn population (1720–1874). *Human Nature* 6:33–50. [1]

Voland, Eckart, and Claudia Engel. 1989. Women's reproduction and longevity in a premodern population (Ostfriesland, German, 18th century). In A. Rasa et al. (eds.), *The sociobiology of sexual and reproductive strategies,* pp. 194–205. London: Chapman and Hall. [1]

———. 1990. Female choice in humans: A conditional mate selection strategy of the Krummhörn women (Germany, 1720–1874). *Ethology* 84:144–54. [1]

Voland, Eckart, Eva Siegelkow, and Claudia Engel. 1991. Cost/benefit oriented parental investment by high status families: The Krummhörn case. *Ethology and Sociobiology* 12:105–18. [1]

Vom Saal, F. S., and C. E. Finch. 1988. Reproductive senescence: Phenomena and mechanisms in mammals and selected vertebrates. In E. Knobil et al. (eds.), *The physiology of reproduction,* pp. 2351–413. New York: Raven Press. [13]

Von Clauzewitz, C. 1968. *On war.* Harmondsworth: Penguin. [9]

Von Grunebaum, Gustave E. 1954. *Medieval Islam,* 2d ed. Chicago: University of Chicago Press. [29]

Waal, Frans B. de. 1982. *Chimpanzee politics.* New York: Harper and Row. [26]

Waal, Frans B. de, and L. M. Luttrell. 1988. Mechanisms of social reciprocity in three primate species: Symmetrical relationship characteristics or cognition? *Ethology and Sociobiology* 9:101–18. [26]

Wade, Michael J. 1979. Sexual selection and variance in reproductive success. *American Naturalist* 114:742–47. [35]

Wade, Michael J., and S. J. Arnold. 1980. The intensity of sexual selection in relation to male sexual behavior, female choice, and sperm precedence. *Animal Behaviour* 28:446–61. [33]

Wagley, C. 1977. *Welcome of tears.* New York: Academic Press. [39]

Waldman, Bruce, P. Frumhoff, and P. Sherman. 1988. Problems of kin recognition. *Trends in Ecology and Evolution* 3:8–13. [15]

Walker, P. L., and Barry S. Hewlett. 1990. Dental health diet and social status among central African foragers and farmers. *American Anthropologist* 92:383–98. [1]

Wallace, A. 1986. *Homicide: The social reality.* Sydney: New South Wales Bureau of Crime Statistics and Research. [17]

Wallace, Alfred Russel. 1913. *Social environment and moral progress.* London: Cassell and Company. [32]

Wallace-Hadrill, Andrew. 1988. The social structure of the Roman house. *Papers of the British School at Rome* 56:43–97. [37]

———. 1991. Houses and households: Sampling Pompeii and Herculaneum. In B. Rawson (ed.), *Marriage, divorce and children in ancient Rome.* Oxford: Clarendon. [37]

Waller, R. 1986. Ecology, migration, and expansion in East Africa. *African Affairs* 85:347–70. [11]

Wallinga, J. H., and H. Baker. 1978. Effects of long-term selection for litter size in mice on lifetime reproduction. *Journal of Animal Science* 46:1563–71. [13]

Walters, Sally, and Charles B. Crawford. 1994. The importance of mate attraction for intrasexual competition in men and women. *Ethology and Sociobiology* 15:5–30. [1]

Wang, X. T. 1996. Evolutionary hypotheses of risk-sensitive choice: Age differences and perspective change. *Ethology and Sociobiology* 17:1–16. [1]

Wang, X. T. and Victor Johnston. 1993. Changes in cognitive and emotional processing with reproductive status. *Brain, Behavior and Evolution* 42:39–47. [1]

———. 1995. Perceived social context and risk preference: A re-examination of framing effects in a life-death decision problem. *Journal of Behavioral Decision Making* 8:279–93. [1]

Washburn, Sherwood L. 1981. Longevity in primates. In J. March and J. McGaugh (eds.). *Aging, biology and behavior.* New York: Academic Press. [13]

Wason, P. 1966. Reasoning. In B. M. Foss (ed.), *New horizons in psychology.* Harmondsworth: Penguin. [26]

———. 1983. Realism and rationality in the selection task. In J. St. B. T. Evans (ed.), *Thinking and reasoning: Psychological approaches.* London: Routledge and Kegan Paul. [26]

Watson, Alan. 1987. *Roman slave law.* Baltimore, Md.: Johns Hopkins University Press. [37]

Watson, Paul, and Randy Thornhill. 1994. Fluctuating asymmetry and sexual selection. *Trends in Ecology and Evolution* 9:21–25. [1]

Weaver, P. R. C. 1972. *Familia Caesaris: A social study of the emperor's freedmen and slaves.* Cambridge: Cambridge University Press. [37]

———. 1986. The status of children in mixed marriages. In B. Rawson (ed.). *The family in ancient Rome: New perspectives.* Ithaca, N.Y.: Cornell University Press. [37]

———. 1991. Children of freemen (and freedwomen). In B. Rawson (ed.), *Marriage, divorce, and children in ancient Rome.* Oxford: Clarendon. [37]

Webb, Eugene, Donald T. Campbell, Richard Schwartz, and Lee Sechrest. 1966. *Unobtrusive measures: Nonreactive research in the social sciences.* Chicago: Rand McNally. [21]

Webster, M. S. 1991. Male parental care and polygyny in birds. *American Naturalist* 137:274–80. [12]

Wedekind, Claus, Thomas Seebeck, Florence Bettens and Alexandra Paepke. 1995. MHC-dependent mate preference in humans. *Proceeding of the Royal Society of London, B* 260:245–49. [1]

Weiner, Jonathan. 1994. *The beak of the finch: A story of evolution in our time.* New York: Knopf. [1]

Weinrich, J. D. 1988. The periodic table model of the gender transpositions. Part II: Limerent and lusty sexual attractions and the nature of bisexuality. *Journal of Sex Research* 24:113–29. [20]

Weischhoff, H. A. 1940. Artifical stimulation of lactation in primitive cultures. *Bulletin of the History of Medicine* 8:1403–15. [39]

Weisner, T. 1987. Socialization for parenthood in sibling caretaking societies. In J. Lancaster et al. (eds.), *Parenting across the lifespan.* Hawthorne NY: Aldine–de Gruyter. [39]

Weiss, Kenneth. 1981. Evolutionary perspectives on human aging. In P. Amoss and S. Harrell (eds.), *Other ways of growing old.* Stanford, Calif.: Stanford University Press. [13]

Weissner, Polly. 1982. Risk, reciprocity and social influences on !Kung San economics. In E. Leacock and R. B. Lee (eds.), *Politics and history in band societies.* Cambridge: Cambridge University Press. [26]

Wenegrat, Brent. 1990. *Sociobiological psychiatry.* Lexington, Mass.: Lexington Books. [1]

West-Eberhard, Mary Jane. 1975. The evolution of social behavior by kin selection. *Quarterly Review of Biology* 50:1–33. [1, 5]

———. 1978. Temporary queens in *Metapolybia* wasps: Nonreproductive helpers without altruism? *Science* 200:441–3. [38]

———. 1981. Intragroup selection and the evolution of insect societies. In R. D. Alexander and D. W. Tinkle (eds.), *Natural selection and social behavior,* pp. 3–17. New York: Chiron Press. [38]

Westermann, W. 1955. *The slave systems of Greek and Roman antiquity.* Philadelphia: American Philosophical Society. [37]

Westneat, David, Paul Sherman, and M. L. Morton. 1990. The ecology and evolution of extra-pair copulations in birds. In D. Power (ed.), *Current ornithology,* pp. 331–69. New York: Plenum Press. [12]

White, Douglas R. 1988. Rethinking polygyny: Co-wives, codes, and cultural systems. *Current Anthropology,* 29:529–58. [11, 33]

———. 1989. Polygyny. *American Anthropologist* 90:177–79. [11]

Whitehead, Hal, and Patricia L. Hope. 1991. Sperm whalers off the Galápagos Islands and in the western North Pacific, 1830–1850: Ideal free whalers? *Ethology and Sociobiology* 12:147–61. [1]

Whiting, Beatrice, and C. P. Edwards. 1973. A cross-cultural analysis of sex differences in the behavior of children aged three through eleven. *Journal of Social Psychology* 91:171–88. [33]

———. 1988. *Children of different worlds: The formation of social behavior.* Cambridge, Mass.: Harvard University Press. [33]

Whiting, Beatrice, and John Whiting. 1975. *Children of six cultures: A psychological analysis.* Cambridge, Mass.: Harvard University Press. [33]

Whiting, John. 1981. Environmental constraints on infant care practices. In R. Munroe et al. (eds.), *Handbook of cross-cultural human development.* New York: Garland. [31]

Whittaker, C. R. 1987. Circe's pigs. In M. Finley (ed.) *Classical slavery.* London: Frankicass. [37]

Whitten, Pat. 1982. Female reproductive strategies among vervet monkeys. Ph.D. diss. Dept. of Anthropology, Harvard University. Ann Arbor, Mich.: University Microfilms International. [39]

Whyte, Martin K. 1978. Cross-cultural codes dealing with the relative status of women. *Ethnology* 17:211–37. [11, 33, 34]

———. 1979. *The status of women in preindustrial society.* Princeton NJ: Princeton University Press. [34]

Wiedemann, Thomas. 1981. *Greek and Roman slavery.* Baltimore, Md.: Johns Hopkins University Press. [37]

———. 1985. The regularity of manumission at Rome. *Classical Quarterly,* 35:162–75. [37]

———. 1987. *Slavery.* Oxford: Clarendon. [37]

———. 1989. *Adults and children in the Roman Empire.* London: Routledge. [37]

Wiederman, Michael W. 1993. Evolved genders differences in mate preferences: Evidence from personal advertisements. *Ethology and Sociobiology* 14:331–52. [1, 23]

Wiederman, Michael W., and Elizabeth Rice Allgeier. 1992. Gender differences in mate selection criteria: Sociobiological or socioeconomic explanation? *Ethology and Sociobiology* 13:115–24. [1]

———. 1993. Gender differences in sexual jealousy: Adaptationist or social learning explanation? *Ethology and Sociobiology* 14:115–40. [1]

Wilkinson, Gerald. 1988. Reciprocal altruism in bats and other mammals. *Ethology and Sociobiology* 9:85–100. [26]

———. 1990. Food sharing in vampire bats. *Scientific American* 163:76–82. [26]

Willerman, L. 1979. *The psychology of individual and group differences.* New York: Freeman. [18]

Williams, George C. 1957. Pleiotropy, natural selection, and the evolution of senescence. *Evolution* 11:32–39. [1, 13]

———. 1966a. *Adaptation and natural selection: A critique of some current evolutionary thought.* Princeton, N.J.: Princeton University Press. [1, 3, 9, 16, 22, 26, 27, 33]

———. 1966b. Natural selection, the costs of reproduction, and a refinement of Lack's principle. *American Naturalist* 100:687–90. [1]

———. 1975. *Sex and evolution.* Princeton, N.J.: Princeton University Press. [1, 18]

———. 1985. A defense of reductionism in biology. *Oxford Surveys in Evolutionary Biology* 2:1–27. [24, 26]

———. 1989. A sociobiological expansion of *Evolution and ethics.* In J. Paradis and G. C. Williams (eds.), *T. H. Huxley's* Evolution and ethics *with new essays on its Victorian and sociobiological context.* pp. 179–214. Princeton, N.J.: Princeton University Press. [1]

———. 1992. *Natural selection: Domains, levels, challenges.* New York: Oxford University Press. [1, 15, 34]

——— 1996. *Plan and purpose in nature.* New York: Basic Books, [1]

Williams, George C., and Dorris C. Williams. 1957. Natural selection of individually harmful social adaptations among sibs with special reference to social insects. *Evolution* 11:32–39. [1, 26]

Williams, J. E., and D. L. Best. 1982. *Measuring sex stereotypes.* Beverly Hills, Calif.: Sage. [22]

Wilmott, William E. 1961. The Eskimo community at Port Harrison, P.Q. Ottawa: Department of Northern Affairs and Natural Resources. [5]

Wilson, David Sloan. 1994. Adaptive genetic variation and human evolutionary psychology. *Ethology and Sociobiology* 15:219–35. [15]

Wilson, Edward O. 1971. *The insect societies.* Cambridge, Mass.: Harvard University Press. [26]

———. 1975. *Sociobiology: The New Synthesis.* Cambridge, Mass.: Harvard University Press. [1, 9, 20, 29]

———. 1978. *On human nature.* Cambridge, Mass.: Harvard University Press. [1, 9].

Wilson, G. D. 1987. Male-female differences in sexual activity, enjoyment, and fantasies. *Personality and Individual Differences* 2:343–46. [20]

Wilson, G. D., and R. J. Lang. 1981. Sex differences in sexual fantasy. *Personality and Individual Differences* 2:343–46. [20]

Wilson, M. 1957. *Rituals of kinship among the Nyakyusa.* Oxford: Oxford University Press. [13]

Wilson, Margo, and Martin Daly. 1985. Competitiveness, risk taking, and violence: The young male syndrome. *Ethology and Sociobiology* 6:59–73. [1]

———. 1987. Risk of maltreatment of children living with stepparents. In R. Gelles and J. Lancaster (eds.), *Child abuse and neglect: Biosocial dimensions.* New York: Aldine–de Gruyter. [16, 17]

———. 1992. The man who mistook his wife for a chattel. In J. Barkow et al. (eds.), *The Adapted Mind,* pp. 289–322. New York: Oxford University Press. [26]

Wilson, Margo, Martin Daly, and Antonietta Daniele. 1995. Familicide: The killing of spouse and children. *Aggressive Behavior* 21:275–91. [17]

Wilson, Margo, Martin Daly, and Suzanne Weghorst. 1980. Household composition and the risk of child abuse and neglect. *Journal of Biosocial Science* 12:333–40. [16, 17]

———. 1983. Differential maltreatment of girls and boys. *Victimology* 6:249–61. [16]

Wilson, W. C. 1975. The distribution of selected sexual attitudes and behaviors among the adults of the United States. *Journal of Sex Research* 11:46–64. [20]

Winget, C., M. Kramer, and R. Whitman. 1972. Dreams and demography. *Canadian Psychiatric Association Journal* 17:203–8. [20]

Winterhalder, Bruce. 1981. Foraging strategies in the boreal environment: An analysis of Cree hunting and gathering. In B. Winterhalder and E. A. Smith (eds.), *Hunter-gatherer foraging strategies,* pp. 66–98. Chicago: University of Chicago Press. [1]

———. 1986. Diet choice, risk, and food sharing in a stochastic environment. *Journal of Anthropological Archaeology* 5:367–92. [6]

———. 1987. The analysis of hunter-gatherer diets: Stalking an optimal foraging model. In M. Harris and E. Ross (eds.), *Food and evolution,* pp. 311–39. Philadelphia: Temple University Press. [6]

———. 1990. Open field, common pot: Harvest variability and risk avoidance in agricultural and foraging societies. In E. Cashdan (ed.), *Risk and uncertainty in tribal and peasant economies,* pp. 67–87. Boulder, Colo.: Westview Press. [6]

Winterhalder, Bruce, W. Baillargeon, F. Cappelletto, J. I. Randolph Daniel, and C. Prescott. 1988. The population ecology of hunter-gatherers and their prey. *Journal of Anthropological Archaeology* 7:289–328. [1]

Wittenberger, James. 1981a. *Animal social behavior.* Boston: Duxbury Press. [30, 33]

———. 1981b. Male quality and polygyny: The "sexy son" hypothesis revisisted. *American Naturalist* 117:329–42. [11]

Wittenberger, James, and R. Tilson. 1980. The evolution of monogamy: Hypotheses and evidence. *Annual Review of Ecology and Systematics* 11:197–232. [37]

Wood, James W. 1989. Fertility and natural fertility in humans. *Oxford Reviews of Reproductive Biology* 11:61–109. [37]

———. 1990. Fertility in anthropological populations. *Annual Review of Anthropology* 19:211–42. [13]

———. 1994. *Dynamics of human reproduction.* Hawthorne, N.Y.: Aldine–de Gruyter. [1]

Wood, James W., D. Lai, P. L. Johnson, Kenneth Campbell, and I. A. Maslar. 1985. Lactation and birth spacing in highland New Guinea. *Journal of Biosocial Science* supplement 9:159–73. [1]

Worthman, Carol, C. L. Jenkins, J. F. Stallings, and D. Lai. 1993. Attenuation of nursing-related ovarian suppression and high fertility in well-nourished, intensively breastfeeding Amele women of lowland Papua New Guinea. *Journal of Biosocial Science* 25:425–43. [1]

Wrangham, Richard. 1982. Mutualism, kinship and social evolution. In King's College Sociobiology Group (eds.), *Current Problems in Sociobiology,* pp. 269–89. Cambridge: Cambridge University Press. [5]

Wright, Q. 1965. *A study of war.* Chicago: University of Chicago Press. [9]

Wright, Robert. 1990. The intelligence test. *New Republic* 202:28–36. [1]

———. 1994. *The moral animal.* New York: Pantheon. [1]

Wright, Sewall. 1922. Coefficients of inbreeding and relationship. *American Naturalist* 56:330–345. [9]

Wrigley, E. Anthony. 1969. *Population and history.* Cambridge: Cambridge University Press. [4]

Yalman, Nur. 1963. On the purity of women in the castes of Ceylon and Malabar. *Journal of the Royal Anthropological Society* 93:25–58. [29]

Yarshater, Latifeh. 1967. Iran. In R. Patai (ed.), *Women in the modern world,* pp. 61–73. New York: Free Press. [29]

Yengoyan, A. A. 1981. Infanticide and birth order: An empirical analysis of preferential female infanticide among Australian aboriginal populations. *Anthropology UCLA* 7:255–73. [39]

Zahavi, Amotz. 1975. Mate selection: A selection for a handicap. *Journal of Theoretical Biology* 53:205–14. [28]

Zappa, Frank. 1989. *The real Frank Zappa book.* New York: Simon and Schuster. [1]

Zhisui, Li. 1994. *The private life of Chairman Mao.* New York: Random House. [38]

Zuk, Marlene. 1992. The role of parasites in sexual selection: Current evidence and future directions. *Advances in the Study of Behavior* 21:39–68. [1]

Index

Abortion, 3, 13n. 8, 14n. 13, 121, 316, 421n. 17. *See also* Child abandonment; Child abuse and neglect; Infanticide

Ache of Paraguay, 7, 10, 16n. 30, 17n. 45, 33, 63–64, 71, 83, 85, 119 20, 122, 124–34, 136n. 3–4, 140–43, 282–84, 286, 403, 408, 414, 417, 419, 421n. 16

Achuar of Ecuador, 293

Adoption, 14n. 13, 168, 300–301, 316, 396, 404, 407. *See also* Fosterage

Adultery. *See* Promiscuity

Aging. *See* Senescence

Aka of the Central African Republic, 14n. 24, 17n. 49

Akhenaten, 377, 400

Alatalo, R. V., 106

Albert, Bruce, 100

Albuquerque, New Mexico, 7–8

Ales, Catherine, 100

Alexander, Richard, 14n. 24, 17n. 49, 47–48, 96n. 1, 96n. 4–6, 115, 152, 155–57, 227, 235, 351, 356, 364, 372, 401n. 4

Allergy, 13n. 10

Allgeier, Elizabeth, 15n. 26

Altruism. *See* Nepotism; Reciprocity

Alvard, Michael, 17n. 45

Alyawara of Australia, 17n. 45

Andaman Islanders, 407

Anderson, Judith, 14n. 20

Andersson, M., 27

Androgens. *See* Testosterone

Antonovics, J., 147

Antoun, Richard, 311, 315–16

Arbuthnott, John, 331, 338

Aristotle, 323, 392

Arnqvist, Göran, 240

Arunta of Australia, 408

Ashante of African Gold Coast, 7, 16n. 30

Atahuallpa, 377

Attachment, 194

Augustine of Hippo, 375, 386

Augustus, 378–79, 381, 383, 385, 396, 398

Aunger, Robert, 17n. 49

Aurelius, Marcus, 380, 383, 396–97

Austin, Jane, 410

Australians, 179, 181–82, 184, 186 87. *See also* Alywara of Australia; Arunta of Australia; Meriam of Australia; Murngin of Australia; Tiwi of Australia

Ax fighting, 14n. 13, 88

Axelrod, Robert, 13n. 4, 14n. 17, 17n. 43, 97n. 20, 246, 251–52

Ayoreo of Bolivia, 13n. 8, 160, 169, 414, 417–19

Aztecs of Mexico, 7, 9, 375–77, 400

Babylonians, 322–23, 375, 377, 400. *See also* Middle East

Bachrach, C. A., 159, 167

"Backward" Approach, 25, 147–53, 157

Badcock, Christopher, 13n. 5

Bailey, F. G., 96n. 3

Bailey, Michael, 14n. 23

Bailey, Robert, 13n. 8, 16n. 30, 150, 417–18

Baker, Robin, 8, 14n. 15, 16n. 35

Bakkarwal of India, 7, 16n. 30

Balsdon, J., 382

Bantu of East and South Africa, 405, 418

Barash, David, 96n. 4

Barclay, A. M., 195

Bari of Columbia, 17n. 45

Barkow, Jerome, 17n. 49

Barnes, Michael, 14n. 23, 15n. 29, 215–16

Barry, H., 351–53, 356, 358, 360–61